Lee Goldberg

17.50

ECONOMIC
DEVELOPMENT
IN
THE
THIRD
WORLD

ECONOMIC DEVELOPMENT IN THE THIRD WORLD

THIRD EDITION

Michael P. Todaro

Longman

New York & London

The author and publisher gratefully acknowledge the kind permission to reprint from the following:

The United States and World Development: Agenda 1979 by Martin M. McLaughlin and the staff of the Overseas Development Council. Copyright © 1979 Overseas Development Council. Reprinted by permission of Praeger Publishers and the Overseas Development Council.

The United States and the Third World: Agenda 1982 by Roger D. Hansen and contributors. Copyright © 1982 Overseas Development Council. Reprinted and altered by permission of Praeger Publishers.

U.S. Foreign Policy and the Third World: Agenda 1983 by John P. Lewis and Vallerieana Kallab. Copyright © 1983 Overseas Development Council. Reprinted and adapted by permission of Praeger Publishers and the Overseas Development Council.

Other acknowledgments are given in citations throughout the book or in the Acknowledgments section.

ECONOMIC DEVELOPMENT IN THE THIRD WORLD, Third Edition

Longman Inc., 1560 Broadway, New York, N.Y. 10036
Associated companies, branches, and representatives throughout the world.

Copyright © 1977, 1981, and 1985 by Michael P. Todaro

Developmental Editor: Irving E. Rockwood
Editorial Supervisor: Thomas Bacher
Production Supervisor: Ferne Y. Kawahara
Illustrations: K & S Graphics/Hal Keith
Composition: The Saybrook Press, Inc.
Printing and Binding: The Alpine Press, Inc.

Library of Congress Cataloging in Publication Data

Todaro, Michael P.
   Economic development in the Third World.

   Bibliography: p.
   Includes index.
   1. Economic development. 2. Developing countries—
Economic policy. I. Title.
HD82.T552 1985   338.9′009172′4   84-9722
ISBN 0-582-28500-3

Manufactured in the United States of America
Printing: 9 8 7 6 5 4 3 2 1   Year: 93 92 91 90 89 88 87 86 85

For
Donna Renée
and
Lenora Jean

CONTENTS

I   PRINCIPLES AND CONCEPTS   1

1   Economics, Institutions, and Development Studies: A Global Perspective   3

2   Diverse Structures and Common Characteristics of Developing Nations   21

II PROBLEMS AND POLICIES—DOMESTIC   133

5 Growth, Poverty, and Income Distribution   137

LIST OF FIGURES

LIST OF TABLES

PREFACE

In the four years since the publication of the second edition of this book, there have been many significant developments that have affected the international economy and the economic well-being of Third World nations. Whereas the late 1970s witnessed an intensification of the global energy crisis and the spread of worldwide inflation, the 1980s have been characterized by massive Third World debt problems, a persistent global recession (especially in the developing world), a curtailment of international trade and foreign public and private lending, and a worsening of the chronic food, unemployment, and poverty problems of many poor nations. These and other factors have combined to generate a sense of pessimism and even despair about the prospects for rapid economic and social development in the next two decades. The global economic expansion of the 1960s and 1970s which enabled many Third World nations to record significant advances in their economic aggregates appears unlikely to be repeated in the 1980s and 1990s. The implications for improving the material conditions of the world's poor—a major theme of this book—are not very positive.

Turning to the literature on economic development, the first half of the 1980s also witnessed a subtle but significant shift in emphasis (primarily among some Western economists and international agencies like the World Bank) toward a more "free market" approach to development problems. The literature of the 1970s had emphasized issues of poverty and distribution within the context of a growing world economy; that of the eighties seemed to turn once again toward growth and efficiency within the context of a stagnating world economy. And yet within the Third World itself there were still calls for a restructuring of the domestic and international economies so that the many hundreds of millions of people struggling to survive can preserve some hope that their situation might change. These calls have assumed a new urgency. If anything, the major problems of Third World development identified and analyzed in this book—poverty, inequality, unemployment, rural neglect, population increase, overurbanization, trade imbalances, public and private sector inefficiencies, etc.—have *intensified* since the last edition was put into print.

I am extremely gratified by the enthusiasm with which the earlier editions of this book were received, both by peer-group reviewers and by the very large number of instructors at universities throughout the United States, Canada, and Europe—not to mention those of the developing world—

who chose to adopt this book for their economic development courses. This was particularly gratifying to me because the book represents a fundamentally new approach to the teaching of development economics with its emphasis on the analysis of critical development problems from a combined theoretical, empirical, and policy-oriented perspective. I trust that this new edition will also be well received by instructors and students alike.

Although the overall orientation and organization of the book remain unchanged, this third edition contains a signficant amount of new material reflecting theoretical and empirical developments in the 1980s. As an aid to the reader, the major changes in the new edition are indicated here:

1. In response to numerous reader suggestions, the section on "theories of development" in Chapter 3 has been extensively revised and expanded. It now compares and contrasts four major development models—linear stages, two-sector surplus labor, long-term structural change, and international dependence theories.
2. Many new sections discussing topics not covered in earlier editions have been interspersed throughout the chapters and appendixes of the book. These include, among others, sections on:
   (a) The debt problem and IMF stabilization policies
   (b) International migration and the global refugee problem
   (c) The economic impact of rising military expenditures
   (d) Women and development, with special emphasis on poverty, fertility, migration, and agriculture
   (e) The urban informal sector
   (f) The role of Central Banks and their alternatives
   (g) The use and measurement of social indicators
   (h) The aid and other implications of OPEC's declining influence in the world economy
   (i) Recent Chinese economic reforms
   (j) The new debate over the relative merits of free markets versus government intervention
   (k) The performance of state-owned enterprises and the role of the public sector
3. Almost every statistical table and figure has been updated, and many new tables, charts, and figures have been added.
4. Also updated are the textual statistics relating to the major domestic and international development problems analyzed in Parts II and III, as well as the initial overviews, in Chapter 2, of the diverse structure and common characteristics of developing countries.
5. The conceptual and policy aspects of problem-oriented chapters have been revised wherever new theories and/or evidence have emerged to alter perceptions about the analytical nature of and possible policy approaches to problems.
6. The readings sections at the ends of chapters have been thoroughly updated and emphasize readily accessible, recently published books and articles.
7. Also revised and updated is the comprehensive bibliography at the end of the book in which readings—in addition to those suggested at the end of each chapter—are listed and organized in accordance with the major themes of each chapter.

I trust that this book (in conjunction with the companion reader I have edited, *The Struggle for Economic Development: Readings in Problems and Policies* [New York: Longman, 1983]), will provide an accurate reflection of the multidimensional nature of development problems in the 1980s and stimulate instructors and students to explore in depth the theoretical, quantitative, and policy-oriented complexities of contemporary development issues. My indebtedness and gratitude to the many individuals who have helped shape this book cannot adequately be conveyed in a few sentences. I will therefore leave it to the Acknowledgments to mention specific names and only record here my substantial indebtedness to my many colleagues in both developed and developing countries who are engaged in research efforts to understand better and perhaps eventually help find solutions to the profound human problems of Third World development.

MICHAEL P. TODARO
New York, October 1984

PREFACE TO FIRST EDITION

The field of development economics has undergone profound changes during the 1970s. Old clichés and shibboleths about necessary conditions and historical determinants have been replaced by a healthy agnosticism and a refreshing willingness to focus on specific problems and real issues. The very meaning of the term "development" has been altered from an almost exclusive association with aggregate economic growth to a much broader interpretation that encompasses questions of poverty, inequality, and unemployment also. If nothing else, the 1970s will be remembered as a decade during which the problems of domestic and international poverty and income distribution rose to the top of the agenda of the development debate. Moreover, the 1970s ushered in a new era of international instability and global economic disorder which shattered the complacency and security of the developed world and forced it to take seriously its pious rhetoric about global interdependence. Whatever else happens, the system of economic relationships between the developed and the underdeveloped world will never be quite the same again; nor will the field of development economics.

In a constantly changing world, outmoded and outdated textbooks have a special proclivity for survival. Long after academic researchers have discarded irrelevant or incorrect theories and have thoroughly reoriented their discipline toward new issues and problems, many leading textbooks continue to focus on discarded concepts and inappropriate models. Nowhere is this more evident than in the rapidly changing field of development economics.[1] It is precisely in the hope of rectifying this situation that the present book has been conceived and structured. (See the Introduction, pp. xxxiii–xxxvi, for a detailed description of the organization and orientation of the text.)

MICHAEL P. TODARO
New York, January 1977

NOTE

1. In his major survey of the recent evolution of development theory and policy, for example, Derek Healey concluded that "there can be little doubt that a thorough survey of opinion on the problem of economic development would show that at the end of the 1960s and the beginning of the 1970s a new consensus began to emerge. Like all new attitudes, it arose not in a vacuum but in response to the demonstrable

failure of past beliefs and practices. For it is difficult to alter accepted notions—we have invested too much intellectual capital in them. It is difficult to admit that what once appeared axiomatic is in fact subject to the limitations of time and space and must now be doubted." Derek T. Healey, "Development policy: New thinking about an interpretation," *Journal of Economic Literature* (September 1972), 792–794.

ACKNOWLEDGMENTS

I am indebted to a great number of friends (far too many to mention individually) in both the developing and the developed world who have directly and indirectly helped to shape my ideas about development economics and how an economic development text should be structured. To my former students in Africa and the United States and my colleagues in Latin America and Asia, I owe a particular debt of gratitude for their probing and challenging questions. Two good friends and colleagues, Edgar O. Edwards and Lloyd G. Reynolds, were particularly helpful at an earlier stage. Kenneth W. Thompson, a close friend and in many ways my mentor in the field of international relations while we both were at the Rockefeller Foundation, indirectly provided much of the inspiration for this book.

Extremely useful suggestions for improving the second and third editions were received from A. G. Blomquist, William Butz, Bruce Bolnick, Ray Canterbury, Michael Conroy, W. M. Corden, Peter Cornelisse, Gary Fields, Patrick J. Gormely, Donald Huddle, Holland Hunter, Gerald Meier, Gus Ranis, Charles Ratliff, David Vail, Thomas Weisskopf, John Wong, and many anonymous respondents to a questionnaire sent out to users of the book in over 200 universities by the publisher, Longman, Inc. Lydia Maruszko, my research assistant, was extremely helpful with early drafts of various new sections and with statistical updating and bibliography preparation. Kate Venet provided her usual valuable assistance in pulling together the various pieces of the third edition manuscript. Kate has been especially helpful as my secretary over the past eight years in keeping diverse files and wide-ranging correspondence in impeccable order. I should also like to express my gratitude to the Compton Foundation and its successive chairmen, Randolf and Jim Compton, for their support of my ongoing research in the area of human resources, population, and development.

Finally, to my lovely wife, Donna Renée, who typed the entire first edition manuscript and provided me with the spiritual and intellectual inspiration to persevere under difficult circumstances, I can do no more than reaffirm my eternal devotion.

We are grateful to the following for permission to reproduce copyrighted material:

American Economic Association and author Derek T. Healey for table from "Development policy: New thinking about an interpretation," *Journal of Economic Literature*, 10. no. 3 (September 1972); Cambridge University

Press and author David Morawetz for table from "Employment implications of industrialization in developing countries," *Economic Journal* 84 (September 1974), and for tables 10.4 and 10.5 by Celso Furtado from *Economic Development in Latin America* © 1970; Columbia University Press for table from *Peasant to Farmer: A Revolutionary Strategy for Development* by R. Weitz (1971) and table John G. Gurley, in "Rural development in China, 1949–1972, and the lessons to be learned from it" from *Employment in Developing Nations*, ed. K. O. Edwards (1974); Elsevier North-Holland, Inc., for tables 8.2. and 8.4. by G. Psacharopoulos from *The Returns to Education: An International Comparison* © 1972; the Ford Foundation for table 2 by Edgar O. Edwards from *Employment in Developing Countries* © 1973; *Development Digest* for extract by Clifton Wharton from "Risk, uncertainty and the subsistence farmer," vol. 7, No. 2 © 1969; Cambridge University Press for table 4.1 by Brinley Thomas from *Migration and Economic Growth* (1974); International Labor Organization for table 3 and appendix by Yves Sabolo in "Employment and unemployment, 1960–90" from *International Labor Review* (Geneva), vol. 112, no. 6 (December 1975) © International Labour Organizations, December 1975; International Labor Office for table 15 by P. Bairoch from *Urban Unemployment in Developing Countries*, © International Labor Organization, Geneva © 1973; Johns Hopkins University Press and IBRD (World Bank) for table D.5 by S. Reutlinger and M. Selowsky from *Malnutrition and Poverty: Magnitude and Policy Options*, Johns Hopkins University Press © 1976, and table by P. A. Coombs and Munzoor Ahmed from *Attacking Rural Poverty: Nonconformed Education Can Help*, Johns Hopkins University Press © 1974; North-Holland Publishing Company, Amsterdam, for tables 1 and 2 by M. S. Ahluwalia, N. Carter, and H. Chenery from *Growth and Poverty in Developing Countries* 6 (September 1979), and table by Edwin P. Reubens from *The Brain Drain and Taxation*, ed. J. N. Bhagwati © 1976; McGraw-Hill for extract by Carr-Saunders from *Population Problems* by Thompson, used with permission of McGraw-Hill Company © 1965; *Journal of Modern African Studies* for "Taxation for economic development," in vol. 1, no. 1 © 1963 by N. Kaldor; Oxford University Press for annex tables 1, 3, 17, 18, 19, 23, 24 by International Bank for Reconstruction and Development from *World Development Report 1979*; Penguin Books, Ltd. for extracts from *International Trade and Economic Development* © 1972 G. K. Helleiner 1972 (Penguin Educ. 1972); Pergamon Press, Ltd., for extracts from articles in *World Development* by Sartaj Aziz, vol. 2, no. 2, 1974, Frances M. Foland, vol. 2, no. 4, 1974, K. Griffin, vol. 3, no. 11, 1973, Felipe Pazos, vol. 1, no. 7, 1973, P. P. Streeten, vol. 1, no. 6, 1973, all reprinted with permission: the Population Council for tables by Tomas Frejka from *The Future of Population Growth* (1973); Atheneum Publishers for extract from *The Cruel Choice: A New Concept in the Theory of Development* by Denis Goulet © 1971 by D. Goulet, reprinted by permission of Atheneum Publishers; Pantheon Books, a division of Random House, Inc., for permission to reprint an extract from *The Challenge of World Poverty* by Gunnar Myrdal © 1970; Sage Publications for statistics by J. Gugler from *Internal Migration*, ed. Anthony Richmond and David Kubat © 1976; *Siglo 21* for extract from "The crisis of development theory and the problem of dependence in Latin America," by T. Dos Santos © 1969; the World Bank for diagram by John Simmons from "Investments in education: National strategy options for developing countries," *Working Paper* 196 (February 1975), for extract from "Education, Poverty and Development," *Staff Working Paper No. 10* © 1974 by John Simmons, and for tables 1 and 2 in "Dimensions of the problem," by M. Ahluwalia from *Redistribution with Growth: An Approach to Policy*, ed. Chenery, Duloy, and Jolly © 1973. While every effort has been made to trace the owners of copyrights in a few cases this has proved impossible and we take this opportunity to offer our apologies to any authors and/or publishers whose rights may have been unwittingly infringed.

INTRODUCTION

THE NATURE, SCOPE, AND ORGANIZATION OF THE TEXT

This book is designed for use in courses that focus on the economics of development in Africa, Asia, and Latin America, regions often collectively referred to as the Third World.[1] It is structured and written both for students who have had some basic training in economics and for those with little or no formal economics background. For the latter group, those essential principles and concepts of economics that appear to be of particular relevance for analyzing and reaching policy conclusions about specific development problems are explained at appropriate points throughout the text. Thus, the book should be of special value for those undergraduate development courses that attract students from a variety of disciplines.[2] Yet the material is also sufficiently broad in scope and rigorous in coverage to satisfy most undergraduate and some graduate economics requirements in the field of development.

In terms of its organization and orientation this book is unique among development texts. Furthermore, the book incorporates a number of important pedagogical innovations that also make it a significant improvement over other books in the field. Among these innovations, the following are perhaps the most signficant.

First, the book is oriented exclusively toward the teaching of economic development within the context of a major set of problems and issues faced by Third World nations; *the focus is on "real world" development problems* like poverty, inequality, unemployment, and rural stagnation rather than on abstract and often unrealistic models of how countries develop or sterile debates about comparative aggregate economic performances.

Second, it focuses on a wide range of developing countries not only in their capacity as independent nation-states but also in relation to one another and in their interaction with rich nations, both capitalist and socialist.

Third, it recognizes the necessity of treating the problems of development and underdevelopment from an *institutional* and *structural* (i.e., a "noneconomic") as well as an economic perspective, with appropriate modifications of the received "general" economic principles, theories, and policies. It thus attempts to combine relevant theory with realistic institutional analyses.

Fourth, it views development and underdevelopment in both domestic and global contexts, stressing the increasing *interdependence of the world economy* in areas such as food, energy, natural resources, technology, and financial flows.

Fifth, it takes a *problem- and policy-oriented approach* to the teaching of development economics on the dual assumption that (a) students can best grasp and eventually apply important economic concepts when these are explicated in the context of actual development problems, and (b) a central objective of any development economics course should be the fostering of a student's ability to understand contemporary Third World economic problems and to reach independent judgments and policy conclusions about their possible resolution

Sixth, it approaches development problems systematically by following a *standard procedure* with regard to their analysis and exposition. Each chapter begins by stating the general nature of a problem (e.g., population, poverty, rural development, education, income distribution, unemployment), in its principal issues, and how it is manifested in the various developing countries. It goes on to discuss main goals and possible objectives, the role of economics in illuminating the problem, and some possible policy alternatives and their likely consequences. I believe that this approach will not only assist students to think systematically about major current development issues but, more importantly, will provide them with a methodology and operating procedure for analyzing and reaching policy conclusions about other contemporary and future development problems.

Seventh, it starts from the premise that it is possible to design and structure a broadly based development economics textbook that simultaneously utilizes the best available cross-section data from Africa, Asia, and Latin America and appropriate theoretical tools to illuminate common Third World problems. Although obviously these problems will differ in both scope and magnitude when we deal with such diverse countries as India, Indonesia, Kenya, Nigeria, Brazil, Mexico, and Guatemala, the fact remains that they all *do* face similar development problems. Widespread poverty and growing income and asset inequalities, rapid population growth, low levels of literacy and nutritional intake, rising levels of urban unemployment and underemployment, stagnating agriculture and relative rural neglect, inadequate and often inappropriate educational and health delivery systems, inflexible institutional and administrative structures, significant vulnerability to external economic, technological, and cultural forces of dominance and dependence, and the difficult choices regarding tradeoffs between "modernization" and cultural preservation—these and other problems are a pervasive phenomenon and, in fact, often define the nature of underdevelopment in Third World nations.

Finally, it views the many economic, social, and institutional problems of underdevelopment as *highly interrelated* and requiring *simultaneous and coordinated approaches to their solution at both the national and international levels.* It is based on the premise that economic development, even when defined in terms of *both* the rapid growth and more equitable distribution of national incomes and opportunities, is a *necessary* but not *sufficient* condition for "development." The problem is that one simply cannot talk about economics for development without placing economic variables squarely in the context of sociopolitical systems and institutional realities. To ignore "noneconomic" factors in an analysis of so-called economic problems such as poverty, unemployment, and inequality, both within and between nations, would do students a great disservice.

ORGANIZATION AND ORIENTATION

The book is organized into four parts. Part I focuses on the nature and meaning of underdevelopment and its various manifestations in Third World nations. It also examines the historical growth experience of the now developed countries and ascertains the degree to which this experience is relevant to contemporary developing nations.

Parts II and III form the core of the book. They focus on major development problems and policies, both domestic and international. Topics of analysis and review include economic growth, poverty and income distribution, population, unemployment, migration, urbanization, technology, agricultural and rural development, education, international trade and finance, foreign aid, and private foreign investment. Finally, Part IV reviews the possibilities and prospects for Third World development. After discussing the theory and practice of development planning and the role and limitations of public policy in the development process, it analyzes the evolving world economy of the 1980s and the place of less developed nations in an increasingly interdependent but highly unequal global system.

All four parts of the book ask fundamental questions: What kind of development is most desirable? And how can Third World nations best achieve these economic and social objectives either individually or, better, in cooperation with one another and, it is to be hoped, with appropriate and meaningful assistance from the more developed countries of the world?

The discussion and analysis of critical development problems includes the diverse and often conflicting viewpoints of development economists, other social scientists, planners, and those actually on the "firing line" in Third World government ministries or departments. If there is any bias, it is probably in trying always to put forward the viewpoints of Third World social scientists and development practitioners who began in the 1970s to articulate their shared perceptions of the meaning of development as never before.[3]

The locus of intellectual influence on development thinking is rapidly shifting from the First (advanced capitalist) and Second (advanced socialist) Worlds to the Third World. These nations must find the ultimate answers and formulate appropriate strategies. The nationals of these countries will increasingly exert the major influence on the form and content of these strategies. Yet, unless students from economically advanced nations possess a broad knowledge and understanding of the real meaning of underdevelopment and its various manifestations in diverse Third World nations, the probability of enlightened developed country policies toward the plight of the world's poor, who comprise over three-quarters of our global population, will be even more remote than at present.

One further introductory comment seems in order. In the final analysis we must realize that the development of *every* person depends directly or indirectly on the development of *all* persons. Third World nations are an integral part of the ever-shrinking global economic and political organism.

Their economic role and influence are likely to increase over the coming decades. A thorough understanding, therefore, of the unique nature of their economic problems and aspirations, as well as of the direct and indirect linkages between these problems and aspirations and the economic well-being of people in developed nations, should be an essential component in the education of all economics students. It is my hope that the present book contributes in some small way to this broadening of student perspectives and that it will lead to a better understanding of the contemporary problems, possibilities, and prospects for economic and social development in the nations of Africa, Asia, and Latin America.

NOTES

1. The 143 African, Asian, and Latin American member countries of the United Nations often collectively refer to themselves as the Third World. They do this primarily to distinguish themselves from the economically advanced capitalist (First World) and socialist (Second World) countries. Although the precise origin of the term "Third World" is obscure, it has become widely accepted and utilized by *economically poor nations themselves*, especially in their negotiations with economically rich nations on critical international controversies relating to trade, aid, energy, natural resource depletion, and dwindling world food supplies. While it is unfortunate that numbers such as First, Second, and Third occasionally bear the regrettable connotation of superiority and inferiority when used in reference to different groups of nations, the fact remains that the term "Third World" is widely used among developing nations primarily in an effort to generate and represent a new sense of common identity and a growing unity of purpose. Accordingly, we will often use the expression "Third World" when referring to the developing countries as a whole with the clear understanding that it is being used in this positive sense of a common identity and a growing unity of purpose.

2. A glossary at the end of the book provides a quick source of information on the meaning of various economic development concepts and institutional acronyms (e.g., IBRD, ILO) used in the text.

3. See, for example, Padma Desai, "Third World social scientists in Santiago," *World Development* 1, no. 9 (1973); "Self-reliance and international reform," *Overseas Development Council Communiqué* no. 24 (1974); Mahbub ul Haq, "Crisis in development strategies," *World Development* no. 1 (1973); and finally, the first communiqué of 50 leading economists from developing nations who met as members of the Third World Forum in Karachi, Pakistan, in January 1975.

I

PRINCIPLES AND CONCEPTS

1

ECONOMICS, INSTITUTIONS, AND DEVELOPMENT STUDIES

A GLOBAL PERSPECTIVE

The Third World, with [76] percent of the world population, subsists on only [27] percent of the world income—and even this meager income is so mal-distributed internally as to leave the bulk of its population in abject poverty.
Santiago Declaration of Third World Economists

Human needs have to be seen in a global framework.
Communiqué of Third World Social Scientists

HOW THE OTHER THREE-QUARTERS LIVE

As people throughout the world awake each morning to face a new day, they do so under very different circumstances. Some live in comfortable homes with many rooms. They have more than enough to eat, are well clothed and healthy, and have a reasonable degree of financial security. Others, and these constitute more than three-fourths of the earth's 4.8 billion people, are much less fortunate. They may have little or no shelter and an inadequate food supply. Their health is poor, they cannot read or write, they are unemployed, and their prospects for a better life are bleak or uncertain at best. An examination of these global differences in living standards is revealing.

If, for example, we looked first at an average family in North America, we would probably find a "nuclear" family of four with an annual income of approximately $20,000 to $25,000. They would live in a reasonably comfort-

3

able city apartment or a suburban house with a small garden. The dwelling would have many comfortable features including a separate bedroom for each of the two children. It would be filled with numerous consumer goods and electrical appliances, many of which were manufactured outside North America in countries as far away as South Korea, Argentina, and Taiwan. There would always be three meals a day, and many of the food products would be imported from overseas: coffee from Brazil, Kenya, or Colombia; canned fish and fruit from Peru, Japan, and Australia; and bananas and other tropical fruits from Central America. Both children would be healthy and attending school. They could expect to complete their secondary education and probably go to a university, choose from a variety of careers to which they are attracted, and live to an average age of 72 to 75 years.

On the surface, this family, which is typical of families in many rich nations, appears to have a reasonably good life. The parents have the opportunity and the necessary education or training to secure regular employment; to shelter, clothe, feed, and educate their children; and to save some money for later life. But against these "economic" benefits, there are always "noneconomic" costs. The competitive pressures to "succeed" financially are very strong, and, during inflationary or recessionary times, the mental strain and physical pressure of trying to provide for a family at levels that the community regards as desirable can take its toll on the health of both parents. Their ability to relax, to enjoy the simple pleasures of a country stroll, to breathe clean air and drink pure water, and to see a crimson sunset is rapidly disappearing with the onslaught of economic progress and environmental decay. But, on the whole, theirs is an economic status and life-style toward which many millions of other less fortunate people throughout the world seem to be aspiring.

Now let us examine a typical "extended" family in rural Asia. The Asian household is likely to comprise ten or more people, including parents, five to seven children, two grandparents, and some aunts and uncles. They have a combined annual income, both in money and in "kind" (i.e., they consume a share of the food they grow), of from $150 to $200. Together they live in a one-room poorly constructed house as tenant farmers on a large agricultural estate owned by an absentee landlord who lives in the nearby city. The father, mother, uncle, and the older children must work all day on the land. None of the adults can read or write; of the five school-age children only one attends school regularly, and he cannot expect to proceed beyond three or four years of primary education. There is only one meal a day; it rarely changes and it is rarely sufficient to alleviate the constant hunger pains experienced by the children. The house has no electricity, sanitation, or fresh water supply. There is much sickness, but qualified doctors and medical practitioners are far away in the cities attending to the needs of wealthier families. The work is hard, the sun is hot, and aspirations for a better life are constantly being snuffed out. In this part of the world the only relief from the daily struggle for physical survival lies in the spiritual traditions of the people.

Shifting to another part of the world, suppose we now were to visit a large and beautiful city situated along the coast of South America. We would immediately be struck by the sharp contrasts in living conditions from one section of this sprawling metropolis to another. There is a modern stretch of tall buildings and wide, tree-lined boulevards along the edge of a gleaming white beach; just a few hundred meters back and up the side of a steep hill, squalid shanties are pressed together in precarious balance.

If we were to examine two representative families—one a wealthy family from the local ruling class and the other of peasant background—we would no doubt also be struck by the wide disparities in their individual living conditions. The wealthy family lives in a multiroom complex on the top floor of a modern building overlooking the sea, while the peasant family is cramped tightly into a small makeshift shack in a *favella*, or squatter slum, on the hill behind that seafront building.

For illustrative purposes, let us assume that it is a typical Saturday evening at an hour when the families should be preparing for dinner. In the penthouse apartment of the wealthy family a servant is setting the table with expensive imported china, high-quality silverware, and fine linen. Russian caviar, French hors d'oeuvres, and Italian wine will constitute the first of several courses. The family's eldest son is home from his university in North America, and the other two children are on vacation from their boarding schools in France and Switzerland. The father is a prominent surgeon trained in the United States; his clientele consists of wealthy local and foreign dignitaries and buisnessmen. In addition to his practice, he owns a considerable amount of land in the countryside. Annual vacations abroad, imported luxury automobiles, and the finest food and clothing are commonplace amenities for this fortunate family in the penthouse apartment.

And what about the poor family living in the dirt-floored shack on the side of the hill? They too can view the sea but, somehow, it seems neither scenic nor relaxing. The stench of open sewers makes such enjoyment rather remote. There is no dinner table being set; in fact, there is no dinner—only a few scraps of stale bread. Most of the seven illiterate children spend their time out on the streets begging for money, shining shoes, or occasionally even trying to steal purses from unsuspecting people who stroll along the boulevard. The father migrated to the city from the rural hinterland a few years ago, and the rest of the family recently followed. He has had part-time jobs over the years but nothing permanent. The family income is less than $150 per year. The children have been in and out of school many times, as they have to help out financially in any way they can. Occasionally the eldest teenage daughter, who lives with friends across town, seems to have some extra money—but no one ever asks where it comes from or how it is obtained.

One could easily be disturbed by the sharp contrast between these two ways of life. However, had we looked at almost any other major city in Latin America, Asia, and Africa, we would have seen much the same contrast (although the extent of inequality might have been less pronounced).

As a final aspect of this brief view of living conditions around the world, imagine that you are in the eastern part of Africa where many small clusters of tiny huts dot a dry and barren land. Each cluster contains a group of extended families, all participating in and sharing the work. There is no money income here because all food, clothing, shelter, and worldly goods are made and consumed by the people themselves—theirs is a subsistence economy. There are no roads, schools, hospitals, electric wires, or water supplies, and life here seems to be much as it must have been thousands of years ago. In many respects it is as stark and difficult an existence as that of the people in that Latin American *favella* across the ocean. Yet, perhaps it is not as psychologically troubling because there is no luxurious penthouse by the sea to emphasize the relative deprivation of the very poor. Life here seems to be eternal and unchanging—but not for much longer.

One hundred kilometers away a road is being built that will pass near this village. No doubt it will bring with it the means for prolonging life through improved medical care. But it will also inexorably bring information about the world outside along with the gadgets of modern civilization. The possibilities of a "better" life will be promoted, and the opportunities for such a life will become feasible. Aspirations will be raised, but so will frustrations. In short, the "development" process will have been set in motion.

Before long, exportable tropical fruits and vegetables will probably be grown in this now sparsely settled region. They may even end up on the dinner table of the rich South American family in the seaside penthouse. Meanwhile, transistor radios made in Southeast Asia and playing music recorded in northern Europe will become a prized possession in this African village. Throughout the world, remote subsistence villages such as this one are gradually but inexorably being linked up with modern civilization. The process is now well under way and will become even more intensified in the coming years.

This first fleeting glimpse at life in different parts of our planet is sufficient to raise various questions. Why does such obvious affluence coexist with such dire poverty not only across different continents but also within the same country or even the same city? How can traditional, low-productivity, subsistence societies be transformed into modern, high-productivity, high-income nations? To what extent are the development aspirations of poor nations helped or hindered by the economic activities of rich nations? By what process and under what conditions do rural subsistence farmers in the remote regions of Nigeria, Brazil, or the Philippines evolve into successful commercial farmers? These and many other questions concerning international and national differences in standards of living in areas including health and nutrition, education, employment, population growth, and life expectancies might be posed on the basis of even this very superficial look at life around the world.[1]

This book is designed to help students obtain a better understanding of the major problems and prospects for economic development by focusing specifically on the plight of the three-quarters of the world's population for whom poverty and low levels of living are a fact of life. However, as we shall soon discover, the development process in Third World nations cannot be analyzed realistically without also considering the role of economically developed nations in directly or indirectly promoting or retarding that development. Perhaps even more important to students in the developed nations is a fact that we noted in the introduction, namely that as our earth shrinks with the spread of modern transport and communications, the futures of *all* peoples on this small planet are becoming increasingly interdependent. What happens to the health and economic welfare of the poor rural family and many others in Southeast Asia, Africa, the Middle East, or Latin America will in one way or another, directly or indirectly, affect the health and economic welfare of families in Europe and North America, and vice versa. The hows and whys of this growing economic interdependence will unfold in the remaining chapters. But it is within this context of a common future for all mankind in the rapidly shrinking world of the 1980s that we now commence our study of economic development.

ECONOMICS AND DEVELOPMENT STUDIES

The study of economic development is one of the newest, most exciting, and most challenging branches of the broader disciplines of economics and political economy. Although one could claim that Adam Smith was the first "development economist" and that his *Wealth of Nations*, written in 1776, was the first treatise on economic development, the systematic study of the problems and processes of economic development has emerged only over the past three decades. Yet there are some who would still claim that development economics is not really a distinct branch of economics in the same sense as is, say, macroeconomics and microeconomics or public finance and monetary economics. Rather, they would assert, it is simply an amalgamation of all these traditional fields, but with a specific focus on the individual economies of Africa, Asia, and Latin America.

This viewpoint is erroneous. While development economics may draw on certain principles and concepts from other branches of economics in either a traditional or modified form, for the most part it is a field of study that is rapidly evolving its own distinctive theoretical and methodological structure. The awarding of the 1979 Nobel Prize in economics to two eminent development economists, Sir Arthur Lewis of Princeton University and Professor Theodore Schultz of the University of Chicago, provided dramatic confirmation of the status of economic development as a separate field within the economics discipline. We begin, therefore, by contrasting modern development economics with "traditional" Western economics and then devote the bulk of this initial chapter to an analysis of those economic, institutional, and structural factors, both domestic and international, that form an essential part of any analysis of development problems and prospects.

The Nature of Development Economics

Traditional economics is concerned primarily with the efficient, least-cost allocation of scarce productive resources and with the optimal growth of these resources over time so as to produce an ever expanding range of goods and services. (By "traditional economics" we simply mean the classical and neoclassical economics taught in American and British textbooks. See below for a further elaboration.) Political economy goes beyond traditional economics to study, among other things, the social and institutional processes through which certain groups of economic and political elites influence the allocation of scarce productive resources now and in the future either exclusively for their own benefit or for their own benefit plus that of the larger population. Political economy is therefore concerned with the relationship between politics and economics, with a special emphasis on the role of power in economic decision making.

Development economics has an even greater scope. In addition to being concerned with the efficient allocation of existing scarce (or idle) productive resources and with their sustained growth over time, it must also deal with the *economic, social,* and *institutional* mechanisms, both public and private, necessary for bringing about rapid (at least by historical standards) *and large-scale improvements in levels of living* for the masses of poverty-stricken, malnourished, and illiterate peoples of Africa, Asia, and Latin America. Thus, development economics to a greater extent than traditional economics or even political economy is concerned with the economic and political processes necessary for affecting *rapid structural and institutional transformations of entire societies in a manner that will most efficiently bring the fruits of economic progress to the broadest segments of their populations.* As such, a government role and some degree of coordinated economic planning and broad-based domestic and international economic policies are usually viewed as essential components of development economics.

Why Study Development Economics? Some Critical Questions

An introductory course in development economics should help students gain a better understanding of a number of critical questions about the economies of Third World nations. The following is a sample list of 17 such questions; they illustrate the kinds of issues faced by almost every developing nation and, indeed, every development economist.

1. What is the real meaning of "development" and how can certain economic principles and theories contribute to a better understanding of the development process?
2. What are the sources of national and international economic growth? Who benefits most from such growth and why? Why do some countries and groups of people continue to get richer while others remain abjectly poor?
3. What has been the impact of the rapid rise in international oil prices in the 1970s and the economic recession of the early 1980s on the economies of the non-oil-exporting developing nations?
4. How did Third World nations get into such serious foreign debt problems and what are the implications of this debt for the economies of developed nations?
5. Is rapid population growth threatening the economic progress of developing nations? Do large families make economic sense in an environment of widespread poverty and financial insecurity?
6. Why is there so much unemployment in the Third World, especially in the cities, and why do people continue to migrate to the cities from rural areas even though their chances of finding a job are very slim?
7. What is development planning all about? Why plan at all?
8. Should foreign private multinational corporations be encouraged to invest in the economies of poor nations and, if so, under what conditions?
9. What about the impact of foreign aid from rich countries? Should developing countries continue to seek such aid, under what conditions, and for what purposes? On the other hand, should developed countries continue to offer aid, under what conditions, and for what purposes?
10. Should exports of primary products such as agricultural commodities be promoted or should all less developed countries (LDCs) attempt to industrialize by developing their own heavy manufacturing industries as rapidly as possible?
11. When and under what conditions should Third World governments adopt a policy of exchange control, raise tariffs, and/or set quotas on the importation of certain "nonessential" goods in order to ameliorate chronic balance of payments problems?

12. Is international trade desirable from the point of view of the development of poor nations? Who really gains from trade and how are the advantages distributed among nations?
13. Since 70 or 80% of many LDC populations still reside in rural areas, how can agricultural and rural development best be promoted?
14. How does the spread of recession and unemployment among rich nations affect the levels of living of people in poor nations? Do poor nations have any recourse, or must they be passive and vulnerable spectators at an international economic power game?
15. Will there be chronic world food shortages? If so, which nations will be most adversely affected and how might such shortages best be avoided in the future?
16. Do Third World educational systems really promote economic development or are they simply a mechanism to enable certain select groups or classes of people to maintain positions of wealth, power, and influence?
17. What is the origin and basis of recent Third World demands for a "new international economic order?" Is such a new world economic order possible and, if so, what might be its main features and how might it affect the economies of developed nations?

These and many similar questions are analyzed and explored in the following chapters. The answers are often more complex than one might think. Remember that the ultimate purpose of any course in economics, including development economics, is to help students *think systematically* about economic problems and issues and formulate judgments and conclusions on the basis of relevant analytical principles and reliable statistical information. Since the problems of Third World development are in many cases unique in the modern world and often not easily understood through the use of traditional Western economic theories, we may often need unconventional approaches to what may appear to be conventional economic problems. Traditional Western economic principles can play a useful role in enabling us to improve our understanding of development problems; but they should not blind us to the realities of local conditions in these countries. Traditional theories of economic growth and development often require modification in both assumptions and procedures before they can shed light adequately on complicated and economically unprecedented development issues. We shall have more to say about the role and limitations of traditional economic theory later in the chapter.

The Important Role of Values in Development Economics

Economics is a social science. It is concerned with human beings and the social systems by which they organize their activities to satisfy basic material needs (e.g., food, shelter, clothing) and nonmaterial wants (e.g., education, knowledge, spiritual fulfillment). Because they are social scientists, economists face the somewhat unusual situation in which the objects of their studies—human beings in the ordinary business of life—and their own activities are rooted in the same social context. Unlike the physical sciences, the social science of economics can claim neither scientific laws nor universal truths. In economics there can only be "tendencies," and even these are subject to great variations in different countries and cultures and at different times. Many so-called general economic models are based on a set of implicit assumptions about human behavior and economic relationships that may have little or no connection with the realities of developing economies.

To this extent, their generality and objectivity may be more assumed than real. Economic investigations and analyses cannot simply be lifted out of their institutional, social, and political context, especially when one must deal with the human dilemmas of hunger, poverty, and ill health which plague more than two-thirds of the world's population.

It is necessary, therefore, to recognize from the outset that ethical or normative value premises about what is or is not desirable are central features of the economic discipline in general and of development economics in particular. The very concepts of economic development and modernization represent implicit as well as explicit value premises about desirable goals for achieving what Mahatma Gandhi once called the "realization of the human potential." Concepts or goals such as economic and social equality, the elimination of poverty, universal education, rising levels of living, national independence, modernization of institutions, political and economic participation, grass-roots democracy, self-reliance, and personal fulfillment all derive from subjective value judgments about what is good and desirable and what is not. So also, for that matter, do opposite values—for example, the sanctity of private property and the right of individuals to accumulate unlimited personal wealth, the preservation of traditional social institutions and rigid, inegalitarian class structures, and the supposed "natural right" of some to lead while others follow.

When we deal in Parts II and III with such major issues of development as poverty, inequality, unemployment, population growth, rural stagnation, and international dependence, the mere indentification of these topics as problems conveys the value judgment that their improvement or elimination is desirable and therefore good. That there is widespread agreement among many different groups of people—politicians, academics, and ordinary citizens—that these are desirable goals does not alter the fact that they arise not only out of a reaction to an objective empirical or positive analysis of what is, but ultimately from a subjective or normative value judgment with regard to what should be.

It follows that value premises, however carefully disguised, are an integral component both of economic analysis and economic policy. Economics cannot be value free in the same sense as, say, physics or chemistry. Thus, the validity of economic analysis and the correctness of economic prescriptions should always be evaluated in light of the underlying assumptions and/or value premises. Once these subjective values have been agreed on by a nation or, more specifically, by those who are responsible for national decision making, then specific development goals (e.g., greater income equality) and corresponding public policies (e.g., taxing higher incomes at higher rates) based on "objective" theoretical and quantitative analyses can be pursued. However, where serious value conflicts and disagreements exist among decision makers, the possibility of a consensus about desirable goals or appropriate policies is considerably diminished. In either case, it is essential that one's value premises, especially in the field of development economics, always be made clear.[2]

The Nature of Western Economic Theory

To analyze the range of critical development problems some basic understanding of general economic concepts and principles is needed. Unfortunately, many fundamental concepts and principles of traditional economics, because they are derived from and related to the special economic, institutional, and structural characteristics of advanced industrial nations, are neither relevant nor appropriate to the understanding or resolution of problems of developing countries.

Let us, therefore, quickly review economic theory and briefly sketch the reasons why many of the so-called Western economic models and theories are inappropriate for the study of Third World development. Having done this, we will be in a better position to appreciate the distinctive nature of modern development economics.

Economic theory represents the way in which economists conceptually organize the interdependent components of economic life including production, consumption, incomes, prices, employment, exports, imports, savings, and investment. While economics as a discipline is concerned with the way in which scarce human and material resources are most efficiently employed for the social good, economic theory consists of a generally accepted body of concepts and principles about economic behavior that, if properly formulated and correctly arranged, can help us understand and explain better the workings of an economic system. The method or "thought process" of economic theory is largely deductive in nature—that is, on the basis of a known or assumed set of facts about the essential characteristics of an economy, a hypothesis is established and a "model" is set up. The model may be simple or complex, but the essence of all models is that they are simplifications of reality. Conclusions about the functioning of an economy or an economic system can then be logically deduced either from the characteristics of the model or from experiments within the model. To be worthwhile, however, models need to be tested constantly against reality through the use of statistics and statistical methods.

The first essential of any economic theory or model is that it should be capable of explaining the economic realities of nations and regions. Any theory or set of principles must of necessity be based on simplifying *assumptions* and *abstractions*; but what these should be cannot be decided in a vacuum. *The assumptions and abstractions made must fit the realities of nations and must be appropriate to the characteristic features of economic life as revealed by observation and experience.* Moreover, theories and principles that might be valid and appropriate for one economy in a given region or at a given moment may not be valid for other societies at the same or at different times. This brings us to an important point about economics and development, one that provides a principal rationale for the structure and design of this book.

THE LIMITED RELEVANCE OF TRADITIONAL THEORY

Many development economists agree that what has come to be known as traditional or Western neoclassical and neo-Keynesian economic theory is in itself of limited relevance for understanding the characteristic features of the economies and economic processes of many Third World nations. Perhaps the Nobel Prize winning Swedish economist Gunnar Myrdal best stated the case against the uncritical use of traditional economic concepts and theories in poor nations when he observed:

Economic theorists, more than any other social scientists, have long been disposed to arrive at general propositions and then postulate them as valid for every time, place, and culture. There is a tendency in contemporary economic theory to follow this path to the extreme. . . . when theories and concepts designed to fit the special conditions of the Western world—and thus containing the implicit assumptions about social reality by which this fitting was accomplished—are used in the study of underdeveloped countries, where they do not fit, the consequences are serious.[3]

Professor Paul Streeten of Boston University was even more succinct when he noted that "the whole paraphernalia of contemporary neoclassical economics seems to have become suddenly obsolete."[4]

Although we shall not at this point get into specific details concerning the extensive criticism of Western economic models as guides to understanding and ameliorating conditions of underdevelopment, a few general comments are needed.

Neoclassical economics as taught in developed nations and, through the importation of Western textbooks, in developing nations has traditionally been divided into three broad categories: microeconomics, macroeconomics, and international economics. Microeconomics focuses on the behavior and activities of individual economic units, primarily producers and consumers. Macroeconomics looks at the economy as a whole in terms of aggregate or "macro" economic variables such as consumption, saving, investment, the money supply, gross domestic product, employment, and the overall price level. International economics examines the trading and financial relationships between nation-states both as producers of exports and consumers of imports. It thus represents a mixture of elements of both micro- and macroeconomic theory.

The conceptual framework and behavioral assumptions that unite these broad areas of traditional neoclassical economic analysis are the threefold "ideals" of consumer sovereignty, perfect competition, and profit maximization. *Neoclassical economics is the economics of equilibrium and stability that needs to be modified for a developing world of disequilibrium and instability.* It is the economics of marginal choice, of "a little more or a little less," that is often inappropriate for a developing world where major fundamental choices must be made to secure "a lot more" in as short a time period as possible.

In microeconomic theory, the basic questions of what and how much to produce are assumed to be determined by the aggregate preferences of all consumers as revealed by their market demand curves for different goods and services. Producers are assumed simply to respond to these "sovereign" consumer preferences and, motivated by the desire to maximize profits, they are assumed to compete with each other *on equal terms* in the purchase of resources and the sale of their products. The neoclassical economist's notion of "perfect competition" is central to this whole process. It assumes that all prices, wages, interest rates, and the like, are determined by the free play of the forces of supply and demand and that each of the millions of consumers and thousands of producers is so small in relation to total demand and supply that they cannot individually influence to any extent the market prices and quantities of goods, services, and resources bought and sold. The ultimate rationale for this theory or model of economic activity is Adam Smith's famous notion of the "invisible hand" of capitalism: If each individual consumer, producer, and supplier of resources pursues self-interest, he or she will, "as if by an invisible hand," be promoting the overall interests of society.

Unfortunately, the facts of economic life in the less developed nations of the world are such as to render much of traditional microeconomic theory of limited importance for either analysis or policy.[5] Competitive markets simply do not exist nor, given the institutional, cultural, and historical context of most LDCs, would they necessarily be desirable from a long-term economic and social perspective. Consumers as a whole are rarely sovereign about anything, let alone about what goods and services are to be produced, in what quantities, and for whom. Producers, whether private or public, have great power in determining market prices and quantities sold. The ideal of competition is typically just that—an ideal with little relation to reality.[6] Finally, the so-called invisible hand often acts not to promote the general welfare but to lift up those who are already well-off while pushing down that vast majority. While much can be learned from micro theory with regard to the importance of "correct" prices for efficient production and resource allocation (see Chapters 8–10), the institutional and political structures of many Third World economies—not to mention their differing value systems and ideologies—often make the attainment of such appropriate prices an exceedingly difficult endeavor.

The limitations of macroeconomic theory are much more pronounced. Briefly, macroeconomic theory (whether in its "Keynesian" or "monetarist" form) also views the economy and its institutions through competitive equilibrium, supply and demand spectacles. Here, however, one is dealing with the determinants of aggregate supply and demand for national output. The greater the level of aggregate demand, the higher the level of equilibrium employment and prices in the economy. Policy prescriptions for government intervention in the economy flow naturally from this theory. For example, in the Keynesian model unemployment is due to insufficient aggregate demand for the "potential" output of a nation (i.e., the goods and services the nation as a whole could produce at maximum capacity). By increasing aggregate demand, therefore (e.g., by expanding government expenditures and/or lowering taxes), governments can accelerate economic activity and consequently induce higher levels of employment. Conversely, when aggregate demand exceeds the productive capacity (aggregate supply) of the economy so that inflation results, the role of government is to spend less and tax people more in order to reduce consumer demand and thus curtail general price increases.

Even more than micro theory, traditional Keynesian macro theory reveals many inadequacies when applied to the realities of economic life in the developing world.[7] This is particularly true in those economies with highly fragmented product, resource, and financial markets. Such market fragmentation typically results from the coexistence of modern and traditional ways of doing things in both agriculture and industry. It is compounded by inadequate and malfunctioning credit systems and a general LDC vulnerability to powerful foreign economic influences.

This fundamental irrelevance of traditional Keynesian macroeconomics for Third World development should not be surprising. The general theory was in fact formulated in response to the *special* Western economic and institutional circumstances of the Great Depression of the 1930s. Indeed, a good deal of Keynesian macro theory is considered irrelevant even in developed nations, where the major problem of the 1970s was no longer simply unemployment or inflation but "stagflation" (i.e., unemployment accompanied by structural as well as demand inflation; see Chapter 8). Manipulating aggregate supply and demand curves by general government monetary and fiscal policies appeared to have lost much of its effectiveness. As a result, Keynesian economics came under increasing criticism even from many of its formerly ardent proponents in the developed nations.[8]

If such a gap between macro theory and economic reality exists in the industrial nations, how much more irrelevant the theory must seem for the underdeveloped countries whose institutions and economic systems don't even approximate those of the developed nations, now or in the past! In fact, as we shall see in Chapter 9, the traditional Keynesian policy for alleviating industrial unemployment—the creation of more urban jobs through expanded government-induced aggregate demand—may under certain real-world conditions in poor countries actually *increase* the level of urban unemployment as a result of induced rural-urban migration. It may simultaneously exacerbate domestic inflationary pressures. And, as we shall also see in Part II, this is not an isolated case of "perverse" results that may occur when standard Western theory is applied uncritically to the problems of Third World development. Many other phenomena that might at first appear to be theoretical paradoxes of development economics become less surprising when the traditional theories are considered in light of the unique characteristics of developing nations.

Finally, in Chapter 12, we will discover that much of the traditional theory of international trade, based as it is on the same competitive assumptions of microeconomics, offers only limited guidance for an understanding of the actual mechanics of international economic relations between rich and poor nations in the 1980s. Who benefits most from trade, how the gains are distributed, and how international commodity prices are determined often bears little resemblance to the dictates of traditional models of trade and growth.

ECONOMIES AS SOCIAL SYSTEMS: THE NEED TO GO BEYOND SIMPLE ECONOMICS

The preceding introductory comments about traditional neoclassical economics were confined largely to questions of its nature, scope, and limitations for dealing with the complex and multidimensional problems of Third World development. But economics and economic systems, especially in the Third World, need to be viewed in a much broader perspective: within the context of the overall social system of a country. By a "social system" is meant the interdependent relationships between so-called economic and noneconomic factors. The latter include attitudes toward life, work and authority, public and private bureaucratic and administrative structures, patterns of kinship and religion, cultural traditions, systems of land tenure, the authority and integrity of government agencies, the degree of popular participation in development decisions and activities, and the flexibility or rigidity of economic and social classes.

Throughout this book we shall discover that resolving development problems and achieving development is a much more complicated task than some people would lead us to believe. Increasing national production, raising levels of living, and promoting widespread employment opportunities are all as much a function of the values, incentives, attitudes and beliefs, and the institutional and power arrangements of a society as they are the direct outcomes of the manipulation of strategic economic variables such as savings, investment, and foreign exchange rates. Just as some economists occasionally make the mistake of confusing their science with universal truth, so they also sometimes mistakenly dismiss these noneconomic variables as "nonquantifiable" and therefore of dubious importance.

But, as we shall see in Parts II, III, and IV, many of the failures of development policies in Third World nations have occurred precisely because these noneconomic factors (e.g., the role of traditional property rights in allocating resources and distributing income or the influence of religion on attitudes toward modernization and family planning) were intentionally or unintentionally excluded from the analysis. While the main focus of this book is on the nature of development economics and its usefulness in understanding problems of economic and social progress in poor nations, we will also continually see the way in which values, attitudes, and institutions play a crucial role in the overall development process.

THIRD WORLD SOCIAL SYSTEMS AS PART OF AN INTERDEPENDENT INTERNATIONAL SOCIAL SYSTEM

We can extend the above analysis even further. Just as the economic life of a developing nation is inevitably linked with its social, political, and cultural life, so these domestic social systems are interconnected with the international social system: the organization and rules of conduct of the global economy. An important aspect of this linkage is the phenomenon of the *dominance* and *dependence* that exists between many developed and less developed nations (see Chapter 3). Such dominance and dependence relationships are indeed pervasive. They are found in a wide range of international economic affairs—including foreign aid, private foreign investment, the debt problem, and the transfer of technology—where the LDCs as a group often appear to be at the mercy of the global power of rich nations and their multinational corporations. And they exist in the political, intellectual, and cultural spheres as well. Here many of the values, ideas, symbols, laws, attitudes, and institutions of rich nations permeate, influence, and shape the social systems of Third World countries.

Conversely, the developed nations are beginning to recognize their own ultimate economic dependence on the developing countries, both as a market for their products and as a major source of raw material and natural resource imports. For example, about 41% of U.S. exports go to developing countries. Of the 20 largest trading partners of the United States, 11 are Third World nations. In fact, 1 out of every 6 jobs in the U.S. manufacturing sector exists to produce goods to export to developing countries. On the import side, developed country dependence on Third World oil production is well known, with the United States still dependent on developing nations for 80% of its fuel imports. Europe and Japan's energy dependence is even greater.

Oil is not the only resource where formerly dependent economies can begin to exert influence on the rich industrial nations. A substantial amount of the world's raw material resources are located in Third World countries, even if in many cases their control and management still resides primarily with powerful multinational corporations. For example, Zambia, Chile, Peru, and a few other Third World countries supply almost 80% of the world's copper. Malaysia and Sri Lanka supply over 50% of the world's natural rubber. Bolivia, Malaysia, and Thailand account for 85% of world trade in tin. Third World countries including Jamaica, Surinam, and Guyana supply almost 90% of developed nation imports of bauxite. Other critical minerals for which Third World nations are major suppliers include manganese (Gabon, Brazil, and Zaire), iron ore (Venezuela and India), and lead (Peru, Mexico, and others).

In commodity exports almost the entire world supply of coffee is produced by Brazil, Colombia, Kenya, the Ivory Coast, Uganda, and El Salvador; most of the world's cocoa is produced by Brazil and Ghana; most of the world's tea comes from India, Sri Lanka, East Africa, and China; and over two-thirds of the world's jute is from India, Pakistan, Bangladesh, Thailand, and Nepal. The Persian Gulf Arab states alone control almost 60% of the world's known oil reserves although they constitute less than 1% of the world's population.

These statistics underscore the now widely recognized fact that the economies of the world today are becoming more and more interdependent. Such interdependence is likely to be even more characteristic in the future. Nevertheless, Third World nations as a whole have always been and still on balance remain much more dependent on the economic and political policies of the dominant rich countries. It is impossible to talk about Third World development without dealing with this dependence phenomenon, even though, in recognition of this fact, many developing countries are attempting either singularly or collectively to pursue more self-reliant development strategies while pressing their demands for a new international economic order (see Chapter 17). In the 1970s, as international political disputes moved away from the cold war politics of the 1950s and 1960s and began to focus more on a growing competition for increasingly scarce natural resources, many of which are located in Third World nations, the possibility of North–South (i.e., rich country–poor country) economic confrontation took on an added importance. In the 1980s this international competition for dwindling natural resources has assumed an even greater significance. We discuss this and related issues further in Part IV.

Any study of development economics, therefore, that does not recognize and deal with this dual phenomenon of the persistent LDC economic, technological, and institutional dependence on rich nations and the growing rich country dependence on Third World export markets and resource policies would be overlooking one of the most important elements in the long-run success or failure of diverse development efforts. Consequently, in the chapters that follow, and especially in Parts II and III, the discussions of critical development problems such as poverty, inequality, and unemployment will be framed not only within the broad context of the social systems of individual developing countries but also within an international context in which developing nations are part of an increasingly interdependent but still highly unequal global economic system. We shall discover that many common forces are at work in this system and that many apparent economic paradoxes become understandable when problems of underdevelopment are viewed, as they should be, in both a domestic *and* a global context.

SUMMARY AND CONCLUSIONS

Development economics is a distinct yet very important extension of both traditional economics and political economy. While necessarily also concerned with efficient resource allocation and the steady growth of aggregate output over time, development economics focuses primarily on those economic, social, and institutional mechanisms necessary to bring about *rapid and large-scale* improvements in levels of living for the masses of poor people in Third World nations. As such, *development economics must be concerned with the formulation of appropriate public policies designed to affect major economic, institutional, and social transformations of entire societies in the shortest possible time.* Otherwise the gap between aspiration and reality will continue to widen with each passing year. It is for this reason that the public sector assumes a much broader and more determining role in development economics than it does in traditional (Western) economic analysis.

As a social science, economics is concerned with people and how best to provide them with the material means to help them realize their full human potentials. But what constitutes the good life is a perennial question and, as such, economics necessarily involves values and value judgments. Our very concern with promoting development represents an implicit value judgment about good (development) and evil (underdevelopment). But "development" may mean a lot of different things to a lot of different people. Therefore, the nature and character of that development and the meaning we attach to it need to be carefully spelled out. This will be our task in Chapter 3 and elsewhere throughout the book.

The central economic problems of all societies include traditional questions such as what, where, how, how much, and for whom goods and services should be produced. But they should also include the fundamental question at the national level about who or which groups actually make or influence economic decisions and for whose principal benefit these decisions are made. Finally, at the international level, it is necessary to consider the question of which nations and which powerful groups within nations exert the most influence with regard to the use and deployment of scarce global food and mineral resource supplies. Moreover, for whom do they exercise this power?

Any realistic analysis of development problems necessitates the supplementation of strictly economic variables such as income, investment, and saving with equally relevant noneconomic factors including the nature of land tenure arrangements; the influence of social and class stratifications; the structure of credit; education and health systems; the organization and motivation of government bureaucracies; the machinery of public administration; the nature of popular attitudes toward work, leisure, and self-improvement; and the values, roles, and attitudes of political and economic elites. Economic development strategies that seek to raise agricultural output, create employment, and eradicate poverty have often failed in the past because economists and other policy advisers neglected to view the economy as an interdependent social system where economic and noneconomic forces are continually interacting, in ways that are at times self-reinforcing and at other times contradictory.

It is important to view these internal social systems of developing nations within the broader context of the international social system of all nations, rich and poor. Here, the phenomenon of small power groups, mostly from rich nations, influencing global strategies and the corresponding "vulnerability" of Third World nations caught in a dominance and dependence relationship vis-à-vis the industrial nations of East and West is often emphasized. An analogous vulnerability and dominance–dependence relationship often also exists between the great masses of people and the relatively small but powerful elites within the developing nations themselves.

Nevertheless, the raw material and resource scarcities of the 1970s as well as the foreign debt problems and declining export markets of the 1980s underlined, as no other events had previously, the increasing dependence of rich nations on poor ones and thus the growing interdependence of all nations and peoples within the international social system. What happens to life in Caracas, Cairo, and Calcutta will in one way or another have important implications for life in New York, London, and Moscow. It was once said that "when the United States sneezes, the world catches pneumonia." A more fitting expression for the 1980s would perhaps be that "the world is like the human body: if one part aches, the rest will feel it; if many parts hurt, the whole will suffer."

Third World nations constitute these "many parts" of the global organism. The nature and character of their future development, therefore, should be a major concern of *all* nations irrespective of their political, ideological, or economic orientations. In the latter part of the twentieth century and in the twenty-first, there can no longer be two futures—one for the few rich and the other for the very many poor. In the words of a poet, "there will be only one future, or none at all."

NOTES

1. Two excellent descriptions of life in Third World nations are provided by Denis Goulet and the Brandt Commission report, which are printed as Readings 1 and 2 in my book of readings designed to complement this text. See M. P. Todaro (ed.), *The Struggle for Economic Development: Readings in Problems and Policies* (New York: Longman, 1983). Further references to this collection in later chapters will identify it simply as *The Struggle for Economic Development*.

2. For an excellent dissection of the role of values in development economics, see Gunnar Myrdal, *The Challenge of World Poverty* (New York: Pantheon, 1970). Chapter 1. A more general critique of the idea that economics can be "value free" is to be found in Robert Heilbroner's "Economics as a 'value free' science," *Social Research* 40 (Spring 1973): 129–143.

3. Gunnar Myrdal, *Asian Drama: An Inquiry into the Poverty of Nations* (New York: Pantheon, 1968), pp. 16–17.

4. Paul Streeten, *World Development* 2, nos. 4 and 5 (1974): 83.

5. For a critique of the relevance of neoclassical economics, even for Western developed economies, by three well-known economists, see E. Phelps-Brown, "The underdevelopment of economics"; G. D. N. Worswick, "Is progress in economic science possible?"; and N. Kaldor, "The irrelevance of equilibrium economics." All are in *Economic Journal, 82,* No. 325 (March 1972).

6. Although monopolies of resource purchase and product sale are a pervasive phenomenon in most developing nations, the traditional theory of monopoly offers little insight into the day-to-day activities of these public, parastatal, and private corporations. Decision rules can vary widely with the social setting so that profit maximization may be a low-priority objective in comparison with, say, employment creation or the replacement of expatriate managers with local personnel (see Chapter 16).

7. One of the earliest and most powerful critiques of the relevance of Keynesian economics for developing nations can be found in Dudley Seers' seminal paper, "The limitations of the special case," *Bulletin of the Oxford Institute of Economics and Statistics,* May 1965.

8. See, for example, J. K. Galbraith, "Power and the useful economist," *American Economic Review, 63,* No. 1 (March 1973): 1–11; and W. Leontief, "Theoretical assumptions and nonobserved facts," *American Economic Review, 61,* No. 1 (March 1971): 1–7. However, for a staunch defense of Keynesian economics and Keynesian policies for developed countries, see W. Heller, "What's right with economics," *American Economic Review, 65,* No. 1 (March 1975): 1–26.

CONCEPTS FOR REVIEW

Traditional (Western) economics	"Laws" versus "tendencies"
Political economy	Values and value premises
Development economics	Social system
Economic theory	Noneconomic variables
Economic model	Interdependence
Consumer sovereignty	Economic and social institutions
Western economic theory	Economic system, domestic and
First World	international
Second World	Subsistence economy
Third World	Dominance–dependence relationships
Social science	

QUESTIONS FOR DISCUSSION

1. Why do you think economics is so central to an understanding of the problems of Third World development?

2. Do you think that the concept of the Third World is a useful one? Why or why not?

3. Why should one be skeptical about any claims of universal applicability of traditional Western economic theories? Explain.

4. What is the meaning of the assertion that although assumptions and propositions of economic theories may differ from one society to the next, the "thought processes" of economics should be similar? Can you give some examples of common thought processes?

5. Do you think that the wide diversity of living conditions found by our brief trip around the world can also be found within most Third World countries? What do we mean by the notion of different "levels of living"?

6. What do you hope to gain from this course in development economics (i.e., besides a passing grade!)?

7. Why are values and value premises so important in economics? Can economics ever be truly "value free"? Why or why not?

8. Why is it important to view economies as social systems and to go beyond simple economic factors in analyzing development problems?

9. What do you think is meant by the expression "interdependent international social system?" In what ways are national economies becoming more interdependent as we approach the end of the twentieth century?

FURTHER READINGS

For an enjoyable and lively layman's exposition of the nature of neoclassical economics see Robert A. Mundell, *Man and Economics* (New York: McGraw-Hill, 1968), Chapters 1–3. In addition to the articles in Note 5 and the Seers article referred to in Note 7, an extensive critique of assumptions, methodology, and relevance of contemporary neoclassical economics can be found in J. Kornai, *Anti-Equilibrium: On Economic Systems, Theory and the Tasks of Research* (Amsterdam: North-Holland, 1971); and, especially, in M. Hollis and E. J. Neil, *Rational Economic Man: A Philosophical Critique of Neo-Classical Economics* (New York: Cambridge University Press, 1975). On the role of values, institutions, and theories in traditional economics and their limited relevance for Third World countries, see Gunnar Myrdal, *The Challenge of World Poverty* (New York: Pantheon, 1970), Part I.

Additional readings can be found on p. 613.

2

DIVERSE STRUCTURES AND COMMON CHARACTERISTICS OF DEVELOPING NATIONS

Of course there must be differences between developing countries . . . [but] to maintain that no common ground exists is to make any discussion outside or across the frontiers of a single country meaningless.
Julian West, Oxford University

The Third World is important because of the massiveness of its poverty.
Padma Desai, Delhi School of Economics and Harvard University

SIMILARITY WITHIN DIVERSITY

It is hazardous to try to generalize too much about the 143 member countries of the United Nations (UN) that constitute the Third World. While almost all are poor in money terms, they are diverse in culture, economic conditions, and social and political structures. Thus, for example, low-income countries include India with over 740 million people and 17 states as well as Belize with less than 100,000 people, fewer than most large towns in the United States. Large size entails complex problems of national cohesion and administration while offering the benefits of relatively large markets, a wide range of resources, and the potential for self-sufficiency and economic diversity. In contrast, for many small countries the situation is reversed, with problems including limited markets, shortages of skills, scarce physical resources, weak bargaining power, and little prospect of significant economic self-reliance.

In attempting to classify countries, some analysts, using the UN classification system, prefer to distinguish among three major groups within the Third World: the 42 poorest countries designated by the United Nations as "least developed,"[1] the 88 non-oil-exporting "developing nations,"[2] and the 13 petroleum-rich OPEC countries whose national incomes increased dramatically during the 1970s. Others follow the classification system established by the Organization for Economic Cooperation and Development (OECD) in Paris, which divides the Third World (including countries and territories not in the UN system) into 62 low-income countries (LICs) (i.e., those with a 1980 per capita income of less than $600, including 29 least-developed countries, or LLDCs), 73 middle-income countries (MICs), 11 newly industrializing countries (NICs), and the 13 members of OPEC. Table 2.1 provides a complete listing of the 159 countries included in the OECD classification scheme.[3]

Finally the International Bank for Reconstruction and Development (IBRD), more commonly known as the World Bank, has its own classification system. It divides all countries (both developing and developed) into six categories: low income, middle income, upper middle income, high-income oil exporters, industrial market economies, and East European non-market economies. The first four groups comprise the 143 countries of the Third World while the last two represent the 29 so-called First and Second World nations. Table A2.2, at the end of this chapter, provides a complete listing of these 172 developing and developed countries based largely on the World Bank's classification system with relevant economic and social data for each.

Despite the obvious diversity of countries and classification schemes, however, most Third World nations share a set of common and well-defined goals. These include the reduction of poverty, inequality, and unemployment; the provision of minimum levels of education, health, housing, and food to every citizen; the broadening of economic and social opportunities; and the forging of a cohesive nation-state. Related to these economic, social, and political goals are the common problems shared in varying degrees by most developing countries: widespread and chronic absolute poverty; high and rising levels of unemployment and underemployment; wide and growing disparities in the distribution of income; low and stagnating levels of agricultural productivity; sizable and growing imbalances between urban and rural levels of living and economic opportunities; antiquated and inappropriate educational and health systems; severe balance of payments and international debt problems; and substantial and increasing dependence on foreign and often inappropriate technologies, institutions, and value systems. It therefore *is* possible and useful to talk about the similarities of critical development problems and to analyze these problems in a broad Third World perspective. This will be our task in Parts II and III.

For the present, we attempt to identify some of the most important structural *differences* among developing countries and then provide relevant data to delineate some of their most *common* characteristic features. In spite of obvious physical, demographic, historical, cultural, and structural differences, most Third World nations share a common set of economic and social dilemmas that define their state of underdevelopment.

Table 2.1 Developing Countries and Territories by Income Group: OECD Classification System

LICs: 62 low-income countries		MICs: 73 middle-income countries	
* Afghanistan	* Maldives	Bahamas	Malta
Angola	* Mali	Bahrain	Martinique
* Bangladesh	Mauritania	Barbados	Mauritius
* Benin	Mayotte	Belize	Morocco
* Bhutan	Mozambique	Bermuda	Nauru
Bolivia	* Nepal	Botswana	Netherlands Antilles
Burma	* Niger	Brunei	New Caledonia
* Burundi	Pakistan	Cameroon	Nicaragua
* Cape Verde	* Rwanda	Chile	Niue Island
* Central African Republic	St. Helena	Colombia	Oman
China	Sao Tome and Principe	Congo	Pacific Islands (U.S.)
* Chad	Senegal	Cook Islands	Panama
* Comoros	Sierra Leone	Costa Rica	Papua New Guinea
Djibouti	Solomon Islands (Br.)	Cuba	Paraguay
Egypt	* Somalia	Cyprus	Peru
El Salvador	Sri Lanka	Dominican Republic	Philippines
Equatorial Guinea	* Sudan	Falkland Islands	Polynesia, French
* Ethiopia	* Tanzania	Fiji	Reunion
* Gambia	Togo	Gibraltar	St. Pierre and Miquelon
Ghana	Tokelau Islands	Guadeloupe	Seychelles
* Guinea	Tonga	Guatemala	Surinam
* Guinea-Bissau	Tuvalu	Guiana, French	Swaziland
* Haiti	* Uganda	Guyana	Syria
Honduras	* Upper Volta	Israel	Thailand
India	Vanuatu	Ivory Coast	Trinidad and Tobago
Kampuchea	Viet Nam	Jamaica	Tunisia
Kenya	* Yemen, North	Jordan	Turkey
* Laos	* Yemen, South	Kiribati	Uruguay
* Lesotho	Zaire	Lebanon	Wallis and Futuna
Liberia	Zambia	Macao	Western Samoa
Madagascar		Malaysia	West Indies
* Malawi			Zimbabwe

NICS: 11 newly industrializing countries	OPEC: 13 Organization of Petroleum Exporting Countries	
Argentina	Algeria	Libya
Brazil	Ecuador	Nigeria
Greece	Gabon	Qatar
Hong Kong	Indonesia	Saudi Arabia
South Korea	Iran	United Arab
Mexico	Iraq	Emirates
Portugal	Kuwait	Venezuela
Singapore		
Spain		
Taiwan		
Yugoslavia		

* LLDC (29 least-developed countries).

AN OVERVIEW OF THE DIVERSE STRUCTURE
OF THIRD WORLD ECONOMIES

With regard to structural diversity of developing nations, we can list the following seven major components:

1. The size of the country (geographic, population, and income)
2. Historical evolution
3. Physical and human resource endowments
4. The relative importance of public and private sectors
5. The nature of the industrial structure
6. The degree of dependence on external economic and political forces
7. The distribution of power and the institutional and political structure within the nation

Let us briefly consider each component, focusing on some similarities and differences among countries in Africa, Asia, and Latin America.

Size and Income Level

Obviously, the sheer physical size of a country, the size of its population, and its level of national income per capita are important determinants of its economic potential and major factors differentiating one Third World nation from another. Of the 143 developing countries that are full members of the United Nations, 104 have less than 15 million people and 75 less than 5 million. Large and populated nations like Brazil, India, Egypt, and Nigeria exist side by side with small countries like Paraguay, Nepal, Jordan, and Chad. Large size usually presents advantages of diverse resource endowment, large potential markets, and a lesser dependence on foreign sources of materials and products. But it also creates problems of administrative control, national cohesion, and regional imbalances. As we shall see in Chapter 5, there is no necessary relationship between a country's size, its level of per capita national income, and the degree of equality or inequality in its distribution of that income. Even excluding the wealthy OPEC oil states, India with a population of over 740 million has an annual per capital income level of less than $265 while nearby Singapore with less than 2.6 million people has an annual GNP per capita of over $5,900.

Historical Background

Most African and Asian nations were at one time or another colonies of Western European countries, primarily Britain and France but also Belgium, the Netherlands, Germany, Portugal, and Spain. The economic structures of these nations as well as their educational and social institutions have typically been modeled on those of their former colonial rulers. Countries like those in Africa that only recently gained their independence are therefore likely to be more concerned with consolidating and evolving their own national economic and political structures than with simply promoting rapid economic development. Their policies (e.g., the rapid Africanization of former colonial-held civil service jobs) may consequently reflect a greater interest with these immediate political issues.

In Latin America, a longer history of political independence plus a more shared colonial heritage (i.e., Spanish and Portuguese) has meant that in spite of geographical and demographic diversity, the countries possess relatively similar economic, social, and cultural institutions and face similar problems. In Asia, different colonial heritages and the diverse cultural traditions of the indigenous peoples have combined to create different institutional and social patterns in countries such as India (British), the Philippines (Spanish and American), Viet Nam (French), and Indonesia (Dutch).

Physical and Human Resource Endowments

A country's potential for economic growth is greatly influenced by its physical resource endowment (its land, minerals, and other raw materials) and by its endowment of human resources (i.e., both numbers of people and their level of skills). The extreme case of favorable physical resource endowments is, of course, the Persian Gulf oil states. At the other extreme are countries like Chad, Yemen, Haiti, and Bangladesh where endowments of raw materials and minerals as well as fertile land are relatively minimal.

In the realm of human resource endowments, not only are sheer numbers of people and their skill levels important but so also are their cultural outlooks, attitudes toward work, and desire for self-improvement. Moreover, the level of administrative skills will often determine the ability of the public sector to alter the structure of production and the time in which such structural alteration can occur. Here one gets involved with the whole complex of interrelationships between culture, tradition, religion, and ethnic and tribal fragmentation or cohesion. Thus the nature and character of a country's human resources are important determinants of its economic structure (see Chapter 11), and these clearly differ from one region to the next.

Relative Importance of Public and Private Sectors

Most Third World countries have "mixed" economic systems; there is both public and private ownership and use of resources. The division between the two and their relative importance is mostly a function of historical and political circumstances. Thus, in general, Latin American nations have larger private sectors than do Asian and especially African nations. The degree of foreign ownership in the private sector is another important variable to consider when differentiating among LDCs. A large foreign-owned private sector usually creates economic and political opportunities as well as problems not found in countries where foreign investors are less prevalent. Often countries like those in Africa with severe shortages of skilled human resources tend to put greater emphasis on public sector activities and state-run enterprises on the assumption that limited skilled manpower can be best used by coordinating rather than fragmenting administrative and entrepreneurial activities. The widespread economic failures and financial difficulties of many of these public concerns in countries such as Ghana, Senegal, Kenya, and Tanzania raise questions, however, about the validity of this assumption.

Economic policies, for example those designed to promote more employment, will naturally be different for countries with large public sectors from those with sizable private sectors. In economies dominated by the public sector, direct government investment projects and large rural works programs will take precedence, whereas in private-oriented economies special tax allowances designed to induce private businessmen to employ more workers might be more common. Thus, although the problem (widespread unemployment) may be similar, the solution can differ in countries with significant differences in the relative importance of their public and private sectors.

Industrial Structure

The vast majority of developing countries are agrarian in economic, social, and cultural outlook. Agriculture, both subsistence and commercial, is the principal economic activity in terms of the occupational distribution of the labor force, if not in terms of proportionate contributions to the gross national product. As we shall see in Chapter 10, farming is not only an occupation but a way of life for most people in Asia, Africa, and Latin America. Nevertheless, there are great differences between the structure of agrarian systems and patterns of land ownership in Latin America and Africa. Asian agrarian systems are somewhat closer to those of Latin America in terms of patterns of land ownership, but the similarities are lessened by substantial cultural differences.

It is in the relative importance of both the manufacturing and service sectors that we find the widest variation among developing nations. Most Latin American countries, having a longer history of independence and, in general, higher levels of national income than African or Asian nations, possess more advanced industrial sectors. But in the 1960s and 1970s countries like Taiwan, South Korea, Hong Kong, and Singapore greatly accelerated the growth of their manufacturing outputs and are rapidly becoming industrialized states. In terms of sheer size, India has one of the largest manufacturing sectors in the Third World, but this sector is nevertheless small in relation to its enormous rural population. Table 2.2 provides information on the percentage distribution of labor force and gross domestic product (GDP) between agriculture and manufacturing in 17 developing countries as well as in the United States and the United Kingdom. The contrasts among the industrial structures of these countries is striking, especially in terms of the relative importance of agriculture.

In spite of common problems, therefore, Third World development strategies may vary from one country to the next depending on the nature, structure, and degree of interdependence among its primary (agriculture, forestry, and fishing), secondary (mostly manufacturing), and tertiary (commerce, finance, transport, and services) industrial sectors.

External Dependence: Economic, Political, and Cultural

The degree to which a country is dependent on foreign economic, social, and political forces will be related to its size, resource endowment, and political history. For most Third World countries, this dependence is substantial. In

Table 2.2 Industrial Structure in 17 Developing Countries, the United States, and the United Kingdom, 1982

	Percentage of labor force		Percentage of gross domestic product	
	Agriculture	*Manufacturing*	*Agriculture*	*Manufacturing*
Africa				
Tanzania	83	6	52	9
Kenya	78	10	32	13
Nigeria	54	19	23	6
Uganda	83	6	75	4
Zaire	75	13	32	3
Asia				
Bangladesh	74	11	54	8
India	69	13	37	18
Indonesia	55	15	24	12
Philippines	46	17	23	25
Sri Lanka	54	14	28	16
South Korea	34	29	17	28
Latin America				
Mexico	36	26	8	22
Guatemala	55	21	—	—
Colombia	26	21	27	21
Brazil	30	24	13	27
Peru	39	18	9	25
Venezuela	21	18	27	15
United States	2	32	3	23
United Kingdom	2	42	2	20

SOURCE: International Bank for Reconstruction and Development, *World Development Report, 1984* (New York: Oxford University Press, 1984), Annex Tables 3 and 21. (Subsequent references to this source are given simply as *World Development Report* with appropriate year.)

some cases, it touches almost every facet of life. Most small nations are very dependent on their foreign trade with the developed world (see Chapter 12). Almost all small nations are dependent on the importation of foreign and often inappropriate technologies of production (Chapter 8). This fact alone exerts an extraordinary influence on the character of the growth process in these dependent nations.

But even beyond the strictly economic manifestations of dependence in the form of the international transfer of goods and technologies is the international transmission of institutions (most notably systems of education and health care), values, patterns of consumption, and attitudes toward life, work, and self. Later chapters show that this transmission phenomenon brings mixed blessings to most LDCs and especially to those with the greatest potential for more self-reliance. A country's ability to chart its own economic and social destiny is significantly affected by its degree of dependence on these and other external forces.

Political Structure, Power, and Interest Groups

In the final analysis, it is often not the correctness of economic policies alone that determines the outcome of national approaches to critical development problems. The political structure and the vested interests and allegiances of ruling elites (e.g., large landowners, urban industrialists, bankers, foreign manufacturers, the military, trade unionists) will typically determine what strategies are possible and where the main roadblocks to effective economic and social change may lie.

The constellation of interests and power among different segments of the populations of most developing countries will itself be the result of their economic, social, and political histories and is likely to differ from one country to the next. Nevertheless—whatever the specific distribution of power among the military, the industrialists, and the large landowners of Latin America; the politicians and high-level civil servants in Africa; the oil sheiks and financial moguls of the Middle East; or the landlords, money-lenders, and wealthy industrialists of Asia—most developing countries are ruled directly or indirectly by small and powerful elites to a greater extent than are the developed nations.

Effective social and economic change requires, therefore, either that the support of elite groups be enlisted through persuasion or coercion or that they be pushed aside by more powerful forces. Either way, and this point will be repeated often throughout this book, *economic and social development will often be impossible without corresponding changes in the social, political, and economic "institutions" of a nation* (e.g., land tenure systems, educational structures, labor market relationships, property rights, the distribution and control of physical and financial assets, laws of taxation and inheritance, and provision of credit).

COMMON CHARACTERISTICS OF DEVELOPING NATIONS

The preceding section should have demonstrated why it is sometimes risky to generalize too much about such a diverse set of nations as those in Africa, Asia, and Latin America. Nevertheless, common characteristic economic features of developing countries permit us to view them in a broadly similar framework. In this section we will attempt to identify these similarities and provide illustrative data to demonstrate their existence. For convenience, we can classify these common characteristics into six broad categories:

1. Low levels of living
2. Low levels of productivity
3. High rates of population growth and dependency burdens
4. High and rising levels of unemployment and underemployment
5. Significant dependence on agricultural production and primary product exports
6. Dominance, dependence, and vulnerability in international relations

Low Levels of Living

In developing nations, general levels of living tend to be very low for the vast majority of people. This is true not only in relation to their counterparts in rich nations but often also in relation to small elite groups within their own societies. These low levels of living are manifested quantitatively and qualitatively in the form of low incomes (poverty), inadequate housing, poor health, limited or no education, high infant mortality, low life and work expectancy, and in many cases, a general sense of malaise and hopelessness. Let us look at some recent statistics comparing certain aspects of life in the underdeveloped countries and in the more economically advanced nations. Although these statistics are national aggregates, often have substantial errors of measurement, and in some cases are not strictly comparable due to exchange rate variations, they do provide at least a summary indication of relative levels of living in different nations.

Per Capita National Incomes

The gross national product (GNP) per capita is often used as a summary index of the relative economic well-being of people in different nations. The GNP itself is the most commonly used measure of the overall level of economic activity. For example, by 1984, the total national product of all the nations of the world was valued at more than U.S. $12,500 billion of which more than $9,750 billion originated in the economically developed regions while less than $2,750 billion were generated in the less developed nations. When one takes account of the distribution of world population, this means that approximately 78% of the world's total income is produced in the economically developed regions by less than one-fourth of the world's people. More than three-fourths of the world's population, therefore, is producing only 22% of total world output. More importantly, on the income side, the Third World, with almost 76% of the world's population, subsists on less than 27% of the world's income. The collective *per capita* incomes of the underdeveloped countries average less than one-twelfth of the per capita incomes of rich nations.

As an illustration of the per capita income gap between rich and poor nations, look at Figure 2.1. Notice that in 1982 Switzerland had over 100 times the per capita income of one of the world's poorest countries, Bangladesh, and over 60 times that of one of the world's largest nations, India. Table A2.2 gives per capita income figures as well as other pertinent social and economic indicators of development for all nations of the world.[4]

Relative Growth Rates of National and Per Capita Incomes

In addition to having very much lower levels of per capita income, many Third World countries have experienced slower GNP growth than the developed nations. For example, the poorest countries (excluding India and China), designated by the UN classification system as "least developed," showed an average annual GNP growth rate amounting to only 1.1% between 1960 and 1982. The member nations classified by the UN as "developing" showed an average growth rate of approximately 3.2% during this same period. Taken together, non-oil-producing Third World nations showed an average GNP growth rate of approximately 3.1% per annum.

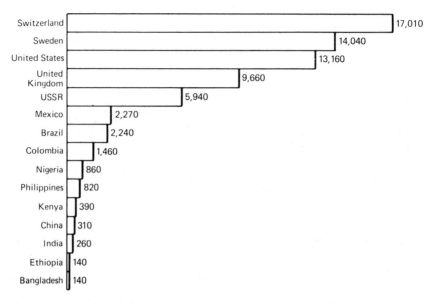

Figure 2.1. Per capita gross national product in selected countries, 1982. *Source: World Development Report, 1984*, Annex Table 1.

The average annual growth rate among all developed countries during this same period was approximately 3.4%. This means that the income gap between rich and least developed nations widened at a rate of 2.3% a year. Even though developing countries as a whole (including members of OPEC) grew at a faster rate than industrialized nations (3.8 compared to 3.4%), since the former started at a much lower base, the absolute income gap between all rich and poor nations continued to widen. Moreover, when one considers that the overall average annual rate of population growth in the developing countries as a whole is approximately 2.1% while that of the developed world is only 0.5% (see below), the actual gap between *per capita incomes* in all developed and non-OPEC less developed countries widened at an annual rate of 1.9%.[5] What is even more striking is the fact that there was little improvement in per capita income levels among the poorest Third World countries (i.e., their populations grew at almost the same rate as GNP) during the 1960s and 1970s—the first two "development decades."[6] No wonder one often hears the expression "the rich get richer, while the poor get children!"

Table 2.3 provides recent data on comparative trends in the growth of gross national product per capita between 1960 and 1982 for the same group of 17 developing countries as in Table 2.2.

The Distribution of National Income

The growing gap between per capita incomes in rich and poor nations is not the only manifestation of the widening economic disparity between the world's rich and poor. To appreciate the breadth and depth of Third World poverty, it is also necessary to look at the growing gap between rich and poor

Table 2.3 Growth Rates of GNP per capita,
Percentage Average Annual Growth, 1960−1982

Africa		Asia		Latin America	
Tanzania	1.9	Bangladesh	0.3	Mexico	3.7
Kenya	2.8	India	1.3	Guatemala	2.4
Nigeria	3.3	Indonesia	4.2	Colombia	3.1
Uganda	1.1	Philippines	2.8	Brazil	4.8
Zaire	−0.3	Sri Lanka	2.6	Peru	1.0
		South Koria	6.6	Venezuela	1.9

SOURCE: *World Development Report, 1984*, Annex Table 1.

within individual less developed countries. We discuss the question of income distribution and equity more fully in Chapter 5, but a few remarks at this point seem appropriate.

First, all nations of the world show some degree of inequality. One finds large disparities between incomes of the rich and poor in both developed and underdeveloped countries. Nevertheless, the gap between rich and poor is generally greater in less developed nations than in developed nations. For example, if we compare the share of national income that accrues to the poorest 40% of a country's population with that of the richest 20% as an arbitrary measure of the degree of inequality, we discover that countries like Brazil, Ecuador, Colombia, Peru, Mexico, Venezuela, Kenya, Sierra Leone, Philippines, and Malaysia have substantial income inequality; others like India, Tanzania, Chile, France, Denmark, and West Germany have moderate inequality; and yet others like Taiwan, Libya, Israel, Yugoslavia, Canada, Japan, the United States, and Czechoslovakia have relatively lesser inequalities in their overall income distribution. Moreover, there is no obvious relationship or correlation between levels of per capita income and degree of income inequality. The Philippines, with the same *low* per capita income as Taiwan, has a much wider income disparity between the top 20% and bottom 40% of the population. Similarly, Venezuela, with almost the same *high* per capita income as Japan, has a much lower percentage of its income distributed to the bottom 40% of its population.[7] This phenomenon underlines the important point that *economic development cannot be measured solely in terms of the level and growth of overall income or income per capita; one must also look at how that income is distributed among the population—that is, at who benefits from development.*

Extent of Poverty

The magnitude and extent of poverty in any country depend on two factors: (a) the average level of national income and (b) the degree of inequality in its distribution. Clearly, for any given level of national per capita income, the more unequal the distribution, the greater the incidence of poverty. Similarly, for any given distribution, the lower the average income level, the greater the incidence of poverty. But how is one to measure poverty in any meaningful quantitative sense?

During the 1970s, as interest in problems of poverty increased, development economists took the first step in measuring its magnitude within and across countries by attempting to establish a common poverty line. They went even further and devised the now widely used concept of "absolute poverty." It is meant to represent a specific minimum level of income needed to satisfy the basic physical needs of food, clothing, and shelter in order to assure "continued survival." A problem, however, arises when one recognizes that these minimum subsistence levels will vary from country to country and region to region, reflecting different physiological as well as social and economic requirements. Economists have therefore tended to make conservative estimates of world poverty in order to avoid unsubstantiated exaggerations of the problem. One common methodology has been to establish an "international poverty line" at, say, 75 constant U.S. dollars (based, for example, on the value of the 1970 dollar) and then attempt to estimate the "purchasing power equivalent" of that sum of money in terms of a developing country's own currency.

Table 2.4 presents some estimates of both the extent of absolute poverty (the proportion of a country's population with real incomes below the international poverty line) and its numerical magnitude (the actual number of people who can be classified as "absolutely poor"). The data are drawn up for 35 developing countries from Latin America, Asia, and Africa using 1983 population figures and 1975 poverty estimates from a well-known study by Ahluwalia, Carter, and Chenery. Using conservative estimates, the authors concluded that almost 40% of Third World populations were attempting to survive at absolute poverty levels. The proportions are much higher in a number of heavily populated low-income countries like Bangladesh (60%), India (46%), and Indonesia (62%). In terms of total numbers, we see from Table 2.4 that over 1,046 million Asians, 74 million Latin Americans, and 171 million Africans from our sample are barely achieving minimum subsistence incomes. If we then multiply the last figure in Column 3, representing the average proportion of Third World populations below the poverty line (35%), by the total population of developing countries in 1983 (3.5 billion), we arrive at the staggering figure of 1.2 billion people who may be classified as suffering from absolute poverty in the early 1980s! The figure is more likely to be around 873 million if one accepts China's claims that it has been able to abolish poverty (see Chapter 10). This is also the most recent and reliable World Bank estimate. Nevertheless, it still represents almost 27% of the total world population in 1983!

Finally, we can note once again from Table 2.4 that high per capita incomes do not necessarily preclude the existence of substantial absolute poverty. Since the degree of inequality of income distribution varies widely among countries, poverty can be equally serious in countries with very different per capita income levels. For example, if we compare Mexico with South Korea in Table 2.4, we discover that even though Mexico had a higher per capita GNP in 1981, it still had a considerably greater percentage of its population below the poverty line than did Korea (10% compared with 6%). Pakistan, with approximately the same income level as Sri Lanka, nevertheless had over three times the proportion of its population below the poverty line (34% compared with 10%). Even adjusting for measurement errors, these results are striking.

Table 2.4 Population below the Poverty Line in 35 Developing Countries, 1983

	Per capita gross national product, 1981 ($)	Population, 1983 (millions)	Percentage of population in poverty[1]	Number of people in poverty (millions)
Latin America (all countries)	**2,063**	**390.0**	**19**	**74.1**
Argentina	2,560	29.1	3	0.9
Brazil	2,220	131.3	8	10.5
Chile	2,770	11.5	9	1.0
Colombia	1,380	27.7	14	3.8
Guatemala	1,140	7.9	10	0.8
Mexico	2,250	75.7	10	7.6
Peru	1,170	19.2	15	2.9
Venezuela	4,220	18.0	5	.9
Asia (all countries except Japan)	**968**	**2,616.0**	**40**	**1,046.4**
Bangladesh	140	96.5	60	57.8
Burma	190	37.9	56	21.2
India	260	730.0	46	335.8
Indonesia	530	155.6	62	96.4
Iran	N/A	42.5	8	3.4
Malaysia	1,840	15.0	8	1.2
Pakistan	350	95.7	34	32.5
Philippines	790	52.8	29	15.3
South Korea	1,700	41.3	6	2.5
Sri Lanka	300	15.6	10	1.6
Taiwan	2,360	18.9	4	0.8
Thailand	770	50.8	23	11.7
Turkey	1,540	49.2	11	5.4
Africa (all countries)	**783**	**513.0**	**33**	**171.0**
Egypt	650	45.9	14	6.4
Ethiopia	140	31.3	62	19.4
Ghana	400	13.9	19	2.6
Ivory Coast	1,200	8.9	14	1.2
Kenya	420	18.6	48	8.9
Morocco	860	22.9	16	3.7
Nigeria	870	84.2	29	22.7
Senegal	430	6.1	29	1.8
Sudan	380	20.6	47	9.7
Tanzania	280	20.5	46	9.4
Tunisia	1,420	6.8	9	0.6
Uganda	220	13.8	45	6.2
Zaire	210	31.3	49	15.3
Zambia	600	6.2	7	0.4
All developing countries	**728**	**3,519.0**	**35**	**1,232.0**

[1]Note that the poverty percentages in Column (3) are for 1975 as estimated by Ahluwalia, *et al.* They are then applied to the 1983 population figures to calculate the 1983 poverty number estimates of Column (4).

SOURCE: Columns (1) and (2): Population Reference Bureau, *1983 World Population Data Sheet* (Washington, D.C., 1983); Column (3): M.S. Ahluwalia, N. Carter, and H. Chenery, "Growth and poverty in developing countries," *Journal of Development Economics* 6 (September 1979): Tables 1 and 2.

Health

In addition to struggling on low income, many people in Third World nations fight a constant battle against malnutrition, disease, and ill health. In the least developed countries of the world, life expectancy in 1984 averaged approximately 49 years compared with 57 years among other Third World countries and 72 years in developed nations. Infant mortality rates (i.e., the number of children who die before their first birthday out of every 1,000 live births) average about 124 in the least developed countries compared with approximately 86 in other less developed countries and 18 in developed countries. The rates for some specific countries are shown in Figure 2.2.

Table 2.5 is even more revealing. Over one billion people, almost half the population of the developing world (excluding China) in 1975, were living on diets deficient in essential calories. One-third of them were children under 2 years of age. These people were concentrated in the poorest countries and, within these poor countries, in the lowest income groups. In both Asia and Africa, over 60% of the population barely met minimum caloric requirements necessary to maintain adequate health. Moreover, it has been estimated that this caloric deficit amounted to less than 2% of the world cereal production in the 1970s. This contradicts the widely held view that malnutrition is the inevitable result of an imbalance between world population and world food supplies. The more likely explanation can be found in the enormous imbalance in world income distribution. Thus, malnutrition and poor health in the developing world are perhaps even more a matter of poverty than of food production, even though the two factors are indirectly interrelated.

Another often used measure of malnutrition is per capita daily protein consumption, which can vary from as high as 97 grams per day in the United

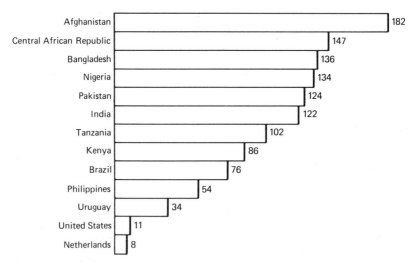

Figure 2.2. Infant mortality rates in selected countries, 1984 (per 1,000 live births). *Source:* Population Reference Bureau, *1984 World Population Data Sheet.*

Table 2.5 Population with Consumption below
Caloric Requirements, 1975

Region	People (millions)	Percentage of population
Latin America	112	36
Asia	707	63
Middle East	61	33
Africa	193	61
Total	1,073	55

SOURCE: S. Reutlinger and M. Selowsky, *Malnutrition and Poverty: Magnitude and Policy Options* (Baltimore: Johns Hopkins University Press, 1976). Published for The World Bank by The Johns Hopkins University Press.

States to 63, 48, and 43 grams per day in Brazil, India, and Ghana, respectively. In terms of world grain consumption, in the 1970s average annual consumption per person was approximately 650 kg in developed countries as contrasted with 180 kg in less developed countries.

Finally, medical care is an extremely scarce social service in many parts of the developing world. Recent data reveal that in the early 1980s the number of doctors per 100,000 people averaged only 9.7 in the least developed countries compared with 158 in the developed countries. The ratio of hospital beds to population is similarly divergent between these two sets of nations. Moreover, when one realizes that most of the medical facilities in developing nations are concentrated in urban areas where only 25% of the population resides, then the woefully inadequate provision of health care to the masses of poor people becomes strikingly clear. For example, in India 80% of the doctors practice in urban areas where only 20% of the population resides. In Bolivia, only one-third of the population lives in cities but 90% of the health facilities are found there. Finally, in Kenya, the population to doctor ratio is 672 to 1 for the capital city of Nairobi and 20,000 to 1 in the rural countryside where 87% of the Kenyan population lives.

Education

As a final illustration of the very low levels of living that are pervasive in Third World nations, consider the spread of educational opportunities. The attempt to provide primary school educational opportunities has probably been the most significant of all LDC development efforts. In most countries, education takes the largest share of the government budget. And yet, in spite of some impressive quantitative advances in school enrollments, literacy levels remain strikingly low compared with the developed nations. For example, among the least developed countries, literacy rates average only 37% of the population (see Table A2.2). The corresponding rates for other Third World nations and the developed countries are approximately 63 and 97% respectively. Moreover, as will be pointed out in Chapter 11, much of the education provided for those children who are able to attend school is ill suited and often irrelevant to the development needs of the nation.

Summarizing our discussion so far, we can list the following common characteristics of developing countries:

1. Low relative levels and, in many countries, slow growth rates of national income.
2. Low levels and, in many countries, stagnating rates of income per capita growth.
3. Highly skewed patterns of income distribution with the top 20% of the population often receiving five to ten times as much income as the bottom 40%.
4. As a result of (1)–(3) above, great masses of Third World populations suffering from absolute poverty, with anywhere from 850 to 1,200 million people living on subsistence incomes of less than $100 per year.
5. Large segments of the populations suffering from ill health, malnutrition and debilitating diseases—with infant mortality rates running as high as ten times those in developed nations.
6. In education, low levels of literacy, significant school dropout rates, and inadequate and often irrelevant educational curricula and facilities.

Most important is the interaction of *all* the above characteristics, which tends to reinforce and perpetuate the pervasive problems of "poverty, ignorance, and disease" that restrict the lives of so many people in the Third World.

Low Levels of Productivity

In addition to low levels of living, developing countries are characterized by relatively low levels of labor productivity. The concept of a production function systematically relating outputs to different combinations of factor inputs for a given technology is often used to describe the way in which societies go about providing for their material needs. But the technical, engineering concept of a production function needs to be supplemented by a broader conceptualization that includes among its "other" inputs managerial competence, worker motivations, and institutional flexibilities. Throughout the developing world, levels of labor productivity (output per worker) are extremely low compared with those in developed countries. This can be explained by a number of basic economic concepts.

For example, the principle of diminishing marginal productivity states that if increasing amounts of a variable factor (labor) are applied to fixed amounts of other factors (e.g., captial, land, materials), then beyond a certain number the extra or marginal product of the variable factor declines. Low levels of labor productivity can, therefore, be explained by the absence or severe lack of "complementary" factor inputs such as physical capital and/or experienced management.

To raise productivity, according to this argument, domestic *savings* and foreign *finance* must be mobilized to generate new investment in physical capital goods and also to build up the stock of human capital (e.g., managerial skills) through investment in education and training. Institutional changes are also necessary to maximize the potential of this new physical and human investment. These changes might include such diverse activities as the reform of land tenure, corporate tax, credit, and banking structures; the creation or strengthening of an independent, honest, and efficient administrative service; and the restructuring of educational and training programs to make them more appropriate to the needs of the developing societies. These and other noneconomic inputs into the "social" production function must be taken into account if strategies to raise productivity are to succeed. An old proverb says that "you can lead a horse to water, but you cannot make him drink." In underdeveloped nations it is equally true that "you can create the economic opportunities for self-improvement, but without the proper institutional and structural arrangements you cannot succeed."

One must also take into account the impact of worker and management *attitudes* toward self-improvement; their degree of alertness, adaptability, ambition, and general willingness to innovate and experiment; and their attitudes toward manual work, discipline, authority, and exploitation. Added to all these must be the physical and mental capacity of the individual to do the job satisfactorily.

The area of physical health most clearly reveals the close *linkage* that exists between low levels of income and low levels of productivity in developing nations. It is well known, for example, that poor nutrition in childhood can severely restrict the mental as well as the physical growth of individuals.[8] Poor dietary habits, inadequate foods, and low standards of personal hygiene in later years can cause further deterioration in a worker's health and, therefore, can adversely influence his attitudes toward his job and the people around him. His low productivity may be due in large part to physical lethargy and the inability, both physical and emotional, to withstand the daily pressures of competitive work.

We may conclude, therefore, that *low levels of living and low productivity are self-reinforcing social and economic phenomena in Third World countries and, as such, are the principal manifestations of and contributors to their underdevelopment.* Myrdal's well-known theory of "circular and cumulative causation" in underdeveloped countries is based on these interactions between low living levels and low productivity.[9]

High Rates of Population Growth and Dependency Burdens

Of the world's population of approximately 4.8 billion people in 1985, more than three-fourths live in Third World countries and less than one-fourth in the more developed nations. Both birth and death rates are strikingly different between the two groups of countries. Birthrates in less developed countries are generally at very high levels, on the order of 35–40 per 1,000, while those in the developed countries are less than half that figure. Indeed, as shown in Table 2.6 the crude birthrate (the yearly number of live births per 1,000 population) is probably one of the most efficient ways of distinguishing the less developed from the more developed countries. There are few less developed countries with a birthrate below 30 per 1,000 and no developed nation with a birthrate above it.

Death rates (the yearly number of deaths per 1,000 population) in Third World countries are also high relative to the more developed nations, but because of improved health conditions and the control of major infectious diseases, the LDC-DC death rate differences are substantially smaller than the corresponding differences in birthrates. As a result, the average rate of population growth is now about 2.1% per year in Third World countries

Table 2.6 Crude Birthrates throughout the World

	Country
50	Ethiopia, Mali, Kenya, Togo, Liberia, Zambia, Ivory Coast, Yemen, Nigeria, Bangladesh
45	Zaire, Sierra Leone, Uganda, Morocco, Sudan, Congo, Bolivia, Pakistan, Saudi Arabia
40	Lesotho, Burma, Iran, Ecuador, Peru, South Africa, Kampuchea, Egypt
35	India, Venezuela, Paraguay
30	Colombia, Malaysia, Turkey, Jamaica, Panama, Albania, Indonesia, Brazil, North Korea
25	Israel, South Korea
20	Poland, U.S.S.R., China, Ireland, Uruguay
15	United States, Canada, Australia, France, Greece, Cuba, Spain
10	Switzerland, Austria, Germany, Hungary, Japan

SOURCE: Population Reference Bureau, *1984 World Population Data Sheet.*

(2.4% excluding China) compared with population growth rates of 0.6% per year in the industrialized world.

A major implication of high LDC birthrates is that children under age 15 make up almost one-half of the total population in these countries, as opposed to approximately one-quarter of the total population in the developed countries. Thus in most developing countries the active labor force has to support proportionally almost twice as many children as it does in richer countries. On the other hand, the proportion of people over the age of 65 is much greater in the developed nations. Older people as well as children are often referred to as an economic "dependency burden" in the sense that they are nonproductive members of society and therefore must be supported financially by a country's labor force (usually defined as those between the ages of 15 and 64). The overall dependency burden (i.e., both young and old) represents only about one-third of the populations of developed countries compared with half of the populations of the less developed nations. Moreover, in the latter countries, over 90% of the dependents are children, whereas only 66% are children in the richer nations.

We may conclude, therefore, that not only are Third World countries characterized by higher rates of population growth, but they also must contend with greater dependency burdens than rich nations. The circumstances and conditions under which population growth becomes a deterrent to economic development is a critical issue and will be examined carefully in Chapter 7.

High and Rising Levels of Unemployment and Underemployment

One of the principal manifestations of and factors contributing to the low levels of living in developing nations is their relatively inadequate or inefficient utilization of labor in comparison with the developed nations.

Underutilization of labor is manifested in two forms. First, it occurs as underemployment—those people, both rural and urban, who are working less than they could (daily, weekly, or seasonally). Underemployment also includes those who are normally working full-time but whose productivity is so low that a reduction in hours would have a negligible impact on total output. The second form is open unemployment—those people who are able and often eager to work but for whom no suitable jobs are available.

Current rates of open unemployment in Third World areas average from 10 to 15% of the urban labor force. But this is only part of the story. Unemployment among young people aged 15 to 24, many of whom have a substantial education, is typically almost twice as high as the overall average. Table 2.7 provides some rough estimates of unemployment by age for eight selected Third World urban areas.

The data shown in Table 2.7 represent only the tip of the iceberg of LDC labor underutilization. When the *underemployed* are added to the openly unemployed, *almost 30% of the combined urban and rural labor forces in Third World nations is unutilized* (see Table 8.1).

Given recent and current birthrates in LDCs, their labor supply will be expanding rapidly for some time to come. This means that jobs will have to be created at equivalent rates simply to keep pace. Moreover, in urban areas where rural – urban migration is causing the labor force to grow at explosive annual rates of 5–7% in many countries (especially those in Africa), the prospects for coping effectively with rising levels of unemployment and underemployment and for dealing with the frustrations and anxieties of an increasingly vocal, educated, but unemployed youth are, to say the least, frighteningly poor. We will further examine the dimensions and implications of the unemployment and migration problem in Chapters 8 and 9.

Substantial Dependence on Agricultural Production and Primary Product Exports

The vast majority of people in Third World nations live and work in rural areas. Almost 80% are rurally based, compared with less than 35% in

Table 2.7 Rates of Urban Unemployment by Age: Selected Urban Areas of LDCs

Urban area	Ages 15–24	Ages 15 and over (total)
Ghana, large towns	21.9	11.6
Bogota, Colombia	23.1	13.6
Buenos Aires, Argentina	6.3	4.2
Chile, urban areas	12.0	6.0
Caracas, Venezuela	37.7	18.8
Bangkok, Thailand	7.7	3.4
Philippines, urban areas	20.6	11.6
Singapore	15.7	9.2

SOURCE: Edgar O. Edwards, *Employment in Developing Countries* (New York: Ford Foundation, 1973), Table 2.

economically developed countries. Similarly, 66% of the labor force is engaged in agriculture, compared with only 21% in developed nations. Agriculture contributes about 32% of the GNP of developing nations versus only 8% of the GNP of developed nations.

Small-Scale Agriculture

Table 2.8 provides a breakdown of population, labor force, and agricultural production by regions of the developed and the less developed world. Note in particular the striking difference between the proportionate size of the agricultural population in Africa and South Asia (68–63%) versus North America (5%). In terms of actual numbers, there were almost 685 million agricultural labor force members in Asia and Africa producing an annual volume of output valued at U.S. $189 million in 1984.[10] On the other hand, in North America, less than 1% of this total number of agricultural workers (4.5 million) produced over a quarter as much total output ($55 million). This means that the average productivity of agricultural labor expressed in U.S. dollars is almost 35 times greater in North America than in Asia and Africa combined. While international comparative figures such as these are often of extremely dubious quality both with regard to their precision and methods of measurement, they nevertheless give us rough orders of magnitude. Even adjusting them for, say, undervaluing Third World nonmarketed agricultural output, the differences in agricultural labor productivity would still be very sizable.

The basic reason for the concentration of people and production in agricultural and other primary production activities in developing countries is the simple fact that at low income levels the first priorities of any person are for food, clothing, and shelter. Agricultural productivity is low not only because of the large numbers of people in relation to available land but also

Table 2.8 Population, Labor Force, and Production in 1984: Developed and Less Developed Regions

	Population (millions)	Urban (%)	Rural (%)	Labor force in agriculture (%)	Agricultural share of GNP (%)
World	4,762	40	60	45	—
Less developed	3,596	32	68	60	26
Developed	1,166	71	29	7	4
Africa	531	29	71	68	28
South Asia	1,539	27	73	63	37
East Asia	1,243	29	71	51	23
Latin America	397	65	35	32	14
Europe	491	72	28	22	8
U.S.S.R.	274	64	36	32	22
North America	262	74	26	5	3
Japan	120	76	24	21	7

SOURCE: Population Reference Bureau, 1984 World Population Data Sheet; *World Development Report, 1984,* Annex Tables 3 and 19.

because LDC agriculture is often characterized by primitive technologies, poor organization, and limited physical and human capital inputs. Thus, technological backwardness arises because Third World agriculture is predominantly noncommercial peasant farming. In many parts of the world, especially in Asia and Latin America, it is characterized further by land tenure arrangements in which peasant proprietors usually rent rather than own their small plots of land. As we shall see in Chapter 10, such land tenure arrangements take away much of the economic incentive for output expansion and productivity improvement. Even where land is abundant, primitive techniques and the use of hand plows, drag harrows, and animal (oxen, buffalo, donkeys) or raw human power necessitate that typical family holdings be not more than 5−8 hectares (12−20 acres). In fact, in many countries average holdings can be as low as 1−3 hectares. The number of people this land must support both directly (through on-the-farm consumption) and indirectly (through production for urban and nonfarm rural food consumption) often runs as high as 10−15 people per hectare. It is no wonder, therefore, that efforts to improve the efficiency of agricultural production and increase the average per hectare yields of rice, wheat, maize, soybeans, and millet are now and will continue to be top-priority development objectives.

Dependence on Exports

Most economies of less developed countries are oriented toward the production of primary products as opposed to secondary (manufacturing) and tertiary (service) activities. These primary commodities form their main exports to other nations (both developed and less developed). For example, as Figure 2.3 shows, in 1980 for all Third World countries, these primary products (food, raw materials, fuels, and base metals) accounted for almost 80 percent of all exports. But except in those few countries blessed with abundant supplies of petroleum and other valuable mineral resources, basic foodstuffs and raw materials alone account for most LDC exports.

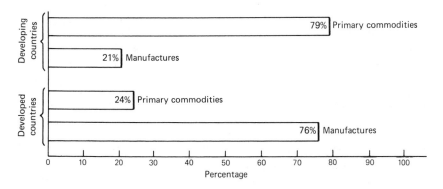

Figure 2.3. Composition of world exports, 1980 (percentages of primary and manufactured products). *Source:* Based on data in Overseas Development Council, *U.S. Foreign Policy and the Third World, Agenda 1983* (New York: Praeger, 1983), Table E-5.

As we shall see in Chapter 14, most poor countries need to obtain foreign exchange in addition to domestic savings in order to finance priority development projects. While private foreign investment flows, plus foreign aid, are a significant source of such foreign exchange, exports of primary products typically account for 60—75% of the annual flow of total foreign currency earnings into the developing world.

Even though exports loom so important in many developing nations, over the past twenty years export growth (excluding oil exports) has not kept pace with that of developed countries. Consequently, even in their best years, the non-oil-exporting developing nations have been losing ground in terms of their share of total world trade to the more developed countries. In 1950, for example, their share was nearly 33%. It has fallen in almost every year since, and by 1980 had fallen to nearly 21%. At the same time, the developed countries have increased their share of world trade (mostly by trading with each other) from 60 to 72%. Moreover, the percentage of total Third World exports going to each other dropped from 28 in 1960 to 25 by 1979. Thus, the less developed countries have become even more dependent on the rich countries for outlets for their products while their overall share of the world trade has been declining.[11]

This growing LDC dependence on rich country economies for flows of foreign exchange brings us to the last major common characteristic of Third World nations—their dependence on and occasional dominance by rich nations in the world economy.

Dominance, Dependence, and Vulnerability in International Relations

For many less developed countries, a significant factor contributing to the persistence of low levels of living, rising unemployment, and growing income inequality is the highly unequal distribution of economic and political power between rich and poor nations. As we shall see later, these unequal strengths are manifested not only in the dominant power of rich nations to control the pattern of international trade but also in their ability often to dictate the terms in which technology, foreign aid, and private capital are transferred to developing countries.

But other equally important aspects of the international transfer process serve to inhibit the development of poor nations. One subtle but nonetheless very significant factor contributing to the persistence of underdevelopment has been the transfer of First and Second World values, attitudes, institutions, and standards of behavior to Third World nations. Examples include the transfer of often inappropriate educational structures, curricula, and school systems; the formation of Western-style trade unions; the organization and orientation of health services in accordance with the Western model; and finally, the importation of inappropriate structures and procedures for public bureaucratic and administrative systems. Of even greater potential significance may be the influence of rich-country social and economic standards on developing-country salary scales, elite life-styles, and general attitudes toward the private accumulation of wealth. Such attitudes can often breed corruption and economic plunder by a privileged minority. Finally, the penetration of rich-country attitudes, values, and standards also contributes to a problem widely recognized and referred to as the "international brain drain"—the migration of professional and skilled personnel, who were often educated in the developing country at great expense, to the various developed nations. Examples include doctors, nurses, engineers, and economists.

The net effect of all these factors is to create a situation of "vulnerability" among Third World nations in which forces largely outside their control can have decisive and dominating influences on their overall economic and social well-being. Many countries—most of the 42 least developed certainly—are small, and their economies are dependent, with very little prospect for self-reliance. Their withdrawal from the world economy is virtually impossible. But, as we shall see in Chapter 13, hope can be found in their joining forces economically to promote some form of collective self-reliance. Such cooperation can also strengthen the joint bargaining power of small nations and enable them to scrutinize more carefully and be more selective about foreign investment and technical assistance.

For Third World nations that possess greater assets and relatively more bargaining power, the phenomenon of dominance becomes manifested more in the general tendency of the rich to get richer, often at the expense of the poor. But, as mentioned, this is not simply a matter of rich nations growing at a faster pace than poor nations. It is also a matter of the rich and dominating sectors or groups *within* the LDC economy (e.g., the modern industrial or agricultural sector; landlords, trade union leaders, industrialists, politicians, bureaucrats, and civil servants in positions of power) growing richer often at the expense of the much larger but politically and economically less powerful masses of poor people. This dual process of rich nations and powerful groups within poor nations prospering while others stagnate is by no means an isolated phenomenon. We shall see that it is a rather common characteristic of international economic relations when we discuss the concept of dualism and dual societies in the next chapter.

CONCLUSION

The phenomenon of underdevelopment needs to be viewed in a national and an international context. Economic and social forces, both internal and external, are responsible for the poverty, inequality, and low productivity that characterize most Third World nations. The successful pursuit of economic and social development will require not only the formulation of appropriate strategies within the Third World but also a modification of the present international economic order to make it more responsive to the development needs of poor nations. But in order to formulate such domestic strategies and to suggest such international modifications, it is essential that we start with a fairly clear idea about what we mean when we use the words "development" and "underdevelopment." This will be our objective in Chapter 3.

NOTES

1. These countries are sometimes even referred to as the Fourth World to underline their situation as the "poorest of the poor" Third World countries and their special

need for international assistance. For a description and analysis, see H.C. Low and J.W. Howe, "Focus on the Fourth World," in *The US and World Development: Agenda for Action 1975*, published for the Overseas Development Council by Praeger (New York, 1975), pp. 35–54.

2. Whether most of these countries are actually developing is an open question. It all depends on one's definition of development (see Chapter 3). However, for expository convenience and in order to avoid semantic confusion we will use the adjectives "developing," "less developed," and "underdeveloped" interchangeably throughout the text when referring to Third World countries as a whole. To do otherwise would unnecessarily complicate the discussion.

3. The well-known Brandt Commission report (see Reading 2 in my reader, *The Struggle for Economic Development*) has adopted a classification system similar to that of the OECD by dividing Third World countries into three groups: low-income countries, newly industrializing countries (NICs) and oil exporters. [The NICs again include countries like Brazil, Argentina, South Korea, Taiwan, Mexico, and Singapore, which are rapidly developing a diversified manufacturing and industrial capability.]

4. By the end of the 1974–1975 oil price boom, countries like Kuwait, Qatar, and the United Arab Emirates all had per capita incomes greatly in excess of that of the United States. Yet in terms of total "wealth" (i.e., accumulated physical and financial assets) the United States is still far ahead of the rest of the world even though, according to the 1984 edition of the *World Development Report* in per capita terms, Switzerland ($17,010), Norway ($14,280), and Sweden ($14,040) had surpassed the United States ($13,160).

5. Recall that the rate of growth of per capita income is simply measured as the difference between GNP growth and population growth.

6. Naturally, within the group of Third World nations there are instances of much better and much worse economic performances than the overall average (see Table A2.2).

7. For specific country-by-country data, see Hollis Chenery *et al.*, *Redistribution with Growth* (London: Oxford, 1974), pp. 8–9.

8. See, for example, Alan Berg *et al.* (eds.), *Nutrition, National Development and Planning* (Cambridge, Mass.: MIT Press, 1973), Parts 1 and 2.

9. See, for example, Gunnar Myrdal, *Asian Drama* (New York: Pantheon, 1968), Appendix 2.

10. The total value of actual agricultural output was probably somewhat higher than this figure since much of the food output in LDCs is consumed directly by farm families and, therefore, not always estimated in aggregate production figures.

11. The share has risen slightly since 1973 but this has been due solely to the spectacular increase in export earnings of OPEC nations. For the rest of the Third World, there has been a continuing decline in their share of world trade (see Chapter 12).

CONCEPTS FOR REVIEW

Per capita income	Labor productivity
Income gap	Crude birthrate
Income inequality	Death rate
Absolute poverty	Dependency burden
Levels of living	Open unemployment
Infant mortality	Underemployment
Malnutrition	Exports
Literacy	Foreign exchange

QUESTIONS FOR DISCUSSION

1. Explain the many ways in which Third World countries may differ in their economic, social, and political structures. They are linked together by a range of common

problems. What are these common problems? Which do you think are the most important? Why?

2. Explain the distinction between low levels of living and low per capita incomes. Can there exist low levels of living simultaneous with high levels of per capita income? Explain and give some examples.

3. What are some common characteristics of less developed countries? Can you think of others not mentioned in the text?

4. What are the advantages and disadvantages of using a concept such as an international poverty line? Do you think that a real annual income of $150 in, say, Mexico has the same meaning as in, say, Nigeria or Thailand? Explain your answer.

5. Do you think that there is a strong relationship between health, labor productivity, and income levels? Explain.

6. What is meant by the statement that many Third World nations are subject to "dominance, dependence, and vulnerability" in their relations with rich nations? Can you give some examples?

FURTHER READINGS

1. For a concise but very informative summary of the diverse structures and the major economic characteristics of Third World Nations, see Lester Pearson *et al.*, *Partners in Development: Report of the Commission on International Development* (New York: Praeger, 1969), Annex I, pp. 231 – 353. See also J.A. Raffaele, *The Economic Development of Nations* (New York: Random House, 1971). For regional surveys, see Gunnar Myrdal, *Asian Drama* (New York: Pantheon, 1968); P. Robson and D. Lury (eds.), *The Economies of Africa* (London: Allen and Unwin, 1969); and Celso Furtado, *Economic Development in Latin America* (London: Cambridge University Press, 1970). More recent material can be found in 3 volumes of readings and statistics edited by Pradip K. Ghosh and entitled *Developing South Asia, Developing Africa,* and *Developing Latin America* (Westport, Conn.: Greenwood Press, 1984).

2. Information on current economic trends within individual Third World countries and regions can best be obtained from the annual *World Development Report* published by the World Bank and from various United Nations publications including the annual *Statistical Yearbook* and the regular publications of the UN Economic Commission for Latin America (ECLA), for Africa (ECA), and for Asia and the Pacific (ESCAP). Concise statistical summaries can also be obtained from the annual *World Bank Atlas.* The World Bank (IBRD) and International Monetary Fund (IMF) also carry out studies of individual countries—see their current publications list for the most recent titles.

Additional readings can be found on pp. 613 – 615.

APPENDIX 2.1

STATISTICAL RANKINGS OF THIRD WORLD COUNTRIES

Table A2.1 Relative Ranking of 14 Third World Countries by Various Indices of Development, 1982–1984

I. Per capita income levels (highest to lowest)	II. Per capita growth rates (highest to lowest)	III. Income distribution ratio: bottom 40% to top 20% of population (highest to lowest)
1. Mexico	1. South Korea	1. Bangladesh
2. Brazil	2. Brazil	2. South Korea
3. South Korea	3. Thailand	3. India
4. Colombia	4. Mexico	4. Thailand
5. Peru	5. Nigeria	5. Philippines
6. Nigeria	6. Colombia	6. Mexico
7. Philippines	7. Kenya	7. Kenya
8. Thailand	8. Pakistan, Philippines	8. Peru
9. Zambia	9. India	9. Brazil
10. Kenya	10. Peru	10. n/a: Pakistan, Zambia, Colombia, Nigeria, Ghana
11. Ghana	11. Bangladesh	
12. Pakistan	12. Zambia	
13. India	13. Ghana	
14. Bangladesh	14. —	

IV. Literacy (% of population, highest to lowest)	V. Population growth rates (highest to lowest)	VI. Infant mortality rates (lowest to highest)
1. South Korea	1. Kenya	1. South Korea
2. Thailand	2. Nigeria	2. Thailand, Philippines
3. Mexico	3. Zambia, Ghana	3. Mexico
4. Colombia	4. Bangladesh	4. Colombia
5. Peru	5. Pakistan	5. Brazil
6. Brazil	6. Philipppines, Mexico	6. Kenya
7. Philippines	7. Peru	7. Peru
8. Kenya	8. Brazil	8. Ghana
9. Zambia	9. India	9. Zambia
10. India	10. Colombia	10. Pakistan
11. Nigeria	11. Thailand	11. India
12. Bangladesh	12. South Korea	12. Nigeria
13. Pakistan	13. —	13. Bangladesh
14. n/a: Ghana	14. —	14. —

SOURCE: Rankings given in II, III, and IV are from *World Development Report, 1984*, Annex Tables 1, 28; rankings in I, V, and VI are from Population Reference Bureau, *1984 World Population Data Sheet*.

Table A2.2 Economic and Social Indicators of Development, 1981—1984

	Population, mid-1984	Per capita GNP, 1982	Per capita GNP (real) growth rate, 1970—1981	Physical Quality of Life Index (PQLI)[a]	Birth rate per 1,000	Death rate per 1,000
	(millions)	($)	(%)			
Low-income (40) (per capita GNP< $400)	2,353.7	285.2	2.5	56	31	12
(excluding People's Republic of China)	1,319.6	252	1.2	42	39	16
Africa (26)	213.7	260	—0.7	37	47	20
*Benin	3.9	310	1.3	33	49	19
*Burundi	4.7	280	1.6	30	47	21
*Cape Verde	0.3	350	3.8	57	35	8
*Central African Republic	2.6	310	—0.4	34	46	20
*Chad	5.0	80	—5.0	24	44	23
*Comoros	0.5	340	—3.3	50	46	17
Equatorial Guinea	0.3	175	2.8	38	42	18
*Ethiopia	32.0	140	0.7	24	47	23
*Gambia	0.7	360	1.6	20	49	28
*Guinea	5.6	310	0.1	28	47	19
*Guinea-Bissau	0.8	170	0.3	29	42	22
Madagascar	9.8	320	—1.9	49	46	18
*Malawi	6.9	210	2.3	31	51	19
*Mali	7.6	180	2.0	23	46	22
Mozambique	13.4	240	—6.2	38	45	17
*Niger	6.3	310	0.2	23	51	22
*Rwanda	5.8	260	1.8	46	49	18
São Tomé and Principe	0.1	370	0.3	n/a	39	10
Sierra Leone	3.9	390	—1.0	24	39	19
*Somalia	5.7	290	1.0	23	47	21
*Sudan	21.1	400	0.5	34	47	17
*Tanzania, Unit. Rep.	21.2	280	1.6	58	46	14
Togo	2.9	340	—0.6	34	47	18
*Uganda	14.3	230	—4.3	52	46	15
*Upper Volta	6.7	210	1.8	18	48	22
Zaire	32.2	190	—3.1	48	46	17
Asia (13)	2,137.0	287	2.8	58	30	11
*Afghanistan	14.4	170	1.3	17	48	23
*Bangladesh	99.6	140	1.5	35	49	18
*Bhutan	n/a	120	—0.1	23	41	18
Burma	38.9	190	2.3	59	38	14
China, People's Republic	1,034.5	310	4.1	75	21	8

Life expectancy at birth (years)	Infant mortality per 1,000 live births	Literacy (%)	Per capita public education expenditures ($)	Per capita military expenditures ($)	Total exports, FOB 1981 ($ millions)	Total imports, CIF 1981 ($ millions)
56	89	50	10	19	42,303	59,452
49	124	37	6	9	22,414	40,084
45	129	34	10	21	8,490	11,953
47	153	25	14	5	36	886
42	121	23	5	6	71	165
61	81	37	n/a	n/a	4	75
43	147	39	12	6	136	88
40	147	15	3	9	141	137
47	92	58	n/a	n/a	20	33
46	142	38	n/a	24	26	58
40	146	15	3	12	431	842
41	197	15	15	0	25	164
45	164	20	12	0	428	351
42	147	28	n/a	n/a	15	52
47	70	50	17	10	335	494
47	170	25	5	8	380	360
43	153	9	8	6	154	370
47	114	28	3	10	457	773
43	144	5	12	2	297	449
47	106	50	5	59	147	191
n/a	70	n/a	n/a	n/a	13	26
47	206	15	11	11	277	238
43	146	5	7	2	133	405
48	123	20	18	81	820	1,942
52	102	74	14	18	533	1,136
47	108	16	24	15	344	597
54	96	48	9	58	317	395
43	210	9	5	13	133	323
47	111	58	13	5	2,817	1,403
57	85	52	11	19	33,480	46,912
40	182	12	4	4	263	484
47	148	26	2	1	791	2,542
44	149	4	n/a	n/a	n/a	n/a
54	99	70	2	6	515	791
65	35	66	16	32	19,889	19,368

(Continued)

	Population, mid-1984	Per capita GNP, 1982	Per capita GNP (real) growth rate, 1970–1981	Physical Quality of Life Index (PQLI)[a]	Birth rate per 1,000	Death rate per 1,000
	(millions)	($)	(%)			
India	746.4	260	1.6	42	34	14
Kampuchea	6.1	110	0.3	21	38	19
*Lao People's Democratic Republic	3.7	110	−2.0	39	42	18
*Maldives	0.2	400	0.2	n/a	43	13
*Nepal	16.6	170	0.0	28	43	18
Pakistan	97.3	380	2.0	40	43	15
Sri Lanka	16.1	320	3.1	82	28	6
Viet Nam	58.3	190	−0.5	65	34	10
Latin America (1)	**5.5**	**300**	**1.6**	**41**	**36**	**14**
*Haiti	5.5	300	1.6	41	36	14
Lower middle-income (38) (per capita GNP $400–$999)	**544.6**	**716**	**3.1**	**55**	**39**	**14**
Africa (16)	**235.5**	**732**	**2.0**	**44**	**48**	**16**
Angola	7.8	790	−8.4	21	47	22
*Botswana	1.0	900	8.5	44	50	16
Cameroon	9.4	890	3.6	43	44	18
Djibouti	0.3	476	−4.4	n/a	47	21
Egypt	47.0	690	5.5	53	38	11
Ghana	14.3	360	−4.5	41	48	16
Kenya	19.4	390	3.1	55	53	13
*Lesotho	1.5	510	7.8	49	41	12
Liberia	2.2	490	−0.4	40	45	15
Mauritania	1.8	470	−0.5	27	50	22
Morocco	23.6	870	2.4	47	41	12
†Nigeria	88.1	860	2.3	38	49	12
Senegal	6.5	499	0.2	24	48	18
Swaziland	0.6	940	3.5	45	48	16
Zambia	6.6	640	−2.6	46	48	16
Zimbabwe	8.3	850	−1.5	63	47	13
Asia (6)	**273.2**	**676**	**4.4**	**62**	**33**	**13**
†Indonesia	161.6	580	4.6	55	34	13
Mongolia	1.9	780	3.1	81	36	8
Philippines	54.5	820	3.6	73	32	7
Thailand	51.7	790	4.3	76	26	6
*Yemen, Arab Republic	5.9	500	5.5	21	48	21

Life expectancy at birth	Infant mortality per 1,000 live births	Literacy	Per capita public education expenditures	Per capita military expenditures	Total exports, FOB 1981	Total imports, CIF 1981
(years)		(%)	($)	($)	($ millions)	($ millions)
50	125	36	6	6	7,844	15,169
43	201	36	n/a	n/a	43	103
45	128	41	n/a	10	9	85
48	120	82	n/a	n/a	9	36
44	149	19	2	1	63	195
51	124	24	5	12	2,881	5,410
66	37	85	5	2	1,020	1,938
66	100	87	6	17	153	791
52	**113**	**23**	**4**	**3**	**333**	**587**
52	113	23	4	3	333	587
52	**95**	**54**	**21**	**23**	**79,971**	**90,714**
50	**117**	**35**	**28**	**29**	**34,353**	**43,573**
42	153	5	17	0	1,744	1,640
50	82	33	58	35	460	600
47	108	41	19	10	1,862	1,760
n/a	n/a	5	n/a	n/a	32	293
56	80	44	19	46	3,233	8,782
50	102	30	12	5	878	1,184
55	86	50	23	18	1,216	2,121
52	120	52	8	0	45	320
54	153	25	29	7	1,141	1,942
43	142	17	17	47	325	571
57	106	28	49	44	2,160	4,487
49	134	29	34	27	18,727	18,776
43	146	10	18	4	416	1,035
47	134	55	39	11	230	466
50	105	44	26	4	1,170	915
53	73	71	22	52	714	590
53	**80**	**68**	**10**	**16**	**35,016**	**35,091**
49	92	62	6	12	22,101	13,520
64	54	95	50	80	36	26
61	54	75	12	13	5,756	8,864
61	54	84	18	24	6,784	10,330
43	160	8	18	68	39	1,699

 (Continued)

Table A2.2 Economic and Social Indicators of Development, 1981–1984 (*Continued*)

	Population, mid-1984	Per capita GNP, 1982	Per capita GNP (real) growth rate, 1970–1981	Physical Quality of Life Index (PQLI)[a]	Birth rate per 1,000	Death rate per 1,000
	(millions)	($)	(%)			
*Yemen, People's Democratic Republic of	2.1	470	9.6	37	48	19
Latin America (10)	**29.7**	**640**	**−0.3**	**74**	**32**	**10**
Bolivia	6.0	570	1.4	51	42	16
Cuba	9.9	n/a	−1.2	94	16	6
Dominica	n/a	710	−2.6	80	22	5
El Salvador	4.8	700	0.0	70	34	8
Grenada	0.1	760	−0.1	92	24	7
Guyana	0.8	670	0.7	87	28	8
Honduras	4.2	660	0.4	61	44	10
Nicaragua	2.9	920	−3.0	69	47	11
St. Lucia	0.1	720	2.0	83	33	7
St. Vincent	0.1	620	−0.6	87	25	6
Oceania (5)	**4.0**	**785**	**−0.1**	**48**	**43**	**15**
Pacific Island Trust Territory	0.1	920	−2.5	n/a	32	5
Papua New Guinea	3.4	820	−0.4	44	43	14
Solomon Islands	0.3	660	2.6	59	47	11
Tonga	0.1	480	0.9	85	13	2
*Western Samoa	0.2	850	3.1	86	38	8
Europe (1)	**2.9**	**840**	**4.2**	**80**	**28**	**7**
Albania	2.9	840	4.2	80	28	7
Upper middle-income (40) (per capita GNP $1,000–$3,499)	**692.0**	**2,171.2**	**3.7**	**72**	**32**	**9**
Africa (8)	**73.4**	**2,046.4**	**2.1**	**55**	**41**	**13**
†Algeria	21.4	2,350	3.0	49	44	11
Congo	1.7	1,180	1.3	44	44	18
Ivory Coast	9.2	1,050	1.4	41	46	17
Mauritius	1.0	1,240	4.8	81	23	7
Namibia	1.1	1,410	0.3	45	43	14
Seychelles	0.1	1,797	4.4	73	24	8
South Africa	31.7	2,670	1.0	62	35	10
Tunisia	7.0	1,390	5.2	62	33	7
Asia (10)	**171.3**	**2,083**	**4.5**	**72**	**33**	**9**

Life expectancy at birth (years)	Infant mortality per 1,000 live births	Literacy (%)	Per capita public education expenditures ($)	Per capita military expenditures ($)	Total exports, FOB 1981 ($ millions)	Total imports, CIF 1981 ($ millions)
45	144	40	21	56	300	652
62	**64**	**77**	**58**	**38**	**9,371**	**10,417**
50	130	63	20	18	884	1,212
74	17	95	122	79	5,800	6,000
65	12	94	n/a	n/a	29	29
64	44	62	24	10	794	962
70	15	98	n/a	n/a	27	49
70	43	92	58	19	422	416
58	87	60	20	15	846	986
56	89	90	19	23	529	731
70	23	82	n/a	n/a	26	20
65	60	96	n/a	n/a	14	12
51	**95**	**39**	**34**	**10**	**956**	**1,409**
n/a	31	n/a	n/a	n/a	n/a	n/a
52	103	32	34	10	860	1,224
65	70	60	n/a	n/a	68	87
61	21	100	n/a	n/a	11	34
63	40	98	n/a	n/a	17	64
70	**47**	**72**	**34**	**68**	**275**	**224**
70	47	72	34	68	275	224
63	**69**	**73**	**70**	**52**	**210,718**	**278,490**
56	**107**	**49**	**96**	**25**	**32,854**	**37,622**
57	116	35	131	33	14,056	11,505
47	128	50	56	34	1,040	791
47	126	41	97	13	2,586	2,434
65	30	85	68	2	283	543
52	95	38	n/a	n/a	24	103
65	19	58	n/a	n/a	6	69
61	95	57	81	27	12,650	18,254
59	98	62	67	9	2,209	3,923
63	**57**	**69**	**73**	**114**	**78,798**	**103,052**

 (Continued)

	Population, mid-1984	Per capita GNP, 1982	Per capita GNP (real) growth rate, 1970–1981	Physical Quality of Life Index (PQLI)[a]	Birth rate per 1,000	Death rate per 1,000
	(millions)	($)	(%)			
†Iran	43.8	1,940	–0.1	57	44	12
†Iraq	15.0	3,020	6.4	48	47	13
Jordan	3.5	1,623	4.9	69	47	10
Korea, Democratic People's Republic	19.2	1,130	3.8	81	32	8
Korea, Republic of	42.0	1,910	6.9	85	23	5
Lebanon	2.6	1,890	6.0	76	30	8
Macao	0.3	2,500	12.9	n/a	26	8
Malaysia	15.3	1,860	5.2	72	31	7
Syrian Arab Republic	10.1	1,680	5.4	69	46	8
Taiwan	19.2	2,503	7.0	87	23	5
Latin America (17)	**337.4**	**2,199.2**	**3.4**	**76**	**31**	**8**
Argentina	29.1	2,520	0.3	87	24	9
Belize	0.2	1,080	3.5	n/a	32	8
Brazil	134.4	2,240	5.2	72	31	8
Chile	11.9	2,210	0.1	84	24	6
Colombia	28.2	1,460	3.4	76	28	7
Costa Rica	2.5	1,280	2.4	89	31	4
Dominican Republic	6.3	1,330	3.1	58	35	9
†Ecuador	9.1	1,350	4.6	72	41	9
Guatemala	8.0	1,130	2.5	59	42	7
Jamaica	2.4	1,330	–3.0	89	26	6
Mexico	77.7	2,270	3.1	79	32	6
Panama	2.1	2,120	1.1	84	26	5
Paraguay	3.6	1,610	5.4	79	35	8
Peru	19.2	1,310	0.2	68	37	12
Puerto Rico	3.3	3,010	–0.5	92	22	6
Surinam	0.4	2,950	6.4	77	28	8
Uruguay	3.0	2,650	3.3	89	18	9
Oceania (1)	**0.7**	**1,950**	**2.7**	**85**	**29**	**6**
Fiji	0.7	1,950	2.7	85	29	6
Europe (4)	**103.4**	**2,308.4**	**4.4**	**75**	**25**	**10**
Portugal	10.1	2,450	1.8	82	16	10
Romania	22.7	2,560	9.2	91	18	9
Turkey	50.2	1,370	2.5	61	31	10
Yugoslavia	23.0	2,800	4.7	85	16	9

Life expectancy at birth (years)	Infant mortality per 1,000 live births	Literacy (%)	Per capita public education expenditures ($)	Per capita military expenditures ($)	Total exports, FOB 1981 ($ millions)	Total imports, CIF 1981 ($ millions)
55	106	50	111	119	10,169	12,634
56	77	24	84	211	9,372	18,907
60	69	70	53	120	682	3,907
64	34	90	34	70	593	659
66	34	93	52	86	20,224	25,092
66	41	68	n/a	77	1,106	3,946
n/a	18	79	n/a	n/a	638	523
64	31	60	82	57	11,198	11,581
66	61	58	69	238	2,205	4,603
72	9.1	82	66	120	22,611	21,200
63	**64**	**80**	**60**	**20**	**68,741**	**91,183**
70	38	93	75	55	7,905	10,017
70	27	91	n/a	n/a	79	161
63	76	76	64	14	19,732	22,995
68	23	89	70	88	3,911	6,246
63	56	81	20	9	3,103	4,813
72	18	90	92	0	968	1,198
61	67	67	24	18	1,174	1,601
61	81	81	43	24	2,562	2,332
59	66	46	19	12	1,393	1,690
71	28	90	72	9	945	1,372
66	55	81	80	10	21,233	29,132
70	25	78	74	8	317	2,880
65	46	84	14	13	296	600
58	101	80	20	25	3,649	4,200
73	19	88	n/a	n/a	n/a	n/a
68	36	65	n/a	n/a	517	526
70	34	94	48	59	957	1,420
62	**29**	**79**	**86**	**16**	**313**	**551**
62	29	79	86	16	313	551
65	**74**	**75**	**80**	**69**	**30,012**	**46,082**
71	26	70	75	70	4,145	9,762
71	29	98	106	64	10,235	11,542
62	121	60	48	57	4,703	8,961
70	30	85	122	97	10,929	15,817

(Continued)

	Population, mid-1984	Per capita GNP, 1982	Per capita GNP (real) growth rate, 1970−1981	Physical Quality of Life Index (PQLI)[a]	Birth rate per 1,000	Death rate per 1,000
	(millions)	($)	(%)			
High-income (54) (per capita GNP > $3,499)	**1,170.6**	**9,372**	**3.1**	**93**	**16**	**9**
Africa (3)	**4.6**	**7,123**	**−1.1**	**53**	**42**	**14**
†Gabon	1.0	4,000	1.7	30	35	20
†Libya	3.7	8,510	−1.9	55	46	13
Réunion	0.5	4,010	0.2	76	23	6
Asia (11)	**151.8**	**11,301**	**4.2**	**92**	**18**	**7**
Bahrain	0.4	9,280	3.6	66	32	6
Brunei	0.2	17,790	5.7	77	30	4
Hong Kong	5.4	5,340	7.1	95	16	5
•Israel	4.2	5,810	1.2	92	24	7
•Japan	119.9	10,080	3.8	98	13	6
†Kuwait	1.6	19,870	2.8	77	35	3
Oman	1.0	6,090	3.5	35	48	17
†Qatar	0.3	21,880	0.0	56	31	9
†Saudi Arabia	10.8	16,000	8.1	40	42	12
Singapore	2.5	5,910	6.9	86	17	5
†United Arab Emirates	1.5	23,770	1.7	68	30	7
Latin America (7)	**21.8**	**4,377**	**1.9**	**82**	**33**	**5**
Bahamas	0.2	3,830	−2.4	87	25	5
Barbados	0.3	3,500	3.1	92	17	8
Guadeloupe	0.3	4,200	4.6	85	19	6
Martinique	0.3	4,680	4.3	87	18	7
Netherlands Antilles	0.2	5,150	0.9	83	27	6
Trinidad and Tobago	1.2	6,840	4.2	89	25	6
†Venezuela	18.6	4,140	1.7	81	33	5
Oceania (5)	**19.1**	**10,973**	**1.2**	**95**	**16**	**7**
•Australia	15.5	11,140	1.4	96	16	8
French Polynesia	0.2	7,980	1.5	79	32	6
Guam	0.1	7,010	5.2	n/a	29	4
New Caledonia	0.1	7,000	−3.5	83	26	7
•New Zealand	3.2	7,920	0.5	95	16	8
Europe (26)	**704.7**	**7,765**	**3.3**	**93**	**15**	**10**

Life expectancy at birth (years)	Infant mortality per 1,000 live births	Literacy (%)	Per capita public education expenditures ($)	Per capita military expenditures ($)	Total exports, FOB 1981 ($ millions)	Total imports, CIF 1981 ($ millions)
72	20	97	422	356	1,632,160	1,619,895
54	94	45	321	160	18,702	17,120
45	116	12	151	108	2,196	956
57	99	50	358	171	16,391	15,414
65	14	63	n/a	n/a	115	750
74	18	90	497	298	365,999	266,452
69	53	40	186	381	3,541	4,386
66	13	64	230	808	3,565	703
73	10	90	n/a	n/a	21,820	24,772
73	14	88	389	1,464	5,381	9,501
76	7	99	508	83	151,500	142,868
70	23	60	541	705	16,561	8,042
50	127	20	94	902	4,416	2,221
59	53	34	2,667	4,762	3,978	1,571
55	112	16	521	1,837	113,328	35,268
71	11	75	108	194	20,970	27,571
64	53	56	226	1,321	20,939	9,549
66	40	83	136	40	29,893	32,594
69	22	90	n/a	n/a	1,769	5,307
71	23	99	154	7	200	515
70	26	83	n/a	n/a	110	546
70	16	88	n/a	n/a	125	622
62	25	93	n/a	n/a	4,485	9,977
70	26	95	155	13	3,570	2,869
67	42	82	135	42	19,634	12,758
73	12	100	476	196	27,798	32,798
75	10	100	505	213	21,796	26,186
62	41	95	n/a	n/a	28	268
n/a	16	n/a	n/a	n/a	18	155
64	30	91	n/a	n/a	349	450
72	12	99	336	111	5,607	5,739
71	22	98	321	327	883,403	927,785

(Continued)

Table A2.2 Economic and Social Indicators of Development, 1981–1984 (*Continued*)

	Population, mid-1984	Per capita GNP, 1982	Per capita GNP (real) growth rate, 1970–1981	Physical Quality of Life Index (PQLI)[a]	Birth rate per 1,000	Death rate per 1,000
	(millions)	($)	(%)			
•Austria	7.6	9,880	3.4	94	12	12
•Belgium	9.9	10,760	2.5	96	12	11
•Bulgaria	9.0	4,150	5.6	91	14	11
Channel Islands	0.1	6,780	1.1	n/a	11	12
Cyprus	0.7	3,840	5.5	86	22	8
•Czechoslovakia	15.5	5,820	4.1	93	15	12
•Denmark	5.1	12,470	1.7	97	10	11
•Finland	4.9	10,870	2.4	96	14	9
•France	54.8	11,680	2.8	96	15	10
•German Democratic Republic	16.7	7,180	4.7	95	14	14
•Germany, Federal Republic	61.4	12,460	2.6	94	10	12
•Greece	10.0	4,290	3.3	90	14	9
•Hungary	10.7	4,180	4.8	92	12	14
•Iceland	0.2	12,150	2.5	98	18	7
•Ireland	3.6	5,150	1.9	95	20	9
•Italy	57.0	6,840	2.3	95	11	10
•Luxembourg	0.4	14,340	2.9	93	12	12
Malta	0.4	3,800	10.9	89	14	8
•Netherlands	14.4	10,930	1.7	97	12	8
•Norway	4.1	14,280	3.5	97	12	10
•Poland	36.9	3,900	5.2	93	19	9
•Spain	38.4	5,430	2.4	93	13	7
•Sweden	8.3	14,040	1.3	98	11	11
•Switzerland	6.5	17,010	0.4	97	12	9
•USSR	274.0	5,940	4.1	90	20	10
•United Kingdom	56.5	9,660	1.5	95	13	12
North America (2)	**261.4**	**12,906**	**2.0**	**96**	**16**	**9**
•Canada	25.1	11,320	2.5	96	15	7
•United States	236.3	13,160	1.9	96	16	9
Developing countries (143 countries)	**3,596**	**750**	**2.8**	**59**	**33**	**12**
Developed countries (29 countries)	**1,166**	**9,190**	**3.0**	**94**	**15**	**10**
World (172 countries)	**4,762**	**2,800**	**2.9**	**68**	**29**	**11**

Life expectancy at birth (years)	Infant mortality per 1,000 live births	Literacy (%)	Per capita public education expenditures ($)	Per capita military expenditures ($)	Total exports, FOB 1981 ($ millions)	Total imports, CIF 1981 ($ millions)
73	13	99	511	111	15,841	21,034
72	12	99	668	368	55,615	62,067
72	18	91	134	106	10,372	9,650
n/a	11	n/a	n/a	n/a	n/a	n/a
74	17	76	97	56	562	1,166
70	17	99	161	148	14,891	15,148
74	8	99	789	297	16,027	17,565
74	6	100	487	126	14,011	14,174
74	10	99	560	424	106,425	120,951
72	12	99	249	235	17,312	19,082
73	10	99	566	404	176,086	163,911
73	14	84	103	257	4,257	8,592
71	23	98	167	95	8,726	9,159
77	7	99	380	0	895	1,024
73	10	98	300	61	7,789	10,596
73	13	98	259	136	75,284	91,102
72	7	98	827	117	n/a	n/a
71	14	87	86	32	444	873
76	8	99	850	359	68,746	67,298
76	8	99	857	357	17,988	15,637
71	20	98	112	111	16,998	19,089
73	9	90	110	95	20,335	32,153
76	7	99	1,164	408	28,566	28,842
75	8	99	789	324	27,037	30,688
69	32	100	210	433	76,481	68,523
73	11	99	360	342	102,715	99,461
74	**12**	**99**	**680**	**508**	**306,365**	**343,146**
74	10	99	715	174	72,627	69,795
74	11	99	676	543	233,738	273,351
57	**86**	**55**	**27**	**34**	**592,106**	**595,365**
72	**18**	**99**	**428**	**345**	**1,373,046**	**1,453,186**
60	**69**	**66**	**123**	**109**	**1,965,152**	**2,048,551**

[a]See Appendix 3.2 for an explanation of the PQLI index.
*Considered by the United Nations to be one of the 31 least developed countries.
[†]Member of the Organization of Petroleum Exporting Countries (OPEC).
•Considered by the ODC to be a developed country because of its per capita GNP of $3,500 or more and PQLI of 90 or above.

Source: Overseas Development Council, *U.S. Foreign Policy and the Third World, Agenda 1983* (New York: Praeger, 1983), pp. 210–221, and Population Reference Bureau, *1984 World Population Data Sheet* (Wash. D.C., 1984).

3

ALTERNATIVE THEORIES AND
THE MEANING OF DEVELOPMENT

It matters little how much information we possess about development
if we have not grasped its inner meaning.

Denis Goulet, The Cruel Choice

Development must be redefined as an attack on the chief evils of the world
today: malnutrition, disease, illiteracy, slums, unemployment and inequality. Measured in terms of aggregate growth rates, development has been a
great success. But measured in terms of jobs, justice and the elimination of
poverty, it has been a failure or only a partial success.

Paul P. Streeten, Director, World Development Institute

Gone are the early naive illusions of development as an endeavor in social
engineering toward a brave new world. Multiple goals have now replaced
the initial single focus. There is now a greater understanding of the profound interaction between international and national factors in the development process and an increasing emphasis on human beings and the human
potential as the basis, the means, and the ultimate purpose of the development effort.

Soedjatmoko, President, United Nations University, Tokyo

EVERYONE WANTS DEVELOPMENT, BUT WHAT DOES IT MEAN?

Every nation strives after development. While economic progress is an
essential component, it is not the only component. Development is not
purely an economic phenomenon. In an ultimate sense, it must encompass
more than the material and financial side of people's lives. Development
should, therefore, be perceived as a *multidimensional* process involving the
reorganization and reorientation of entire economic and social systems. In

61

addition to improvements in incomes and output, it typically involves radical changes in institutional, social, and administrative structures as well as in popular attitudes and, in many cases, even customs and beliefs. Finally, although development is usually defined in a *national* context, its widespread realization may necessitate fundamental modifications of the *international* economic and social system as well.

This chapter focuses on the meaning of development—its multidimensional nature, its noneconomic as well as economic components. We begin by examining three alternative theories of development and then review the important notion of dualism and dual societies. After looking at some traditional economic measures of development, we attempt to arrive at a working definition of development that encompasses concern for essential material and nonmaterial human needs.

LEADING THEORIES OF ECONOMIC DEVELOPMENT: THREE APPROACHES

The literature on economic development over the past 30 years has been dominated by three major and sometimes competing strands of thought: (a) linear stages of economic growth theories, (b) neoclassical structural change models, and (c) international dependence paradigms.[1]

The thinking of the 1950s and early 1960s focused mainly on the concept of *stages of economic growth* in which the process of development was viewed as a series of successive stages through which all countries must pass. It was primarily an economic theory of development in which the right quantity and mixture of saving, investment, and foreign aid were all that was necessary to enable Third World nations to proceed along an economic growth path that historically had been followed by the more developed countries. Development thus became synonymous with rapid, aggregate economic growth.

This linear stages approach has now been replaced to a great extent by two competing economic (and, indeed, ideological) schools of thought. The first, the *neoclassical structural change models*, uses modern economic theory and statistical analysis in an attempt to portray the internal process of structural change that a "typical" developing country must undergo if it is to succeed in generating and sustaining a process of rapid economic growth. The second, the *international dependence paradigms*, is more radical and political in orientation. It views underdevelopment in terms of international and domestic power relationships, institutional and structural economic rigidities, and the resulting proliferation of dual economies and dual societies both within and among the nations of the world. Dependence theories tend to emphasize external and internal institutional and political constraints on economic development. Emphasis is placed on the need for major new policies to eradicate poverty, to provide more diversified employment opportunities, and to reduce income inequalities. These and other egalitarian objectives are to be achieved within the context of a growing economy, but economic growth per se is not given the exalted status accorded to it by the linear stages and the structural change models. We now look at each of these alternative approaches in greater detail.

The Linear Stages Theory

When the interest in the poor nations of the world really began to materialize following the Second World War, economists in the industrialized nations were caught off guard. They had no readily available conceptual apparatus with which to analyze the process of economic growth in largely peasant, agrarian societies characterized by the virtual absence of modern economic structures. But they did have the recent experience of the Marshall Plan in which massive amounts of U.S. financial and technical assistance enabled the war-torn countries of Europe to rebuild and modernize their economies in a matter of a few years. Moreover, was it not true that all modern industrial nations were once undeveloped peasant agrarian societies? Surely their historical experience in transforming their economies from poor agricultural subsistence societies to modern industrial giants had important lessons for the "backward" countries of Asia, Africa, and Latin America? The logic and simplicity of these two strands of thought—the utility of massive injections of capital and the historical pattern of the now developed countries—was too irresistible to be refuted by scholars, politicians, and administrators in rich countries to whom people and ways of life in the Third World were often no more real than UN statistics or scattered chapters in anthropology books.

Rostow's Stages of Growth

Out of this somewhat sterile intellectual environment, and fueled by the cold war politics of the 1950s and 1960s with the resulting competition for the allegiance of newly independent nations, came the doctrine of the stages of economic growth. Its most influential and outspoken advocate was the American economic historian W. W. Rostow. According to the Rostow doctrine, the transition from underdevelopment to development can be described in terms of a series of steps or stages through which *all* countries must proceed. As Professor Rostow wrote in the opening chapter of his *Stages of Economic Growth*:

> *This book presents an economic historian's way of generalizing the sweep of modern history. . . . It is possible to identify* all *societies, in their economic dimensions, as lying within one of five categories: the traditional society, the pre-conditions for take-off into self-sustaining growth, the drive to maturity, and the age of high mass consumption. . . . These stages are not merely descriptive. They are not merely a way of generalizing certain factual observations about the sequence of development of modern societies. They have an inner logic and continuity. . . . They constitute, in the end, both a theory about economic growth and a more general, if still highly partial, theory about modern history as a whole.[2]*

The advanced countries, it was argued, had all passed the stage of "take-off into self-sustaining growth," and the underdeveloped countries that were still in either the traditional society or the "pre-conditions" stage had only to follow a certain set of rules of development to take off in their turn into self-sustaining economic growth.

One of the principal tricks of development necessary for any takeoff was the mobilization of domestic and foreign savings in order to generate sufficient investment to accelerate economic growth. The economic mechanism by which more investment leads to more growth can be described in terms of the Harrod–Domar growth model.

The Harrod–Domar Growth Model

Every economy must save a certain proportion of its national income if only to replace worn out or impaired capital goods (buildings, equipment, materials). However, in order to grow, new *investments* representing net additions to the capital stock are necessary. If we assume that there is some direct economic relationship between the size of the total capital stock, K, and total GNP, Y—for example, if $3 of capital are always necessary to produce a $1 stream of GNP—then it follows that any net additions to the capital "stock" in the form of new investment will bring about corresponding increases in the "flow" of national output (GNP).

Suppose this relationship, known in economics as the capital/output ratio, is roughly 3 to 1. If we define the capital/output ratio as k and assume further that the national savings ratio, s, is a fixed proportion of national output (e.g., 6%) and that total new investment is determined by the level of total savings, we can construct the following simple model of economic growth:

1. Saving (S) is some proportion, s, of national income (Y) such that we have the simple equation

$$S = s \cdot Y \tag{1}$$

2. Investment (I) is defined as the change in the capital stock, K, and can be represented by ΔK such that

$$I = \Delta K \tag{2}$$

But since the total capital stock, K, bears a direct relationship to total national income or output Y, as expressed by the capital/output ratio, k, then it follows that

$$\frac{K}{Y} = k,$$

$$\text{or} \quad \frac{\Delta K}{\Delta Y} = k,$$

$$\text{or finally,} \quad \boxed{\Delta K = k \, \Delta Y} \tag{2a}$$

3. Finally, since total national savings, S, must equal total investment, I, we can write this equality as

$$S = I \tag{3}$$

But from Equation (1) above we know that $S = s \cdot Y$ and from Equations (2) and (2a) we know that $I = \Delta K = k\Delta Y$.

It therefore follows that we can write the "identity" of saving equaling investment shown by Equation (3) as

$$S = s \cdot Y = k\Delta Y = \Delta K = I \tag{3a}$$

or simply as

$$s \cdot Y = k\Delta Y \tag{3b}$$

Now by dividing both sides of Equation (3b) first by Y and then by k, we obtain the following expression:

$$\frac{\Delta Y}{Y} = \frac{s}{k} \tag{4}$$

Note that the left-hand side of Equation (4), $\Delta Y/Y$, represents the rate of change or rate of growth of GNP (i.e., it is the percentage change in GNP).

Equation (4), which is a simplified version of the famous Harrod–Domar equation in the theory of economic growth,[3] states simply that the rate of growth of GNP ($\Delta Y/Y$) is determined *jointly* by the national savings ratio, s, and the national capital/output ratio, k. More specifically, it says that the growth rate of national income will be directly or "positively" related to the savings ratio (i.e., the more an economy is able to save—and invest—out of a given GNP, the greater will be the growth of that GNP) and inversely or "negatively" related to the economy's capital/output ratio (i.e., the higher is k, the lower will be the rate of GNP growth).

The economic logic of Equation (4) is very simple. In order to grow, economies must save and invest a certain proportion of their GNP. The more they can save and, therefore, invest, the faster they can grow. But the actual rate at which they can grow for any level of saving and investment depends on how productive that investment is. The productivity of this investment—how much additional output can be had from an additional unit of investment—can be measured by the inverse of the capital/output ratio, k, since this inverse, 1/k, is simply the output/capital or output/investment ratio. It follows that multiplying the *rate* of new investment, s = I/Y, by its productivity, 1/k, will give us the rate by which national income or GNP will increase.

Obstacles and Constraints

Returning to the stages of growth theories, and using Equation (4) of our simple Harrod–Domar growth model, we learn that one of the most fundamental "tricks" of economic growth is simply to increase the proportion of national income saved (i.e., not consumed). If we can raise s in Equation (4), then we can increase $\Delta Y/Y$, the rate of GNP growth. For example, if we assume that the national capital/output ratio in some less developed country is, say,

3 and the aggregate saving ratio is 6% of GNP, it follows from Equation (4) that this country can grow at a rate of 2% per year since

$$\frac{\Delta Y}{Y} = \frac{s}{k} = \frac{6\%}{3} = 2\%.$$

Now if the national savings rate can somehow be increased from 6 to, say, 15%—through increased taxes, foreign aid, and/or general consumption sacrifices—then GNP growth can be increased from 2 to 5% since now

$$\frac{\Delta Y}{Y} = \frac{s}{k} = \frac{15\%}{3} = 5\%.$$

In fact, Rostow and others defined the "takeoff" stage precisely in this way. Countries that were able to save 15–20% of their GNPs could grow ("develop") at a much faster rate than those that saved less. Moreover, this growth would then be self-sustaining. The tricks of economic growth and development, therefore, are simply a matter of increasing national savings and investment.

The main obstacle to or constraint on development according to this theory was the relatively low level of new capital formation in most poor countries. But if a country wanted to grow at, say, a rate of 7% per year and if it could not generate savings and investment at a rate of 21% of national income (assuming that *k*, the final aggregate capital/output ratio, is 3) but could only manage to save 15%, then it could seek to fill this "savings gap" of 6% either through foreign aid or private foreign investment.

Thus, the "capital constraint" stages approach to growth and development became a rationale and (in terms of cold war politics) an opportunistic tool for justifying massive transfers of capital and technical assistance from the developed to the less developed nations. It was to be the Marshall Plan all over again, but this time for the underdeveloped nations of the Third World!

Necessary versus Sufficient Conditions:
Some Criticisms of the Stages Model

Unfortunately, the tricks of development embodied in the theory of stages of growth did not always work. And the basic reason why they didn't work was not because more saving and investment isn't a *necessary* condition for accelerated rates of economic growth—it is—but rather because it is not a *sufficient* condition. Once again we are faced with an example of what we discussed in Chapter 1: the inappropriateness and/or irrelevance of many of the *implicit* assumptions of Western economic theory for the actual conditions in Third World nations. The Marshall Plan worked for Europe because the European countries receiving aid possessed the necessary structural, institutional, and attitudinal conditions (e.g., well-integrated commodity and money markets, highly developed transport facilities, well-trained and educated manpower, the motivation to succeed, an efficient government bureaucracy) to convert new capital effectively into higher levels of output. The Rostow–Harrod–Domar models implicitly assume the existence of these same attitudes and arrangements in underdeveloped nations. Yet in many cases they are lacking, as are complementary factors such as managerial competence, skilled labor, and the ability to plan and administer a wide assortment of development projects.

But at an even more fundamental level, the stages theory failed to take into account the crucial fact that contemporary Third World nations are part of a highly integrated and complex international system in which even the best and most intelligent development strategies can be nullified by external forces beyond the countries' control. (The case of Chile under the Allende regime in the early 1970s is a striking, if somewhat extreme, example of this point.) One simply cannot claim, as many economists did in the 1950s and 1960s, that development is merely a matter of "removing obstacles" and supplying various "missing components" like capital, foreign exchange, skills, and management—tasks in which the developed countries could theoretically play a major role. It was because of numerous failures and the growing disenchantment with this strictly economic theory of development (especially among Third World intellectuals) that a more recent approach has emerged, one that attempts to combine economic and institutional factors into a social systems model of international development and underdevelopment. This is the international dependence paradigm which we will review shortly. But first we examine two prominent examples of the current mainstream Western theories of development known as neoclassical structural change models.

Neoclassical Structural Change Models

The theory of structural change focuses on the mechanism by which underdeveloped economies transform their domestic economic structures from a heavy emphasis on traditional subsistence agriculture to a more modern, more urbanized, and more industrially diverse manufacturing and service economy. It employs the tools of neoclassical price and resource allocation theory and modern econometrics to describe how this transformation process takes place. Two well-known representative examples of the structural change approach are the "two-sector surplus labor" *theoretical* model of W. Arthur Lewis and the "patterns of development" *empirical* analysis of Hollis Chenery.

The Lewis Theory of Development

THE BASIC MODEL. One of the best-known early theoretical models of development that focused on the structural transformation of a primarily subsistence economy was that initially formulated by Nobel Laureate W. Arthur Lewis in the mid-1950s and later modified, formalized, and extended by John Fei and Gustav Ranis.[4] The Lewis two-sector model became the received "general" theory of the development process in labor-surplus Third World nations during most of the late 1950s and the 1960s. It still has many adherents today—especially among American development economists.

In the Lewis model, the underdeveloped economy consists of two sectors: (a) a traditional, overpopulated *rural subsistence sector* characterized by zero marginal labor productivity—a situation that permits Lewis to *[handwritten margin notes: "surplus" (dfn) — can be withdrawn fr. rural sector w/no loss in Y]*

classify this labor as "surplus" in the sense that it can be withdrawn from the agricultural sector without any loss of output—and (b) a high-productivity modern *urban industrial sector* into which labor from the subsistence sector is gradually transferred. The primary focus of the model is both on the process of labor transfer and on the growth of output and employment in the modern sector. Both labor transfer and modern sector employment growth are brought about by output expansion in that sector. The speed with which this expansion occurs is determined by the rate of industrial investment and capital accumulation in the modern sector. Such investment is made possible by the excess of modern sector profits over wages on the assumption that "capitalists" reinvest all their profits. Finally, the level of wages in the urban industrial sector is assumed to be constant and determined as a given premium over a fixed average subsistence level of wages in the traditional agricultural sector. (Lewis assumed that urban wages would have to be at least 30% higher than average rural income to induce workers to migrate from their home areas.) At the constant urban wage, the supply curve of rural labor is considered to be perfectly elastic.

[handwritten margin note: $W_{URB} = (130\%) \ W_{RURAL}$]

We can illustrate the Lewis model of modern sector growth in a two-sector economy using Figure 3.1. On the vertical axis of the figure we have the real wage and the marginal product of labor, MP_L (assumed to be equalized in the competitive modern sector labor market) and on the horizontal axis the quantity of labor.

Segment OA represents the average level of real subsistence income in the traditional (i.e., noncompetitive factor and product pricing) rural sector. Segment OW, therefore, is the real wage in the modern capitalist sector. At this wage, the supply of rural labor is assumed to be "unlimited" or perfectly

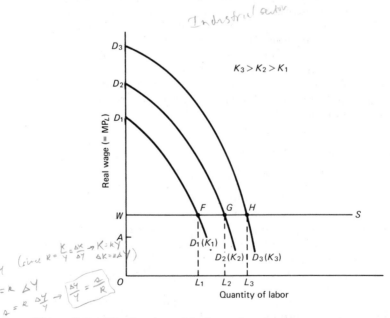

[handwritten margin notes: HD: 1) $S = \delta Y$ 2) $I = \Delta K = R \Delta Y$ (since $R = \frac{K}{Y} = \frac{\Delta K}{\Delta Y} \rightarrow K = kY \ \Delta K = R\Delta Y$) 3) $s = I \Rightarrow \delta Y = R \Delta Y \rightarrow \frac{\Delta Y}{Y} = \frac{\delta}{R}$ 4) $\frac{\delta Y}{Y} = \frac{R\Delta Y}{Y}$]

Figure 3.1. The Lewis model of growth and employment in a dual labor surplus economy.

elastic, as shown by the horizontal labor supply curve WS. In other words, Lewis assumes that at urban wage OW above rural average income OA, modern sector employees can hire as many surplus rural workers as they want without fear of rising wages. Given a fixed supply of capital, K_1, in the initial stage of modern sector growth, the demand curve for labor is determined by labor's declining marginal product and is shown by Curve $D_1(K_1)$. Since profit-maximizing modern sector employers are assumed to hire laborers up to the point where their marginal physical product is equal to the real wage (i.e., the point F of intersection between the labor demand and supply curves), total modern sector employment will be equal to OL_1. Total modern sector output would be given by the area bounded by Points OD_1FL_1. The share of this total output paid to workers in the form of wages would be equal, therefore, to the area of the rectangle $OWFL_1$. The balance of the output shown by the area WD_1F would be the total profits that accrue to the capitalists. Since Lewis assumes that all of these profits are reinvested, the total capital stock in the modern sector will rise from K_1 to K_2. This larger capital stock causes the total product curve of the modern sector to rise, which in turn induces a rise in the marginal product demand curve for labor. This outward shift in the labor demand curve is shown by Line $D_2(K_2)$ in the figure. A new equilibrium modern sector employment level will be established at Point G with OL_2 workers now employed. Total output rises to OD_2GL_2 while total wages and profits increase to $OWGL_2$ and WD_2G respectively. Once again, these larger (WD_2G) profits are reinvested, increasing the total capital stock to K_3, shifting the labor demand curve to $D_3(K_3)$ and raising the level of modern sector employment to OL_3.

The above process of modern sector growth and employment expansion is assumed to continue until all surplus rural labor is absorbed in the new industrial sector. Thereafter, additional workers can be withdrawn from the agricultural sector only at a higher cost of lost food production since the declining labor/land ratio means that the marginal product of rural labor is no longer zero. Thus, the labor supply curve becomes positively sloped as modern sector wages and employment continue to grow. The structural transformation of the economy will have taken place, with the balance of economic activity shifting from traditional rural agriculture to modern urban industry.

CRITICISMS OF THE LEWIS MODEL. Although the Lewis two-sector development model is both simple and roughly in conformity with the historical experience of economic growth in the West, three of its key assumptions do not fit the institutional and economic realities of most contemporary Third World countries.

First, the model implicitly assumes that the rate of labor transfer and employment creation in the modern sector is proportional to the rate of modern sector capital accumulation. The faster the rate of capital accumulation, the higher the growth rate of the modern sector and the faster the rate of new job creation. But what if capitalist profits are reinvested in more sophisticated labor-saving capital equipment rather than just duplicating the existing capital as is implicitly assumed in the Lewis model? (We are, of course, here accepting the debatable assumption that capitalist profits are in fact reinvested in the local economy and not sent abroad as a form of "capital flight" to be added to the deposits of Western banks!) Figure 3.2 reproduces

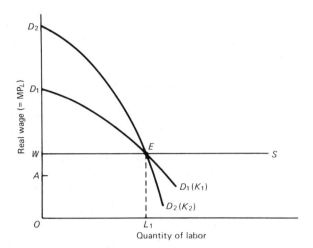

Figure 3.2.   Labor saving capital accumulation modifies the employment implications of the Lewis model.

the basic model, only this time the labor demand curves do not shift uniformly outward but, in fact, cross. Demand Curve $D_2(K_2)$ has a greater negative slope than $D_1(K_1)$ to reflect the fact that additions to the capital stock embody labor-saving technical progress—that is, K_2 technology requires less labor per unit of output than does K_1 technology (see Appendix 5.1 for a more formal analysis of factor-saving technological change).

We see that even though total output has grown substantially (i.e., OD_2EL_1 is significantly greater than OD_1EL_1), total wages ($OWEL_1$) and employment (OL_1) remain unchanged. All of the extra output accrues to capitalists in the form of excess profits. Figure 3.2, therefore, provides an illustration of what some might call "antidevelopmental" economic growth—that is, *all* the extra income and output growth is distributed to the few owners of capital while income and employment levels of the masses of workers remain largely unchanged. Although total GNP would rise, there would be little or no improvement in aggregate social welfare measured, say, in terms of more widely distributed gains in income and employment.

The second questionable assumption of the model is the notion that surplus labor exists in rural areas while there is *full employment in the urban areas*. As we will discover in Chapters 8 and 9, most contemporary research indicates the reverse is more likely true in many Third World countries (i.e., there is substantial unemployment in urban areas but little general surplus labor in rural locations). True, there are both seasonal and geographic exceptions to this rule (e.g., parts of the Asian subcontinent and isolated regions of Latin America where land ownership is very unequal) but, by and large, development economists today seem to agree that the assumption of urban surplus labor is empirically more valid than the opposite Lewis assumption of a general rural surplus labor.

The third unreal assumption is the notion of a competitive modern sector labor market that guarantees the continued existence of *constant* real urban wages until the point where the supply of rural surplus labor is exhausted. Chapter 9 will show that one of the most striking features of urban labor markets and wage determination in almost all developing countries has been the tendency for these wages to rise substantially over time, both in absolute terms and relative to average rural incomes, even in the presence of rising levels of open modern sector unemployment and low or zero marginal productivity in agriculture. Institutional factors such as union bargaining power, civil service wage scales, and multinational corporation hiring practices tend to negate whatever competitive forces might exist in Third World modern sector labor markets.

We conclude, therefore, that when one takes into account the labor-saving bias of most modern technological transfer, the existence of substantial capital flight, the widespread nonexistence of rural surplus labor, the growing prevalence of urban surplus labor, and the tendency for modern sector wages to rise rapidly even where substantial open unemployment exists, then the Lewis two-sector model—while extremely valuable as an early conceptual portrayal of the development process of sectoral interaction and structural change—requires considerable modification in assumptions and analysis to fit the reality of contemporary Third World nations.

Structural Change and Patterns of Development

Like the earlier Lewis model, the "patterns of development" analysis of structural change focuses on the sequential process through which the economic, industrial, and institutional structure of an underdeveloped economy is transformed over time to permit new industries to replace traditional agriculture as the engine of economic growth. However, in contrast to the Lewis model and the original "stages" view of development, increased savings and investment are perceived by "patterns of development" analysts as necessary but not sufficient conditions for economic growth. In addition to the accumulation of capital, both physical and human, a set of interrelated changes in the economic structure of a country are required for the transition from a traditional to a modern economic system. These structural changes involve virtually all economic functions including the transformation of production and changes in the composition of consumer demand, international trade, and resource use as well as changes in socioeconomic factors such as urbanization and the growth and distribution of a country's population.

The empirical structuralists emphasize both domestic and international constraints on development. The domestic ones include economic constraints such as a country's resource endowment and its physical and population size as well as institutional constraints such as government policies and objectives. International constraints on development include access to external capital, technology, and international trade. Differences among developing countries in their level of development are largely ascribed to these domestic and international constraints. However, it is the international constraints that make the transition of currently developing countries differ from that of the now industrialized countries. To the extent that developing countries have access to the opportunities presented by the industrial countries as sources of capital, technology, and manufactured imports as well as markets for exports, they can make the transition at an even faster rate than those that were achieved by the industrial countries during the early periods of their economic development. Thus, unlike the earlier stages model, the structuralist model recognizes the fact that developing countries are part of a highly integrated international system which can promote (as well as hinder) their development.

The structuralist model is based largely on the empirical work of Harvard economist Hollis Chenery, who examined patterns of development for numerous Third World countries during the postwar period 1950–1973.[5] His empirical studies, both cross-sectional (i.e., among countries at a given point in time) and time-series (i.e., over long periods of time), of countries at different levels of per capita income led to the identification of several characteristic features of the development process.

CHENERY'S EMPIRICAL FINDINGS. One of the most pervasive features identified by Chenery and his colleagues in the countries they studied is the transformation of the structure of production. As per capita incomes rise, they found that there was a shift from agricultural production to industrial production. This initial structural change is illustrated in Figure 3.3, which shows the share of industrial output in GDP rising and the share of agricultural (primary) output declining as per capita national incomes increase. For example, Chenery found that countries with a per capita income of $200 in 1976 dollars had on the average primary production valued at 45% of GDP and industrial production at approximately 15% (see

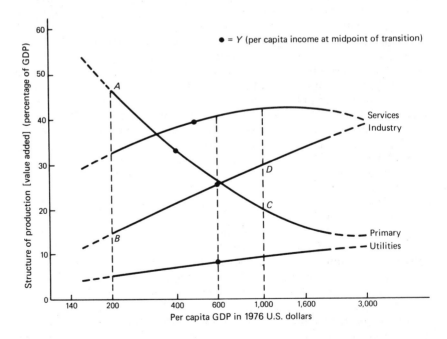

Figure 3.3. Transformation of production. *Source:* Hollis Chenery and Moses Syrquin, *Patterns of Development, 1950–70* (London: Oxford University Press, 1975), Figure 5.

Points *A* and *B* in Figure 3.3). However, at an income of $1,000, primary output had fallen to 20% and industry risen to 28% of GDP (Points *C* and *D*). Note that the declining share of agricultural output in GDP does not necessarily imply that the absolute level of agricultural output falls. Instead, there may be a relative decline in agricultural production.

Structural changes in production can be divided into an earlier and a later phase by measuring the halfway point in the development process at which the shares of agriculture and industry are about equal. In Figure 3.3 this occurs at a per capita income level (*Y*) of $600 measured in 1976 dollars. Countries below this level of income are typically viewed by Chenery and others as in the early phase of development or as "underdeveloped" while those above $600 but below the industrialized level of income of $3,000 are viewed as in the later or "transitional" phase of development. The early phase of development is characterized by dependence (although diminishing) on agricultural production as a source of income and growth while the later phase involves dependence on industrial production. In this sense the patterns of development model is similar to that proposed by Lewis.

Associated with the rising share of industrial output in GDP is the accumulation of physical and human capital. Figure 3.4 shows the shares of savings, investment, and government revenue in GDP and indexes of school enrollment. The graph reveals a substantial increase in investment and school enrollment (representing investment in human capital) taking place in the early phase of the development transition.

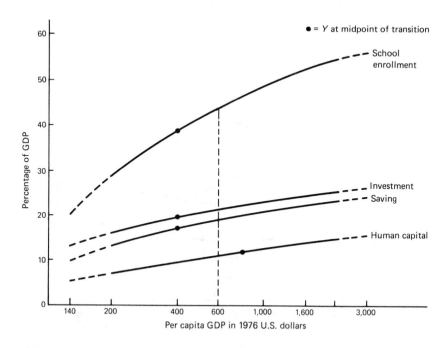

Figure 3.4. Capital accumulation. *Source:* Hollis Chenery and Moses Syrquin, *Patterns of Development, 1950–70* (London: Oxford University Press, 1975), Figures 1, 2, 3.

Corresponding to structural changes in production and the accumulation of physical and human capital are changes in the composition of domestic demand, as shown in Figure 3.5. The most uniform change over countries is the decline in food consumption from over 40% to only 17% of total domestic demand. This allows the other major components of demand—nonfood consumption, government consumption, and investment—to increase their shares of total demand.

While changes in the pattern of international trade are the most variable among countries, in general Chenery found that there is a rise in both total imports and exports over the course of transition, with a relative rise in the share of industrial products in total exports and a relative decline in their share of total imports. These changes are illustrated in Figure 3.6.

With regard to changes in factor use, there is a shift of labor out of the

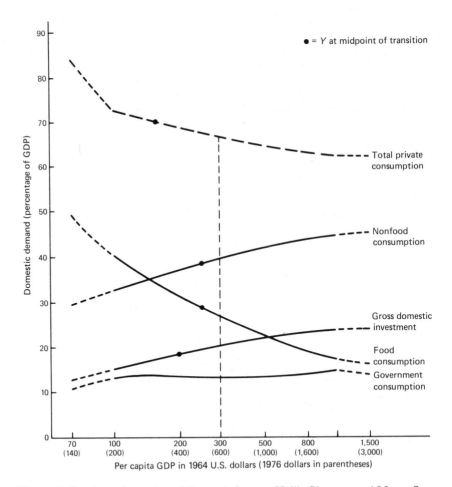

Figure 3.5. Transformation of demand. *Source:* Hollis Chenery and Moses Syrquin, *Patterns of Development, 1950–70* (London: Oxford University Press, 1975), Figure 4.

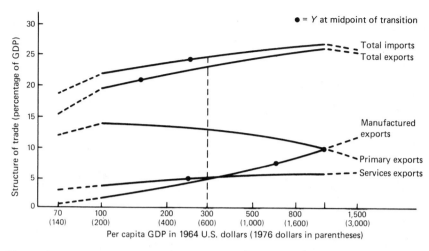

Figure 3.6. Transformation of trade. *Source:* Hollis Chenery and Moses Syrquin, *Patterns of Development, 1950–70* (London: Oxford University Press, 1975), Figure 6.

agricultural sector into the industrial and service sectors, although this shift lags behind the structural change in production (see Figure 3.7). As a consequence of this lag, the agricultural sector plays a large role in generating employment in both the early and later phases of development; the industrial sector finally matches employment in the agricultural sector at a per capita income level of $1,600, or well into the later phase of development. Labor productivity in the agricultural sector grows slowly in the early phase and equals that of the industrial sector only on completion of the transition (see Figure 3.8). However, total labor productivity rises in the economy as a whole.

There are changes in socioeconomic processes during the course of transition as well. The most common trend found among countries is the phenomenon of increasing urbanization caused by the rise of industry and the accelerated migration of people from farm to city. Chenery found that the urban population typically exceeds the rural population above a per capita income level of $1,000. But industrialization and urbanization were also found to contribute to a worsening distribution of income, with the bulk of increases in income being concentrated in the urban modern sector. Nevertheless, certain other structural changes such as the spread of educational opportunities, the lowering of population growth, and the reduction of economic dualism (see below) were associated with a more even distribution of income. This enabled certain countries (e.g., Japan, South Korea, and Taiwan) to pursue policies that spread the benefits of industrialization more equally. The final dimension of transition identified by Chenery is the reduction of both mortality and fertility rates as national income rises, although as Chenery has noted, there is nothing inevitable about the long time lag between mortality and fertility declines that characterizes most developing countries.

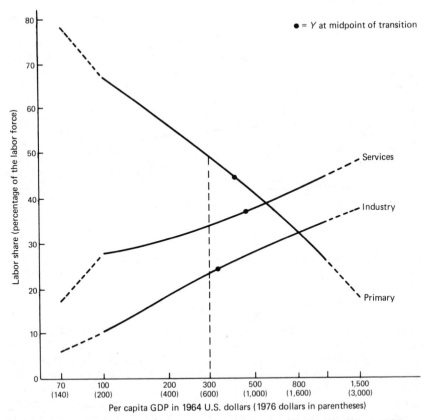

Figure 3.7. Transformation of employment. *Source:* Hollis Chenery and Moses Syrquin, *Patterns of Development, 1950–70* (London: Oxford University Press, 1975), Figure 8.

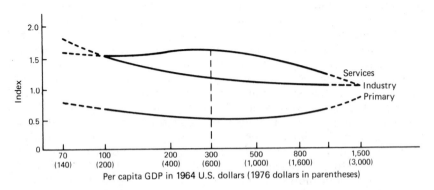

Figure 3.8. Productivity of labor sector. *Source:* Hollis Chenery and Moses Syrquin, *Patterns of Development, 1950–70* (London: Oxford University Press, 1975), Figure 9.

CONCLUSIONS AND IMPLICATIONS. The set of structural changes that have been described are the "average" patterns of development Chenery and colleagues observed among countries in time-series and cross-sectional analyses. *The major hypothesis of the structuralist model is that development is an identifiable process of growth and change whose main features are similar in all countries.* However, as mentioned earlier, the model does recognize that differences can arise among countries in the pace and exact pattern of development depending on their particular set of circumstances. Factors influencing the development process include a country's resource endowment and size, its government's policies and objectives, the availability of external capital and technology, and the international trade environment.

In general, large countries (e.g., India, China, and Brazil) have a more diversified resource base and a larger internal demand. This larger demand is due to their greater population size, and it enables these countries to industrialize earlier and to exploit economies of scale without the need to penetrate export markets. Smaller countries (e.g., Taiwan, South Korea, and Singapore) usually have a smaller internal demand and must therefore rely on external demand and foreign markets to stimulate their general economic growth. Smaller countries that also lack a favorable resource base for the promotion of primary product exports tend to industrialize at an earlier stage, whereas the resource-rich smaller countries tend to delay industrialization and to rely on primary production well into higher levels of per capita income.

However, variations among individual countries are substantial. For example, Malaysia and Venezuela were found to delay their industrialization even longer than the resource-rich smaller country norm due to their especially favorable primary exports (or favorable international trade climate). Brazil and Israel, on the other hand, were found to industrialize at an even earlier stage than would be indicated by the norm for either a large or a resource-deficient small country. The explanation of the deviation was the availability of large amounts of external capital and technology that both Brazil and Israel were able to attract. Moreover, a rapidly growing country specializing in primary production can easily have a greater increase in industrial output per capita than a more slowly growing country specializing in modern industry—comparing the cases of, say, Malaysia (tin and rubber) with India, or Venezuela (oil) with Argentina.

In summary, empirical studies of the process of structural change lead to the conclusion that the pace and pattern of development can vary according to both domestic and international factors, many of which lie outside the control of an individual developing nation. Yet, despite this variation, structural change economists argue that one can identify certain patterns occurring in almost all countries during the development process. And these patterns, they argue, may be affected by the choice of development policies pursued by LDC governments as well as the international trade and foreign assistance policies of developed nations. Hence structuralists are basically optimistic that the "correct" mix of economic policies will generate beneficial patterns of self-sustaining growth. The international dependence school, in contrast, is much less sanguine and, in many cases, is downright pessimistic. They argue that the statistical averages that structuralist economists calculate from a diverse range of rich and poor countries are not only of limited practical value in identifying the critical factors in a particular nation's development process but, more importantly, they divert attention from the real factors in the global economy that maintain and perpetuate the poverty of Third World nations. Let's now see what this dependence theory is all about.

International Dependence Models

In recent years international dependence models have gained increasing support, especially among Third World intellectuals, as a result of a growing disenchantment with both the stages and the structural change models. Essentially, international dependence models view Third World countries as beset by institutional, political, and economic rigidities, both domestic and international, and caught up in a dependence and dominance relationship to rich countries. Within this general approach there are two major streams of thought.

The Neocolonial Dependence Model

The first major stream, which we call the "neocolonial dependence model," is an indirect outgrowth of Marxist thinking. It attributes the existence and continuance of Third World underdevelopment primarily to the historical evolution of a highly unequal international capitalist system of rich country−poor country relationships. Whether because rich nations are intentionally exploitative or unintentionally neglectful, the coexistence of rich and poor nations in an international system dominated by such unequal power relationships between the *center* (the developed countries) and the *periphery* (the LDCs) renders attempts by poor nations to be self-reliant and independent in their development efforts difficult and sometimes even impossible.[6] Certain groups in the developing countries (e.g., landlords, entrepreneurs, military rulers, merchants, salaried public officials, and trade union leaders) who enjoy high incomes, social status, and political power constitute a small elite ruling class whose principal interest, whether knowingly or not, is in the perpetuation of the international capitalist system of inequality and conformity by which they are rewarded. Directly and indirectly, they serve (are dominated by) and are rewarded by (dependent on) special interest international power groups including multinational corporations, national bilateral aid agencies, and multilateral assistance organizations like the World Bank or the IMF which are tied by allegiance and/or funding to the wealthy capitalist countries. The elites' activities and viewpoints often serve to inhibit any genuine reform efforts that might benefit the wider population and in some cases actually lead to even lower levels of living and to the perpetuation of underdevelopment. In short, the neo-Marxist, neocolonial view of underdevelopment attributes a large part of the Third World's continuing and worsening poverty to the existence and policies of the industrial capitalist countries of the northern hemisphere and their extensions in the form of small but powerful elite or *comprador* groups in the less developed countries.[7] Revolutionary struggles or at least major restructurings of the world capitalist system are therefore required to free dependent Third World nations from the direct and indirect economic control of their First World and domestic oppressors.

One of the most forceful statements of the international dependence school of thought is that of Theotonio Dos Santos:

> *Underdevelopment, far from constituting a state of backwardness prior to capitalism, is rather a consequence and a particular form of capitalist development known as dependent capitalism . . . dependence is a conditioning situation in which the economies of one group of countries are conditioned by the development and expansion of others. A relationship of interdependence between two or more economies or between such economies and the world trading system becomes a dependent relationship when some countries can expand through self-impulsion while others, being in a dependent position, can only expand as a reflection of the expansion of the dominant countries, which may have positive or negative effects on their immediate development. In either case, the basic situation of dependence causes these countries to be both backward and exploited. Dominant countries are endowed with technological, commercial, capital and socio-political predominance over dependent countries—the form of this predominance varying according to the particular historical moment—and can therefore exploit them, and extract part of the locally produced surplus. Dependence, then, is based upon an international division of labor which allows industrial development to take place in some countries while restricting it in others, whose growth is conditioned by and subjected to the power centers of the world.[8]*

Various components of the neo-Marxist dependence argument will be explored in greater detail when we discuss problems of poverty, income distribution, unemployment, international trade, and foreign assistance in Parts II and III of the book. However, for those with a deeper interest in the subject, Appendix 3.1 attempts to summarize the central arguments of the neo-Marxist theory of underdevelopment.

The False Paradigm Model

A second and a less radical international dependence approach to development, which we might call the "false paradigm" model, attributes Third World underdevelopment to faulty and inappropriate advice provided by well-meaning but often uninformed international "expert" advisers from developed country assistance agencies and multinational donor organizations. These experts offer sophisticated concepts, elegant theoretical structures, and complex econometric models of development that often lead to inappropriate or simply incorrect policies. Because of institutional factors such as the highly unequal ownership of land and other property rights, disproportionate control by local elites over domestic and international financial assets, and very unequal access to credit, these policies, based as they often are on mainstream Lewis-type surplus labor and/or Chenery-type structural change models, in many cases merely serve the vested interests of existing power groups, both domestic and international.

In addition, according to this argument, leading university intellectuals, trade unionists, future high-level government economists, and other civil servants all get their training in developed country institutions where they are unwittingly served an unhealthy dose of alien concepts and elegant but inapplicable theoretical models. Having little or no really useful knowledge to enable them to come to grips in an effective way with real development problems, they often tend to become unknowing or reluctant apologists for the existing system of elitist policies and institutional structures. In university economics courses, for example, this typically entails the perpetuation of the teaching of false, or at least irrelevant, Western concepts and models, while in government policy discussions too much emphasis is placed on attempts to measure capital/output ratios, to increase savings and investment ratios, or to maximize GNP growth rates. As a result, desirable institutional and structural reforms, many of which we have discussed in previous sections, are neglected or given only cursory attention.

Conclusions and Implications

Whatever their ideological differences, the advocates of both the neocolonial dependence and false paradigm models reject the exclusive emphasis on traditional Western economic models designed to accelerate the growth of GNP as the principal index of development. They question the validity of Lewis-type two-sector models of modernization and industrialization in light of their unreal assumptions and recent Third World history. They further reject the claims made by Chenery and others that there exist well-defined empirical patterns of development that should be pursued by most poor countries on the periphery of the world economy. Instead, dependency and false paradigm theorists place more emphasis on international power imbalances and on needed fundamental economic, political, and institutional reforms, both domestic and worldwide. In extreme cases, they call for the outright expropriation of privately owned assets in the expectation that public asset ownership and control will be a more effective means to help eradicate absolute poverty, provide expanded employment opportunities, lessen income inequalities, and raise the general levels of living (including health, education, and cultural enrichment) of the masses of people. While a few radical neo-Marxists would even go so far as to say that economic growth and structural change do not matter, the majority of thoughtful observers recognize that the most effective way to deal with these diverse social problems is to accelerate the pace of economic growth through domestic and international reforms accompanied by a judicious mixture of both public and private economic activity. The ultimate goal is to generate rapid economic growth while altering its *character*, so that all segments of Third World populations can participate in and benefit from its realization. In Chapter 5 we will explore ways of achieving these twin objectives of greater growth with greater equity.

DUALISM AND THE CONCEPT OF DUAL SOCIETIES

Implicit in structural change theories and explicit in international dependence theories is the notion of a world of dual societies—of rich nations and poor nations, and in the developing countries pockets of wealth within broad areas of poverty. "Dualism" is a concept widely discussed in development economics. It represents the existence and persistence of *increasing divergences* between rich and poor nations and rich and poor peoples on various levels. Specifically, the concept of dualism embraces four key elements:[9]

1. *Different sets of conditions* of which some are "superior" and others "inferior" can *coexist* in a given space. Examples of this element of dualism include the Lewis notion of the coexistence of modern and traditional methods of production in urban and rural sectors; the coexistence of wealthy, highly educated elites with masses of illiterate poor people; and the dependence notion of the coexistence of powerful and wealthy industrialized nations with weak, impoverished peasant societies in the international economy.
2. *This coexistence is chronic* and not merely transitional. It is not due to a temporary phenomenon, in which case time could eliminate the discrepancy between superior and inferior elements. In other words, the international coexistence of wealth and poverty is *not* simply a historical phenomenon that will be rectified in time. Although both the stages of growth theory and the structural change models implicitly make such an assumption, the facts of growing international inequalities seem to refute it.
3. Not only do the degrees of superiority or inferiority fail to show any signs of diminishings, they even have an inherent *tendency to increase.* For example, the productivity gap between workers in developed countries and their counterparts in most LDCs seems to widen with each passing year.
4. The interrelations between the superior and inferior elements are such that *the existence of the superior elements does little or nothing to pull up the inferior element.* In fact, it may actually serve to push it down—to "develop its underdevelopment."

International Dualism

These four principal components of dualism provide an appropriate description of the contemporary situation in the international economic system. First, there are, as we have seen in Chapter 2, great differences in per capita incomes and levels of living currently coexisting between different countries, races, continents, and climatic zones of the world. Second, these differences are clearly not short term but chronic. The disparity between levels of living in, say, England and France on the one hand and India and sub-Saharan Africa on the other have persisted not for decades but for centuries. Third, these differences show signs of increasing rather than decreasing. We saw how growth rates of GNP and especially GNP per capita had widened in favor of the developed countries during the past two decades. Fourth and finally, the interrelations between the rich and poor countries in the international economy, at least in the judgment of most members of the dependence school of development, contain many elements that make the rapid growth of the former only marginally helpful and, in some cases, absolutely harmful to the development of the latter. These so-called international backwash effects inhibiting the sustained development of Third World nations include, among others, the following forces of international dominance and dependence:

1. The power of strong countries to control and manipulate world resource and commodity markets to their advantage
2. The spread of international capitalist domination of domestic LDC economies through the foreign investment activities of private multinational corporations
3. The privileged access of rich nations to scarce raw materials
4. The export of unsuitable and inappropriate science and technology protected by an exploitative patent and licensing system

5. The ability of industrialized countries to "impose" their products on fragile Third World markets behind import-substituting tariff barriers that protect the monopolistic practices of multinational corporations
6. The transfer of outmoded and irrelevant systems of education to societies where education is perceived as a key component in the development process
7. The ability of rich countries to disrupt efforts at industrialization by poor countries by "dumping" cheap products in these controlled markets
8. Harmful international trade theories and policies that lock Third World countries into primary product exports with declining international revenues
9. Harmful aid policies that often merely serve to perpetuate and exacerbate internal dualistic economic structures by focusing on large-scale modern-sector "showpiece" projects
10. The creation and support of privileged elite groups whose economic and ideological allegiance is to the external world, whether capitalist or socialist
11. The transfer of unsuitable methods of university training and unrealistic, often irrelevant professional standards, such as the externally conceived degree requirements for doctors, engineers, technicians, and economists
12. The capacity of rich countries to lure skilled and professional personnel away from LDCs with attractive financial rewards (the international brain drain)
13. The demoralizing "demonstration effect" of luxury consumption on the part of the wealthy both at home and abroad as propagated, for example, in imported foreign movies and magazine advertisements

As pointed out earlier, it is unrealistic to attempt to lay the blame for all the evils of underdevelopment at the international doorstep of rich nations. Clearly, the continued economic growth of rich nations helps to make it possible for poor countries to maintain growth rates of output that are high by historical standards. On the other hand, it is equally naive to believe that many of the serious problems of underdevelopment do not in part originate abroad. It would be difficult to refute Professor Singer's observation that

> *the very forces which are set in motion by the rapid growth of the richer countries—specifically the development of even more sophisticated, costly and capital-intensive technologies, and of mortality-reducing health improvements and disease controls—are such as to create forces within the poorer countries—specifically a population explosion, rising unemployment and inability to develop their own technological capacities, which may in fact assure that they will not have the time needed for the continued maintenance of current growth rates, let alone their acceleration, so as to result in acceptable levels of development.*[10]

Domestic Dualism

Our fourfold definition of dualism is equally descriptive of the internal economic structures of many Third World countries. First, standards of living vary greatly between the top 20% and bottom 40% of the population, with ratios as high as 6 and 12 to 1 being quite representative (see Chapter 5). The majority of those few with very high incomes live in urban areas while the great clusters of mass poverty are generally to be found in rural regions. However, even within most Third World urban areas one typically finds pockets of great wealth coexisting with spreading slums

But this initial element of dualism—the coexistence of "superior" with "inferior" phenomena—is not limited to the distribution of wealth, income, and power. It also exists in the technological nature of Third World industrial production. Small enclaves of modern industries (mostly urban manufacturing) using modern imported capital-intensive production methods to produce sophisticated products in large quantities coexist with traditional labor-intensive, small-scale activities catering to limited local needs.

Second, the coexistence of a small group of "progressive" wealthy elites with masses of traditionally oriented poor shows no sign of disappearing. A large proportion of Third World peoples seems today as untouched by "development" as they were, say, 10 or 15 years ago.

Third, the gap between the rich and poor and between modern and traditional methods of production shows signs of growing even wider not only within individual LDCs but also among the developing countries as a group. Countries such as Brazil, Venezuela, Costa Rica, Singapore, Taiwan, Thailand, Korea, Cyprus, Sierra Leone, and Kenya have experienced relatively high rates of per capita income growth for a number of years now; in contrast, Bangladesh, Haiti, Mali, the Sudan, Ghana, India, Peru, and many others have shown little or no per capita growth at all over the past decade. The widening gap within nations is especially evident in those Third World countries with markedly dualistic industrial structures, including Brazil, Mexico, the Philippines, Venezuela, Peru, Kenya, Zambia, and India.

Finally, the "spread effects" between the rising wealth of modern enclaves and the improvement in the levels of living of the traditional society are less than obvious in most LDCs. In fact, there seem to be little or no spread effects whatsoever. Many observers claim with some justification that it is the very growth of the stronger or "superior" component of dualistic societies that pushes down, or at least is achieved at the expense of, the weaker or inferior element. We shall see how this can come about when we discuss the problems of poverty, income distribution, unemployment, rural development, education, trade, aid, and technology transfer in Parts II and III.

WHAT DO WE MEAN BY "DEVELOPMENT"?

Let us now try to pull together many of the threads of previous sections of this chapter and, indeed, of previous chapters in an attempt to define what we really mean by "development."

Traditional Economic Measures

In strictly economic terms, "development" has traditionally meant the capacity of a national economy, whose initial economic condition has been more or less static for a long time, to *generate* and *sustain* an annual increase in its gross national product at rates of perhaps 5–7% or more. An alternative common economic index of development has been the use of rates of growth of per capita GNP to take into account the ability of a nation to expand its output at a rate faster than the growth rate of its population. Levels and rates of growth of "real" per capita GNP (i.e., monetary growth of GNP per capita minus the rate of inflation) are normally used to measure in a broad sense the overall economic well-being of a population—that is, how much of real goods and services is available for consumption and investment for the average citizen.

Economic development in the past has also been typically seen in terms of the planned alteration of the structure of production and employment so that agriculture's share of both declines, whereas that of the manufacturing and service industries increases. This, of course, is the essence of theories of structural change. Development strategies, therefore, have usually focused on rapid industrialization, often at the expense of agriculture and rural development. Finally, these principal economic measures of development have often been supplemented by casual reference to noneconomic social indicators: gains in literacy, schooling, health conditions and services, and provision of housing, for instance. A description of various attempts to generate these "social indicators" of development to supplement GNP and GNP per capita is presented for the interested student in Appendix 3.2 at the end of this chapter.

But, on the whole, development in the 1960s and 1970s was nearly always seen as an economic phenomenon, in which rapid gains in overall and per capita GNP growth would either "trickle down" to the masses in the form of jobs and other economic opportunities or create the necessary conditions for the wider distribution of the economic and social benefits of growth. Problems of poverty, unemployment, and income distribution were of secondary importance to "getting the growth job done."

The New Economic View of Development

The experience of the 1950s and 1960s, when a large number of Third World nations *did* achieve the overall UN growth targets but the levels of living of the masses of people remained for the most part unchanged, signaled that something was very wrong with this narrow definition of development. An increasing number of economists and policy makers now clamored for the "dethronement of GNP" and the elevation of direct attacks on widespread absolute poverty, increasingly inequitable income distributions, and rising unemployment. In short, *during the 1970s economic development came to be redefined in terms of the reduction or elimination of poverty, inequality, and unemployment within the context of a growing economy.* "Redistribution from Growth" became a common slogan. Professor Dudley Seers posed the basic question about the meaning of development succinctly when he asserted:

> *The questions to ask about a country's development are therefore: What has been happening to poverty? What has been happening to unemployment? What has been happening to inequality? If all three of these have declined from high levels then beyond doubt this has been a period of development for the country concerned. If one or two of these central problems have been growing worse, especially if all three have, it would be strange to call the result "development" even if per capita income doubled.[11]*

The above assertion is not idle speculation nor the description of a hypothetical situation. There were a number of developing countries that experienced relatively high rates of growth of per capita income during the 1960s and 1970s but that showed little or no improvement or even an actual decline in employment, equality, and the real incomes of the bottom 40% of their populations. By the earlier "growth" definition, these countries were "developing." By the more recent poverty, equality, and employment criteria, they were not. The situation in the early 1980s worsened further as GNP growth rates turned negative for many LDCs and governments were forced to cut back on their already limited social and economic programs.

But the phenomenon of development or the existence of a chronic state of underdevelopment is not only a question of economics or even of quantitative measurement of incomes, employment, and inequality. Underdevelopment is a real fact of life for over 2 billion people in the world—a state of mind as much as a state of national poverty. As Denis Goulet has so forcefully portrayed it:

> Underdevelopment is shocking: the squalor, disease, unnecessary deaths, and hopelessness of it all! No man understands if underdevelopment remains for him a mere statistic reflecting low income, poor housing, premature mortality or underemployment. The most empathetic observer can speak objectively about underdevelopment only after undergoing, personally or vicariously, the "shock of underdevelopment." This unique culture shock comes to one as he is initiated to the emotions which prevail in the "culture of poverty." The reverse shock is felt by those living in destitution when a new self-understanding reveals to them that their life is neither human nor inevitable. . . . The prevalent emotion of underdevelopment is a sense of personal and societal impotence in the face of disease and death, of confusion and ignorance as one gropes to understand change, of servility toward men whose decisions govern the course of events, of hopelessness before hunger and natural catastrophe. Chronic poverty is a cruel kind of hell, and one cannot understand how cruel that hell is merely by gazing upon poverty as an object.[12]

The condition of underdevelopment in its totality is thus a consciously experienced state of deprivation rendered especially intolerable as more and more people acquire information about the development of other societies and realize that technical and institutional means for abolishing poverty, misery, and disease do indeed exist.

Development must, therefore, be conceived of as a multidimensional process involving major changes in social structures, popular attitudes, and national institutions, as well as the acceleration of economic growth, the reduction of inequality, and the eradication of absolute poverty. Development, in its essence, must represent the whole gamut of change by which an entire social system, tuned to the diverse basic needs and desires of individuals and social groups within that system, moves away from a condition of life widely perceived as unsatisfactory and toward a situation or condition of life regarded as materially and spiritually "better."

Three Core Values of Development

Is it possible to define or broadly conceptualize what we mean when we talk about development as the sustained elevation of an entire society and social system toward a "better" or "more humane" life? The question, What constitutes the good life? is as old as philosophy and humankind. It is a timeless and perennial question that needs to be reevaluated and freshly answered with the changing environment of world society. The appropriate answer for Third World nations in the last two decades of the twentieth century is not necessarily the same as it would have been in previous decades. But we believe with Professor Goulet and others that at least three basic components or core values should serve as a conceptual basis and practical guideline for understanding the "inner" meaning of development. These core values are *life-sustenance, self-esteem,* and *freedom,* representing common goals sought by all individuals and societies.[13] They relate to fundamental human needs that find their expression in almost all societies and cultures at all times. Let us, therefore, examine each in turn.

Life-Sustenance: The Ability to Provide Basic Needs

All people have certain basic needs without which life would be impossible. These "life-sustaining" basic human needs include food, shelter, health, and protection.[14] When any of these is absent or in critically short supply, we may state without reservation that a condition of "absolute underdevelopment" exists. *A basic function of all economic activity, therefore, is to provide as many people as possible with the means of overcoming the helplessness and misery arising from a lack of food, shelter, health, and protection.* To this extent, we may claim that economic development is a *necessary* condition for the improvement in the "quality of life" which is "development." Without sustained and continuous economic progress at the individual as well as the societal level, the realization of the human potential would not be possible. One clearly has to "have enough in order to be more."[15] Rising per capita incomes, the elimination of absolute poverty, greater employment opportunities, and lessening income inequalities, therefore, constitute the *necessary* but not the *sufficient* conditions for development.[16]

Self-Esteem: To Be a Person

A second universal component of the good life is self-esteem—a sense of worth and self-respect, of not being used as a tool by others for their own ends. All peoples and societies seek some basic form of self-esteem, although they may call it authenticity, identity, dignity, respect, honor, or recognition. The nature and form of this self-esteem may vary from society to society and from one culture to another. However, with the proliferation of the "modernizing values" of developed nations, many societies in Third World countries that previously may have possessed a profound sense of their own worth suffer from serious cultural confusion when they come in contact with economically and technologically advanced societies because national prosperity has become an almost universal measure of worth. Because of the significance attached to material values in developed nations, worthiness and esteem are nowadays increasingly conferred only on those countries who possess economic wealth and technological power— those that have "developed." Again, we may quote Professor Goulet:

> The relevant point is that underdevelopment is the lot of the majority of the world's population. As long as esteem or respect was dispensed on grounds other than material achievement, it was possible to resign oneself to poverty without feeling disdained. Conversely, once the prevailing image of the better life includes material welfare as one of its essential ingredients it becomes difficult for the materially "underdeveloped" to feel respected or

esteemed. . . nowadays the Third World seeks development in order to gain
the esteem which is denied to societies living in a state of disgraceful "under-
development." . . . Development is legitimized as a goal because it is an
important, perhaps even an indispensable, way of gaining esteem.[17]

Freedom from Servitude: To Be Able to Choose

A third and final universal value that we suggest should constitute the
meaning of development is the concept of freedom. Freedom here is not to be
understood in the political or ideological sense (e.g., the free world), but in
the more fundamental sense of freedom or emancipation from alienating
material conditions of life and from social servitude to nature, ignorance,
other people, misery, institutions, and dogmatic beliefs. Freedom involves
the expanded range of choices for societies and their members together with
the minimization of external constraints in the pursuit of some social goal
we call development. W. Arthur Lewis stressed the relationship between
economic growth and freedom from servitude when he concluded that "the
advantage of economic growth is not that wealth increases happiness, but
that it increases the range of human choice."[18] Wealth can enable a person
to gain greater control over nature and his physical environment (e.g.,
through the production of food, clothing, and shelter) than he would have if
he remained poor. It also gives him the freedom to choose greater leisure, to
have more goods and services, or to deny the importance of these material
wants and live a life of spiritual contemplation.

The Three Objectives of Development

We may conclude that *development is both a physical reality and a state of
mind* in which society has, through some combination of social, economic,
and institutional processes, secured the means for obtaining a better life.
Whatever the specific components of this better life, development in all
societies must have at least the following three objectives:

1. To increase the availability and widen the distribution of basic life-sustaining goods
   such as food, shelter, health, and protection
2. To raise levels of living including, in addition to higher incomes, the provision of more
   jobs, better education, and greater attention to cultural and humanistic values, all of
   which will serve not only to enhance material well-being but also to generate greater
   individual and national self-esteem
3. To expand the range of economic and social choices available to individuals and nations
   by freeing them from servitude and dependence not only in relation to other people and
   nation-states but also to the forces of ignorance and human misery

We may therefore reformulate and broaden Professor Seers' questions
about the meaning of development as follows:

1. Have general levels of living within a nation risen to the point that there has been a
   lessening of absolute poverty (i.e., deprivation of life-sustaining goods) and of inequality in income distribution, as well as improvements in the level of employment and the
   nature and quality of educational, health, and other social and cultural services?

2. Has economic progress enhanced individual and group esteem both internally vis-à-vis one another and externally vis-à-vis other nations and regions?

3. Finally, has economic progress expanded the range of human choice and freed people from external dependence and internal servitude to other men and institutions, rather than merely substituting one form of dependence (e.g., economic) for another (e.g., cultural)?

If for a given nation the answer to each of the above three questions is yes, then clearly that nation has undergone development. If the first question (which is equivalent to Seers' three questions) can be answered affirmatively but the other two remain negative, then the country may properly be designated as "economically more developed" yet it remains underdeveloped in a more fundamental sense. In this context, it is more appropriate to refer to the rich nations of the world as economically developed and reserve judgment as to whether or not they are actually developed in a more thoroughgoing social, political, and cultural analysis. To paraphrase Seers, if the second and third of these central questions evoke negative responses (i.e., if people feel less self-esteem, respect, or dignity and/or if their freedom to choose has been constrained), then even if the provision of life-sustaining goods and improvements in levels of living are occurring, it would be misleading to call the result development.

UNDERDEVELOPMENT AND DEVELOPMENT: A MULTIDIMENSIONAL SCHEMATIC SUMMARY

Figure 3.9 is a schematic attempt to portray and summarize some of the main economic and noneconomic aspects of what we mean by underdevelopment. In the bottom half our three primary components of underdevelopment—low levels of living (life-sustenance), low self-esteem, and limited freedom—are given in rectangular boxes with arrows indicating general lines of causation. The upper half of the chart, relating to the determinants of levels of living, portrays the principal economic aspects of underdevelopment. The two boxes at the very bottom of the chart—self-esteem and a freedom to choose—are typically referred to as noneconomic aspects of development.

In fact, economic forces impinge on all three boxes, while important noneconomic factors like attitudes and institutions are also vital components of the determinants of levels of living. *It is simply not possible to separate economic from noneconomic phenomena when dealing with real-world development problems.* But in order fully to understand the concepts and processes portrayed in our schematic framework of underdevelopment, let us look briefly at each of the three components.

First, we see that low levels of living (insufficient life-sustaining goods and inadequate or nonexistent education, health, and other social services) are all related in one form or another to low incomes. These low incomes result from the low average productivity of the *entire* labor force, not just those working. Low labor force productivity can result from a variety of factors, including on the supply side poor health, nutrition, and work attitudes, high population growth, and high unemployment and underemployment. On the demand side inadequate skills, poor managerial

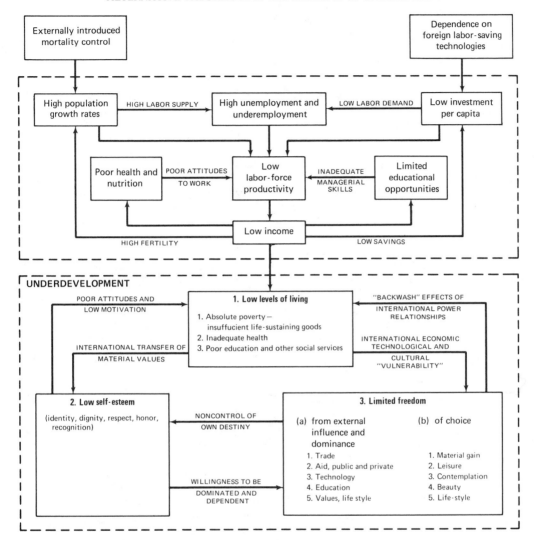

Figure 3.9. Underdevelopment: A multidimensional schematic framework.

talents, and overall low levels of worker education may, along with the importation of developed-country labor-saving techniques of production, result in the substitution of capital for labor in domestic production. The combination of low labor demand and large supplies results in the wide-spread underutilization of labor. Moreover, low incomes lead to low savings and investment which also restrict the total number of employment opportunities. Finally, as we shall see in Chapter 6, low incomes are also thought to be related to large family size and high fertility since children provide one of the few sources of economic and social security in old age for very poor families.

Note that the arrows in the upper half of Figure 3.9, the productivity-income relationship, form a series of continuous "loops," indicating that a process of "circular causation," or vicious circles, is in operation. For example, on the outer right loop we see that low incomes result in low savings, which means low investment, limited labor demand, high unemployment, low productivity, and therefore low incomes. On the inner right loop we have low incomes leading to restricted educational opportunities (both at the state and family level) and inadequate managerial skills. The result is that a relatively unskilled labor force is compelled to produce at low levels of productivity, which in turn serves to perpetuate low incomes. The inner left loop shows low incomes leading to poor health and worker nutrition due to a lack of food, sanitation, etc., which in turn is a primary factor in the worker's poor performance and his attitudes toward promptness, discipline, and self-improvement. Finally, the outer left loop shows the linkage between low incomes, high fertility, rapid population growth, high labor supply, high unemployment, low per capita labor productivity, and, lastly, the perpetuation of chronically low incomes.

The important point to remember from all these loops and arrows is that *low productivity, low incomes, and low levels of living are mutually reinforcing phenomena.* They constitute what Myrdal has called a process of "circular and cumulative causation" in which low incomes lead to low levels of living (income plus poor health, education, etc.) which keeps productivity low, which in turn perpetuates low incomes, and so on.[19]

But low levels of living, broadly defined, do not by themselves define underdevelopment. They only reflect one, although we would argue the most crucial, component of the inner meaning of development and underdevelopment. Boxes (2) and (3) in Figure 3.9—low self-esteem and limited freedom of choice—comprise the two other poles of the tripod of underdevelopment. Both are strongly influenced by low levels of living; both in turn contribute to these low levels. For example, there is nothing inherent in low levels of living to cause low esteem or a lack of dignity among the very poor *except* when their identity and worth in other people's eyes are largely determined by their material well-being. Thus the international transfer of material-oriented values from rich nations (through the movies, television, newspapers, magazines, tourists, educational systems, foreign "experts," and community developers, etc.) can and usually does alter the determinants of self-esteem so that low living levels cause individuals to feel a low sense of worthiness. Conversely, low self-respect can contribute to low levels of living as a result of poor attitudes toward life, work, cleanliness, punctuality, and self-improvement. These relationships are captured by the arrows that connect Boxes (1) and (2).

Low levels of living also influence and are influenced by limited freedom—Box (3) and arrows between Boxes (1) and (3). They make people and nations vulnerable to, dependent on, and often dominated by those who are materially better off. This greatly limits the range of choice regarding national and personal life-styles. Conversely, limited freedom greatly weakens nations and people and forces them to accept an international economic order in which the progress of the rich may have a chronic "backwash" effect perpetuating the low living levels of the poor.

Finally, note that Boxes (2) and (3) are also connected by arrows showing cause and effect. Limited freedom means that nations and individuals have little or no control over their own destinies. They are therefore likely to have a lower opinion of themselves and to lose some respect in the eyes of others. Conversely, nations and people with low self-esteem often do not have the economic, psychological, or physical strength to resist domination and a loss of their freedom to choose.

Taken together, the three boxes in Figure 3.9 present a concise portrait of the nature and inner meaning of underdevelopment. While low levels of living, low self-esteem, and limited freedom all work in a cumulative cause-and-effect process to perpetuate underdevelopment, it is clear that without improving the level of living of people within a nation, the prospects for development are practically nonexistent. *It follows that the first priority of moving from a chronic state of underdevelopment to one of development must be the improvement of people's levels of living. For this reason economics must play a central role in the development process.* However, the impact of that role will be greatly diminished, even nullified, if at the same time the importance of attending to the determinants of national and personal esteem and of striving to broaden society's freedom to choose are not also afforded priority attention by Third World politicians and planners alike.

NOTES

1. In addition to this section on theories of development, the student is encouraged to consult readings 3, 4, and 5 by Papanek, Henriot, and Lisk in my collection, *The Struggle for Economic Development*, pp. 17–54.

2. W. W. Rostow, *The Stages of Economic Growth, A Non-Communist Manifesto* (London: Cambridge University Press, 1960), pp. 1, 3, 4, and 12. For an extensive and critical review of the Rostow stages doctrine from a Marxist perspective see P. Baran and E. Hobsbaum, "The stages of economic growth," *Kyklos* 14 (1961): 234–242.

3. This model is named after two economists, Sir Roy Harrod of England and Professor Evesey Domar of the United States, who separately but concurrently developed a variant of it in the early 1950s.

4. W. A. Lewis, "Economic development with unlimited supplies of labour," *Manchester School*, 1954; and J. C. H. Fei and G. Ranis, *Development of the Labor Surplus Economy: Theory and Policy* (Homewood, Ill: Irwin, 1964).

5. See, for example, Hollis Chenery, *Structural Change and Development Policy* (Baltimore: Johns Hopkins University Press, 1979); "Industrialization and growth," *World Bank Staff Working Papers No. 539* (1982); and Hollis Chenery and Moises Syrquin, *Patterns of Development, 1950–70* (London: Oxford University Press, 1975).

6. For one of the most comprehensive introductions to the neo-Marxist view of international development and underdevelopment, see Paul Baran, *The Political Economy of Neo-Colonialism* (London: Heinemann, 1975).

7. A provocative and well-documented application of this argument to the case of Kenya can be found in Colin Leys, *Underdevelopment in Kenya: The Political Economy of Neo-Colonialism* (London: Heinemann, 1975).

8. Theotonio Dos Santos, "The crisis of development theory and the problem of dependence in Latin America," *Siglo* 21 (1969). See also Benjamin J. Cohen, *The Question of Imperialism: The Political Economy of Dominance and Dependence* (New York: Basic Books, 1973).

9. Hans Singer, "Dualism revisited: A new approach to the problems of dual societies in developing countries," *Journal of Development Studies* 7, no. 1 (1970):60−61.

10. *Ibid*, p. 62.

11. Dudley Seers, "The meaning of development," *Eleventh World Conference of the Society for International Development*, New Delhi (1969), p. 3.

12. Denis Goulet, *The Cruel Choice: A New Concept in the Theory of Development* (New York: Atheneum, 1971), p. 23. Part of Chapter 1 of the Goulet book is reprinted as reading 1 in *The Struggle for Economic Development*.

13. *Ibid*, pp. 87−94.

14. For a description of the "basic needs" approach see Franklyn Lisk, "Conventional development strategies and basic needs fulfilment," reprinted as Reading 5 in *The Struggle for Economic Development* and P.K. Ghosh (ed.), *Third World Development: A Basic Needs Approach* (Westport, Conn.: Greenwood, 1984).

15. *Ibid.*, p. 124.

16. For a recent attempt to specify and quantify the concept of basic needs, see ILO, *Employment, Growth and Basic Needs* (Geneva: International Labor Organization, 1976). A similar view with a focus on the notion of "entitlements" can be found in Amartya Sen, "Development: Which way now?" *The Economic Journal* 93 (December 1983):754−757.

17. Denis Goulet, *Cruel Choice*, pp. 89, 90. For an even more provocative discussion of the meaning of individual self-esteem and respect in the context of Latin American development see Paulo Freire, *Pedagogy of the Oppressed* (Harmondsworth, England: Penguin, 1972).

18. W. Arthur Lewis, "Is economic growth desirable?" in *The Theory of Economic Growth* (London: Allen & Unwin, 1963), p. 420.

19. See Gunnar Myrdal, *Asian Drama* (New York: Pantheon, 1968), Appendix 4.

CONCEPTS FOR REVIEW

Development	Structural change models
Underdevelopment	Lewis two-sector model
Spread effects	Surplus labor
Dominance	Labor-saving capital accumulation
Dependence	Patterns of development analysis
Vulnerability	Institutional wage
Stages of growth theory of development	Neocolonial dependence model
Capital/output ratio	*Comprador* groups
Capital stock	False paradigm model
Savings ratio	Dualism
Center and periphery	Life sustenance, self-esteem, freedom
Harrod−Domar equation	Vicious circle
Necessary and sufficient conditions	Circular cumulative causation

QUESTIONS FOR DISCUSSION

1. Explain the essential distinctions between the stages of growth theory of underdevelopment, the structural change models of Lewis and Chenery, and the theory of international dependence in both its neo-Marxist and false paradigm conceptualizations. Which model do you think provides the best explanation of the situation in most Third World nations? Explain.

2. Explain the meaning of dualism and dual societies. Do you think that the concept of dualism adequately portrays the development picture in most Third World countries? Explain.

3. Some people claim that international dualism and domestic dualism are merely different manifestations of the same phenomenon. What do you think they mean by this and is it a valid conceptualization? Explain.

4. Briefly describe the various definitions of the meaning of "development" encountered in the text. What are the strengths and weaknesses of each approach? Do you think that there are other dimensions of development not mentioned in the text? If so, please describe them. If not, please explain why you believe that the textual description of the meaning of development is adequate.

5. Why is a strictly economic definition of development inadequate? What do you understand "economic" development to mean? Can you give hypothetical or real examples of situations in which a country may be developing economically but still be underdeveloped?

6. Why is an understanding of the meaning of development crucial to policy formulation in Third World nations? Do you think it is possible for a nation to agree on a rough definition of development and orient its strategies for achieving these objectives accordingly? What might be some of the roadblocks or constraints in realizing these development objectives—both economic and noneconomic?

FURTHER READINGS

1. On the complex question of what the real meaning of development and underdevelopment is, see Dudley Seers, "The meaning of development," in Nancy Bastor (ed.), *Measuring Development* (London: Frank Cass, 1972); Gunnar Myrdal, *The Challenge of World Poverty* (New York: Pantheon, 1970), Chapters 1–4; Celso Furtado, *Development and Underdevelopment* (Berkeley and Los Angeles: University of California Press, 1964), especially Chapter 4; Denis Goulet, *The Cruel Choice: A New Concept on the Theory of Development* (New York: Atheneum, 1971), Chapter 2; Mahbub ul Haq, "Crisis in development strategies," *World Development* (1973); Irma Adelman, "Development economics: A reassessment of goals," *American Economic Review* 65, no. 2 (1975); the various readings in Henry Bernstein (ed.), *Underdevelopment and Development: The Third World Today* (Harmondsworth, England: Penguin, 1973); M.D. Morris, *Measuring the Condition of the World's Poor: The Physical Quality of Life Index* (New York: Pergamon, 1979); and Norman Hicks and Paul Streeten, "Indicators of development: The search for a basic needs yardstick," *World Development* 7, no. 6 (1979).

2. For a survey of various theories of development as well as a review of alternative development strategies see articles by Papanek, Henriot, and Lisk, readings 3, 4, and 5 in *The Struggle for Economic Development*. Another thoughtful and provocative analysis can be found in Amartya Sen, "Development: Which way now?" *The Economic Journal* 93 (December 1983):745–762.

3. For an excellent summary statement of the concept of dualism and dual societies, see Hans Singer, "Dualism revisited: A new approach to the problems of dual society in developing countries," *Journal of Development Studies* 7, no. 1 (1970).

4. Among a number of recent surveys of the dependence literature as applied to problems of underdevelopment the following are perhaps the best: S. Amin, *Imperialism and Unequal Development* (New York: Monthly Review Press, 1977); F. H. Cardoso, "Dependence and development in Latin America," *New Left Review*, July–August 1972, pp. 83–95; P. O'Brien, "A critique of Latin American theories of dependency," in I. Oxaal *et al.* (eds.), *Beyond the Sociology of Development* (London: Routledge and Kegan Paul, 1975); Sanjaya Lall, "Is 'dependence' a useful concept in analysing underdevelopment?" *World Development* 3, nos. 11 and 12 (1975): 799–810; G. Kay, *Development and Underdevelopment: A Marxist Analysis* (London: Macmillan, 1975); Gabriel Palma, "Dependency: A formal theory of underdevelopment or a methodology for the analysis of concrete situations of underdevelopment." *World Development* 6 (1978); and Ronald H. Chilcote, *Theories of Development and Underdevelopment* (Boulder: Westview Press, 1984). See also bibliography to Appendix 3.1.

Additional readings can be found on pp. 616–618.

APPENDIX 3.1

THE NEO-MARXIST THEORY AND CRITIQUE OF ECONOMIC DEVELOPMENT[1]

In this appendix we present a brief exposition of the neo-Marxists' views on economic development. Neo-Marxist theory rests on two foundations: the *theory of monopoly capitalism* and the *theory of imperialism*. Although in many ways the theory of imperialism follows from the theory of monopoly capitalism, the former does not entirely determine the latter. In other words, the specific forms that imperialism will take as a relationship of domination of the poor countries of the "periphery" by the rich countries of the "center" cannot be fully anticipated. This "indeterminacy" is enhanced in view of two factors: (a) the predominance of politics over economics in international relations and the greater difficulty in predicting political decisions; and (b) by the fact that neither the center nor the periphery are homogeneous, so that there can be a multitude of kinds of domination and dependence. Thus, the neo-Marxist model purports to show only the general characteristics of this relationship, while allowing enough room for a wide variety of specific situations.

The fundamental thesis of the neo-Marxists regarding the relationship between rich and poor countries is that the center is actually inimical to the development of peripheral countries and that a capitalist development of LDCs is *impossible* today. This is one of two major departures of the neo-Marxists from the writings of Marx, Engels, and the classical writers on imperialism. It can be explained, in very general terms, by means of their other major departure: the need under monopoly capitalism for a system of external sources of demand and profitable outlets for investment, a need that is greater because of the operation of the Marxian law of the "rising surplus," which makes monopoly capitalism more expansive and outwardly aggressive than its predecessor, competitive capitalism.

According to neo-Marxists, the relationship between the center and periphery is, by virtue of the nature of the structural needs of the center, necessarily one of *exploitation*: surplus or profit is transferred, through various channels, from the periphery to the center. This, in turn, aggravates the surplus-absorption difficulties of the center and induces further outward expansion. Thus, the LDCs are caught in the explosive vicious spiral of the center's surplus-absorption problem; at the same time, the *surplus drain* they are subjected to and other factors (to be explained below) make their economic development an impossibility.

There are some important differences on this point: while the founders of the neo-Marxist school—Baran, Sweezy, and Magdoff—see this ever-present surplus drain as the decisive factor and a sufficient condition for the *impossi-*

bility of LDC development, Amin and Thomas (see bibliography at the end of this appendix for specific references), emphasizing the "other" factors that led to the development of an inappropriate economic structure in the LDCs, are led to question the absolute validity of the "impossibility thesis." Thus, according to these neo-Marxists, a distinction must be made between the "impossibility" and the "inappropriate pattern" of LDC development.

This difference is crucial. Because of their emphasis on the surplus drain (which they assume to be of crippling magnitude), the early neo-Marxists saw imperialism as a system that created a necessary *polarity* between an extremely poor periphery and a prospering center. Poverty and wealth were thus seen as the two faces of the same coin. This view, implying as it does the impossibility of capitalist development of LDCs, is, in its resemblance to a zero-sum game, unrealistic, dogmatic, and subject to damaging criticism. Quite arbitrarily, the early neo-Marxists assumed (a) that a very large part of the surplus is drained, and (b) that the part of the surplus not drained is not utilized in a way conducive to local development. Thus, for them, even if the proportion of drained to not-drained is low, there is no growth.

By being more realistic on these two points, Amin and Thomas tried to replace the dogmatic "impossibility thesis" by that of the *necessary inappropriateness of the pattern of LDC development*. Using Marx's terminology, Amin has called the surplus drain the "continuing primitive accumulation" by the center, but he allows both for a residue of surplus left in the hands of local LDC elites and for the possibility of the rational utilization of this surplus toward the development of LDCs. In this way, the neo-Marxist model's ability to fit the facts is thought to be greatly enhanced. The inappropriateness of the LDC's pattern of development is then seen as the necessary consequence of its inclusion in the periphery of the world capitalist system.

The neo-Marxists also reject the "vicious circle" arguments of the early mainstream development literature. These theories, they claim, have served as ideological weapons for the creation of a climate of dependency, fatalism, and resignation in poorer nations, thus helping to perpetuate their poverty and their habit of looking for outside help for their development. Baran's criticism of the vicious circle theories is most often quoted. He argues:

> *It would seem that we are faced with a vicious circle. There can be no modernization of agriculture without industrialization, and there can be no industrialization without an increase of agricultural output and surplus. Yet, as is usual in the universe of social and economic relations, the interlocking of factors appears thus stringent, and the circularity of a constellation thus compelling, only so long as it is considered merely abstractly—merely "speculatively," as Marx would have said. In a concrete historical situation there are a number of elements that enter the process and permit a breakthrough where in the "grayness of theory" an exit appears impossible.*[2]

The implication, according to neo-Marxists, is that a vicious circle theory is the necessary outcome of a mode of thinking that refuses to recognize the historical specificity of the concrete situation, where an outside stimulus to growth is usually found. In the early development of capitalism, Baran further argues, this necessary outside stimulus was furnished by what Marx has called "primitive accumulation," especially the looting of colonies. In Soviet Russia, the extreme privations imposed on the population by Stalin's tyranny cut the Gordian knot of underdevelopment; an economic surplus was created that was utilized in the development of industry and agriculture in a roughly simultaneous process.

For Baran, the real problem in LDCs is not the presence of the vicious circle—a phenomenon whose existence is acknowledged—but the lack of a significant stimulus to development aggravated by the surplus drain. Here again we have a polar view, something like a zero-sum game, in which the continuing primitive accumulation by the center implies a simultaneous *negative* primitive accumulation for the periphery. Surplus transfers, then, create and perpetuate underdevelopment in the LDCs, a phenomenon Frank has called "the development of underdevelopment."

Amin, too, adopts Frank's motto, but with an altered meaning; for Amin, it means a "dependent development," that is, an inappropriate pattern of growth imposed upon the country through its ties with the center—literally, through its being included in the world capitalist system. This view in turn allows for the possibility of growth of aggregate income, an observed fact in many LDCs.

The crucial problem of how the available surplus is utilized in LDCs leads the neo-Marxists to the examination of *local elites*. Although writers like Baran and Sweezy become extremely contemptuous at times, their contempt is more a political posture than a moral judgment: it seeks to make plain that no local development is to be expected from such elites. On the contrary, the elites are by their nature a factor contributing to underdevelopment. The analysis is based on the "objective situation" in which these elites find themselves. Their economic behavior—conspicuous consumption, investments in real estate and extreme risk-aversion, the export of their savings to be deposited with foreign banks for security, their avoidance of investments in industry—is, from the standpoint of private advantage, essentially a rational response to the circumstances in which they find themselves. Their fear of foreign competition were they to invest in more productive activities is seen as fully justified. Most elite members lack the capital required for the establishment of enterprises able to compete with foreign oligopolies. Also lacking are entrepreneurial skills and attitudes to work and innovation conducive to growth.

Amin offers the view that local elites are *not*, in fact, "exploited" by the elites of the center. What happens is simply that their field of independent activity and initiative is severely curtailed by these elites. Anyway, many members of LDC elites profit, too, from foreign activities in their country. What enables Amin to say this is his adoption of Emmanuel's theory of unequal exchange, in which the level of wages is the major determining factor. That wages are lower in LDCs means that the labor force of these countries carries the burden of exploitation both by its local capitalist class and by the capitalist class at the center. It is burdened by the "regular" exploitation of the home capitalists and the "primitive accumulation" of the capitalist class at the center. The higher wages that the center's working class enjoys are in turn attributed solely to its higher productivity; it does *not* partake of the proceeds of the continuing primitive accumulation.

That there is also a disheartening lack of *entrepreneurial and administrative talent* in the countries of the Third World the neo-Marxists do not deny. But they view those who place this fact at the center of their explanations of underdevelopment as being eclectic and arbitrary. They claim that entrepreneurial and administrative skills will be found or created as soon as the "objective conditions" that will make their utilization possible and necessary appear—conditions that cannot exist in an environment of dependence. This problem, they claim, is secondary; it is a consequence of the fundamental problem, which is the discouragement and systematic sabotaging (or, for Amin and Thomas, the guiding into wrong paths) of local development efforts by the center.

From this view of the economic impotence of the elites at the periphery, the neo-Marxists are led to the conclusion that in LDCs only *the state* can mobilize the surplus in a way conducive to the country's development. This could be done in two ways. First, the state could itself become a capitalist and finance industrialization with state-owned enterprises. Within the context of world capitalism, however, such a role for the state is necessarily limited. Second, the state could put sufficient funds in the hands of capable members of the local elite in the form of long-term loans. This common practice is behind the view of LDC states as *instruments of class creation*. Once the existence of a local industrial capitalist class is seen as a necessary precondition of growth, the state tries to create such a class out of an existing elite that is exclusively commercial, bureaucratic, and landed. But the state is soon caught in a contradiction: an indigenous industrial capitalist class is likely to find itself pitted against more powerful foreign competitors—to whose needs the state typically caters in a servile manner—and also against the local commercial capitalist, bureaucratic, and landed interests, who are as servile to the foreign interests as the state. Usually, then, the state invests in sectors not competing with the foreign interests, such as infrastructural investments and tourism.

The relatively high investment in *infrastructures*, mainly *transport and communications*, that the neo-Marxists believe characteristic of LDCs, are seen either as the result of the full-employment policies of LDC "New Deal" governments with no other investment choices because of foreign competition or as a "natural" policy for *comprador* regimes that aid by local means in the exploitation of the country by foreign capital. As proof of this last thesis, it is asserted that roads are built in such a way as to serve not the needs of the indigenous population but those of foreign companies: access to trade centers, ports, and locations of multinational companies.

The second area of high local investment, *tourism*, is seen with wrathful scorn. This, neo-Marxists claim, is the direct result of dependence, an easy solution to chronic LDC problems. It brings in foreign exchange, creates employment, and raises the level of construction activities—construction being one of the few industries not usually taken over by foreigners. But the resulting ills are greater than the benefits. Contact with foreign habits (often the habits of a wealthy class) disrupts the indigenous culture and creates consumption patterns and tastes likely to worsen the country's balance of payments and its saving ability. "Demonstration effects" become very significant in LDCs: foreign consumption patterns are symbols of status.

Just as large oligopolistic firms are seen as dominating the domestic market of the center, so too are the foreign branches of these companies seen as the main instruments of domination of the Third World by the center. *Multinational corporations* (MNCs) are seen by neo-Marxists as the power units of modern imperialism, while the role of the state of the imperialist country is merely that of an assistant and supporter.

The views of neo-Marxists as to the effects of the operations of MNCs on their host countries of the Third World thus show an overwhelming unidirectionality: they see only negative effects, or, at the most, positive effects that are either offset by negative ones or are of trivial importance. (See Chapter 14 for a more balanced discussion of the pros and cons of MNCs in the Third World.)

Since the profit motive is assumed to remain the central dominant motive under monopoly capitalism, the MNC's essential role, as viewed by neo-Marxist writers, is to be an instrument in the transfer of economic surplus (profits) from the periphery to the center. Therefore, the *raison d'être* of MNCs, their essential function, makes them deleterious to the development of their host countries of the Third World. For neo-Marxists, MNCs are essentially deleterious to the development of the Third World because they are instruments of the profit motive. And for Marx, there can be no rationalization for profits: they represent theft, pure and simple. Thus, the neo-Marxists' theses on MNCs are the result of their method (predominance of profit motive), their view of profit as theft, and their view of the MNC as an instrument of the profit motive. Unfortunately, this leads them to play down the importance of some observable beneficial effects of MNCs on LDCs.

The same *radicalism* inherent in the neo-Marxists' view of MNCs can also be found in their views on foreign investment, aid, trade, and international relations in general. *Foreign investment*, whether public or private, is seen as *the* major instrument of penetration of the periphery by the center. Since the choice of projects to be undertaken is left to foreign investors, in real terms their role is to make the peripheral economies an appendage to those of the center. Even when the power of making decisions is not totally in the hands of foreign investors (with regard to specific projects), the international price structure, reflecting as it does the preferences and scarcities of the center, and the neoclassical planning method of project evaluation (recommended to LDCs by international organizations, aid agencies, etc.—see Chapter 15) based on these center prices brings almost the same effect. Thus the center is accused of imposing on peripheral economies a growth pattern incompatible with local needs. But it is also seen as undermining to a significant extent the possibility and speed of this growth since an initial inflow of foreign capital will induce a much higher outflow in the following years in the form of payment of interest, amortization, repatriated profits, and *flight capital*—the local elites' savings exported for security.

According to the theory of monopoly capital, therefore, foreign investment is a consequence of the center's desperate search for profitable investment outlets. Any such outlet is likely to be exploited by the center. Early neo-Marxists held, for example, that the preferred area of foreign investment was raw materials extraction (particularly energy-related raw materials). This process was seen as a reflection of the postwar scarcity that the center faced with regard to crucial raw materials and as a calculated attempt to reverse its own dependence on such supplies from the countries of the periphery by creating a "dependency" in the opposite direction. It can be argued, however, that the more relevant question is what happens in *real* terms in the time interval between the investment of foreign capital and the repatriation of profits. Traditionalists, for example, argue that the building of factories and the creation of local skills could not have been created without foreign investment. Therefore, they claim that in some cases it may pay to be exploited. The foreign investor's profits thus represent the price paid for such external benefits. But such a view of profits is totally incompatible with Marx's (and the neo-Marxists') view of them as "exploitation" and theft.

Aid is seen by neo-Marxists in a role complementary to that of foreign investment. Either indirectly, when the aid funds are used by the LDC government for infrastructural investments, or directly, when the use of the aid funds is specified by the donor country, aid opens the country up to foreign capital and oils the mechanisms of surplus transfer. Since it is predominantly public, aid is seen by neo-Marxists as the government expenditures component in the process of exploitation of LDCs by private investment.

Strategic considerations make aid an invaluable foreign policy tool. Much aid is given to avert political crises unfavorable to the center, and a large component of aid is for military purposes; for example, for rent for U.S. military bases. The result of such aid is said to be the transfer of decision-making power from the local authorities to the state of the donor country. Thus, aid is seen as an instrument in the service of the motives for control and profit. The structure of the system has no specific, permanent, and necessary place for humanitarian aid; hence such aid is negligible. It is further assumed by neo-Marxists that even the small amount of humanitarian aid that is given is used in the same way as public aid, since it is given through the same channels.

Similar arguments are presented by neo-Marxists for *multilateral* aid, whose "multilaterality" is seen as a device for minimizing risks. Thus, the anger of the exploited poor of the Third World cannot find a concrete target. The international institutions that administer such aid (e.g., the World Bank, the IMF) under the banner of philanthropism are seen as mere accomplices in the exploitation by the center.

Finally, some neo-Marxists criticize the current *dualist* theories of development as misleading because these theories neglect what, according to them, is the basic fact, the "compulsive" and intentional transfer of surplus from the traditional to the modern sector and from the periphery to the center. For them nothing short of political and social revolution can alter the current state of affairs and bring about self-reliant development.

This completes our examination of the neo-Marxists' critique of contemporary economic development. At its core is a rigid ideology and an extremely demanding goal of economic development together with the brutal realization of its necessity; a necessity, it is claimed, that grows out of the great moral and economic evils of dependence, even of "dependent development," and because of the irrationality of the current international system that fosters these evils.

Other less radical observers, however, while agreeing with much of the neo-Marxist analysis (though disputing fundamental propositions), would argue that change *can* be initiated from within and outside the present system—and need not be revolutionary in character. They point out that the neo-Marxists have no prescriptions beyond revolution and note that revolutionary movements have a tendency to substitute one kind of exploitation (political, religious, and social) for another (economic).

But whatever the relative merits of the neo-Marxist and various structuralist and traditionalist theories, one can be sure that the debate among them will rage on in the coming years as the North–South confrontation intensifies.

NOTES

1. The assistance of my student, George Yannacogeogos, in the preparation of this appendix is much appreciated.
2. P. Baran, *The Political Economy of Growth* (New York: Monthly Review Press, 1968), p. 277.

FURTHER READINGS

Amin, Samir. *Accumulation on a World Scale: A Critique of the Theory of Underdevelopment.* Trans. Brian Pearce. New York: Monthly Review Press, 1974.

Amin, Samir. *Unequal Development: An Essay on the Social Formations of Peripheral Capitalism.* Trans. Brian Pearce. New York: Monthly Review Press, 1976.

Baran, Paul. *The Political Economy of Growth.* New York: Monthly Review Press, 1968.

Baran, Paul. *The Longer View: Essays toward a Critique of Political Economy.* Ed. John O'Neill. New York: Monthly Review Press, 1971.

Baran, Paul, and Sweezy, Paul. *Monopoly Capital: An Essay on the American Economic and Social Order.* New York: Monthly Review Press, 1968.

Barraclough, Geoffrey. *An Introduction to Contemporary History.* Baltimore: Penguin, 1967.

Barratt-Brown, Michael. *The Economics of Imperialism.* Baltimore: Penguin, 1976.

Brenner, Robert. "The origins of capitalist development: A critique of neo-Smithian Marxism." *New Left Review,* July–August 1977, pp. 25–92.

Cardoso, Fernando Henrique. "Dependence and development in Latin America." *New Left Review,* July–August 1972, pp. 83–95.

Emmanuel, Arghiri. *Unequal Exchange: An Essay on the Imperialism of Trade.* New York: Monthly Review Press, 1972.

Frank, Andre Gunder. "The development of underdevelopment." *Monthly Review* 18, no. 4 (1966).

Jalée, Pierre. *The Pillage of the Third World.* Trans. Mary Klopper. New York: Monthly Review Press, 1968.

Laclau(h), Ernesto. "Feudalism and capitalism in Latin America." *New Left Review,* May–June 1971, pp. 19–38.

Lall, Sanjaya. "Is 'dependence' a useful concept in analysing underdevelopment?" *World Development* 3, nos. 11 and 12 (1975):799–810.

Magdoff, Harry. *The Age of Imperialism: The Economics of U.S. Foreign Policy.* New York: Monthly Review Press, 1969.

Magdoff, Harry, and Sweezy, Paul. *The Dynamics of U.S. Capitalism: Corporate Structure, Inflation, Credit, Gold and the Dollar.* New York: Monthly Review Press, 1974.

Mills, C. Wright. *The Marxists.* New York: Dell, 1975.

Palma, Gabriel. "Dependency: A formal theory of underdevelopment or a methodology for the analysis of concrete situations of underdevelopment?" *World Development* 6 (1978): 881–924.

Radice, Hugo (ed.). *International Firms and Modern Imperialism.* Baltimore: Penguin, 1975.

Rhodes, Robert I. *Imperialism and Underdevelopment: A Reader.* New York: Monthly Review Press, 1970.

Schumpeter, Joseph. *Imperialism/Social Classes: Two Essays.* New York: New American Library, 1974.

Sweezy, Paul M. *The Theory of Capitalist Development.* New York: Monthly Review Press, 1970.

Sweezy, Paul M. *Modern Capitalism and Other Essays.* New York: Monthly Review Press, 1972.

Thomas, Clive Y. *Dependence and Transformation: The Economics of the Transition to Socialism.* New York: Monthly Review Press, 1974.

Warren, Bill. "Imperialism and capitalist industrialization." *New Left Review,* September–October 1973, pp. 3–44.

APPENDIX 3.2

SOCIAL INDICATORS AS ALTERNATIVE MEASURES OF DEVELOPMENT

The problems associated with using per capita GNP as a measure of development are well known. Among the major objections to this measure are its failure to include non-marketed (and, therefore, non-priced) subsistence production including much of women's household work and to incorporate welfare and income distribution considerations. As a result, there have been numerous efforts both to remedy its defects and to create other composite indicators that could serve as complements or alternatives to this traditional measure.[1] Basically, such indicators fall into two groups—those that seek to measure development in terms of a "normal" or "optimal" pattern of interaction among social, economic, and political factors and those that measure development in terms of the quality of life.

One of the major studies on the first group of composite indicators was carried out by the United Nations Research Institute on Social Development (UNRISD) in 1970.[2] The study was concerned with the selection of the most appropriate indicators of development and an analysis of the relationship between these indicators at different levels of development. The result was the construction of a composite social development index. Originally, 73 indicators were examined. However, only 16 core indicators (9 social indicators and 7 economic indicators) were ultimately chosen (see Table A3.1). These indicators were selected on the basis of their high intercorrelation to form a development index using weights derived from their various degrees of correlation. The development index was found to correlate more highly with individual social and economic indicators than per capita GNP correlated with the same indicators. Rankings of some countries under the development index differed from per capita GNP rankings. It was also found that the development index was more highly correlated with per capita GNP for developed countries than for developing ones. The study concluded that social development occurred at a more rapid pace than economic development up to a level of $500 per capita (1960 prices).

Another study that sought to measure development in terms of a pattern of interaction among social, economic, and political factors was that made by Adelman and Morris which classified 74 developing countries according to 41 variables, listed in Table A3.2.[3] Factor analysis was used to examine the interdependence between social and political variables and the level of economic development. They found numerous correlations between certain key variables and economic development.

Table A3.1 UNRISD List of Core Indicators of Socioeconomic Development

Expectation of life at birth
Percentage of population in localities of 20,000 and over
Consumption of animal protein, per capita, per day
Combined primary and secondary enrollment
Vocational enrollment ratio
Average number of persons per room
Newspaper circulation per 1,000 population
Percentage of economically active population with electricity, gas, water, etc.
Agricultural production per male agricultural worker
Percentage of adult male labor in agriculture
Electricity consumption, kw per capita
Steel consumption, kg per capita
Energy consumption, kg of coal equivalent per capita
Percentage GDP derived from manufacturing
Foreign trade per capita, in 1960 U.S. dollars
Percentage of salaried and wage earners to total economically active population

SOURCE: UNRISD, *Contents and Measurement of Socioeconomic Development* (Geneva, 1970), p. 63.

The major criticism of these studies is that they seek to measure development in terms of structural change rather than in terms of human welfare. There is also the implicit assumption that developing countries must develop along the lines of the developed countries, as illustrated by researchers' use of indicators such as animal protein consumption per capita or energy consumption per capita.

Furthermore, there is usually an emphasis on measuring inputs, such as the number of doctors or hospital beds per 1,000 population or enrollment rates in schools to measure health and education, when outputs, such as life expectancy and literacy, are the actual objectives of development. In response to these criticisms, several studies have sought to develop composite indicators that measure development in terms of meeting the basic needs of the majority of the population or in terms of the "quality of life."

One well-known endeavor in this area was the development of the Physical Quality of Life Index (PQLI) undertaken by Morris.[4] Three indicators—life expectancy at age one, infant mortality, and literacy—were used to form a simple composite index (PQLI). For each indicator, the performance of individual countries is rated on a scale of 1 to 100, where 1 represents the "worst" performance by any country and 100 the "best" performance. For life expectancy, the upper limit of 100 was assigned to 77 years (achieved by Sweden in 1973) and the lower limit of 1 was assigned to 28 years (the life expectancy of Guinea Bissau in 1950). Within these limits, each country's life expectancy figure is ranked from 1 to 100. For example, a life expectancy of 52, midway between the upper and lower limits of 77 and 28, would be assigned a rating of 50. Similarly for infant mortality, the upper limit was set at 9 per 1,000 (achieved by Sweden in 1973) and the lower limit at 229 per 1,000 (Gabon, 1950). Literacy rates, being measured as percentages of from 1 to 100, provide their own direct scale. Once a country's performance in life expectancy, infant mortality, and literacy has been rated on the scale of 1 to 100, the composite

Table A3.2 Social, Political, and Economic Variables: Adelman and Morris

Size of the traditional agricultural sector
Extent of dualism
Extent of urbanization
Character of basic social organization
Importance of the indigenous middle class
Extent of social mobility
Extent of literacy
Extent of mass communication
Degree of cultural and ethnic homogeneity
Degree of social tension
Crude fertility rate
Degree of modernization of outlook
Degree of national integration and sense of national unity
Extent of centralization of political power
Strength of democratic institutions
Degree of freedom of political opposition and press
Degree of competitiveness of political parties
Predominant basis of the political party system
Strength of the labor movement
Political strength of the traditional elite
Political strength of the military
Degree of administrative efficiency
Extent of leadership commitment to economic development
Extent of political stability
Per capita GNP in 1961
Rate of growth of real per capita GNP: 1950/51 – 1963/64
Abundance of natural resources
Gross investment rate
Level of modernization of industry
Change in degree of industrialization since 1950
Character of agricultural organization
Level of modernization of techniques in agriculture
Degree of improvement in agricultural productivity since 1950
Level of adequacy of physical overhead capital
Degree of improvement in physical overhead capital since 1950
Level of effectiveness of the tax system
Degree of improvement in the tax system since 1950
Level of effectiveness of financial institutions
Degree of improvement in human resources
Structure of foreign trade

SOURCE: Irma Adelman and Cynthia Taft Morris, *Society, Politics, and Economic Development* (Baltimore: Johns Hopkins University Press, 1967).

index (PQLI) for the country is calculated by averaging the three ratings, giving equal weight to each.

While the study found that countries with low per capita GNPs tended to have low PQLIs and countries with high per capita GNPs tended to have high PQLIs, the correlations between GNP and PQLI were not substantially close. Some countries with high per capita GNPs had very low PQLIs—even below the average of the poorest countries. Other countries with very low per capita

GNPs had PQLIs that were higher than the average for the upper-middle-income countries. Table A3.3 provides a sample of Third World countries ranked both by per capita incomes and PQLIs in the early 1980s. The data seem to indicate that significant improvements in the basic quality of life can be achieved before there is any great rise in per capita GNP, or conversely, that a higher level of per capita GNP is not a guarantee of a better quality of life. Note in particular the wide PQLI variations for countries with similar levels of per capita income such as Angola and Zimbabwe, China and India, Tanzania and Gambia, Taiwan and Iraq, and Costa Rica and Brazil. A particularly striking contrast is that between Saudi Arabia and Sri Lanka.

The PQLI appears on the surface to be free of the major problems associated with using GNP as a measure of development. It aims directly at incorporating welfare considerations through measuring the ends of development in terms of the quality of human life. It also incorporates distributional considerations by using three indicators that reflect distributional characteristics in the sense that countries cannot achieve high national averages of life expectancy, infant mortality, and literacy unless the majorities of their populations are receiving the benefits of progress in each of these areas. Moreover, there is general agreement that improvements in these areas are an important part of development progress. And, like GNP, the PQLI can be used to make inter-country comparisons. In contrast to the other alternative indicators discussed, it has the major advantage of being a simple measure with data being easily available.

One of the major criticisms of the PQLI, however, is that it is a limited measure, failing to incorporate many other social and psychological characteristics suggested by the term "quality of life"—security, justice, human rights, and so on. A much more serious criticism is the lack of a rationale for

Table A3.3 A Comparison of Per Capita GNP and the Physical Quality of Life Index (PQLI) for Selected LDCs, 1981

Country	Per Capita GNP ($)	PQLI
Gambia	348	20
Angola	790	21
Sudan	380	34
Pakistan	349	40
Saudi Arabia	12,720	40
India	253	42
Iraq	3,020	48
Qatar	27,790	56
Tanzania	299	58
Zimbabwe	815	63
Brazil	2,214	72
China	304	75
Sri Lanka	302	82
Singapore	5,220	86
Taiwan	2,503	87
Costa Rica	1,476	89

SOURCE: John P. Lewis and Veleriana Kellab (eds.), *U.S. Foreign Policy and the Third World, Agenda 1983* (New York: Praeger, 1983), Table C-3.

giving equal weight to each of the indicators used in forming the index and the possibility that measures such as life expectancy and infant mortality are both reflecting similar phenomena.

Nevertheless, despite its limitations, the PQLI appears to be a useful indicator of development, making up for some of the deficiencies in the GNP measure. As such, it can serve as an instructive complement to GNP statistics.

NOTES

1. Two excellent surveys of social indicators, which this section draws on, are Nancy Bastor, "Development indicators: An Introduction," in Nancy Bastor (ed.), *Measuring Development: The Role and Adequacy of Development Indicators* (London: Frank Cass, 1972), and Norman Hicks and Paul Streeten, "Indicators of development: The search for a basic needs yardstick," *World Development* 7, no. 6 (June 1979):567–580.
2. UNRISD, *Contents and Measurements of Socioeconomic Development* (Geneva: United Nations Research Institute on Social Development, 1970).
3. Irma Adelman and Cynthia Taft Morris, *Society, Politics, and Economic Development* (Baltimore: Johns Hopkins University Press, 1967).
4. Morris D. Morris, *Measuring the Condition of the World's Poor: The Physical Quality of Life Index* (London: Frank Cass, 1979).

4

HISTORIC GROWTH AND CONTEMPORARY DEVELOPMENT

LESSONS AND CONTROVERSIES

The growth position of the less developed countries today is significantly different in many respects from that of the presently developed countries on the eve of their entry into modern economic growth.

Simon Kuznets, Nobel Laureate, Economics

THE GROWTH GAME

For the past two decades a primary focus of world economic attention has been on ways to accelerate the growth rate of national incomes. Economists and politicians from all nations, rich and poor, capitalist, socialist, and mixed, have worshipped at the shrine of economic growth. At the end of every year, statistics are compiled for all countries of the world showing their relative rates of GNP growth. "Growthmanship" has become a way of life. Governments can rise or fall if their economic growth performance ranks high or low on this global scorecard. As we have seen, Third World development programs are often assessed by the degree to which their national outputs and incomes are growing. In fact, for many years the conventional wisdom equated development with the rapidity of national output growth.

In view of the central role this concept has assumed in worldwide assessment of relative national economic performance, it is important to understand the nature and causes of economic growth. In this chapter, therefore, we start by examining some of the basic concepts of the theory of economic growth, using the simple production possibility framework to portray the level, composition, and growth of national output. After looking briefly at the historical record of economic growth in contemporary rich nations, we then isolate six principal economic, structural, and institutional components that appear to have characterized all growing economies. We conclude by asking the question, Of what relevance is the historical growth experience of contemporary developed countries to the plans and strategies of present-day Third World nations?

THE ECONOMICS OF GROWTH: CAPITAL, LABOR, AND TECHNOLOGY

The major factors in or components of economic growth in any society are:

1. Capital accumulation, including all new investments in land, physical equipment, and human resources
2. Growth in population and thus, although delayed, growth in the labor force
3. Technological progress[1]

Let us look briefly at each.

Capital Accumulation

Capital accumulation results when some proportion of present income is saved and invested in order to augment future output and income. New factories, machinery, equipment, and materials increase the physical "capital stock" of a nation (i.e., the total "net" real value of all physically productive capital goods) and make it possible for expanded output levels to be achieved. These directly productive investments are supplemented by investments in what is often known as social and economic "infrastructure"—roads, electricity, water and sanitation, communications, etc.—which facilitate and integrate economic activities. For example, investment by a farmer in a new tractor may increase the total output of the vegetables he can produce, but without adequate transport facilities to get this extra product to local commercial markets, his investment may not add anything to national food production.

There are other less direct ways to invest in a nation's resources. The installation of irrigation facilities may improve the quality of a nation's agricultural land by raising productivity per hectare. If 100 hectares of irrigated land can produce the same output as 200 hectares of nonirrigated land using the same other inputs, then the installation of such irrigation is the equivalent of doubling the quantity of unirrigated land. Use of chemical fertilizers and the control of insects with pesticides may have equally beneficial effects in raising the productivity of existing farmland. All these forms of investment are ways of improving the quality of existing land resources. Their effect in raising the total "stock" of productive land is, for all practical purposes, indistinguishable from the simple clearing of hitherto unused but usable land.

Similarly, investment in human resources can improve its quality and thereby have the same or even a more powerful effect on production as an increase in human numbers. Formal schooling, vocational and on-the-job training programs, and adult and other types of "informal" education may all be made more effective in augmenting human skills and resources as a result of direct investments in buildings, equipment, and materials (e.g., books, film projectors, personal computers, science equipment, vocational tools and machinery such as lathes and grinders). The advanced and relevant training of teachers, as well as good textbooks in economics, may make an enormous difference in the quality, leadership, and productivity of a given labor force. The concept of investment in human resources is therefore analogous to that of improving the quality and thus the productivity of existing land resources through strategic investments.

All the above phenomena and many others are forms of investment that lead to "capital accumulation." Capital accumulation may add new resources (e.g., the clearing of unused land) or upgrade the quality of existing resources (e.g., irrigation, fertilizer, pesticides), but its essential feature is that it involves a tradeoff between present and future consumption—giving up a little now so that more can be had later.

Population and Labor Force Growth

Population growth and the associated, although delayed, increase in the labor force has traditionally been considered a positive factor in stimulating economic growth. A larger labor force means more productive manpower, while a larger overall population increases the potential size of domestic markets. However, it is questionable whether rapidly growing manpower supplies in "labor surplus" developing countries exert a positive or negative influence on economic progress (see Chapter 6 for a lengthy discussion of the pros and cons of population growth for economic development). Obviously it will depend on the ability of the economic system to absorb and productively employ these added workers—an ability largely associated with the rate and kind of capital accumulation and the availability of related factors, such as managerial and administrative skills.

Given an initial understanding of these first two fundamental components of economic growth and disregarding for a moment the third (technology), let us see how they interact via the production-possibility curve to expand society's potential total output of *all* goods. Recall that for a given technology and a given amount of physical and human resources, the production-possibility curve portrays the *maximum* attainable output combinations of any two commodities, say rice and radios, when all resources are fully and efficiently employed.

Suppose now that with unchanged technology the quantity of physical and human resources were to double, as a result of either investments that improved the quality of the existing resources or investment in new resources—land, capital, and, in the case of larger families, labor. Figure 4.1 shows that this doubling of total resources will cause the entire production-possibility curve to shift uniformly outward from $P-P$ to $P'-P'$. More radios and more rice can now be produced.

Since these are assumed to be the only two goods produced by this economy, it follows that the gross national product (i.e., the total value of all goods and services produced) will be higher than before. In other words, the process of economic growth is under way.

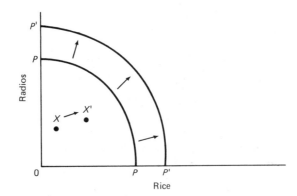

Figure 4.1. The effect of increases in physical and human resources on the production-possibility frontier.

Note that even if the country in question is operating with underutilized physical and human resources as at Point X in Figure 4.1, a growth of productive resources can result in a higher total output combination as at Point X', even though there may still be widespread unemployment and underutilized or idle capital and land. But note also that there is nothing deterministic about resource growth leading to higher output growth. This is not an economic law, as is attested by the poor growth record of many contemporary developing countries. Nor is resource growth even a necessary condition for *short-run* economic growth since the better utilization of idle existing resources can raise output levels substantially, as portrayed in the movement from Point X to X' in Figure 4.1. Nevertheless, in the *long run*, the improvement and upgrading of the quality of existing resources and new investments designed to expand the quantity of these resources are principal means of accelerating the growth of national output.

Now, instead of assuming the proportionate growth of *all* factors of production, let us assume that, say, only capital or only land is increased in quality and quantity. Diagrams *(a)* and *(b)* of Figure 4.2 show that if radio manufacturing is a *relatively* large user of capital equipment while rice production is a *relatively* land-intensive process, then the shifts in society's production-possibility curve will be more pronounced for radios when capital grows rapidly (Figure 4.2a) and for rice when the growth is in land quantity or quality (Figure 4.2b). However, since under normal conditions both products will require the use of both factors as productive inputs, albeit in different combinations, the production-possibility curve still shifts slightly outward along the rice axis in *(a)*, when only capital is increased, and along the radio axis in *(b)*, when only the quantity and/or quality of land resources are expanded.

Technological Progress

It is now time to consider the third, and to many economists the most important, source of economic growth—technological progress. In its sim-

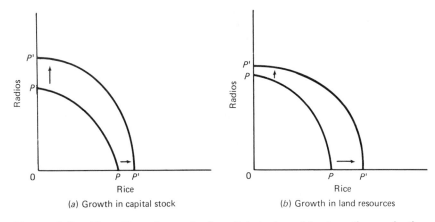

Figure 4.2. The effect of growth of capital stock and land on the production-possibility frontier.

plest form, *technological progress results from new and improved ways of accomplishing traditional tasks* such as growing maize, making clothing, or building a house. There are three basic classifications of technological progress: neutral, labor saving, and capital saving.

"Neutral" technological progress occurs when higher output levels are achieved with the same quantity and combinations of factor inputs. Simple innovations like those that arise from the division of labor can result in higher total output levels and greater consumption for all individuals. In terms of production-possibility analysis, a neutral technological change which, say, doubles total output is conceptually equivalent to a doubling of all productive inputs. The outward shifting production-possibility curve of Figure 4.1, therefore, could also be a diagrammatic representation of neutral technological progress.

On the other hand, technological progress may either be labor saving or capital saving (i.e., higher levels of output can be achieved with the same quantity of labor or capital inputs). The use of electronic computers, automated textile looms, high-speed electric drills, tractors, and mechanical ploughs—these and many other kinds of modern machinery and equipment can be classified as labor saving. As we shall discover in Chapter 8, the history of technological progress in the twentieth century has been largely one of rapid advances in labor-saving technologies of producing anything from beans to bicycles to bridges.

Capital-saving technological progress is a much rarer phenomenon. But this is primarily because almost all of the world's scientific and technological research is conducted in developed countries where the mandate is to save labor, not capital. In the labor-abundant (capital-scarce) countries of the Third World, however, capital-saving technological progress is what is most needed. Such progress results in more efficient (i.e., lower cost) labor-intensive methods of production—for example, hand- or rotary-powered weeders and threshers, foot-operated bellows pumps, and back-mounted mechanical sprayers for small-scale agriculture.[2] As we show in Chapter 8, the indigenous LDC development of low-cost, efficient, labor-intensive (capital saving) techniques of production is one of the essential ingredients in any long-run employment-oriented development strategy.

Technological progress may also be labor- or capital-augmenting. *Labor-augmenting technological progress* occurs when the quality or skills of the labor force are upgraded—for example, by the use of videotapes, televisions, and other electronic communications media for classroom instruction. Similarly, capital-augmenting technological progress results in the more productive use of existing capital goods as, for example, the substitution of steel for wooden plows in agricultural production.

We can use our production-possibility curve for rice and radios to examine two very specific examples of technological progress as it relates to output growth in developing countries. In the 1960s, agricultural scientists at the International Rice Research Institute in the Philippines developed a new and highly productive hybrid rice seed, known as IR-8, or "miracle rice." These new seeds, along with later further scientific improvements, enabled some rice farmers in parts of Southeast Asia to double and triple their per hectare yields in a matter of a few years. In effect, this technological progress was "embodied" in the new rice seeds (one could also say it was "land augmenting"), which permitted higher output levels to be achieved with essentially the same complementary inputs (although more fertilizer and pesticides were recommended). In terms of our production-possibility analysis, the higher-yielding varieties of hybrid rice could be depicted as in Figure 4.3 by an outward shift of the curve along the rice axis with the intercept on the radio axis remaining essentially unchanged (i.e., the new rice seeds could not be directly used to increase radio production).

In terms of the technology of radio production, the invention of transistors probably has had as significant an impact on communications as did the discovery of the steam engine on transportation. Even in the remotest parts of Africa, Asia, and Latin America, the transistor radio has become a prized possession. The introduction of the transistor, by obviating the need for

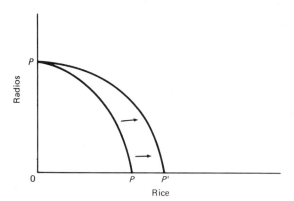

Figure 4.3. The effect of technological change in the agricultural sector on the production-possibility frontier.

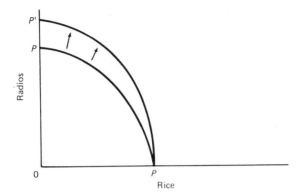

Figure 4.4. The effect of technological change in the industrial sector on the production-possibility frontier.

complicated, unwieldy, and fragile tubes, led to an enormous growth of radio production. The production process became less complicated, and workers were able to increase significantly their total productivity. Figure 4.4 shows that, as in the case of higher-yielding rice seeds, the technology of the transistor can be said to have caused the production-possibility curve to rotate outward along the vertical axis. For the most part, the rice axis intercept remains unchanged (although perhaps the ability of rice paddy workers to listen to music on their transistor radio while working may have made them more productive!).

Conclusion

We may summarize the discussion so far by saying that the sources of economic progress can be traced to a variety of factors, but by and large, *investments that improve the quality of existing physical and human resources, that increase the quantity of these same productive resources, and that raise the productivity of all or specific resources through invention, innovation, and technological progress have been and will continue to be primary factors in stimulating economic growth in any society.* The production-possibility framework conveniently allows us to analyze the production choices open to an economy, to understand the output and "opportunity cost" implications of idle or underutilized resources, and to portray the effects on economic growth of increased resource supplies and improved technologies of production.

Having provided this introduction to the simple economics of growth, we can now look more carefully at the historical experience of contemporary developed nations in order to analyze in detail the nature of those economic and noneconomic factors that were basic to their long-term growth. We shall then see what relevance all this has for the growth prospects of developing countries.

THE HISTORICAL RECORD: KUZNETS' SIX CHARACTERISTICS OF MODERN ECONOMIC GROWTH

Professor Simon Kuznets, who received the Nobel Prize in economics in 1971 for his pioneering work in the measurement and analysis of the historical growth of national incomes in developed nations, has defined a country's economic growth as "a long-term rise in capacity to supply increasingly diverse economic goods to its population, this growing capacity based on advancing technology and the institutional and ideological adjustments that it demands."[3] All three principal components of this definition are of great importance.

1. The *sustained rise in national output* is a manifestation of economic growth, and the ability to provide a wide range of goods is a sign of economic maturity.
2. *Advancing technology* provides the basis or preconditions for continuous economic growth—a necessary but not sufficient condition.
3. In order to realize the potential for growth inherent in new technology, *institutional, attitudinal, and ideological adjustments* must be made. Technological innovation without concomitant social innovation is like a light bulb without electricity—the potential exists but without the complementary input nothing will happen.

In his exhaustive analysis Professor Kuznets has isolated six characteristic features manifested in the growth process of almost every developed nation. They include the following:

TWO AGGREGATE ECONOMIC VARIABLES:
1. High rates of growth of per capita output and population
2. High rates of increase in total factor productivity, especially labor productivity

TWO STRUCTURAL TRANSFORMATION VARIABLES:
3. High rates of structural transformation of the economy
4. High rates of social and ideological transformation

TWO FACTORS AFFECTING THE INTERNATIONAL SPREAD OF GROWTH:
5. The propensity of economically developed countries to reach out to the rest of the world for markets and raw materials
6. The limited spread of this economic growth to only a third of the world's population

Let us briefly examine each of these six characteristics.

High Rates of Per Capita Output and Population Growth

In the case of both per capita output and population growth, all contemporary developed countries have experienced large multiples of their previous historical rates during the epoch of modern economic growth—roughly from around 1770 to the present. For the non-Communist developed countries, annual growth rates over the past 200 years averaged almost 2% for per capita output and 1% for population, therefore 3% for total output (i.e., real GNP). These rates, which imply a doubling time of roughly 35 years for per capita output, 70 years for population, and 24 years for real GNP, were far greater than those experienced during the entire era before the start of the industrial revolution in the late eighteenth century. For example, per capita output during the last two centuries has been estimated to be at almost

10 times that of the premodern era; population has grown at a multiple of 4 or 5 times its level in the earlier period, and the acceleration in the growth rate of total output or GNP is therefore estimated to have been some 40 or 50 times as large as that experienced before the nineteenth century!

High Rates of Productivity Increase

The second aggregate economic characteristic of modern growth is the relatively high rate of rise in total factor productivity (i.e., output per unit of all inputs). In the case of the major productive factor (labor), rates of productivity increase have also been large multiples of the rates in the premodern era. For example, it has been estimated that rates of productivity increase account for anywhere from 50 to 75% of the historical growth of per capita output in developed countries. In other words, *technological progress including the upgrading of existing physical and human resources accounts for most of the measured historical increase in per capita GNP.* We shall discuss the crucial role technological advance played in generating and sustaining economic growth shortly.

High Rates of Economic Structural Transformation

The historical growth record of contemporary developed nations reveals a third important characteristic: the high rate of structural and sectoral change inherent in the growth process. Some of the major components of this structural change include the gradual shift away from agricultural to nonagricultural activities and, more recently, away from industry to services; a significant change in the scale or average size of productive units (i.e., away from small family and personal enterprises to the impersonal organization of huge national and multinational corporations); and finally, a corresponding shift in the spatial location and occupational status of the labor force away from rural, agricultural, and related nonagricultural activities toward urban-oriented manufacturing and service pursuits. For example, in the United States the proportion of the total labor force engaged in agricultural activities was 53.5% in 1870. By 1960 this figure had declined to less than 7%. Similarly, in a European country like Belgium, the agricultural labor force dropped from 51% of the total in 1846 to 12.5% in 1947 and less than 7% in 1970. In view of the fact that it took many centuries for agricultural labor forces to drop to even approximately 50% of the total labor supply prior to the nineteenth century, a drop of 40 to 50 points in the last 100 years in countries such as the United States, Japan, Germany, Belgium, and Great Britain underlines the rapidity of this structural change.

High Rates of Social, Political, and Ideological Transformation

For a significant economic structural change to take place in any society concomitant transformations in *attitudes, institutions,* and *ideologies* are often necessary. Obvious examples of these social transformations include the general urbanization process and the adoption of the ideals, attitudes, and institutions of what has come to be known as "modernization." Gunnar

Myrdal has provided a lengthy list of these modernization ideals in his seminal treatise on underdevelopment in Asia.[4] They include the following:

1. *Rationality:* the substitution of modern methods of thinking, acting, producing, distributing, and consuming for age-old, traditional practices. According to the first Indian prime minister, Jawaharlal Nehru, what underdeveloped nations need is "a scientific and technological society. It employs new techniques whether it is in the farm, in the factory or in transport. Modern technique is not a matter of just getting a tool and using it. Modern technique follows modern thinking. You can't get hold of a modern tool and have an ancient mind. It won't work."[5] The quest for rationality implies that opinions about economic strategies and policies should be logically valid inferences rooted as deeply as possible in knowledge of relevant facts.
2. *Planning:* the search for a rationally coordinated system of policy measures that can bring about and accelerate economic growth and development (see Chapter 15).
3. *Social and economic equalization:* the promotion of more equality in status, opportunities, wealth, incomes, and levels of living.
4. *Improved institutions and attitudes:* Such changes are envisaged as necessary to increase labor efficiency and diligence; promote effective competition, social and economic mobility, and individual enterprise; permit greater equality of opportunities; make possible higher productivity; raise levels of living; and promote development. Included among social institutions needing change are outmoded land tenure systems, social and economic monopolies, educational and religious structures, and systems of administration and planning. In the area of attitudes, the concept of "modern man" embodies such ideals as efficiency, diligence, orderliness, punctuality, frugality, honesty, rationality, change-orientation, integrity and self-reliance, cooperation, and willingness to take the long view.

In Part II we will look more carefully at some of these characteristics of modernization as they relate to contemporary Third World countries to see how and in what manner they fit into a development-oriented economic strategy.

International Economic Outreach

The last two characteristics of modern economic growth deal with the role of developed countries in the international arena. The first of these relates to the historical and ongoing propensity of rich countries to reach out to the rest of the world for primary products and raw materials, cheap labor, and lucrative markets for their manufactured products. Such outreach activities are made feasible by the increased power of modern technology, particularly in transport and communication. These had the effect of unifying the globe in ways that were not possible before the nineteenth century. They also opened the possibilities for political and economic dominance of poor nations by their more powerful neighbors to the north. In the nineteenth and early twentieth centuries, the establishment of colonies and the opening up or partitioning of previously inaccessible areas such as sub-Saharan Africa and parts of Asia and Latin American provided the expanding economies of the Northern Hemisphere with cheap raw materials and with export markets for their growing manufacturing industries.

Limited International Spread of Economic Growth

In spite of the enormous increases in world output over the past two centuries, the spread of modern economic growth is still largely limited to less than one-third of the world's population. As we discovered in Chapter 2, this minority of the world's population enjoys almost 75% of the world's income. Moreover, as we saw later in that chapter, unequal international power relationships between developed and underdeveloped countries have a tendency to exacerbate the gap between the rich and poor. The further economic growth of the former is often achieved at the expense of the growth of the latter.[6]

Conclusions: The Interdependence of Growth Characteristics

The six characteristics of modern growth reviewed here are highly interrelated and mutually reinforcing. High rates of per capita output result from rapidly rising levels of labor productivity. High per capita incomes in turn generate high levels of per capita consumption, thus providing the incentives for changes in the structure of production (since as incomes rise the demand for manufactured goods and services rises at a much faster rate than the demand for agricultural products). Advanced technology needed to achieve these output and structural changes causes the scale of production and the characteristics of economic enterprise units to change in both organization and location. This in turn necessitates rapid changes in the location and structure of the labor force and in status relations among occupational groups (e.g., the income shares of landlords and farmers decline while those of manufacturers and industrialists tend to rise). It also means changes in other aspects of society including family size, urbanization, and the material determinants of self-esteem and dignity. Finally, the inherent dynamism of modern economic growth coupled with the revolution in the technology of transportation and communication necessitates an international outreach on the part of those countries that developed first. But the poor countries affected by this international outreach may for institutional, ideological, or political reasons either not be in a position to benefit from the process or may simply be weak victims of the policies of rich countries designed to exploit them economically.

If the common ingredient and linkage in all these interrelated growth characteristics is, as Professor Kuznets suggests, the "mass application of technological innovations," then the rapid growth that makes possible the economic surplus to finance further progress in scientific research has a built-in tendency to be self-generating. In other words, *rapid economic growth makes possible basic scientific research, which in turn leads to technological inventions and innovations, which propel economic growth even further.*

We have an important hint here why the growth process seems to benefit the already rich nations disproportionately in relation to the poor ones: almost 98% of all scientific research is undertaken in rich countries and on their problems. This research and the resulting technological progress are of little direct benefit to poor nations whose resource and institutional conditions differ greatly from those of the developed nations. Wealthy nations can afford basic scientific research; poor ones cannot. Developed countries can therefore provide a continuous mechanism for self-sustaining technological and economic advance that is beyond the financial and technical capabilities of most developing countries. This is one of the real underlying economic reasons why the gap between rich and poor nations seems to widen every year.

Some Lessons and Implications

A basic question emerging from our discussion of the six characteristics of modern economic growth is: Why did the growth experience of the more developed nations not spread more rapidly to the less developed nations? Two broad explanations come immediately to mind. The first relates to the initial internal conditions of most Third World countries and the other to the contemporary nature of international economic and political relationships between rich and poor nations.

Economic growth, as we have seen, results not only from the growth in quantity and quality of resources and improved technology but also from a social and political structure that is conducive to such change. Growth demands a stable but flexible social and political framework that is capable of accommodating and even encouraging rapid structural change. It also requires a social environment capable of resolving the inevitable interest group and sectoral conflicts that accompany such structural change. Consider, for example, the transition from a land-based, rural agrarian society to a highly skilled, urban-oriented industrial and service economy. Conflicts of interest would arise with the concomitant shift in relative power and influence from, say, the large landowners to the new urban industrialists.

In short, unless local attitudes and institutional conditions exist that are amenable to structural change and, without holding back the growth-promoting groups in society, still provide opportunities for wider segments of the population to participate in the fruits of economic progress, efforts to stimulate growth through narrowly conceived economic policies are likely to fail. As we shall discover in many of the chapters in Part II, the apparent failure of some developing countries to generate more rapid rates of economic growth despite heavy investments in human and physical resources and the importation of sophisticated technological practices can be traced largely to the inflexibility of their social and political institutions and to the reactionary power of certain vested interest groups.

The second, and not unrelated, explanation for the limited spread effects of modern economic growth derives from the economic and political policies of the developed countries themselves vis-à-vis the developing nations. As we discovered in Chapter 2, the dominant power of rich nations collectively to influence and control the conditions of their international trading relationships with poor countries and to transfer their economic, social, political, and cultural values and institutions as well as their technology to these societies in opportunist ways may have greatly inhibited the latter's economic progress. There are three reasons why this may have been so. First, such wholesale transfers tend to create and perpetuate dominance and dependence relationships between rich and poor, in which the latter remain largely incapable of controlling their economic destiny or evolving an indigenous ethos of self-reliance. Second, the transfers themselves may be largely inappropriate and counterproductive to the development aspirations of many Third World countries. Finally, it may simply not be in the private long-run economic and political interests for the one-fourth of the world's population who now control three-quarters of the world's production to share this abundance with the other three-fourths. A world of increasingly scarce resources and commodities may not be compatible with a more equitable global economic expansion, especially when the relative distribution of power is so unequal.

The analogy here between, on the one hand, inflexible and reactionary domestic social structures and elite power groups which inhibit national economic growth and, on the other, inflexibilities and reactionary policies among a small group of elite nations is an obvious one. Just as the economic growth of individual nations required flexible social and political institutions capable of resolving conflicts and promoting structural change, so too any realistic notion of world development must accept that without an analogous flexibility at the international level (i.e., a genuine commitment on the part of developed nations to assist or at least not impede the economic progress of poor societies), global economic progress will probably never occur. Without flexible global institutions (e.g., flexible world trade and aid relationships) and an international rather than provincial outlook on the part of world leaders, it is not unreasonable to anticipate the emergence of growing conflict and perhaps even worldwide violence between those few who prosper with the many who do not. In the face of inflexible social and political structures, domestic civil wars have often broken out to resolve economic conflicts in the developed nations; the American Civil War in the 1860s is an example. More recently, violent conflicts related to struggles between small elites and the masses of poor, usually represented by other elites, have occurred with growing frequency in a number of developing countries (Sri Lanka, Pakistan, Algeria, Libya, Nigeria, Angola, Thailand, Chile, Haiti, Ethiopia, Vietnam, Cambodia, Laos, Sudan, Mozambique, and, most recently, Iran, El Salvador, and Nicaragua). Again, an analogy may be drawn between the domestic and international arenas. In the absence of a more equitable distribution of the fruits of world economic growth and more flexible international institutions, Third World nations may well grow impatient with the present international system and begin as a group to exercise their own potential power. The outcome may or may not be violent. But the underlying conditions for such violence seem to grow with each passing year. (In Chapter 17 we will examine the question of prospects for international cooperation or conflict in the context of the Third World's demands for a "new international economic order.")

THE LIMITED VALUE OF THE HISTORICAL GROWTH EXPERIENCE: DIFFERING INITIAL CONDITIONS

One of the principal failures of development economics of the 1950s and 1960s was its inability to recognize and take into account the limited value of the historical experience of economic growth in the West for charting the development path of contemporary Third World nations. Stages of economic growth theories and related models of rapid industrialization gave too little emphasis to the very different and less favorable initial economic, social, and political conditions of today's developing countries. The fact is that the growth position of these countries today is in many important ways significantly different from that of the currently developed countries as they embarked on their era of modern economic growth. We can identify at least eight significant differences in initial conditions—differences that require a much amended analysis of the growth prospects and requirements of modern economic development:

1. Resource endowments, physical and human
2. Per capita incomes and levels of GNP in relation to the rest of the world
3. Climate
4. Population size, distribution, and growth
5. Historical role of international migration
6. International trade benefits
7. Basic scientific and technological research and development capabilities
8. Stability and flexibility of political institutions

Each of these conditions is discussed below with a view to formulating a more realistic set of requirements and priorities for generating and sustaining economic growth in the 1980s and 1990s.

Resource Endowments, Physical and Human

Contemporary Third World countries are on the whole often less well endowed with natural resources than were the currently developed nations when they began their modern growth. (*Note:* We are not here talking about the present very depleted natural resource situation of many rich countries, but what they possessed on the eve of their development.) With the exception of those few Third World nations blessed with abundant supplies of petroleum, other minerals, and raw materials with growing world demands, most less developed countries, like those in Asia where almost one-third of the world's population resides, are poorly endowed with natural resources. Moreover, in parts of Latin America and especially in Africa where natural resources are more plentiful, heavy investments of capital are needed to exploit them. Such finance is not easy to come by without sacrificing substantial autonomy and control to the powerful developed-country multinational corporations that alone are at present capable of large-scale, efficient resource exploitation.

The difference in skilled human resource endowments is even more pronounced. The ability of a country effectively to exploit natural resources is dependent on, among other things, the managerial and technical skills of its people. The populations of today's Third World nations are on the whole less educated, less experienced, and less skilled than were their counterparts in the early periods of economic growth in the West (or, for that matter, the Soviet Union and Japan at the outset of their more recent growth processes).

Relative Levels of Per Capita Income and GNP

The three-fourths of the world's population at present living in developing countries have on the average a much lower level of real per capita income than their counterparts had in nineteenth-century Russia and Japan. As we discovered in Chapter 2, well over 70% of the population of Third World countries is attempting to subsist at bare minimum levels. Obviously, the average standard of living in, say, early nineteenth-century England was nothing to envy or admire. But it was not as economically debilitating and precarious as it is today for most people in the Third World, especially those in the 40 or so least developed countries.

Second, at the beginning of their modern growth era, today's developed nations were economically in advance of the rest of the world. They could therefore take advantage of their relatively strong financial positions to widen the income gaps between themselves and other less fortunate countries. On the other hand, today's LDCs begin their growth process at the low end of the international per capita income scale. Their relatively weak position in the world economy is analogous to that of a 1,500-meter race between a young athlete and an old man where the former is given a 1,000-meter start. Such backwardness is not only economically difficult to overcome or even reduce but, psychologically, it creates a sense of frustration and a desire to "grow" at any cost. This can in fact inhibit the long-run improvement in national levels of living.

Climatic Differences

Almost all Third World countries are situated in tropical or subtropical climatic zones. *It is a historical fact that almost every successful example of modern economic growth has occurred in a temperate zone country.* Such a dichotomy cannot simply be attributed to coincidence; it must bear some relation to the special difficulties caused directly or indirectly by differing climatic conditions.

One obvious climatic factor directly affecting conditions of production is that in general the extremes of heat and humidity in most poor countries contribute to deteriorating soil qualities and the rapid depreciation of many natural goods. They also contribute to the low productivity of certain crops, the weakened regenerative growth of forests, and the poor health of animals. Finally, and perhaps most important, extremes of heat and humidity not only cause discomfort to workers but can also weaken their health, reduce their desire to engage in strenuous physical work, and generally lower their levels of productivity and efficiency.

Population Size, Distribution, and Growth

In Chapter 6 we will examine in detail some of the development problems and issues associated with rapid population growth. At this point it is sufficient to note that Third World population size, density, and growth constitute another important difference between less developed and developed countries. Before and during their early growth years, Western nations experienced a very slow rise in population growth. As industrialization proceeded, population growth rates increased primarily as a result of falling death rates but also because of slowly rising birthrates. However, *at no time during their modern growth epoch did European and North American countries have natural population growth rates in excess of 2% per annum.*

By contrast, the populations of most Third World countries have been increasing at annual rates in excess of 2.5% over the past few decades, and some are rising even faster today. Moreover, the concentration of these large and growing populations in a few areas means that most LDCs today start with considerably higher person/land ratios than did the European countries in their early growth years. Finally, in terms of comparative absolute size, it is a fact that with the exception of the USSR, no country that embarked on a long-term period of economic growth approached the present-day population size of India, Egypt, Pakistan, Indonesia, Nigeria, or Brazil. Nor, as we have just seen, were their rates of natural increase anything like that of present-day Mexico, Kenya, the Philippines, Bangladesh, Zaire, or Guatemala. In fact, many observers even doubt whether the industrial revolution and the high long-term growth rates of contemporary developed countries could have been achieved or proceeded so fast and with such minimal setbacks and disturbances, especially for the very poor, had their populations been expanding so rapidly.

The Historical Role of International Migration

Of perhaps equal historical importance to the differing rates of natural population increase is the fact that in the nineteenth and early twentieth centuries there was a major outlet for excess rural populations in international migration.

As Table 4.1 reveals, international migration was both widespread and large in scale. In countries such as Italy, Germany, and Ireland, periods of severe famine or pressure on the land often combined with limited economic opportunities in urban industry to "push" unskilled rural workers toward the labor-scarce nations of North America and Australasia. Thus, as Brinley Thomas argues in his treatise on migration and economic growth in the nineteenth century, the "three outstanding contributions of European labor to the American economy—1,187,000 Irish and 919,000 Germans between 1847 and 1855, 418,000 Scandinavians and 1,045,000 Germans between 1880 and 1885, and 1,754,000 Italians between 1898 and 1907— had the character of evacuations."[7]

Whereas the main thrust of international emigration up to the First World War was both long-distant and permanent in nature, the period since the Second World War has witnessed a resurgence of international migration within Europe itself, which is essentially over short distances and to a large degree temporary in nature. However, the economic forces giving rise to this migration are basically the same; that is, during the 1950s and especially the 1960s surplus rural workers from southern Italy, Greece, and Turkey flocked into areas of labor shortages, most notably West Germany and Switzerland. Table 4.2 gives an example of the magnitude and direction of Italian migration between 1960 and 1964.

The fact that this contemporary migration from regions of surplus labor in southern and southeastern Europe is of both a permanent and a nonpermanent nature provides a valuable dual benefit to the relatively poor areas from which these unskilled workers migrate. The home governments are relieved of the costs of providing for people who in all probability would remain unemployed, and because a large percentage of the workers' earnings are sent home they receive a valuable and not insignificant source of foreign exchange.[8]

In view of the above discussion, one might reasonably ask why the large numbers of impoverished peoples in Africa, Asia, and Latin America do not follow the example of workers from southeastern Europe and seek temporary or permanent jobs in areas of labor shortage. Historically, at least in the case of Africa, migrant labor both within and between countries was rather common and did provide some relief for locally depressed areas. Even today, considerable benefits accrue and numerous potential problems are avoided by the fact that thousands of unskilled laborers in Upper Volta are able to find temporary work in neighboring Ivory Coast. The same is true for Egyptians, Pakistanis, and Indians in Kuwait and Saudi Arabia; Tunisians, Moroccans, and Algerians in Europe; Colombians in Venezuela; and Mexicans in the United States. With these possible exceptions, however, the fact remains that *there is very little scope for reducing the pressures of over-population in Third World countries today through massive international emigration.* The reasons for this relate not so much to a lack of local knowledge about opportunities in other countries but to the combined effects of geographical (and thus economic) distance and, more important, to the very restrictive nature of immigration laws in modern developed countries. Moreover, the irony of international migration today is not merely that this historical outlet for surplus people has effectively been closed, but that a large percentage of those people who do, in fact, migrate from poor to richer lands are the very ones whom the less developed countries cannot afford to lose: the highly educated and skilled. Since the great majority of these migrants move on a permanent basis, this perverse "brain drain" not only represents a loss of valuable human resources but could prove to be a serious constraint on the future economic progress of Third World nations. For example, during the 1960s and 1970s the emigration of high-level professional and technical manpower from the developing to the developed countries of the United States, Canada, and the United Kingdom alone amounted to over 400,000 skilled workers (see Table 11.5). The fundamental point remains, however, that the possibility of legal international migration of *unskilled* workers on a scale resembling that of the nineteenth and early twentieth centuries no longer exists to provide an effective "safety valve" for the contemporary surplus populations of Africa, Asia, and Latin America. (We will discuss recent trends in Third World international migration and the growing problems of illegal migration and global refugees in detail in Chapter 9.)

The Growth Stimulus of International Trade

International trade has often been referred to as the "engine of growth" that propelled the development of the currently economically advanced nations during the nineteenth and early twentieth centuries. Rapidly expanding export markets provided an additional stimulus to growing local demands that led to the establishment of large-scale manufacturing industries. Together with a relatively stable political structure and flexible social institutions, these increased export earnings enabled the developing country of the nineteenth century to borrow funds in the international capital market at

Table 4.1 Average Annual Overseas Emigration from Europe, 1846–1939 (in tens of thousands)

	Total European overseas emigration	Total	British Isles	Ireland	Germany	Norway, Sweden, Denmark
1846–1850	256.6	254.3	199.1	(118.8)	35.5	4.3
1851–1855	342.3	331.3	231.7	(139.0)	74.9	6.9
1856–1860	197.1	184.7	123.5	(43.7)	49.4	4.5
1861–1865	219.3	202.9	143.6	(39.1)	43.5	9.7
1866–1870	354.9	308.4	170.8	(47.8)	83.4	39.3
1871–1875	370.7	310.1	193.9	(59.0)	79.0	22.1
1876–1880	258.0	192.8	114.9	(28.4)	46.2	23.2
1881–1885	661.3	480.7	228.0	(67.1)	171.5	58.4
1886–1890	737.7	407.2	214.8	(62.0)	97.0	60.8
1891–1895	674.8	273.9	128.4	(45.5)	80.5	48.1
1896–1900	543.3	137.5	81.0	(30.2)	24.9	22.1
1901–1905	1,038.9	253.0	156.0	(36.8)	28.4	53.9
1906–1910	1,436.7	322.2	234.6	(31.0)	26.4	43.7
1911–1915	1,365.3	325.6	265.7	(38.4)	15.8	28.6
1916–1920	405.5	123.9	101.1	—	2.4	11.2
1921–1925	629.5	295.2	197.7	—	58.9	26.2
1926–1930	555.6	253.5	163.3	—	54.0	23.9
1931–1935	130.8	50.0	30.4	—	12.7	3.1
1936–1939	147.4	60.4	30.3	—	17.3	4.2

SOURCE: Dudley Kirk, *Europe's Population in the Interwar Years* (Princeton: League of Nations, 1946), p. 279. For Ireland, Brinley Thomas, *Migration and Economic Growth* (Cambridge, England: Cambridge University Press, 1954), p. 284.

Table 4.2 Italian Emigration, 1960–1964

Region	1960	1961	1962	1963	1964
European Economic Community	170,580	175,266	158,900	107,578	113,200
Total Europe	309,876	329,597	313,400	235,134	236,600
North America	34,219	29,754	27,876	26,492	26,466
Central and South America	18,823	10,252	6,568	3,837	3,322
Australasia	19,629	16,379	14,411	11,539	10,890
Africa	1,283	1,022	706	589	1,128
Asia	78	119	255	20	178
Grand total	383,908	387,123	363,216	277,611	278,584

SOURCE: "Italian emigration: Some aspects of migration in 1964," *International Migration* 4, no. 2 (1966): 122.

Switzer- land, France, Low Countries	Total	Italy	Austria, Hungary, Czecho- slovakia	Russia, Poland, Lithuania, Finland	Spain, Portugal	Balkans
14.4	2.3	0.2	1.6	0.1	0.4	
17.8	11.0	0.7	4.0	0.2	6.1	
7.3	12.5	4.2	2.2	0.2	5.9	
6.1	16.4	8.2	2.2	0.3	5.9	
14.9	37.4	18.7	5.7	0.6	12.4	
15.1	60.6	23.3	10.5	5.0	21.8	
8.5	65.2	28.9	11.8	7.2	17.3	
22.8	180.6	64.0	34.6	17.1	64.5	0.4
34.6	330.5	134.2	52.5	45.5	96.7	1.6
16.9	400.9	150.2	67.6	72.2	108.9	2.0
9.5	405.7	165.7	77.2	55.8	102.4	4.6
14.7	785.9	320.6	203.0	143.4	97.4	21.3
17.6	1,114.3	402.4	265.4	211.6	185.4	49.5
15.5	1,039.5	312.2	243.6	216.8	220.2	46.7
9.2	281.8	126.6	11.5	7.8	121.3	14.6
12.2	334.4	130.9	23.8	56.8	96.3	26.5
13.3	302.2	89.4	23.0	75.5	74.7	39.6
3.8	81.0	28.2	5.1	20.9	19.6	7.2
5.6	87.2	23.6	6.3	20.8	27.4	9.1

very low interest rates. This capital accumulation in turn stimulated further production, made possible increased imports, and led to a more diversified industrial structure. In the nineteenth century, European and North American countries were able to participate in this dynamic growth of international exchange largely on the basis of relatively free trade, free capital movements, and the unfettered international migration of unskilled surplus labor.

Today, the situation is very different. With the exception of a few very successful East Asian and Latin American countries, the *non-oil exporting (and, indeed, some oil exporting) developing countries face formidable difficulties in trying to generate rapid economic growth on the basis of world trade.* Ever since the First World War, most developing countries have experienced a deteriorating trade position. Their exports have expanded but usually not as fast as the exports of developed nations. Their terms of trade (i.e., the price they receive for their exports relative to the price they have to pay for imports) have declined steadily. Export volume has therefore had to grow faster just to earn the same amount of foreign currencies as in previous years. Moreover, the developed countries are so far ahead of the LDCs economically that they can afford through their advanced science and technology to remain more competitive, develop more new products (often synthetic substitutes for traditional LDC primary commodity exports), and obtain international finance on much better terms. Finally, where developing countries are successful at becoming lower-cost producers of competitive products with the developed countries (e.g., textiles, clothing, shoes, some light manufactures), the latter have typically resorted to various forms of tariff and nontariff barriers to trade, including import quotas, sanitary requirements, and special licensing arrangements.

We will discuss the economics of international trade and finance in detail in Chapters 12–14. For the present, it is sufficient to point out that the so-called international engine of growth that roared across the Northern Hemisphere in the nineteenth century has for the most part, for lack of sufficient fuel and need of repairs, struggled and crawled for most newcomers to the growth game in the twentieth century.

Basic Scientific and Technological Research and Development Capabilities

A recurrent theme throughout this chapter has been the crucial role played by basic scientific research and technological development in the modern economic growth experience of contemporary developed countries. Their high rates of growth have been sustained by the interplay between mass applications of many new technological innovations based on a rapid advancement in the stock of scientific knowledge and further additions to that stock of knowledge made possible by growing surplus wealth. And even today the process of scientific and technological advance in all its stages—from basic research to product development—is heavily concentrated in the rich nations. We saw earlier that almost 98% of all world research and development expenditures originate in these countries. Moreover, as we also saw, research funds are spent on solving the economic and technological problems of concern to rich countries in accordance with their own economic priorities and resource endowments. Rich countries are mainly interested in the development of sophisticated products, large markets, and technologically advanced production methods using large inputs of capital and high levels of skills and management while economizing on their relatively scarce supplies of labor and raw materials. The poor countries by contrast are much more interested in simple products, simple designs, saving of capital, use of abundant labor, and production for smaller markets. But they have neither the financial resources nor the scientific and the technological know-how at present to undertake the kind of research and development that would be in their best long-term economic interests. Their dependence on "inappropriate" foreign technologies creates and perpetuates the internal economic dualism that we discussed in Chapter 3.

We may conclude, therefore, that in the important area of scientific and technological research, contemporary Third World nations are in an extremely disadvantageous competitive position vis-à-vis the developed nations. In contrast, when the latter countries were embarking on their early growth process they were scientifically and technologically greatly in advance of the rest of the world. They could consequently focus their attention on staying ahead by designing and developing new technology at a pace dictated by their long-term economic growth requirements.

Stability and Flexibility of Political and Social Institutions

The final distinction between the historical experience of developed countries and the situation faced by contemporary Third World nations relates to the nature of social and political institutions. One very obvious difference between the now developed and the underdeveloped nations is that well before their industrial revolutions the former were independent consolidated nation-states able to pursue national policies on the basis of a general consensus of popular opinions and attitudes toward "modernization." As Professor Myrdal has correctly pointed out:

> . . . they [the now developed countries] formed a small world of broadly similar cultures, within which people and ideas circulated rather freely. . . . Modern scientific thought developed in these countries (long before their industrial revolutions) and a modernized technology began early to be introduced in their agriculture and their industries, which at that time were all small-scale.[9]

In contrast to those preindustrial, culturally homogeneous, materially oriented, and politically unified societies with their emphasis on rationalism and modern scientific thought, many Third World countries of today have only recently gained their political independence and have yet to become consolidated nation-states with an effective ability to formulate and pursue national development strategies. Moreover, the modernization ideals embodied in the notions of rationalism, scientific thought, individualism, social and economic mobility, the work ethic, and dedication to national material and cultural values are concepts largely alien to many contemporary Third World societies, except perhaps for their educated ruling elites. Until stable and flexible political institutions can be consolidated with broad public support, the present social and cultural fragmentation of many developing countries is likely to inhibit their ability to accelerate national economic progress.

Conclusions

In view of the preceding discussion we may conclude that due to very different initial conditions, the historical experience of Western economic growth is of only limited relevance for contemporary Third World nations. Nevertheless, one of the most significant and relevant lessons to be learned from this historical experience is the critical importance of concomitant and complementary technological, social, and institutional changes, which must take place if long-term economic growth is to be realized. Such transformations must occur not only within individual developing countries but, perhaps more importantly, within the international economy as well. In other words, unless there is some major structural, attitudinal, and institutional reform in the world economy, one that accommodates the rising aspirations and rewards the outstanding performances of individual developing nations, internal economic and social transformation within the

Third World may be insufficient. This realization provides one of the principal rationales for Third World demands for a "new international economic order." We will take up this important issue once again in Part III and finally in Chapter 17.

NOTES

1. Algebraically, these components can be written in the standard neoclassical "production function" format as $Y = f(L, K, t)$ where Y is national output, L is labor, K is capital, and t is technological progress.
2. For a more formal classification of neutral, labor- and capital-saving innovation in the context of neoclassical economics, see Appendix 4.1.
3. Simon Kuznets, "Modern economic growth: Findings and reflections," Nobel lecture delivered in Stockholm, Sweden, December 1971 and published in the *American Economic Review* 63, no. 3 (1973). Much of the information and analysis in this section is based on Kuznets' trailblazing work. The full Kuznets article is reprinted as Reading 6 in my *Struggle for Economic Development*.
4. Gunnar Myrdal, *Asian Drama* (New York: Pantheon, 1971), pp. 57−69.
5. Jawaharlal Nehru, "Strategy of the Third Plan," in *Problems in the Third Plan: A Critical Miscellany*, Ministry of Information and Broadcasting, Government of India, 1961, p. 46.
6. For a Third World view of the impact of international outreach in fostering the dependence of developing nations, see Theotonio Dos Santos, "The structure of dependence," Reading 7 in *The Struggle for Economic Development*.
7. Brinley Thomas, *Migration and Economic Growth* (London: Cambridge University Press, 1954), p. viii.
8. For a description and analysis of the economic implications of international migration from the Mediterranean area to Western Europe, see W. R. Böhnung, "Some thoughts on emigration from the Mediterranean area," *International Labour Review* 14 (1975).
9. Gunnar Myrdal, *The Challenge of World Poverty* (New York: Pantheon, 1970), pp. 30−31.

CONCEPTS FOR REVIEW

Capital accumulation

Technological progress

Neutral, labor-saving, and capital-saving technological progress

Labor augmenting and capital augmenting technological progress

Inventions versus innovations

Economic growth

Social and institutional innovations

Economic structural transformation

Modernization ideals

Rationality

Resource endowment

Economies of scale

Trade as an "engine of growth"

Flexible versus rigid political and social institutions

Relation between "basic science" and technological innovation

Research and development (R & D)

QUESTIONS FOR DISCUSSION

1. How would you describe the economic growth process in terms of the production-possibility analysis? What are the principal sources of economic growth and how can they be illustrated using $P-P$ frontier diagrams?
2. What does the historical record reveal about the nature of the growth process in the now developed nations? What were its principal ingredients?
3. Of what relevance is the historical record of modern economic growth for contemporary Third World nations? How important are differences in "initial conditions"? Give

some examples of the initial conditions in a Third World country with which you are familiar that make it different from most contemporary developed nations at the beginning of their modern growth experience.

4. What is meant by the statement "social and institutional innovations are as important for economic growth as technological and scientific inventions and innovations"? Explain your answer.

5. What do you think were the principal reasons why economic growth spread rapidly amongst the now developed nations during the nineteenth and early twentieth centuries, but has failed to spread to an equal extent to contemporary less developed nations?

FURTHER READINGS

On the historical record of economic growth the classic study is that of the Nobel Prize—winning Harvard economist Simon Kuznets, whose lifetime work is best revealed in two volumes: *Modern Economic Growth: Rate, Structure, and Spread* (New Haven: Yale University Press, 1966) and *Economic Growth of Nations: Total Output and Production Structure* (Cambridge, Mass.: Harvard University Press, 1971). A concise summary of his findings is given in Simon Kuznets, "Modern economic growth: findings and reflections," *American Economic Review* 63 no. 3 (1973): 247–258, reprinted as Reading 6 in the *Struggle for Economic Development*. *See also* Barry E. Supple (ed.), *The Experience of Economic Growth* (New York: Random House, 1963), especially Part 2, for a comparison of the growth experience in a number of contemporary developed countries. For the most comprehensive general statement of the nature of economic growth as applied to less developed countries, see W. Arthur Lewis' classic work, *Theory of Economic Growth* (London: Unwin, 1955).

An extensive critique of the historical growth record of developed nations as applied to Third World countries can be found in Gunnar Myrdal, *The Challenge of World Poverty* (New York: Pantheon, 1970), Chapter 2, and in his *Asian Drama* (New York: Pantheon, 1968), Chapter 14. See also Louis Lefeber, "On the paradigm for economic development," *World Development* 2, no. 1 (1974), and Keith Griffin, "Underdevelopment in history," in C. Wilber (ed.), *The Political Economy of Development and Underdevelopment* (New York: Random House, 1979), Chapter 6. A somewhat different view, stressing what can be learned from the historical growth experience and applied to contemporary developing nations, can be found in A. J. Youngson (ed.), *Economic Development in the Long Run* (New York: St. Martin's, 1973) and, especially, Lloyd G. Reynolds, "The spread of economic growth to the Third World," *Journal of Economic Literature* 21 (September 1983):941–980.

Additional readings can be found on pp. 618–619.

APPENDIX 4.1

THE CLASSIFICATION OF INNOVATIONS

The classification of inventions and innovations as labor saving, capital saving, or neutral can be demonstrated with the use of elementary isoquant analysis. For those unfamiliar with this concept, an "isoquant" or "equal-product line" is a locus of all combinations of, say, capital (K) and labor (L) that, for a given structure of technology, result in an *identical* level of physical output. Consider Figure A4.1.

We start with a given isoquant, Y_0, representing an output level of, say, 60 units. Assume that the current factor price ratio is such that the minimum cost point is at P with K_0 capital and L_0 labor being used. Technological progress can then be represented by a new isoquant which passes through P, but now denoting an output level of, say, 100 units. In Figure A4.1, three such new 100 unit isoquants are depicted; dotted lines Y_2 and Y_3 as well as solid line Y_1 which coincides with the original Y_0. Technological progress is classified according to whether the slope of the new isoquant at Point P (i.e., the new ratio of marginal physical products) is

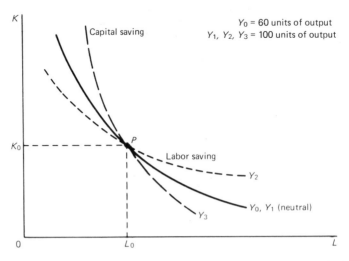

Figure A4.1.   Technological progress: Neutral, labor saving, and capital saving.

(1) unchanged $\quad \dfrac{MP_L}{MP_K}(Y_1) = \dfrac{MP_L}{MP_K}(Y_0) \quad$ denoting neutral progress

(2) lower $\quad \dfrac{MP_L}{MP_K}(Y_2) < \dfrac{MP_L}{MP_K}(Y_0) \quad$ denoting labor-saving progress

or

(3) higher $\quad \dfrac{MP_L}{MP_K}(Y_3) > \dfrac{MP_L}{MP_K}(Y_0) \quad$ denoting capital-saving progress

For purposes of illustration we have assumed the existence of conventional, continuous, convex neoclassical isoquants in Figure A4.1. This implies an infinite choice of techniques, ranging from very labor intensive (low K/L ratios) to very capital intensive (high K/L ratios). In actual practice, most developing countries face a very limited range of technical choice, largely dictated by the availability of foreign technology and the influence of multinational corporations (see Chapter 8).

II

PROBLEMS AND POLICIES

DOMESTIC

A note to the student on the organizational structure and operating procedure for analyzing development problems in Parts II and III

In Part I of this text, we examined the major characteristics of Third World nations, reviewed some basic concepts of development economics, and explored the nature and meaning of economic growth and development. In Parts II and III we analyze a number of critical problems which are priority issues in almost all developing countries. Our task here is not only to describe the nature of these problems but also to demonstrate how economic analysis can contribute to their ultimate resolution. It is of little value to understand basic economic concepts and principles if one is not able to apply them to real-world development problems.

Accordingly, the problem-focused chapters in Parts II and III are, in general, organized around a common five-stage operating procedure. This procedure, I would argue, provides a convenient methodology for analyzing and solving any problem, whether in economics or any other field. The five stages of problem analysis are:

1. Problem statement and principal issues
2. Relative importance of the problem in diverse developing countries
3. Possible goals and objectives
4. Role of economics
5. Policy alternatives and consequences

133

Step No. 1: Statement of problem

Each discussion begins with an analysis of what it is we are trying to understand (e.g., population growth, unemployment, poverty). Basically, four questions are asked:

1. What is the problem all about?
2. Why is it a problem?
3. How important is it?
4. What are the principal issues?

The purpose of this first step is to clarify the nature and importance of the problem so that the student can recognize why it receives so much attention in newspapers, development plans, political speeches, and international writings of scholars and journalists.

Step No. 2: Significance and variations of problems in developing countries

Using the most recent available data, we attempt here to provide a capsule statistical summary of the relative importance of the particular problem under review in diverse developing nations. How does it vary from one country to the next and what, if any, are the qualitative as well as quantitative differences in Africa, Asia, and Latin America? It is clear, for example, that while rising unemployment is a common phenomenon in developing nations, the nature, extent, and significance of the problem may be quite different in sub-Saharan Africa than in, say, Latin America or South Asia. Our purpose is not to overload the student with comparative Third World statistics. Rather, it is to give the student a feel for the ubiquitous nature of certain development problems while advising the student that the significance and principal manifestations of the problem may vary from country to country and region to region. As a result, policy approaches designed to cope with the problem can and often do differ in their scope and content.

Step No. 3: Possible goals and objectives

Our next step is to set out the likely development goals and objectives as they relate to this particular issue. Here unavoidably we must deal with value judgments and priorities. For example, if greater equality is an overall objective of government policy, then factors such as the distribution of income, the spread of educational opportunities, and the role of labor-intensive rural development projects become significant. If, however, the objective is maximum growth of GNP irrespective of its distribution, then these factors may be less important. The point is that any attempt to deal with real-world development problems must be based on explicit economic and social value premises about what is desirable and what the priorities are among different desirable goals. In fact, the very selection of specific problems to be discussed and analyzed in Parts II and III (e.g., poverty, inequality, unemployment, population growth, education, rural development, trade, aid, technology) reflects a value judgment on the part of the author, albeit one that seems to be rooted in the consensus opinion of the majority of those who study or act on Third World development problems.

Step No. 4: The role of economics and economic principles

After setting forth a possible set of goals and objectives to a specific development problem, we ask the following pertinent questions for economists:

1. What are the economic components of the problem?
2. How can economic concepts and principles help us to understand better and possibly solve the problem?
3. Do the economic components dominate the problem and, regardless of whether they do or don't, how might they be related to the noneconomic components?

Step No. 5: Policy alternatives and consequences

The final step in our problem-solving procedure is to set forth alternative economic policy approaches and their possible consequences for the problem under review. Policy options expounded at the end of each chapter are intended primarily to stimulate group discussion and individual analysis. Students are encouraged, therefore, to formulate their own conclusions and to feel free to disagree with those put forward by the author. The nature of the policy options available to governments depends on the economic aspects of the overall problem. Each policy alternative needs to be evaluated in light of a variety of priority development objectives. As a result, the possibility of tradeoffs between goals must always be considered. For example, the goal of rapid GNP growth may or may not be compatible with the elimination of unemployment or the eradication of rural poverty. Similarly, the encouragement of private foreign investment may not be compatible with the desire to be more self-reliant. In either case, when such a conflict of goals becomes apparent, choices have to be made on the basis of priorities and the socioeconomic consequences of giving up or curtailing one objective in favor of another. It is at this final stage of evaluating the *indirect* ways in which a policy designed to eliminate one problem might exacerbate other problems that the wisdom of the broad-gauged development economist can be most important.

By following the above five-step problem-solving procedure, students will not only secure a more comprehensive understanding of critical development issues but, more important, they will be better able to approach and reach independent judgments about other contemporary or future development problems. In the long run, we believe that the possible "costs" of trying to analyze all problems within a somewhat rigid five-step framework rather than following a less tightly organized discussion will be greatly outweighed by the benefits.

5

GROWTH, POVERTY, AND INCOME DISTRIBUTION

No society can surely be flourishing and happy, of which by far the greater part of the numbers are poor and miserable.

Adam Smith, 1776

A society that is not socially just and does not intend to be puts its own future in danger.

Pope John Paul II, Brazil, 1980

THE GROWTH CONTROVERSY

The 1970s witnessed a remarkable change in public and private perceptions about the ultimate nature of economic activity. In both rich and poor countries there was a growing disillusionment with the idea that the relentless pursuit of growth was the principal economic objective of society. In the developed countries, the major emphasis seemed to shift toward more concern for the "quality of life," a concern which was manifested principally in the environmental movement. There was an outcry against the concomitants of industrial growth: the pollution of air and water, the depletion of natural resources, and the destruction of many natural beauties. An influential book, *The Limits to Growth*, appeared in 1972 and purported to document the fact, first expounded in the early nineteenth century by Ricardo and especially by Malthus, that the earth's finite resources could not sustain a continuation of high growth rates without major economic and social catastrophes. It is a testimony to the mood of the times that in spite of obvious flaws in logic and many dubious assumptions, this book became widely publicized and acclaimed.

137

In the poor countries the main concern focused on the question of growth versus income distribution. Many Third World countries that had experienced relatively high rates of economic growth by historical standards in the 1960s began to realize that such growth had brought little in the way of significant benefits to their poor. For those hundreds of millions of people in Africa, Asia, and Latin America, levels of living seemed to stagnate and, in some countries, even to decline in real terms. Rates of rural and urban unemployment and underemployment were on the rise. The distribution of incomes seemed to become less equitable with each passing year. Many people felt that rapid economic growth had failed to eliminate or even reduce widespread absolute poverty, which remained a fact of economic life in all Third World nations. In both the developing and developed worlds the call for the "dethronement of GNP" as the major objective of economic activity was widely heard. In its place concern for the problems of poverty and equality became the major theme of the second development decade. Mahbub ul Haq of Pakistan seemed to speak for a great number of observers when he succinctly asserted that "we were taught to take care of our GNP as this will take care of poverty. Let us reverse this and take care of poverty as this will take care of the GNP."[1]

Since the elimination of widespread poverty and growing income inequalities is at the core of all development problems and, in fact, defines for many the principal objective of development policy, we begin Part II of this book by focusing on the nature of the poverty and inequality problem in Third World countries. Although our principal focus is on economic inequalities in the distribution of incomes and assets, it is important to keep in mind that these are only a small part of the broader inequality problem in the developing world. Of parallel or even greater importance are inequalities of power, prestige, status, recognition, job satisfaction, conditions of work, degree of participation, freedom of choice, and many other dimensions of the problem that relate more to our second and third components of the meaning of development—self-esteem and freedom to choose. But as in most social relationships, one cannot really separate the economic from the noneconomic manifestations of inequality. Each reinforces the other in a complex and often interrelated process of cause and effect.

Our basic problem-solving approach will be as outlined in the Introduction to Parts II and III. First, we define the nature of the poverty and income distribution problem and consider its quantitative significance in various Third World nations. We then set forth possible goals and objectives, examine in what ways economic analyses can shed light on the problem, and, finally, explore alternative possible policy approaches directed at the elimination of poverty and the reduction of excessively wide disparities in Third World distributions of income. A thorough understanding of these two fundamental economic manifestations of underdevelopment provides the basis for analysis in subsequent chapters of more specific development issues including population growth, unemployment, rural development, education, international trade, and foreign assistance.

WHO GETS HOW MUCH OF WHAT? A SIMPLE ILLUSTRATION

A simple and convenient way to approach the twin problems of poverty and income distribution is to utilize once again the production-possibility framework. To illustrate our point, however, let us divide production in our hypothetical developing economy into two classes of goods. First, there are necessity goods such as staple foods, simple clothing, and minimum shelter—goods essential to basic subsistence. The second class of goods, luxuries, might include expensive cars and houses, sophisticated consumer goods, fashionable clothes, and specialty foods. Assuming for the present that production occurs on the possibility frontier (i.e., that all resources are fully and efficiently employed), the question arises as to what combination of economic necessities and luxuries will actually be chosen by the society in question. Who will do the choosing and how?

Figure 5.1 illustrates the issue. On the vertical axis are aggregated all luxury goods and on the horizontal axis all necessities. The production-possibility curve, therefore, portrays the maximum combinations of both kinds of goods that this economy could produce by making efficient use of all available resources with the prevailing technological know-how. But it does *not* tell us precisely which combination among the many possible ones will actually be chosen. For example, the same real GNP would be represented at Points A and B in Figure 5.1. At Point A many luxury goods and very few necessities are being produced, while at Point B few luxuries and many necessities are being supplied to the population. One would normally expect the actual production combination in low-income countries to be somewhere in the vicinity of Point B. But in market and mixed economies, as opposed to "command" economies where production and distribution decisions are centrally planned, the basic determinant of output combinations is the level of effective aggregate demand exerted by all consumers. This is because the position and shape of society's aggregate demand curve for different products is determined primarily by the level and especially the distribution of national income.

Take, for example, the simple case of an economy consisting only of two consumers and two goods, luxuries and necessities. We know from both historical and cross-country expenditure studies that individuals or families with low incomes spend very high proportions of their incomes on basic necessities such as food, clothing, and simple shelter. On the other hand, relatively rich people spend a low proportion of their income on these

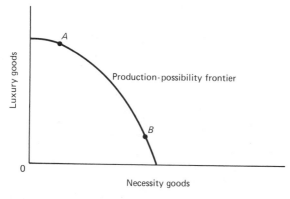

Figure 5.1. Choosing what to produce: Luxuries versus necessities.

necessities and a relatively high proportion on what we have called luxury goods—luxurious at least in the context of what poor societies can afford. For our illustration, let us suppose that a person is poor if he has 5 units or less of income per year. Such a person might spend 90% of his income on necessities—that is, his "propensity to consume" necessities will be 0.9, which when multiplied by his income level will show his total consumption or expenditure on necessities. The remaining 10% will be spent on luxuries, a propensity to consume of 0.10. On the other hand, a rich person—one who has more than, say, 5 units per year—will spend on the average only 20% of his income on necessities (a propensity to consume of 0.2) and 80% (or a propensity of 0.8) on luxuries. We are assuming, therefore, for simplicity that all income is expended on these two goods.

Now suppose that the total GNP is 8 units and that this income is divided *equally* into 4 units of personal income for each of our two individuals, where Y stands for the level of personal income. According to our definition these two individuals are poor. Table 5.1 shows that in such a situation each individual, having a propensity to spend 90% of his 4 units of income on necessities, will allocate 3.6 units of his income ($0.9 \times 4 = 3.6$) to these goods so that the total demand for necessity goods will be 7.2 units. On the other hand, each person will spend only 0.4 (i.e., 0.1×4) on luxuries so that a total of only 0.8 units of income will be spent on luxury goods. If this demand is translated into production, the point on the production-possibility curve where this economy will be operating will be in the vicinity of B in Figure 5.1.

Now, assume that this same national income of 8 units is distributed *very unequally*, with Individual no. 1 getting 7 units and Individual no. 2 only 1 unit. Table 5.2 shows that in the case of the coexistence of relative wealth and extreme poverty, total demand for necessity goods will amount only to 2.3 units (i.e., the rich person will spend 1.4 and the poor person 0.9 units respectively) while the total demand for luxury goods is 5.7 units (5.6 for the rich individual and 0.1 for the poor one). Production will take place in the vicinity of A in Figure 5.1.

We see, therefore, that in spite of the relative poverty of the country as a whole, the very unequal distribution of income means that the rich individual can dictate the overall pattern of production since his demand preferences carry more weight in the consumer goods market than those of the poor person. In both examples GNP (8) and per capita income (4) were exactly the same. But, given the very different distribution of this income, significant differences in production and consumption patterns ensued.

Tables 5.1 and 5.2 illustrate a basic point about the relationship between income distribution and the pattern of demand. Two countries with the same levels of GNP and income per capita may have entirely different production and consumption structures (i.e., they may be operating at different points on the same production-possibility curve) depending on whether or not personal incomes are distributed equitably. *For a given low level of GNP and per capita income, the more unequal the distribution of income, the more aggregate demand and production will be influenced by the consumption preferences of the rich.* In spite of the fact that they may constitute only a small proportion of the population, the rich can control a very disproportionately large share of national resources. Their dominant

Table 5.1 Expenditure and Production Patterns for a Hypothetical Two-Person, Two-Good Economy with Equal Incomes

		Individual no. 1	Individual no. 2
Personal income (Y)		$Y = 4$	$Y = 4$
Propensity to consume and expenditures on			
1. Necessities	($0.9 \times Y$ if $Y \le 5$)	3.6($= 0.9 \times 4$)	3.6
or	($0.2 \times Y$ if $Y > 5$)		
2. Luxuries	($0.1 \times Y$ if $Y \le 5$)	0.4($= 0.1 \times 4$)	0.4
or	($0.8 \times Y$ if $Y > 5$)		
Total demand for			
1. Necessities	$= 7.2$ ($= 3.6 + 3.6$)		
2. Luxuries	$= 0.8$ ($= 0.4 + 0.4$)		
Total expenditure	$= 8.0$ (per capita		
($=$ total GNP)	income $= 4.0$)		

purchasing power can bias production and imports toward manufactured luxury goods even while the masses of people are barely subsisting. This provides a good example of a situation in which the traditional theory of consumer sovereignty, as manifested in market demand curves, represents in fact the sovereignty not of all consumers but of the very few rich ones who dominate the market and determine what goods should be produced.

As a result of highly unequal income distributions, we find a number of low-income Third World countries devoting a sizable proportion of their financial, technical, and administrative resources to the production of sophisticated consumption goods with large import contents (e.g., television sets, stereophonic equipment, automobiles) to cater to the demands of a very small but economically powerful minority located mostly in urban areas. If

Table 5.2 Expenditure and Production Patterns for a Hypothetical Two-Person, Two-Good Economy with Highly Unequal Incomes

		Individual no. 1	Individual no. 2
Personal income (Y)		$Y = 7$	$Y = 1$
Propensity to consume and expenditures on			
1. Necessities	($0.9 \times Y$ if $Y \le 5$)		0.9 ($= 0.9 \times 1$)
or	($0.2 \times Y$ if $Y > 5$)	1.4 ($= 0.2 \times 7$)	
2. Luxuries	($0.1 \times Y$ if $Y \le 5$)		0.1 ($= 0.1 \times 1$)
or	($0.8 \times Y$ if $Y > 5$)	5.6 ($= 0.8 \times 7$)	
Total demand for			
1. Necessities	$= 2.3$ ($= 1.4 + 0.9$)		
2. Luxuries	$= 5.7$ ($= 5.6 + 0.1$)		
Total expenditure	$= 8.0$ (per capita		
($=$ total GNP)	income $= 4.0$)		

incomes were more equitably distributed, the pattern of demand would be geared more toward the production of basic foods and other necessities, which would further help to eliminate rural poverty and raise levels of living for broader segments of the population. An additional implication (to be discussed in Chapter 8) of a demand pattern biased toward expensive consumption goods is that these products normally require relatively sophisticated capital-intensive production techniques compared with the relatively more labor-intensive technology of necessity goods production. As a result, fewer jobs are available, profits (including those of resident foreign corporations) are higher, and the distribution of income tends to widen even further.

For the remainder of this chapter we will examine the following five critical questions about the relationship between economic growth, income distribution, and poverty:

1. What is the extent of relative inequality in Third World countries and how is this related to the extent of absolute poverty?
2. Who are the poor and what are their economic characteristics?
3. What determines the "character" of economic growth (i.e., who benefits)?
4. Are rapid economic growth and more equitable distributions of income compatible or conflicting objectives for low-income countries? To put it another way, is rapid growth achievable only at the cost of greater inequalities in the distribution of income or can a lessening of income disparities contribute to higher growth rates?
5. What kinds of policies are required to reduce the magnitude and extent of absolute poverty?

SOME BASIC CONCEPTS: SIZE AND FUNCTIONAL DISTRIBUTIONS OF INCOME

We can get some idea of the answers to Questions 1 and 2 relating to the extent and character of inequality and poverty in developing countries by pulling together some recent evidence from a variety of sources. In this section, we define the dimensions of the income distribution and poverty problems and identify some similar elements that characterize the problem in many Third World nations. But first we should be clear about what we are measuring when we speak about the distribution of income.

Economists usually like to distinguish between two principal measures of income distribution both for analytical and quantitative purposes: (a) the "personal" or "size" distribution of income, and (b) the "functional" or "distributive factor share" distribution of income.

Size Distributions

The *personal or size distribution of income* is the measure most commonly used by economists. It simply deals with individual persons or households and the total incomes they receive. The way in which that income was received is not considered. What matters is how much each earns irrespective of whether the income was derived solely from employment or came also from other sources such as interest, profits, rents, gifts, or inheritance. Moreover, the locational (urban or rural) and occupational sources of the income (e.g., agriculture, manufacturing, commerce, services) are neglected.

If Mr. X and Mr. Y both receive the same annual personal income, they are classified together irrespective of the fact that Mr. X may work 15 hours a day on his farm while Mr. Y doesn't work at all but simply collects interest on his inheritance.

Economists and statisticians, therefore, like to arrange all individuals by ascending personal incomes and then divide the total population into distinct groups, or "sizes." A common method is to divide the population into successive quintiles (i.e., five groups) or deciles (ten groups) according to ascending income levels and then determine what proportion of the total national income is received by each income group. For example, Table 5.3 shows a hypothetical but fairly typical distribution of income for a developing country. In this table 20 individuals (more commonly, households), representing the entire population of the country, are arranged in order of ascending annual personal incomes ranging from the individual household with the lowest income (0.8 units) to the one with the highest (15 units). The total or national income of all individuals amounts to 100 units and is the sum of all entries in Column 2. In Column 3 the population is grouped into quintiles of 4 individuals each. The first quintile represents the bottom

Table 5.3 A Hypothetical (but Typical) Size Distribution of LDC Personal Income by Income Shares—Quintiles and Deciles

Individuals	Personal income (money units)	Percentage share in total income	
		Quintiles	*Deciles*
1	0.8		
2	1.0		1.8
3	1.4		
4	1.8	5	3.2
5	1.9		
6	2.0		3.9
7	2.4		
8	2.7	9	5.1
9	2.8		
10	3.0		5.8
11	3.4		
12	3.8	13	7.2
13	4.2		
14	4.8		9.0
15	5.9		
16	7.1	22	13.0
17	10.5		
18	12.0		22.5
19	13.5		
20	15.0	51	28.5
Totals 20 (National income)	100.0	100	100

Measure of inequality →Ratio of bottom 40% to top 20% = 14/51 = 0.28

20% of the population on the income scale. This group receives only 5% (i.e., a total of 5 money units) of the total national income. The second quintile (Individuals 5–8) receives 9% of the total income. Alternatively, the bottom 40% of the population (quintiles one plus two) is receiving only 14% of the income, while the top 20% (the fifth quintile) of the population receives 51% of the total income.

A common measure of income inequality that can be derived from Column 3 is the ratio of the incomes received by the bottom 40% and top 20% of the population. This ratio is often used as a measure of the degree of inequality between the two extremes of very poor and very rich in a country. In our example, this inequality ratio is equal to 14 divided by 51 or approximately 1 to 3.7, or 0.28.

To provide a more detailed breakdown of the size distribution of income, decile (10%) shares are listed in Column 4. We see, for example, that the bottom 10% of the population (the two poorest individuals) is receiving only 1.8% of the total income while the top 10% (the two richest individuals) receives 28.5%. Finally, if we wanted to know what the top 5% receives, we would divide the total population into 20 equal groups of individuals (in our example, this would simply be each of the 20 individuals) and calculate the percentage of total income received by the top group. In Table 5.3, we see that the top 5% of the population (the 20th individual) receives 15% of the income, a higher share than the combined shares of the lowest 40%.

Lorenz Curves

Another common way to analyze personal income statistics is to construct what is known as a Lorenz curve.[2] Figure 5.2 shows how it is done. The numbers of income recipients are plotted on the horizontal axis, not in absolute terms but in *cumulative percentages*. For example, at point 20 we have the lowest (poorest) 20% of the population, at point 60 we have the bottom 60%, and at the end of the axis all 100% of the population has been accounted for. The vertical axis portrays the share of total income received by each percentage of population. It also is cumulative up to 100%, so that both axes are equally long. The entire figure is enclosed in a square, and a diagonal line is drawn from the lower-left-hand corner (the origin) of the square to the upper-right-hand corner. At every point on that diagonal, the percentage of income received is *exactly equal* to the percentage of income recipients—for example, the point halfway along the length of the diagonal represents 50% of the income being distributed to exactly 50% of the population. At the three-quarter point on the diagonal, 75% of the income would be distributed to 75% of the population. In other words, the diagonal line in Figure 5.2 is representative of "perfect equality" in size distribution of income. Each percentage group of income recipients is receiving that same percentage of the total income; for example, the bottom 40% receives 40% of the income, while the top 5% receives only 5% of the total income.[3]

The Lorenz curve shows the *actual* quantitative relationship between the percentage of income recipients and the percentage of the total income they did in fact receive during, say, a given year. In Figure 5.2 we have plotted this Lorenz curve using the decile data contained in Table 5.3. In other words, we have divided both the horizontal and vertical axes into 10

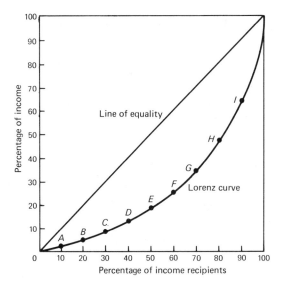

Figure 5.2.   The Lorenz curve.

equal segments corresponding to each of the 10 decile groups. Point A shows that the bottom 10% of the population receives only 1.8% of the total income. Point B shows that the bottom 20% is receiving 5% of the total income—and so on for each of the other 8 cumulative decile groups. Note that at the halfway point, E, 50% of the population is in fact receiving only 19.8% of the total income.

The more the Lorenz line curves away from the diagonal (perfect equality), the greater the degree of inequality represented. The extreme case of perfect inequality (i.e., a situation in which one person receives *all* of the national income while everybody else receives nothing) would be represented by the coexistence of the Lorenz curve with the bottom horizontal and the right-hand vertical axes. Since no country exhibits either perfect equality or perfect inequality in its distribution of income, the Lorenz curves for different countries will lie somewhere to the right of the diagonal in Figure 5.2. The greater the degree of inequality, the more "bend" and the closer to the bottom horizontal axis will be the Lorenz curve. Two representative distributions are shown in Figure 5.3, one for a relatively equal distribution (5.3a) and the other for a more unequal distribution (5.3b). (Can you explain why the Lorenz curve could not lie above or to the left of the diagonal at any point?)

Gini Coefficients and Aggregate Measures of Inequality

A final and very convenient shorthand summary measure of the relative degree of income inequality in a country can be obtained by calculating the ratio of the "area" between the diagonal and the Lorenz curve divided by the total area of the half-square in which the curve lies. In Figure 5.4 this is the

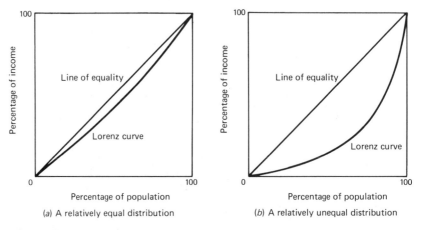

Figure 5.3.   The greater the curvature of the Lorenz line, the greater the relative degree of inequality.

ratio of the shaded area A to the total area of the triangle BCD. This ratio is known as the "Gini Concentration Ratio," or more simply, the *Gini coefficient*, after the Italian statistician C. Gini who first formulated it in 1912.

Gini coefficients are aggregate inequality measures and can vary anywhere from 0 (perfect equality) to 1 (perfect inequality). In actual fact, as we shall soon discover, the Gini coefficient for countries with highly unequal income distributions typically lies between 0.50 and 0.70, while for coun-

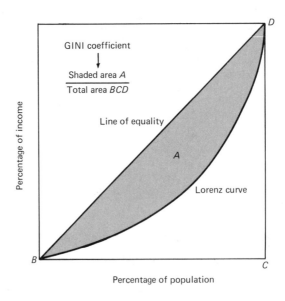

Figure 5.4.   Estimating the GINI coefficient.

tries with relatively equitable distributions, it is of the order of 0.20 to 0.35. The coefficient for our hypothetical distribution of Table 5.3 and Figure 5.2 is approximately 0.61—a relatively unequal distribution.

Functional Distributions

The second common measure of income distribution used by economists, the *functional* or *factor share distribution*, attempts to explain the share of total national income that each factor of production receives. Instead of looking at individuals as separate entities, the theory and measure of functional income distribution inquires into the percentage that "labor" receives as a whole and compares this with the percentages of total income distributed in the form of rent, interest, and profit (i.e., the returns to land and financial and physical capital). Although specific individuals may receive income from all these sources, it is not a matter of concern for the functional approach.

A sizable body of theoretical literature has been built up around the concept of functional income distribution. It attempts to explain the income of a factor of production by the contribution that this factor makes to production. Supply and demand curves are assumed to determine the unit prices of each productive factor. When these unit prices are multiplied by quantities employed on the assumption of efficient (i.e., minimum cost) factor utilization, one gets a measure of the total payment to each factor. For example, the supply of and demand for labor are assumed to determine its market wage. When this wage is then multiplied by the total level of employment, one gets a measure of total wage payments, also sometimes called the total wage bill.

Figure 5.5 provides a simple diagrammatic illustration of the traditional theory of functional income distribution. We assume that there are only two

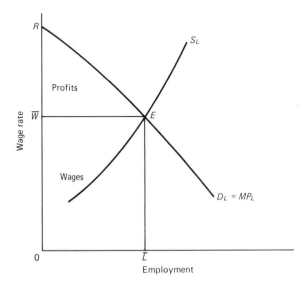

Figure 5.5.   Functional income distribution in a market economy: An illustration.

factors of production: capital, which is a fixed (given) factor, and labor, which is the only variable factor. Under competitive market assumptions, the demand for labor will be determined by labor's marginal product (i.e., additional workers will be hired up to the point where the value of their marginal product equals their real wage). But, in accordance with the principle of diminishing marginal products, this demand for labor will be a declining function of the numbers employed. Such a negatively sloped labor demand curve is shown by Line D_L in Figure 5.5. With a traditional neoclassical upward sloping labor supply curve S_L the "equilibrium" wage will be equal to $0\overline{W}$ and the equilibrium level of employment will be $0\overline{L}$. Total national output (= total national income) will be represented by the area $0\overline{REL}$.[4] This national income will be distributed in two shares—$0\overline{WEL}$ going to workers in the form of wages, and $\overline{W}RE$ remaining as capitalist profits (i.e., the return to owners of capital). In a competitive market economy with constant returns to scale production functions, therefore, factor prices are determined by factor supply and demand curves, while factor shares always combine to exhaust the total national product. Income is distributed by "function"—laborers receive wages, owners of land receive rents, and capitalists obtain profits. It is all a very neat and logical theory since each and every factor gets paid only in accordance with what it contributes to national output—no more, no less. In fact, as you may recall from Chapter 3, this model of income distribution is at the core of the Lewis theory of modern sector growth based on the reinvestment of rising capitalist profits.

Unfortunately, the relevance of the functional theory is greatly diminished by its failure to take into account the important role and influence of nonmarket forces such as power in determining these factor prices—for example, the role of collective bargaining between employers and trade unions in the setting of "modern sector" wage rates and the power of monopolists and wealthy landowners to manipulate prices on capital, land, and output to their own personal advantages. Later in the chapter we shall have more to say about the relative strengths and weaknesses of the size and functional approaches to analyzing income distribution. But first let us review some empirical data to get a better idea of the magnitude of the problems of inequality and poverty in a wide range of developing nations.

A REVIEW OF EVIDENCE: INEQUALITY AND ABSOLUTE POVERTY IN THIRD WORLD COUNTRIES

Inequality: Variations among Countries

As a first step in determining the significance of the income distribution and poverty problems in Third World countries, let us look at recent data collected from 15 countries on the percentage shares in total national income going to different percentile groups. This is done in Table 5.4. Though methods of collection, degree of coverage, and specific definitions of personal income may vary from country to country, the figures recorded in Table 5.4 give a first approximation of the magnitude of income inequalities in these developing countries. For example, we see from the last row by averaging income shares for different percentile groups among all 15 countries that on average the *poorest* 20% of the population receives only 5.8% of

Table 5.4 Some Income Distribution Estimates

	Lowest 20%	2nd Quintile	3rd Quintile	4th Quintile	Highest 20%	Highest 10%	Year
Argentina	4.4	9.7	14.1	21.5	50.3	35.2	1970
Brazil	2.0	5.0	9.4	17.0	66.6	50.6	1972
Sri Lanka	7.5	11.7	15.7	21.7	43.4	28.2	1970
Chile	4.4	9.0	13.8	21.4	51.4	34.8	1968
Costa Rica	3.3	8.7	13.3	19.9	54.8	39.5	1971
Egypt	4.2	9.8	15.5	23.5	47.0	n.a.	
Hong Kong	5.4	10.8	15.2	21.6	41.6	31.3	1980
India	7.0	9.2	13.9	20.5	49.8	33.6	1975
Kenya	2.6	6.3	11.5	19.2	60.4	n.a.	1976
South Korea	5.7	11.2	15.1	22.4	45.3	n.a.	1976
Mexico	2.9	7.0	12.0	20.4	57.7	40.6	1977
Peru	1.9	5.1	11.0	21.0	61.0	42.9	1972
Philippines	5.2	9.0	12.8	19.0	54.0	38.5	1971
Tanzania	5.8	10.2	13.9	19.7	50.4	35.6	1969
Venezuela	3.0	7.3	12.9	22.8	54.0	35.7	1970
Averages	5.8	8.7	13.4	20.7	51.4	36.9	

Source: *World Development Report, 1984*, Annex Table 28; Overseas Development Council, *U.S. Foreign Policy and the Third World, Agenda 1983* (New York: Praeger, 1983), Table C-10.

the income while the *highest* 10 and 20 percentile groups receive 36.9 and 51.4% respectively.

Now, consider the relationship, if any, between levels of per capita income and degrees of inequality for a large sample of both developed and less developed countries. Table 5.5 presents a cross-classification of these countries into three groups. The groupings correspond to high, moderate, and low degrees of inequality as measured by specified ranges of the Gini coefficients and to high, middle, and low income levels in accordance with specified ranges of real GNP per capita. As an alternative inequality measure to the Gini coefficient, Table 5.5 also provides a measure of the degree of concentration of incomes at the lowest and highest levels of the distribution scale by showing for each country the ratio of the income share of the lowest 40% to the highest 20% of the population.

A number of specific and interesting conclusions emerge from a careful examination of Table 5.5.

1. All countries, whether capitalist, socialist, or "mixed," show some degree of inequality. This is important because we need to have some idea of what kinds of distributions are practical and feasible in order to establish some reasonable benchmarks (targets) toward which a country might strive rather than to attempt to achieve the idealized, impractical, and perhaps undesirable goal of perfect equality.
2. Socialist countries such as Czechoslovakia, Hungary, Poland, and Bulgaria have the highest degree of equality in their distributions of incomes (e.g., they have the lowest Gini coefficients).
3. Developed countries on the whole exhibit a relatively more equal distribution than *most* Third World countries. This is primarily because most economically advanced countries have been able to develop effective mechanisms over the years to transfer

Table 5.5 Classification of Countries by Income Levels and Inequality

High inequality (Gini > 0.50)

Income	Country*	Year	Per capita income†	Ratio‡	Gini
Low income < U.S. $300	Brazil§	1970	231	6.5/66.7	0.61
	Colombia§	1970	251	9.4/59.5	0.54
	Ecuador§	1970	202	6.4/73.5	0.66
	Gabon§	1960	261	6.0/71.0	0.65
	Honduras§	1967–68	224	7.3/67.5	0.61
	Iraq§	1956	172	6.8/68.0	0.61
	Madagascar§	1960	93	13.5/61.0	0.52
	Peru	1970–71	297	6.5/60.0	0.57
	Rhodesia§	1968	214	8.2/69.0	0.62
	Senegal§	1960	171	10.0/64.0	0.56
Middle income U.S. $300–750	Jamaica	1958	388	8.2/61.5	0.56
	Lebanon	1955–60	454	13.0/61.0	0.52
	Mexico§	1968	464	10.2/65.8	0.58
	Panama§	1969	560	9.4/59.3	0.54
	South Africa§	1965	530	6.2/58.0	0.56
	Venezuela	1962	750	9.7/58.0	0.52

Moderate inequality (Gini = 0.40–0.50)

Income	Country*	Year	Per capita income†	Ratio‡	Gini
Low income < U.S. $300	Dahomey§	1959	65	15.5/50.0	0.44
	El Salvador§	1969	248	12.7/52.0	0.45
	Guyana	1955–56	272	14.0/45.7	0.40
	India	1961–64	84	14.0/54.0	0.46
	Philippines	1965	150	11.6/55.4	0.50
	Sudan	1963	91	14.2/50.3	0.43
	Tanzania	1967	70	14.0/57.0	0.48
	Thailand	1962	92	12.9/57.7	0.50
	Tunisia§	1961	156	10.5/55.0	0.50
	Zambia	1959	150	14.6/57.0	0.49
Middle income U.S. $300–750	Argentina§	1961	681	17.3/52.0	0.42
	Chile	1968	427	13.0/56.8	0.49
	Costa Rica	1971	423	14.7/50.6	0.43
	Uruguay	1967	460	14.3/47.4	0.42
High income > U.S. $750	Denmark	1968	1,838	13.6/47.6	0.42
	Finland	1962	1,193	11.1/49.3	0.45
	France	1962	1,373	9.5/53.7	0.50
	West Germany§	1964	1,614	15.4/52.9	0.45
	Netherlands§	1967	1,437	13.6/48.5	0.43
	Puerto Rico	1963	988	13.7/50.6	0.44

Low inequality (Gini < 0.40)

Income	Country*	Year	Per capita income†	Ratio‡	Gini
Low income < U.S. $300	Ceylon	1969–70	155	17.0/46.0	0.37
	Taiwan	1964	201	20.4/40.1	0.32
	Chad	1958	63	18.0/43.0	0.35
	Ivory Coast	1959	139	17.5/55.0	0.43
	South Korea	1970	180	18.0/45.0	0.36
	Libya	1962	220	23.5/37.0	0.26
	Malaysia	1957–58	208	17.7/43.9	0.36
	Niger§	1960	73	18.0/42.0	0.36
	Pakistan (E/W)	1963–64	83	17.5/45.0	0.37
	Uganda§	1969–70	110	17.1/47.1	0.38
Middle income U.S. $300–750	Bulgaria§	1962	407	26.8/33.2	0.21
	Greece§	1957	341	21.0/49.5	0.37
	Israel§	1957	686	20.2/39.4	0.30
	Poland§	1964	649	23.4/36.0	0.25
	Spain	1964–65	572	17.0/45.2	0.38
	Surinam	1962	311	21.7/42.6	0.31
	Yugoslavia	1968	451	18.5/41.5	0.33
High income > U.S. $750	Canada	1965	2,057	20.0/40.2	0.32
	Czechoslovakia§	1964	880	27.6/31.0	0.18
	Hungary§	1969	870	24.0/33.5	0.24
	Japan	1963	780	20.7/40.0	0.31
	New Zealand§	1968–69	1,800	15.5/42.0	0.37
	Norway§	1963	1,609	16.6/40.5	0.35
	Sweden§	1963	2,220	14.0/44.0	0.39
	United Kingdom	1968	1,599	18.8/39.0	0.32
	United States§	1970	3,603	19.7/38.8	0.31

*The data on countries without the section mark is based on household size distribution.
†Per capita income is in 1964 U.S. $ to the closest 2 years.
‡Ratios are ratio of bottom 40% to top 20%.
§The data is based on active workers income distribution.

SOURCE: Montek Ahluwalia, "Dimensions of the problem," in H. Chenery, Duloy, and Jolly (eds.), *Redistribution with Growth: An Approach to Policy* (Washington, D.C.: IBRD, 1973) (mimeo). Reprinted by permission of The World Bank and Oxford University Press.

some proportion of their incomes from rich to poor. For example, progressively higher income tax rates combined with public expenditures, social security payments, unemployment compensation, food stamps, and outright welfare payments to the very poor are methods used to temper the wide income disparities that might normally result in the course of private economic activity. Such income transfer mechanisms are still either largely nonexistent or ineffectively administered in most developing countries.

4. Third World countries have a significant variation in their degree of inequality as shown by the wide range of their Gini coefficients.
5. Perhaps more important, there seems to be no apparent relationship between levels of per capita income and the degree of income concentration. Even within the group of very low income countries (i.e., those with per capita incomes of less than $300) we see from Table 5.5 that the share of income accruing to the bottom 40% varies from 6.5% (Brazil) to over 20% (Taiwan).

Absolute Poverty: Extent and Magnitude

Now let's switch our attention from relative income shares of various percentile groups within a given population to the more significant question of the extent and magnitude of "absolute poverty" in developing countries. In Chapter 2, remember, we said the extent of absolute poverty can be defined by the number of people living below a specified minimum level of income—an imaginary "international poverty line." Such a line knows no national boundaries and is independent of the level of national per capita income. Absolute poverty can and does exist, therefore, as readily in New York City as it does in Calcutta, Cairo, Lagos, or Bogota, although its magnitude is likely to be much lower in terms of total numbers or percentages of the total population. In a recent paper focused on the dimensions of Third World poverty and its relationship to economic growth, Ahluwalia, Carter, and Chenery concluded that "almost 40 percent of the population of the developing countries live in absolute poverty defined in terms of income levels that are insufficient to provide adequate nutrition. The bulk of the poor are in the poorest countries: in South Asia, Indonesia, and sub-Saharan Africa. These countries account for two-thirds of the total (world) population and well over three-fourths of the population in poverty. The incidence of poverty is 60 percent or more in countries having the lowest level of real GNP."[5]

Table 5.6 shows the authors' estimate of absolute poverty levels with projections to the year 2000 for 36 Third World countries divided into low (less than $150 per capita incomes measured in 1970 U.S. dollars), medium (between $150 and $325), and high ($325 to $1,300) per capita income levels. Note that they project substantial declines in absolute poverty— though by no means an eradication of it—by the turn of the century. However, this projection is based on several optimistic assumptions regarding future trends in real economic growth and the distribution of its benefits. The year 2000 projections can be taken, therefore, as lying at the optimistic end of the spectrum of possibilities—especially in view of the severe economic showdown of the 1980s.

One final point, analogous to Conclusion (5) above regarding the apparent absence of any necessary relationship between levels of per capita income and the distribution of that income, needs to be mentioned. It is that *high per capita incomes per se do not guarantee the absence of significant*

Table 5.6 Income Growth and Poverty in 36 Developing Countries, 1975 and 2000 (projected)

Country	1975 GNP per capita	GNP growth rates		Share of lowest 40%		Percentage of population in poverty, 1975	Number of people in poverty (millions)	
		1960–1975	*1975–2000*	*1975 estimate*	*2000 projection*		*1975 estimate*	*2000 projection*
Group A (under $150)								
Bangladesh	72	2.4	4.6	20.1	17.4	60	52	56
Ethiopia	81	4.3	4.1	16.8	15.0	62	19	25
Burma	88	3.2	2.5	15.7	15.2	56	20	29
Indonesia	90	5.2	5.5	16.1	12.7	62	76	30
Uganda	115	4.0	3.2	14.4	14.0	45	6	12
Zaire	105	4.3	4.8	14.6	12.7	49	11	13
Sudan	112	3.0	6.0	14.5	12.0	47	10	8
Tanzania	118	6.8	5.4	14.3	12.3	46	8	9
Pakistan	121	5.6	5.2	16.5	14.5	34	32	26
India	108	3.6	4.5	17.0	14.6	46	277	167
Subtotal	99	3.8	4.7	16.7	13.9	49	510	375
Group B ($150–$325)								
Kenya	168	7.0	5.9	8.9	7.7	48	7	11
Nigeria	176	7.1	5.2	13.0	11.8	27	27	30
Philippines	182	5.6	7.3	11.6	10.3	29	14	6
Sri Lanka	185	4.2	3.8	19.3	18.2	10	2	2
Senegal	227	1.5	4.0	9.6	8.9	29	1	2
Egypt	238	4.2	6.1	13.9	13.5	14	7	5
Thailand	237	7.5	6.7	11.5	10.9	23	13	4
Ghana	255	2.7	2.1	11.2	11.9	19	2	6

Morocco	266	4.4	6.2	13.3	10.9	16	4	2
Ivory Coast	325	7.7	5.8	10.4	10.4	14	1	1
Subtotal	209	5.5	5.8	12.0	10.1	24	81	70
Group C ($325–$1,300)								
South Korea	325	9.3	8.1	16.9	19.1	6	3	1
Chile	386	2.3	6.0	13.1	14.3	9	1	1
Zambia	363	3.4	4.9	13.0	12.9	7	0	1
Colombia	352	5.6	7.4	9.9	11.5	14	5	2
Turkey	379	6.4	6.3	9.3	10.4	11	6	4
Tunisia	425	6.1	7.5	11.1	13.3	9	1	0
Malaysia	471	6.7	6.7	11.1	13.3	8	1	1
Taiwan	499	9.1	6.2	22.3	24.4	4	1	0
Guatemala	497	6.1	6.0	11.3	12.4	9	1	1
Brazil	509	7.2	7.0	9.1	11.9	8	16	7
Peru	503	5.7	6.3	7.3	8.8	15	3	2
Iran	572	9.5	7.2	8.2	11.0	8	5	2
Mexico	758	6.8	6.8	8.2	10.8	10	8	6
Yugoslavia	828	5.8	6.1	18.8	23.9	4	1	0
Argentina	1,097	4.0	4.5	15.1	18.5	3	1	1
Venezuela	1,288	5.8	6.8	8.5	12.9	5	1	1
Subtotal	577	6.4	6.9	9.9	10.0	8	54	30
Total	237	5.4	6.2	9.8	6.5	35	644	475

SOURCE: M.S. Ahluwalia, N. Carter, and H. Chenery, "Growth and poverty in developing countries," *Journal of Development Economics* 6 (September 1979), Tables 1 and 2.

numbers of absolute poor. Since the share of income accruing to the lowest percentile of a population can vary widely from one country to another, it is possible for a country with a high per capita income to have a larger percentage of its population below an international poverty line than a country with a lower per capita income. Thus, for example, if we look at Table 5.6, we see that Taiwan and Guatemala had approximately the same level of real per capita income in 1975 even though the proportion of Guatemala's population below the poverty line was more than twice as large as that of Taiwan. Similarly, Korea has 60% of the per capita income level of Peru, but the proportion of its people below the poverty line is only 40% of the figure for Peru (6 compared with 15% of their respective populations). This simply shows that problems of poverty and highly unequal distributions of income are not just the result of natural economic growth processes. Rather, they depend on the *character* of that economic growth and the political and institutional arrangements according to which rising national incomes are distributed among the broad segments of a population.

ECONOMIC CHARACTERISTICS OF POVERTY GROUPS

So far, we have painted a broad picture of the income distribution and poverty problem in developing countries.[6] We argued that the magnitude of absolute poverty results from a combination of low per capita incomes and highly unequal distributions of that income. Clearly, for any given distribution of income, the higher the level of per capita income, the lower will be the numbers of the absolutely poor. But, as we have seen, higher levels of per capita income are no guarantee of lower levels of poverty. An understanding of the nature of the size distribution of income, therefore, is central to any analysis of the poverty problem in low-income countries.

But painting a broad picture of Third World poverty is not enough. Before we can formulate effective policies and programs to attack poverty at its source, we need some specific knowledge of who these poverty groups are and what are their economic characteristics. As we show in a later section when we deal with alternative policies to combat poverty, it is *not* sufficient simply to focus on raising growth rates of GNP in the expectation or hope that this national income growth will "trickle down" to improve levels of living for the very poor. On the contrary, direct attacks on poverty by means of poverty-focused policies and plans appear to be more effective both in the short and longer runs. And one cannot attack poverty directly without detailed knowledge of its location, extent, and characteristics.

Perhaps *the most valid generalization about the poor is that they are disproportionately located in the rural areas* and that they are primarily engaged in agricultural and associated activities. Data from a broad cross-section of Third World nations supports this generalization. We find, for example, that about two-thirds of the very poor scratch out their livelihood from subsistence agriculture either as small farmers or as low-paid farm workers. Some of the remaining one-third are also located in rural areas but engaged in petty services, others are located on the fringes and marginal areas of urban centers where they engage in various forms of self-employment such as street-hawking, trading, petty services, and small-scale commerce. On the average, we may conclude that *in Africa and Asia about*

75—80% of all target poverty groups are located in the rural areas, as are about 70% in Latin America.

It is interesting to note in the light of the rural concentration of absolute poverty that the largest share of most LDC government expenditures over the past two decades has been directed toward the urban area and, within that area, toward the relatively affluent modern manufacturing and commercial sectors. Whether in the realm of directly productive economic investments or in the fields of education, health, housing, and other social services, this urban modern sector bias in government expenditures is at the core of many of the development problems that will be discussed in succeeding chapters. We need only point out here that in view of the disproportionate numbers of the very poor who reside in rural areas, any policy designed to alleviate poverty must necessarily be directed to a large extent toward rural development in general and the agricultural sector in particular (see Chapter 9).

Women and Poverty

Another important generalization about poverty is that it affects a disproportionate number of women. In virtually every country, there are more women than men at the lowest levels of income. Moreover, there is an increasing incidence of poverty in households headed by women. Of the world's total households, an estimated 17—28% are headed by women. In some areas, like the Caribbean and South Africa, this figure exceeds 40%. Generally, households headed by women are among the poorest groups in society.

Poverty lays a particularly heavy burden on women because of their dual roles in the economy. Women often work both inside and outside the home. At home, they are usually responsible for housework, food preparation, and child care. And for poor women "home production" can also include such grueling chores as gathering firewood and carrying water; weeding, sowing, and harvesting food crops on family plots; grinding and milling grains; and caring for animals. Poor women also tend to have more children, which adds considerably to their chores. Outside the home, these women are relegated to working in the agricultural and informal urban sectors where labor is hard, hours are long, and wages are low. In an arena of low technology, virtually no capital, and marginal wages, many of these women seek to provide the sole means of survival for their families while yet others try to make up for the shortfalls in their males' sub-subsistence wages.

Time is the primary resource of poor women; they generally work longer and harder hours as a result of their dual roles. This leaves them little time for leisure, and in fact, as incomes decline, women give up their leisure time rather than home time to earn extra income outside the home. When these working hours are assigned an economic value and added to the household's cash income, the contribution of women and children can be greater than that of poor men.

The facts suggest that the poverty of households headed by women and the poverty of women in general is directly related to their status. Women are usually less educated, have fewer employment opportunities, and receive lower wages than men. Furthermore, they have less access to land, capital, and technology, and this lack of access greatly diminishes the efficiency of production both inside and outside the home.

Clearly, if policies aimed at eliminating absolute poverty are to be successful, efforts must be made to improve the status of women. Such efforts should include the provision of education and employment opportunities as well as improved access to factors of production, all of which can enhance the productivity and income of women. In fact, this may be the most direct means of improving the incomes of the most impoverished households where women's income is either the only means of survival or a major component of household income.

The urban-industrial bias of development policies has led to a widening of the gap in income between men and women, as such policies usually provide for the employment and training of men rather than women. And several trends related to this bias have had similar consequences. Thus the increasing urbanization further widens the gap in income as women have fewer income-earning opportunities in the urban sector. The migration of male workers also results in a loss of income for rural households if remittances are not forthcoming, and the decline of agriculture results in the loss of employment for women who traditionally have generated income from that sector (see Chapter 10 for a further discussion of women's economic role in agriculture).

ECONOMIC GROWTH AND THE EXTENT OF POVERTY

We have already discussed the fact that exclusive reliance on the natural forces of economic growth to reduce significantly the extent of absolute poverty in most developing countries would probably be insufficient. This issue is so central to development theory and policy that it warrants further examination. The basic question is the following: Does the pursuit of economic growth along traditional GNP-maximizing lines tend to improve, worsen, or have no necessary effect on the distribution of income and the extent of poverty in developing countries? Unfortunately, economists do not at present possess any definitive knowledge of the specific factors that affect changes in the distribution of income over time for individual countries. Professor Kuznets, to whom we owe so much for his pioneering analysis of the historical growth patterns of contemporary developed countries, has suggested that in the early stages of economic growth the distribution of income will tend to *worsen* while at later stages it will improve. Although long-run data for Western nations do seem to support this proposition, a look at recent data from developing nations is less convincing, as is shown by Figure 5.6.[7]

In Figure 5.6 we have plotted rates of growth of GNP for some 13 developing countries on the horizontal axis and the growth rate of income of the lowest 40% of their population along the vertical axis. The data are for two points in time, shown in parentheses after each country, and the scatter is intended to reveal any obvious relationships between growth rates of GNP and improvements in income levels for the very poor. Each country's data, therefore, are plotted in the figure at a point reflecting its combination of GNP growth and the income growth of the lowest 40% of its population. Countries above the 45° line are those countries where the distribution of

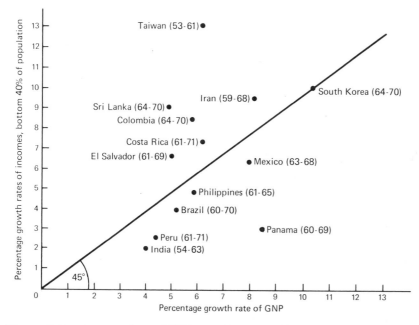

Figure 5.6. A comparison of GNP growth rates and income growth rates of the bottom 40% in selected LDCs.

income has improved—i.e., the incomes of the bottom 40% grew faster than the overall GNP growth rate—whereas countries below the 45° line have experienced a worsening of their income distributions over the indicated period.

The scatter of points in Figure 5.6 does *not* reveal any strong or obvious relationship between GNP growth and the distribution of income. High growth rates do not necessarily worsen the distribution of income, as some have suggested. Indeed, countries like Taiwan, Iran, and Korea have experienced relatively high rates of GNP growth and showed improved, or at least unchanged, distributions of income. Nevertheless, countries like Mexico and Panama have grown just as fast but experienced a deterioration of their income distribution. On the other hand, there does not seem to be a necessary relationship between low GNP growth and improved income distribution. In developing countries like India, Peru, and the Philippines low rates of GNP growth appear to have been accompanied by a deterioration of the relative income shares of the bottom 40%. And yet, Sri Lanka, Colombia, Costa Rica, and El Salvador with similarly low GNP growth rates managed to improve the relative economic well-being of their low-income populations.

Although admittedly sketchy and limited to a short period of time, these data suggest once again that it is the "character" of economic growth (i.e., how it is achieved, who participates, which sectors are given priority, what institutional arrangements are designed and emphasized, etc.) that determines the degree to which that growth is or is not reflected in the improved living standards of the very poor. Clearly, it is not the mere fact of rapid growth per se that determines the nature of its distributional benefits.

This "character of economic growth" argument is further reinforced by an extensive empirical study of 43 developing nations which analyzed the relationship between the shares of income accruing to the poorest 60% of the population and a country's aggregate economic performance.[8] It was found that the principal impact of economic development on income distribution has been, on average, to *decrease* both the absolute and the relative incomes of the poor. There was no evidence of any automatic "trickle down" of the benefits of economic growth to the very poor. On the contrary, the growth process experienced by these 43 LDCs has typically led to a "trickle up" in favor of the small middle class and especially the very rich. The authors, therefore, conclude that "economic structure, not level or rate of economic growth, is the basic determinant of patterns of income distribution."[9]

REDEFINING DEVELOPMENT GOALS: GROWTH WITH IMPROVED INCOME DISTRIBUTION

The necessity of reorienting development priorities away from exclusive preoccupation with maximizing rates of GNP growth and toward broader social objectives such as the eradication of poverty and the reduction of excessive income disparities is now widely recognized throughout the Third World. The gap between problem redefinition and specific action can, however, be quite enormous. There are, of course, serious political, institutional, and power structure problems involved in any reorientation of development strategy toward greater concern for the very poor. Moreover, economics itself has very little in the way of a received theory of either how developing economies grow or what investment strategies can maximize economic growth rates. There is relatively little consensus among economists on what strategies should be followed and whether any strictly economic strategy can eliminate or greatly reduce the incidence of poverty. Quite simply, the theoretical determinants of income distribution are very poorly understood with respect to the developed countries toward which the bulk of existing theory has been directed—let alone with respect to the underdeveloped countries, where much of this theory is irrelevant.

But the history of economics has been marked by theories and concepts that have evolved as responses to specific real-world economic problems and not merely as a natural organic process, unrelated to the world at large. The Malthusian theory of population, the Marxist theory of the increasing misery of the masses, the neoclassical theory of maximizing behavior and atomistic competition, the Keynesian theory of income and employment determination, and the Harrod–Domar theories of economic growth all represented direct responses to what were perceived to be the principal economic and social problems of the times. Given the recent emphasis on problems of poverty and income distribution, therefore, it is not unreasonable to anticipate that as economists increasingly turn away from exclusive concern with growth, new and better theories and policies will emerge to comprehend and cope with these very serious problems that are the daily scourge of hundreds of millions of people.

Although rapid economic growth does not automatically provide the answer, it nevertheless remains an essential ingredient in any realistic poverty-focused program of development. Moreover, rapid economic growth and more equitable distributions of income are not necessarily incompatible as development objectives. The choice is not between more growth and more equality but about the type of economic growth Third World countries wish to pursue—one that principally benefits the very rich or one in which the benefits are more widely distributed. In the next section we will look at some of the economic arguments why growth and equality are not in conflict. For present purposes, however, we may conclude that *development strategy requires not only a concern with accelerating economic growth but also a direct concern with improving the material standards of living for those very sizable segments of Third World populations who have been largely bypassed by the economic growth of the last two decades.*

A principal development objective, therefore, should be to generate a desired pattern of overall and broad-based income growth with special emphasis on accelerating the growth of incomes of "target" poverty groups. Such an aim requires a very different strategy from one that is simply oriented toward maximizing the growth rate of GNP, irrespective of the distributional consequences.

THE ROLE OF ECONOMIC ANALYSIS: REDISTRIBUTION FROM GROWTH

Growth versus Income Distribution

The Traditional Argument: Factor Shares, Savings, and Economic Growth

Although much of economic analysis has been strangely silent on the relationship between economic growth and the resulting distribution of income, a large body of theory in essence asserts that highly *unequal* distributions are *necessary* conditions for generating rapid growth.[10] In fact, in the 1960s and early 1970s, the explicit and implicit acceptance of this proposition by economists from both developed and underdeveloped countries tended to turn their collective and individual attentions away from problems of poverty and income distribution. If wide inequalities are a necessary condition of maximum growth and if in the long run maximum growth is a necessary condition of rising standards of living for all, through the natural "trickle-down" processes of competitive and mixed economic systems, then it follows that direct concern with the alleviation of poverty would be self-defeating. Needless to say, such a viewpoint, whether correct or not, provided a psychological, if not conscious, rationalization for the accumulation of wealth by powerful elite groups.

The basic economic argument to justify large income inequalities was that high personal and corporate incomes were necessary conditions of saving, which made possible investment and economic growth through a mechanism such as the Harrod–Domar model described in Chapter 3. If the rich save and invest significant proportions of their incomes while the poor spend all their income on consumption goods, and if GNP growth rates are directly related to the proportion of national income saved, then apparently an economy characterized by highly unequal distributions of income would save more and grow faster than one with a more equitable distribution of income. Eventually, it was assumed that national and per capita incomes would be high enough to make sizable redistributions of income possible through tax and subsidy programs. But until such a time is reached, any attempt to redistribute incomes significantly would only serve to lower growth rates and delay the time when a larger income pie could be cut up into bigger slices for all population groups.[11]

A Counterargument[12]

There are four general reasons why many development economists now believe the above argument to be incorrect and *why greater equality in developing countries may in fact be a condition for self-sustaining economic growth.*

First, common sense supported by a wealth of recent empirical data bears witness to the fact that unlike the historical experience of the now developed countries, the rich in contemporary Third World countries are *not* noted for their frugality nor for their desire to save and invest substantial proportions of their incomes in the *local* economy. Instead, landlords, businessmen, politicians, and other rich elites are known to squander much of their incomes on imported luxury goods, expensive houses, foreign travel, and investment in gold, jewelry, and foreign banking accounts. Such "savings" and "investments" do not add to the nation's productive resources. In fact, they represent substantial drains on these resources in that the income so derived is extracted from the sweat and toil of common, uneducated, and unskilled laborers. In short, the rich do not necessarily save and invest significantly larger proportions of their incomes (in the real economic sense of "productive" domestic saving and investment) than do the poor.[13] Therefore, a growth strategy based on sizable and growing income inequalities may in reality be nothing more than an opportunistic myth designed to perpetuate the vested interests and maintain the status quo of the economic and political elites of Third World nations, often at the expense of the great majority of the general population. Such strategies might better be called "antidevelopmental."[14]

Second, the low incomes and low levels of living for the poor, which are manifested in poor health, nutrition, and education, can lower their economic productivity and thereby lead directly and indirectly to a slower-growing economy. Strategies to raise the incomes and levels of living of, say, the bottom 40% would therefore contribute not only to their material well-being but also to the productivity and income of the economy as a whole.

Third, raising the income levels of the poor will stimulate an overall increase in the demand for locally produced necessity products like food and clothing. On the other hand, the rich tend to spend more of their additional incomes on imported luxury goods. Rising demands for local goods provide a greater stimulus to local production, local employment, and local investment. Such demands thus create the conditions for rapid economic growth and a broader popular participation in that growth.[15]

Fourth, and finally, a more equitable distribution of income achieved through the reduction of mass poverty can stimulate healthy economic expansion by acting as a powerful material and psychological incentive to widespread public participation in the development process. On the other hand, wide income disparities and substantial absolute poverty can act as powerful material and psychological disincentives to economic progress. They may even create the conditions for an ultimate rejection of progress by the masses of frustrated and politically explosive people, especially those with considerable education.

GNP as a Biased Index of National Development and Welfare

We have already criticized reliance on GNP and its growth rate as the principal indicator of development and economic well-being. Figures for GNP per capita give no indication of how national income is actually distributed and who is benefiting most from the growth of production. We have seen, for example, that a rising level of absolute and per capita GNP can camouflage the fact that the poor are no better off than before.

Although many people (including some economists) are unaware of this fact, the calculation of the rate of GNP growth is largely a calculation of the rate of growth of the incomes of the upper 40% of the population who receive a disproportionately large share of the national product. Therefore, GNP growth rates should *not* be used as an index of improved welfare. To give an extreme example, suppose that an economy consisted of only 10 people and that 9 of them had no income at all and the 10th received 100 units of income. The GNP for this economy would therefore be 100 and per capita GNP would be 10. Now suppose that everyone's income increases by 20% so that GNP rises to 120 while per capita income grows to 12. For the 9 individuals with no income before and still no income now (i.e., $1.20 \times 0 = 0$), such a rise in per capita income provides no cause for rejoicing. The one rich individual still has all the income. And GNP, instead of being a welfare index of society as a whole, is merely measuring the welfare of a single individual!

The same line of reasoning applies to the more realistic situation where incomes are very unequally distributed although not perfectly unequal as in the above example. Taking the figures from Table 5.3, where we divided the population into quintiles which received 5, 9, 13, 22, and 51% income shares respectively, we found that these income shares are a measure of the relative economic welfare of each income class and that the rate of income growth in each quintile is a measure of the economic welfare growth of that class. We can approximate the growth in total welfare of society as the simple weighted sum of the growth of income in each class. This in fact is what the rate of GNP growth measures—where the weights applied to each income class, however, are their respective shares of national income. To be specific, in the case of a population divided into quintiles according to rising income levels, we would have[16]

$$G = w_1 g_1 + w_2 g_2 + w_3 g_3 + w_4 g_4 + w_5 g_5 \tag{1}$$

where G = a weighted index of growth of social welfare,
   g_i = the growth rate of income of the ith quintile (where the i quintiles are ordered 1, 2, 3, 4, and 5 in our example),
and w_i = the "welfare weight" of the ith quintile (i.e., in our example $w_1 = 0.05$, $w_2 = 0.09$, $w_3 = 0.13$, $w_4 = 0.22$, and $w_5 = 0.51$).

As long as the weights add up to unity and are nonnegative, our overall measure of the growth of social welfare, G, must fall somewhere between the maximum and minimum income growth rates in the various quintiles. In the extreme case of all income accruing to one individual or one group of individuals in the highest quintile and where the "welfare weights" are the income shares (as they are with GNP growth calculations), Equation (1) would be written as

$$G = 0g_1 + 0g_2 + 0g_3 + 0g_4 + 1.0g_5 = 1.0g_5 \qquad (2)$$

The growth of social welfare would, therefore, be associated exclusively with the growth of incomes of the top quintile of the population!

In the example derived from Table 5.3, the GNP income share weighted index of social welfare would be written as

$$G = 0.05g_1 + 0.09g_2 + 0.13g_3 + 0.22g_4 + 0.51g_5 \qquad (3)$$

Now suppose the income growth rate of the bottom 60% of the population is zero (i.e., $g_1 = g_2 = g_3 = 0$) while that of the top 40% is 10% (i.e., $g_4 = g_5 = 0.10$). Equation (3) could therefore be written as

$$G = 0.05(0) + 0.09(0) + 0.13(0) + 0.22(0.10) + 0.51(0.10) = 0.073$$

and the social welfare index would rise by over 7%, which is the rate of growth of GNP (i.e., GNP would rise from 100 in Table 5.3 to 107.3 if the incomes of the 4th and 5th quintiles grew by 10%). Thus, we have an illustration of a case where GNP rises by 7.3%, implying that social well-being has increased by this same proportionate amount even though 60% of the population is no better off than before. These bottom 60% still have only 5, 13, and 22 units of income respectively. Clearly, the distribution of income would be worsened (the relative shares of the bottom 60% would fall) by such a respectable growth rate of GNP.

The numerical example given by Equation (3) illustrates our basic point. The use of the growth rate of GNP as an index of social welfare and as a method of comparing the development performance of different countries can be very misleading, especially where countries have markedly different distributions of income. The "welfare weights" attached to the growth rates of different income groups are very unequal, with a heavy social "premium" being placed on the income growth of the highest quintile groups. In the example of Equation (3), a 1% growth in the income of the top quintile carries over 10 times the weight of a 1% growth in the lowest quintile (i.e., 0.51 compared with 0.05) because it implies an absolute increment that is 10 times larger. In other words, *using the measure of GNP growth as an index of improvements in social welfare and development accords to each income group a "welfare valuation" that corresponds to their respective income shares* (i.e., a 1% increase in the income of the richest 20% of the population is implicitly assumed to be over 10 times as important to society as a 1% increase in the income of the bottom 20%). It follows that the best way to maximize social welfare growth is to maximize the rate of growth of the incomes of the rich while neglecting the poor! If ever there was a case for *not* equating GNP growth with development, the preceding example should provide a persuasive illustration.

Constructing a Poverty-Weighted Index of Social Welfare

An alternative to using a simple rate of GNP growth ("distributive share") index of social welfare would be to construct an "equal-weights" or even a "poverty-weighted" index. The latter two indexes might be especially relevant for those countries concerned with the elimination of poverty as a major development objective. As its name indicates, an equal-weights index weighs the growth of income in each income class not by the proportion of total income in that class but rather by the proportion of the total population—that is, all people are treated ("weighted") equally. In an economy divided into quintiles, such an index would give a weight of 0.2 to the growth of income in each quintile. Thus a 10% increase in the income of the lowest 20% of the population would have the same bearing on the overall measure of social welfare improvement as a 10% increase in the top 20% group or in any other quintile group, even though the absolute increase in income for the bottom group will be much smaller than for the upper groups.

Using an equal-weights index in our example of a 10% income growth of the top two quintiles with the bottom three remaining static, we would have

$$G = 0.20g_1 + 0.20g_2 + 0.20g_3 + 0.20g_4 + 0.20g_5 \qquad \textbf{(4)}$$

or, inserting growth rates for g_1 through g_5,

$$G = 0.20(0) + 0.20(0) + 0.20(0) + 0.20(0.10) + 0.20(0.10) = 0.04$$

Social welfare will have increased by only 4%, compared to the 7.3% increase recorded by using the distributive shares or GNP growth rate index. Even though recorded GNP still grows by 7.3%, this alternative welfare index of development shows only a 4% rise.

Finally, consider a developing country that is genuinely and solely concerned with improving the material well-being of, say, the poorest 40% of its population. Such a country might wish to construct a poverty-weighted index of development, which places "subjective" social values *only* on the income growth rates of the bottom 40%. In other words, it might arbitrarily place a welfare weight on w_1 of 0.60 and on w_2 of 0.40 while giving w_3, w_4, and w_5 zero weights. Using our same numerical example, the social welfare growth index for this country would be given by the expression

$$G = 0.60g_1 + 0.40g_2 + 0g_3 + 0g_4 + 0g_5 \qquad \textbf{(5)}$$

which, when substituting $g_1 = g_2 = g_3 = 0$ and $g_4 = g_5 = 0.10$, becomes

$$G = 0.60(0) + 0.40(0) + 0(0) + 0(0.10) + 0(0.10) = 0$$

The poverty-weighted index therefore records *no* improvement in social welfare (i.e., no development) even though recorded GNP has grown by 7.3%!

Although the choice of welfare weights in any index of development is purely arbitrary, it does represent and reflect important social value judgments about goals and objectives for a given society. It would certainly be interesting to know, if this were possible, what are the *real* implicit welfare weights of the various development strategies of different Third World countries. Our main point, however, is that as long as the growth rate of GNP is explicitly or implicitly used to compare development performances, we know that a "wealthy weights" index is actually being employed.

To put some real-world flavor into the preceding discussion of alternative indexes of improvements in economic welfare and to illustrate the usefulness of different weighted growth indices in evaluating the economic performance of various countries, consider the data in Table 5.7 presented in a paper by Chenery and Ahluwalia. The table shows the growth of income in 14 countries as measured first by the rate of growth of GNP, second by an equal-weights index, and third by a poverty-weights index where the actual weights assigned to income growth rates of the lowest 40%, the middle 40%, and the top 20% of the population are 0.6, 0.4 and 0.0 respectively. Some interesting conclusions emerge from a review of the last three columns of Table 5.7.

1. Economic performance as measured by equal- and poverty-weighted indexes is notably worse in some otherwise high GNP growth countries like Brazil, Mexico, and Panama. Since these countries all experienced a deterioration in their income distribution and a growing concentration of income growth in the upper groups over this period, the equal- and poverty-weights indexes naturally show a less impressive development performance than does the simple GNP measure.

2. In five countries (Colombia, El Salvador, Costa Rica, Sri Lanka, and Taiwan) the weighted indexes show a better performance than GNP growth because the relative income growth of lower-income groups proceeded more rapidly over the period in question in those five countries than that of the higher-income groups.

3. In four countries (Korea, Peru, the Philippines, and Yugoslavia) little change in income distribution during the period in question results in little variation between the GNP measure and the two alternative weighted indexes of social welfare.

We may conclude, therefore, that *a useful summary measure of the degree to which economic growth is biased toward the relative improvement of high-income or low-income groups is the positive or negative divergence between a weighted (equal or poverty) social welfare index and the actual growth rate of GNP.*

Finally, our analysis leads us to conclude that the presumed tradeoff between rapid economic growth and a more equitable distribution of income is in reality better expressed as a tradeoff between income growth rates among different income groups. If a weighted welfare index is used to measure economic development, then it is not only possible but may even be desirable for a lower growth rate of GNP to be associated with a higher rate of economic development, at least in terms of the value judgments of an egalitarian society.

Combining the Economics of Growth and Distribution

The reformulation of indexes of development to take account of alternative social premiums for different income groups takes us a long way toward a better understanding of the relationship between economic growth and

Table 5.7 Income Distribution and Growth

Country	Period	I. Income growth			II. Annual increase in welfare		
		Upper 20%	Middle 40%	Lowest 40%	(A) GNP weights	(B) Equal weights	(C) Poverty weights
South Korea	1964–1970	12.4	9.5	11.0	11.0	10.7	10.5
Panama	1960–1969	8.8	9.2	3.2	8.2	6.7	5.2
Mexico	1963–1968	8.8	5.8	6.0	7.8	6.5	5.9
Taiwan	1953–1961	4.5	9.1	12.1	6.8	9.4	11.1
Costa Rica	1961–1971	4.5	9.3	7.0	6.3	7.4	7.8
Canada	1961–1965	7.0	5.3	6.5	6.2	6.1	6.1
Colombia	1964–1970	5.2	7.9	7.8	6.2	7.3	7.8
El Salvador	1961–1969	3.5	9.5	6.4	5.7	7.1	7.4
Philippines	1961–1965	5.0	6.7	4.4	5.5	5.4	5.2
Brazil	1960–1970	6.7	3.1	3.7	5.2	4.1	3.5
United States	1960–1966	5.6	5.2	4.1	5.2	4.8	4.5
Finland	1952–1962	6.0	5.0	2.1	5.1	4.0	3.1
Sri Lanka	1963–1970	3.1	6.3	8.3	5.0	6.5	7.6
Yugoslavia	1963–1968	5.0	5.0	4.3	4.9	4.7	4.5
France	1956–1962	5.6	4.5	1.4	4.8	3.5	2.4
Peru	1961–1971	3.9	6.7	2.4	4.6	4.4	3.8
India	1954–1963	5.3	3.5	2.0	4.2	3.3	2.5

SOURCE: M. Ahluwalia and H. Chenery, "A conceptual framework for economic analysis," in H. Chenery, Duloy, and Jolly, *Redistribution with Growth: An Approach to Policy* (Washington, D.C.: IBRD, 1973), (3), p. 5. Reprinted by permission of The World Bank and Oxford University Press.

income distribution. For one thing, the use of such indexes underlines the importance of focusing on the *direct* improvement in living standards for the lowest income groups rather than worrying about nonexistent conflicts between growth and distribution or about the overall pattern of income distribution in Third World countries. On the other hand, the recognition that real development entails direct attacks on the sources of poverty within a country is useless without a better understanding of the factors that determine income shares and the relative rates of growth within different income groups. Unfortunately, economic theory offers little guidance, since it has always been concerned not with the size distribution of income (i.e., who gets what) but rather with the determinants of the functional distribution of income (i.e., how much of the total GNP is attributable to the total productivity of labor, capital, land, etc.). Even if the traditional theory of the determinants of functional income distribution had relevance for understanding the economic processes of contemporary developing nations (which, as we saw in a previous section, it does not, due to unreal assumptions about factor pricing, competitive markets, and the influence of power), knowledge of how incomes are functionally distributed would not help us to understand how and why incomes tend to be concentrated in certain population groups. For this we need to know how income-earning factors of production are distributed among different groups of people. We know, for example, that personal income consists not only of income derived from the supply of an individual's labor but also, and primarily for upper-income groups, from an individual's control over other income-earning assets such as land and capital (both physical and financial).

When we analyze the real determinants of highly unequal distributions of income, *it is the very unequal distribution of the ownership of productive assets such as land and capital within different segments of Third World populations that largely accounts for the wide income divergence between rich and poor.* The concentration of physical and financial capital as well as land in the hands of small economic and political elites enables them to expand their stock of human capital through education and thereby to control even greater shares of the national product. As in the international sphere, it is another case of the rich getting richer while the poor stagnate. Any attempt to improve the living standards of the poor significantly must therefore focus not only on increasing the economic returns to the limited factors they possess (i.e., raising the returns to their labor through more employment) but also on progressively altering the existing pattern of concentration of both physical and human capital toward low-income groups. Such redistribution can probably best be achieved in a growing economy. This leads us directly to our concluding sections on alternative policy approaches.

THE RANGE OF POLICY OPTIONS: SOME BASIC CONSIDERATIONS

Those developing countries that aim to reduce poverty and excessive inequalities in their distribution of income need to know how best to achieve their aim. What kinds of economic and other policies might LDC governments adopt to reduce poverty and inequality while maintaining or even accelerating economic growth rates? Since we are concerned here with moderating the size distribution of incomes in general and raising the income levels of, say, the bottom 40% of the population in particular, it is important to understand the various determinants of the distribution of income in an economy and see in what ways government intervention can alter or modify their effect.

Areas of Intervention

We can identify *four broad areas of possible government policy intervention*, which correspond to the following four major elements in the determination of a developing economy's distribution of income:

1. Functional distribution: the returns to labor, land, and capital as determined by factor prices, utilization levels, and the consequent shares of national income that accrue to the owners of each factor.
2. Size distribution: the functional income distribution of an economy can be translated into the size distribution by knowledge of how ownership and control over productive assets and labor skills are concentrated and distributed throughout the population. The distribution of these asset holdings and skill endowments ultimately determines the distribution of personal income.
3. Moderating (reducing) the size distribution at the upper levels through progressive taxation of personal income and wealth. Such taxation increases government reve-

nues and converts a market-determined level of personal income into a fiscally corrected, "disposable" personal income. An individual or family's disposable income is the actual amount available for expenditure on goods and services and for saving.

4. Moderating (increasing) the size distribution at the lower levels through public expenditures of tax revenues to raise the incomes of the poor either directly (e.g., by outright money transfers) or indirectly (e.g., through public employment creation, the provision of free or subsidized primary education). Such public policies raise the real income levels of the poor above their market-determined personal income levels.

Policy Options

Third World governments have many options and alternative possible policies to operate in the four broad areas of intervention outlined above. Let us briefly identify the nature of some of them.[17]

Altering the Functional Distribution of Income through Policies Designed to Change Relative Factor Prices

Factor-Price Distortions

Altering the functional distribution represents the traditional economic approach. It is argued that as a result of institutional constraints and faulty policies, the relative price of labor (basically, the wage rate) is higher than that which would be determined by the free interplay of the forces of supply and demand. For example, the power of trade unions to raise minimum wages to artificially high levels (i.e., higher than those which would result from supply and demand) even in the face of widespread unemployment is often cited as an example of the "distorted" price of labor. From this it is argued that measures designed to reduce the price of labor relative to capital (e.g., through lower wages in the public sector or public wage subsidies to employers) will cause employers to substitute labor for capital in their production activities. Such factor substitution increases the overall level of employment and ultimately raises the incomes of the poor, who typically possess only their labor services.

On the other hand, it is often also correctly pointed out that the price of capital equipment is "institutionally" set at artificially low levels (i.e., below what supply and demand would dictate) through various public policies such as investment incentives, tax allowances, subsidized interest rates, overvalued exchange rates, and low tariffs on capital good imports such as tractors and automated equipment. If these special privileges and capital subsidies were removed so that the price of capital would rise to its true "scarcity" level, producers would have a further incentive to increase their utilization of the abundant supply of labor and lower their uses of very scarce capital. Moreover, owners of capital (both physical and financial) would not receive the artificially high economic returns they now enjoy. Their personal incomes would thereby be reduced.

Since factor prices are assumed to function as the ultimate signals and incentives in any economy, "getting these prices right" (i.e., lowering the relative price of labor and raising the relative price of capital) would not only increase productivity and efficiency but would also reduce inequality by providing more wage-paying jobs for currently unemployed or underemployed unskilled and semiskilled workers. It would also lower the artificially high incomes of owners of capital. Removal of such factor-price distortions would, therefore, go a long way toward combining more growth, efficiently generated, with higher employment, less poverty, and greater equality.

We deal more extensively with the important question of factor-price distortions, employment generation, and choice of "appropriate" production techniques in Chapter 8. For the present we may conclude that there is much merit to the traditional factor-price distortion argument and that "getting the prices right" should contribute to a reduction in poverty and an improved distribution of income. How much it actually contributes will depend on the degree to which firms and farms switch to more labor-intensive production methods as the relative price of labor falls and the relative price of capital rises (i.e., on the elasticity of factor substitution). This is an important empirical question, the answer to which will vary from country to country. But some improvement can be expected.

Modifying the Size Distribution through Progressive Redistribution of Asset Ownership

Given resource prices and utilization levels for each type of productive factor (labor, land, and capital), we can arrive at estimates for the total earnings of each asset. But in order to translate this functional income into personal income, we need to know the *distribution* and *ownership concentration* of these assets among and within various segments of the population. Here we come to what is probably the most important fact about the determination of income distribution within an economy. *The ultimate cause of the very unequal distribution of personal incomes in most Third World countries is the very unequal and highly concentrated patterns of asset ownership within these countries.* The principal reasons why less than 20% of their populations receive over 50% of the national income is that this 20% probably owns and controls well over 70% of the productive resources, especially physical capital and land but also human capital in the form of better education. Correcting factor prices is certainly not sufficient to reduce income inequalities substantially nor to eliminate widespread poverty where physical asset ownership and education are highly concentrated.

It follows that the *second and perhaps more important line of policy to reduce poverty and inequality is to focus directly on reducing the concentrated control of assets, the unequal distribution of power, and the unequal access to educational and income-earning opportunities that characterize many developing countries.* A classic case of such redistribution as it relates to the rural poor, who comprise 70–80% of the target poverty group, is *land reform.* The basic purpose of land reform is to transform tenant cultivators into smallholders who will then have an incentive to raise production and improve their incomes. But as we shall see in Chapter 10, land reform may be a weak instrument of income redistribution if other institutional and price distortions in the economic system prevent small farmholders from securing access to much needed critical inputs such as credit, fertilizers, seeds, marketing facilities, and agricultural education.

In addition to the redistribution of existing productive assets, "dynamic" redistribution policies could be gradually pursued. For example, Third World governments could transfer a certain proportion of annual savings and investments to low-income groups so as to bring about a more gradual and perhaps politically more acceptable redistribution of *additional* assets as they accumulate over time. This is what is often meant by the expression "redistribution from growth." Whether such a gradual redistribution from growth is any more possible than a redistribution of existing assets is a moot point, especially in the context of very unequal power structures. But some form of asset redistribution, whether static or dynamic, seems to be a necessary condition for any significant reduction of poverty and inequality in most Third World countries.

Human capital in the form of education and skills is another example of the unequal distribution of productive asset ownership. Public policy, therefore, should promote a wider access to educational opportunities as a means of increasing income-earning potentials for more people. But, as in the case of land reform, the mere provision of greater access to education is no guarantee that the poor will be any better off, unless complementary policies—for example, the provision of more productive employment opportunities for the educated—to capitalize on this increased human capital are adopted. The relationship between education, employment, and development is discussed further in Chapter 11.

Modifying (Reducing) the Size Distribution at the Upper Levels through Progressive Income and Wealth Taxes

Any national policy attempting to improve the living standards of the bottom 40% must secure sufficient financial resources to transform paper plans into program realities. The major source of such development finance is the direct and progressive taxation of both income and wealth. Direct progressive income taxation focuses on personal and corporate incomes, with the rich required to pay a progressively larger percentage of their total income in taxes than the poor. Taxation on wealth (i.e., the stock of accumulated assets and income) typically involves personal and corporate property taxes but may also include progressive inheritance taxes. In either case, the burden of the tax is designed to fall most heavily on the upper income groups.

Unfortunately, in many developing countries (and developed countries as well) the gap between what is supposed to be a progressive tax structure and what different income groups actually pay can be substantial. Progressive tax structures on paper often turn out to be regressive in practice, that is to say, the lower- and middle-income groups pay a proportionately larger share of their incomes in taxes than do the upper-income groups. The reasons for this are simple. The poor are often taxed at the source of their incomes or expenditures (by withholding taxes from wages, general poll taxes, or "indirect" taxes levied on the retail purchase of goods such as cigarettes and beer). On the other hand, the rich derive by far the largest part of their incomes from the return on physical and financial assets, which often go unreported. They often also have the power and ability to avoid paying taxes without fear of government reprisal. Policies to enforce progressive rates of direct taxation on income and wealth, especially at the highest levels, are what is most needed in this area of redistribution activity (see Chapter 16 for a further discussion of taxation for development).

Modifying (Increasing) the Size Distribution at the Lower Levels through Direct Transfer Payments and the Public Provision of Goods and Services

The direct provision of tax-financed public consumption goods and services to the very poor is another potentially very important instrument of a comprehensive policy designed to eradicate poverty. Examples include public health projects in rural villages and urban fringe areas, school lunches and preschool nutritional supplementation programs, and the provision of clean water and electrification to remote rural areas. Direct money transfers and subsidized food programs for the urban and rural poor, as well as direct government policies to keep the price of essential foodstuffs low, represent additional forms of public consumption subsidies. All these policies have the effect of raising the real personal income levels of the very poor beyond their actual market-derived monetary incomes.

Summary and Conclusions: The Need for a Package of Policies

To summarize our discussion of alternative policy approaches to the problem of growth, poverty, and inequality in Third World countries, the need is not for one or two isolated policies but for a "package" of complementary and supportive policies, including the following three basic elements:

1. A policy or set of policies designed to *correct factor-price distortions* so as to ensure that market or institutionally established prices provide accurate (i.e., socially correct) signals and incentives to both producers and resource suppliers. "Getting the price right" should help to contribute to greater productive efficiency, more employment, and less poverty. Equally important may be the promotion of indigenous technological research and development of efficient, labor-intensive methods of production (see Chapter 8).
2. A policy or set of policies designed to bring about far-reaching *structural changes in the distribution of assets, power, and access to education and associated income-earning (employment) opportunities.* Such policies go beyond the narrow realm of economics and touch upon the whole social, institutional, cultural, and political fabric of the developing world. But without such radical structural changes and asset redistributions, whether immediately achieved (e.g., through public sector expropriation) or gradually introduced over time (through redistribution from growth), the chances of improving significantly the living conditions of the masses of rural and urban poor will be highly improbable, perhaps even impossible.
3. A policy or set of policies designed to *modify the size distribution of income* at the upper levels through the enforcement of legislated progressive taxation on incomes and wealth and at the lower levels through direct transfer payments and the expanded provision of publicly provided consumption goods and services.

A Final Question

The above policy package would provide a comprehensive agenda for any national attack on the pervasive problems of mass poverty and income inequality. Within the context of such a comprehensive three-pronged national policy, however, it is necessary to ask a final but far from trivial question: Can Third World countries actively pursue policies to reduce poverty and promote equality while remaining open to and dependent on the public financial resources, private investments, imported technology and products, and, most importantly, the values, symbols, ideals, attitudes, and institutions of advanced industrial countries? In other words: Can growth with equity be realistically pursued in isolation (as in the case of China) or, if not, can Third World countries collectively become more self-reliant masters of their own economic and social destinies while still actively participating in an increasingly interdependent yet highly unequal global system? It is a difficult and perplexing question, but one that every developing nation and every thoughtful individual needs to ponder. We will raise it again and attempt to arrive at some possible answers in the concluding chapters of the book.

NOTES

1. Mahbub ul Haq, "Employment and income distribution in the 1970s: A new perspective," *Development Digest*, October 1971, p. 7.
2. The Lorenz curve is named after Conrad Lorenz, an American statistician who in 1905 devised this convenient and widely used diagram to show the relationship between population groups and their respective income shares.
3. A more precise definition of perfect equality would take into account the age structure of a population and expected income variations over the "life cycle" of all households within that population. See M. Paglin, "The measurement and trend of inequality: A basic revision," *American Economic Review*, September 1975.
4. The summation of each worker's "marginal" product must equal total national product (GNP), which will be distributed as the national income. For the mathematically inclined, total product is simply the integral of the marginal product curve between 0 and $\bar{L}$. This is because the marginal product function is the derivative of the total product curve—i.e., $TP = f(L,K); MP_L = f'(L)$.
5. M. S. Ahluwalia, N. Carter, and H. Chenery, "Growth and poverty in developing countries," *Journal of Development Economics* 6 (September 1979):306.
6. For an additional analysis of the nature and dimension of the poverty problem see the World Bank report *Poverty, Growth, and Human Development*, extracted as Reading 8 in *The Struggle for Economic Development*.
7. Note that the Kuznets hypothesis focuses on the relationship between per capita income levels and distribution, while Figure 5.6 examines GNP growth rates with income distribution. Thus, it is not a strict test of the Kuznets hypothesis per se. See the Chenery article "Poverty and progress," Reading 9 in *The Struggle for Economic Development*, for a more detailed look at the Kuznets hypothesis for LDCs and Ashwani Saith, "Development and distribution: A critique of the cross-country U-hypothesis," *Journal of Development Economics* 13 (1983), p. 367−382 for a skeptical view.
8. I. Adelman and C. T. Morris, *Economic Growth and Social Equity in Developing Countries* (Stanford, Calif.: Stanford University Press, 1973).
9. *Ibid.*, p. 186. Some contrary evidence, however, in the case of Brazil is presented in an article by Gary Fields, "Who benefits from economic development? A reexamination of Brazilian growth in the 1960s," *American Economic Review* 67 (September 1977).
10. One of the earliest and best-known articles on the subject is that of Walter Galenson and Harvey Leibenstein, "Investment criteria, productivity and economic development," *Quarterly Journal of Economics*, August 1955, pp. 343−370.
11. The formal neoclassical growth model most often used to justify this argument is briefly described and illustrated in Appendix 5.1.
12. For an additional argument, drawn from the experiences of Taiwan and Korea, against the notion that growth and equity are necessarily in conflict, see Gustav

Ranis, "Development and the distribution of income: Some counterevidence," *Challenge*, September–October 1977.

13. See, for example, various UN studies on sources of savings in Third World nations which show that small farmers and individuals seem to be among the highest savers. Also see Gustav Ranis, "Investment criteria, productivity and economic development: An empirical comment," *Quarterly Journal of Economics*, May 1962; and K.L. Gupta, "Personal saving in developing countries: Further evidence," *Economic Record*, June 1970.

14. For empirical support of this argument with regard to rural saving and investment, see Keith Griffin, "Rural development: The policy options," in E. O. Edwards (ed.), *Employment in Developing Nations* (New York: Columbia University Press, 1974), pp. 190–191.

15. A recent empirical study of variables explaining LDC growth during the 1960–1973 period provides strong econometric confirmation of our argument that policies designed to promote better distribution and reduce poverty are, on balance, growth stimulating rather than growth retarding. See Norman L. Hicks, "Growth vs. basic needs: Is there a trade-off?" *World Development* (1979):985–994; reprinted as Reading 10 in *The Struggle for Economic Development*.

16. This illustration is derived from M.S. Ahluwalia and H. Chenery, "A conceptual framework for economic analysis," in H. Chenery, Duloy, and Jolly, *Redistribution with Growth: An Approach to Policy* (Washington, D.C.: IBRD, 1973), pp. 2–4.

17. A more comprehensive review of policy options is contained in Reading 11 in *The Struggle for Economic Development*, an article by Charles R. Frank, Jr., and Richard Webb entitled "Policy choices and income distribution in less developed nations."

CONCEPTS FOR REVIEW

Luxury versus necessity goods
Consumer demand and income
   distribution
"Size" distribution of income
"Functional" distribution of income
Quintiles and deciles
Highly skewed distribution of income
Income inequality
Lorenz curve
GINI coefficient
Absolute poverty
"Scatter" diagram
"Character" of economic growth

"Trickle down" theory of development
Welfare index
GNP growth rate index
Equal-weights index
Poverty-weighted index
Asset ownership
Factor-price distortions
Redistribution policies
Progressive income and wealth taxes
Regressive tax
Indirect tax
Subsidy
"Package" of policies

QUESTIONS FOR DISCUSSION

1. Most development eonomists now seem to agree that the level and rate of growth of GNP and per capita income do not provide sufficient or even accurate measures of a country's development. What is the essence of their argument? Give some examples.

2. Distinguish between "size" and "functional" distributions of income in a nation. Which do you feel is the more appropriate concept? Explain.

3. What is meant by "absolute" poverty? Why should we be concerned with the measurement of absolute poverty in Third World nations?

4. What are the principal economic characteristics of poverty groups? What do these characteristics tell us about the possible nature of a poverty-focused development strategy?

5. In the text, when we examined statistics from a wide range of Third World countries, we found *no* direct relationship (positive or negative) between a country's level of GNP, GNP per capita, and rate of economic growth and its extent of absolute

poverty or the degree of equality in its distribution of income. Assuming that these data are indeed correct, what do they tell us about the importance of the character of a nation's growth process, and about its institutional structure?

6. What is the relationship between a Lorenz curve and a Gini coefficient? Give some examples of how Lorenz curves and Gini coefficients can be used as summary measures of equality and inequality in a nation's distribution of income.

7. In the text it is asserted that the major determinant of a country's income distribution is its distribution of productive and income-earning assets. Explain the meaning of this statement, giving examples of different kinds of productive and income-earning assets.

8. Are rapid economic growth (either GNP or per capita GNP) and a more equitable distribution of personal income necessarily conflicting objectives? Summarize the arguments both for and against the presumed conflict of objectives and state and explain your own view.

9. GNP is said to be a biased index of national development and economic welfare. Explain the meaning of this statement, giving a specific hypothetical or real example of such "bias."

10. What is the value of constructing an equal-weights or especially a poverty-weighted index of social welfare? Under what conditions will these welfare indexes differ from GNP? Explain your answer.

11. Economic growth is said to be a "necessary but not sufficient condition" to eradicate absolute poverty and reduce inequality. What is the reasoning behind this argument?

12. Outline the range of major policy options available to LDC governments to alter and modify the size distribution of their national incomes. Which policy or policies do you believe are absolutely essential and which are important but not crucial? Explain your answer.

FURTHER READINGS

A comprehensive description of the various meanings and measurements of income distribution can be found in Jan Pen, *Income Distribution* (Harmondsworth, England: Penguin, 1971), Chapters 1–3. See also A. B. Atkinson, *The Economics of Inequality* (New York: Oxford University Press, 1975) and A. K. Sen, "Three notes on the concept of poverty," International Labor Office, *World Employment Programme Research Paper #65*, January 1978.

For summaries of the poverty and income distribution problem in LDCs using cross-country data with appropriate analysis and alternative policy strategies, see H. Chenery *et al.*, *Redistribution with Growth* (London: Oxford University Press; and Washington, D.C.: IBRD, 1974); Mahbub ul Haq, *The Assault on World Poverty* (Baltimore: Johns Hopkins University Press, 1975); M. S. Ahluwalia, N. G. Carter, and H. B. Chenery, "Growth and poverty in developing countries," *Journal of Development Economics* (September 1979); H. B. Chenery, *Structural Change and Development Policy* (London: Oxford University Press, 1980); and Gary S. Fields, *Poverty, Inequality and Development* (Cambridge, England: Cambridge University Press, 1980).

Other useful readings include William R. Cline, *Income Distribution and Economic Development: A Survey and Tests for Selected Latin American Cities* (Washington, D.C.: Brookings Institution, 1973); G. Ranis, J.C.H. Fei, and G. Fields, "Growth, employment and the size distribution of income: A progress report," *Discussion Paper No. 208*, Yale Economic Growth Center, June 1974; D.B. Keesing, "Income distribution from outward-looking development policies," *Research Memorandum No. 59*, Williams College, Williamstown, Massachusetts, April 1974; Gunnar Myrdal, "Equity and growth," *World Development* 1, no. 11 (1973); Felix Paukert, "Income distribution at different levels of development: A survey of evidence," *International Labor Review*, August–September 1973; A.B. Atkinson, "On the measurement of inequality," *Journal of Economic Theory*, September 1970; I. Adelman and C.T. Morris, "An anatomy of income distribution patterns in developing nations," *Development Digest*, October 1971; Arun Shourie, "Growth, poverty and inequalities," *Foreign Affairs* 51, no. 2 (1973); Roger D. Hansen, "The emerging challenge: Global distribution of income and economic opportunity," in Overseas Development Council, *Agenda for Action 1975* (New York: Praeger, 1975); D.L. Meadows *et al.*, *The Limits to Growth* (New York: Universe, 1972); and World Bank, *World Development Reports, 1978 and 1980* (New York: Oxford University Press, 1978, 1980).

Additional readings can be found on pp. 619–622.

APPENDIX 5.1

FACTOR SHARES, SAVINGS, AND GROWTH: A DIAGRAMMATIC ILLUSTRATION

The traditional argument presented in the text that unequal incomes will best promote savings (and thus growth) is typically illustrated by using the standard neoclassical (i.e., variable factor proportions) growth model.[1] Assume the existence of an aggregate production function in the form of

$$Y = f(K, L, t) \tag{A5.1}$$

where K is the capital stock, L the labor force, and t a trend variable denoting technological change. Assuming neutral technological progress, production function (A5.1) can be rewritten as

$$Y = A(t)f[K, L], \tag{A5.2}$$

where $A(t)$ is some constant such as 1.06 per year. Finally, it is assumed that the production function is linear, homogeneous so that $\alpha Y = A(t)[\alpha K, \alpha L]$. Setting $\alpha = 1/L$, then, we obtain

$$\frac{Y}{L} = A(t)f\left[\frac{K}{L}, 1\right] = A(t)f\left[\frac{K}{L}\right] \tag{A5.3}$$

Equation (A5.3) can be used to portray graphically the *theoretical* relationship between output per worker (Y/L), and thus by inference output per capita, and technological change and changes in the capital/labor ratio (K/L). It can also be used to depict the two-way relationship between functional income shares and economic growth under the assumed savings conditions. This is done in Figure A5.1.

In the upper-right-hand quadrant is the production function as given by Expression (A5.3) for any given level of technology; changes in technology shift this function upward. Since we have designated the Y-axis below the origin as constituting the amount of labor input, the area $OQRS$ is the amount of capital stock employed ($OS \cdot RS = K/L \cdot L = K$). Similarly, the x-axis to the left of zero measures labor input (OST being an isosceles triangle) while the total

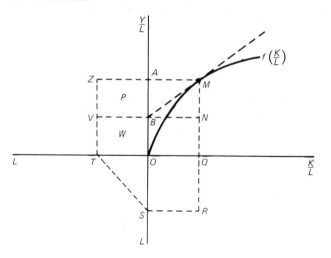

Figure A5.1. Economic growth and income distribution.

area $OAZT$ in the upper-left quadrant is the amount of real output produced $(OT \cdot OA = L \cdot Y/L = Y)$.

Now let us define P as "profit," or the share of national output which is a return to capital, and W as labor's share of national output, so that

$$\frac{P}{K} = \frac{Y - W}{K} = \frac{Y/L - W/L}{K/L} = \frac{f(K/L) - W/L}{K/L} \qquad \textbf{(A5.4)}$$

According to some writers, producers may be expected to adopt a capital/labor ratio (K/L) which maximizes the profit per unit of capital employed, (P/K). This presumably does, or could, maximize "business saving" and "reinvestment" over some time period, increasing potential output over that period, with resources that at the end of this (indefinite) time period shifted to consumption and so maximizing consumption *at that point in time*. This is the essence of the argument underlying the "big push" theory of economic development, as advanced, for example, by Galenson and Leibenstein.[2] Let us see what this implies.

If we differentiate Expression (A5.4) for (P/K) with respect to (K/L) and set it equal to zero, we have

$$\frac{d(P/K)}{d(K/L)} = \frac{(K/L) \cdot f'(K/L) - f(K/L)}{(K/L)^2} + \frac{W/L}{(K/L)^2} = 0, \qquad \textbf{(A5.5)}$$

or

$$f(K/L) = Y/L = (K/L) \cdot f'(K/L) + W/L, \qquad \textbf{(A5.6)}$$

where $f'(K/L)$ is the derivative of the function $f(K/L)$. But since $(Y/L) - (W/L) = (P/L)$, which then from the above is equal to $(K/L) \cdot f'(K/L)$, the distance $AB =$

MN in Figure A5.1 must equal (P/L); the tangent to the production function at M is $f'(K/L) = (P/L) \div (K/L) = (P/K)$ for any point M along the production function. By definition, then, if distance AB is (P/L), distance OB must be (W/L). Thus, the point where the tangent to the production function intersects the Y-axis can be used to show the relative income share going to wage earners, OB/OA, and that going to those who contribute capital to the productive process, BA/OA.

From all this it can be seen that rates of return plus relative and absolute shares of income going to labor and capital depend on the relative growth rates of labor and capital. If they grow evenly, the rates of return and relative income shares will be unchanged, while the absolute shares increase. If labor grows faster than the capital stock so that (K/L) falls, the rate of return to labor falls, but the rate of return to capital may rise or fall. Technological change which shifts the production function upward will be "neutral" if the ratio W/L/P/K is unchanged (i.e., if the distance OB relative to MN/BN is unchanged).

To maximize $f'(K/L) = P/K$ at any point in time involves maximizing the slope of BM, which ostensibly will occur where point B is at point O in Figure A5.1—that is, where the absolute share of income going to labor (OBVT, or Area W) is zero! Of course neoclassical growth economists recognize that this is absurd. Clearly workers must be paid at least a subsistence wage. But their point is that holding wages at this level, and so maximizing P/K with this constraint, will maximize saving over some time period and therefore consumption at some (unspecified) future point in time.[3]

NOTES

1. See Robert Solow, "Technical progress and the aggregate production function," *Review of Economics and Statistics*, August 1957, pp. 312–320.
2. Walter Galenson and Harvey Leibenstein, "Investment criteria, productivity and economic development," *Quarterly Journal of Economics*, August 1955, pp. 343–370. The authors suggest, for example, that "successful economic development under present conditions . . . hinges largely upon the introduction of modern technology on as large a scale as possible." What is needed, therefore, is "up-to-date equipment and relatively high initial capital/labor ratios" (p. 370).
3. See, however, the section on "Growth versus Income Distribution" in this chapter for a criticism of this neoclassical growth model.

6

THE POPULATION DEBATE

The central issue of our time may well turn out to be how the world
addresses the problem of ever expanding human numbers.
James Grant, Director General, UNICEF

What governments and their people do today to influence our demographic future will set the terms for development strategy well into the
next century.
A. W. Clausen, President, World Bank, 1984

NUMBERS AND CONTROVERSIES

As the decade of the 1980s reached its midpoint, the world's population was estimated to be almost 4.9 billion people. Optimistic projections by the United Nations placed the figure at more than 6.1 billion
by the end of the twentieth century. Over four-fifths of that population
will inhabit the developing world. What will be the economic and
social implications for levels of living, national and personal esteem,
and freedom of choice—that is, for "development"—if such quantitative projections are realized? Are such projections inevitable, or will
they depend on the success or failure of Third World development
efforts? Finally, and more significantly, is rapid population growth per
se as serious a problem as many in the developed world believe, or is it
a manifestation of more fundamental problems of underdevelopment
and the unequal utilization of global resources between rich and poor
nations, as many others (mostly in the developing world) believe?

These and other questions lie at the core of the current worldwide
interest in and debate about world population growth and human welfare.
The main elements of this debate were clearly evident at the first World
Population Conference held in Bucharest in 1974 and then reiterated, al-

though less stridently, at the second conference held in Mexico City in August 1984. The first half of the present chapter, therefore, attempts to analyze the nature and context of the current population debate both as it relates to the domestic concerns of many developing countries and in its worldwide context. In Chapter 7 we will look more closely at the economics of population and examine various policies that both the developing and the developed world might pursue in a joint effort to deal with the global population dilemma.

THE BASIC ISSUE: POPULATION GROWTH AND THE QUALITY OF LIFE

Every year over 80 million people are being added to a world population of almost 5 billion. Over 70 million of these additional people per year will be born in Third World countries. These increases are unprecedented in history. But the problem of population growth is not simply a problem of numbers. It is a problem of human welfare and of development as defined in Chapter 3. Rapid population growth can have serious consequences for the well-being of humanity worldwide. If development entails the improvement in people's levels of living—their incomes, health, education, and general well-being—and if it also encompasses their self-esteem, respect, dignity, and freedom to choose, then the really important question about population growth is: *How does the contemporary population situation in many Third World countries contribute to or detract from their chances of realizing the goals of development, not only for the current generation but also for future generations? Conversely, how does development affect population growth?*

Among the major issues relating to this basic question are the following:

1. Will Third World countries be capable of improving the *levels of living* for their people with the current and anticipated levels of population growth? To what extent does rapid population increase make it more difficult to provide essential social services including housing, transport, sanitation, and security?
2. How will the developing countries be able to cope with the vast increases in their labor forces over the coming decades? Will *employment opportunities* be plentiful or will it be a major achievement just to keep unemployment levels from rising?
3. What are the implications of higher population growth rates among the world's poor for their chances of overcoming the human misery of *absolute poverty*? Will *world food supply* and its distribution be sufficient not only to meet the anticipated population increase in the coming decades but also to improve nutritional levels to the point where all humans can have an adequate diet?
4. Given the anticipated population growth, will developing countries be able to extend the coverage and improve the quality of their *health and educational systems* so that everyone can at least have the chance to secure adequate health care and a basic education?
5. To what extent are low levels of living an important factor in limiting the *freedom of parents to choose* a desired family size? Is there a relationship between poverty and family size?
6. To what extent is the *growing affluence* among the economically more developed nations an important factor preventing poor nations from accommodating their growing populations? Is the inexorable pursuit of increasing affluence

among the rich an even more detrimental force to rising living standards among the poor than the absolute increase in their numbers?

In view of the above questions, it becomes essential to frame the population issue not simply in terms of numbers, or densities, or rates, or movements but, as Bernard Berelson, former president of the Population Council, has said, with full consideration of

> *the qualities of human life: prosperity in place of poverty, education in place of ignorance, health in place of illness and death, environmental beauty in place of deterioration, full opportunities for the next generations of children in place of current limitations. . . . Population trends, if favorable, open man's options and enlarge his choices. Thus, population policy is not an end, but only a means—a means to the better life. That is what the concern about population is about, or ought to be.[1]*

A REVIEW OF NUMBERS: POPULATION GROWTH—PAST, PRESENT, AND PROSPECTIVE[2]

World Population Growth through History

Throughout most of the 2 million years of human existence on earth, humanity's numbers have been few. When people first started to cultivate food through agriculture some 12,000 years ago, the estimated world population was no more than 5 million, less than the number of people living today in Mexico City, Lagos, Buenos Aires, or Bangkok (see Table 6.1). At the beginning of the Christian era nearly 2,000 years ago, world population had grown to nearly 250 million, less than a quarter of the population of China today. From A.D. 1 to the beginning of the industrial revolution around 1750 it increased twofold to 728 million people, less than the total number of those

Table 6.1 Estimated World Population Growth through History

Year	Estimated population	Estimated annual increase in the intervening period
Circa 10,000 B.C.	5,000,000	
A.D. 1	250,000,000	0.04
1650	545,000,000	0.04
1750	728,000,000	0.29
1800	906,000,000	0.45
1850	1,171,000,000	0.53
1900	1,608,000,000	0.65
1950	2,486,000,000	0.91
1970	3,632,000,000	2.09
1985	4,890,000,000	1.70

SOURCE: Based on V. Carr-Saunders in W.S. Thompson and D.T. Lewis, *Population Problems*, 5th ed. (New York: McGraw-Hill, 1965), p. 384; United Nations, *Demographic Yearbook for 1971*; and Population Reference Bureau, *1984 World Population Data Sheet*.

living in India today. During the next 200 years (1750–1950), an additional 1.7 billion people were added to the earth's numbers. But in the last 35 years (1950–1985) world population has almost doubled again, bringing the total figure at the beginning of 1985 to almost 4.9 billion. If this trend continues, by the year 2000 the world's population will be almost 6.2 billion.

Turning from absolute numbers to percentage growth rates, we can see from Table 6.2 that for almost the whole of humankind's existence on earth until approximately 300 years ago, the human population grew at an annual rate not much greater than zero (i.e., 0.002% or 20 per million). Naturally, this overall rate has not been steady; there were many ups and downs in the earth's numbers as a result of natural catastrophes and variations in growth rates among regions. By 1750, the population growth rate had accelerated by 150 times from 0.002 to 0.3% per year. By the 1950s, the rate had again accelerated, this time by threefold to about 1.0% per year. Today, less than three decades later, the world's population growth rate has almost doubled to a rate of 1.7% per year.[3]

The relationship between annual percentage increases and the time it takes for a population to double in size is shown in the last column of Table 6.2. We see that before 1650 it took nearly 35,000 years, or about 1,400 generations, for the world population to double. Today, in less than 45 years, little more than one generation, world population will double.[4] Moreover, whereas it took almost 1,750 years to add 480 million people to the world's population between A.D. 1 and the onset of the industrial revolution, at current growth rates this same number of people are being added to the earth's population every 6 years!

The reason for the sudden change in overall population trends is that for almost all of recorded history the rate of population change, whether up or down, had been strongly influenced by the combined effects of famine, disease, malnutrition, plague, and war—conditions that resulted in high and fluctuating death rates. Now, in the twentieth century, such conditions are coming increasingly under technological and economic control. As a result, human mortality (the death rate) is lower than at any other point in human existence. It is this decline in mortality resulting from rapid technological advances in modern medicine and the spread of modern sanitation

Table 6.2 World Population Growth Rates and Doubling Times: A Historical Review

Period	Approximate growth rate (%)	Doubling time (years)
Appearance of man to early historical times	0.002	35,000
1650–1750	0.3	240
1850–1900	0.6	115
1930–1950	1.0	70
Present (1980s)	1.7	43

SOURCE: Carr-Saunders, op. cit., p. 384, and Population Reference Bureau, op. cit.

measures throughout the world, particularly within the last 30 years, that has resulted in the unprecedented increases in world population growth—especially in Third World countries. For example, death rates in Africa, Asia, and Latin America have fallen by as much as 50% during the last 20–30 years (see Table 6.5 below) while birthrates have only recently begun to decline.

In short, *population growth today is primarily the result of a rapid transition from a long historical era characterized by high birth and death rates to one in which death rates have fallen sharply whereas birthrates, especially in developing countries, are only just beginning to fall from their historic high levels.*

The Structure of the World's Population

Geographic Region

The world's population is very unevenly distributed by geographic region, by fertility and mortality levels, and by age structures. Of the world's total population in 1985, more than three-quarters lived in developing countries and less than one-quarter in the economically developed nations. Figure 6.1 shows the regional distribution of the world's population as it existed in 1984 and as it is projected for the year 2000.

Given current population growth rates in different parts of the world (significantly higher in the LDCs), the regional distribution of the world's population will inevitably change by the year 2000. By that time it is likely there will be about 4 billion more people on the earth than in 1950 and more than 1.8 billion more than in 1980. However, it is estimated that over 60% of

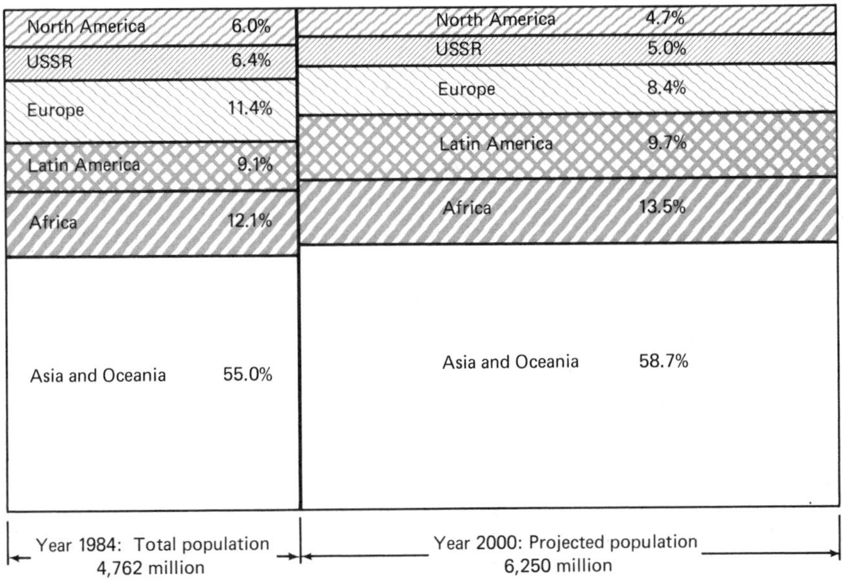

North America	6.0%	North America	4.7%
USSR	6.4%	USSR	5.0%
Europe	11.4%	Europe	8.4%
Latin America	9.1%	Latin America	9.7%
Africa	12.1%	Africa	13.5%
Asia and Oceania	55.0%	Asia and Oceania	58.7%
Year 1984: Total population 4,762 million		Year 2000: Projected population 6,250 million	

Figure 6.1. World population by region: 1984 and 2000 (projection). *Source:* Population Reference Bureau, *1984 World Population Data Sheet.*

the added people will be in Asia, where overall population size will have increased by some 300% since 1950. The corresponding increases in Africa and Latin America are estimated at almost 400% with an addition of almost 1 billion people. Together these three Third World continents will probably constitute over 80% of the world's population by the year 2000 as contrasted with 70% in 1950 and 76% in 1980. Correspondingly, the proportion of the world's population living in Europe, the Soviet Union, and North America will have fallen from 30 to less than 20% of the total.

Consider finally the distribution of national populations. Table 6.3 lists the 15 largest countries in the world in 1984. Together they account for over 70% of the world's population. While these countries come from all the continents and from both developed and underdeveloped regions, it is instructive to note that in terms of annual increases in world population, countries such as India, Indonesia, Brazil, Bangladesh, Pakistan, and Nigeria all add more to the world's annual population increase than do most of the economically more developed countries. For example, Nigeria, ranked 10th in size, adds almost twice as many people to the absolute growth of the world's population than does the United States, ranked as the 4th largest country. Similarly, Brazil, ranked 6th, adds more people annually than does the Soviet Union, ranked 3rd.

Table 6.3 The 15 Largest Countries and Their Annual Population Increases, 1984

Country	Total population 1984 (millions)	Percentage rate of natural increase 1984	Annual increase (millions)
China	1034.5	1.3	13.45
India	746.4	2.0	14.92
USSR	274.0	1.0	2.70
United States	236.3	0.7	1.65
Indonesia	161.6	2.1	3.39
Brazil	134.4	2.3	3.09
Japan	119.9	0.7	0.70
Bangladesh	99.6	3.1	3.09
Pakistan	97.3	2.8	2.72
Nigeria	88.1	3.2	2.82
Mexico	77.7	2.6	2.02
West Germany	61.4	−0.2	−0.12
Vietnam	58.3	2.3	1.34
Italy	57.0	0.2	0.13
United Kingdom	56.5	0.1	0.05

SOURCE: Population Reference Bureau, *1984 World Population Data Sheet.*

Fertility and Mortality Trends

The *rate of population increase* is quantitatively measured as the percentage yearly net relative increase (or decrease, in which event it is negative) in population size due to *natural increase* and *net international migration*. Natural increase simply measures the excess of births over deaths or, in more technical terms, the difference between *fertility* and *mortality*. Net international migration is of negligible, though growing, importance today (although in the nineteenth and early twentieth centuries it was an extremely important source of population increase in North America, Australia, and New Zealand and corresponding decrease in Western Europe). Population increases in Third World countries, therefore, depend almost entirely on the difference between their birth and death rates.

The difference between developing and developed nations in terms of their rates of population growth can be explained simply by the fact that birthrates (fertility) in developing countries are generally much higher than in the rich nations. Third World death rates (mortality) are also higher. However, these death-rate differences are substantially smaller than the differences in birthrates. As a result, the average rate of population growth in the developing countries is now about 2.1% per year (2.4 percent excluding China) whereas most of the economically developed countries have annual growth rates of only 0.4–0.7%. Figure 6.2 shows recent and projected trends in population growth for both developed and less developed nations. Note that the overall population growth rate in developing countries appears to have peaked at an annual rate of 2.35% in the early 1970s and is now slowly declining.

As just noted, the major source of difference in population growth rates between the less developed and the more developed countries is the sizable difference in their birthrates. Recall from Chapter 2 that most Third World nations have birthrates ranging from 30 to 50 per 1,000. By contrast, in almost all developed countries the rate is less than 20 per 1,000 (see Table 2.3). Moreover, LDC birthrates today are substantially higher than they were

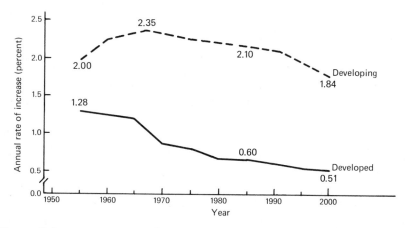

Figure 6.2. Population growth rates in developed and developing countries, 1950–2000.

in preindustrial Western Europe. This is largely because of early and almost universal marriage in contemporary Third World countries. But there are signs of the beginnings of a substantial decline in LDC fertility, especially in countries like Taiwan, South Korea, Singapore, and Hong Kong where rapid economic and social development have taken place. Table 6.4 records the recent and projected declines in Third World birthrates to the end of the century. Note, in particular, the recent declines reported for East and South Asia and the expectation that currently high birthrates in Africa will persist at least until the 1990s.

On the other hand, there has been a narrowing of the gap in mortality rates between developed and less developed countries. The primary reason is undoubtedly the rapid improvement in health conditions throughout the Third World. Modern vaccination campaigns against malaria, smallpox, yellow fever, and cholera as well as the proliferation of public health facilities, clean water supplies, improved nutrition, and public education have all worked together over the past 25 years to lower death rates by as much as 50% in parts of Asia and Latin America and by over 30% in much of Africa and the Middle East. Nevertheless, the average life span remains almost 20 years greater in the developed countries. But even this gap has been sharply reduced over the last 25 years. For example, in 1950 life expectancy at birth for people in Third World countries averaged 35–40 years compared with 62–65 years in the developed world. By 1980 the difference had fallen to 16 years as life expectancy in the LDCs increased to 56 years (a gain of 42%) while in the industrial nations it had risen to 72 years (an increase of 13%). Today, because of still relatively high infant mortality rates, Africa has the lowest life expectancy, 49 years, while the most favorable region is Europe where life expectancy at birth now averages about 73 years. Table 6.5 shows the rapid decline in Third World death rates between 1950 and 1980.

Age Structure and Dependency Burdens

World population today is very youthful, particularly in the Third World. Children under the age of 15 constitute almost half the total population of Third World countries but only a quarter of the population of developed nations. For example, 48 and 50% of the population of Nigeria and Kenya were below 15 years in 1983; for Mexico the comparable figure was 44% and for Syria, Pakistan, and India it was 48, 45 and 39% respectively. In countries with such an age structure, the youth dependency ratio—that is, the proportion of youths (below 15 years) to economically active adults (ages 15–64)—is very high. Thus the working force in developing countries must support almost twice as many children as they do in the wealthier countries. For example, in Sweden and the Soviet Union the working force age group (15–64) amounts to almost 65% of the total population. This work force has to support only 21 and 27% respectively of the population who are its youthful dependents. By contrast, in countries like Nigeria, Bangladesh, and Ghana the economically active work forces and the child dependents are each about 50% of the total population. In general, the more rapid the population growth rate, the greater will be the proportion of dependent children in the total population and the more difficult it becomes for those who are working to support those who are not.

Table 6.4 Crude Birthrates, 1950–2000 (per 1,000 population)

	1950–1955	1960–1965	1970–1975	1980–1985	1990–1995	1995–2000
World total	35.6	34.0	30.3	28.1	25.4	23.8
Developed countries	22.7	20.3	16.7	15.9	15.2	14.9
Developing countries	41.8	40.0	35.5	32.1	28.3	26.2
Africa	48.1	47.6	46.1	45.0	40.1	36.9
Middle East	47.9	48.0	46.3	44.2	40.0	36.9
Latin America	41.4	39.9	36.3	34.4	31.3	29.6
China	39.8	33.8	26.0	20.1	18.0	17.4
East Asia	36.6	38.3	30.1	26.1	22.4	20.3
South Asia	43.2	44.1	40.5	36.9	31.0	27.8

SOURCE: UN, *World Population Trends and Prospects, 1955–2000* (New York: United Nations, 1979), Tables 2-A and 2-B.

Birthrates: Their Relationship to Income Levels, GNP Growth Rates, and Income Distribution

Whatever the line of causality, high birthrates are generally associated with national poverty. However, it would be a mistake simply to claim that since high birthrates are generally associated with countries having low per capita incomes (the less developed nations) and low birthrates with countries having high per capita incomes (the more developed nations), then a rise in per capita income will lead to lower birthrates.

Consider, for example, Table 6.6. Twelve Third World countries are listed according to their 1981 per capita income levels, their per capita GNP growth rates from 1960 to 1981, their income distribution ratios measuring

Table 6.5 Crude Death Rates, 1950–2000 (per 1,000 population)

	1950–1955	1960–1965	1970–1975	1980–1985	1990–1995	1995–2000
World total	18.3	14.4	12.0	10.6	9.2	8.7
Developed countries	10.1	9.0	9.2	9.7	10.1	10.1
Developing countries	22.2	16.8	13.2	10.9	9.0	8.3
Africa	26.9	22.4	18.8	15.4	12.0	10.6
Middle East	25.3	20.9	16.6	13.4	10.4	9.2
Latin America	14.5	11.5	9.3	7.7	6.5	6.0
China	20.1	13.6	9.4	8.3	7.8	7.7
East Africa	30.0	11.8	8.7	7.4	6.7	6.6
South Asia	24.6	19.8	15.8	12.5	9.9	8.8

SOURCE: UN, *World Population Trends and Prospects, 1950–2000* (New York: United Nations, 1979) Tables 2-A and 2-B.

Table 6.6 The Relationship between National Per Capita Incomes, Growth Rates, Income Distribution, and Birthrates: Selected Third World Countries

	Birthrate 1981 (per 1,000)	Per capita GNP 1981 ($)	Per capita GNP growth rate 1960–1981(%)	% change in crude birthrate (1960–1981)	Income distribution ratio of top 20% to bottom 40%
Brazil	30	2,220	5.1	−28.6	9.5
Colombia	29	1,380	3.2	−32.2	6.8
Costa Rica	30	1,430	3.0	−36.5	4.6
India	35	260	1.4	−18.8	3.1
Mexico	36	2,250	3.8	−20.6	5.0
Peru	36	1,170	1.0	−20.2	8.7
Philippines	34	790	2.8	−27.4	3.8
Senegal	48	430	−0.3	0.1	6.4
South Korea	24	1,700	6.9	−43.7	2.7
Sri Lanka	27	300	2.5	−24.3	2.3
Taiwan[a]	21	1,170	6.2	−41.8	3.8
Thailand	30	770	4.6	−32.1	3.3

[a]1977 figures for Taiwan.
SOURCE: *World Development Report, 1983*, Annex Tables 1, 20, 27.

the income multiple of the top 20% to the bottom 40% of the income scale, and the magnitude of their crude birthrates.

The three diagrams in Figure 6.3 graphically portray the relationship, or nonrelationship, between each of the three major income variables and the birthrate as shown in Table 6.6. Figure 6.3a plots the birthrate for each country against its *level of per capita income* to test the widely held hypothesis that there exists a close negative association between birthrates and per capita incomes. In Figure 6.3b these same country birthrates are plotted against *growth rates* in per capita incomes to see if more rapid rates of income growth are closely associated with lower fertility levels. Finally in Figure 6.3c birthrates are plotted against *income distribution* ratios to see if lower ratios (i.e., more equal distributions of income) are associated with lower birthrates.

Taking Figure 6.3a first, it is immediately evident that there is no apparent direct or inverse relationship between levels of per capita income and birthrates, at least for the 12 countries under consideration. Countries with similar relatively high birthrates like the Philippines, India, Peru, and Mexico have widely varying levels of per capita income. Similarly, countries with close but relatively low birthrates like Sri Lanka, South Korea, and Taiwan have national incomes varying from U.S. $300 to $1,700 per capita. So, we can reject the simple hypothesis that higher per capita incomes necessarily are associated with lower birthrates, at least over the range of incomes represented by the 12 LDCs in our sample.

Looking now at Figure 6.3b, we see that there appears to be a negative relationship between growth rates of GNP per capita and birth levels. How-

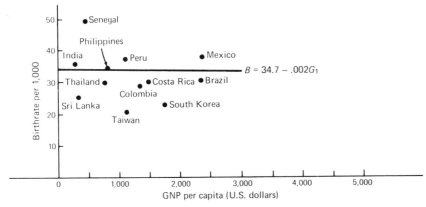

(a) Birthrates and GNP per capita

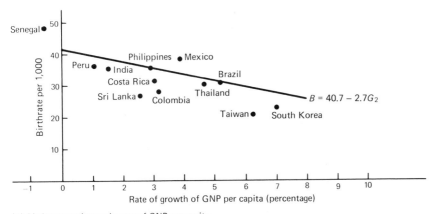

(b) Birthrates and growth rates of GNP per capita

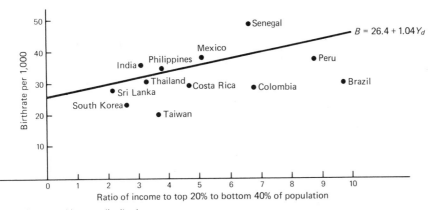

(c) Birthrates and income distribution

Figure 6.3. The relationship between incomes and birthrates in twelve Third World countries. Note: G_1 is GNP per capita; G_2 is the growth rate of GNP per capita; Y_d is the income distribution ratio; B is the birthrate; 1977 figures for Taiwan.

ever, note that countries with similarly high birthrates like Peru, India, the Philippines, and Mexico have wide variations in their income growth performances (ranging from a rate of 1.0% per annum in Peru to 3.8% in Mexico). Also, countries with the same relatively low birthrates (like Sri Lanka and South Korea) have variations of over 200% in their respective GNP growth rates (2.5% for Sri Lanka compared to 6.9% for South Korea).[5] Thus, the link between per capita income growth rates and birthrate declines may be tenuous.

Finally, if we compare relative birthrates with relative degrees of income inequality as in Figure 6.3c we discover that there *does* appear to be some relationship between lower (higher) birthrates and less (more) inequality in the distribution of income. Our 12 countries seem to fall roughly into two distinct groups—those with relatively low inequality ratios and relatively low birthrates (Taiwan, Sri Lanka, and South Korea) and others with moderate to high inequality ratios and relatively higher birthrates (India, Thailand, the Philippines, Mexico, Senegal, Colombia, Peru, and Brazil).

We may tentatively conclude, therefore, that *countries that strive to lessen the inequality in their distribution of income, or, alternatively, attempt to spread the benefits of their economic growth to a wider segment of the population may be better able to begin to lower their birthrates than countries where the benefits of growth are more unevenly shared,* even though these latter countries may have *both* higher levels and faster growth rates of per capita income.[6] However, given a development policy oriented toward a more equitable pattern of income distribution, higher rates of GNP growth are likely to result in even greater reductions in fertility—contrast, for example, South Korea and Taiwan with, say, Brazil and Thailand.

The reason why direct attacks on poverty and low levels of living are probably more effective measures to lower birthrates than simple growth maximization is that higher levels of living provide the necessary *motivations* for families to *choose* to limit their size. Widespread poverty tends to sustain high birthrates for the obvious reason that families living without adequate incomes, employment, health, education, and social services have little security for the future other than reliance on their children. They are caught in an "underdevelopment trap" vis-à-vis their family size not only because their levels of living are low but also because their self-esteem and dignity may thereby be questioned and their freedom to choose a desired family size is constrained by their poverty and economic uncertainty.

The Hidden Momentum of Population Growth

Perhaps the least understood aspect of population growth is its tendency to continue even after birthrates have declined substantially. Population growth has a built-in tendency to continue, a powerful *momentum* which, like a speeding automobile when the brakes are applied, tends to keep going for some time before coming to a stop. In the case of population growth this momentum can persist for decades after birthrates drop.

There are two basic reasons for this hidden momentum. First, high birthrates cannot be altered substantially overnight. The social, economic, and institutional forces that have influenced fertility rates over the course of centuries do not simply evaporate at the urging of national leaders. We know from the experience of European nations that such reductions in birthrates can take many decades. Consequently, even if developing countries assign top priority to the limitation of population growth, it will still take many years to lower national fertility to desired levels.

The second and less obvious reason for the hidden momentum of population growth relates to the age structure of LDC populations. We saw earlier in the chapter that nations with high birthrates have large proportions of children and adolescents in their population, sometimes as high as 50%. In such a high-fertility population, young people greatly outnumber their parents, and when their generation reaches adulthood the number of potential parents will inevitably be much larger than at present. It follows that even if these new parents have only enough children to replace themselves (two per couple as compared with their parents, who may have had four children), the fact that the total number of couples having two children is much greater than the number of couples who previously had four children means that the total population will still increase substantially before leveling off.

To illustrate, suppose that country X has a total population of 600: 100 married couples, each with 4 children (2 girls and 2 boys). When these 400 children grow up, suppose they all marry, forming 200 new couples of childbearing age. Assume now that instead of 4 children per family, these new couples have only 2 children each (1 boy and 1 girl). Assuming the death of the first generation of parents, the total population of country X will have grown from 600 to 800 people (i.e., 200 families with 4 people in each family). Now when the children of these 2-child families grow up and get married, if they too have only 2 children per couple, then there will again be 200 families with 4 people in each for a total population of 800 people. Country X will, therefore, have been able to stabilize its population *only* after two generations or approximately 50 years! This is why it takes many years to curtail population growth in high-fertility countries. Too often politicians, planners, and even economists are unaware of the mathematics of population momentum. They assume incorrectly that population growth rates can be manipulated in the short-run with the same ease as the manipulation of, say, saving and investment rates or the levels and rates of taxation.

Suppose that during the period of 1980–1985 fertility rates in all developing countries had actually declined to the "replacement" levels now characteristic of most developed countries (roughly two children per family). Even if this had happened, the population of the Third World would still continue to grow for many decades. In fact, it would not level off until it had reached a size fully 88% greater than its 1970 level (i.e., an increase of more than 2.2 *billion* people!). And heavily populated countries like Mexico, India, Bangladesh, Indonesia, Nigeria, and others would all also experience very substantial increases as a result of the momentum *already* built into the age structure of their current populations.

If we now assume that LDC fertility declines to "replacement levels" by 2000–2005, we obtain an entirely different set of figures. In this case the population of the Third World would not level off until its built-in momentum had resulted in an overall increase of 158% and an additional 4 billion people had been born. This would be more than the total world population in 1975! These figures emphasize dramatically the importance to eventual population size of the date at which countries are able to lower their fertility levels. In the above example, a mere 20 years meant an additional 1.8 billion people, almost two-thirds of the present population of the entire Third World.

Table 6.7 strikingly illustrates the "arithmetic" of population momentum using actual data and projections for a number of developing countries. We see that countries like Bangladesh, Mexico, the Philippines, and Nigeria with high current birthrates have the highest built-in momentum of population growth. Note also that even though a country like India has approximately the same percentage growth momentum as Egypt, its current size means that it stands to gain almost 750 million more people than Egypt even if both achieve replacement birthrates by the year 2000.

These illustrations vividly demonstrate the extent to which most Third World countries are *already* virtually assured of substantial population increases, whatever happens to fertility levels. As they set goals for desirable future population sizes, they may as well accept the fact that increases on the order of 80–125% are coming *regardless of what policy strategies are adopted.* But this should not be a cause for despair or a diminished commitment on the part of those countries that genuinely believe that slowing down population growth is in their best national interest. For, as we have seen from the above example, every year that passes without a reduction in fertility means a larger multiple of the present total population size before it can eventually level off.

Table 6.7 Population "Momentum" and Projected Population Increases under Two Alternative (Optimistic) Fertility Assumptions

Country	Population circa 1970 (millions)	Eventual population size in 2050 (millions)		Increase from 1970 level (%)	
		Replacement by			
		1980–1985	*2000–2005*	*1980–1985*	*2000–2005*
India	534	1,002	1,366	88	156
Brazil	94	192	266	104	183
Bangladesh	69	155	240	125	248
Nigeria	65	135	198	108	205
Pakistan	57	112	160	96	181
Mexico	51	111	168	118	229
Philippines	38	79	119	108	213
Egypt	34	64	92	88	171
All LDCs	2,530	4,763	6,525	88	158
All developed countries	1,122	1,482	1,610	32	44
World	3,652	6,245	8,135	71	123

SOURCE: Tomas Frejka, reference tables to *The Future of Population Growth* (New York: Population Council, 1973).

THE POPULATION DEBATE: SOME CONFLICTING OPINIONS

Before discussing specific goals and objectives, we must recognize that there is substantial disagreement, particularly between the developed and the developing world, about how serious a problem rapid population growth really is. Nowhere was this conflict more evident nor the debate more vocal than at the first World Population Conference held in Bucharest in 1974.[7] On the one hand, one must recognize that population growth is not the only, or even the primary, source of low levels of living, eroding self-esteem, and limited freedom in Third World nations. On the other hand, it would be equally naive to think that rapid population growth in many countries and regions is not a serious *intensifier* and multiplier of our three integral components of underdevelopment, especially the first and third. The following summary of some of the main arguments for and against the idea that rapid population growth is a serious development problem forms the basis for considering whether some consensus of opinion can be reached so that specific goals and objectives can be postulated.[8]

Population Growth Is Not a Real Problem

We can identify three general lines of argument on the part of those individuals, primarily from Third World countries, who assert that:

1. The problem is not population growth but, rather, other issues.
2. Population growth is a false issue deliberately created by dominant rich-country agencies and institutions to keep LDCs in their underdeveloped, dependent condition.
3. For many developing countries and regions, population growth is, in fact, desirable.

Some Other Issues

Many knowledgeable people from both rich and poor nations argue that the real problem is not population growth per se but one or all of the following issues.

Underdevelopment. If correct strategies are pursued and lead to higher levels of living, greater esteem, and expanded freedom, population will take care of itself. Eventually, it will disappear as a problem as it has in all of the present economically advanced nations. According to this argument *underdevelopment is the real problem, and development should be the only goal.* With it will come economic progress and social mechanisms that will more or less automatically regulate population growth and distribution. As long as the vast majority of people in Third World countries remain impoverished, uneducated, and physically and psychologically weak, the large family will constitute the only real source of "social security" (i.e., parents will continue to be denied the freedom to choose a small family, if they so desire). Proponents of the underdevelopment argument then conclude that birth control programs will surely fail, as they have in the past, when there is no motivation on the part of poor families to limit their size.

World resource depletion. Population can only be an economic problem in relation to the availability and utilization of scarce natural and material resources. The fact is that developed countries, with only one-quarter of the world's population, consume almost 80% of the world's resources. For example, the average North American or European consumer uses up, directly and indirectly, almost 16 times as much of the world's food, energy, and material resources as his counterpart in Third World countries. In terms of the depletion of the world's limited resources, therefore, the addition of another child in the developed countries is as significant as the birth of 16 additional children in the underdeveloped countries. According to this argument, *developed* nations should curtail their excessively high consumption standards instead of asking less developed nations to restrict their population growth. The latter's high fertility is really due to their low levels of living, which in turn are largely the result of the "overconsumption" of the world's scarce resources by rich nations. This combination of rising affluence and extravagant, selfish consumption habits in rich countries and among rich people in poor countries should be the major world concern, *not* population growth.

Population distribution. According to this third argument, it is not the number of people per se that is causing population problems but their *distribution* in space. Many regions of the world (e.g., sub-Saharan Africa) and many regions within countries (e.g., the northeast and Amazon regions of Brazil) are in fact *underpopulated* in terms of available or potential resources. Others simply have too many people concentrated in too small an area (e.g., central Java or most urban concentrations in LDCs). Governments, therefore, should strive not to moderate the rate of population growth but rather to reduce rural–urban migration and to bring about a more natural spatial distribution of the population in terms of available land and other productive resources.

A Deliberately Contrived False Issue

The second main line of argument denying the significance of population growth as a major development problem is closely allied to the neocolonial dependence theory of underdevelopment discussed in Chapter 3. Basically, it is argued that the frenetic overconcern in the rich nations with the population growth of poor nations is really an attempt by the former to hold down the development of the latter in order to maintain an international status quo that is favorable to their self-interests. Rich nations are pressuring poor nations to adopt aggressive population control programs even though they themselves went through a period of sizable population increase that accelerated their own development processes.

A radical neo-Marxist version of this argument views population control efforts by rich countries and their allied international agencies as racist or genocidal attempts to reduce the relative or absolute size of those poor, largely nonwhite populations of the world who may someday pose a serious threat to the welfare of the rich, predominantly white societies. Worldwide birth control campaigns are seen as manifestations of the fears of the developed world in the face of a possible radical challenge to the international order by the people who are its first victims.

Population Growth Is Desirable

A more conventional economic argument is that of population growth as an essential ingredient to stimulate economic development.[9] Larger populations provide the needed consumer demand to generate favorable economies of scale in production, to lower production costs, and to provide a sufficient and low-cost labor supply to achieve higher output levels. More-over, it is argued that many rural regions in the Third World are in reality *underpopulated* in the sense that much unused but arable land could yield large increases in agricultural output if only more people were available to cultivate it. Many regions of tropical Africa and Latin America and even parts of Asia are said to be in this situation.

With respect to Africa, for example, it has even been argued that many regions had *larger* populations in the remote past than exist today.[10] Their rural depopulation resulted not only from the slave trade but also from compulsory military service, confinement to "reservations," and the forced-labor policies of former colonial governments. For example, the sixteenth-century Congo Kingdom is said to have had a population of approximately 2 million. But by the time of the colonial conquest, which followed 300 years of slave trade, the population of the region had fallen to less than one-third of that figure. Today's Zaire has barely caught up to the sixteenth-century numbers.[11] Other regions of western and eastern Africa provide similar examples—at least in the eyes of those who advocate rapid population growth in Africa.

In terms of ratios of population to arable land (i.e., land under cultivation, fallow land, pastures, and forests), Africa south of the Sahara is said by these supporters of population expansion to have a total of 1,400 million arable hectares. Land actually being cultivated amounts to only 170 million hectares, or about 1 hectare per rural inhabitant. Thus, only 12% of all potential arable land is under cultivation, and this very low rural population density is viewed as a serious drawback to raising agricultural output.[12] Similar arguments have been expounded with regard to such Latin American countries as Brazil and Argentina.

Three other noneconomic arguments, each found to some degree in a wide range of developing countries, complete the "population-growth-is-desirable" viewpoint. First, many countries claim a need for population growth to protect currently underpopulated border regions against expansionist intentions of neighboring nations. Second, there are many ethnic, racial, and religious groups within less developed countries whose attitudes favoring large family size have to be protected for both moral and political reasons. Finally, military and political power are often seen as dependent on a large and youthful population.

Many of these arguments have a certain realism about them; if not in fact, then at least in the perceptions of vocal and influential individuals within the developing world. Clearly, some of the arguments have greater validity for some Third World countries than others. The important point is that they represent a considerable range of opinions and viewpoints within the Third World and therefore need to be seriously weighed against the counterarguments of those (mostly in the developed world) who believe that rapid population growth is indeed a real and important problem for under-developed countries. Let us now look at some of these counterarguments.

Population Growth Is a Real Problem

Positions supporting the need to curtail population growth through special programs and policies are typically based on one or more of the following four arguments.[13]

The Population "Hawk" Argument

The extreme version of the population-as-a-serious-problem position attempts to attribute almost all of the world's economic and social evils to excessive population growth. Unrestrained population increase is seen as the major crisis facing mankind today. It is regarded as the principal cause of poverty, low levels of living, malnutrition, and ill health, of environmental degradation, and of a wide array of other social problems. Value-laden and incendiary words such as the "population bomb" or "population explosion" are tossed around at will. Indeed, dire predictions of world food catastrophes and ecological disaster are attributed almost entirely to the growth in world numbers.[14] Such an extreme position leads some of its advocates to assert that "world" (i.e., LDC) population stabilization or even decline is the most urgent contemporary task even if it requires severe and coercive measures such as compulsory sterilization to "control" family size in some of the most populated Third World countries like India and Bangladesh.

The Provision of Family-Planning Services

A much less extreme and draconian anti-population-growth argument asserts that many families in Third World countries would *like* to limit their size if only they had the *means* to do so. Hence, the main problem is to provide modern means of birth control such as the pill, the intrauterine device (IUD), and increasingly, "voluntary" sterilization through male vasectomy. Third World countries need to establish family-planning programs with many local clinics both to educate people about modern methods of fertility control and to provide them with cheap and safe means to practice it.

Human Rights

At a UN convention held in Teheran, Iran, in 1968 a resolution was adopted asserting that "it is a fundamental human right for each person to be able to determine the size of his or her own family." A current version of this position, at least in more affluent societies, asserts that every woman has the fundamental right to the control of her own reproductive processes, including the right to legal abortion as well as contraception. Since maternal and child health are also related to the ability of parents to space their children at greater intervals, the human rights position bases its "freedom to choose" advocacy of family planning on grounds of health as well as family size.

Development Plus Population Programs

The development-plus-population-programs position is by far the principal stance among those who hold that a too rapid population growth should be a real concern of Third World countries. Advocates start from the basic proposition that population growth intensifies and exacerbates the economic, social, and psychological problems associated with the condition of underdevelopment. Population growth retards the prospects for a better life for those already born. It also severely draws down limited government revenues simply to provide the most rudimentary economic, health, and social services to the additional people. This in turn further reduces the prospects for any improvement in the levels of living of the existing generation.

As we have seen, widespread absolute poverty and low levels of living are a major cause of large family size, due in part to parental desires for economic security when they grow old. It follows that economic and social development are *necessary* conditions for bringing about an eventual slowing down or cessation of population growth at low levels of fertility and mortality. But, according to this argument, it is not a *sufficient* condition—that is, development provides people with the *incentives* and *motivations* to limit their family size, but family-planning programs are needed to provide them with the technological *means* to avoid unwanted pregnancies. Even though countries like France, Japan, the United States, Great Britain, and, more recently, Taiwan and South Korea were able to reduce their population growth rates without widespread family-planning clinics, it is argued by advocates of the development-plus-population-program position that the provision of these services will enable other countries desiring to control excessive population growth to do so more *rapidly* than if these family-planning services were not available.

GOALS AND OBJECTIVES: TOWARD A CONSENSUS

In spite of what may appear to be diametrically opposing arguments about the causes and significance of population growth, during the late 1970s and early 1980s there emerged a more common ground, an intermediate position, that many on both sides of the debate could agree upon. This was especially evident at the Second World Population Conference held in Mexico City in August 1984. The ethical values that provided the basis for this consensus are rooted in what was termed in Chapter 3 the "inner meaning" of development taken in conjunction with the UN human rights declaration of 1968 referred to in the previous section. The following four propositions constitute the essential components of this intermediate or consensus opinion:

1. *Population growth is not the primary cause of low levels of living, gross inequalities, or the limited freedom of choice that characterize much of the Third World.* The fundamental causes of these problems must be sought, rather, in the "dualistic" nature of the domestic and international economic and social order.
2. *The problem of population is not simply one of numbers but involves the quality of life and material well-being.* Thus, LDC population size must be viewed *in conjunction with developed country affluence* in relation to the quantity, distribution, and utilization of world resources, not just in relation to "indigenous" resources of the LDCs.
3. *But rapid population growth does serve to intensify problems of underdevelopment* and make prospects for development that much more remote. As we have seen, the momentum of growth means that barring catastrophe, the population of developing countries will increase dramatically over the coming decades, no matter what fertility control measures are adopted now. It follows that high population growth rates, while not the principal cause of underdevelopment, are nevertheless important contributing factors in specific countries and regions of the world.
4. *Many of the real problems of population arise not from its overall size but from its concentration,* especially in urban areas as a result of accelerated rural–urban migration (see Chapter 9). A more rational and efficient spatial *distribution* of national populations thus becomes an alternative, in some countries, to the slowdown of overall population growth.

In view of the above propositions and the development and human rights value premises implicit in them, we may conclude that the following three *goals* and *objectives* might be included in any realistic approach to the issue of population growth in many developing countries.

1. In countries or regions where the population size, distribution, and growth are viewed as an existing and/or potential problem, the primary objective of any strategy to limit its further growth must deal not only with the population variable per se but also with the underlying social and economic conditions of *underdevelopment*. Problems such as absolute poverty, gross inequality, widespread unemployment (especially among females), limited female access to education, malnutrition, and poor health facilities need to be given high priority. Their amelioration is both a necessary concomitant of development and a fundamental motivational basis for the expanded *freedom* of the individual to choose an optimal—and, in many cases, smaller—family size.

2. In order to bring about smaller families through development-induced motivations, family-planning programs providing both the education and the technological means to regulate fertility *for those who wish to regulate it* need to be established.

3. Developed countries need to assist developing countries to achieve their lowered fertility and mortality objectives not only by providing contraceptives and funding family-planning clinics but, more importantly, *(a) by curtailing their own excessive depletion of nonrenewable world resources* through programs designed to cut back on the unnecessary consumption of products that intensively utilize such resources; *(b) by making genuine commitments* to eradicating poverty, illiteracy, disease, and malnutrition in Third World countries as well as their own; and *(c)* by recognizing in both their rhetoric and their international economic and social dealings that *"development" is the real issue, not simply population control.*

With these observations in mind, we can now turn to a more specific analysis of the "economics" of population in Chapter 7. We would encourage readers, however, to reach their own independent judgment about the validity of the various arguments presented in this chapter as part of the continuing worldwide debate on the pros and cons of population growth.

NOTES

1. Bernard Berelson, "World Population: Status Report 1974," *Reports on Population and Family Planning, No. 15* (January 1974):47.

2. The information in this section is derived primarily from Berelson, *ibid.*, pp. 3–20. An additional valuable source of information on recent demographic trends as well as a review of current issues and strategies can be found in G. McNicoll and M. Nag, "Population growth: Current issues and strategies," Reading 12 in *The Struggle for Economic Development.*

3. However, the decade of the 1970s may represent a watershed in the history of world population growth. By the end of the decade there were increasing signs that rates were beginning to decline in a growing number of developing countries and the world population growth may have finally peaked. For some evidence of this possible turning point, see B. Berelson, W. Parker Mauldin, and Sheldon Segal, "Population: Current status and policy options," *Social Science and Medicine*, Part C, Health and Population in Developing Countries, 14C, May 1980, and, especially, World Bank, *World Development Report 1984* (New York: Oxford University Press, 1984), Part II, Ch. 4.

4. For those interested, a convenient shorthand method of calculating "doubling times" is simply to divide any growth rate into the number 70. For example, something (an

asset, population, GNP, etc.) growing at 2% per year will double its value in approximately 35−36 years.

5. For further statistical evidence of the lack of any clear relationship between rates of population growth and rates of GNP per capita growth for a sample of 79 Third World nations, see Derek T. Healey, *Population Growth and Real Output Growth in Developing Countries: A Survey and Analysis,* Department of Economics, University of Adelaide, South Australia (mimeo), 1974.

6. For empirical support of the proposition that reducing income inequality will tend to lower fertility levels in developing nations, see A. K. Bhattacharyya, "Income inequality and fertility: A comparative view," *Population Studies* 29, no. 1 (1975):5−19; David Morawetz, "Basic needs policies and population growth," *World Development* 6, No. 11/12 (1978):1251−1259; and especially Robert Repetto, *Economic Equality and Fertility in Developing Countries* (Baltimore: Johns Hopkins University Press, 1979).

7. For an analysis of this conflict, see J. Finkle and B. Crane, "The politics of Bucharest: Population, development and the new international economic order," *Population and Development Review* 1, no. 1 (1975): 87−114. Although this conflict was less visible in the Second World Population Conference held in Mexico City in August 1984, it still remained prominent in the thoughts and discussions of many Third World delegates.

8. For a more detailed discussion of these divergent opinions, see Michael Teitelbaum, "Population and development: Is a consensus possible?" *Foreign Affairs,* July 1974, pp. 749−757.

9. See, for example, Colin Clark, "The 'population explosion' myth," *Bulletin of the Institute of Development Studies,* Sussex, May 1969.

10. See Samir Amin, "Underpopulated Africa," paper given at the African Population Conference, Accra, December 1971.

11. *Ibid.,* fn. 2.

12. *Ibid.,* p. 3.

13. Teitelbaum, "Population and Development" pp. 752−753.

14. For example, see Paul R. and Anne H. Ehrlich, *Population, Resources and Environment: Issues in Human Ecology,* 2nd ed. (San Francisco: Freeman, 1972), and Lester R. Brown, *In the Human Interest: A Strategy to Stabilize World Population* (New York: Norton, 1974).

CONCEPTS FOR REVIEW

Doubling time	Life expectancy at birth
Rate of population increase	Youth dependency ratio
Rate of natural increase	Age structure of population
General fertility rate	Hidden momentum of population growth
Crude birthrate	Replacement fertility
Crude death rate	Population distribution
Infant mortality rate	

QUESTIONS FOR DISCUSSION

1. Population growth in Third World nations has proceeded at unprecedented rates over the past few decades. Compare and contrast the present rate of population growth in less developed countries with that of the modern developed nations during their early growth years. What has been the major factor contributing to rapid Third World population growth since the Second World War? Explain.

2. What is the relationship between the age structure of a population and its dependency burden? Is the so-called dependency burden higher or lower in Third World countries? Why?

3. Does there appear to be any distinctive statistical relationship between Third World birthrates and (a) levels of per capita GNP, (b) rates of per capita GNP growth, and/or

(c) degree of equality or inequality in income distributions? If so, explain why you think such a relationship might exist.

4. Explain the meaning of the notion of the "hidden momentum" of population growth. Why is this an important concept for projecting future population trends in different Third World nations?

5. Outline and comment briefly on some of the arguments *against* the idea that population growth is a serious problem in Third World nations.

6. Outline and comment briefly on some of the arguments *in favor* of the idea that population growth is a serious problem in Third World nations.

FURTHER READINGS

For an analysis and quantitative review of recent trends in world population growth see the World Bank's *World Development Report 1984* (New York: Oxford University Press, 1984). A handy statistical summary is found in the annual *World Population Data Sheet*, Population Reference Bureau, Washington, D.C.

An excellent survey article on the various interrelationships between population and economic development can be found in R. H. Cassen, "Population and development: A survey," *World Development* 4, nos. 10–11 (October 1976). Two additional volumes of readings on the subject are Ronald Ridker (ed.), *Population and Development: The Search for Selective Interventions* (Baltimore: Johns Hopkins University Press, 1976), and Richard Easterlin (ed.), *Population and Economic Change in Developing Countries* (Chicago: University of Chicago Press for the National Bureau of Economic Research, 1980). The best overall reviews, however, are those of Nancy Birdsall, "Analytical approaches to the relationship of population growth and development," reprinted as Reading 13 in *The Struggle for Economic Development*, and Geoffrey McNicoll, "Consequences of rapid population growth: An overview and assessment," *Population and Development Review* 10, no. 2 (June 1984).

For a concise and informative summary of the debate on population and development, see Michael S. Teitelbaum, "Population and development: Is a consensus possible?" *Foreign Affairs*, July 1974.

Additional readings can be found on pp. 622–623.

7

ECONOMICS OF POPULATION
AND DEVELOPMENT

The basis for an effective solution of population problems is, above all,
socioeconomic transformation.
First World Population Plan of Action, Bucharest, 1974

Economic development is a central factor in the solution of population and
interrelated problems. . . . national and international efforts should give
priority to action programmes integrating population and development.
Second World Population Plan of Action, Mexico City, 1984

In recent years economists have begun to focus increasingly on the relationship between economic development and population growth. The most
difficult problem for such an analysis, however, is to be able somehow to
separate cause from effect. Does economic development accelerate or retard
population growth rates; or does rapid population growth contribute to or
retard economic development? What are the linkages, how strong are they,
and in what direction do they operate? In this chapter we examine three
major approaches to the economics of population analysis: the theory of
demographic transition, the Malthusian "population trap," and the new
"microeconomics" of fertility. Our aim is to assess the degree to which these
various approaches shed light on the main goals and objectives enumerated
in the previous chapter. We conclude with an analysis of alternative policy
approaches for dealing with global population problems in the dual context
of developing and developed countries.

THE THEORY OF DEMOGRAPHIC TRANSITION

The theory of demographic transition attempts to explain why all contemporary developed nations have more or less passed through the same three

"stages" of modern population history. Before their economic modernization, these countries for centuries had stable or very slow growing populations as a result of a combination of *high birthrates* and almost equally *high death rates*. This was Stage I. Stage II began to occur when modernization, associated with improved public health methods, better diets, higher incomes, etc., led to a marked reduction in mortality that gradually raised life expectancy from under 40 years to over 60 years. However, the decline in death rates was not immediately accompanied by a decline in fertility. As a result, the growing divergence between *high birthrates* and *falling death rates* led to sharp increases in population growth compared to past centuries. Stage II thus marks the beginning of the demographic transition (i.e., the transition from stable or slow-growing populations first to rapidly increasing numbers and then to declining rates). Finally, Stage III was entered when the forces and influences of modernization and development caused the beginning of a decline in fertility; eventually, *falling birthrates converged with lower death rates*, leaving little or no population growth.

Figure 7.1 roughly depicts the three historical stages of the demographic transition in Western Europe. Before the early nineteenth century, birthrates hovered around 35 per 1,000 while death rates fluctuated around 30 per 1,000. This resulted in population growth rates of around 5 per 1,000, or less than one-half of 1% per year. Stage II, the beginning of Western Europe's demographic transition, was initiated around the first quarter of the nineteenth century by slowly falling death rates as a result of improving economic conditions and the gradual development of disease and death control through modern medical and public health technologies. The decline in birthrates (Stage III) did not really begin until late in the nineteenth century, with most of the reduction concentrated in the current century—many decades after modern economic growth had begun and long after death rates began their descent. But since the initial level of birthrates was generally low in Western Europe as a result of either late marriage or celibacy, overall rates of population growth seldom exceeded the 1% level, even at their peak. By the end of Western Europe's demographic transition in the second half of the

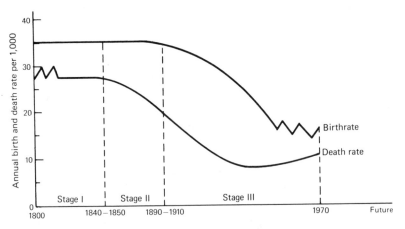

Figure 7.1.   The demographic transition in Western Europe.

twentieth century, the relationship between birth and death rates that marked the early 1800s had reversed with birthrates fluctuating and death rates remaining fairly stable or slightly rising. This latter phenomenon is simply due to the older age distributions of contemporary European populations.

Figure 7.2 shows the population histories of contemporary Third World countries, which contrast with those of Western Europe and fall into two patterns.

Birthrates in most underdeveloped countries today are considerably higher than they were in preindustrial Western Europe. This is because women tend to marry at an earlier age. As a result there are both more families for a given population size and more years in which to have children. Beginning in the 1940s and especially in the 1950s and 1960s, Stage II of the demographic transition occurred throughout most of the Third World. The application of highly effective imported modern medical and public health technologies caused LDC death rates to fall much more rapidly than in nineteenth-century Europe. Given their historically high birthrates (over 40 per 1,000 in many countries), this has meant that Stage II of the LDC demographic transition has been characterized by population growth rates well in excess of 2.0–2.5% per annum.

With regard to Stage III, we can distinguish between two broad classes of developing countries. In Case A in Figure 7.2 modern methods of death control *combined with rapid and widely distributed rises in levels of living* have resulted in death rates falling as low as 10 per 1,000 and birthrates also falling rapidly, to levels between 20 and 30 per 1,000. These countries, most notably Taiwan, South Korea, Costa Rica, China, Cuba, and Sri Lanka, have

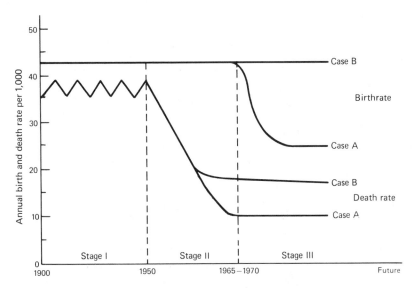

Figure 7.2. The beginning of a demographic transition in Third World countries. *Source:* Based on *The Growth of World Population*, National Academy of Sciences Publication 1091 (Washington, D.C.: National Academy of Sciences, 1963), p. 15.

thus entered Stage III of their demographic transition and have experienced rapidly falling rates of overall population growth. In the late 1970s several other countries including Colombia, Indonesia, the Dominican Republic, Thailand, Malaysia, and the Philippines appeared to be entering a period of sustained fertility decline consistent with Case A.

On the other hand, the majority of Third World countries fall into Case B of Figure 7.2. After an initial period of rapid decline, death rates have failed to drop further, largely because of the persistence of widespread absolute poverty and low levels of living. Moreover, the continuance of high birthrates as a result of these low levels of living causes overall population growth rates to remain relatively high. These countries, including most of those in sub-Saharan Africa and the Mideast, are still in Stage II of their demographic transition.

The important question, therefore, is, When and under what conditions are Third World nations likely to experience falling birthrates and a slower expansion of population? To address this issue many traditional and modern economic theories of population and development have been appealed to. Two of the best known are the traditional Malthusian "population trap" and the most recent "microeconomic" theory of fertility.

THE MALTHUSIAN POPULATION TRAP

The Basic Model

More than 175 years ago, the Reverend Thomas Malthus put forward a theory of the relationship between population growth and economic development that still survives today. Writing in 1798 in his *Essay on the Principle of Population*, and drawing on the concept of diminishing returns, Malthus postulated a universal tendency for the population of a country, unless checked by dwindling food supplies, to grow at a geometric rate, doubling every 30–40 years.[1] At the same time, because of diminishing returns to the fixed factor, land, food supplies could only expand roughly at an arithmetical rate. In fact, as each member of the population would have less land to work, his marginal contribution to food production would actually start to decline. Since the growth in food supplies could not keep pace with the burgeoning population, per capita incomes (defined in an agrarian society simply as per capita food production) would have a tendency to fall so low as to lead to a stable population existing barely at or slightly above the subsistence level. Malthus therefore contended that the only way to avoid this condition of chronic low levels of living or "absolute poverty" was for people to engage in "moral restraint" and limit the numbers of their progeny. Thus, one might regard Malthus as the father of the modern birth control movement.

Modern economists have given a name to the Malthusian idea of a population inexorably forced to live at subsistence levels of income. They have called it the "low-level—equilibrium population trap," or more simply, the "Malthusian population trap." Diagrammatically, the basic Malthusian model can be illustrated by comparing the shape and position of curves representing population growth rates and aggregate income growth rates when these two curves are each plotted against levels of per capita income. This is done in Figure 7.3.

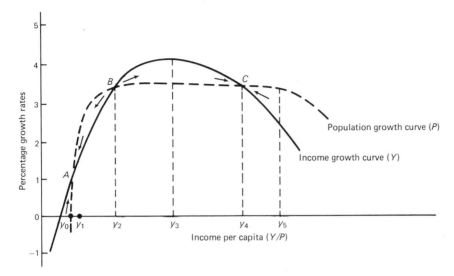

Figure 7.3. The Malthusian "population trap."

On the vertical axis we plot numerical percentage changes, both positive and negative, in the two principal variables under consideration (i.e., total population and aggregate income). On the horizontal axis are levels of per capita income. Look first at the dashed curve P portraying the assumed relationship between rates of population growth (measured vertically) and levels of per capita income, Y/P (measured horizontally). At a very low level of per capita income, y_0, the rate of population change will be nil so that there exists a stable population. Thus, y_0 might represent our concept of "absolute poverty." Birth and death rates are equal and the population is barely holding its own absolute level. The situation is analogous to Stage I of the demographic transition theory. At per capita income levels beyond (to the right of) y_0, it is assumed that population size will begin to increase under the pressure of falling death rates. Higher incomes mean less starvation and disease. And, with birthrates always assumed to be at the biological maximum, falling death rates provide the impetus for an expanding population (i.e., Stage II).

In Figure 7.3, population growth achieves its maximum rate, roughly 3.3% at a per capita income level of y_2. It is assumed to remain at that level until much higher per capita income levels are realized. Thereafter (i.e., beyond y_5), in accordance with Stage III of the demographic transition, birthrates will begin to decline and the population growth rate curve becomes negatively sloped and once again approaches the horizontal axis.

The other part of the Malthusian theory requires us to plot a relationship between the growth rate of aggregate income (in the absence of population growth) and levels of per capita income. We can then compare the two rates (i.e., aggregate income and total population). If aggregate income (total product) is rising faster, per capita income by definition must be increasing; if total population is growing faster than total income, per capita income must be falling. In Figure 7.3 the rate of aggregate income growth (also measured vertically) is assumed at first to be positively related to levels of per capita income; that is, the higher the level of per capita income, the higher the rate of increase in aggregate income. The economic reason for this positive relationship is the assumption that savings vary positively with income per capita. Countries with higher per capita incomes are assumed to be capable of generating higher savings rates and thus more investment. Given a Harrod-Domar type model of economic growth (see Chapter 3), higher savings rates mean higher rates of aggregate income growth. Beyond a certain per capita income point (y_3), however, the income growth rate curve is assumed to level off and then begin to decline as new investments and more people are required to work with fixed quantities of land and natural resources. This is the point of diminishing returns in the Malthusian model (note that the possibility of technological progress is not considered). The aggregate income growth curve therefore is conceptually analogous to the total product curve in the basic theory of production.

Observe that in Figure 7.3 the curves are drawn so that they intersect at three points: A, B, and C. Point A represents the point at which the Malthusian population trap level of per capita income (y_1) is attained. It is a stable equilibrium point—any small movement to the left or right of Point A will cause the per capita income equilibrium point to return to y_1. For example, as per capita income rises from y_1 toward y_2, the rate of population increase will exceed the rate of aggregate income growth (i.e., the P curve is vertically higher than the Y curve). We know that whenever population is growing faster than income, per capita income must fall. The arrow pointing in the direction of A from the right, therefore, shows that per capita income must fall back to its very low level at y_1 for all points between y_1 and y_2. Similarly, to the left of Point A incomes grow faster than population, causing the equilibrium per capita income level to rise to y_1.

According to Malthus and the neo-Malthusians, poor nations will never be able to rise much above their subsistence levels of per capita income unless they initiate "preventive" checks (i.e., birth control) on their population growth. In the absence of such preventive checks, "positive" checks (starvation, disease, wars) on population growth will inevitably provide the restraining force.

Completing our description of the population trap portrayed in Figure 7.3, we see that Point B is an "unstable" equilibrium point. If per capita income can somehow jump rapidly from y_1 to y_2 (e.g., as a result of "big push" investment and industrialization programs) before Malthusian positive checks take their toll, it will continue to grow until the other stable equilibrium Point C at per capita income level y_4 is reached. Point B is an unstable equilibrium point in the sense that any movement to the left or right will continue until either A or C is reached.

Criticisms of the Model

The Malthusian population trap provides a simple and in many ways appealing theory of the relationship between population growth and economic development. Unfortunately it is based on a number of simplistic assumptions and hypotheses that do not stand the test of empirical verification. We can criticize the population trap on two major grounds.

First, and most important, the model (and, indeed, Malthus) assumes away or does not take into account the enormous impact of technological progress in offsetting the growth inhibiting forces of rapid population increases. As we discovered in Chapter 4, the history of modern economic growth has been most closely associated with rapid technological progress in the form of a continuous series of scientific, technological, and social inventions and innovations. Increasing rather than decreasing returns to scale have been a distinguishing feature of the modern growth epoch. While Malthus was basically correct in assuming a limited supply of land, he did not, and in fairness could not at that time, anticipate the manner in which technological progress could augment the availability of land by raising its quality (i.e., productivity) even though its quantity might remain roughly the same.

In terms of the population trap, rapid and continuing technological progress can be represented by an upward shift of the income growth (total product) curve so that *at all levels of per capita income* it is vertically higher than the population growth curve. This is shown in Figure 7.4. As a result, per capita income will grow steadily over time. All countries, therefore, have the potential of escaping the Malthusian population trap.

The second basic criticism of the trap focuses on its assumption that national rates of population increase are directly (positively) related to the level of national per capita income. According to this assumption, at relatively low levels of per capita income we should expect to find population growth rates increasing with increasing per capita incomes. However, as we discovered in the preceding chapter, there appears to be no clear correlation between population growth rates and levels of per capita income among Third World nations. As a result of modern medicine and public health

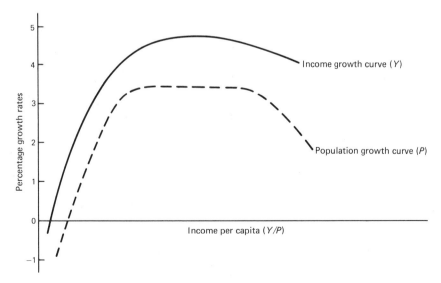

Figure 7.4. Technological (and social) progress allows nations to avoid the population trap.

programs, death rates have fallen rapidly and have become less dependent on the level of per capita income in most Third World nations. And as we discovered in Figure 6.2a, birthrates seem to show no definable relationship with per capita income levels. Our conclusion, therefore, is that it is not so much the *aggregate* level of per capita income that matters for population growth but, rather, how that income is *distributed*. The social and economic institutions of a nation and its philosophy of development are probably greater determinants of population growth rates than are aggregate economic variables and simplistic models of macroeconomic growth.

We can thus largely reject the Malthusian and neo-Malthusian theories as applied to contemporary Third World nations on the following grounds:

1. They do not take adequate account of the role and impact of technological progress.
2. They are based on a hypothesis about a macro relationship between population growth and levels of per capita income that does not stand up to empirical testing.
3. They focus on the wrong variable, per capita income, as the principal determinant of population growth rates. A much better and more valid approach to the question of population and development centers on the microeconomics of family-size decision making in which individual, and not aggregate, levels of living become the principal determinant of a family's decision to have more or fewer children.

THE MICROECONOMIC THEORY OF FERTILITY

General Considerations

In recent years economists have begun to look more closely at the microeconomic determinants of family fertility in an attempt to provide a better theoretical and empirical explanation for the observed falling birthrates associated with Stage III of the demographic transition. In doing this, they have drawn on the traditional neoclassical theory of household and consumer behavior for their basic analytical model, and have utilized the principles of economy and optimization to explain family-size decisions.

The conventional theory of consumer behavior assumes that an individual with a given set of tastes or preferences for a range of goods (i.e., a "utility function") tries to maximize the satisfaction derived from consuming these goods subject to his own income constraint and the relative prices of all goods. In the application of this theory to fertility analysis, children are considered as a special kind of consumption (and in LDCs, investment) good so that fertility becomes a rational economic response to the consumer's (family's) demand for children relative to other goods. The usual income and substitution effects are assumed to apply. That is, if other factors are held constant, the desired number of children can be expected to vary directly with household income (this direct relationship may not hold for poor societies; it depends on the strength of demand for children relative to other consumer goods and to the sources of increased income, e.g., female employment, see below), inversely with the price (cost) of children, and inversely with the strength of tastes for other goods relative to children. Mathematically, these relationships can be expressed as follows:

$$C_d = f\left(Y, P_c, P_x, t_x\right) \qquad x = 1, \ldots, n$$

where C_d is the demand for surviving children (an important consider-
           ation in low-income societies where infant mortality rates
           are high)
          Y is the given level of household income
          P_c is the "net" price of children (i.e., the difference between
           anticipated "costs," mostly the "opportunity cost" of a
           mother's time, and "benefits,"potential child income and
           old-age support)
          P_x are the prices of all other goods
          t_x are the tastes for goods relative to children

Under normal (i.e., neoclassical) conditions we would expect that

$\dfrac{\partial C_d}{\partial Y} > 0;$ the higher the household income, the greater the demand
                   for children (since the partial derivative of C_d with respect
                   to Y, $\partial C_d/\partial Y$, is *positive*)

$\dfrac{\partial C_d}{\partial P_c} < 0;$ the higher the net price of children, the lower the quan-
                   tity demanded (since the partial derivative of C_d with re-
                   spect to P_c is *negative*)

$\dfrac{\partial C_d}{\partial P_x} > 0;$ the higher the prices of all other goods relative to chil-
                   dren, the greater the quantity of children demanded

$\dfrac{\partial C_d}{\partial t_x} < 0;$ the greater the strength of tastes for goods relative to children,
                   the fewer children demanded

Figure 7.5 provides a simplified diagrammatic presentation of the microeconomic theory of fertility. The number of desired (surviving) children, C_d,
is measured along the horizontal axis and the total quantity of goods consumed by the parents, G_p, is measured on the vertical axis.

Household desires for children are expressed in terms of an indifference
map representing the subjective degree of satisfaction derived by the parents
for all possible combinations of commodities and children. Each individual
indifference curve portrays a locus of commodity–children combinations
that yield the same amount of satisfaction. Any point (or combination of
goods and children) on a "higher" indifference curve—that is, on a curve
farther out from the origin—represents a higher level of satisfaction than any
point on a lower indifference curve. But each indifference curve is a
"constant statisfaction" locus.

In Figure 7.5 only four indifference curves, I_1 to I_4, are shown; in theory
there exists an entire set of such curves, filling the whole quadrant and
covering all possible commodity–children combinations. The household's
ability to "purchase" alternative combinations of goods and children is
shown by the budget constraint line, ab. Thus, all combinations on or below
Line ab (i.e., within the triangular area oab) are financially attainable by the
household on the basis of its perceived income prospects and the relative
prices of children and goods, as represented by the slope of the ab budget
constraint. The steeper the slope of the budget line, the higher the price of
children relative to goods.

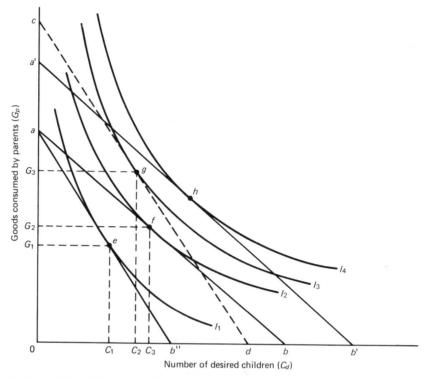

Figure 7.5. Microeconomic theory of fertility: An illustration.

According to the demand-based theory of fertility, the household chooses from among all attainable combinations that one combination of goods and children which maximizes family satisfaction on the basis of its subjectively determined preferences. Diagrammatically, this optimal combination is represented by Point f, the tangency point between the budget constraint, ab, and Indifference Curve $I_2{}^2$. Therefore, C_3 children and G_2 goods will be demanded.

A rise in family income, represented in Figure 7.5 by the parallel outward shift of the budget line from ab to $a'b'$, enables the household to attain a higher level of satisfaction (Point h on Curve I_4) by consuming more of both commodities and children—that is, if children, like most commodities, are assumed to be "normal" goods, an important "if" in low-income countries where children are often demanded primarily as a source of future financial security.

Similarly, an increase in the price (opportunity cost) of children relative to other goods will cause households to substitute commodities for children. Other factors (namely, income and tastes) being constant, a rise in the relative price of children causes the household utility-maximizing consumption combination to occur on a lower indifference curve, as shown by the movement of the equilibrium point from f to e when the budget line rotates around Point a to ab''.

Note, finally, that if there is a simultaneous increase in household income and net child price as a result, say, of expanding female employment opportunities and/or a rise in wages coupled with a tax on children beyond a certain number per family, there will be *both* an outward shift and a downward rotation of the budget constraint line of Figure 7.5 to, say, dashed line *cd*. The result is a new utility-maximizing combination that includes fewer children per family (Point g compared with Point *f*). In other words, higher levels of living for low-income families in combination with a relative increase in the price of children (whether brought about directly by fiscal measures or indirectly by expanded female employment opportunities) will *motivate* households to have fewer children while still improving their welfare. This is just one example of how the economic theory of fertility can shed light on the relationship between economic development and population growth as well as suggest possible lines of policy.

The Demand for Children in Developing Countries

As we have seen, the economic theory of fertility assumes that the household demand for children is determined by family preferences for a certain number of surviving (usually male) children (i.e., in regions of high mortality, parents may produce more children than they actually desire in the expectation that some will not survive), by the price or "opportunity cost" of rearing these children, and by levels of family income. Children in poor societies are seen partially as economic investment goods in that there is an "expected return" in the form of both child labor and the provision of financial support for parents in old age. As Professor Kuznets has noted in an exhaustive empirical study,

> they [the LDCs] are prolific because under their economic and social conditions large proportions of the population see their economic and social interests in more children as a supply of family labor, as a pool for a genetic lottery, and as a matter of economic and social security in a wealthy organized, non-protecting society.[3]

On the other hand, in many developing countries there is a strong intrinsic psychological and cultural determinant of family size so that the first two or three children should be viewed as "consumer" goods for which demand may not be very responsive to relative price changes.

The choice mechanism in the economic theory of fertility as applied to LDCs is assumed, therefore, to exist primarily with regard to the additional or marginal children who are considered as investments. In deciding whether or not to have *additional* children, parents are assumed to weigh economic benefits against costs, where the principal benefits are, as we have seen, the expected income from child labor, usually on the farm, and their financial support for elderly parents. Balanced against these benefits are the two principal elements of cost:

1. The "opportunity cost" of the mother's time (i.e., the income she could earn if she were not at home caring for her children)
2. The cost (both opportunity and actual) of educating children, that is, the financial tradeoff between having fewer "high-quality," high-cost, educated children with

high-income-earning potentials versus more "low-quality," low-cost, uneducated children with much lower earnings prospects

Using the same "thought processes" as in the traditional theory of consumer behavior, the theory of family fertility as applied to LDCs concludes that when the price or cost of children rises as a result, say, of increased educational and employment opportunities for women, or a rise in school fees, or the establishment of minimum-age child labor laws, or the provision of publicly financed old-age social security schemes and so on, parents will demand *fewer* "additional" children, substituting, perhaps, quality for quantity or a mother's employment income for her child-rearing activities. It follows that one way to induce families to desire fewer children is to raise the "price" of child rearing, by, say, providing greater educationai opportunities and a wider range of higher-paying jobs for young women.

Some Empirical Evidence

Statistical studies in countries like Chile, the Philippines, Taiwan, and Thailand have given a certain credence to the economic theory of fertility. For example, it has been found that high female employment opportunities outside the home and greater female and male school attendance, especially at the primary and early years of secondary schooling, are associated with lower levels of fertility.[4] As women become better educated, they tend to earn a larger share of household income and to produce fewer children. Moreover, these studies have confirmed the strong association between declines in child mortality and the subsequent decline in fertility. Assuming that households desire a target number of surviving children, increased incomes and higher levels of living can decrease child mortality and therefore increase the chances that the firstborn will survive. As a result, fewer births may be necessary to attain the same number of surviving children. This fact alone underlines the importance of improved public health and child nutrition programs in ultimately reducing Third World fertility levels.

Finally, while increased income may enable the family to support more children, the evidence seems to show that with higher incomes parents will tend to substitute child "quality" for "quantity" by investing in fewer, more educated children whose eventual earning capacity will be much higher. Additionally, it is argued that more income may also tend to lower fertility because the status effect of increased incomes raises the relative desire for material goods, especially among low-income groups whose budget constraints previously precluded the purchase of these goods. In other words, additional children beyond a socially accepted or minimum desired number may be "inferior goods" in low-income countries, that is, above some threshhold subsistence level, higher incomes may induce families to desire fewer children.

The Implications for Development and Fertility

All the above can be summarized by saying that *the effect of social and economic progress in lowering fertility in developing countries will be the greatest when the majority of the population and especially the very poor share in its benefits.* Specifically, birthrates among the very poor are likely to fall where there is

1. An increase in the education of women and a consequent change in their role and status
2. An increase in female nonagricultural wage employment opportunities, which raises the price or "cost" of their traditional child-rearing activities
3. A rise in family income levels through the increased direct employment and earnings of husband and wife and/or through the redistribution of income and assets from rich to poor
4. A reduction in infant mortality through expanded public health programs and better nutritional status for both parent and child
5. The development of old age and other social security systems outside the extended family network to lessen the economic dependence of parents on their offspring

In short, expanded efforts to make jobs, education, and health more broadly available to poverty groups in Third World countries will not only contribute to their economic and psychic well-being (i.e., to their "development"), but can also contribute substantially to their *motivation* for smaller families (i.e., their "freedom to choose"), which is vital to reducing population growth rates. Where such motivation exists, well-executed family-planning programs can then be an effective tool.

SOME POLICY APPROACHES

In view of the above analysis and in terms of the broad goals and objectives discussed in Chapter 6, what kinds of economic and social policies might developing and developed country governments and international assistance agencies consider in order to bring about long-term reductions in the overall rate of world population growth? Three areas of policy can have important direct and indirect influences on the well-being of present and future world populations:

1. Those general and specific policies that developing country governments can initiate to influence and perhaps even "control" their population growth and distribution
2. Those general and specific policies that developed country governments can initiate in their own countries to lessen their disproportionate consumption of limited world resources and promote a more equitable distribution of the benefits of global economic progress
3. Those specific ways in which developed country governments and international assistance agencies can help developing countries to achieve their population policy objectives, whatever they may be, in shorter periods of time

Let us deal with each of these areas in turn.

What Developing Countries Can Do[5]

As we have seen from both the cross-country data presented in Chapter 6 and the analytical and empirical content of the microeconomic theory of fertility, the principal variables influencing the demand for children at the family level are those which are most closely associated with the concept of development as we have defined it in Part I of this book. Thus, certain development policies are particularly crucial in the transition from a high-growth to a low-growth population. These policies aim at eliminating absolute poverty; lessening income inequalities; expanding educational opportunities, especially for women; providing increased job opportunities for both men and women; bringing the benefits of modern preventive medicine and public health programs, especially the provision of clean water and sanitation, to the rural and urban poor; improving maternal and child health through more food, better diets, and improved nutrition so as to lower infant mortality; and finally, creating a more equitable provision of other social services to wider segments of the population. Again, it is not numbers per se nor parental irrationality that is at the root of the LDC "population problem." Rather, it is the pervasiveness of absolute poverty and low levels of living that provides the economic rationale for large families and burgeoning populations.

While such broad long-run development policies are essential to ultimate population stabilization, there are some more specific policies that LDC governments might try to adopt in order to lower birthrates in the short run. Basically, governments can attempt to "control" fertility in six ways:

1. They can, through the *media* and the *educational process*, both formal (school system) and informal (adult education), try to persuade people to have smaller families.
2. They can establish *family-planning programs* to provide health and contraceptive services in order to encourage the desired behavior. Such publicly sponsored or officially supported programs now exist in 47 Third World countries covering almost 90% of LDC populations (see Table 7.1). Today only a few large countries such as Burma, Ethiopia, Nigeria, and Zaire do not have such publicly sponsored or officially endorsed family-planning programs.
3. They can deliberately *manipulate economic incentives and disincentives* for having children, for example, through the elimination or reduction of maternity leaves and benefits, the reduction or elimination of financial incentives and/or the imposition of financial penalties for having children beyond a certain number, the establishment of old-age social security provisions and minimum-age child labor laws, the raising of school fees and the elimination of heavy public subsidies for secondary and higher education, and finally, the subsidization of smaller families through direct money payments. Although some form of population related incentive and/or disincentive schemes now exist in over 30 LDCs, Singapore, India, Taiwan, Korea, and China are especially prominent in experimenting with various incentive – disincentive policies to reduce family size. For example, Singapore allocates scarce public housing without giving preference to family size. It is also limiting paid maternity leave to a maximum of two children, scaling the delivery fee according to child numbers, and reducing income tax relief from five to three children. In 1984, it even went so far as to give special priority in school admission to all children born to women holding university degrees while still penalizing non-degree women with more than two children. The presumed, but dubious, rationale was that university women have brighter children whose births should be encouraged while discouraging the less educated (and presumably less intelligent) women from bearing more children.

    In India, a tea estate has experimented with making deposits into savings accounts for individual female workers during their periods of nonpregnancy. The deposits are scaled according to the number of children, and the whole account can be canceled if a woman bears too many children. These accumulated savings are then paid out when the woman reaches the non-childbearing age of 45, as a form of social security in the place of children. In Taiwan there is an experiment in a rural township

Table 7.1 Countries Adopting Family-Planning Programs to Reduce Rates of Population Growth, 1960–1984

	Before 1960	1960–1964	1965–1969	1970–1974	1975–1979	1980–1984
Asia	India	China Fiji South Korea Pakistan	Indonesia Iran Malaysia Nepal Singapore Sri Lanka Taiwan Turkey	Bangladesh Hong Kong Philippines Thailand	Vietnam	Yemen

Latin America			Barbados
			Dominican
			  Republic
			Jamaica
			Trinidad &
			  Tobago
				Colombia
				El Salvador
				Mexico
				Puerto Rico
					Guatemala	Haiti
						Honduras
						Peru
						Brazil

Africa			Egypt Ghana Kenya Mauritius Morocco Tunisia	Botswana		Algeria Burundi Gambia Lesotho Rwanda Senegal Uganda Zimbabwe
Total	1	4	18	9	2	13

SOURCE: Population Council, *Data Bank*, November 1984.

in which the local government is depositing funds into bank accounts for young couples to cover the costs of educating their first two children. However, if the couple has a third child, part of this money is forfeited. It is *all* forfeited at the birth of the fourth child. The program is expressly designed to encourage families to have fewer but more educated children. South Korea has also initiated a national system of rewards and penalties to encourage small family size. It offers educational allowances and free medical care to all two-child families provided one of the parents has been sterilized.

China has by far the most comprehensive set of state enforced incentives and disincentives. In 1980 it initiated a tough new drive on births with a goal of lowering the annual birthrate to 1% during the decade. Stringent and often draconian measures to achieve that goal were introduced in 1982–1983 as the Chinese government adopted a policy of one child per family. Social and political pressures to limit family size to one child have included requiring women to appeal to the neighborhood committee or commune for formal permission to become pregnant. Although first births are routinely approved, second births are usually approved only if the first child has a serious birth defect or if the woman has remarried. Economic pressures include giving priority to one-child families in housing, medical care, and education. Mothers of two or more children are often denied promotions, and steep fines, sometimes in excess of 10 times China's per capita income, are levied for second and third children. Given such rigid national policies and a strong preference for male children, there have been reports of an alarming increase in female infanticide.

Early results seem to indicate that many of these economic and social experiments are achieving their goals. For a while in the mid-1970s India also had a major vasectomy program under way, in which men were given a direct cash payment, transitor radios, or even free tickets to championship soccer matches if they agreed to undergo "voluntary" sterilization. But the program had a negative political effect that set back governmental family-planning efforts for a number of years. The impact of the new Chinese population control programs, however, is more uncertain. Only time will tell whether the benefits of reduced population growth achieved through severe social and economic pressures for one-child families will be worth the costs of a harsh break with traditional family norms and perceptions regarding the value of children. Resistance in rural areas, where 80% of the population still resides, has apparently been widespread.

4. Countries can attempt to *redirect their populations away from the rapidly growing urban areas* by eliminating the current imbalance in economic and social opportunities in urban versus rural areas. As we shall see in Chapter 10, rural development programs are increasingly being emphasized in contemporary Third World development strategies, in part to stem the rising tide of rural–urban population movements and thus to promote a more geographically balanced distribution of the population.

5. Governments can attempt to *forcibly coerce people into having smaller families* through the power of state legislation and penalties. For obvious reasons, a few governments would attempt to engage in such coercion; not only is it often morally repugnant and politically unacceptable, but it is also almost always extremely difficult to administer. The defeat of Indira Gandhi's government in the Indian elections of March 1977 was largely due to the popular backlash against the government's forced sterilization program. Her return to power in 1980 and until her assasination in 1984 was accompanied by a commitment not to reintroduce coercive birth control policies. China's current policy, however, borders on overt coercion.

6. Finally, no policy measures will be successful in controlling fertility unless efforts are made to *raise the social and economic status of women* and hence create conditions favorable to delayed marriage and lower marital fertility. A crucial ingredient in any program designed to lower fertility rates is the creation of employment for women outside the home. The availability of income-earning opportunities can lead young women to delay marriage by enabling them to become economically self-sufficient and therefore in a better position to exercise control over the choice of partner and the timing of marriage. It can also reduce family pressures for early marriage by allowing women to make a contribution to parental household income. An independent source of income also secures a stronger position for married women in the household, reducing their dependence on other family members, particularly male offspring, for economic security. Furthermore, it enables women to consider the opportunity costs of additional children when childbearing competes with income-generating activities. In general, the availability of outside sources of income offers women genuine alternatives to early marriage and frequent childbearing, which are often motivated by women's lack of resources. An additional benefit of employment outside the home is that it reduces women's isolation which is often an impediment to the provision of family-planning services. The work place can provide a site for the distribution of birth control information and devices as well as for social support from women co-workers for delaying marriage and reducing childbearing. China provides an extreme example of this phenomenon.

What the Developed Nations Can Do in Their Own Countries

When we view the problems of population from a global perspective, as we should, the question of the relationship between population size and distribution and the depletion of many nonrenewable resources in developed and underdeveloped countries assumes major importance. In a world where 6% of the population, located in one country, the United States, accounts for 40% of annual world resource use and where slightly over 20% of the population accounts for 80% of annual resource use, we clearly are not dealing only or even primarily with a problem of numbers. We must also be concerned with the impact of rising affluence and the very unequal world-wide distribution of incomes on the depletion of many nonrenewable resources such as petroleum, certain basic metals, and other raw materials essential for economic growth.

In terms of food consumption, basic grains like wheat, corn, and rice are by far the most important source of man's direct food energy supply (52%). Consumed indirectly (e.g., grain fed to livestock, which are then consumed as beef, poultry, pork, and lamb or indirectly as milk, cheese, and eggs) they make up a significant share of the remainder. In resource terms, more than 70% of the world's cropland goes into grain production. And yet, the average North American directly and indirectly consumes 5 times as much grain and the corresponding agricultural resources—land, fertilizer, water, etc.—as his counterpart in India, Nigeria, or Colombia. With regard to energy, probably the second most essential resource to modern society, consumption of energy fuels (fossil-oil and coal, nuclear, and hydroelectric) by the average American in 1984 was 25 times the average Brazilian, 60 times the average Indian, 191 times the average Nigerian, and 351 times the average Ethiopian consumption level! The use of this energy to power private automobiles, operate home and office air conditioners, and activate electric toothbrushes in the developed nations means that there is potentially that much less to fertilize small family farms in the less developed nations. Alternatively, it means that poor families will have to pay more to obtain these valuable resource inputs.

Many other similar examples could be given of the gross inequalities in resource use. Perhaps more importantly, one could cite innumerable instances of the unnecessary and costly wastage of many scarce and nonrenewable resources by the affluent developed nations. The point, therefore, is that *any worldwide program designed to engender a better balance between resources and people by limiting Third World population growth through social intervention and family planning must also include the responsibility of rich nations systematically to simplify their own consumption demands and life-styles.* Such changes would free resources which could then be used by poor nations to generate the social and economic development essential to slower population growth.

In addition to simplifying life-styles and consumption habits, one other very positive but unlikely internal policy that rich nations could adopt to mitigate current world population problems would be to liberalize the legal conditions for the international emigration of poor, unskilled workers and their families from Africa, Asia, and Latin America to North America,

Europe, and Australia. The international migration of peasants from western and southern Europe to North America, Australia, and New Zealand in the nineteenth and early twentieth centuries was a major factor in moderating the problems of underdevelopment and population pressure in European countries. No such "safety valve" or outlet exists today for Third World countries. Yet, clearly, many underpopulated regions of the world and many labor-scarce societies could benefit economically from international migration (see Chapter 19).

How Developed Countries Can Assist Developing Countries in Their Varied Population Programs

There are also a number of ways in which the governments of rich countries and multilateral donor agencies can assist the governments of developing countries to achieve their population policy objectives in shorter periods of time. The most important of these concerns the willingness of rich countries (including now the wealthy Arab oil states) to be of genuine assistance to poor countries in their development efforts. Such genuine support would consist not only of expanded public and private financial assistance but also of improved trade relations, more appropriate technological transfers, assistance in developing indigenous scientific research capacities, better international commodity pricing policies, and a more equitable sharing of the world's scarce natural resources. (These and other areas of international economic relations between rich and poor countries will be examined in Parts III and IV.)

There are two other activities more directly related to fertility moderation where rich country governments and international donor agencies can play an important assisting role. The first of these is the whole area of research into the technology of fertility control, the contraceptive pill, modern intrauterine devices (IUDs), voluntary sterilization procedures, etc. Research has been going on in this area for a number of years, almost all of it financed by international donor organizations, private foundations, and aid agencies of developed countries. Further efforts to improve the effectiveness of this contraceptive technology while minimizing the health risks need to be encouraged.

The second area includes financial assistance from developed countries for family-planning programs, public education, and national population policy research activities in the developing countries. This has been the traditional and principal area of developed country assistance in the field of population. Total resources devoted to these activities have risen dramatically from around $2 million in 1960 to almost $3,000 million by the early 1980s. It remains an open question, however, whether such resources (especially those allocated to premature family-planning programs) might not have been more effectively used to achieve their fertility goals had they instead been devoted directly to assisting LDCs to raise the levels of living of their poorest people. As we have seen, it is of little value to have sophisticated family-planning programs when people are not motivated to reduce family size.

CONFLICTS, TRADEOFFS, AND CHOICES AMONG ALTERNATIVE POLICIES AND COMPETING OBJECTIVES: SOME FINAL OBSERVATIONS

Our discussion of possible policy options for curtailing population growth in Third World countries and freeing scarce world resources for development activities on the part of rich countries was intended principally to illustrate the range of alternatives that might be followed in the light of stated objectives. However, diverse policies need to be weighed against alternative and often conflicting goals. For example, two common population objectives are the lowering of fertility in order to slow down overall population growth and the reduction of rural–urban migration to avoid excessive urban concentrations and improve the spatial distribution of a given population. It turns out, however, as we shall see in Chapter 9, that one of the principal strategies for lowering fertility—more education, especially for women—happens to be an important factor stimulating the movement of people from rural to urban areas. Thus, while more education might decrease family size, it might also increase rural–urban migration and urban population congestion with its attendant social, physical, and psychological problems. In such a situation a simultaneous policy to develop rural areas would be needed. This would provide expanded rural job opportunities and improved health, cultural, and social amenities so that more educated men and women will remain in rural areas, adding to total production and having fewer children as their levels of living increase.

In addition to analyzing possible goal conflicts and tradeoffs, policymakers in developing countries, even more so than in developed nations, are faced with severe budgetary constraints. They therefore have to choose among alternative policies in terms of some social benefit–cost framework. Would an extra rupee, bhat, or shilling of expenditure be more effective in lowering fertility if it went toward family-planning programs, nutritional supplementation projects, educational expansion, employment creation, or direct incentive and disincentive schemes? Unfortunately, the problem does not end here, for many *other* goals and objectives of development may take precedence over fertility reduction. Choices always have to be made not only on the basis of fundamental economic concepts such as the principles of economy and optimization but also in terms of explicit value judgments about what is desirable and what the priorities are among alternative goals.

While it might be an important objective in certain densely populated Third World nations, direct attempts to reduce population growth rates—for example, through massive expenditures on sophisticated family-planning programs—need not be a primary development objective. A decrease in population growth is more likely to be the natural consequence of policies directly designed to raise levels of living among the poverty-stricken masses of Asia, Africa, and Latin America. True development will normally motivate people to have fewer children. Well-conceived and well-executed family-planning and other direct population programs can *then* play an important and useful role. But their widespread success can occur *only* within the context of a successful poverty-focused strategy of national and regional development. Not only does this appear to be the consensus opinion of development economists, but it also represents the *unanimous* position of the more than 100 nations that participated in the First World Population Conference in Bucharest when they asserted that "the basis for an effective solution of population problems is, above all, socio-economic transformation."[6]

NOTES

1. A geometric progression is simply a doubling or some other multiple of each previous number, like 1, 2, 4, 8, 16, 32, 64, 128, 256, 512, 1,024, ... etc. Like compound interest, geometric progressions have a way of attaining large numbers very rapidly.

2. At Point f and only at Point f will the marginal utility per last unit of expenditure on goods and children be equal—the condition for utility maximization in the traditional theory of consumer behavior. See, among other texts, P.W. Bell and M.P. Todaro, *Economic Theory* (Nairobi: Oxford University Press, 1969), pp. 41−55.

3. Simon Kuznets, "Fertility differentials between less developed and developed regions: Components and implications," *Discussion Paper No. 217*, Economic Growth Center, Yale University, November 1974, pp. 87−88.

4. See T. Paul Schultz, *Fertility Determinants: A Theory, Evidence and Application to Policy Evaluation* (Santa Monica, Calif.: Rand Corporation, 1974).

5. A valuable review of the population policy experience in a number of Third World countries including Brazil, China, South Korea, Taiwan, and Sri Lanka is found in G. McNicoll and M. Nag, "Population growth: Current issues and strategies," Reading 12 in *The Struggle for Economic Development*.

6. *World Population Plan of Action*, Bucharest, August 1974, paragraph A.I.

CONCEPTS FOR REVIEW

Family-planning programs
Demographic transition
Malthusian population trap
"Macro" population−development
  relationship
Marginal utility
Microeconomic theory of fertility
"Opportunity cost" of a woman's time

Economic incentives and disincentives
  for fertility reduction
Private versus social benefits and costs
  of fertility reduction
Education and fertility relationship
"Investment" in children

QUESTIONS FOR DISCUSSION

1. Describe briefly the theory of the demographic transition. At what stage in this transition do most developing countries seem to be? Explain.

2. How does the so-called microeconomics of fertility relate to the theory of consumer choice? Do you think that economic incentives and disincentives do influence family-size decisions? Explain your answer, giving some specific examples of such incentives and disincentives.

3. "The world population problem is not just a matter of expanding numbers but also one of rising affluence and limited resources. It is as much a problem caused by developed nations as it is one deriving from Third World countries." Comment on this statement.

4. Outline and comment briefly on the various policy options available to Third World governments in their attempt to modify or limit the rate of population growth.

FURTHER READINGS

On the general relationship between population growth and economic development broadly defined see Nancy Birdsall, "Analytical approaches to the relationship of population growth and development," *Population and Development Review* 3, nos. 1 and 2 (March/June 1977), reprinted in my *Struggle for Economic Development* as Reading 13;

Simon Kuznets, "Population trends and modern economic growth: Notes toward an historical perspective," *Discussion Paper No. 191*, Yale Economic Growth Center, November 1973; Simon Kuznets, "Fertility differentials between less developed and developed regions: Components and implications," *Discussion Paper No. 217*, Yale Economic Growth Center, November 1974; Derek T. Healey, *Population Growth and Real Output Growth in Developing Countries: A Survey and Analysis*, University of Adelaide (mimeo), (1974); William Rich, "Smaller families through social and economic progress," *Monograph No. 7*, Overseas Development Council, January 1973; and Léon Tabah (ed.), *Population Growth and Economic Development in the Third World* (Belgium: Ordina, 1976).

On the new microeconomics of fertility, see Harvey Leibenstein, "An interpretation of the economic theory of fertility: Promising path or blind alley?" *Journal of Economic Literature* 12, no. 2 (1974); T. Paul Schultz, "Fertility determinants: A theory, evidence, and an application to policy evaluation," *Rand Corporation Monograph R−106*, January 1974; Richard A. Easterlin, "An economic framework for fertility analysis," *Studies in Family Planning*, Population Council, March 1975; Marc Nerlove, "Household and economy: Toward a new theory of population and economic growth," *Journal of Political Economy* 82, no. 2, Pt 2 (1974); and Susan H. Cochrane, "A review of some microeconomic models of fertility," *Population Studies* 29, no. 3 (1975).

Finally, an excellent comprehensive survey of population policies in developing countries can be found in World Bank, *World Development Report 1984* (New York: Oxford University Press, 1984), Chapters 4 and 8.

Additional readings can be found on pp. 622−623.

8

UNEMPLOYMENT: ISSUES, DIMENSIONS, AND ANALYSES

The cities are filling up and urban unemployment steadily grows . . . the "marginal men," the wretched strugglers for survival on the fringes of farm and city, may already number more than half a billion, by 1990 two billion. Can we imagine any human order surviving with so gross a mass of misery piling up at its base?

Robert McNamara, former President of World Bank

THE EMPLOYMENT PROBLEM: SOME BASIC ISSUES

Historically, the economic development of Western Europe and North America has often been described in terms of the continuous transfer of economic activity and people from rural to urban areas, both within and between countries. As urban industries expanded, new employment opportunities were created; and over the same period, labor-saving technological progress in agriculture reduced rural manpower needs. The combination of these two phenomena made it possible for Western nations to undergo an orderly and effective rural-to-urban transfer of their human resources.

On the basis of this shared experience, many economists concluded that economic development in the Third World, too, necessitated a concentrated effort to promote rapid urban industrial growth. They tended to view cities, therefore, as the "growth centers" and focal points of an expanding economy. Unfortunately, this strategy of rapid industrialization has, in many instances, failed to bring about the desired results predicted by historical experience.

Today, many developing countries are plagued by a historically unique combination of massive rural-to-urban population movements, stagnating agricultural productivity, and growing urban and rural unemployment and

223

underemployment. Substantial unemployment in LDC economies is probably one of the most striking symptoms of their inadequate development. In a wide spectrum of poor countries open unemployment, especially in urban areas, now affects 10–20% of the labor force. The incidence of unemployment is much higher among the young and increasingly more educated in the 15–24 age bracket. Even larger fractions of both urban and rural labor forces are "underemployed" (see Table 8.1 below). They have neither the complementary resources (if they are working full-time) nor the opportunities (if they work only part-time) for increasing their very low incomes to levels comparable with those in modern manufacturing, commerce, and the service sector. Because of its relationship to the problem of Third World poverty, the employment issue occupies a central place in the study of underdevelopment.

But the dimensions of the employment problem go beyond the simple shortage of work opportunities or the underutilization and low productivity of those who work long hours. It also includes the growing divergence between inflated attitudes and job expectations, especially among the educated youth, and the actual jobs available in urban and rural areas. In particular, the growing aversion to manual and agricultural work fostered in urban- and "white-collar"-oriented educational systems creates severe strains for poor societies attempting to accelerate national development.

The employment problem in Third World countries, therefore, has a number of facets that make it historically unique and thus subject to a variety of unconventional economic analyses. There are three major reasons for this:

1. Unemployment and underemployment regularly and chronically affect much larger proportions of LDC labor forces than did unemployment in the industrialized countries, even during the worst years of the Great Depression.
2. Third World employment problems have much more complex causes than employment problems in the developed countries. They therefore require a variety of policy approaches that go far beyond simple Keynesian-type policies to expand aggregate demand.
3. Whatever the dimensions and causes of unemployment in Third World nations, it is associated with human circumstances of abject poverty and low levels of living such as have rarely been experienced in the now developed countries. There is an urgent need for concerted policy action by both the less developed and the more developed nations. As we shall see, the LDCs need to readjust domestic policies to include employment creation as a major social and economic objective, while the developed countries need to review and readjust their traditional economic policies vis-à-vis the Third World, especially in the areas of trade, aid, and technology transfer.

Since it is impossible to do justice to the many complexities and nuances of employment problems in diverse Third World countries, our focus in this and the next chapter will be on two major questions that face almost all LDCs:

1. Why has rapid industrial growth failed in many developing countries to generate substantial new employment opportunities?
2. Why do great numbers of people continue to migrate from diverse rural areas into the crowded and congested cities despite high and rising levels of urban unemployment?

In investigating these two issues, we will see why the urbanization process in less developed countries has differed so markedly from the historical experience of the now developed countries, and why growing unemployment and underemployment are not, as many economists believed, merely self-correcting, "transitory" phenomena present in the early stages of economic growth. We will see why they are, instead, symptoms of more far-reaching economic and social disturbances both within LDCs and in their relationship with developed countries.

Our purpose in this chapter is to examine the dimensions as well as the analytics of the employment problem in developing nations. The chapter begins with a quantitative profile of current and anticipated trends in Third World unemployment. It then focuses on the nature and characteristics of the employment problem and the linkages among unemployment, poverty, and income distribution. Unemployment in its simplest dimension results from a relatively slow growth of labor demand in both the modern, industrial sector and in traditional agriculture combined with a rapidly growing labor supply, especially as a result of accelerated population growth and high levels of rural–urban migration. Demand factors are examined in this chapter in the form of both traditional and contemporary models of employment determination, and the supply factors are analyzed in Chapter 9 where we look at the problem of urban population growth and the economics of both rural–urban and international migration. Chapter 9 then concludes with an analysis of alternative policy approaches to cope with diverse LDC employment problems.

DIMENSIONS OF THIRD WORLD UNEMPLOYMENT: EVIDENCE AND CONCEPTS

First let us look at some of the quantitative and qualitative dimensions of the unemployment problem in developing nations.

Employment and Unemployment: Trends and Projections

During the 1970s, increased interest in the widespread and growing problem of Third World unemployment and underemployment—on the part of individual development economists, national planning authorities, and international assistance agencies alike—led to a much broader and more precise picture of the quantitative dimensions of the problem. In particular, at the beginning of the decade the International Labor Organization (ILO) launched its ambitious World Employment Program with a series of detailed case studies of the employment problem in such diverse countries as Colombia, Kenya, Sri Lanka, Iran, and the Philippines. These and similar studies in other countries documented the seriousness of the existing problem and the likelihood that it would worsen over the coming years.

Table 8.1 provides a summary picture of employment and unemployment trends since 1960 with projections to the year 1990 both for developing countries as a whole and for Africa, Asia, and Latin America. We see first that unemployment grew from approximately 36.5 million in 1960 to over 54 million workers in 1973, an increase of 46%. This averages out to an

Table 8.1 Employment and Unemployment in Developing Countries, 1960–1990 (in thousands)

Indicator	1960	1970	1973	1980	1990
All developing countries[*]					
Employment[†]	507,416	617,244	658,000	773,110	991,600
Unemployment	36,466	48,798	54,130	65,620	88,693
Unemployment rate (%)	6.7	7.4	7.6	7.8	8.2
Combined unemployment and underemployment rate (%)[‡]	25	27	29		
Africa	31	39	38		
Asia	24	26	28		
Latin America	18	20	25		
All Africa					
Employment[†]	100,412	119,633	127,490	149,390	191,180
Unemployment	8,416	12,831	13,890	15,973	21,105
Unemployment rate (%)	7.7	9.6	9.8	9.8	9.9
All Asia[*]					
Employment[†]	340,211	413,991	441,330	516,800	660,300
Unemployment	24,792	31,440	34,420	43,029	59,485
Unemployment rate (%)	6.8	7.1	7.2	7.7	8.3
All Latin America					
Employment[†]	66,793	83,620	89,180	106,920	140,120
Unemployment	3,258	4,527	5,820	6,618	8,103
Unemployment (%)	4.7	5.1	6.1	5.8	5.5

[*] Excluding China.
[†] Including underemployment.
[‡] Not calculated for 1980 and 1990.

SOURCE: Yves Sabolo, "Employment and unemployment, 1960–90," *International Labor Review* 112, no. 6 (1975), Table 3 and Appendix.

annual rate of increase of 3%, which is higher than the annual rate of employment growth during this same period. Thus, in the developing world as a whole unemployment was growing faster than employment.

When we also consider that the "underemployed" in 1973 comprised approximately an additional 250 million people, then the combined unemployment and underemployment rate reaches a staggering 29% for all developing countries, with Africa experiencing a labor underutilization rate of 38%. Moreover, with rapid labor force growth (see below), the marginal unemployment rate (i.e., the proportion of new labor force entrants unable to find regular jobs) is likely to be even higher than the average figures shown in Table 8.1. Although the extent of labor underutilization is lower in Asia and Latin America than in Africa, the quantitative and qualitative dimensions of the problem are just as serious. For example, even though Asia may have a lower rate of unemployment than Africa, the absolute numbers involved are many times larger (34.4 million in 1973 compared with 13.9 million for Africa).

Projections to 1990 indicate that the rate of Third World unemployment will rise steadily and that the total numbers unemployed will reach almost 90 million. Adding projections for the underemployed could give a figure as high as 600 million workers in the mid-1980s who are either unemployed, employed part-time, or whose productivity is very low. Although these figures are only rough estimates, they do strikingly underline the seriousness of the problem.

Labor Force: Present and Projected

The number of people searching for work in a less developed country depends primarily on the size and age composition of its population. Among the numerous processes relating trends in overall population growth to the growth of indigenous labor forces, two are of particular interest. First, whatever the overall magnitude of the population growth rate, its fertility and mortality components have a separate significance. A 3% (or 30 per 1,000) natural growth rate has different labor force implications when crude birth and death rates are, say, 50 and 20 as opposed to 40 and 10. This is because the *age structure* of the population will be different for a high birth and death rate economy than for a low birth and death rate one, even though the natural rate of increase is the same for both. Since birthrates obviously affect only the numbers of newly born while death rates affect (although unevenly) all age groups, a high birth and death rate economy will have a greater percentage of the total population in the dependent age group (i.e., 1–15 years) than will a low birth and death rate economy. The rapid reductions in death rates recently experienced by most LDCs, therefore, have expanded the size of their present labor forces, while continuous high birthrates create high present dependency ratios and rapidly expanding future labor forces.

Second, the impact of fertility decline on labor force size and age structures operates only with very long lags, even when the decline is rapid. The reason is the phenomenon of population momentum described in Chapter 6. For example, a 50% fall in LDC fertility rates by 1985 will reduce the male labor force by only 13% by the year 2000, a reduction from about 1.27 to 1.11 billion workers. This is certainly not a trivial reduction, and its long-run impact would clearly be substantial. Nevertheless, the essential fact remains that those who will enter the labor force over the next 15 years have *already been born* and the size of the labor force two decades hence is largely determined by current fertility rates.

Present labor force projections suggest annual increases on the order of 2.2% for all less developed regions during the present decade and approximately 2.1% for the 1990s (see Table 8.2). Within the Third World, Latin American countries are likely to experience the greatest rates of labor force growth over the next 25 years. But in terms of actual numbers, which demonstrate the prospective magnitude of the LDC employment problem more dramatically than percentage rates of growth, reasonable projections for the year 2000 indicate that there will be over 920 million more job seekers

Table 8.2   Growth of the Labor Force, 1960–2000

	Average annual percentage growth rate			
	1960–1970	*1970–1980*	*1980–1990*	*1990–2000*
Developing countries	1.8	2.2	2.2	2.1
Developed countries	1.2	1.2	0.7	0.5
Asia and Pacific	2.4	2.6	2.3	2.0
Latin America	2.4	2.7	3.0	2.7
Middle East and North Africa	1.9	2.6	2.9	2.2
Sub-Saharan Africa	2.2	2.2	2.5	2.6

SOURCE: *World Development Report 1979*, Table 27. Reprinted by permission of Oxford University Press.

than in 1970 with nearly 50% of these concentrated in South Asia and 25% in East Asia (Table 8.3).

Labor Underutilization: Some Definitional Distinctions

To get a full understanding of the significance of the employment problem, we must take into account, in addition to the openly unemployed, those larger numbers of workers who may be visibly active but in an economic sense are grossly underutilized. As Professor Edgar O. Edwards has correctly pointed out in his comprehensive survey of employment problems in developing countries:

> *In addition to the numbers of people unemployed, many of whom may receive minimal incomes through the extended family system, it is also necessary to consider the dimensions of (1) time (many of those employed would like to work more hours per day, per week or per year), (2) intensity of work (which brings in considerations of health and nutrition), and (3) productivity (lack of which can often be attributed to inadequate comple-*

Table 8.3   Labor Force Projections, 1970–2000

	Labor force in millions (and percentage of total)			
	1970	*1980*	*1990*	*2000*
Developed countries	498.3 (33)	554.7 (30)	593 (28)	649 (25)
Less developed countries	1013.5 (67)	2180.9 (70)	1547 (72)	1933 (75)
Regions				
South Asia	430.1 (43)	549.0 (43)	691 (45)	886 (46)
East Asia	379.6 (37)	467.3 (37)	519 (33)	602 (31)
Africa	125.8 (12)	160.3 (12)	212 (14)	277 (14)
Latin America	76.2 (8)	102.0 (8)	129 (8)	172 (8)

SOURCE: Based on data from International Labor Office, Statistical Branch, as reported in ODC *Agenda 1979*, Table A-13.

mentary resources with which to work). Even these are only the most obvious dimensions of effective work, and factors such as motivation, attitudes, and cultural inhibitions (as against women, for example) must also be considered.[1]

Edwards, therefore, distinguishes among the following five forms of underutilization of labor:

1. *Open unemployment:* both voluntary (people who exclude from consideration some jobs for which they could qualify, implying some means of support other than employment) and involuntary.
2. *Underemployment:* those working less (daily, weekly, or seasonally) than they would like to work.
3. *The visibly active but underutilized:* those who would not normally be classified as either unemployed or underemployed by the above definitions, but who in fact have found alternative means of "marking time," including,

   a. *Disguised underemployment.* Many people seem occupied on farms or employed in government on a full-time basis even though the services they render may actually require much less than full time. Social pressures on private industry may result also in substantial amounts of disguised underemployment. If available work is openly shared among those employed, the disguise disappears and underemployment becomes explicit.

   b. *Hidden unemployment.* Those who are engaged in "second choice" nonemployment activities, perhaps notably education and household chores, primarily because job opportunities are not available (i) at the levels of education already attained or (ii) for women, given social mores. Thus, educational institutions and households become "employers of last resort." Moreover, many of those enrolled for further education may be among the less able as indicated by their inability to compete successfully for jobs before pursuing further education.

   c. *Premature retirement.* This phenomenon is especially evident, and apparently growing, in the civil service. In many countries, retirement ages are falling at the same time that longevity is increasing, primarily as a means of creating promotion opportunities for some of the large numbers pressing up from below.
4. *The impaired:* those who may work full-time but whose intensity of effort is seriously impaired through malnutrition or lack of common preventive medicine.
5. *The unproductive:* those who can provide the human resources necessary for productive work but who struggle long hours with inadequate complementary resources to make their inputs yield even the essentials of life.[2]

Although all the above manifestations of the underutilization of labor in LDCs are highly interrelated and each in its own way is of considerable significance, we shall for convenience limit our discussion throughout the remainder of this chapter to the specific problems of unemployment and underemployment.

Linkages among Unemployment, Poverty, and Income Distribution

There is a close relationship between high levels of unemployment and underemployment, widespread poverty, and unequal distributions of income. For the most part, those without regular employment or with only scattered part-time employment are also among the very poor. Those with regular paid employment in the public and private sector are typically among the middle- to upper-income groups. But it would be wrong to assume that everyone who does not have a job is necessarily poor or that all those who work full-time are relatively well off. There may be unemployed urban workers who are "voluntarily" unemployed in the sense that they are searching for a very specific kind of job, perhaps because of high expectations based on their presumed educational or skill qualifications. They refuse to accept jobs they feel to be inferior and are able to do this because they have outside sources of financial support (e.g., relatives, friends, or local money lenders). Such people are unemployed by definition, but they may not be poor. By the same token, many individuals may work full-time in terms of hours per day but may nevertheless earn every little income. Many self-employed workers in the so-called urban "informal" sector (e.g., traders, hawkers, petty service providers, workers in repair shops) may be so classified. Such people are by definition fully employed, but often they are still very poor (see Appendix 9.2).

In spite of the above reservations about a too literal linkage between unemployment and poverty, it still remains true that one of the major mechanisms for reducing poverty and inequality in less developed nations is the provision of adequate paying, productive employment opportunities for the very poor. As we have seen in Chapter 5, the creation of more employment opportunities should not be regarded as the sole solution to the poverty problem. More far-reaching economic and social measures are needed. But the provision of more work and the wider sharing of the work that is available would certainly go a long way toward solving the problem. Employment, therefore, must be an essential ingredient in any poverty-focused development strategy.

The Lag between Industrial Output and Employment Growth: The Misplaced Emphasis of the 1950s and 1960s

During the 1950s and 1960s one of the major doctrines of the development literature was that successful economic development could be realized only through the twin forces of substantial capital accumulation and rapid industrial growth. By concentrating their efforts on the development of a modern industrial sector to serve the domestic market and to facilitate the absorption of "redundant" or "surplus" rural laborers in the urban economy, less developed countries, it was argued, could proceed most rapidly toward the achievement of considerable economic self-sufficiency. As we will discover in Chapter 9, an inevitable consequence of this emphasis has been the extraordinary growth of urban centers resulting from an accelerated influx of rural, unskilled workers in search of urban jobs.

Unfortunately, optimistic predictions regarding the ability of the modern industrial sector to absorb these migrants have not been realized. In fact, the failure of modern urban industries to generate a significant number of employment opportunities is one of the most obvious failures of the development process over the past two decades. For example, as Table 8.4 shows, for many developing countries the growth of manufacturing output, even during the rapid growth years of the 1960s, exceeded the growth of employment by a factor of 3 or 4 to 1.

Too much emphasis, however, cannot be placed on the expansion of the modern industrial sector to solve the unemployment problem. The reason is that in most Third World countries it employs only 10–20% of the total labor force. For example, if the manufacturing sector employs, say, 20% of the country's labor force, it would need to increase employment by 15% per year just to absorb the increase in a total work force growing at 3% per year (i.e., $0.2 \times 0.15 = 0.03$). None of the countries in Table 8.4 has been able to achieve such a high rate of employment growth in its manufacturing sectors. In fact, such industrial employment growth is virtually impossible to achieve in any economy.

Again the contrast between the present urban situation in LDCs and the historical situation in the now more developed countries is worth noting. In nineteenth-century Western Europe, the pace of industrialization was much faster than that of urbanization. The percentage of the working force in industry was always higher than that of the population living in cities. For example, in France in 1856 only 10% of the total population lived in cities of 20,000 inhabitants and over, while 20% of the working force was engaged in manufacturing. In Germany in 1870 the corresponding figures were 12 and 30% respectively. Since the labor forces of both France and Germany were growing at no more than 1% per annum over this period, the manufacturing sector needed to grow at a rate of only 3.3% to absorb the *total* yearly labor force increases.

Table 8.4 Industrialization and Employment in
Developing Countries, 1963–1969

Region/countries	Manufacturing annual output growth	Manufacturing employment growth
Africa		
Ethiopia	12.8	6.4
Kenya	6.4	4.3
Nigeria	14.1	5.3
Egypt (UAR)	11.2	0.7
Asia		
India	5.9	5.3
Pakistan	12.3	2.6
Philippines	6.1	4.8
Thailand	10.7	−12.0
Latin America		
Brazil	6.5	1.1
Colombia	5.9	2.8
Costa Rica	8.9	2.8
Dominican Republic	1.7	−3.3
Ecuador	11.4	6.0
Panama	12.9	7.4

SOURCE: David Morawetz, "Employment implications of industrialization in developing countries," *Economic Journal* 84 (September 1974). Reprinted by permission of Cambridge University Press.

By contrast, the pace of industrialization in less developed countries has been much slower than that of urbanization. In almost all Third World countries the percentage of populations living in cities greatly *exceeds* the proportion engaged in manufacturing. For example, in 1980 Brazil had over 52% of its population living in urban areas of 500,000 or more, while only 20% were engaged in manufacturing. Colombia had an urbanization rate of almost 51% with only 17% engaged in manufacturing. Given these very different demographic and structural economic circumstances, it would be totally unrealistic to rely solely on accelerated modern sector industrial growth to solve the problems of growing unemployment, even if such growth were to have a substantial labor-using bias, which it usually doesn't.

ECONOMIC MODELS OF EMPLOYMENT DETERMINATION

Over the years economists have formulated a number of economic models of employment determination. The majority of these models have focused on or been derived from the social, economic, and institutional circumstances of the developed nations. They have, nevertheless, often been uncritically and inappropriately applied to the unique circumstances of employment problems in developing countries. In recent years, the use of more relevant and realistic models of employment and development has often led to policy conclusions diametrically opposite to those of the traditional theories.

In this section we review four major economic models of employment determination. The first two, the classical and Keynesian models, form the substance of the traditional theory of employment. Neither has much relevance for understanding the particular employment problems of developing countries. The third and fourth models, like the Keynesian model, grew out of the more recent neoclassical tradition of economics. The first, the output–employment macro model, focuses on the relationship between capital accumulation, industrial output growth, and employment generation; the second, the price-incentive micro model, considers the impact of distorted factor prices on resource (especially labor) utilization. Both the output–employment and price-incentive models, again like the Keynesian model, concentrate exclusively on the demand side of the employment equation: they focus on policies to increase labor demand. A fifth model or group of models, which we designate as "two-sector labor transfer" or "rural–urban migration" models, focus on the determinants of both demand and supply. These will be the subject of Chapter 9. Even more than neoclassical equilibrium models (although still in the same tradition), the disequilibrium labor-transfer migration models seek to take purposeful account of the institutional and economic realities of Third World nations.

We conclude this chapter, therefore, by examining the first four of the above five models of employment determination and then devote some considerable space in the next chapter to the fifth.

The Traditional Competitive Free Market Model

Flexible Wages and Full Employment

In traditional Western economics characterized by consumer sovereignty, individual utility and profit maximization, perfect competition, and economic efficiency with very many "atomistic" producers and consumers, none of whom is large enough to influence prices or wages, the level of employment and the "wage rate" are determined simultaneously with all other prices and factor uses in the economy by the forces of demand and supply. Producers demand more workers as long as the value of the marginal product produced by an additional worker (i.e., his physical marginal product multiplied by the market price of the product he produces) exceeds his cost (i.e., the going wage rate). Since the law of diminishing marginal product is assumed to apply and since product prices are fixed by the market, the value of labor's marginal product and thus the demand curve for labor will be negatively sloped as shown in Figure 8.1. More workers will be hired only at successively lower wage rates.

On the supply side, individuals are assumed to operate on the principle of utility maximization. They will therefore divide their time between work and leisure in accordance with the relative marginal utility of each. A rise in wage rates is equivalent to an increase in the price (or opportunity cost) of leisure. When the price of any item rises, in general its quantity demanded will decrease and other items will be substituted. It follows that more labor services will be supplied at successively higher wage rates, so that the aggregate supply curve of labor will be positively sloped. This supply curve is also depicted in Figure 8.1.

We see from Figure 8.1 that only at one point, the "equilibrium" wage rate W_e, will the amount of work that individuals are *willing* to supply just equal the amount that employers will demand. At any higher wage, like W_2, the supply of labor will exceed its demand and competitive pressures among workers will force the wage rate down to W_e. At any lower price, like W_1, the

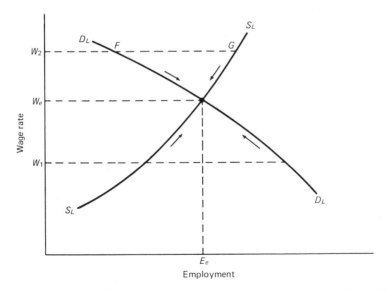

Figure 8.1. Wage and employment determination by demand and supply: The traditional approach.

labor quantity demanded will exceed the quantity supplied and competition among producers will drive the wage rate up until it reaches its equilibrium level at W_e. At W_e total employment will be E_e on the horizontal axis. *By definition, this will be full employment*—that is, at the equilibrium wage and only at this wage will all those willing to work be able to obtain jobs so that there is no involuntary unemployment. In other words, in the idealized flexible wages world of traditional equilibrium economics, there can never be unemployment!

Limitations of the Competitive Model for Developing Countries

The traditional competitive model offers little insight into the realities of wage and employment determination of Third World countries. Wage rates are typically not flexible downward since they are largely determined by "institutional" forces including trade union pressures, legislated government salary scales, and multinational corporation hiring practices. There are many more laborers seeking employment at the going wage than there are jobs available. Involuntary unemployment (and, especially, underemployment) is pervasive. For example, if the wage were institutionally set at W_2 in Figure 8.1, there would be an *excess* supply of labor equal to Line *FG*. The automatic adjustment mechanism of the market would not work to push wages down to W_e—the equilibrium or "shadow" wage. But, as we show below and in later chapters, this concept of the "shadow price" for a factor of production such as labor, even though it may differ from actual factor prices, still has important analytical meaning for development policy. The classical model, therefore, is useful to the extent that it gives comparative baselines for examining price distortions that can cause unemployment in developing countries.[3]

The Keynesian Model

Insufficient Demand and the Employment Gap: The Simple Model

The 1930s ushered in a Great Depression in the Western world, the like of which had not been experienced by the developed countries during their entire modern growth era. Widespread and seemingly chronic unemployment and low levels of national output shook economists out of the complacency of their idealized classical world. Clearly, there was something very inadequate about the traditional theory of wage and employment determination.

Two major theoretical responses emerged to explain what apparently was going on. At the micro level, the theory of "imperfect competition" associated with Professors Joan Robinson of England and Edward H. Chamberlain of the United States was developed to explain the nature and implications of markets dominated by one (monopoly) or a few sellers of products (oligopoly) or by one or more purchasers of resources (monopsony and oligopsony). In each of these cases of imperfect competition, it was demonstrated, resources (including labor) would be underutilized and total production would be less than what would occur if product and resource markets were characterized by perfect competition. Such "market failures" often provided the theoretical justification and economic rationale for increased government intervention in the economic system to offset the negative output and employment effects of monopoly and other forms of concentrated selling power. In Chapter 15 we discuss in more detail the market failure argument, among others, as a basis for development planning in Third World nations.

The other and by far the more influential theory that emerged in response to the harsh economic realities of the Great Depression was macro oriented. This is the famous Keynesian general theory of income and employment determination. What may have appeared to be a "general" theory of employment at the time, however, has now been recognized, especially in the less developed countries, as a "special" theory of unemployment for the developed countries.[4] Let us briefly review the simple Keynesian model to see why this is so.

Basically, Keynesian theory explains the determination of national output and employment in terms of the level of "aggregate demand" in relation to an economy's "potential output"—what it could produce if resources were fully and efficiently utilized given the prevailing technology. In its simplest form aggregate demand for a "closed" economy consists of three fundamental components: (a) the total demand for all goods and services by private consumers (C for consumption); (b) the total demand for investment goods by private industry (I for investment); and (c) the demand for goods and services, both consumption and investment, by the government (G for government). The level of national income or GNP (Y) is then defined as national income (Y) = consumption (C) + investment (I) + government expenditure (G), or simply

$$Y = C + I + G \qquad (1)$$

For an "open" economy with foreign trade, one would need to add expressions for exports (X) and imports (M), the difference constituting either a "surplus" balance of trade (i.e., $X - M > 0$) and thus an additional positive component of aggregate demand, or a "deficit" trade balance ($X - M < 0$), which would lower national income. Thus, for an open economy, Equation (1) would be rewritten as

$$Y = C + I + G + (X - M) \qquad (2)$$

For illustrative purposes, however, let's use only Equation (1). National income and/or expenditure (Y) is determined by the level of aggregate demand (i.e., $C + I + G$). This level of national output is assumed to be uniquely associated with a level of national employment (N) as expressed, for example, in a national production function, $Y = f(N, \bar{K}, t)$ where $f'_N > 0$ and $f''_N < 0$. For any given technology (t) and stock of fixed land and capital ($\bar{K}$), total national output (real GNP) will be uniquely and positively associated with a different level of employment; that is, higher levels of national output (Y) are associated with higher levels of employment (N). But since for any given society total employment is limited by the size of the active labor force, there will be some unique level of *maximum national output* that can be achieved only at full employment. This full-employment level of national income, sometimes called "potential output," may be denoted Y_F.

The main thrust of Keynesian theory, and the factor that distinguished it from the classical model, was the contention that nothing inherent in a market economy would guarantee that the actual level of national income (Y) would be exactly equal to the potential full-employment level (Y_F). Everything depends on the level of total aggregate demand ($C + I + G$). This is shown in Figure 8.2. In Diagram (a) the combined sums of C plus I plus G yield a level of national output (Y_1) that is *less* than the potential full-employment output level (Y_F). As a result, the level of unemployment will be given by the "gap" between N_F and N_1 in the aggregate production function of Diagram (b). It follows, therefore, that if consumption and investment are already determined by the existing level of national income, the only way that aggregate demand can be increased is for the government to increase its level of total expenditure from G to G'. Government "deficit" expenditure thus becomes necessary to fill in the gap between actual and

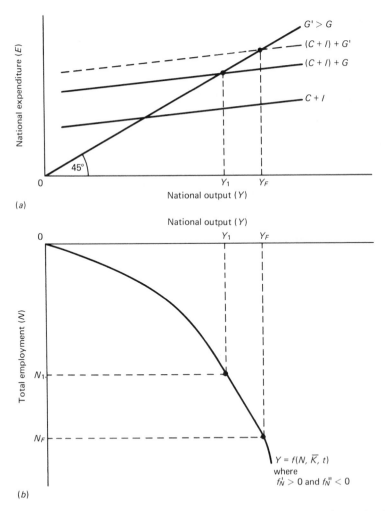

Figure 8.2. The simple Keynesian model of employment determination.

potential GNP so as to increase the level of national output and consequently eliminate unemployment.

The Keynesian prescription for reducing or eradicating unemployment is therefore quite simple: increase aggregate total demand through direct increases in government expenditure or by government policies that indirectly encourage more private investment (e.g., low interest rates on business loans, tax allowances, investment subsidies). As long as there is unemployment and excess capacity in the economy, the supply of goods and services will respond automatically to this higher demand. A new equilibrium will be established with more income and higher levels of employment.

Limitations of the Model in the Development Context

Without enumerating all the shortcomings of the Keynesian model as applied to the economics of Third World nations, we must draw attention to two of its major deficiencies in this respect. First, since the model is derived from advanced country economies, it is implicitly based on the institutional and structural assumption of well-functioning product, factor, and money markets, which are characteristic of these countries. Specifically, it is based on the assumption, correct for developed nations but not for LDCs, that firms and farms can respond quickly and effectively to increases in the demand for their products by rapidly expanding output and employment. But in most Third World countries, the major bottleneck to higher output and employment levels typically is not insufficient demand but structural and institutional constraints on the supply side. Shortages of capital, raw materials, intermediate products, skilled and managerial human resources, combined with poorly functioning and inefficiently organized commodity and loan markets, poor transport and communications, shortages of foreign exchange, and import-dominated consumption patterns among the rich—all of these, and many other structural and institutional factors, militate against the simple notion that expanded government and private demand will be effective measures to solve employment (and poverty) problems in most Third World countries. In fact, under conditions of severe constraints on the supply side (i.e., where the aggregate supply curve of national output is price inelastic), expanding aggregate demand through deficit-financed government expenditure may merely result in higher prices and chronic inflation. This was the common experience of many Latin American countries during the 1950s and 1960s and again in the 1980s. The worldwide inflation of the 1970s can also be attributed largely to supply constraints, especially in the areas of raw materials, energy resources, and food products.

The second major limitation of the Keynesian model for most LDCs also relates to conditions of supply in developing countries, this time to the supply of labor to the urban industrial sector. As we show in Chapter 9 when we discuss the economics of rural–urban migration, the creation of additional modern sector urban jobs through increased aggregate demand is likely to attract many additional migrants from rural areas. Since urban wages are typically much higher than average rural incomes, every urban job created may induce three or four new job seekers to migrate from the countryside. The net result may be that the creation of additional urban jobs through traditional Keynesian demand-oriented policies designed to reduce unemployment in fact causes urban unemployment to rise. Moreover, since many rural migrants were productive farmers or low-paid farm workers, *the overall level of national employment and output may be reduced by Keynesian policies designed to increase employment and output!*

We may conclude that for many reasons, but especially because of structural and institutional supply constraints and the phenomenon of induced rural–urban migration, the Keynesian macro model of employment determination has limited analytical relevance for understanding and dealing with employment problems in developing nations.

Output and Employment Growth: Conflict or Congruence?

Growth Models and Employment Levels: The Conflict Argument

A natural extension of the Keynesian model that dominated many theories of development in the 1950s and 1960s (and was evident again in the "supply side" environment of the early 1980s) focused on policies to increase the levels of national output rapidly through accelerated capital formation. Since the "static" Keynesian model associated levels of employment uniquely with levels of GNP, it followed that by maximizing the rate of growth of GNP, Third World countries could also maximize their rate of labor absorption. The principal theoretical tool used to describe the growth process was the simple Harrod–Domar model described in Chapter 3. Although many sophisticated variants of this model appeared later, the basic idea remained the same. Economic growth is explained as the combined result of the rate of saving and the resultant physical capital accumulation on the one hand and the capital–output ratio (i.e., the physical productivity of new investment) on the other. For a given aggregate capital–output ratio, therefore, the rate of national output and employment growth could be maximized by maximizing the rate of saving and investment. A natural and inevitable outgrowth of this neo-Keynesian view was the emphasis on generating domestic savings and foreign exchange to make possible heavy capital investments in the growing industrial sector. The "big push" for rapid industrialization thus became the code word for development and growth.

But as we saw in Table 8.4, in spite of relatively impressive rates of industrial output growth in many less developed countries, the rate of employment growth has lagged significantly behind. In a number of cases it has even stagnated. Why has rapid industrial output growth failed to generate correspondingly rapid rates of employment growth?

Basically, the answer lies in the growth in labor productivity. By definition, the rate of growth in output (Q) minus the rate of growth in labor productivity (Q/N) approximately equals the rate of growth of employment (N), that is,

$$\frac{dQ}{Q} - \frac{d(Q/N)}{Q/N} = \frac{dN}{N}$$

It follows that if output is growing at 8% per year while employment is expanding by only 3%, the difference is due to the rise in labor productivity.

The original Harrod–Domar model did not specifically incorporate technological change (although later modifications did). It was a "fixed coefficient" model (i.e., it assumed a fixed relationship between changes in output levels and changes in the capital stock). This constant capital–output ratio was then paralleled in early versions of the model by a constant output–labor ratio (i.e., a fixed labor coefficient). It follows from this constant labor productivity assumption that a 10% increase in national output (GNP) will always be accompanied by a 10% increase in employment. In reality, if labor productivity is rising, so that fewer workers are required to produce any given level of total output, a 10% output growth may only result in, say, a 3% increase in employment.

The phenomenon of rising labor productivity associated with higher capital–labor ratios can be explained better (at least, theoretically better) with the aid of a variable proportions neoclassical growth model like the one described in Appendix 5.1. Recall that this model of savings, capital accumulation, and economic development—the latter term defined simply as maximum output growth—purports to demonstrate that higher capital–labor ratios (i.e., more capital-intensive production methods) will generate larger profit shares, higher savings rates, and thus higher rates of growth. The "optimal" savings rate—that is, the one which leads to maximum output growth—can be generated only by relatively capital-intensive methods of production. Maximum output and maximum employment growth are, therefore, seen as conflicting objectives.

Growth and Employment: The Congruence Argument

In general, increases in labor productivity are desirable. But what is really desirable are increases in total factor productivity: output per unit of *all* resources. The productivity of labor can increase for a variety of reasons, some good and some not so good. Improved education, better training, and better management are all desirable reasons for increased productivity. But increases as a result of the substitution of capital for labor in production processes or as a result of the importation of sophisticated and expensive labor-saving machinery and equipment (e.g., tractors, power tools, fully automated textile machinery, heavy construction equipment) may be less satisfactory in heavily populated nations. Not only can such capital accumulation waste valuable domestic financial resources and foreign exchange, but it can also curtail the growth of new employment opportunities. Moreover, the importation of inappropriate and expensive labor-saving capital equipment may in fact *reduce* total factor productivity and thereby *increase* average costs of production even though it increases labor productivity. In other words, even though average labor costs fall, the average total costs of production may rise because of the underutilized productive capacity that often results when expensive mechanical equipment designed for large-scale production in developed countries is imported into less developed countries where the local market is too small for its efficient utilization.

Our conclusion, therefore, is that typical Harrod–Domar and neoclassical models of capital accumulation and economic growth, and the kinds of economic policies they imply, can and often do lead to rapid output growth but with lagging employment creation. If the overriding development objective is to maximize the rate of GNP growth, these approaches may be the right ones. But if it is equally or more important to create jobs, then different policies (e.g., focusing on the promotion of labor-intensive industries such as small-scale agriculture and manufacturing) may be better.

Moreover, it is far from self-evident that higher levels of employment must necessarily be achieved *at the expense of* output growth. Just as there is now widespread disagreement with the conventional wisdom of the 1950s and 1960s which assumed that income growth and more equitable distributions of income were mutually exclusive objectives, so too many economists have now come around to the view that an employment-oriented (and therefore, indirectly, a poverty-oriented) development strategy is likely also to be one which *accelerates* rather than retards overall economic progress.[5] This is especially true with regard to the growth and development of the rural and small-scale urban sectors. More employment means more income for the poor, which in turn implies a greater demand for locally produced basic consumption goods. Since these products tend to be more labor intensive than many of those produced by large-scale industry, both domestic and foreign, it follows that more jobs and higher incomes can become self-reinforcing phenomena. They ultimately lead to higher growth rates of both national output and aggregate employment. But in order to achieve this dual objective, a complementary policy of removing factor-price distortions and promoting labor-intensive technologies of production may be required. This leads us to the fourth model of employment determination.

Appropriate Technology and Employment Generation: The Price-Incentive Model

Choice of Techniques: An Illustration

We briefly discussed the question of factor-price distortions and their impact on poverty and employment in Chapter 5 and at other points in earlier chapters. However, since the neoclassical price-incentive school of thought has occupied such a prominent place in the debate about employment problems in developing countries, it is important to reintroduce it here.

The basic proposition of the price-incentive model is quite simple and in the best tradition of the neoclassical theory of the firm. Following the principle of economy, producers (firms and farms) are assumed to face a given set of relative factor prices (e.g., of capital and labor) and to utilize that combination of capital and labor which minimizes the cost of producing a desired level of output. They are further assumed to be capable of producing that output with a variety of technological production processes, ranging from highly labor-intensive to highly capital-intensive methods. Thus, if the price of capital is very expensive relative to the price of labor, a relatively labor-intensive process will be chosen. On the other hand, if labor is relatively expensive, our economizing firm or farm will utilize a more capital-intensive method of production—that is, it will economize on the use of the expensive factor, which in this case is labor.

The conventional economics of technical choice is portrayed in Figure 8.3. Assume that the firm, farm, industry, or economy in question has only two techniques of production from which to choose: technique or

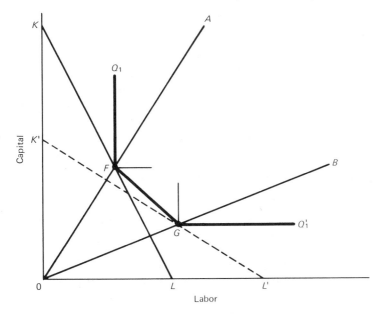

Figure 8.3. Choice of techniques: The price-incentive model.

process $0A$, which requires larger inputs of (homogeneous) capital relative to (homogeneous) labor; and technique or process $0B$, which is relatively labor intensive. Points F and G represent *unit* output levels for each process, and the line $Q_1FGQ'_1$ connecting F and G is therefore a unit-output iso-quant. (Note that in the traditional neoclassical model, an infinite number of such techniques or processes are assumed to exist so that the isoquant takes on its typical convex curvature, as for example in Figure 4.5.)

According to this theory, optimum (least cost) capital–labor combina-tions (i.e., efficient or "appropriate" technologies) are determined by rela-tive factor prices. Assume for the moment that market prices of capital and labor reflect their scarcity or "shadow" values and that the desired output level is Q_1 in Figure 8.3. If capital is cheap relative to labor (Price Line KL), production will occur at Point F using capital-intensive process $0A$. Alternatively, if the market prices of labor and capital are such that labor is the relatively cheap (abundant) factor (Line $K'L'$), optimal production will occur at Point G with the labor-intensive technique, $0B$, chosen. It follows that for any technique of production currently in use, a fall in the relative price of labor, *ceteris paribus*, will lead to a substitution of labor for capital in an optimal production strategy. (Note that if capital-intensive process $0A$ "dominates" labor-intensive process $0B$—that is, if technology $0A$ requires less labor *and* less capital than $0B$ *for all levels of output*—then for any factor price ratio, the capital-intensive technique will be chosen.[6] See below for further discussion.)

Factor-Price Distortions and Appropriate Technology

Given that most Third World countries are endowed with abundant sup-plies of labor but possess very little capital, either financial or physical, one would naturally expect production methods to be relatively labor intensive. But, in fact, one often finds production techniques in both agriculture and industry to be heavily mechanized and capital intensive. Large tractors and combines dot the rural landscape of Asia, Africa, and Latin America while people stand idly by. Gleaming new factories with the most modern and sophisticated automated machinery and equipment are a common feature of urban industries while idle workers congregate outside the factory gates. Surely, this phenomenon could not be the result of a lesser degree of economic rationality on the part of Third World farmers and manufacturers.

The explanation, according to the price-incentive school, is simple. Because of a variety of structural, institutional, and political factors, the actual market price of labor is higher and that of capital lower than their respective true scarcity, or shadow, values would dictate. In Figure 8.3 the shadow price ratio would be given by Line $K'L'$ whereas the actual (distorted) market price ratio is shown by Line KL. Market wage structures are relatively high because of trade union pressure, politically motivated minimum wage laws, an increasing range of employee fringe benefits, and the high-wage policies of multinational corporations. In former colonial nations high-wage structures are often relics of expatriate remuneration scales based on European levels of living and "hardship" premiums. On the other hand, the price of (scarce) capital is kept artificially low by a combination of liberal capital depreciation allowances, low or even negative real interest rates, low or negative effective rates of protection (see Chapter 13) on capital good imports, tax rebates, overvalued foreign exchange rates (see Chapter 13), etc.

The net result of these distorted factor prices is the encouragement of inappropriate capital-intensive methods of production in both agriculture and manufacturing. Note that from the private cost-minimizing viewpoint of individual firms and farms, the choice of a capital-intensive technique is correct. It is their rational response to the existing structure of price signals in the market for factors of production. However, from the viewpoint of society as a whole, the social cost of underutilized capital and, especially, labor can be very substantial. Government policies designed to "get the prices right"—that is, to remove factor-price distortions—would contribute not only to more employment but also to a better overall utilization of scarce capital resources through the adoption of more appropriate technologies of production.[7]

The Possibilities of Labor–Capital Substitution

The actual employment impact of removing factor-price distortions will depend, however, on the degree to which labor can be substituted for capital in the production processes of various Third World industries. Economists refer to this as the "elasticity of substitution" and define it roughly as the ratio of the percentage change in the proportion of labor used relative to capital (i.e., the labor–capital or L/K ratio) compared to a given percentage change in the price of capital relative to labor (i.e., P_k/P_L). Algebraically, the elasticity of substitution can be defined as

$$\eta_{LK} = -d\left(\frac{L}{K}\right) \Big/ \frac{L}{K} \div d\left(\frac{P_K}{P_L}\right) \Big/ \frac{P_K}{P_L}$$

For example, if the relative price of capital rises by 1% in the manufacturing sector and the labor–capital ratio rises as a result by, say, 1.5%, the elasticity of substitution in the manufacturing industry will be equal to 1.5. If P_k/P_L falls by, say, 10% while L/K falls by only 6%, then the elasticity of substitution for that industry would be 0.6. Relatively high elasticities of substitution (e.g., ratios greater than, say, 0.7) are indicative that factor-price adjustments can have a substantial impact on levels and combinations of factor utilization. In such cases, factor-price modifications may be an important means of generating more employment opportunities.

In general, most empirical studies of the elasticity of substitution for manufacturing industries in less developed countries reveal coefficients in the range of 0.5–1.0.[8] These results indicate that a relative reduction in wages (either directly or by holding wages constant while letting the price of capital rise) of, say, 10% will lead to a 5–10% increase in employment. But, given the fact that the organized wage and manufacturing sector in most LDCs employs only a small proportion of the total labor force, the *total* impact of even a 10% increase in industrial employment will not be sufficient to solve the employment problem. It can, however, make a contribution to the ultimate solution. Policies to eliminate factor-price distortions, therefore, do have an important role to play in any overall employment-oriented development strategy.

NOTES

1. Edgar O. Edwards, *Employment in Developing Countries: Report on a Ford Foundation Study* (New York: Columbia University Press, 1974), p. 10.
2. *Ibid.*, pp. 10–11.
3. There are many who would also argue that this flexible wages model provides a useful depiction of LDC labor market interactions in small-scale industry (the so-called urban informal sector; see Appendix 9.2) and agriculture. While it is true that wages are more flexible and competitively determined in urban informal and rural traditional industry, the classical concept of full employment is hardly adequate for these purposes.
4. See, for example, Dudley Seers, "The limitations of the special case," *Bulletin of the Oxford Institute of Economics and Statistics*, May 1965.
5. For one of the best-known arguments that output growth and employment creation are congruent rather than conflicting development objectives, see P. Streeten and F. Stewart, "Conflicts between output and employment objectives in developing countries," *Oxford Economic Papers*, July 1971, pp. 145–168, reprinted as reading 15 in *The Struggle for Economic Development*.
6. This argument as applied to LDCs was first expounded in R.S. Eckaus's seminal article, "The factor proportions problem in underdeveloped areas," *American Economic Review*, September 1955.
7. For an extensive analysis of this issue from a theoretical, empirical, and policy perspective, see Howard Pack, "Policies to encourage the use of intermediate technology," Reading 16 in *The Struggle for Economic Development*.
8. For a useful summary of evidence on this issue, see David Morawetz, "Employment implications of industrialization in developing countries," *Economic Journal*, September 1974. Additional data is contained in Howard Pack, *ibid*.

CONCEPTS FOR REVIEW

Complementary resources
Urbanization
Labor force
Underutilization of labor
Open unemployment
Underemployment
Disguised underemployment
Hidden unemployment
Voluntary unemployment
Industrialization
Employment gap
Total factor productivity
Small-scale industry
Output—employment lag

Classical model
Equilibrium wage rate
Flexible wages
Shadow price
Keynesian employment model
Aggregate demand
Full employment
Potential output
Deficit expenditure
Fixed input coefficients
"Big push" theory of development
Neoclassical price-incentive model
Elasticity of (factor) substitution
Appropriate technology

QUESTIONS FOR DISCUSSION

1. Discuss the nature of the employment problem in Third World countries. Include in your discussion a review of the various manifestations of the underutilization of labor.
2. Why should we be so concerned with unemployment and underemployment? Why is it a serious development problem?
3. Compare and contrast the contemporary urbanization process in Third World countries with the historical experience of Western Europe and North America. What are the major differences and how did they arise?
4. What is the relationship, if any, between unemployment (and underemployment) and the problems of poverty and inequality?
5. What are the principal economic reasons for the widespread failure of rapid LDC industrial growth to generate equally rapid employment growth? Is such a large output—employment lag an inevitable result of the process of modern industrial growth? Explain your answer.
6. The Keynesian model of employment determination seems to offer some simple policy prescriptions for generating full employment which, by and large, have proven successful over the past 25 years in the industrially developed countries. What are the principal limitations of utilizing this same approach for solving Third World employment problems? Is it possible that Keynesian policy prescriptions could actually *worsen* the problem of urban unemployment? Explain your answer.

FURTHER READINGS

The literature on Third World employment problems has grown to voluminous proportions over the past few years. Out of many excellent surveys, the following are perhaps the best: Edgar O. Edwards (ed.), *Employment in Developing Nations* (New York: Columbia University Press, 1974); David Turnham and Ian Jaeger, *The Employment Problem in Less Developed Countries* (Paris: OECD, 1970); Richard Jolly *et al.*, (eds.), *Third World Employment: Problems and Strategy* (Harmondsworth, England: Penguin, 1973); *Employment in Africa: Some Critical Issues* (Geneva: International Labor Office, 1974); Paul Bairoch, *Urban Unemployment in Developing Countries* (Geneva: International Labor Office, 1973); Lyn Squire, *Employment Policy in Developing Countries: A Survey of Issues and Evidence* (New York: Oxford University Press, 1981); and ILO, *World Labor Report I* (Geneva: International Labor Office, 1984).

For comparative and comprehensive country studies of Colombia, Kenya, Sri Lanka, and the Philippines, see the various ILO expert mission reports available from the International Labor Office in Geneva and its various UN distributional outlets in Africa, Asia, and Latin America.

On the question of technology and employment, see especially Frances Stewart, "Technology and employment in LDCs," in Edwards, *Employment*, pp. 83–132; Amartya Sen, *Employment, Technology, and Development* (London: Oxford University Press, 1975); and P.K. Ghosh (ed.), *Appropriate Technology in Third World Development* (Westport, Conn.: Greenwood, 1984).

Additional readings can be found on pp. 623–625.

9

URBANIZATION AND MIGRATION: INTERNAL AND INTERNATIONAL

In the final quarter of this century the number of people living in the cities and towns of these [developing] nations is projected to increase by nearly a billion, from about 650 million in 1975 to over 1,600 million in 2000.
World Development Report, 1979

We are firmly persuaded that the most fundamental and promising attack on employment problems in developing countries is in efforts to redress the present urban bias in development strategies.
Edgar O. Edwards,
Report on Employment in Developing Countries

THE MIGRATION AND URBANIZATION DILEMMA

In this chapter we focus on one of the most perplexing dilemmas of the development process: the phenomenon of massive and historically un-precedented movements of people from the rural countryside to the burgeon-ing cities of Africa, Asia, and Latin America. In Chapter 6 we documented the extraordinary increase in world and especially Third World population over the past few decades. By the year 2000 world population could range anywhere from 6 to 7 billion people, although the lower estimate is more likely to be accurate given recent fertility declines. But, whatever the figure eventually reached, one thing is clear: nowhere will population growth be more dramatic than in the major cities of the developing world.

After reviewing trends and prospects for urban population growth, we examine in this chapter a well-known theoretical model of rural–urban labor transfer in the context of rapid growth and high urban unemployment. We then turn to the related problem of international migration and the dilemma of global refugees. In the final section we evaluate various policy options that LDC governments may wish to pursue in their attempts to curtail the heavy flow of rural to urban migration and to ameliorate the serious unemployment problems that continue to plague their crowded cities.

Urbanization: Trends and Projections

One of the most significant of all postwar demographic phenomena and the one that promises to loom even larger in the future is the rapid growth of cities in developing countries. In 1950, 275 million people were living in Third World cities, a mere 38% of the 724 million total urban population. According to UN estimates, the world's urban population had reached 1.56 billion by 1975, with more than half of these living in metropolitan areas of developing countries. In the year 2000 the UN estimates that over 2.12 billion, or 66%, of the urban dwellers of the world will reside in less developed regions (note that this figure is higher than the World Bank's 1979 estimate quoted at the beginning of this chapter since the UN's estimate includes China while the bank's does not). This will represent an overall increase of 166%, or 1.32 billion new urbanites in Africa, Asia, and Latin America. Depending on the nature of development strategies pursued, the final total could be substantially higher or lower than the 2.12 billion estimate. Figure 9.1 provides a statistical breakdown of the projected growth of urban populations in four Third World regions and China between 1950 and the year 2000; Table 9.1 includes a more detailed country-specific breakdown.

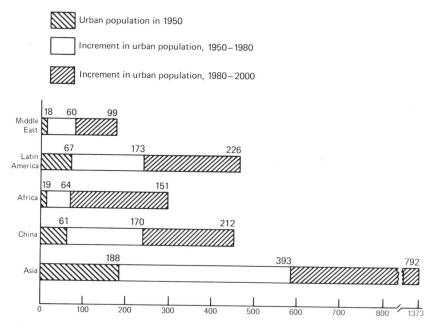

Figure 9.1. Urban population estimates and projections, 1950–2000 (in millions).

Table 9.1 Size of Urban Population in Major World Regions and Selected Developing Countries, 1950–2000 (in thousands)

	1950	1960	1970	1975	1980	1990	2000
World total	724147	1012084	1354357	1560860	1806809	2422293	3208028
More developed regions	448929	572730	702876	767302	834401	969226	1092470
Less developed regions	275218	439354	651481	793558	972408	1453067	2115558
Africa	31818	49506	80373	103032	132951	219202	345757
Algeria	1948	3287	6529	9024	12065	19714	28021
Egypt	6532	9818	14080	16346	19119	26604	37048
Ethiopia	761	1284	2315	3273	4562	8555	15140
Ghana	727	1575	2511	3193	4104	6830	10843
Kenya	336	597	1145	1592	2223	4314	8125
Morocco	2345	3412	5236	6551	8265	13126	19704
Nigeria	3595	5642	9009	11449	14811	25665	45041
Senegal	563	704	930	1070	1265	1896	3002
South Africa	5261	7424	10281	11934	14154	20417	30109
Sudan	572	1212	2571	3722	5305	10014	16551
Zambia	428	742	1290	1704	2235	3802	6260
Latin America	67511	106559	162355	198366	240592	343304	466234
Argentina	11205	15172	18616	20436	22300	25818	28875
Brazil	19064	32996	53253	66621	82172	119271	163027
Chile	3558	5145	7048	8044	9116	11390	13460
Colombia	4334	7665	13209	16946	21212	31102	41779
Ecuador	911	1490	2384	2971	3707	5735	8564
Guatemala	921	1317	1889	2269	2763	4193	6384
Mexico	11348	18458	29706	37318	46660	71069	102293
Nicaragua	397	609	930	1163	1457	2256	3396
Paraguay	474	631	853	1003	1205	1800	2708
Peru	2811	4265	7605	9619	11942	17498	24132
Venezuela	2739	5084	8048	9795	11776	16364	21125
Asia	217595	341738	482032	573994	688579	991212	1411847
Bangladesh	1786	2649	5150	6838	9531	18192	32095
India	59247	76575	106994	127177	154524	235837	360688
Indonesia	9362	13522	20395	25079	31293	49477	76612
Iran	4087	7249	11601	14959	19209	30162	43138
Iraq	1819	2937	5461	7272	9414	14525	20366
Nepal	183	285	440	550	708	1245	2275
Philippines	5695	8350	12387	15244	18902	29198	43988
South Korea	4347	6843	12766	16682	20921	29915	37807
Sri Lanka	1106	1772	2736	3359	4108	6090	8660
Syria	1071	1677	2708	3393	4290	6776	10105
Turkey	4441	8181	13536	17106	21482	32684	45482

SOURCE: UN, *Patterns of Urban and Rural Population Growth* (New York: United Nations, 1980), ST/ESA/Series A.68, Tables 4 and 48.

With regard to particular cities, current rates of urban population growth range from under 1% per annum in two of the world's largest cities, New York and London, to over 7% per annum in many African cities including Nairobi, Lagos, and Accra. In Asia and Latin America, many cities are growing at rates in excess of 5%. Table 9.2 shows the explosive growth of the Third World's 15 largest cities. Of these, 13 will more than double in size from 1975 to 2000. In fact, some, like Jakarta and Bogota, will almost triple in size, growing at rates in excess of any experienced by cities in developed countries over a similarly short time span.[1]

Along with the rapid spread of urbanization has come the prolific growth of huge slums and shantytowns. From the *favellas* of Rio de Janeiro and the *pueblos jovenes* of Lima to the *bustees* of Calcutta and the *bidonvilles* of Dakar, such makeshift communities have been doubling in size every 5–10 years. Today slum settlements represent over one-third of the urban population in all developing countries; in many cases they account for more than 60% of the urban total (see Table 9.3). Most of the settlements are without clean water, sewerage systems, or electricity. For example, metropolitan Cairo is attempting to cope with a population of 10 million people with a water and sanitation system built to service 2 million.

The extent of Third-World government concern and even alarm at current and projected trends in urban population growth was vividly revealed in a 1978 United Nations report on population policies in the world.[2] It showed that out of a total of 158 countries, 73 countries, the vast majority of which (68) were developing nations, considered the geographic distribution of their population to be "highly unacceptable." Another 66 countries, 42 of them developing, considered their urban population size to be "unacceptable to a degree." Only 6 developing countries considered their distribution to be acceptable. Almost all countries dissatisfied with the size and growth of their urban population believed that internal, rural–urban migration was the most prominent factor contributing to city growth. Statistics show that rural migrants constitute anywhere from 35 to 60% of recorded urban population growth (see Table 9.4). Accordingly, 90 out of 116 developing countries responding to the 1978 UN survey indicated that they had initiated policies to either slow down or reverse their accelerating trends in rural–urban migration.

Given the widespread dissatisfaction with rapid urban growth in developing countries, the critical issue that needs to be addressed is the degree to which national governments can indeed formulate development policies that can have a definite impact on trends in urban growth. It is clear that the unquestioning pursuit of the orthodox development strategies of the 1950s and 1960s, with their emphasis on industrial modernization, technological sophistication, and metropolitan growth, created a substantial geographic imbalance in economic opportunities and contributed significantly to the steadily accelerating influx of rural migrants into urban areas. Is it possible and/or even desirable now to attempt to reverse these trends by pursuing a different set of population and development policies? With birthrates beginning to decline in some Third World countries, the serious and worsening problem of rapid urban growth and accelerated rural–urban migration will undoubtedly be one of the most important development and demographic issues of the 1980s and 1990s.

Table 9.2 The 15 Largest Third World Cities (1975) and Their Projected Growth to the Year 2000

City	1975 population (millions)	2000 projected population	Projected overall growth rate (%) 1975–2000
Mexico City, Mexico	11.9	31.0	160
Shanghai, China	11.6	22.7	96
Sao Paulo, Brazil	10.7	25.8	141
Buenos Aires, Argentina	9.3	12.1	30
Rio de Janeiro, Brazil	8.9	19.0	113
Beijing, China	8.7	19.9	129
Calcutta, India	7.8	16.7	114
Bombay, India	7.0	17.1	144
Seoul, South Korea	6.8	14.2	109
Cairo, Egypt	6.4	13.1	104
Jakarta, Indonesia	5.7	16.6	191
Manila, Philippines	4.5	12.3	173
Delhi, India	4.4	11.7	166
Teheran, Iran	4.3	11.3	162
Bogota, Colombia	4.0	11.7	193

SOURCE: UN, *Population Studies No. 68*, Table 4.7.

Table 9.3 Slums and Squatter Settlements as a Percentage of Urban Total Populations

City	Slums as percentage of city population
Latin America	
Bogota, Colombia	60
Mexico City, Mexico	46
Caracas, Venezuela	42
Middle East and Africa	
Addis Ababa, Ethiopia	79
Casablanca, Morocco	70
Kinshasa, Zaire	60
Cairo, Egypt	60
Ankara, Turkey	60
Asia	
Calcutta, India	67
Manila, Philippines	35
Seoul, South Korea	29
Jakarta, Indonesia	26

SOURCE: Population Crisis Committee, "World Population Growth and Global Security" Report No. 13, (Washington, D.C., September 1983), p. 2.

Table 9.4 The Importance of Rural–Urban Migration as a Source of Urban Population Growth: Selected Developing Countries (1970s)

Country	Annual urban growth (%)	Share of growth due to migration (%)
Argentina	2.0	35
Brazil	4.5	36
Colombia	4.9	43
India	3.8	45
Indonesia	4.7	49
Nigeria	7.0	64
Philippines	4.8	42
Sri Lanka	4.3	61
Tanzania	7.5	64
Thailand	5.3	45

SOURCE: K. Newland, *City Limits: Emerging Constraints on Urban Growth*. Worldwatch Paper No. 38 (Washington, D.C., August 1980), p. 10.

Urban Unemployment and Underemployment

One of the major consequences of the rapid urbanization process has been the burgeoning supply of urban job seekers. In many developing countries the supply of workers far exceeds the demand, the result being extremely high rates of unemployment and underemployment in urban areas. Table 9.5 provides some detailed data on urban and rural unemployment for 34 countries. Note that the table focuses solely on rates of open unemployment. It thus excludes the very many more people who are chronically underemployed. The problem is therefore much more serious than even these data suggest. Also, since these statistics are from the 1960s, they are likely to show unemployment rates considerably below current levels. Nevertheless, the table indicates that even in the 1960s developing countries had very high rates of open urban unemployment. Nine out of 36 countries had rates above 15%, while 22 countries had rates in excess of 10%.

With the exception of Iran, recorded unemployment was higher in urban areas than in rural areas. For the vast majority of the countries, the urban rate was at least twice as high as the rural rate; in 47% of the countries it was three times as high. This is in marked contrast to the situation in developed countries where urban unemployment has been much lower and where the general tendency has been for urban rates to be lower than rural rates. If we had included scattered information on the very substantial numbers of the urban labor force who were underemployed in part-time service activities, then the overall figures for urban "surplus labor" (both openly unemployed and underemployed) would well exceed 30% in many developing countries. Moreover, had we focused on those in the 15-to-24 age bracket (the majority of whom are recent migrants), the rate would typically exceed 50%. Since a major contributing factor to both high rates of urban growth and high rates of unemployment is rural–urban migration, it is essential to investigate this critical issue in some detail.

MIGRATION AND DEVELOPMENT

Only a few years ago, rural–urban migration was viewed favorably in the economic development literature. Internal migration was thought to be a natural process in which surplus labor was gradually withdrawn from the rural sector to provide needed manpower for urban industrial growth. The process was deemed socially beneficial since human resources were being shifted from locations where their social marginal products were often assumed to be zero to places where this marginal product was not only positive but also rapidly growing as a result of capital accumulation and technological progress. This process was formalized in the Lewis theory of development discussed in Chapter 3. As Richard Jolly, former director of the Institute of Development Studies at the University of Sussex, has noted, "Far from being concerned with measures to stem the flow, the major interest of these economists (i.e. those who stressed the importance of labor transfer) was with policies that would *release* labor to *increase* the flow. Indeed, one of the reasons given for trying to increase productivity in the agricultural sector was to release *sufficient* labor for urban industrialization. How irrelevant most of this concern looks today!"[3]

In contrast to this viewpoint, it is now abundantly clear from recent LDC experience that rates of rural–urban migration continue to exceed rates of urban job creation and to surpass greatly the absorption capacity of both industry and urban social services. No longer is migration viewed by economists as a beneficent process necessary to solve problems of growing urban labor demand. On the contrary, migration today must be seen as the major factor contributing to the ubiquitous phenomenon of urban surplus labor, as a force that continues to exacerbate already serious urban unemployment problems caused by economic and structural imbalances between urban and rural areas.

Migration exacerbates these rural–urban structural imbalances in two direct ways. First, on the supply side, internal migration disproportionately increases the growth rate of urban job seekers relative to urban population growth, which itself is at historically unprecedented levels, because of the high proportion of well-educated young people in the migrant system. Their presence tends to swell the growth of urban labor supply while depleting the rural countryside of valuable human capital. Second, on the demand side, urban job creation is generally more difficult and costly to accomplish than rural employment creation because of the need for substantial complementary resource inputs for most jobs in the industrial sector. Moreover, the pressures of rising urban wages and compulsory employee fringe benefits in combination with the unavailability of "appropriate," more labor-intensive production technologies means that a rising share of modern sector output growth is accounted for by increases in labor productivity. Together this rapid supply increase and lagging demand growth tend to convert a short-run problem of manpower imbalances into a long-run situation of chronic and rising urban surplus labor.

But the impact of migration on the development process is much more pervasive than its obvious exacerbation of urban unemployment and underemployment. In fact, the significance of the migration phenomenon in most developing countries is not necessarily in the process itself or even in its impact on the sectoral allocation of human resources. Rather, its signifi-

Table 9.5 Rates of Urban and Rural Unemployment
(percentage of the active population)

Country	Year	Town(s)	Urban unemployment	Rural unemployment
Africa				
Algeria	1966	urban areas	26.6	—
Benin	1968	urban areas	13.0*	—
Burundi	1963	capital city	18.7*	—
Ghana	1960	large towns	12.0	—
	1970	2 large cities	.9.0*	—
Ivory Coast	1963	capital city	15.0*	—
Kenya	1968–69	capital city	10.0*	—
	1968–69	second largest city	14.0*	—
Morocco	1960	urban areas	20.5	5.4
Nigeria	1963	urban areas	12.6	—
Sierra Leone	1967	capital city	15.0	—
Cameroon	1962	largest city	13.0*	—
	1964	capital city	17.0*	—
Tanzania	1965	urban areas	7.0	3.9
	1971	7 towns	5.0*	—
Zaire	1967	capital city	12.9	—
Latin America				
Argentina	1968	capital city	5.4	—
Bolivia	1966	urban areas	13.2	—
Chile	1968	urban areas	6.1	2.0
Colombia	1967	urban areas	15.5	—
Costa Rica	1966–67	capital city	5.6	—
El Salvador	1961	capital city	6.6	—
Guatemala	1964	capital city	5.4	—

cance lies in its implications for economic growth in general and for the character of that growth, particularly its distributional manifestations.

We must recognize at the outset, therefore, that migration in excess of job opportunities is both a symptom of and a contributor to Third World underdevelopment. Understanding the causes, determinants, and consequences of internal and international migration is thus central to understanding the nature and character of the development process and to formulating policies to influence this process in socially desirable ways. A simple yet crucial step in underlining the centrality of the migration phenomenon is to recognize that *any economic and social policy that affects rural and urban real incomes will directly and/or indirectly influence the migration process. This process in turn will itself tend to alter the pattern of sectoral and geographic economic activity, income distribution, and even population growth.* Since all economic policies have direct and indirect effects on the level and growth of *either* urban or rural incomes or of *both*, they *all* will have a tendency to influence the nature and magnitude of the migration

Table 9.5 (*Continued*)

Country	Year	Town(s)	Urban unemployment	Rural unemployment
Latin America (continued)				
Guyana	1965	capital city	20.5	—
Honduras	1961	capital city	7.8	—
Jamaica	1960	capital city	19.0	12.4
Panama	1960	urban areas	15.5	3.6
	1967	urban areas	9.3	2.8
Peru	1964	capital city	4.2	—
	1969	capital city	5.2	—
Uruguay	1963	urban areas	10.9	2.3
Venezuela	1961	urban areas	17.5	4.3
	1968	urban areas	6.5	3.1
Asia				
India	1961–62	urban areas	3.2	1.7
Indonesia	1961	urban areas	9.5	—
Iran	1966	urban areas	5.5	11.3
Korea	1963–64	urban areas	7.0	1.8
Malaysia (West)	1967	urban areas	11.6	7.4
Philippines	1967	urban areas	13.1	6.9
Singapore	1966	urban areas	9.1	—
Sri Lanka	1959–60	urban areas	14.3	10.0
Syria	1967	urban areas	7.3	—
Thailand	1966	urban areas	2.8	—

*Men only.

SOURCE: P. Bairoch, *Urban Unemployment in Developing Countries* (Geneva: Internal Labor Office, 1973), p. 49; J. Gugler, *Internal Migration: The New World and the Third World*, ed. A. Richmond and D. Kubat (California: Sage, 1976), p. 185.

stream. Although some policies may have a more direct and immediate impact (e.g., wages and income policies and employment promotion programs), there are many others which, though less obvious, may in the long run be no less important. Included among these policies, for example, would be land tenure arrangements; commodity pricing; credit allocation; taxation; export promotion; import substitution; commercial and exchange rate policies; the geographic distribution of social services; the nature of public investment programs; attitudes toward private foreign investors; the organization of population and family-planning programs; the structure, content, and orientation of the educational system; the functioning of labor markets; and the nature of public policies toward international technological transfer and the location of new industries. There is thus a clear need to recognize the central importance of internal and, for many countries, even international migration and to integrate the two-way relationship between migration and population distribution on the one hand and economic variables on the other into a more comprehensive framework designed to improve development policy formulation.

In addition, we need to understand better not only why people move and what factors are most important in their decision-making process but also what the *consequences* of migration are for rural and urban economic and social development. If all development policies affect and are affected by migration, which are the most significant and why? What are the policy options and tradeoffs among different and sometimes competing objectives (e.g., curtailing internal migration and expanding educational opportunities in rural areas)? Part of our task in the following sections will be to seek answers to these and other questions relating to migration, unemployment, and development.

INTERNAL MIGRATION IN DEVELOPING NATIONS: SOME GENERAL FACTS

An understanding of the causes and determinants of rural–urban migration and the relationship between migration and relative economic opportunities in urban and rural areas is central to any analysis of Third World employment problems. Since migrants comprise a significant proportion of the urban labor force in many developing nations, the magnitude of rural–urban migration has been and will continue to be a principal determinant of the supply of new job seekers. And if migration is a key determinant of the urban labor supply, then the migration process must be understood before the nature and causes of urban unemployment can be properly understood. Government policies to ameliorate the urban unemployment problem must be based, in the first instance, on knowledge of who comes to town and why.

The Migration Process

The factors influencing the decision to migrate are varied and complex. Since migration is a *selective process* affecting individuals with certain economic, social, educational, and demographic characteristics, the relative influence of economic and noneconomic factors may vary not only between nations and regions but also within defined geographic areas and populations. Much of the early research on migration tended to focus on social, cultural, and psychological factors while recognizing, but not carefully evaluating, the importance of economic variables. Emphasis has variously been placed, for example, on

1. *Social factors* including the desire of migrants to break away from traditional constraints of social organizations
2. *Physical factors* including climate and meteorological disasters like floods and droughts
3. *Demographic factors* including the reduction in mortality rates and the concomitant high rates of rural population growth
4. *Cultural factors* including the security of urban "extended family" relationships and the allurement of the "bright city lights"
5. *Communication factors* including improved transportation, urban-oriented educational systems, and the "modernizing" impact of the introduction of radio, television, and the cinema

All these noneconomic factors are of course relevant. However, there now seems to be widespread agreement among economists and noneconomists alike that *rural−urban migration can be explained primarily by the influence of economic factors.* These include not only the standard "push" from subsistence agriculture and "pull" of relatively high urban wages, but also the potential "pushback" toward rural areas as a result of high urban unemployment.

Migrant Characteristics

It is convenient to divide the main characteristics of migrants into three broad categories: demographic, educational, and economic.

Demographic characteristics. Urban migrants in Third World countries tend to be young men and women between the ages of 15 and 24. Various studies in Africa and Asia have provided quantitative evidence of this phenomenon in countries such as Kenya, Tanzania, Ghana, Nigeria, India, Thailand, Korea, and the Philippines. In recent years the proportion of migrating women has increased as their educational opportunities have expanded. This increase, substantial in many countries, has been particularly evident in Latin America, Southeast Asia, and West Africa. In fact, women now constitute the majority of the migration stream in Latin America, largely as a result of its relatively advanced state of urbanization compared with other developing continents.[4] Basically, there are two types of female migration—the "associational" migration of wives and daughters accompanying the "primary" male migrant and the migration of unattached females. It is the latter type of migration that is increasing most rapidly.

Educational characteristics. One of the most consistent findings of rural−urban migration studies is the positive correlation between educational attainment and migration. There seems to be a clear association between the level of completed education and the propensity to migrate—those with more years of schooling, everything else being equal, are more likely to migrate than those with fewer. In Barnum and Sabot's comprehensive study of migration in Tanzania, for example, the relationship between education and migration is clearly documented, especially in terms of the impact of declining urban employment opportunities on the educational characteristics of migrants.[5] High school dropouts were found to constitute a rising proportion of the migration stream. The explanation offered by Barnum and Sabot is that limited urban employment opportunities were being rationed by educational levels and only those workers with at least some secondary education had a chance of finding a job. Those with only primary school education were finding it very difficult to secure employment, and their proportionate numbers in the migrant stream had therefore begun to decline.

Economic characteristics. For many years the largest percentage of urban migrants were poor, landless, and unskilled individuals whose rural opportunities were for the most part nonexistent. In colonial Africa, seasonal migration was predominant, with migrants from various income levels seeking short-term urban jobs. Recently, however, with the emergence of a stabilized, modern industrial sector in most urban areas of the less developed countries, the situation has changed. Migrants, both male and female, seem to come from all socioeconomic strata, with the majority being very poor only because most rural inhabitants are poor.

TOWARD AN ECONOMIC THEORY OF RURAL–URBAN MIGRATION

As we saw in Chapter 4, the economic development of Western Europe and the United States was closely associated with, and in fact defined in terms of, the movement of labor from rural to urban areas. For the most part, with a rural sector dominated by agricultural activities and an urban sector focusing on industrialization, overall economic development in these countries was characterized by the gradual reallocation of labor out of agriculture and into industry through rural–urban migration, both internal and international. Urbanization and industrialization were in essence synonymous. This historical model served as a blueprint for the development of Third World nations, as evidenced, for example, by the original Lewis theory of labor transfer (see Chapter 3).

But the overwhelming evidence of the 1960s and 1970s, when Third World nations witnessed a massive migration of their rural populations into urban areas despite rising levels of urban unemployment and underemployment, lessens the validity of the Lewis two-sector model of development. An explanation of the phenomenon, as well as policies to address the resulting problems, must be sought elsewhere. In a series of articles, I have attempted to develop a theory of rural–urban migration to explain the apparently paradoxical relationship (at least to economists) of accelerated rural–urban migration in the context of rising urban unemployment.[6]

A Verbal Description of the Todaro Model

Starting from the assumption that migration is primarily an economic phenomenon which for the individual migrant can be a quite rational decision despite the existence of urban unemployment, the Todaro model postulates that migration proceeds in response to urban–rural differences in *expected rather than actual earnings*. The fundamental premise is that migrants consider the various labor market opportunities available to them in the rural and urban sectors and choose the one which maximizes their "expected" gains from migration. Expected gains are measured by the *difference in real incomes between rural and urban work* and the *probability of a new migrant obtaining an urban job*. A schematic framework showing how the varying factors affecting the migration decision interact is given in Figure 9.2.

In essence, the theory assumes that members of the labor force, both actual and potential, compare their "expected" incomes for a given time horizon in the urban sector (i.e., the difference between returns and costs of migration) with prevailing average rural incomes and migrate if the former exceeds the latter.

Consider the following illustration. Suppose the average unskilled or semiskilled rural worker has a choice between being a farm laborer (or working his own land) for an annual average real income of, say, 50 units or migrating to the city where a worker with his skill or educational background can obtain wage employment yielding an annual real income of 100 units. The more commonly used economic models of migration, which place exclusive emphasis on the income differential factor as the determinant of the decision to migrate, would indicate a clear choice in this situa-

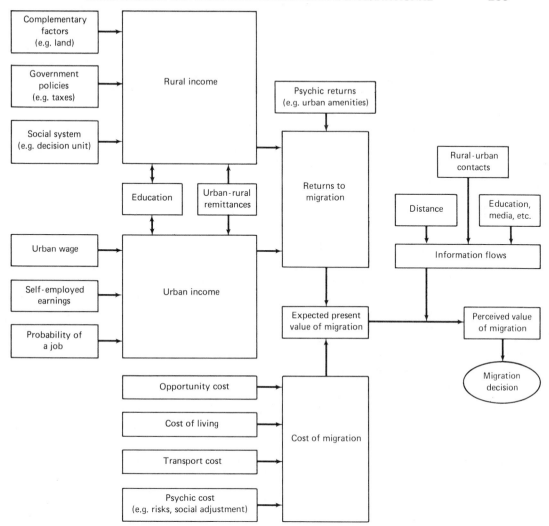

Figure 9.2. A schematic framework for the analysis of the migration decision. *Source:* D. Byerlee, "Rural-Urban Migration in Africa: Theory, Policy and Research Implications,"*International Migration Review*, 1974.

tion. The worker should seek the higher-paying urban job. It is important to recognize, however, that these migration models were developed largely in the context of advanced industrial economies and, as such, implicitly assume the existence of full or near-full employment. In a full-employment environment the decision to migrate can be based solely on the desire to secure the highest-paid job wherever it becomes available. Simple economic theory would then indicate that such migration should lead to a reduction in wage differentials through the interaction of the forces of supply and demand, both in areas of emigration and in points of immigration.

Unfortunately, such an analysis is not realistic in the context of the institutional and economic framework of most of Third World nations. First, these countries are beset by a chronic and serious unemployment problem with the result that a typical migrant cannot expect to secure a high-paying urban job immediately. In fact, it is much more likely that on entering the urban labor market many migrants will either become totally unemployed or will seek casual and part-time employment as vendors, hawkers, repairmen, and itinerant day laborers in the urban "traditional" or "informal" sector where ease of entry, small scale of operation, and relatively competitive price and wage determination prevails (see Appendix 9.2 for more detailed analysis of the urban informal sector). Consequently, in his decision to migrate the individual must balance the probabilities and risks of being unemployed or underemployed for a considerable period of time against the positive urban−rural real income differential. The fact that a typical migrant can expect to earn twice the annual real income in an urban area than in a rural environment may be of little consequence if the actual probability of his securing the higher-paying job within, say, a one-year period is one chance in five. Thus, the actual probability of his being successful in securing the higher-paying urban job is 20% and therefore his expected urban income for the one-year period is in fact 20 units and not the 100 units that an urban worker in a full-employment environment would expect to receive. So with a "one-period" time horizon and a probability of success of 20% it would be irrational for this migrant to seek an urban job even though the differential between urban and rural earnings capacity is 100%. On the other hand, if the probability of success were, say, 60% and the expected urban income therefore 60 units, it would be entirely rational for our migrant with his one-period time horizon to try his luck in the urban area even though urban unemployment may be extremely high.

If we now approach the situation by assuming a considerably longer time horizon—a more realistic assumption, especially in view of the fact that the vast majority of migrants are between the ages of 15 and 24—the decision to migrate should be represented on the basis of a longer-term, more "permanent" income calculation. If the migrant anticipates a relatively low probability of finding regular wage employment in the initial period but expects this probability to increase over time as he is able to broaden his urban contacts, it would still be rational for him to migrate even though expected urban income during the initial period or periods might be lower than expected rural income. As long as the "present value" of the net stream of expected urban income over the migrant's planning horizon exceeds that of the expected rural income, the decision to migrate is justifiable. This, in essence, is the process portrayed in Figure 9.2.

Rather than equalizing urban and rural wage rates as would be the case in a competitive model, we see that rural−urban migration in our model acts as an equilibrating force that equates rural and urban *expected* incomes. For example, if average rural income is 60 and urban income is 120, then a 50% urban unemployment rate would be necessary before further migration would no longer be profitable. Since expected incomes are defined in terms of *both* wages and employment probabilities, it is possible to have continued migration despite the existence of sizable rates of urban unemployment. In the above numerical example, migration would continue even if the urban unemployment rate were 30 or 40%.

To sum up, the Todaro migration model has four basic characteristics:

1. *Migration is stimulated primarily by rational economic considerations* of relative benefits and costs, mostly financial but also psychological.
2. *The decision to migrate depends on "expected" rather than actual urban − rural real wage differentials*, where the expected differential is determined by the interaction of two variables, the actual urban − rural wage differential *and* the probability of successfully obtaining employment in the urban sector.
3. *The probability of obtaining an urban job is inversely related to the urban unemployment rate.*
4. *Migration rates in excess of urban job opportunity growth rates are not only possible but rational* and even likely in the face of wide urban − rural *expected* income differentials. High rates of urban unemployment are therefore inevitable outcomes of the serious *imbalance* of economic opportunities between urban and rural areas of most underdeveloped countries. (For a mathematical presentation of the Todaro model, see Appendix 9.1.)

Some Policy Implications[7]

While the above theory might at first seem to devalue the critical importance of rural − urban migration by portraying it as an adjustment mechanism by which workers allocate themselves between rural and urban labor markets, it does have important policy implications for development strategy with regard to wages and incomes, rural development, and industrialization.

The Need to Reduce Imbalances in Urban − Rural Employment Opportunities

Since migrants are assumed to respond to differentials in expected incomes, it is vitally important that imbalances between economic opportunities in rural and urban sectors be minimized. Permitting urban wage rates to grow at a greater pace than average rural incomes will stimulate further rural − urban migration in spite of rising levels of urban unemployment. This heavy influx of people into urban areas not only gives rise to socioeconomic problems in the cities but may also eventually create problems of labor shortages in rural areas, especially during the busy seasons.

Urban Job Creation is an Insufficient Solution for the Urban Unemployment Problem

The traditional (Keynesian) economic solution to urban unemployment (i.e., the creation of more urban modern-sector jobs without simultaneous attempts to improve rural incomes and employment opportunities) can result in the paradoxical situation where more urban *employment* leads to higher levels of urban *unemployment!* Once again, the imbalance in expected income-earning opportunities is the crucial concept. Since migration rates are assumed to respond positively to *both* higher urban wages and higher urban employment opportunities (or probabilities), it follows that for any given positive urban − rural wage differential (in most LDCs urban wages are typically three to four times as large as rural wages), higher urban employment rates will widen the expected differential and induce even higher rates of rural–urban migration. For every new job created, two or three migrants who were productively occupied in rural areas may come to the city. Thus, if 100 new jobs are created, there may be as many as 300 new migrants and, therefore, 200 more urban unemployed. A policy designed to reduce urban unemployment, therefore, may lead not only to the higher levels of urban unemployment but also to lower levels of agricultural output.

Indiscriminate Educational Expansion Will Lead to Further Migration and Unemployment

The Todaro model also has important policy implications for curtailing investment in excessive educational expansion, especially at the higher levels. The heavy influx of rural migrants into urban areas at rates much in excess of new employment opportunities has necessitated a rationing device in the selection of new employees. Although within each educational group such selection may be largely random, many observers have noted that employers tend to use educational attainment or number of years of completed schooling as the typical rationing device. For the same wage, they will hire those with more education in preference to those with less even though extra education may not contribute to better job performance. Jobs that could formerly be filled by those with primary education (sweepers, messengers, filing clerks, etc.) now require secondary training; those formerly requiring a secondary certificate (clerks, typists, bookkeepers, etc.) now necessitate a university degree. It follows that for any given urban wage, if the probability of success in securing a modern sector job is higher for those with more education, their expected income differential will also be higher and they will be more likely to migrate to the cities. The basic Todaro model, therefore, provides an economic rationale for the observed fact in most LDCs that rural inhabitants with more education are more likely to migrate than those with less.

From the viewpoint of educational policy, it is safe to predict that as job opportunities become scarce in relation to the number of applicants, students will experience increasing pressure to proceed further up the educational ladder. The private demand for education, which in many ways is a "derived demand" for urban jobs, will continue to exert tremendous pressure on governments to invest in postprimary school facilities. But for many of these students, the specter of joining the ranks of the "educated unemployed" becomes more of a reality with each passing year. Government overinvestment in postprimary educational facilities thus often turns out to be an investment in idle human resources. Chapter 11 will focus on this and other issues related to the economics of education in greater detail.

Wage Subsidies and Traditional Scarcity Factor Pricing Can Be Counterproductive

As we have seen in Chapter 8, a standard economic policy prescription for generating urban employment opportunities is to eliminate factor-price distortions by using "correct" prices perhaps implemented by wage subsidies (i.e., fixed government subsidies to employers for each worker employed) or direct government hiring. Since actual urban wages generally exceed the market or "correct" wage as a result of a variety of institutional factors, it is often correctly argued that the elimination of wage distortions through price adjustments or a subsidy system will encourage more labor-intensive modes of production. But while such policies can generate more urban employment opportunities, they can also lead to higher levels of unemployment in accordance with the argument above about induced migration. The overall welfare impact of a wage-subsidy policy when both the rural and urban sectors are taken into account is not immediately clear. Much will depend on the level of urban unemployment, the size of the urban–rural expected income differential, and the magnitude of induced migration as more urban jobs are created.

Programs of Integrated Rural Development Should Be Encouraged

Policies that operate only on the demand side of the urban employment picture, such as wage subsidies, direct government hiring, elimination of factor-price distortions, and employer tax incentives, are probably far less effective in the long run in alleviating the unemployment problem than are policies designed directly to regulate the supply of labor to urban areas. Clearly, however, some combination of both kinds of policies is most desirable.

Policies of rural development are crucial to this aim. Many informed observers of Third World development agree on the central importance of rural and agricultural development if the urban unemployment problem is to be solved. Most proposals call for the restoration of a proper balance between rural and urban incomes and for changes in government policies that currently give development programs a strong bias toward the urban industrial sector (e.g., policies in the provision of health, educational, and social services).

Given the political difficulties of reducing urban wage rates, the need continuously to expand urban employment opportunities through judicious investments in small- and medium-scale labor-intensive industries, and the inevitable growth of the urban industrial sector, every effort must be made to broaden the economic base of the rural economy at the same time. The present unnecessary economic incentives for rural–urban migration need to be minimized through creative and well-designed programs of integrated rural development. These should focus on income generation, both farm and nonfarm, employment growth, health delivery, educational improvement, infrastructure development (electricity, water, roads, etc.), and the provision of other rural amenities. Successful rural development programs adapted to the socioeconomic and environmental needs of particular countries and regions seem to offer the only viable long-run solution to the problem of excessive rural–urban migration.

To assert, however, that there is an urgent need for policies designed to curb the excessive influx of rural migrants is not to imply an attempt to reverse what some have called "inevitable historical trends." Rather, the implication of the Todaro migration model is that there is a growing need for a "policy package" that does not *exacerbate* these historical trends toward urbanization by *artificially* creating serious imbalances in economic opportunities between urban and rural areas.

International Migration and Global Refugees

Trends and Estimates of International Migration

People migrate in search of better economic opportunities not only from rural to urban areas within Third World nations, but also between countries, both developing and developed. In fact, following the Second World War, open-door migration policies coupled with improvements in air travel and international communications permitted workers from developing countries to migrate to countries in the industrialized world in search of better jobs and a new life. With the emergence of different levels of income within the Third World, this process was expanded into other developing countries where wages were higher and jobs were more plentiful.

At present, there are six major regions into which international labor migration takes place: Western Europe, North America, Oceania, the Middle East, southern Africa, and a few countries in South America. There are substantial differences in the types of migration to the various regions. Migration to the industrial countries from the developing ones includes both temporary and permanent migration. In Europe, the bulk of migration is temporary and is increasingly composed of dependents admitted for family reunification purposes. In North America and Oceania, international migration is primarily of a permanent nature, although it is declining dramatically. More significant is the growth of substantial illegal migration, particularly into the United States. In the few countries in South America, migration is permanent but largely on a selective basis either as a means of settling underpopulated areas or attracting needed skills. In the Middle East and southern Africa, the major emphasis is on temporary migration to provide much-needed manpower.

There are also differences in the patterns of migration. Migration to the industrial countries from the developing ones originates from diverse parts of the world, while migration from one developing nation to another is largely confined to neighboring states. For example, migration to the OPEC countries is largely from their Arab neighbors and migration to southern Africa (South Africa and Zimbabwe) is from Botswana, Lesotho, Swaziland, Zambia, Mozambique, and Malawi. Furthermore, some developing countries are both recipients and senders of migrant workers. Examples of this kind are Argentina, which attracts manual laborers from surrounding countries and exports professionals to them, and the Dominican Republic, which exports workers to Venezuela, the United States, and Canada and imports contract workers from Haiti for its sugar cane fields.

Numerical estimates of the current migrant population are difficult to make since they vary considerably from one statistical source to another. The reason for the difficulty lies in the substantial amount of illegal migration now taking place, a type of migration that is almost impossible to estimate. In absolute terms, however, the largest number of recorded (i.e., legal) migrant workers are in Europe and the Middle East. By 1973, there were 6.5 million foreign workers employed in Western European countries, particularly West Germany, France, and Great Britain.[8] After the 1973 oil shock, however, there was a substantial decline in their numbers as Western economies slid into a recession. At the same time, the Middle Eastern countries emerged as major importers of labor although this did not benefit many of the migrants who had sought employment in Western Europe. While Turkish and Arab migrants were easily reabsorbed into the new Middle Eastern labor markets, the southern Europeans—Greeks, Yugoslavs, Italians, and Spaniards—had to be painfully reabsorbed domestically.

The total number of migrants in the Middle East was estimated at 2.7 million in 1980.[9] They come primarily from Eygpt, North Yemen, South Yemen, Pakistan, Bangladesh, and India. Foreign Arab workers comprise almost 70% of migrants in the Middle East, although their proportion has been on a steady decline in recent years as a result of increasing numbers of Asian migrants. The largest proportion of the latter group are Indians and Pakistanis, who together comprise 23% of foreign workers in the region. The remainder are from Malaysia, the Philippines, and South Korea. In most Middle Eastern importers of labor, immigrants now form the majority of the work force and in some countries, like Kuwait and the United Arab Emirates, the majority of the population as well. As a result, the Middle Eastern countries strongly discourage permanent migration, restricting family immigration and making little effort to extend economic and social benefits, not to mention political rights, to their foreign workers.

Other areas of migration are less significant, although there has been a steady decrease in the traditionally large amount of permanent migration to North America (both the United States and Canada) and Oceania (Australia and New Zealand) since the onset of economic problems following the first oil shock. Temporary migration to North America comes primarily from Latin America and the Caribbean, while to Oceania it comes mainly from Southeast Asia and the Pacific Islands. With the large amount of temporary, illegal migration taking place in North America, it is difficult to estimate the total migrant population. However, it is far from insignificant in the United States. Migration to southern Africa is also mostly temporary and usually from neighboring countries. There were about a third of a million foreign workers in South Africa, with the majority employed in mining. Migration to the few countries in South America is of a much smaller magnitude though it too is mostly temporary and from neighboring countries.

In the countries that export labor, migration has become an important feature of the economy. Such countries include North Yemen, Pakistan, and Jordan in the Middle Eastern region, Lesotho and Botswana in southern Africa, and the Dominican Republic in the Caribbean Basin. For example, Jordan and North Yemen had 28.2 and 20.3% of their work force, respectively, living abroad in 1975. Similarly, in 1976–1977, Lesotho and Botswana had 33.3 and 20.0% of their total workers abroad. The Dominican Republic had somewhere between 6 and 10% of its total population living in the United States in 1982.

Economic Effects of International Migration

According to the neoclassical model of international factor mobility, the process of labor migration should benefit both the labor-sending and the labor-receiving countries, or at least make one better off and the other no worse off.[10] The appearance of higher wages for labor in one country relative to another is a sign that labor is relatively scarce in the country with the higher wages and relatively abundant in the country with the lower wages. The free movement of labor from the low-wage to the high-wage country would thus benefit all parties concerned. The labor-importing country would receive an addition to its relatively scarce stock of labor. The laborers themselves would get higher wages. The labor-exporting country, if it was faced with unemployment, would be relieved of that problem. If it was operating at full employment, it would experience a drop in GDP but not in GNP as remittance income from abroad would cover the drop in domestic output caused by the workers' departure. If the workers migrated permanently and did not send back remittances, the labor-exporting country would experience a drop in absolute GNP but not in per capita GNP and hence would be neither worse off nor better off in per capita terms.

A more sophisticated version of this analysis recognizes the structural problems of developing countries and espouses the benefits of international labor migration in helping to provide a solution to these problems in the labor-exporting country. According to this version there are five major benefits that accrue to the sending country. The first is the *reduction of domestic unemployment*. Second, the remittances sent to families by overseas migrants cause an increase in local consumer demand and savings, thereby providing an incentive and a source of foreign exchange for *physical capital formation* which would spur long-run economic growth. Third, the outflow of redundant labor from the rural sector would raise the land–labor ratio, improving labor productivity and, hence, raising rural incomes and stimulating the *rural sector's growth*. Fourth, returning migrant workers would bring back skills learned in more prosperous countries, thereby contributing to increased *human capital formation* without the need for expensive domestic training programs. Finally, by allowing disadvantaged sections of the population to proceed abroad and earn higher wages, international migration is supposed to help improve *income distribution* in the sending country.

In general, as long as jobs are plentiful the economic benefits of international migration for the labor-importing country are not the subject of much debate (except perhaps in the United States), although there may be considerable social costs arising from the presence of foreign workers. Similarly, there is little disagreement that migration generally benefits the individual migrant who receives higher wages and attains a better standard of living. There is, however, considerable controversy over the purported benefits to the labor-exporting country as a whole. Indeed, in the case of almost all of the points made above, a deeper look into the realities of developing countries reveals that these benefits can be illusory and that certain factors can negate them. Let's therefore examine each of the five presumed benefits of international migration.

Reduction in Unemployment

It is generally accepted that the emigration of unskilled and unemployed workers relieves pressure on scarce employment opportunities in the labor-exporting country. In the Dominican Republic, for example, it has been estimated that the return of half its overseas workers would double the open unemployment rate. However, it is not always the unskilled workers who migrate in search of better income-earning opportunities. Indeed, many developing countries are suffering from the contemporary problem of "brain drain," whereby their doctors, engineers, and other professionals have migrated to the industrial and OPEC countries in search of higher wages. Even in the blue-collar work force, a considerable proportion of emigrating workers may be highly skilled. In the Middle East, for example, the ongoing construction boom of the oil-rich states has siphoned off many skilled construction workers from Egypt, Pakistan, and India. As a result, some of these labor-exporting countries are suffering shortages of skilled construction workers while unemployment for other types of workers continues. Furthermore, skilled workers are often complementary to unskilled workers. Each skilled worker may work with one or two unskilled assistants. Thus, the departure of such a worker, if it leads to a shortage in that skill category, can aggravate the unemployment situation for unskilled workers as well.

Capital Formation

The role of remittances in promoting long-run economic growth through capital formation is being viewed with increasing skepticism. The reason is that remittances are often used for private consumption by the emigrants' households with very little going into savings. For example, in Pakistan, 82% of all remittances were found to be used for direct consumption or real estate acquisitions. Although most remittances increase consumer demand, there may not be a corresponding increase in supply, at least in the short run. In order to expand supply, new projects must be undertaken with increased capital formation which in turn requires foreign exchange to import the necessary machinery and equipment. However, at this point, the unsatisfied consumer demand itself can become an obstacle by competing with investment for the scarce foreign exchange that is also needed to import many consumer goods. If the government steps in and attempts to restrict consumer imports, prices will spiral upwards because of the excess demand.

The economic impact of remittances varies across countries, depending on each country's ability to absorb excess demand through domestic production. The preceding argument is therefore most applicable to those low-income countries which have experienced repeated inflationary spirals and excessive consumer spending with little real economic growth.

Rural Sector Growth

It is argued in the Lewis model and others that the rural sector in developing countries suffers from both underemployment and unemployment as a result of its large labor–land ratio, which leads to low productivity and low average incomes. Emigration from this sector should, therefore, be an unmixed blessing—allowing redundant workers to leave and find well-paid jobs overseas while easing the pressure on scarce land for those remaining. For the latter, higher incomes would result from the higher land–labor ratio, permitting greater productivity per worker. Higher incomes might induce the remaining workers to make improvements to their land, thereby raising productivity and incomes even further.

But two factors may well militate against these benefits. First, if the rural sector emigrants remit substantial income to their families, this income may lead to some substitution of leisure for labor, with the result that there may be only a small increase in agricultural output or possibly even a fall, depending on social custom. In societies where economic activity by women is frowned on, traditional restrictions on their participation in the labor force may be strengthened by the inflow of remittance income from abroad, leading to declines in the agricultural output which is currently produced in large part by rural women (i.e., because of the absence of local male workers).

Second, there is the possibility that once a rural area is substantially experiencing the emigration of its young, able-bodied workers, the process may go beyond the dictates of the local employment situation. As long as expected income remains higher overseas, there is little reason for workers to remain at home even if local incomes are rising as a result of declining labor pressure. From the extreme of abundant labor and scarce land, the rural sector may swing to the other extreme of abundant land and scarce labor. Indeed, this has already happened in Oman, North Yemen, and Jordan, all of which have suffered a decline in agricultural output as a result of excessive emigration of their rural workers. Jordan, in fact, has actually had to import farm workers to make up for the departure of its own farmers.

Human Capital Formation

The argument that migrant workers acquire skills while working abroad and later use these skills on returning home makes two critical assumptions. First, it is assumed that emigrants find overseas employment that involves greater skill than they used at home and hence become more skilled. Second, it is assumed that the workers will return home and will be able to apply their new skills domestically.

In many cases, however, these assumptions have little basis in reality. Unskilled workers simply don't get skilled jobs while overseas. Furthermore, even skilled workers may move down the occupational ladder, ending up as janitors or garbage collectors in host countries where menial jobs often pay considerably more than do skilled jobs at home. As a result, far from obtaining new skills, workers may be "deskilled." With regard to the second assumption, it is more realistic to assume that migrants who do manage to move up the occupational ladder and obtain better skills are the least likely to return home, as for them the chance of steady advancement may be better overseas. This alternative assumption is particularly valid for those who migrate to the industrial countries, which both attract and sanction the largest number of skilled permanent immigrants. Moreover, migrants who do eventually return home may discover that their new skills are not applicable to the level of technology used there. They have become "overskilled" with respect to domestic production.

Distribution of Income

The benefits argument assumed that overseas migrants are usually drawn from the most disadvantaged sections of the population. In reality, it is probably the middle-income households that make up the most significant migration streams. This is explained by the fact that the emigration of a worker involves an initial investment (e.g., recruiting agency fees, airline tickets, taxes), which may be beyond the reach of the poorest families. Hence, poorer households may be left out of the process, and remittance income would flow to the middle-income families, making them even richer. In real terms, those households that are unable to afford to send a worker may be even worse off if remittance inflows fuel domestic price inflation in food staples and consumer household goods.

Conclusion

In addition to the preceding critique of the presumed benefits of international migration for the exporting country, there are a number of related reservations that deserve mention. First, while the labor-importing country can turn off the "valve" of labor migration whenever it so desires, the labor-exporting country has no power to turn it back on. As a result, international migration implies a dependence of the labor-exporting country on the labor-importing country. If, in the long run, the labor-exporting country cannot find ways to expand employment opportunities at home, it may be faced with an overwhelming influx of workers should they suddenly be repatriated by the host country—a not unlikely occurrence in view of the recent experience of such important host countries as Saudi Arabia, Kuwait, Germany, and Switzerland. Absorbing the returning workers at short notice would be difficult for a country that had failed to follow a policy of gradually reducing dependence on international migration. Second, it has been suggested that by allowing the industrial countries to import their workers, developing countries may have gained individually but have lost collectively. Given the relative scarcity of labor in capital-rich countries, the labor-intensive firms in these countries might have in fact relocated themselves in developing countries had not the developing countries so willingly supplied cheap labor. Such relocation could conceivably provide even more employment for local labor than that created by international migration, while simultaneously increasing LDC productive capacity.

In conclusion it appears that the social as opposed to the private benefits of international migration may not be as great as suggested by advocates of free factor mobility, particularly for the labor-exporting countries. In fact, it may cause even more harm than good for the labor-exporting country if it leads to a drain of skilled workers, excess consumer demand, a reduction in agricultural output, a worsening of the distribution of income, or any of the other pitfalls discussed above. It falls on the governments that sanction emigration, therefore, to play a more active role in controlling its consequences.

The Growing Refugee Problem

One form of migration, both internal and international, that is not primarily motivated by economic but by political, ideological, and religious or ethnic factors is that of the ever growing number of global refugees. According to recent estimates, there are 12.6 million refugees living throughout the world today, with over a third of these people being displaced within their own country. Africa contains 6.3 million refugees, half of the world's total. It is followed by Asia, including the Middle East, with 5.8 million refugees. In total, the developing countries account for almost 98% of the world's refugees, both in terms of origin and place of asylum. By origin, Ethiopian (3.8 million), Palestinian (1.8 million), and Afghan (1.5 million) refugees comprise the largest groups. Other prominent sources are Kampuchea, Lebanon, Iran, Uganda, Chad, and South Africa. As places of asylum for foreign refugees, Somalia (1.5 million Ethiopians), Pakistan (1.4 Afghans), and Jordan (716,400 Palestinians) numerically bear the largest burden. As a ratio of the total population, foreign refugees are most significant in Somalia (1:3), Jordan (1:5), and Djibouti (1:10). Countries with a per capita GNP of less that $500 harboring significant numbers of refugees include Somalia, Djibouti, Cameroon, Sudan, Pakistan, and Zaire. In essence, the refugee problem is a major developing country problem, with many of the poorest nations bearing a disproportionate share of the burden of sheltering these unfortunate people.[11]

Providing some assistance to countries sheltering refugee populations are a handful of international and private relief agencies, supplemented by individual governments and regional organizations. Of the international organizations, the largest are the United Nations High Commissioner for Relief (UNHCR) and the United Nations Relief and Works Administration (UNRWA) which assists primarily Palestinians. Other UN agencies, such as UNICEF and UNESCO, have begun playing a more active role recently. The combined budget of these specialized relief agencies was about $700 million in 1981. Private and voluntary agencies include the Red Cross Society, the Red Crescent Society, the International Council on Voluntary Agencies, and numerous other religious and secular groups. Regional bodies like the European Economic Community (EEC) and the Organization of African Unity (OAU) have also helped to some extent.

There are, however, major problems with the current global refugee policy. First, this policy generally follows the UN official definition of a refugee as "a person, who owing to well-founded fear of being persecuted for reasons of race, religion, nationality, membership of a particular social group or political opinion, is outside the country of his nationality and is unable or, owing to such fear, is unwilling to avail himself of the protection of that country." This definition had its origin in the problems of European refugees following the Second World War and, for two reasons, can no longer be considered applicable:

1. Many Third World refugees who are outside their country did not leave out of a "well-founded fear of being persecuted" as individuals directly, although they may have left a climate of war, civil strife, or general terror and repression. However, if these individuals are denied refugee status, they may well suffer persecution on being *returned* to their country, for reasons of "betrayal."
2. Many refugees fleeing the ravages of war or civil strife may be displaced *within* their own country and are as worthy of assistance as those crossing the border.

The UN definition ignores both of these possibilities, and as a result, many refugees are denied assistance from international organizations. Furthermore, the UN definition is often used for political purposes by individual governments. Governments will often ignore the definition in welcoming exiles from a "hostile" country as bonafide refugees but then invoke it to deny refugee status to people who flee a "friendly" country. The UN itself has been hamstrung in some cases, like Kampuchea, in providing relief to refugees because of political infighting between its member governments.

Second, current global refugee policy is directed at providing relief for refugees in their initial place of asylum until they can be resettled in a third country, usually an industrial country, which can afford to absorb them. The problem with this approach is that it also dates back to the Second World War, when assistance was given to European refugees to resettle in Western countries in which they were welcomed and could assimilate easily. Third World refugees, on the other hand, are not as readily welcomed by Western countries and must wait long periods of time before resettlement in the West takes place. At the current rate of resettlement, most of today's refugees will never be resettled. Moreover, those refugees who are finally resettled in Western countries find themselves placed in localities that bear little resemblance to their own and whose populations can frequently be hostile and where survival itself depends on possessing skills or education that most will lack.

In response to these two major problems in global refugee policy, two basic reforms have been proposed: (a) a change in the official definition of a refugee, and (b) the adoption of a development-oriented policy regarding refugee assistance.

Official definition of a refugee. Critics of the present UN definition of a refugee have advocated the adoption of a new definition that will cover the diverse nature of today's refugee problems. Specifically, it has been proposed that the definition (a) cover refugees who are internally displaced as well as those who cross borders and (b) apply to all people who leave their country out of a *general* sense of fear arising from war, political turmoil, or repression. The inclusion of people who flee poverty and economic chaos that stems from government mismanagement and/or corruption has also been proposed. Individual governments in Europe have already implemented such a definition, in deed if not in word, by granting quasi-refugee or B-refugee status to people who flee their country as a result of a general climate of oppression or who seek opportunities not available at home due to mismanagement by their government.

A development-oriented strategy. As opposed to the present policy of relief and resettlement in a third country, an alternative strategy calls for development-oriented aid to the country of initial asylum and/or to the country of origin. It is hoped that by offering additional development aid to the country of initial asylum, which currently harbors refugees indefinitely, that country will be able to assimilate the refugees constructively within its own economy rather than bearing the burden of operating permanent relief camps. This would eliminate the problems of finding ultimate havens in Western countries and perhaps place refugees in countries with some ethnic similarities, as well as provide an economic stimulus to the asylum country. By offering additional development aid to the country of origin, it is hoped that political solutions may be expedited and refugees reabsorbed more easily into the economy.

There are, however, a number of problems with this approach as well. First, the country of initial asylum may be reluctant to accept such long-term aid if it means permanently legitimizing the presence of foreigners. And the country of origin may be unable or unwilling to implement political solutions, the prospect of aid notwithstanding. Second, countries donating aid may find it politically more useful to continue committing money to more immediate, humanitarian relief rather than to long-run development assistance which has low visibility. Third, such a policy may allow the industrial countries to dodge their responsibilities in helping refugees, by excusing them from physically accepting these global migrants.

Whatever policy decisions are made, however, one can be sure that the combined effects of rapid population growth, rising unemployment, and continued social and political unrest will make the global refugee problem even more serious in the coming years.

SUMMARY AND CONCLUSIONS: THE SHAPE OF A COMPREHENSIVE MIGRATION AND EMPLOYMENT STRATEGY

At various points throughout this and the previous chapter, we have looked at possible policy approaches designed to improve the very serious migration and employment situation in Third World countries. We conclude with a summary of what appears to be the "consensus" opinion of most economists on the shape of a comprehensive migration and employment strategy.[12] This would appear to have *six key elements:*

1. *Creating an appropriate rural–urban economic balance.* A more appropriate balance between rural and urban economic opportunities appears to be indispensable to ameliorating both urban and rural unemployment problems in developing countries and to slowing the pace of rural–urban migration. The main thrust of this activity should be in the integrated development of the rural sector, the spread of small-scale industries throughout the countryside, and the reorientation of economic activity and social investments toward the rural areas.
2. *Expansion of small-scale, labor-intensive industries.* The composition or "product mix" of output has obvious effects on the magnitude (and, in many cases, the location) of employment opportunities since some products (often basic consumer goods) require more labor per unit of output and per unit of capital than others. Expansion of these mostly small-scale and labor-intensive industries in both urban and rural areas can be accomplished in two ways: *directly* through government investment and incentives, particularly for activities in the urban informal sector, and *indirectly* through income redistribution (either directly or from future growth) to the rural poor whose structure of consumer demand is both less import-intensive and more labor-intensive than the rich.
3. *Elimination of factor-price distortions.* There is ample evidence to demonstrate that correcting factor-price distortions primarily by eliminating various capital subsidies and curtailing the growth of urban wages would increase employment opportunities and make better use of scarce capital resources. But by how much and how quickly these policies would work is not clear. Moreover their migration implications would have to be ascertained. Surely correct pricing policies by themselves are insufficient to alter significantly the present employment situation for the reasons described in Chapter 8.
4. *Choosing appropriate labor-intensive technologies of production.* One of the principal factors inhibiting the success of any long-run program of employment creation both in urban industry and rural agriculture is the almost complete technological dependence of Third World nations on imported (typically labor-saving) machinery and equipment from the developed countries. Both domestic and international efforts must be made to reduce this dependence by developing technological research and adaptation capacities in the developing countries themselves. Such efforts might first be linked to the development of small-scale, labor-intensive rural and urban enterprises. They could also focus on the development of low-cost, labor-intensive methods of providing rural infrastructure needs including roads, irrigation and drainage systems, and essential health and educational services. Clearly this is an area where

scientific and technological assistance from the developed countries could prove extremely fruitful.

5. *Modifying the direct linkage between education and employment.* The emergence of the phenomenon of the "educated unemployed" in many developing countries is calling into question the appropriateness of massive quantitative expansion of educational systems, especially at the higher levels. Formal education has become the rationing tunnel through which all prospective jobholders must pass. As modern sector jobs multiply more slowly than the numbers leaving the educational tunnel, it becomes necessary to extend the length of the tunnel and to narrow its exit. While a full discussion of educational problems and policies must await Chapter 11, we may point out that one way to moderate the excessive demand for additional years of schooling (which in reality is a demand for modern sector jobs) would be for governments, often the largest employers, to base their hiring practices and their wage structures on other criteria. Moreover, the creation of attractive economic opportunities in rural areas would make it easier to redirect educational systems toward the needs of rural development. At present, many Third World educational systems, being transplants of Western systems, are oriented toward preparing students to function in a small modern sector employing at the most 20−30% of the labor force. Many of the necessary skills for development, therefore, remain largely neglected.

6. *Internalizing the domestic benefits of international migration.* As we discussed in Chapter 4, international migration historically has served as a "safety value" permitting countries with excess, unemployed, or low-paid labor to export these workers to labor-scarce, higher-wage nations. Today international migration from developing countries to both developed and other Third World nations is significant in volume but not nearly as significant in economic or quantitative terms as it was for Europe in the nineteenth century. While the benefits of international migration to the individual migrant and his or her family in the sending country are clearly positive, it is not at all apparent that the net benefits (i.e., benefits minus costs, both actual and opportunity) that accrue to the sending country are all that positive. Much will depend on the degree to which sending nations are able to internalize the potential social benefits of international migration through their ability to prevent excessive drains of highly skilled and professional workers, to control excess consumer demand arising from migrant remittances, to prevent losses of agricultural output to the extent that international migrants represent important elements of the rural economy, and to offset whatever negative employment and income distribution effects might result from the age, skill, and income class composition of international migrants. Finally, refugees represent a different category of global migrants, one whose plight requires more political and humanitarian rather than economic policy responses.

A Comment on Population

The reader may have noted that an active population policy is not among our major migration and employment-oriented strategies. Reducing excessive population growth is undoubtedly critical to the ultimate amelioration of both the urbanization and the employment problems, for the simple reason that it would reduce the future size and growth of new urban and international job seekers. However, we know that for the next 15 to 25 years the size of the LDC domestic labor force has already been determined by existing fertility rates. This does not negate the need to lower fertility rates as soon as possible, especially in heavily populated developing nations. The reason we have not included an active, government-sponsored family-planning program among our priority policy areas is simply that, as should be clear from the discussion in Chapter 7, each of the policies suggested here will contribute indirectly to lowering levels of fertility by raising living standards for the very poor, especially in rural areas.

NOTES

1. For additional information on the problems of rapid urban population growth, see Michael P. Todaro, "The urbanization dilemma," Reading 17 in *The Struggle for Economic Development,* and Bertrand Renaud, *National Urbanization Policy in Developing Countries* (New York: Oxford University Press, 1981).

2. United Nations Economic and Social Council, Population Commission, Twentieth Session, *Concise Report on Monitoring of Population Policies* E/CN.9/338, December 1978, pp. 27–28.

3. Richard Jolly, "Rural-urban migration: Dimensions, causes, issues and policies," in *Prospects for Employment Opportunities in the Nineteen Seventies* (Cambridge: Cambridge University Press, 1970), p. 4.

4. Pamela Brigg, "Migration to urban areas," *World Bank Staff Working Papers* No. 107 (1971).

5. H.N. Barnum and R.H. Sabot, *Migration, Education and Urban Surplus Labour,* OECD Development Center Employment Series Monograph, October 1975 (mimeo).

6. See, for example, Michael P. Todaro, "An analysis of industrialization, employment and unemployment in LDCs," *Yale Economic Essays* 8, no. 2 (1968): 329–492, and "A model of labor migration and urban unemployment in less developed countries," *American Economic Review* 59, no. 1 (1969): 138–148.

7. A comprehensive review of what governments in diverse developing countries have tried to do to stem the tide of rural–urban migration can be found in Alan B. Simmons, "A review and evaluation of attempts to constrain migration to selected urban centers and regions," Reading 19 in *The Struggle for Economic Development.*

8. United Nations, *International Migration: Policies and Programs* (New York: United Nations, 1983), p. 20.

9. *Ibid*, p. 40.

10. See, for example, J. S. Birks and C. A. Sinclair, *International Migration and Development in the Arab Region,* (Geneva: International Labor Office, 1980).

11. For an excellent and concise review of the refugee problem, both statistical and policy based, see Charles Keely, *Global Refugee Policy: The Case for a Development Oriented Strategy* (New York: Population Council, 1982). The data referred to in this section are from the Keely monograph.

12. See, for example, Edgar O. Edwards (ed.), *Employment in Developing Nations* (New York: Ford Foundation, 1974), pp. 1–46.

CONCEPTS FOR REVIEW

Push and pull migration factors	Present values
Job probabilities	Income differentials
Migrant time horizon	Urban–rural economic imbalances
Institutional urban wage	Induced migration
Demand curve for labor	Economic and social infrastructure
Expected income	Wage subsidy
Informal sector	Refugee

QUESTIONS FOR DISCUSSION

1. Why might the problem of rapid urbanization turn out to be a more significant "population policy" issue than curtailing Third World population growth rates over the next two decades? Explain.

2. Describe briefly the essential assumptions and major features of the Todaro model of rural−urban migration. One of the most significant implications of this model is the paradoxical conclusion that government policies designed to create more urban employment may in fact lead to more urban unemployment. Explain the reasons why such a paradoxical result might be forthcoming.

3. "The key to solving the serious problem of excessive rural−urban migration and rising urban unemployment and underemployment in Third World countries is to restore a proper balance between urban and rural economic and social opportunities." Discuss the reasoning behind this statement and give a few specific examples of government policies that will promote a better balance between urban and rural economic and social opportunities.

4. For many years the conventional wisdom of development economics assumed that there existed an inherent *conflict* between the objectives of maximizing output growth and promoting rapid industrial employment growth. Why might these two objectives be mutually supportive rather than conflicting? Explain.

5. What is meant by the expression "getting prices right"? Under what conditions will liminating factor-price distortions generate substantial new employment opportunities? Be sure to include in your discussion a brief definition of what is meant by "factor-price distortions."

6. Distinguish between the economic determinants and consequences of international migration and the political and economic background to the global refugee problem. What types of policies might be required to deal with these separate issues?

FURTHER READINGS

Four useful surveys of urbanization issues in developing nations are Philip Hauser et al., *Population and the Urban Future* (New York: State University of New York Press, 1982); Alan Gilbert and Josef Gugler, *Cities, Poverty and Development* (New York: Oxford University Press, 1982); Helen I. Safa (ed.), *Towards a Political Economy of Urbanization in Third World Countries* (Delhi: Oxford University Press, 1982); and P. K. Ghosh (ed.), *Urban Development in the Third World* (Westport, Conn.: Greenwood, 1984).

Among the many readings on the critical problem of rural−urban migration in developing countries, the following are perhaps the most comprehensive: D. Byerlee, "Rural−urban migration in Africa: Theory, policy and research implications," *International Migration Review,* 1974; P. Brigg, "Migration to urban areas: A survey," *World Bank Staff Working Papers* No. 107 (1971); N. Carynnyk-Sinclair, "Rural to urban migration in developing countries, 1950−1970: A survey of the literature," *Working Paper WEP 2−19,* International Labor Organization, February 1974; J. R. Harris and M. P. Todaro, "Migration, unemployment and development: A two-sector analysis," *American Economic Review,* March 1970, reprinted as Reading 18 in *The Struggle for Economic Development;* M. P. Todaro, *Internal Migration in Developing Countries: A Review of Theory, Evidence, Methodology and Research Priorities* (Geneva: International Labor Organization, 1976); Sally Findlay, *Planning for Internal Migration* (Washington, D.C.: U.S. Department of Commerce, 1977); and "Migration, population growth and development," *Population Reports,* Series M, No. 7, September 1983 (Johns Hopkins University).

For a suggested national and international strategy to combat Third World poverty and unemployment, see ILO, *Employment, Growth and Basic Needs: A One-World Problem* (Geneva: International Labor Organization, 1976); Lyn Squire, *Employment Policy in Developing Countries: A Survey of Issues and Evidence* (New York: Oxford University Press, 1981); and S. Kannappan, *Employment Problems and the Urban Labor Market in Developing Nations* (Ann Arbor: University of Michigan Press, 1983).

Two excellent sources of information on international migration and refugees are UN, *International Migration: Policies and Programs* (New York: United Nations, 1983), and Charles Keely, *Global Refugee Policy* (New York: Population Council, 1982).

Additional readings can be found on pp. 625−627.

APPENDIX 9.1

A MATHEMATICAL FORMULATION OF
THE TODARO MIGRATION MODEL

Consider the following mathematical formulation of the basic Todaro model discussed in this chapter. Individuals are assumed to base their decision to migrate on considerations of income maximization and what they perceive to be their expected income streams in urban and rural areas. It is further assumed that the individual who chooses to migrate is attempting to achieve the prevailing average income for his level of education or skill attainment in the urban center of his choice. Nevertheless, he is assumed to be aware of his limited chances of immediately securing wage employment and the likelihood that he will be unemployed or underemployed for a certain period of time. It follows that the migrant's expected income stream is determined both by the prevailing income in the modern sector and by the probability of being employed there, rather than being underemployed in the urban informal sector or totally unemployed.

If we let $V(0)$ be the discounted present value of the expected net urban–rural income stream over the migrant's time horizon; Y_u, $Y_r(t)$ the average real incomes of individuals employed in the urban and the rural economy; n the number of time periods in the migrant's planning horizon; and r the discount rate reflecting the migrant's degree of time preference, then the decision to migrate or not will depend on whether

$$V(0) = \int_{t=0}^{n} [p(t)Y_u(t) - Y_r(t)]e^{-rt}\, dt - C(0)$$

is positive or negative,

where $C(0)$ represents the cost of migration, and
$p(t)$ is the probability that a migrant will have secured an urban job at the average income level in period t.

In any one time period, the probability of being employed in the modern sector, $p(t)$, will be directly related to the probability π of having been selected in that or any previous period from a given stock of unemployed or underemployed job seekers. If we assume that for most migrants the selection procedure is random, then the probability of having a job in the modern sector within x periods after migration, $p(x)$, is

$$p(1) = \pi(1)$$

and

$$p(2) = \pi(1) + [1 - \pi(1)]\pi(2)$$

so that

$$p(x) = p(x - 1) + [1 - p(x - 1)]\pi(x)$$

or

$$p(x) = \pi(1) + \sum_{t=2}^{x} \pi(t) \prod_{s=1}^{t-1} [1 - \pi(s)]$$

where $\pi(t)$ equals the ratio of new job openings relative to the number of accumulated job aspirants in period t.

It follows from this probability formulation that for any given level of $Y_u(t)$ and $Y_r(t)$, the longer the migrant has been in the city the higher his probability p of having a job and the higher, therefore, is his expected income in that period.

Formulating the probability variable in this way has two advantages:

1. It avoids the "all or nothing" problem of having to assume that the migrant either earns the average income or earns nothing in the periods immediately following migration; consequently, it reflects the fact that many underemployed migrants will be able to generate some income in the urban informal or traditional sector while searching for a regular job.
2. It modifies somewhat the assumption of random selection since the probability of a migrant having been selected varies directly with the time he has been in the city. This permits adjustments for the fact that longer-term migrants usually have more contacts and better information systems so that their expected incomes should be higher than those of newly arrived migrants with similar skills.

Suppose we now incorporate this behavioristic theory of migration into a simple aggregate dynamic equilibrium model of urban labor demand and supply in the following manner. We once again define the probability π of obtaining a job in the urban sector in any one time period as being directly related to the rate of new employment creation and inversely related to the ratio of unemployed job seekers to the number of existing job opportunities, that is:

$$\pi = \frac{\lambda N}{S - N} \tag{A9.1}$$

where λ is the net rate of urban new job creation
N is the level of urban employment and
S is the total urban labor force.

If w is the urban real wage rate and r represents average rural real income, then the "expected" urban–rural real income differential d is

$$d = w \cdot \pi - r \qquad \textbf{(A9.2)}$$

or, substituting (A9.1) into (A9.2),

$$d = w \cdot \frac{\lambda N}{S - N} - r \qquad \textbf{(A9.3)}$$

The basic assumption of our model once again is that the supply of labor to the urban sector is a function of the urban–rural *expected* real income differential, i.e.:

$$S = f_S(d) \qquad \textbf{(A9.4)}$$

If the rate of urban job creation is a function of the urban wage w and a policy parameter a (e.g., a concentrated governmental effort to increase employment through a program of import substitution), both of which operate on labor demand, we have

$$\lambda = f_d(w, a) \qquad \textbf{(A9.5)}$$

where it is assumed that $\partial \lambda / \partial a > 0$. If the growth in the urban labor demand is increased as a result of the governmental policy shift, the increase in the urban labor supply is

$$\frac{\partial S}{\partial a} = \frac{\partial S}{\partial d} \cdot \frac{\partial d}{\partial \lambda} \cdot \frac{\partial \lambda}{\partial a} \qquad \textbf{(A9.6)}$$

Differentiating (A9.3) and substituting into (A9.6), we obtain

$$\frac{\partial S}{\partial a} = \frac{\partial S}{\partial d} \cdot w \cdot \frac{N}{S - N} \cdot \frac{\partial \lambda}{\partial a} \qquad \textbf{(A9.7)}$$

The absolute number of urban employed will increase if the increase in labor supply exceeds the increase in the number of new jobs created, i.e., if

$$\frac{\partial S}{\partial a} > \frac{\partial (\lambda N)}{\partial a} = \frac{N \partial \lambda}{\partial a} \qquad \textbf{(A9.8)}$$

Combining (A9.7) and (A9.8), we get

$$\frac{\partial S}{\partial d} \cdot w \cdot \frac{N}{S - N} \cdot \frac{\partial \lambda}{\partial a} > \frac{N \partial \lambda}{\partial a} \qquad \textbf{(A9.9)}$$

or

$$\frac{\partial S/S}{\partial d/d} > \frac{d}{w} \cdot \frac{(S-N)}{S} \tag{A9.10}$$

or, finally, substituting for d:

$$\frac{\partial S/S}{\partial d/d} > \frac{w \cdot \pi - r}{w} \cdot \frac{(S-N)}{S} \tag{A9.11}$$

Expression (A9.11) reveals that the absolute level of unemployment will rise if the elasticity of urban labor supply with respect to the expected urban−rural income differential, $\partial S/S/\partial d/d$ (what has elsewhere been called the "migration response function"), exceeds the urban−rural differential as a proportion of the urban wage times the unemployment rate, $S - N/S$. Alternatively, Equation (A9.11) shows that the higher the unemployment rate, the higher must be the elasticity to increase the level of unemployment for any expected real income differential. But note that in most developing nations the inequality (A9.11) will be satisfied by a very low elasticity of supply when realistic figures are used. For example, if the urban real wage is 60, average rural real income is 20, the probability of getting a job is 0.50, and the unemployment rate is 20%, then the level of unemployment will increase if the elasticity of urban labor supply is greater than 0.033, i.e., substituting into (A9.11) we get

$$\frac{\partial S/S}{\partial d/d} = \frac{0 \cdot 50 \times 60 - 20}{60} \times 0.20 = 0.033$$

Much more needs to be known about the empirical value of this elasticity coefficient in different developing nations before it will be possible realistically to predict what the impact of a policy to generate more urban *employment* will be on the overall level of urban *unemployment*.

APPENDIX 9.2

THE URBAN INFORMAL SECTOR

Much discussion on the problems of Third World development has focused on the dualistic nature of developing countries' national economies—the existence of a modern capitalist sector geared toward capital-intensive, large-scale production and a traditional subsistence sector geared toward labor-intensive, small-scale production. In recent years, this dualistic analysis has also been applied specifically to the urban economy, which has been decomposed into a "formal" and an "informal" sector.

The existence of an informal sector was "formally" recognized in the early seventies following observations in several developing countries that massive additions to the urban labor force failed to show up in unemployment statistics. The bulk of new entrants to the urban labor force seemed to create their own employment or to work for small-scale family-owned enterprises. The self-employed were engaged in a remarkable array of activities ranging from hawking, street vending, letter writing, knife sharpening, and junk collecting to selling fireworks, prostitution, drug peddling, and snake charming. Others found jobs as mechanics, carpenters, small artisans, barbers, and personal servants. Subsequent studies revealed that the share of the urban labor force engaged in informal sector activities (legal ones) ranges anywhere from 20 to 70%, the average being around 50% (see Table A9.1). With the unprecedented rate of growth of the urban population in developing countries expected to continue (having increased from 275 million in 1950 to an estimated 2 billion in 2000) and with the increasing failure of the rural and urban formal sectors to absorb additions to the labor force, more attention is being devoted to the role of the informal sector in serving as a panacea for the growing unemployment problem.

The informal sector is characterized by a large number of small-scale production and service activities that are individually or family owned and use labor-intensive and simple technology. The usually self-employed workers in this sector have little formal education, are generally unskilled, and lack capital resources. As a result, worker productivity and income tend to be lower in the informal sector than in the formal sector. Moreover, workers in the informal sector do not enjoy the measure of protection afforded by the formal sector in terms of job security, decent working conditions, and old-age pensions. Most workers entering this sector are recent migrants from rural areas unable to find employment in the formal sector. Their motivation is usually to obtain sufficient income for survival purposes rather than necessarily for profit, relying on their own indigenous resources to create work. As many members of the household as possible are involved in income-generating

Table A9.1 Estimated Share of Urban Labor Force in the Informal Sector in Selected Developing Countries

Area	Share (%)
Africa	
Abidjan, Ivory Coast	31
Lagos, Nigeria	50
Kumasi, Ghana	60–70
Nairobi, Kenya	44
Urban areas, Senegal	50
Urban areas, Tunisia	34
Asia	
Calcutta, India	40–50
Ahmedabad, India	47
Jakarta, Indonesia	45
Colombo, Sri Lanka	19
Urban areas in West Malaysia, Malaysia	35
Singapore	23
Urban areas, Thailand	26
Urban areas, Pakistan	69
Latin America	
Cordoba, Argentina	38
Sao Paulo, Brazil	43
Urban areas, Brazil	30
Rio de Janeiro, Brazil	24
Belo Horizonte, Brazil	31
Urban areas, Chile	39
Bogota, Colombia	43
Santo Domingo, Dominican Republic	50
Guayaquil, Ecuador	48
Quito, Ecuador	48
San Salvador, El Salvador	41
Federal district and State of Mexico	27
Mexico, D.F., Guadalajara, and Monterey	42
Asuncion, Paraguay	57
Urban areas, Peru	60
Urban areas, Venezuela	44
Caracas, Venezuela	40
Kingston, Jamaica	33

SOURCE: S.U. Sethuraman, *The Urban Informal Sector in Developing Countries* (Geneva: International Labor Organization, 1981). Copyright © 1981 International Labour Organization, Geneva.

activities, including women and children; and they often work very long hours. Most inhabit shacks they themselves have built in slums and squatter settlements, which generally lack minimal public services such as electricity, water, drainage, transportation, and educational and health services.

In terms of its relationship with other sectors, the informal sector is linked with the rural sector in that it allows excess labor to escape from rural poverty and underemployment, although under living and working conditions and incomes that are not much better. It is closely connected with the formal urban sector: the formal sector depends on the informal sector for cheap inputs and wage goods for its workers, and the informal sector in turn depends on the growth of the formal sector for a good portion of its income and clientele. A strong case can be made that the informal sector in fact subsidizes the formal sector by providing raw materials and basic commodities for its workers at artificially low prices maintained through the formal sector's economic power and legitimacy granted by the government.

The important role that the informal sector plays in providing income opportunities for the poor is no longer open to debate. There is some question, however, as to whether the informal sector is merely a holding ground for people awaiting entry into the formal sector and, as such, is a transitional phase that must be made as comfortable as possible without perpetuating its existence until it is itself absorbed by the formal sector or whether it is here to stay and should in fact be promoted as a major source of employment and income for the urban labor force.

There seems to be a good argument in support of the latter view. The formal sector in developing countries has a small base in terms of output and employment. In order to absorb future additions to the urban labor force, the formal sector must be able to generate employment at a very high rate of at least 10% per annum, according to estimates made by the ILO. This means that output must grow at an even faster rate, since employment in this sector increases less than proportionately in relation to output. This sort of growth seems highly unlikely in view of current trends. Thus the burden on the informal sector to absorb more labor will continue to grow unless other solutions to the urban unemployment problem are provided.

Moreover, the informal sector has demonstrated its ability to generate employment and income for the urban labor force. As pointed out earlier, it is already absorbing an average of 50% of the urban labor force. Some studies have shown the informal sector generating almost a third of urban income.

Several other arguments can be made in favor of promoting the informal sector. First, scattered evidence indicates that the informal sector generates surplus even under the currently hostile policy environment, which denies it access to the advantages offered to the formal sector such as the availability of credit, foreign exchange, and tax concessions. Thus, the informal sector's surplus could provide an impetus to growth in the urban economy. Second, as a result of its low capital intensity, only a fraction of the capital needed in the formal sector is required to employ a worker in the informal sector, offering considerable savings to developing countries so often plagued with capital shortages. Third, by providing access to training and apprenticeships at substantially lower costs than that provided by formal institutions and the formal sector, the informal sector can play an important role in the formation of human capital. Fourth, the informal sector generates demand for semiskilled and unskilled labor whose supply is increasing in both relative and absolute terms and which is unlikely to be absorbed by the formal sector with its increasing demands for a skilled labor force. Fifth, the informal sector is more likely to adopt appropriate technologies and make use of local resources, allowing for a more efficient allocation of resources. Sixth, the informal sector plays an important role in recycling waste materials, engaging in the collection of goods ranging from scrap metals to cigarette butts, many of which find their way to the industrial sector or provide basic commodities for the poor. Finally, promotion of the informal sector would insure an increased distribution of the benefits of development to the poor, many of whom are concentrated in the informal sector.

Promotion of the informal sector is not, however, without its disadvantages. One of the major disadvantages in promoting the informal sector lies in the strong relationship between rural–urban migration and labor absorption in the informal sector. Migrants from the rural sector have both a lower unemployment rate and a shorter waiting period before obtaining a job in the informal sector. Promoting income and employment opportunities in the informal sector could therefore aggravate the urban unemployment problem by attracting more labor than either the informal or the formal sector could absorb. Furthermore, there is concern over the environmental consequences of a highly concentrated informal sector in the urban areas. Many informal sector activities cause pollution and congestion (e.g., pedi-cabs) or inconvenience to pedestrians (e.g., hawkers and vendors). Moreover, increased densities in slums and low-income neighborhoods, coupled with poor urban services, could cause enormous problems for urban areas. Any policy measures designed to promote the informal sector must be able to cope with these various problems.

There has been little discussion in the literature as to what sorts of measures might be adopted to promote the informal sector. The ILO has made some general suggestions. To begin with, governments will have to dispense with the currently hostile attitude toward the informal sector and maintain a more positive and sympathetic posture. In addition, they might register these small enterprises in an effort to obtain more information about them for planning purposes. Since access to skills plays an important role in determining the structure of the informal sector, governments should facilitate training in those areas that are most beneficial to the urban economy. In this way, the government can play a role in shaping the informal sector so that it contains production and service activities that provide the most value to society. Specifically, such measures might promote legal activities, and discourage illegal ones, by providing proper skills and other incentives.

The lack of capital is a major constraint on activities in the informal sector. The provision of credit would therefore permit these enterprises to expand, produce more profit, and hence generate more income and employment. Access to improved technology would have similar effects. Providing infrastructure and suitable locations for work (e.g., designating specific areas for stalls) could help alleviate some of the environmental consequences of an expanded informal sector. More importantly, better living conditions must be provided, if not directly, then by promoting growth of the sector on the fringes of urban areas or in smaller towns where the population will settle close to its new area of work, away from the urban density. Promotion of the informal sector outside the urban areas may also help with redirecting the flow of rural–urban migration, especially if carried out in conjunction with the policies discussed at the end of Chapter 9.

In conclusion, while there are several convincing arguments for promoting the informal sector's development in an effort to generate employment and income for the urban poor, it should be remembered that this is only one step among many needed to solve the problems of poverty and unemployment in urban areas.

FURTHER READINGS

Readings on the informal sector include Helen I. Safa, *Towards a Political Economy of Urbanization in Third World Countries* (Delhi: Oxford University Press, 1982); A. Gilbert and J. Gugler, *Cities, Poverty and Development* (New York: Oxford University Press, 1982); S. U. Sethuraman, *The Urban Informal Sector in Developing Countries: Employment, Poverty and Environment* (Geneva: ILO, 1981); D. Mazumdar, "The urban informal sector," *World Development* 4, no. 8 (1976); and, especially, Harry W. Richardson, "The role of the informal sector in developing countries: An overview," *Regional Development Dialogue*, Autumn 1984.

10

AGRICULTURAL TRANSFORMATION
AND RURAL DEVELOPMENT

It is in the agricultural sector that the battle for long term economic development will be won or lost.

Gunnar Myrdal, Nobel Laureate, Economics

The main burden of development and employment creation will have to be borne by the part of the economy in which agriculture is the predominant activity: that is, the rural sector.

Francis Blanchard, Director-General,
International Labor Organization

THE IMPERATIVE OF AGRICULTURAL PROGRESS AND RURAL DEVELOPMENT

If migration to the cities in Africa, Asia, and Latin America is proceeding at historically unprecedented rates, a large part of the explanation can be found in the economic stagnation of the outlying rural areas. This is where the people are. Over 1.9 billion people in the Third World grind out a meager and often inadequate existence in agricultural pursuits. Over 2.6 billion people lived in rural areas in the mid-1980s. Estimates indicate that this figure will rise to almost 3.1 billion by the year 2000. In Latin America and Asia people living in the countryside comprise considerably more than half the total populations of such diverse nations as Bolivia, Guatemala, India, Indonesia, Burma, Ecuador, Sri Lanka, Pakistan, the Philippines, and China. In Africa the ratios are much higher, with almost every country having rural dwellers in excess of three-quarters of the total population. In spite of the massive migration to the cities, the absolute population *increase* in rural areas of most Third World nations will continue to be greater than that of urban areas for at least the next decade.

Of greater importance than sheer numbers is the fact that the vast majority (almost 70%) of the world's poorest people are also located in rural areas and engaged primarily in subsistence agriculture. Their basic concern is survival. Many hundreds of millions of people have been bypassed by whatever economic "progress" has been attained. In their daily struggle to subsist, their behavior may often seem irrational to Western economists who have little comprehension of the precarious nature of subsistence living and the importance of avoiding risks. If "development" is to take place and become self-sustaining, it will have to start in the rural areas in general and the agricultural sector in particular. The core problems of widespread poverty, growing inequality, rapid population growth, and rising unemployment all find their origins in the stagnation and often retrogression of economic life in rural areas.

Traditionally, the role of agriculture in economic development has been viewed as largely passive and supportive. Based on the historical experience of Western countries, economic development was seen as requiring a rapid structural transformation of the economy from one predominantly focused on agricultural activities to a more complex modern industrial and service society. As a result, agriculture's primary role was to provide sufficient low-priced food and manpower to the expanding industrial economy, which was thought to be the dynamic, "leading sector" in any overall strategy of economic development. Lewis's famous two-sector model discussed in Chapter 3 is an outstanding example of a theory of development that places heavy emphasis on rapid industrial growth with an agricultural sector fueling this industrial expansion by means of its cheap food and surplus labor.

Today, as we have seen, development economists are less sanguine about the desirability of placing such heavy emphasis on rapid industrialization. Perhaps more importantly, they have come to realize that far from playing a passive, supporting role in the process of economic development, the agricultural sector in particular and the rural economy in general need to be the dynamic and leading elements in any overall strategy—at least for the vast majority of contemporary Third World countries. To a large extent, therefore, the 1970s witnessed a remarkable transition in development thinking—one in which agricultural and rural development came to be seen by many as the *sine qua non* of national development. Without such agricultural and rural development, industrial growth either would be stultified or, if it succeeded, would create such severe internal imbalances in the economy that the problems of widespread poverty, inequality, and unemployment would become even more pronounced.

Five main questions, therefore, need to be asked about Third World agriculture and rural development as these relate to overall national development:

1. How can total agricultural output and productivity per capita be substantially increased in a manner that will directly benefit the average small farmer and the landless rural dweller while providing a sufficient food surplus to support a growing urban, industrial sector?
2. What is the process by which traditional low-productivity subsistence farms are transformed into high-productivity commercial enterprises?

3. When traditional small farmers and peasant cultivators resist change is their behavior stubborn and irrational or are they acting rationally within the context of their particular economic environment?

4. Are economic incentives sufficient to elicit output increases among peasant agriculturalists or are institutional and structural changes in rural farming "systems" also required?

5. Is raising agricultural productivity sufficient to improve rural life or must there be concomitant improvements in educational, medical, and other social services? In other words, what do we mean by "rural development" and how can it be achieved?

Our approach in this chapter is to start with a brief factual account of the relative stagnation of the agricultural sector in most Third World nations over the past two decades. Next, we describe and analyze the basic characteristics of agrarian systems in Latin America, Asia, and Africa to see if we can identify some important similarities and differences. We then look at the economics of subsistence agriculture and discuss the stages of transition from subsistence to commercial farming in Third World Nations. Our focus here is on not only the economic factors but also the social, institutional, and structural requirements of small-farm modernization. We then explore the meaning of rural development and review alternative policies designed to raise levels of living in Third World rural areas. A brief look at the Chinese experience with rural development and the lessons, if any, that this experience affords to other developing nations concludes the chapter.

AGRICULTURAL STAGNATION IN THE DEVELOPMENT DECADES

We have seen that many developing countries experienced respectable rates of GNP growth during the 1960s and 1970s. The greatest proportionate share of this overall growth occurred in the manufacturing and commerce sectors, where recorded rates of annual output growth often exceeded 10%. In contrast, agricultural output growth for most developing regions remained stagnant during these decades so that the share of agricultural output in total GNP declined. Table 10.1 reveals that in spite of the fact that the agricultural sector accounts for most of the employment in developing countries, it accounts for a much lower share of the output. In fact, in no Third World region does agricultural production constitute more than 35% of the total national product. This is in marked contrast to the historical experience of advanced countries where agricultural output in their early stages of growth always contributed at least as much to total output as the share of the labor force engaged in these activities. The fact that contemporary Third World agricultural *employment* is typically twice as large in proportion to the total as is agricultural *output* simply reflects the relatively low levels of labor productivity compared with that in manufacturing and commerce.

The data in Table 10.1 and especially in Chapter 5, where we discussed the sectoral location of absolute poverty, strongly suggest that a direct attack on rural poverty through accelerated agricultural development is necessary to raise rural living standards. Mere concern with maximizing GNP growth is not enough. Unfortunately, the record of the past three decades offers little hope, as can be seen from Table 10.2 and Figure 10.1

Over the two decades that ended in 1970, per capita food production and per capita agricultural production (which includes not only food but

Table 10.1 Output and Employment in Third World Agriculture, 1982

Third World regions	% of labor force in agriculture	Output of agriculture, forestry, and fishing as % of GDP
South Asia	69	35
East Asia (including China)	66	29
Latin America	39	23
Africa	66	31

SOURCE: *World Development Report, 1984*, Annex Tables 3, 21. Reprinted by permission of Oxford University Press.

also nonedible agricultural products like cotton, sisal, and rubber) each increased less than 1% per year in the Third World as a whole. Moreover, as Table 10.2 shows, the rates of growth of both these measures of agricultural performance were much slower in the 1960s than in the 1950s. In fact, the agricultural sector in many developing countries completely stagnated in the 1960s. People on the whole were little or no better off in terms of the *per capita* availability of food at the end of the decade than they were at the beginning. The situation improved somewhat during the 1970s as develop-

Table 10.2 The Growth (and Stagnation) of Per Capita Food and Agricultural Output in Third World Regions, 1950–1980

Region	Growth in per capita food production (%)			Growth in per capita agricultural production (%)		
	1948/52–60	*1960–70*	*1970–80*	*1948/52–60*	*1960–70*	*1970–80*
Latin America	0.4	0.6	0.9	0.2	0.0	0.7
Far East (excluding Japan)	0.8	0.3	0.7	0.7	0.3	0.6
Near East (excluding Israel)	0.7	0.0	0.7	0.8	0.0	0.4
Africa (excluding South Africa)	0.0	−0.7	−1.2	0.3	−0.5	−1.4
All developing countries	0.6	0.1	0.5	0.6	0.0	0.8
Developed capitalist countries	1.1	0.9	1.3	1.0	0.6	1.2

SOURCE: K. Griffin, "Agrarian policy: The political and economic context," *World Development* 1, no. 11 (1973):3; UNCTAD, *1981 Supplement*, Table 6.5A, p. 361–362.

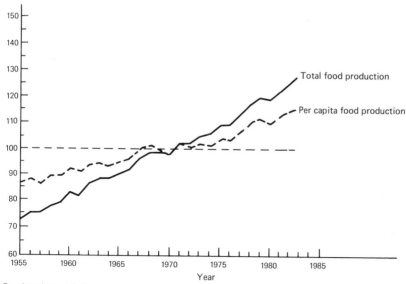

(a) Developed countries[a]

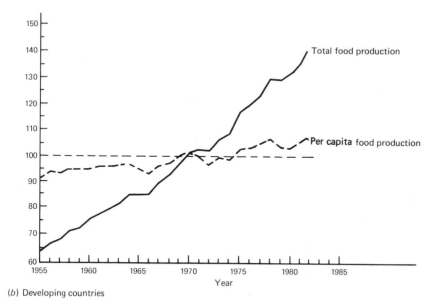

(b) Developing countries

Figure 10.1. Indexes of food production, 1955–1982 (1969–1971 = 100). *Source:* ODC, *U.S. Foreign Policy and the Third World, Agenda 1983* (New York: Praeger, 1983), Table D-1; United Nations, *World Economic Survey 1983*, Table III-12. Note: Data do not include centrally planned economies; inedible fiber products such as cotton, hemp, and wool; or noncaloric products such as tobacco, coffee, tea, and spices. [a]Developed countries = United States, Canada, Japan, South Africa, Europe, Australia, and New Zealand.

ing countries increasingly turned their attention to raising agricultural productivity. As a result, from 1970 to 1980 per capita food production grew at an annual rate of 0.5%—almost matching their 1950s performance. Unfortunately, in the early 1980s per capita production once again slowed down. In contrast, in the more developed countries per capita food production continued to rise at a much more rapid annual rate, primarily because of a much slower population growth.

From Table 10.2 we can also see that these same broad tendencies were at work within each of the major regions of the Third World. In Latin America there was some increase in the growth of per capita food production, but agricultural production in the 1960s as a whole showed no such increase. The picture for Africa is even more dismal. Per capita food production declined sharply in the 1960s and became even worse in the 1970s. This suggests that the average African suffered a *fall* in his level of food consumption during the past two decades. Since food consumption constitutes by far the largest component in a typical African's standard of living, the total decline of almost 15% in per capita food consumption meant that the region as a whole was becoming even more underdeveloped during the period 1960–1980.

The agricultural performance in Asia was only slightly better. In the Near East there was a decline in the rate of growth compared to the pre-1960 period. During the 1960s both per capita food and agricultural production tended to stagnate while in the 1970s food production rose sufficiently to provide slight increases in per capita output. Rates of growth also fell in the Far East though production per capita did increase at about 0.6% per annum during the 1970s.

We may conclude that in spite of some impressive rates of per capita GNP growth recorded in Third World regions during the 1960s and 1970s, growth in the agricultural sector not only showed negligible progress overall but in some regions even declined. Since the vast majority of people in developing countries seek their livelihoods in this sector, the data of Table 10.2 confirm what we discovered in Chapter 5: the magnitude and extent of Third World poverty has probably worsened over the past two decades. This becomes especially apparent when one realizes that per capita aggregates for food consumption mask the inherently unequal distribution of that consumption, just as per capita GNP figures often mask the magnitude of absolute poverty.

Finally, using Figure 10.1 to look at the experience of the early 1980s, we can see that the per capita food production picture for the Third World shows only a very negligible improvement in 1982 compared with the base period of 1969–1971. Even though total food production increased by 41% between 1970 and 1982, rapid population growth in the LDCs meant that per capita food production rose by only 15%. Compounding this production problem along with the persistence of severe droughts and famines in many parts of central Africa and South Asia was the unprecedented rise in world food and fertilizer prices during the 1970s. The combination of growing populations, increased resource scarcities, and rapidly rising food prices has undoubtedly meant a marked deterioration in levels of living for that sizable segment of mankind that spends 80% of its income on food. A doubling in the price of wheat, maize, or rice (as occurred in the early 1970s) cannot possibly be offset by increased expenditures on the part of these already impoverished people. Such an increase, then, can only drive a subsistence diet below the subsistence and survival level.

In sub-Saharan Africa the situation is particularly acute. The United Nations Food and Agriculture Organization (FAO) has repeatedly warned of catastrophic food shortages during the 1980s. In a majority of African countries, the average per capita calorie intake has now fallen below minimal nutritional standards. Of Africa's 465 million people, the FAO estimates that more than 150 million suffer from some form of malnutrition associated with inadequate food supplies. Whereas the severe famine of 1973–1974 took the lives of hundreds of thousands and left many more with permanent damage from malnutrition, its geographic impact was limited to the Sahelian belt that stretches below the Sahara from Cape Verde, off the coast of Senegal in the west, across the continent to Ethiopia. By contrast in 1982–1984, the food crisis became much more widespread, with more than 22 nations threatened by severe famine, including, in addition to the Sahelian nations, Zambia, Tanzania, Zimbabwe, and Angola.

A major reason for the relatively poor performance of Third World agriculture has been the neglect of this sector in the development priorities of the 1950s and 1960s. This neglect of agriculture and the accompanying bias toward investment in the urban industrial economy in turn can be traced largely to the misplaced emphasis on rapid industrialization that permeated development thinking and strategy during these two decades. For example, during the 1950s and throughout most of the 1960s the share of total national investment allocated toward the agricultural sector in a sample of 18 LDCs was approximately 12%, even though agriculture in these countries accounted for almost 30% of the GNP and more than 60% of the total employment.[1] As we saw in Chapter 9, one significant manifestation of this rural neglect and the corresponding emphasis on urban growth has been the massive migration of rural peasants into the teeming cities of Third World nations.

As a result of this disappointing experience and the realization that the future of most underdeveloped countries will depend to a large extent on what happens to their agriculture, there has been a marked shift in development thinking and policymaking. This shift, which began in the late 1970s, has been away from the almost exclusive emphasis on rapid industrialization and toward a more realisitc appreciation of the overwhelming importance of agricultural and rural development for national development. A first step toward understanding what is needed for agricultural and rural development, however, must be a comprehension of the nature of agricultural systems in diverse Third World regions and, in particular, of the economic aspects of the transition from subsistence to commercial agriculture.

THE STRUCTURE OF THIRD WORLD AGRARIAN SYSTEMS

Two Kinds of World Agriculture

When we look at the state of contemporary agriculture in most poor countries, we realize the enormity of the task that lies ahead. A brief comparison between agricultural productivity in the developed nations and the underdeveloped nations makes this clear.[2] World agriculture, in fact, comprises two distinct types of farming: (a) the *highly efficient agriculture of the developed countries*, where substantial productive capacity and high output per worker permits a very small number of farmers to feed entire nations; and (b) the *inefficient and low-productivity agriculture of developing countries*, where in many instances the agricultural sector can barely sustain the farm population, let alone the burgeoning urban population, even at a minimum level of subsistence.

The gap between the two kinds of agriculture is immense. This is best illustrated by the disparities in labor productivity, shown in Table 10.3. In 1960 the agricultural population of the developed nations totaled about 115 million people. They produced a total output amounting to $78 billion, or about $680 per capita of their agricultural population. In contrast, the per capita product of the agricultural population in the underdeveloped countries in 1960 was only $52. In other words, agricultural labor productivity in developed countries was more than 13 times that in the less developed countries. Projections for the end of the century show this productivity gap widening to 40 to 1.

In the developed countries, there has been a steady growth of agricultural output since the mid-eighteenth century. This growth has been spurred by technological and biological improvements, which have resulted in even higher levels of labor and land productivity. The growth rate accelerated after the First World War and particularly after the Second World War. The end result is that fewer farmers are able to produce more food. This is especially the case in the United States where less than 6% of the total work force is agricultural compared with more than 70% in the early nineteenth century. For example, in 1820 the American farmer could produce only 4 times his own consumption. One hundred years later, in 1920, his productivity had doubled and he could provide enough for 8 persons. It took only another 32 years for this productivity to double again, and then only 12 more years for it to double once more. By 1980 a single American farmer could provide enough food to feed almost 75 people. Moreover, during the entire period average farm incomes in North America were rising steadily.[3]

The picture is entirely different when we turn to the agricultural production experience of Third World nations. In many poor countries agricultural production methods have changed relatively slowly over time. Later in this chapter we discover that much of this technological stagnation can be traced to the special circumstances of subsistence agriculture with its high risks and uncertain rewards. Rapid rural population growth has compounded the problem by causing great pressure to be exerted on existing resources. Where fertile land is scarce, especially throughout South and Southeast Asia, but also in many parts of Latin America and Africa, rapid population growth has led to an increase in the number of people living on each unit of land. Given the same farming technology and the use of traditional nonlabor inputs (e.g., simple tools, animal power, traditional seeds), we know from the principle of diminishing returns that as more and more people are forced to work on a given piece of land, their marginal (and average) productivity will decline. The net result is a continuous deterioration in real living standards for rural peasants.

Table 10.3 Agricultural Population and Production in Developed and Less Developed Countries: 1960, 1980, and 2000

	1960		1980		2000	
	Developed nations	*LDCs*	*Developed nations*	*LDCs*	*Developed nations*	*LDCs*
Agricultural population (millions)	115	850	75	1,230	50	1,480
Agricultural production total ($ billions)	78	43	125	77	186	135
Per capita agricultural production ($)	680	52	1,660	63	3,720	91

SOURCE: From Raanan Weitz, FROM PEASANT TO FARMER: A REVOLUTIONARY STRATEGY FOR DEVELOPMENT, a Twentieth Century Fund Study. Copyright © 1971 by the Twentieth Century Fund.

In order to avert massive starvation and raise levels of living for the average rural dweller, agricultural production and the productivity of both labor *and* land must be rapidly increased throughout Asia, Africa, and Latin America. Third World nations need to become more self-sufficient in their food production. But unless some major economic, institutional, and structural changes are made, their dependence, especially on North American food supplies, will increase in the 1980s and 1990s.

Peasant Agriculture in Latin America, Asia, and Africa

In many developing countries, various historical circumstances have led to a concentration of large areas of land in the hands of a small class of powerful land owners. This is especially true in Latin America and parts of the Asian subcontinent. In Africa, both historical circumstances and the availability of relatively more unused land have resulted in a different pattern and structure of agricultural activity; however, in terms of levels of farm productivity there is little to distinguish among the three regions.

A common characteristic of agriculture in all three regions, and for that matter in many developed countries, is the position of the family farm as the basic unit of production. As Professor Weitz points out:

> For the vast number of farm families, whose members constitute the main agricultural work force, agriculture is not merely an occupation or a source of income; it is a way of life. This is particularly evident in traditional societies, where farmers are closely attached to their land and devote long, arduous days to its cultivation. Any change in farming methods perforce brings with it changes in the farmer's way of life. The introduction of biological and technical innovations must therefore be adapted not only to the natural and economic conditions, but perhaps even more to the attitudes, values and abilities of the mass of producers, who must understand the suggested changes, must be willing to accept them, and must be capable of carrying them out.[4]

Thus, in spite of the obvious differences between agricultural systems in Asia, Latin America, and Africa and among individual nations within each region, certain broad similarities enable us to make some generalizations and comparisons. In particular, agrarian systems in many parts of Asia and Latin America show more structural and institutional similarities than differences, and subsistence farmers in all three regions exhibit many of the same economic behavior patterns. We examine first the major features of agricultural systems in Latin America and Asia.

Latin America and Asia: Similarities and Differences

Although Latin America and Asia have very different heritages and cultures, peasant life in these two regions is in many ways similar. Francis Foland has succinctly described these similar features in the following passage:

> *Both the Latin American and Asian peasant is a rural cultivator whose prime concern is survival. Subsistence defines his concept of life. He may strive to obtain his and his family's minimal needs by tilling an inadequate piece of land which is his own or, more often, which is rented from or pawned to a landlord or money lender, or by selling his labour for substandard wages to a commercial agricultural enterprise. Profits which might come to him through the fortunes of weather or market are windfalls, not preconceived goals. Debt rather than profit is his normal fate, and therefore, his farming techniques are rationally scaled to his level of disposable capital: human and animal power rather than mechanized equipment; excrement rather than chemical fertilizers; traditional crops and seeds rather than experimental cultivations.*
>
> *No effective social security, unemployment insurance, or minimum-wage law ease his plight. His every decision and act impinge directly upon his struggle for physical survival. In countries with a high proportion of peasantry, traditional food crops which a rural family can itself convert readily into the daily fare for its grain- or tuber-based diet dominate the agriculture; corn in Mexico, rice in Indonesia, mandioca in Brazil, soybeans in China. India's is typical of peasant agriculture with seventy-five percent of the cropped land devoted to food grains such as rice, wheat, millets, barley and lentils. When these fail, as in Maharashtra in 1972, a peasant is reduced to trading his bullocks for a few bananas.[5]*

Although the day-to-day struggle for survival permeates the lives and attitudes of peasants in both Latin America and Asia (and also Africa, although the rural structure and institutions are considerably different), the nature of their agrarian existence differs markedly. In Latin America, the peasant's plight is rooted in the *latifundio—minifundio* system. In Asia, it lies primarily in fragmented and heavily congested dwarf parcels of land.

The *Latifundio—Minifundio* Pattern and Resource Underutilization in Latin America

In Latin America, as indeed in Asia and Africa, agrarian structures are not only part of the production system but also a basic feature of the entire economic, social, and political organization of rural life. The agrarian structure that has prevailed in Latin America since colonial times and that provides much of the region with its social organization is the pattern of agricultural dualism known as *latifundio—minifundio*. Basically, *latifundios* are very large landholdings. They are defined in Latin America as those farms large enough to provide employment for over 12 people. In contrast, *minifundios* are the smallest farms. They are defined as farms too small to provide employment for a single family (2 workers) with the typical incomes, markets, and levels of technology and capital prevailing in each country or region.

According to the FAO, 1.3% of landowners in Latin America hold 71.6% of the entire area of land under cultivation. If we exclude those countries that have carried out drastic land reforms during the last 60 years (Mexico, Bolivia, and Cuba), Latin America's agrarian structure seems to follow a uniform pattern. This pattern is basically one in which a small number of *latifundios* control a large proportion of the agricultural land while a vast number of *minifundios* must scratch a survival existence on a meager fraction of the occupied land. Moreover, they must be ready to provide unpaid seasonal labor to the *latifundios*.

Table 10.4 provides a dramatic picture of this unequal distribution of land holdings in seven Latin American countries. In no case do *minifundios*, which comprise up to 90% of the total farms, occupy more than 17% of the total agricultural land. In those countries with dense indigenous populations like Ecuador, Guatemala, and Peru, *minifundios* are particularly widespread. In all countries the *latifundios* comprise less than 7% of the total farms. Yet they occupy as much as 82% of the agricultural land. The average size of the *latifundios* in Argentina is 270 times that of the *minifundios* in Guatemala, and the *latifundio* is often as much as 1,732 times the size of the *minifundio*. Countries like Guatemala with large and rapidly growing indigenous populations crowded onto shrinking areas of poor land have even evolved what has come to be known as *microfundios* as a major form of land tenure. For example, at present 75,000 *microfundios* in Guatemala yield an average income that is less than one-third of that provided by its *minifundios* and about one-thousandth of the average incomes realized on its *latifundios*.[6] *Microfundio* peasants cannot even meet their subsistence requirements; they are thus forced to sell their labor at pitiful wages in order to secure a minimum diet for their families.

Table 10.4 *Minifundios* and *Latifundios* in the Agrarian Structure of Selected Latin American Countries

	Minifundios		Latifundios	
	Farms (%)	Occupied land (%)	Farms (%)	Occupied land (%)
Argentina	43.2	3.4	0.8	36.9
Brazil	22.5	0.5	4.7	59.5
Colombia	64.0	4.9	1.3	49.5
Chile	36.9	0.2	6.9	81.3
Ecuador	89.9	16.6	0.4	45.1
Guatemala	88.4	14.3	0.1	40.8
Peru	88.0	7.4	1.1	82.4

SOURCE: Celso Furtado, *Economic Development in Latin America* (New York: Cambridge University Press, 1970), p. 54.

But *latifundios* and *minifundios* do not constitute the entire gamut of Latin American agricultural holdings. A considerable amount of production is also earned on what are known as "family" farms and "medium-sized" farms. The former provides work for 2 to 4 people (recall the *minifundio* could only provide work for fewer than 2 people) while the latter, also sometimes known as "multifamily" farms, employ 4−12 workers (just below the *latifundio*). We see from Table 10.5 that in Argentina, Brazil, and Colombia, these intermediate forms of farm organization account for over 60% of total agricultural output and employ similar proportions of agricultural labor.

The economic and social ramifications of heavy land concentration in the hands of a few large landowners are compounded by the relative inefficiency of *latifundios* in comparison with other Latin American farm organizations. Economists normally assume that large farms (or firms) use productive resources more efficiently than small ones on the grounds that large enterprises can take advantage of economies of large-scale production and thereby lower costs. In terms of agriculture, the efficient utilization of large tractors and combine harvesters requires large tracts of land—otherwise, this capital equipment will be grossly underutilized. Recent evidence from a wide range of Third World countries, however, clearly demonstrates that small farms are more efficient (i.e., lower-cost) producers of most agricultural commodities.[7] For example, *minifundios* in Argentina, Brazil, and Chile yield more than twice the value of output per hectare under cultivation than do the *latifundios* and more than 10 times the value per hectare of total farmland.[8] This finding does not contradict the theory since most large farms in developed countries *are* lower-cost producers than small family farms. Rather, the explanation lies in the poor utilization of productive farm resources in developing nations—especially land resources on *latifundios* in Latin America. In terms of farm yields per unit of land actually under cultivation, the *latifundios* of Argentina, Brazil, Colombia, Chile, and Guatemala are all below not only the *minifundios* but also the medium-sized family farms.[9] Moreover, in Brazil it has been estimated that the *latifundios*, with an average area 31.6 times larger than that of the family farm, invest only 11.0 times as much. A considerable portion of the arable *latifundio* land is thus left idle. The net result is that *total factor productivity* on family farms was twice as high (and, therefore, unit costs twice as low) as on the large *latifundio* tracts of land. It follows that a redistribution of these large unused arable lands to family farms would probably raise national agricultural output and productivity. In terms of simple economic efficiency criteria, the argument for such redistribution is straightforward. However, the pattern of land ownership and control in Latin America is based on much more than economic criteria. It touches the whole social and political fabric of Latin American societies.

Such a concentrated distribution of land ownership is typically accompanied in Latin America, as it is in many parts of Asia, by a feudal-type social system in which the masses of small producers are dependent on the benevolence and goodwill of the large landowner. He has the power backed by local social and political institutions to permit them to make a meager living off his land or deny them even this opportunity, in which case they have no means of subsistence. Small producers pay for this privilege either by giving

Table 10.5 Agrarian Structure Indicators in Selected Latin American Countries

	Minifundios	Family farms	Medium-sized farms	Latifundios
Argentina				
Total farmland (%)	3	46	15	36
Value of agricultural product (%)	12	47	26	15
Labor employed (%)	30	49	15	6
Brazil				
Total farmland (%)	—	6	34	60
Value of agricultural product (%)	3	18	43	36
Labor employed (%)	11	26	42	21
Chile				
Total farmland (%)	—	8	13	79
Value of agricultural product (%)	4	16	23	57
Labor employed (%)	13	28	21	38
Colombia				
Total farmland (%)	5	25	25	45
Value of agricultural product (%)	21	45	19	15
Labor employed (%)	58	31	7	4
Guatemala				
Total farmland (%)	14	13	32	41
Value of agricultural product (%)	30	13	36	21
Labor employed (%)	68	13	12	7

SOURCE: Celso Furtado, *Economic Development in Latin America* (New York: Cambridge University Press, 1970), p. 55.

up to the landowner large proportions of their output (sometimes as much as 80%) or by working his land for no payment at different times of the year. In some cases, these tenant farmers must provide *both* output and free labor to the *patron*. Under such a system, landownership provides not only economic benefits but also, and often more importantly, social status and political power.

In short, a major explanation for the relative economic inefficiency and misuse of fertile land on the *latifundios* in Latin America is simply that the landowners often value these holdings not for their potential contributions to national agricultural output, but rather for the considerable power and prestige that they bring. (And as will be seen, this problem is not unique to Latin America.) It follows, and we discuss this issue later in the chapter, that raising agricultural production and improving the efficiency of Latin American agrarian systems in particular will require much more than direct economic policies that lead to the provision of better seeds, more fertilizer, less distorted factor prices, higher output prices, and improved marketing facilities. It will also require a reorganization of rural social and institutional structures to provide Latin American peasants, who now constitute almost

70% of the total rural population, a real opportunity to lift themselves out of their present state of economic subsistence and social subservience.

The Fragmentation and Subdivision of Peasant Land in Asia

If the major agrarian problem of Latin America can be identified as too much land under the control of too few people, the basic problem in Asia is one of too many people crowded onto too little land. For example, the per capita availability of arable land in India, the People's Republic of China, and Japan is 0.29, 0.20, and 0.07 hectares respectively. Central Java in Indonesia is an extreme example of the pressure of population on limited land that characterizes the Asian agrarian scene. It has the dubious distinction of possessing the world's record population density—over 1,500 persons per square km.[10]

In the course of the twentieth century rural conditions in Asia have deteriorated significantly. Professor Myrdal has identified three major and interrelated forces that have molded the traditional pattern of land ownership into its present fragmented condition: (a) the intervention of European rule; (b) the progressive introduction of monetized transactions and the rise in power of the moneylender; and (c) the rapid growth of Asian populations.[11]

Briefly, the traditional Asian agrarian structure before European colonization was organized around the village community. Local chiefs and peasant families each provided goods and services—produce and labor from the peasants to the chief in return for protection, rights to use community land, and the provision of public services. Decisions on the allocation, disposition, and use of the village's most valuable resource—land—belonged to the tribe or village community, either as a body or through its chief. Land could be redistributed among village members as a result of either population increase or natural calamities like droughts, floods, famines, war, or disease. Within the community, families had a basic right to cultivate land for their own use, and they could be evicted from their land only after a decision by the whole village community.

The arrival of the Europeans (mainly the British, French, and Dutch) led to major changes in the traditional agrarian structure, some of which had already begun. As Myrdal points out, "Colonial rule acted as an important catalyst to change, both directly through its effects on property rights and indirectly through its effects on the pace of monetization on the indigenous economy and on the growth of population."[12] In the area of property rights, European land tenure systems of private property ownership were both encouraged and reinforced by law. One of the major social consequences of the imposition of systems was, as Mydral says, the

> breakdown of much of the earlier cohesion of village life with its often elaborate, though informal, structure of rights and obligations. The landlord was given unrestricted rights to dispose of the land and to raise the tribute from its customary level to whatever amount he was able to extract. He was usually relieved of the obligation to supply security and public amenities because these functions were taken over by the government. Thus his status was transformed from that of a tribute receiver with responsibilities to the community to that of an absolute owner unencumbered by obligations toward the peasants and the public, other than the payment of land taxes.[13]

Contemporary landlords in India and Pakistan are able to avoid much of the taxation on income derived from their ownership of land. Today, the typical landlord in South Asia is an absentee owner who lives in the town and turns over the working of the land to sharecroppers and tenant farmers. In many respects, therefore, his position of power in the economic, political, and social structure of the rural community is analogous to that of the Latin American *patron*. There is a difference in that the former is an absentee owner whereas the latter often lives on his *latifundio*. But the efficiency and productivity implications are the same.

The creation of individual titles to land made possible the rise to power of another dubious "agent of change" in Asian rural socioeconomic structures—the moneylender. Once private property came into effect, land became a negotiable asset that could be offered by peasants as security for loans, and, in the case of default, could be forfeited and transferred to the often unscrupulous moneylender. At the same time, Asian agriculture was being transformed from a subsistence to a commercial orientation, both as a result of rising local demand in new towns and, more importantly, in response to external food demands of colonial European powers. With this transition from subsistence to commercial production, the role of the moneylender changed drastically. In the subsistence economy, his activities had been restricted to supplying the peasant with money to tide him over a crop failure or to cover extraordinary ceremonial expenditures such as family weddings or funerals. Most of these loans were paid in kind (i.e., in the form of food) at very high rares of interest. With the development of commercial farming, however, the peasant's cash needs grew significantly. Money was needed for seeds, fertilizer, and other inputs. It was also needed to cover his food requirements if he shifted to the production of cash crops such as tea, rubber, or jute. Often moneylenders were more interested in acquiring peasant lands as a result of loan defaults than they were in extracting high rates of interest. By charging exorbitant interest rates or inducing peasants to secure larger credits than they could manage, moneylenders were often able to drive the peasants off their land. They could then reap the profits of land speculation by selling this farmland to rich and acquisitive landlords. Alternatively, they often became powerful landlords themselves. At any rate, largely as a consequence of the moneylender's influence, Asian peasant cultivators have seen their economic status deteriorate steadily over time.

The final major force altering the traditional agrarian structure in Asia has been the rapid rate of population growth, especially over the past 30 years. Myrdal notes in reference to the population phenomenon that

> when and where expansion in the cultivated area was not a feasible alternative—whether for physical, technical, social, economic, or institutional reasons—population growth was reflected, in the first instance, in the cumulative subdivision and fragmentation of the acreages already under cultivation. Later this process, in combination with the emergence of private property and the rise of commercial agriculture and moneylending, often contributed to the rise of large landowners, the demise of small peasant proprietors, and the increase of the landless.[14]

The ultimate impoverishment of the peasantry was the inevitable consequence of this process of fragmentation, economic vulnerability, and loss of land to rich and powerful landlords.

To understand the deterioration of rural conditions in some Asian countries during this century, consider the cases of India, Indonesia, and the Philippines. In 1901 there were 286 million Indians. Now there are more than twice that number. The Indonesian population grew from 28.4 million in 1900 to its present level of over 160 million. The population of Central Luzon in the Philippines has increased almost fivefold from its level of 1 million in 1903. In each case, severe fragmentation of landholdings inevitably followed, so that today average peasant holdings in many areas of these countries are less than 1 hectare.

As these holdings shrink even further, production falls below the subsistence level and chronic poverty becomes a way of life. Peasants are forced to borrow even more from the moneylender at interest rates ranging from 50 to 200%. Most cannot repay these loans. They are then compelled to sell their land and become tenants with large debts. Since land is scarce, they are forced to pay high rents. If they are sharecroppers, they typically have to give the landlord 50–80% of their crop. Since labor is abundant, wages are extremely low. Peasants therefore have no source of external income. They are trapped in a vice of chronic poverty from which, in the absence of major rural reconstruction and reform, there is no escape. Like their Latin American counterparts, then, many rural Asians are gradually being transformed from small proprietors to tenant farmers and sharecroppers, then landless rural laborers, then jobless vagrants, and finally migrant slum dwellers on the fringes of modern urban areas. Not only have their levels of living deteriorated but their sense of self-esteem and freedom from exploitation, which may previously have been relatively high despite low incomes, have also vanished. These many hundreds of millions of people in Asia and Latin America are thus caught in a downward spiral of underdevelopment, instead of an upward thrust toward real economic development and social progress. An excerpt from the diary notes of sociologist Mead Cain, who in 1979 returned after a two-year absence to a small rural village, Char Gopalpur, in Bangladesh where he had done earlier research, vividly depicts the precarious existence of a typical peasant farmer's life in South Asia.

This past year has indeed been a poor one economically for Bangladesh, with a succession of poor harvests. . . . The tranquility of the village setting hides an enduring, harsh existence, and a number of persistent degenerative social processes. The recent drought, bringing with it a series of poor harvests, accelerated the process of economic differentiation; the process by which marginal farmers lose their land and eventually become landless, while at the same time, larger farmers accumulate land. A typical example from the village will illustrate the process of economic differentiation and the kinds of effects generated among marginal farmers by this past year's drought. The case is that of Amir Hossain, a man who is about 50 years old, who owns slightly less than two acres of arable land, and who lives with his wife, one married son, the son's wife, and several unmarried children. In a good year, the produce from the two acres will just about provide for the consumption needs of Amir's family. This past year, because of poor harvests, Amir's son had to work as an agricultural wage laborer for a period. In addition, Amir took a loan from a local bank in order to purchase paddy for consumption; he also used part of the loan to purchase paddy, have his wife husk paddy, and then resell the processed rice for a profit. The distress of Amir and his family was compounded when a bull that he had purchased for 900 taka in January contracted a disease and died in April of this year. The combination of the poor harvest, the untimely death of the bull, and the inadequacy of the various supplementary sources of income that the family collectively exploited, forced Amir to sell one tenth of an acre of land.

The experience of Amir Hossain and his family is significant because it is not at all unusual among farmers with similar or smaller land holdings. With as little land as they own, small differences in yield can force such families into debt or the distress sale of land. The case also illustrates the importance of luck and the ominous uncertainty of the environment in which the villagers live. The death of the bull was unrelated to the drought. The value of the bull was 900 taka and the value of the land sold was 1,300 taka. It is unlikely that the family would have been forced to sell the land if the bull had not died. Even in a normal or relatively good agricultural year, the individual experience of particular farmers will vary widely. The distribution among farmers of good and bad experiences in a given year is largely random. However, the ability of families to absorb dips in fortune depends very much on the size of a family's land holdings and on the size and composition of the family. Other things equal, those with smaller holdings and with certain demographic characteristics (e.g., few able-bodied males) are less resilient and are more at risk of enduring loss in times of hardship.[15]

Subsistence Agriculture and Extensive Cultivation in Africa

As in Asia and Latin America, subsistence agriculture on small plots of land is the way of life for the vast majority of African people. However, the organization and structure of African agricultural systems differ markedly from those found in contemporary Asia or Latin America. Except in former colonial settlement areas like White Highlands of Kenya and some of the large sugar, cocoa, and coffee plantations of East and West Africa, the great majority of farm families in tropical Africa still plan their output primarily for their own subsistence. Since the basic variable input in African agriculture is farm family and village labor, African agricultural systems are dominated by three major characteristics: (a) the importance of subsistence farming in the village community; (b) the existence of land in excess of immediate requirements, which permits a general practice of shifting cultivation and diminishes the value of land ownership as an instrument of economic and political power; and (c) the rights of each family (both nuclear and extended) in a village to have access to land and water in the immediate territorial vicinity, excluding from such access use by those families that do not belong to the community even though they may be of the same tribe.

The low-productivity subsistence farming characteristic of most traditional African agriculture results from a combination of three forces restricting the growth of input:

1. In spite of the existence of some unused and potentially cultivable land, only small areas can be planted and weeded by the farm family at a time when it uses only traditional tools such as the short-handled hoe, the axe, and the long-handled knife or panga. In some countries use of animals is impossible on account of the notorious tsetse fly or a lack of fodder in the long dry seasons, and traditional farming practices must rely primarily on the application of human labor to small parcels of land.
2. Second, given the limited amount of land that a farm family can cultivate in the context of a traditional technology and the use of primitive tools, these small areas tend to be intensively cultivated. As a result, they are subject to rapidly diminishing returns

to increased labor inputs. In such conditions, *shifting cultivation* is the most economic method of using limited supplies of labor on extensive tracts of land. Under shifting cultivation, once the minerals are drawn out of the soil as a result of numerous croppings, new land is cleared and the process of planting and weeding is repeated. In the meantime, the fertility is restored to formerly cropped land until eventually it can be used again. Under such a process, manure and chemical fertilizers are unnecessary, although in most African villages some form of manure (mostly animal waste) is applied to nearby plots that are intensively cultivated in order to extend their period of fertility.

3. The third major factor curtailing output increases in traditional African agriculture is the scarcity of labor during the busiest part of the growing season, namely, planting and weeding times. At other times much of the labor is underemployed. Since the time of planting is determined by the onset of the rains and since much of Africa experiences only one extended rainy season, the demand for workers during the early weeks of this rainy season usually exceeds all available rural labor supplies.

The net result of these three forces has been a relatively constant level of agricultural total output and labor productivity throughout much of Africa. As long as population size remained relatively stable, the pattern of low productivity and shifting cultivation enabled most African tribes to meet their subsistence food requirements (with the obvious exception of times of severe and prolonged droughts such as that experienced in much of the Sahelian region during the early 1970s and throughout the whole continent in 1982–1984). But the feasibility of shifting cultivation breaks down as population densities increase, as they have during the past two decades. It tends to be replaced by sedentary cultivation on small owner-occupied plots. As a result, the need for other nonhuman productive inputs grows, especially in the more densely populated agricultural regions of Kenya, Nigeria, Ghana, and Uganda. Moreover, with the growth of towns, the penetration of the monetary economy, and the introduction of land taxes, purely subsistence agricultural practices are no longer viable. Mixed and exclusively commercial farming begin to appear, as indeed they have throughout sub-Saharan Africa.

Conclusions

We may conclude our analysis by noting that although traditional African communal social systems differ markedly from those agrarian structures prevalent throughout much of Asia and Latin America, the contemporary economic status of the small farmer is not very different among the three regions. *Achieving subsistence is still the major objective of Third World peasant agriculture.* Even though the small African farmer may seem to have more room in which to maneuver than his typical Asian or Latin American counterpart, the rapid growth of rural populations in countries like Nigeria, Kenya, and Uganda is creating pressures for the further fragmentation of smallholder agriculture. Unless low-productivity peasant agriculture can be transformed rapidly into higher-productivity farming in Asia and Latin America (primarily through judicious land reform accompanied by concomitant structural changes in socioeconomic institutions) and Africa (basically through improved farming practices), the masses of impoverished rural dwellers face an even more precarious existence in the years immediately ahead.

THE IMPORTANT ROLE OF WOMEN

A major and often overlooked feature of Third World agrarian systems, particularly in Africa and Asia, is the crucial role played by women in agricultural production. In Africa, where subsistence farming is predominant and shifting cultivation is the primary method, nearly all tasks associated with subsistence food production are performed by women. While men who remain home generally perform the initial task of cutting trees and bushes on a potentially cultivable plot of land, women are responsible for all subsequent operations, which include removing and burning felled trees, sowing or planting the plot, weeding, harvesting, and finally preparing the crop for storage or immediate consumption. In her pioneering work on women and development, Ester Boserup examined many studies on African women's participation in agriculture and found that in nearly all cases recorded, women did most of the agricultural work. In some cases they were found to do around 70% and in one case nearly 80% of the total. Typically, these tasks are performed only with the most primitive tools and require many days of long, hard labor simply to produce enough output to meet the family's subsistence requirements, while the men often attempt to generate cash income through work on nearby plantations or in the cities.

In addition to performing virtually all of the subsistence farming in Africa, women may also contribute to the production of cash crops, usually on plantations. Often, they form a reserve labor force available for seasonal or part-time agricultural work such as weeding and harvesting. However, their most important role in plantation production consists in the cultivation of small plots of land to meet the family's subsistence needs. They thus attempt to make up for the shortfalls that occur given the very low male wages typically paid on most plantations.

While African women play the major role in subsistence farming and a lesser role in the production of cash crops, in Asia the situation is reversed: women produce the major share of cash crops and make a smaller contribution to the production of home crops. In Sri Lanka and Kampuchea for example, women account for over 50% of the labor force on plantations. In Malaysia and India their share is over 40%, and in Pakistan and the Philippines it is around 35%. The reason for this role reversal lies primarily in the different methods of farming used on the two continents. In Africa, shifting cultivation permits a smaller labor input per unit of land to meet subsistence needs, which enables women to do virtually all of the subsistence farming while men work at the plantations. In the densely populated regions of Asia, the greater labor input required on the relatively smaller plots of land is insufficient to meet subsistence needs. As a result, the whole family often must migrate to the plantation with every able-bodied member working in cash crop production to generate sufficient income for the family's survival.

In both the African and Asian agricultural sectors, therefore, women have a heavy burden to bear. This burden is compounded by their responsibilities within the home: housework, food preparation, and child care, each of which takes on different meanings from those we are accustomed to. "Housework" may include such difficult chores as hauling water over long distances, gathering heavy loads of firewood, or washing clothes in a stream.

"Food preparation" may include several hours a day of pounding and grinding grain or cooking over a small fire with few utensils. "Child care" usually means caring for several small children and nursing infants at the same time. In both Africa and Asia, then, rural women usually work longer hours than men, working both inside and outside of the home.

One of the major reasons for the heavy burden borne by women in the agricultural sector of many developing countries is the relative inefficiency with which they must perform their tasks due to the lack of capital and technology. Unfortunately, little effort is being made to improve women's productivity. Most development programs are targeted at improving the productivity of the male worker in the agricultural sector. Men are usually given access to credit and are taught modern methods of production while the women continue to rely on traditional methods of farming. As a result, the differences in labor productivity between men and women are growing wider. Given the major role played by women in the production of agricultural output, whether in home crops or cash crops, it is imperative that women share in the improvements in labor productivity that arise as Third World agriculture undergoes a transition from subsistence to commercial and specialized farming.

THE ECONOMICS OF SMALL-SCALE AGRICULTURAL DEVELOPMENT: TRANSITION FROM SUBSISTENCE TO SPECIALIZED FARMING

There are three major stages in the evolution of agricultural production.[16] The first and most primitive is the pure, low-productivity subsistence farm. The second stage is what might be called "diversified" or "mixed" agriculture, where part of the produce is grown for self-consumption and part for sale to the commercial sector. Finally, the third stage represents the "modern" farm, exclusively engaged in high-productivity, "specialized" agriculture geared to the commercial market.

Agricultural modernization in mixed-market developing economies may be described in terms of the gradual but sustained transition from subsistence to specialized production. But such a transition involves much more than reorganizing the structure of the farm economy or applying new agricultural technologies. We have seen that in most traditional societies agriculture is not just an economic activity; it is a way of life. Any government attempting to transform its traditional agriculture must recognize that in addition to adapting the farm structure to meet the demand for increased production, profound changes affecting the entire social, political, and institutional structure of rural societies will often be necessary. Without such changes, agricultural development will either never get started or, more likely, will simply widen the already sizable gap between the few wealthy large landholders and the masses of impoverished tenant farmers, smallholders, and landless laborers.

Before analyzing the economics of agricultural and rural development, therefore, we need to understand the evolutionary process by which traditional subsistence farms are transformed into modern specialized commercial farms, both through the farm family's own efforts and also through supporting activities of governments and local institutions. The three basic stages are outlined below.

Stage I. Subsistence Farming: Risk, Uncertainty, and Survival

In the traditional subsistence farm, output and consumption are identical and one or two staple crops (usually wheat, barley, sorghum, rice, or corn) are the chief sources of food intake. Output and productivity are low and only the simplest tools are used. Capital investment is minimal while land and labor are the principal factors of production. The law of diminishing returns is in operation as more labor is applied to shrinking (or shifting) parcels of land. The failure of the rains, the appropriation of his land, or the appearance of the moneylender to collect outstanding debts are the banes of the peasant's existence and cause him to fear for his survival. Labor is underemployed for most of the year, although workers may be fully occupied at seasonal peak periods such as planting and harvesting. The peasant usually cultivates only as much land as his family can manage without the need for hired labor, although many peasant farmers intermittently employ one or two landless laborers. The environment is harsh and static. Technological limitations, rigid social institutions, and fragmented markets and communication networks between rural areas and urban centers tend to discourage higher levels of production.

Throughout much of the Third World, agriculture is still in this subsistence stage. But in spite of the relative backwardness of production technologies and the misguided convictions of some foreigners who attribute the peasants' resistance to change as a sign of incompetence or irrationality, the fact remains that given the static nature of the peasant's environment, the uncertainties that surround him, the need to meet minimum survival levels of output, and the rigid social institutions into which he is locked, most peasants behave in an economically rational manner when confronted with alternative opportunities. As one informed observer of peasant agricultural systems has noted:

> *Despite the almost infinite variety of village-level institutions and processes to be found around the world, they have three common characteristics which are pertinent to change: 1, they have historically proven to be successful, i.e., the members have survived; 2, they are relatively static, at least the general pace of change is below that which is considered desirable today; and 3, attempts at change are frequently resisted, both because these institutions and processes have proven dependable and because the various elements constitute something akin to an ecological unity in the human realm.*[17]

The traditional two-factor neoclassical theory of production where land (and perhaps capital) is fixed and labor is the only variable input provides some insight into the economics of subsistence agriculture. Specifically, it provides an economic rationale for the observed low productivity of traditional agriculture in the form of the law of diminishing marginal productivity.

Unfortunately, this traditional theory of production does not satisfactorily explain why peasant agriculturalists are often resistant to technological innovation in farming techniques or to the introduction of new seeds or different cash crops. According to the standard theory a rational income or profit-maximizing farm or firm will always choose a method of production that will increase output for a given cost (in this case, the available labor time) or lower costs for a given output level. But the theory is based on the crucial assumption that farmers possess "perfect knowledge" of all input–output relationships in the form of a stable technological production function for their crop. This is the point at which the theory loses a good deal of its validity when applied to the environment of subsistence agriculture in much of Asia, Africa, and Latin America.

Subsistence agriculture is a highly *risky* and *uncertain* venture. It is made even more so by the fact that human lives are at stake. In regions where farms are extremely small and cultivation is dependent on the uncertainties of a highly variable rainfall, average output will be low and in poor years the peasant and his family will be exposed to the very real danger of starvation. In such circumstances, the main motivating force in the peasant's life may be the maximization, *not* of income, but rather *of his family's chances of survival.* Accordingly, when risk and uncertainty are high, a small farmer may be very reluctant to shift from a traditional technology and crop pattern that over the years he has come to know and understand to a new one that promises higher yields but may entail greater risks of crop failure. When sheer survival is at stake, it is more important to avoid a "bad" year (i.e., total crop failure) than to maximize the output in better years. In the jargon of economic statistics, risk-avoiding peasant farmers are likely to prefer a technology of food production that combines a low mean per hectare yield with low variance (i.e., less fluctuations around the average) to alternative technologies and crops that may promise a higher mean yield but also present the risk of a greater variance.

Figure 10.2 provides a simple illustration of how attitudes toward risk among small farmers may militate against apparently economically justified innovations.[18] In the figure levels of output and consumption are measured on the vertical axis and time on the horizontal axis, and two straight lines are drawn. The lower, horizontal line measures the minimum physiological consumption requirements (MCR) necessary for the farm family's physical survival. This may be taken as the starvation minimum fixed by nature: any output below this level would be catastrophic for the peasant and his family. The upper, positively sloped straight line represents the minimum level of food consumption that would be *desirable* (MDCL) given the prevailing cultural factors affecting village consumption standards. It is assumed that MDCL rises over time to reflect rising expectations as traditional societies are opened up to external influences. The producer's attitude toward risk will be largely conditioned by his historic output performance relative to these two standards of reference.

Looking at Figure 10.2, we see that at Time X, Farmer A's output levels have been very close to MCR. He is barely getting by and cannot take a chance of any drops. He will therefore have a greater incentive to minimize risk than will Farmer B, whose output performance has been well above the minimum subsistence level and is close to the culturally determined MDCL. Farmer B will therefore be more likely to innovate and change than will Farmer A.

Many programs to raise agricultural productivity among small farmers have suffered because of failure to provide adequate insurance (both financial credit and physical "buffer" stocks) against the risks of crop shortfalls, whether these risks are real or imagined. An understanding of the major role

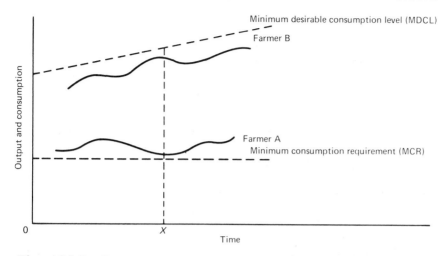

Figure 10.2. Small farmer attitudes toward risk: Why it sometimes is rational to resist innovation and change.

that risk and uncertainty play in the economics of subsistence agriculture would have prevented early and unfortunate characterizations of subsistence or traditional farmers as technologically backward, irrational producers with limited aspirations, or just plain "lazy natives" as in the colonial stereotype. Moreover, in many parts of Asia and Latin America, a closer examination of why peasant farmers have apparently not responded to an "obvious" economic opportunity will often reveal that (a) the landlord secured all the gain, or (b) the moneylender captured all the profits, or (c) the government "guaranteed" price was never paid, or (d) complementary inputs, fertilizer, pesticides, assured supplies of water, adequate nonusurious credit, etc., were never made available to the small farmer.

We may conclude that peasant farmers *do* act rationally and are responsive to economic incentives and opportunities. Where innovation and change fail to occur, we should not assume that peasants are stupid, irrational, or conservative; instead, we should examine carefully the environment in which the small farmer operates to search for the particular institutional or commercial obstacles that may be blocking or frustrating constructive change. As Professor Griffin has pointed out,

> *if peasants sometimes appear to be unresponsive or hostile to proposed technical changes it is probably because the risks are high, the returns to the cultivator are low—for example, because of local custom or land tenure conditions, or because credit facilities and marketing outlets are inadequate and the necessary inputs—including knowledge—are missing.[19]*

Efforts to minimize risk and remove commercial and institutional obstacles to small farmer innovation are, therefore, essential requirements of agricultural and rural development.

Stage II. The Transition to Mixed and Diversified Farming

It is unrealistic to think in terms of instantly transforming a traditional agrarian system that has prevailed for many generations into a highly specialized commercial farming system. Attempts to introduce cash crops indiscriminately in subsistence farms have more often than not resulted in the peasant's loss of land to moneylenders or landlords. Subsistence living is merely substituted for subsistence production. For small farmers exclusive reliance on cash crops can be even more precarious than pure subsistence agriculture, since risks of price fluctuations are added to the uncertainty of nature.

Diversified or mixed farming therefore represents a logical first step in the transition from subsistence to specialized production. In this stage the staple crop no longer dominates farm output since new cash crops such as fruits, vegetables, coffee, tea, and pyrethrum are established, together with simple animal husbandry. These new activities can take up the normal slack in farm workloads during times of the year when "disguised unemployment" is prevalent. This is especially desirable in the vast majority of Third World nations where rural labor is abundantly available for better and more efficient utilization.

For example, if the staple crop occupies the land during only parts of the year, new crops can be introduced in the slack season to take advantage of both idle land and family labor. And where labor is in short supply during peak planting seasons, as in many parts of Africa, simple labor-saving devices (such as small tractors, mechanical seeders, or animal-operated steel plows) can be introduced to free labor for other farm activities. Finally, the use of better seeds, fertilizer, and simple irrigation to increase yields of staple crops like wheat, maize, and rice can free part of the land for cash crop cultivation while assuring an adequate supply of the staple food. The farm operator can thus have a marketable surplus, which he can sell to raise his family's consumption standards and/or invest in farm improvements. Diversified farming can also minimize the impact of staple crop failure and provide a security of income previously unavailable.

The success or failure of such efforts to transform traditional agriculture will depend not only on the farmer's ability and skill in raising his productivity but even more importantly on the social, commercial, and institutional conditions under which he must function. Specifically, if he can have a reasonable and reliable access to credit, fertilizer, water, crop information, and marketing facilities; if he receives a fair market price for his output; and if he can feel secure that he and his family will be the primary beneficiaries of any improvements, then there is no reason to assume that the traditional farmer will not respond to economic incentives and new opportunities to improve his standard of living. Evidence from such diverse countries as Colombia, Mexico, Nigeria, Ghana, Kenya, India, Pakistan, Thailand, and the Philippines shows that under proper conditions small farmers are responsive to incentives and opportunities and will make radical changes in what they produce and how they produce it. Lack of innovation in agriculture, as we have seen, is usually due not to poor motivation or fear of change per se but to inadequate or unprofitable opportunities.

Stage III. From Divergence to Specialization: Modern Commercial Farming

The specialized farm represents the final and most advanced stage of individual holding in a mixed-market economy. It is the most prevalent type of farming in advanced industrial nations. It has evolved in response to and parallel with development in other areas of the national economy. General rises in living standards, biological and technical progress, and the expansion of national and international markets have provided the main impetus for its emergence and growth.

On specialized farms, the provision of food for the family with some marketable surplus is no longer the basic goal. Instead, pure commercial "profit" becomes the criterion of success, and maximum per hectare yields derived from man-made (irrigation, fertilizer, pesticides, hybrid seeds, etc.) and natural resources become the object of farm activity. Production, in short, is entirely for the market. Economic concepts such as fixed and variable costs, saving, investment and rates of return, optimal factor combinations, maximum production possibilities, market prices, and price supports take on quantitative and qualitative significance. The emphasis in resource utilization is no longer on land, water, and labor as in subsistence and often mixed farming. Instead, capital formation, technological progress, and scientific research and development play a major role in stimulating higher levels of output and productivity.

Specialized farms vary in both size and function. They range from intensively cultivated fruit and vegetable farms to the vast wheat and corn fields of North America. In most cases, sophisticated labor-saving mechanical equipment, ranging from huge tractors and combine harvesters to airborne spraying techniques, permits a single family to cultivate many thousands of acres of land.

The common features of all specialized farms, therefore, are their emphasis on the cultivation of one particular crop; their use of capital-intensive and, in many cases, labor-saving techniques of production; and their reliance on economies of scale to reduce unit costs and maximize profits. For all practical purposes, specialized farming is no different in concept or operation from large industrial enterprises. In fact, some of the largest specialized farming operations in both the developed and especially the less developed nations are owned and managed by large "agribusiness" multinational corporate enterprises.

Stages of Farm Evolution: A Summary

Table 10.6 summarizes the basic characteristics of the three stages of farm evolution—subsistence, mixed, and specialized—that parallel the broad stages of national economic growth. Most Third World nations are in the process of transition from subsistence to mixed farming (excluding, of course, the scattered enclaves of large and often foreign-owned specialized plantation agriculture). The further transition from mixed to widespread specialized farming may not always be desirable as an ultimate national goal, especially in view of the serious nature of rural and urban unemploy-

Table 10.6 Distinguishing Characteristics of the Three Stages of Farm Evolution

Characteristic	Subsistence	Mixed	Specialized
Composition of output	One dominant staple crop and auxiliary crops	Diversified	One dominant cash crop and auxiliary crops
Purpose of production	Domestic supply	Domestic and market supply	Market only
Work schedule	Seasonal	Balanced	Seasonal
Capital investment	Low	Medium	High
Income	Low	Medium	High
Income security	Low	High	Medium (price fluctuations)
Ratio of income to value of output	High	Approximately half	Low
Farmer's professional know-how	Specialized	Diverse	Specialized
Dependence on a supporting system	None	Partial	Full

SOURCE: R. Weitz, *From Peasant to Farmer: A Revolutionary Strategy for Development* (New York: Columbia University Press, 1971), p. 20.

ment problems. Moreover, such a transition may be difficult to achieve, depending as it does on the solution of many other short- and intermediate-term problems. The improvement of small-scale mixed farming practices that will not only raise farm incomes and average yields but, if labor intensive, will also effectively absorb underutilized rural labor offers the major immediate avenue toward the achievement of real people-oriented rural development.

TOWARD A STRATEGY OF AGRICULTURAL AND RURAL DEVELOPMENT: SOME MAIN REQUIREMENTS

If the major objective of agricultural and rural development in Third World nations is the progressive improvement in rural levels of living achieved primarily through increases in small-farm incomes, output, and productivity, it is important to identify the principal sources of agricultural progress and the basic conditions essential to its achievement. These are necessarily interrelated, but for purposes of description we may separate them and further divide each into three components:

Sources of small-scale agricultural progress	*Conditions of general rural advancement*
1. Technological change and innovation	1. Modernizing farm structures to meet rising food demands
2. Appropriate government economic policies	2. Creating an effective supporting system

3. Supportive social
    institutions

3. Changing the rural
    environment to improve
    levels of living

Let us look at each of these six interrelated components in turn.

Improving Small-Scale Agriculture

Technology and Innovation

In most developing countries new agricultural technologies and innovations in farm practices are preconditions for sustained improvements in levels of output and productivity. In many parts of Africa and Latin America, however, increased output has been achieved without the need for new technology simply by extending cultivation into unused but potentially productive lands. Most of these opportunities have by now been exploited, however, and there is not much scope for further significant improvement.

Two major sources of technological innovation can increase farm yields. Unfortunately both have somewhat problematic implications for Third World agricultural development. The first is the introduction of "mechanized" agriculture to replace human labor. The introduction of labor-saving machinery (e.g., large tractors) can have a dramatic effect on the volume of output per worker, especially where land is extensively cultivated and labor is scarce. For example, one man operating a huge combine-harvester can accomplish in a single hour the equivalent of hundreds of workers using traditional methods.

But in the rural areas of most developing nations where land parcels are small, capital is scare, and labor is abundant, the introduction of heavily mechanized techniques is not only often ill suited to the physical environment but, more important, often has the effect of creating more rural unemployment without necessarily lowering per unit costs of food production.[20] Importation of such machinery can therefore be "antidevelopmental," since its efficient deployment requires large tracts of land (and thus the expropriation of small holdings by landlords and moneylenders) and tends to exacerbate the already serious problems of rural poverty and unemployment. And if mechanized techniques exclude women, the male–female productivity gap, discussed in the last section, could widen further, with serious repercussions.

By contrast, biological (hybrid seeds) and chemical (fertilizer, pesticides, insecticides, etc.) innovations—the second major source—are far from problematic per se. They are land-augmenting, that is, they improve the quality of existing land by raising yields per hectare. Only indirectly do they increase output per worker. Improved seeds, advanced techniques of irrigation and crop rotation, the increasing use of fertilizers, pesticides, and herbicides, and new developments in veterinary medicine and animal nutrition represent major scientific advances in modern agriculture. These measures are technologically "scale neutral," that is, theoretically they can be applied equally effectively on large and small farms. They do not necessarily require large capital inputs or mechanized equipment. They are therefore particularly well suited for tropical and subtropical regions and offer an enormous *potential* for raising agricultural output in Third World nations.

Institutional and Pricing Policies: Providing the Necessary Incentives

Unfortunately, although the new hybrid seed varieties of wheat, corn, and rice (often collectively referred to as the "miracle seeds" or the basis of the "Green Revolution") are scale neutral and thus offer the potential for small-farm progress, the institutions and government policies that accompany their introduction into the rural economy often are *not* scale neutral. On the contrary, they often merely serve the needs and vested interests of the wealthy landowners. Since the new hybrid seeds require access to complementary inputs like irrigation, fertilizer, insecticides, credit, and agricultural extension services, if these are provided only to a small minority of large landowners, then the effective impact of the Green Revolution can be (and has been in parts of South Asia and Mexico) the further impoverishment of the masses of rural peasants. Large landowners with their disproportionate access to these complementary inputs and support services are able to gain a competitive advantage over smallholders and eventually drive them out of the market. Large-scale farmers obtain access to low-interest government credit, while smallholders are forced to turn to the moneylender. The inevitable result is the further widening of the gap between rich and poor and the increased consolidation of agricultural land in the hands of a very few so-called progressive farmers. A developmental innovation with great potential for alleviating rural poverty and raising agricultural output can thus turn out to be antidevelopmental if public policies and social institutions militate against the active participation of the small farmer in the evolving agrarian structure.[21]

A second critical area calling for major improvements in government policies relates to the pricing of agricultural commodities, especially food grains and other staples produced for local markets. Many LDC governments in their headlong pursuit of rapid industrial and urban development have maintained low agricultural prices in an attempt to provide cheap food for the urban modern sector. Farmers have been paid prices below either world competitive or free market internal prices. The relative internal price ratio between food and manufactured goods thus turned against farmers and in favor of urban manufacturers. With farm prices so low—in some cases below costs of production—there was no incentive for farmers to expand output or invest in new productivity-raising technology. As a result, local food supplies continually fell short of demand and many Third World nations that were formerly self-sufficient in food production had to import the balance of their food needs. This caused further strains on their international balance of payments situation and contributed to the worsening foreign exchange and international debt crisis of the early 1980s (see Chapters 14 and 17 for further analysis of the international trade and debt problems).

Economists, therefore, argue that if Third World governments are to promote increases in agricultural production through new technologies, they must not only make the appropriate institutional and credit market adjustments, but must also provide *incentives* for small- and medium-sized farmers by implementing pricing policies that truly reflect internal market conditions.[22]

Three Conditions for Rural Development

Let us now collect what has already been said to formulate three propositions that in essence constitute the necessary conditions for the realization of a people-oriented agricultural and rural development strategy.[23]

Land Reform

Proposition I: *Farm structures and land tenure patterns need to be adapted to the dual objectives of increasing food production and promoting a wider distribution of the benefits of agrarian progress.*

Agricultural and rural development that benefits the masses of people can succeed only through a joint effort by the government and *all* the farmers, not just the large farmers. A first step in any such effort, especially in Latin America but also in parts of Asia, is the provision of secured tenure rights to the individual farmer. A small farmer's attachment to his land is profound. It is closely bound up with his innermost sense of self-esteem and freedom from coercion. When he is driven off his land or is gradually impoverished through accumulated debts, not only is his material well-being damaged but, more important, his sense of self-worth and his desire for self- and family-improvement can be permanently destroyed.

It is for these human reasons as well as for reasons of greater agricultural output that "land reform" is often proposed as a necessary first condition for agricultural development in many LDCs. *In most countries the highly unequal structure of the land ownership is probably the single most important determinant of the existing highly inequitable distribution of rural income and wealth.* It is also the basis for the character of agricultural development. When land is very unevenly distributed, rural peasants can have little hope for economic advancement.

Land reform usually entails a redistribution of the rights of ownership and/or use of land away from large landowners and in favor of cultivators with very limited or no landholdings. It can take many forms: the transfer of ownership to tenants who already work the land (as in Cuba, Ethiopia, Japan, and Taiwan); transfer of land from large estates to small farms (as in Mexico); the appropriation of large estates for new settlement (as in Kenya); and the improvement or irrigation and subsequent development of large private or state-owned lands into farmer cooperatives (as in China and Tanzania). All go under the heading of land reform and are designed to fulfill one central function: *the transfer of land ownership or control directly or indirectly to those who actually work the land.*

There is widespread agreement among economists and other development specialists on the need for land reform. To Myrdal, land reform holds the key to agricultural development in Asia. The Economic Commission for Latin America (ECLA) has repeatedly identified land reform as a necessary precondition for agricultural and rural progress. A 1970s FAO report concluded that in many Third World regions land reform remains a prerequisite for development. The report argued that such reform was more urgent today than ever before, primarily because (a) income inequalities and unemployment in rural areas have worsened, (b) rapid population growth threatens further to worsen existing inequalities, and (c) recent and potential technological breakthroughs in agriculture (the Green Revolution) can be exploited primarily by large and powerful rural landholders and hence can result in an increase in their power, wealth, and capacity to resist future reform.

If programs of land reform can be legislated and *effectively implemented by the government* (a major problem with many such efforts in Asia and Latin America), then the basis for the transition from subsistence to mixed farming with improved output levels and higher standards of living for rural peasants will be established. But an egalitarian land reform program alone is no guarantee of successful agricultural and rural development. This leads to our second proposition.

Supportive Policies

Proposition II: *The full benefits of small-scale agricultural development cannot be realized unless government support systems are created that provide the necessary incentives, economic opportunities, and access to needed inputs to enable small cultivators to expand their output and raise their productivity.*

While land reform is essential in many parts of Asia and Latin America, it is likely to be ineffective and perhaps even counterproductive unless there are corresponding changes in rural institutions that control production (e.g., banks, moneylenders, seed and fertilizer distributors), in supporting government services (e.g., technical and educational extension services, public credit agencies, storage and marketing facilities, rural transport and feeder roads), and in government pricing policies with regard to both inputs (e.g., removing factor-price distortions) and outputs. Even where land reform is not necessary but where productivity and incomes are low (as in the whole of Africa and much of Southeast Asia), this broad network of external support services along with appropriate governmental pricing policies related to both farm inputs and outputs is an essential condition for sustained agricultural progress.

Integrated Development Objectives

Proposition III: *Rural development, while dependent primarily on small-farmer agricultural progress, implies much more. It encompasses (a) improvement in levels of living, including income, employment, education, health and nutrition, housing, and a variety of related social services; (b) a decreasing inequality in the distribution of rural incomes and a lessening of urban– rural imbalances in incomes and economic opportunities; and (c) the capacity of the rural sector to sustain and accelerate the pace of these improvements over time.*

This proposition is self-explanatory. We need only add that the achievement of its three objectives is vital to national development. This is not only because the majority of Third World populations are located in rural areas but also because the burgeoning problems of urban unemployment and population congestion must find their ultimate solution in the improvement of the rural environment. By restoring a proper balance between urban and rural economic opportunities and by creating the conditions for broad popular participation in national development efforts and rewards, developing nations will have taken a giant step toward the realization of the true meaning of development.

With these thoughts in mind, let us now conclude with a brief look at one unique approach to rural development that in the past decade has attracted considerable attention.

RURAL DEVELOPMENT IN CHINA: A UNIQUE APPROACH[24]

Since the opening up of the People's Republic of China to foreign visitors in the early 1970s, there has been widespread interest in and considerable debate about the Chinese model of rural development. The question most often asked is, Of what relevance is this model to other Third World nations in their attempt to eliminate mass poverty and build a unified and largely self-sufficient social and economic system? We can only hint at the range of possible answers in this brief section, but according to one early observer "the Chinese experiment in rural development has already thrown up some very important truths and principles which every policy-maker or social scientist concerned with rural development should at least begin to think about."[25]

The People's Commune

Until the political and institutional reforms were introduced by Mao Tse-tung's successor, Deng Xiaoping, in 1979 (see Appendix 10.1), rural develop-ment in China was based on the people's commune, a "multi-purpose political, administrative and organizational unit covering the full range of economic, social and administrative activities necessary and feasible in a rural community."[26] The people's commune was started in 1958 and repre-sented the fourth stage in the evolution of China's program of agrarian reform. The first stage was characterized by China's traditional feudal sys-tem of land tenure in which 10% of the rural population (landlords and rich peasants) owned 70–75% of the land. This land was confiscated during the Chinese revolution of 1949 and distributed to the poor and landless peas-ants, who nevertheless found it very difficult to cultivate the land economi-cally on an individual basis without supporting commercial and social services. As a result, "mutual aid teams" were formed between 1949 and 1952, during the second stage of agrarian reform. These groups were still too small to be effective, in terms of both their purchase of inputs and their efficiency in producing outputs. Thus, the third stage was initiated in 1955–1956. It was characterized by the formation of agricultural producers' cooperatives and then by advanced cooperatives ranging from 100 to 500 hectares. Such cooperatives were able to pool their resources effectively and consequently to raise agricultural yields. But they were not equipped to carry out the diverse economic, political, and administrative functions required for sustained progress. As a result, in 1958 the fourth and final stage of agrarian reform was begun by "introducing and regrouping all the Ad-vanced Cooperatives into People's Agricultural Communes and abolishing whatever individual ownership of land still existed in favor of communal ownership."[27] Communal ownership included all land in rural communi-ties, all means of agricultural production, and commune-owned industries.

[handwritten margin notes: commune (9o-50 r people); prodn brigade; work team (= village, 25-30 families)]

Organizationally, each commune was divided into production brigades and each brigade into a number of basic units known as "work teams." Each work team was equal to a village of about 25 – 30 families. It produced both to meet its own needs and to meet quotas allotted to it by the commune. The total land and population in a commune varied anywhere from 3,000 to 12,000 hectares and from 9,000 to 50,000 people. There were approximately 26,000 communes in China in the early 1970s.[28]

Poverty, Employment, and Income Distribution

During the past three decades China has been successful in reducing poverty by providing minimum levels of living for all its people, in lowering unemployment by mobilizing available human resources into production brigades and work teams, and in narrowing disparities in the distribution of personal income and wealth through the virtual abolition of private assets and the use until very recently of a system of fixed wages and prices. As a result of increases, average real income levels of Chinese farmers rose substantially. More significantly, this average is relatively evenly distributed, with the highest income levels said to be only twice as large as the lowest. As we have seen, average income levels in other Third World countries often mask great differences between wealthy landowners and poor subsistence farmers. But, at an even more basic level, Chinese officials have asserted that "the days in which the Chinese were without food and clothing are gone forever. There is no Chinese man or woman today whose basic needs of food, clothing, shelter, education and medical facilities are not met."[29] Even though this statement is probably a substantial exaggeration, there are few other countries in the Third World that can plausibly make a similar claim.

How the Chinese System Worked: Six Important Factors

Before its recent abolition, the Chinese commune system had six central attributes. The first and historically most important factor in the system was its ability to *mobilize the unemployed labor force* for land improvements, building dams and dikes, digging irrigation channels, constructing roads, and cultivating existing land more intensively. As a result, average Chinese farm yields grew quite rapidly. Chinese food grain production increased from 108 million tons in 1949 to 246 million tons in the early 1970s. China is now and has been for several years more than self-sufficient in food production in spite of its enormous population of over one billion people.

The second important factor about the Chinese commune was its ability to *diversify its rural economic activity* from agriculture to forestry, fisheries, and finally small industries. This was done only after a satisfactory base had been established within the agricultural sector itself. According to Aziz, "This continuing diversification in economic activities can be regarded as the most important factor in tackling the problem of rural employment by absorbing the internal additions to the labor force and workers rendered potentially surplus by increasing productivity in agriculture."[30]

The third major element of the system was its ability to *generate rural capital formation and industrialization* through a system of transfers of

15–20% of total commune revenue into an accumulation fund. These funds were then used to invest in productive improvements in commune industries, especially in the form of capital construction but also in mechanized farm equipment. Of perhaps even greater importance from the viewpoint of economic incentives were the Chinese government's deliberate attempts to improve rural standards of living by consciously raising the price of agricultural goods relative to that of industrial goods (i.e., the "terms of trade" between agriculture and industry). As Table 10.7 reveals, between 1950 and 1970 the quantity of industrial goods that a given amount of agricultural produce could purchase increased by almost 67%.

A fourth significant aspect was the commune's role in *providing essential social services to all rural people*, particularly in the areas of education and health. Schools and hospitals were provided out of the commune's own savings. The people were therefore able to realize the direct social benefits of their labor.

The unique system of Chinese *decentralized rural planning*, with its emphasis on the maximum exploitation of local resources to meet local needs, was the fifth strategic aspect of the commune system. Chinese planning differed from that of most other countries by its emphasizing mass participation in the planning process rather than having production targets and industrial or regional preferences determined by out-of-touch central planners.

Sixth, and probably most important, was the strategic position of the commune in *the political and ideological system* of China. Again, we quote Dr. Aziz:

> *The most important factor in the system of the Chinese Commune is its place in the ideological and political system of China. The main objective of the Chinese society is not the most rapid material progress or the creation of a*

Table 10.7 Terms of Trade between Agriculture and Industry, People's Republic of China, 1950–1970

	(1) Agricultural purchase price index	**(2) Industrial retail prices in rural areas index**	**(3) Ratio of (1) to (2)**
1950	100.0	100.0	100.0
1951	119.6	110.2	108.5
1952	121.6	109.7	110.8
1953	132.5	108.2	122.4
1954	136.7	110.3	123.9
1955	135.1	111.9	120.7
1956	139.2	110.8	125.6
1957	146.2	112.1	130.4
1958	149.5	111.2	134.4
1970	n.a.	n.a.	166.7

SOURCE: John G. Gurley, "Rural development in China: 1949–1972, and the lessons to be learned from it," in E.O. Edwards (ed.), *Employment in Developing Nations* (New York: Columbia University Press, 1974), p. 396.

consumer society but the evolution of a classless society in which social inequalities are reduced to the minimum, and where there is a high level of political and ideological consciousness and a pronounced concern for the well-being of every citizen. These goals are radically different from the implicit or express objectives of many other developing countries, where in the name of economic growth or economic development the main pursuits are essentially material in nature and the end result is generally the enrichment of a privileged minority or "a consumer society but without anything to consume." Pecuniary incentives are not absent in China—they have sought to meet everyone's basic needs and provide for a steady increase in real income—but the desire for a larger monetary reward is not the prime mover of the system: it is ideology plus organization.[31]

Implications for Rural Development in Other Third World Nations

Since their formation in 1958, the Chinese rural communes apparently made impressive economic and social strides, among which the following were most significant:

1. The transformation of an impoverished and stratified rural society into viable production units capable of meeting the food and basic material needs of the world's largest population
2. The transformation of the rural economy into a diversified economic system with labor-intensive, small-scale industry functioning in conjunction with labor-intensive agriculture
3. The creation of a social system founded on principles of equality and social justice
4. The development of a decentralized administrative and planning system that is close to the people and based on their perceived needs and requirements

Scholars who visited China in the early 1970s often claimed that in the short period since the 1949 revolution, China, which had effectively isolated itself from the rest of the world, had "already abolished absolute poverty; there is no unemployment in China and no inflation—the three problems which most other developing countries of Asia, Africa and Latin America have failed to deal with so far."[32] Information now available casts serious doubt on these earlier "official" versions of the successes of the agricultural system.[33] Moreover, the restructuring of the agricultural economy in the early 1980s to make it more decentralized with increased private ownership, more competitive, and more price responsive (see Appendix 10.1) indicates the dissatisfaction of the new leaders with the performance of the Chinese rural economy in the late 1970s.

Despite the performance controversy, however, the basic question remains. Of what relevance is the Chinese experience for other Third World nations? Specifically, without the powerful and massively supported political and ideological basis of Chinese society, which contributed so significantly to its achievements in both agricultural production and income redistribution, can other LDCs develop effective rural cooperative efforts within the context of their economic and political systems? Can they eliminate wide disparities in the distribution of wealth and income? Can they content the majority of their populations with only basic necessities such as food, clothing, and shelter plus a few minor luxuries such as bicycles, radios, and clocks, despite their continual exposure to the "demonstration effects" of mass consumption items like cars, fashionable clothes, TV sets, refrigerators, and other luxury goods that are consumed in more developed countries? Is it possible for resource-deficient small countries like most of those in Asia, Africa, and Latin America to shut themselves off from the rest of the world and become totally self-reliant? And finally, can the sense of security and prestige derived from private land ownership—a sense so central to the societies of Asia and Latin America and of increasing importance in Africa—be replaced by a sense of communal commitment and motivation based on a political ideology of equality and social justice? Is it feasible and, more importantly, is it desirable?

These are not easy questions to answer without reference to particular nations and societies. Moreover, the real material benefit that the average Chinese rural dweller has obtained over the past quarter of a century is not without its price: limited private freedom to choose a way of life that may not be in tune with the prevailing ideology. Freedom of choice (e.g., with regard to family size in the context of China's "one-child" campaign) may be relatively unimportant when sheer survival is the major concern, but it tends to assume greater importance as basic material needs become satisfied. With respect to China itself we might ask how long the present ideological and economic system can be sustained as the nation opens itself and its people to outside influences.

But even if most underdeveloped countries have neither the possibility nor the desire to imitate the Chinese system, there is still much to be learned from China's experience of the past two decades. Perhaps most important is the lesson it provides about agricultural output and promoting rural industries through small-scale, labor-intensive activities supported by publicly supplied economic and social services. While the Chinese model may not provide a blueprint for less well endowed or less culturally homogeneous Third World nations, it does provide a rough sketch of how rural development can be achieved. Perhaps more important, it shows that it *can* be achieved, even in a country with over one billion people.

NOTES

1. E.F. Szcepanik, "Agricultural capital formation in selected developing countries," *Agricultural Planning Studies* No. 11, FAO (1970).
2. See Raanan Weitz, *From Peasant to Farmer: A Revolutionary Strategy for Development* (New York: Columbia University Press, 1971), pp. 6–9. Much of the following analysis is drawn from this very informative and thoughtful book.
3. *Ibid.*, pp. 7–8.
4. *Ibid.*, p. 9.
5. Francis M. Foland, "Agrarian unrest in Asia and Latin America," *World Development* 2, nos. 4 and 5 (1974):56.
6. Celso Furtado, *Economic Development in Latin America* (Cambridge: Cambridge University Press, 1970), p. 54.
7. For a summary of the empirical evidence on this point, see R.A. Berry and W. Cline, *Agrarian Structure and Productivity in Developing Countries* (Baltimore: Johns Hopkins University Press, 1979), Chapter 3 and Appendix B.
8. Furtado, *Economic Development*, p. 56.
9. *Ibid.*, pp. 57–58.

10. Foland, "Agrarian unrest," p. 57.

11. Gunnar Myrdal, *Asian Drama* (New York: Pantheon, 1968), pp. 1033–1052.

12. *Ibid.*, p. 1035.

13. *Ibid.*

14. *Ibid.*, p. 1048.

15. Mead Cain, "Char Gopalpur revisited," diary notes, Center for Policy Studies, Population Council, October 1979 (mimeo).

16. See Weitz, *Peasant to Farmer*, pp. 15–28.

17. Clifton R. Wharton, Jr., "Risk, uncertainty and the subsistence farmer," *Development Digest* 7, no. 2 (1969):3, reprinted as Reading 20 in *The Struggle for Economic Development*.

18. See Marvin P. Miracle, "Subsistence agriculture: Analytical problems and alternative concepts," *American Journal of Agricultural Economics*, May 1968, pp. 292–310.

19. K. Griffin, "Agrarian policy: The political and economic context," *World Development* 1, no. 11 (1973):6.

20. For an extensive analysis of these adverse effects of mechanization, see Montague Yudelman et al., *Technological Change in Agriculture and Employment in Developing Countries* (Paris: OEC, 1971).

21. For an analysis of the impact of the Green Revolution in the developing world, see Keith Griffin, *The Political Economy of Agrarian Change* (London: Macmillan, 1974).

22. A provocative discussion of the important role of appropriate pricing policies in stimulating agricultural production can be found in Gilbert T. Brown, "Agricultural pricing policies in developing countries," Reading 21 in *The Struggle for Economic Development*.

23. For a more comprehensive review of integrated programs for rural development, see IBRD, "Rural Development," reprinted as Reading 22 in *The Struggle for Economic Development*.

24. Given the author's lack of firsthand familiarity with the economy of China, much of the factual information in this section is derived from Sartaj Aziz, "The Chinese approach to rural development," *World Development* 2, no. 2 (1974):87–91, and John Gurley, "Rural development in China, 1949–1972, and the lessons to be learned from it," in E.O. Edwards (ed.), *Employment in Developing Nations* (New York: Columbia University Press, 1974), pp. 383–403. Given their sympathy to the Chinese system, the views of these writers may be somewhat biased. Quite the opposite view is given in Steven Mosher, *Broken Earth: The Rural Chinese* (New York: Free Press, 1983), where it is argued that peasants are worse off today— economically and spiritually—than before the revolution of 1949.

25. Aziz, "Chinese approach," p. 87.

26. *Ibid.*, p. 88.

27. *Ibid.*

28. Gurley, "Rural development," p. 391.

29. As quoted in Aziz, "Chinese approach," p. 88; but see Mosher, *Broken Earth*, for a contrary conclusion.

30. Aziz, "Chinese approach," p. 89.

31. *Ibid.*, p. 90.

32. *Ibid.*, p. 91.

33. See, for example, John Wong, "Some aspects of China's agricultural development experience: Implications for developing countries in Asia," in C. Wilber (ed.), *The Political Economy of Development and Underdevelopment*, 2d ed. (New York: Random House, 1979), pp. 241–257, and S. Feuchtwang and A. Hussain, *The Chinese Economic Reforms* (New York: St. Martin's, 1983).

CONCEPTS FOR REVIEW

Per capita food production

Staple foods

The productivity gap

Farm yields

Agrarian systems

Latifundio

Minifundio

Microfundio

Family farm

Medium-sized farm

Landlord, patron

Tenant farmer

Sharecropper

Moneylender

Land tenure systems

Shifting cultivation

Integrated rural development

Subsistence farming

Mixed or diversified farming

Mechanization

Population density

Scale-neutral technological progress

Hybrid seeds

Agricultural extension services

Green Revolution

Land reform

Farmer cooperatives

Government support systems

Chinese people's commune

Risk and uncertainty

Cash crops

Demonstration effects

QUESTIONS FOR DISCUSSION

1. Why should any analysis of Third World development problems place heavy emphasis on the study of agricultural systems, especially peasant agriculture, and the rural sector?

2. What were the principal reasons for the relative stagnation of Third World agriculture during the so-called development decades of the 1960s and 1970s? How can this disappointing performance be improved on in the future? Explain.

3. It is sometimes said that the world consists of two kinds of agriculture. Explain what is meant by this statement and indicate how it might be illustrated both between and within countries.

4. Compare and contrast the nature of peasant or small-scale agriculture in Asia, Africa, and Latin America. How do overall agricultural systems differ among these regions? What are the common characteristics?

5. Explain the meaning of Professor Myrdal's quote at the beginning of this chapter: "It is in the agricultural sector that the battle for long term economic development will be won or lost."

6. It is sometimes asserted that small peasant farmers are backward and ignorant because they seem to resist agricultural innovations that could raise farm yields substantially. Does this resistance stem from an inherent "irrationality" on their part or might it be attributable to some other factors often overlooked by Western economists? Explain your answer.

7. In the chapter we described three stages in the transition from subsistence to specialized agriculture. What are the principal characteristics of these stages?

8. There appears to be widespread agreement that in those regions where the distribution of land ownership is highly unequal (mainly Latin America but also parts of Asia), land reform is a necessary but not sufficient condition for promoting and improving small-scale agriculture. What is meant by this statement and by the concept of land reform? Give some examples of supportive policy measures that might accompany land reform.

9. What is meant by comprehensive or "integrated" rural development? What criteria would you use to decide whether or not such integrated rural development was or was not taking place?

10. The People's Republic of China has apparently evolved a unique approach to promoting rural development. What are the main characteristics of this approach and what have been its supposed achievements?

11.   A crucial issue in the debate on development is whether the Chinese experiment in rural development offers any lessons or strategies that can be adopted in other Third World nations. What relevance, if any, do you think the Chinese experience offers?

FURTHER READINGS

An excellent survey of agrarian systems in developing countries can be found in Dharam Ghai et al. (eds.), *Agrarian Systems and Rural Development* (New York: Holmes and Meier, 1979). There are also a number of studies of agriculture and agrarian systems in specific Third World regions. For Africa see P. Robson and D.A. Lury (eds.), *The Economies of Africa* (London: Allen & Unwin, 1969). For Asia see Gunnar Myrdal, *Asian Drama* (New York: Pantheon, 1968), Chapters 22, 23, and 26. For Latin America see Rodolfo Stavenhagen (ed.), *Agrarian Problems and Peasant Movements in Latin America* (New York: Doubleday, 1970); Celso Furtado, *Economic Development in Latin America* (London: Cambridge University Press, 1970), Chapters 7 and 14; and, especially, Solon Barraclough, *Agrarian Structure in Latin America* (Lexington, Mass.: Lexington Books, 1973). Comparative analyses of landlessness and rural poverty can be found in M.J. Esman, *Landlessness and Near-Landlessness in Developing Countries* (Ithaca, N.Y.: Cornell University Press, 1978), and Erick Eckholm, "The dispossessed of the earth: Land reform and sustainable development," *Worldwatch Paper* No. 13, Washington, D.C., June 1979.

Three outstanding comparative studies of Third World agrarian systems are Guy Hunter, *Modernizing Peasant Societies: A Comparative Study of Asia and Africa* (London: Oxford University Press, 1969); Keith Griffin, *The Political Economy of Agrarian Change* (London: Macmillan, 1974); and, especially, Bruce F. Johnston and Peter Kilby, *Agriculture and Structural Transformation: Economic Strategies in Late Developing Countries* (London: Oxford University Press, 1975).

For a general introduction to the economics of agricultural and rural development in Third World countries see Erik Thorbecke (ed.), *The Role of Agriculture in Economic Development* (New York: Columbia University Press, 1969); Raanan Weitz, *From Peasant to Farmer: A Revolutionary Strategy for Development* (New York: Columbia University Press, 1971); Bruce F. Johnston, "Agriculture and structural transformation in developing countries: A survey of research," *Journal of Economic Literature* 8, no. 2 (1970); John Mellor, *The Economics of Agricultural Development* (Ithaca: Cornell University Press, 1966); A.T. Mosher, *Creating a Progressive Rural Structure* (New York: Agricultural Development Council, 1969); T.W. Schultz, *Transforming Traditional Agriculture* (New Haven: Yale University Press, 1964); Robert d'A. Shaw, *Jobs and Agricultural Development* (Washington, D.C.: Overseas Development Council, 1970); Nurul Islam (ed.), *Agricultural Policy in Developing Countries* (New York: Halsted Press, 1974); World Bank, *Rural Development: Sector Policy Paper* (Washington, D.C.: World Bank, 1975); World Bank, *World Development Report 1982*, where there is an examination of recent and projected trends in Third World agriculture; and C.P. Timmer, W. Falcon, and S. Pearson, *Food Policy Analysis* (Baltimore: Johns Hopkins University Press, 1983).

As mentioned in Note 24, Chinese rural development is dealt with in Sartaj Aziz, "The Chinese approach to rural development," *World Development* 2, no. 2 (1974):87–91, and in John G. Gurley, "Rural development in China, 1949–1972, and the lessons to be learned from it," in E.O. Edwards (ed.), *Employment in Developing Nations* (New York: Columbia University Press, 1974), pp. 383–403. In addition, see Carl Riskin, "Small industry and the Chinese model of development," *China Quarterly*, April–June 1971, pp. 245–273; Keith Buchanan, *The Transformation of the Chinese Earth* (New York: Praeger, 1970); Lloyd G. Reynolds, "China as a less developed economy," *American Economic Review* 65, no. 3 (1975):418–428; and, especially, John Wong, "Some aspects of China's agricultural development: Implications for developing countries in Asia," in Charles Wilber (ed.), *The Political Economy of Development and Underdevelopment* (New York: Random House, 1979). See also notes at the end of Appendix 10.1.

Additional readings can be found on pp. 627–629.

APPENDIX 10.1

RECENT REFORMS IN CHINESE AGRICULTURE[1]

Since the radical changes in agricultural policy introduced by Mao's successor Deng Xiaoping in 1979, including greater decentralization, stronger incentives, and increased use of the market mechanism to allocate resources, there have been substantial improvements in both the standard of living in rural areas and the production and growth of agricultural output. The per capita income of Chinese peasants increased at an annual rate of 10% during the 1978–1982 period. There have been steady increases in the harvest of major field crops such as cotton, jute, sugar, oilseeds, and silkworm cultivation. The 1982 record grain harvest exceeded 344 million tons. The annual growth rate of agricultural output has jumped from 3.5% in 1978 to 7% by the end of the 5-year period.[2]

One of the major changes in agricultural policy has been the newly instituted "zeren zhi," or responsibility system. Under the zeren zhi, a farming household contracts for a given output and any surplus produced over the contracted amount is retained and divided between the family farm and the commune (now called "townships" or "administrative districts"). In recent years, there has been very little accumulation of surplus by the administrative districts, resulting in considerable autonomy for the household in terms of disposing its own surplus. In some areas, the new system has resulted in the virtual privatization of agricultural production. Plots of land have been allocated to individual families, rather than to a collective, on the condition that they pay the state grain tax (which in several cases has been drastically reduced or even waived). Individual houses are free, therefore, to keep and dispose of all surplus above the tax.

Another major change in policy has been the trend toward diversification in the agricultural sector and specialization in labor. For many years, the sole focus of agriculture throughout the country had been on grain production, sometimes even in areas where land was not suitable for such cultivation. Now the government is promoting expansion into non-grain food crops, animal husbandry, fish farming, handicrafts, and other activities appropriate for local conditions. Furthermore, it is encouraging small-scale, rural-based industry in areas including construction, production of farm machinery, repair, and transportation. In addition to enhancing agricultural production, accounting for nearly 40% of the total value of agricultural output, such rural industries are now a major source of employment, absorbing one-tenth of the rural work force or about 30 million workers.[3] With regard to specialization, members of collectives are now being encouraged to specialize in lines of production closest to their area of expertise in a bid to increase labor productivity. Individual members can now spend their full working time on one task, such as raising poultry or caring for the collective's orchard.

A series of reforms in agricultural policy have led to what amounts to direct profit incentives for farmers. First, state purchasing prices for all important commodities, which include several agricultural products, were raised 20–30% by 1979. The purchase price for grain produced in fulfillment of state quotas was raised 20%, while grain sales above quota were offered a premium of 50% over the base price. In addition, farmers are entitled to sell crops and livestock products to state agencies at relatively favorable prices to supplement normal sales proceeds. In order to make certain manufactured goods more available to the rural population, the prices of industrial products have been lowered 10–15%. Second, the ban on rural markets has been lifted, and a virtual barter economy has given way to some 44,000 rural markets where prices are negotiated between buyer and seller. Finally, the system of "work points" has been reinstituted so that less is apportioned to workers as basic rations and more as a return for the quality and quantity of work. Perhaps the most radical change is the current plan to gradually phase out the people's commune, so long a mainstay of Chinese rural life (see text). Some 55,000 communes have been stripped of administrative authority, leaving only their economic functions. Political power is being restored to the "xiang" or rural townships which had been abolished during Mao's reign.

While these numerous changes in agricultural policy have so far brought about a revitalization of the Chinese rural economy, it remains to be seen whether such private enterprise, with its natural tendencies toward increased individual decision making and emerging economic stratification, will be compatible with the long-run political and ideological goals of China's Communist government. For example, the encouragement of private enterprise among individual peasant farmers would appear to be in direct conflict with the government's enormous pressures to limit family size to one child: on private farmland children will once again represent important economic assets (see Chapter 6) and peasant farmers are likely to resist, for economic as well as traditional cultural reasons, the pressures to limit family size. Thus, at least two of China's major development goals—the "one-child" family to limit population growth and the privatization of the rural economy to increase food production—could potentially come into serious conflict.

NOTES

1. For an extensive description and analysis of recent Chinese economic reforms see the special issue, "China's changed road to development," of *World Development* (vol. 11, no. 8, August 1983), as well as Stephen Feuchtwang and Athar Hussain, *The Chinese Economic Reforms* (New York: St. Martin's, 1983) and Thomas B. Wiens, "Price adjustment, the responsibility system and agricultural productivity," *American Economic Review* 73, no. 2 (May 1983).
2. Statistics are from Christopher Wren, "Peking's farm policies beginning to pay off," *New York Times*, April 10, 1983.
3. World Bank, *World Development Report 1982* (New York: Oxford University Press, 1982), Box 5.3.

11

EDUCATION AND DEVELOPMENT

The school in many underdeveloped countries is a reflection and a fruit of the surrounding underdevelopment, from which arises its deficiency, its quantitative and qualitative poverty. But little by little, and there lies the really serious risk, the school in these underdeveloped countries risks becoming in turn a factor of underdevelopment.

Joseph Kizerbo, former Minister of Education,
Upper Volta

Virtually every serious commentator agrees that major reform within Third World education is long overdue.

Richard Jolly, Deputy Director General, UNICEF

EDUCATION AND HUMAN RESOURCES

Most economists would probably agree that it is the human resources of a nation, not its capital or its material resources, that ultimately determine the character and pace of its economic and social development. For example, according to the late Professor Harbison of Princeton University:

> *Human resources . . . constitute the ultimate basis for wealth of nations. Capital and natural resources are passive factors of production; human beings are the active agents who accumulate capital, exploit natural resources, build social, economic and political organizations, and carry forward national development. Clearly, a country which is unable to develop the skills and knowledge of its people and to utilize them effectively in the national economy will be unable to develop anything else.[1]*

The principal institutional mechanism for developing human skills and knowledge is the formal educational system. Most Third World nations have been led to believe or have wanted to believe that it is the rapid *quantitative* expansion of educational opportunities which holds the basic key to national development: the more education, the more rapid the development. All countries have committed themselves, therefore, to the goal of universal primary education in the shortest possible time. This quest has become a politically very sensitive, but often economically costly, sacred cow. Until recently few politicians, statesmen, economists, or educational planners inside or outside of the Third World would have dared publicly to challenge the cult of formal education.

Nevertheless, the challenge is now gathering momentum, and it comes from many sources. It can be found most clearly in the character and results of the development process itself. After almost three decades of rapidly expanding enrollments and hundreds of billions of dollars of educational expenditure, the plight of the average citizen of Asia, Africa, and Latin America seems little improved. Absolute poverty is chronic and pervasive. Economic disparities between rich and poor widen with each passing year. Unemployment and underemployment have reached staggering proportions, with the "educated" increasingly swelling the ranks of those without jobs.

It would be foolish and naive to blame these problems exclusively on the failures of the formal educational system. At the same time, one must recognize that many of the early claims made on behalf of the unfettered quantitative expansion of educational opportunities—that it would accelerate economic growth; that it would raise levels of living especially for the poor; that it would generate widespread and equal employment opportunities for all; that it would acculturate diverse ethnic or tribal groups; and that it would encourage "modern" attitudes—have been shown to be greatly exaggerated and, in many instances, simply false.

As a result there has been a growing awareness in many developing nations that the expansion of formal schooling is not always to be equated with the spread of learning; that the acquisition of school certificates and higher degrees is not necessarily associated with improved ability to undertake productive work; that education oriented almost entirely toward preparation for work in the modern urban sector can greatly distort student aspirations; and that too much investment in formal schooling, especially at the secondary and higher levels, can divert scarce resources from more socially productive activities (e.g., direct employment creation) and thus be a drag rather than a stimulus to national development.

The educational systems of Third World nations strongly influence and are influenced by the whole nature, magnitude, and character of their development process. The role of formal education is not limited to imparting the knowledge and skills that enable individuals to function as economic change agents in their societies. Formal education also imparts values, ideas, attitudes, and aspirations, which may or may not be in the nation's best developmental interests. Education absorbs the greatest share of LDC recurrent government expenditures, occupies the time and activities of the greatest number of adults and children (almost 30% of Third World populations), and carries the greatest psychological burden of development aspirations. We must therefore examine its fundamental economic basis in developing countries and also its social and institutional ramifications.

The economics of education is a vital yet somewhat amorphous component of the economics of development. It is a young subject, having emerged as a separate branch of economics only in the early 1960s. Yet when we recognize the principal motivation or "demand" for education in Third World countries as a desire for economic improvement by means of access to better-paid jobs, we must understand the economic processes through which such aspirations are either realized or frustrated.

In this chapter we explore the relationship (both positive and negative) between development and quantitative and qualitative educational expansion in terms of six basic issues that grow directly out of the discussions of previous chapters:

1. How does education influence the rate, structure, and character of economic growth? Conversely, how do the rate, structure, and character of economic growth influence the nature of the educational system?
2. Does education in general and the structure of Third World educational systems in particular contribute to or retard the growth of domestic inequality and poverty?
3. What is the relationship between education, rural–urban migration, and urban unemployment? Are rising levels of the "educated unemployed" a temporary or chronic phenomenon?
4. Is there a relationship between the education of women and their desired family size?
5. Do contemporary Third World formal educational systems tend to promote or retard agricultural and rural development?
6. What is the relationship, if any, between Third World educational systems, developed country educational systems, and the international migration of highly educated professional and technical manpower from the less developed to the more developed nations?

We begin this chapter with a brief profile of the status of education in a range of Third World countries. In this profile we focus on public expenditure levels, enrollment ratios, literacy levels, dropout rates, and costs and earnings differentials. After then discussing the principal economic and environmental factors affecting the ability to learn, we review some basic concepts in the economics of education, including the determinants of the demand for and supply of school places and the distinction between private and social benefits and costs of investment in education. Next we examine in detail the above six issues to see if we can reach any conclusions about the relationship between education and various key components of the development process. We then end with a review of alternative policy options open to Third World governments in their attempt to evolve an educational system that will more efficiently serve the needs and aspirations of all their people.

A PROFILE OF EDUCATION IN DEVELOPING REGIONS[2]

Public Educational Expenditure

In many developing countries formal education is the largest "industry" and the greatest consumer of public revenues. Poor nations have invested huge sums of money in education. The reasons are numerous. Literate farmers with at least a primary education are thought to be more productive and more responsive to new agricultural technologies than illiterate farmers. Specially trained craftsmen and mechanics who can read and write are assumed to be better able to keep up to date with changing products and materials. Secondary school graduates with some knowledge of arithmetic and clerical skills are needed to perform technical and administrative functions in growing public and private bureaucracies. In former colonial countries many people with such skills are also needed to replace departing expatriates. University graduates with advanced training are needed to provide the professional and managerial expertise necessary for a modernized public and private sector.

In addition to these obvious "manpower planning" needs, the people themselves, both rich and poor, have exerted tremendous political pressure for the expansion of school places in developing countries. Parents have realized that in an era of scarce skilled manpower, the more schooling and certificates their children can accumulate, the better will be their chances of getting secure and well-paid jobs. For the poor, more years of schooling have been perceived as the only avenue of hope for their children to escape from poverty.

As a result of these forces on both demand and supply, there has been a tremendous acceleration in LDC public expenditures on education during the last two decades. Both the proportion of national income and of national budgets spent on education have increased rapidly. In Asia total public expenditures tripled during the 1960s and 1970s. In Africa and Latin America, public educational expenditures more than doubled. In fact, the increase in public expenditure on education in the 1960s and 1970s exceeded increases in any other sector of the economy. By the early 1980s educational budgets in many Third World nations were absorbing anywhere from 20 to 35% of total government recurrent expenditure. While this is a sizable expenditure in terms of overall budget, developing nations nevertheless were spending only $27 per capita on public education as opposed to $428 per capita spent in the developed world.

Enrollments

Between 1960 and 1985 the total number of persons enrolled in the three main levels of education in Africa, Asia, the Middle East, and Latin America rose from 163 million to 455 million—an average annual increase of 5%. Although the largest part of this increase has been in primary education, it is in the secondary and tertiary levels that the greatest proportionate increases have occurred—12.7% and 14.5% per annum respectively. Nevertheless, primary enrollment still accounts for nearly 80% of the total LDC school enrollments.

In terms of the proportion of children of school age actually attending school at the primary, secondary, and tertiary levels, the differential between the developed and the less developed regions and among Third World regions themselves is substantial. African countries lag behind at all levels with, for example, only 55% of their primary-school-age children actually enrolled. Table 11.1 shows comparative data on enrollment ratios at the primary, secondary, and higher education levels for a selected group of low- and middle-income developing countries in 1960 and 1981. The remarkable increases in enrollments at both the primary and secondary levels are strikingly evident from this table.

Table 11.1 Enrollment Ratios in Selected Developing Countries: Primary, Secondary, and Higher Education, 1960 and 1981

	Numbers enrolled as a percentage of age group					
	Primary		Secondary		Higher	
	1960	1981	1960	1981	1960	1981
Low-income LDCs						
Bangladesh	47	62	8	15	1	3
Ethiopia	7	46	1	12	(.)	1
India	61	79	20	30	(3)	(8)
Tanzania	25	98	2	3	(.)	(.)
Sri Lanka	95	100	27	51	1	3
Indonesia	71	100	6	30	1	3
Middle-income LDCs						
Thailand	83	96	13	29	2	20
Philippines	95	100	26	63	13	26
Colombia	77	100	12	48	2	12
South Korea	94	100	27	85	5	18
Brazil	95	93	11	32	2	12
Mexico	80	100	11	51	3	15
Developed countries	100	100	64	90	16	37

SOURCE: *World Development Report, 1984*, Annex Table 25. Reprinted by permission of Oxford University Press.

Dropouts

One of the major educational problems of developing nations is the very high percentage of students who drop out before completing a particular cycle. For example, in Latin America an estimated 60 out of every 100 students who enter primary school drop out before completion. In some Latin American countries, the primary school dropout rate is as high as 75%. In Africa and Asia the median dropout rates are approximately 54% and 20% respectively. But the variation among countries has been wide, with dropout rates as high as 81% and 64% respectively in certain African and Asian nations.

At the secondary level, median dropout rates for those entering in 1975 were 38.7% in Africa and 18% in Latin America and Asia. In Europe the rate was approximately 11.4%. One consequence of this phenomenon, particularly for Africa, is the serious and growing problem of the secondary school dropout who joins the ranks of the educated unemployed.

Literacy

The percentage of adults, persons aged 15 and over, who are illiterate has fallen since 1960 from 60 to 51% of the adult population in developing countries. However, as a result of rapid population growth, the actual number of adult illiterates has risen over this same period by nearly 70 million to an estimated total of over 900 million by 1985. The highest illiteracy rates are found in Africa (73.7) and the Arab states (73.0), followed by Asia (46.8) and Latin America (23.6). In North America and Europe, illiteracy rates are a mere 1.0 and 2.5% respectively. Information on literacy rates for particular countries can be obtained from Appendix 2.2.

Costs and Earnings

There has been growing criticism in recent years of the very serious disproportionate per pupil costs of education at various levels in the LDCs. The imbalance is particularly apparent when one compares secondary and higher educational costs with primary-level costs. While much of the early criticism was based on scattered ad hoc empirical and interpretative information, in the 1970s a highly regarded comparative study provided detailed data on the magnitude of these cost divergences.[3]

Table 11.2 compares the ratio of total costs per student year by educational level for a group of developed and less developed countries. The data reveal that whereas in the three developed countries shown the ratio of total per pupil costs of secondary to primary education is 6.6 to 1 and that of higher to primary education is 17.6 to 1, in the seven LDCs shown these relative costs are 11.9 and 87.9 to 1 respectively. In other words, taking the 87.9 figure, for the equivalent cost of educating 1 university student for a year, 88 primary school children could have received a year of schooling. In many African countries (e.g., Sierra Leone, Malawi, Kenya, and Tanzania) cost ratios per pupil between higher and primary education range as high as 283 to 1. Since in over half of the world's developing countries the ratio of students in primary schools to students in higher education is above 100 to 1 (compared, for example, with ratios of less than 10 to 1 in the developed countries), it follows that LDCs spend large proportions of their educational budgets on a very small proportion of their students enrolled in universities and professional schools.

If one then compares the data in Table 11.3, showing the relative average earnings of individuals by educational level, with those on costs, it becomes clear that relative earnings differentials by educational level are much less than unit cost differentials in the developing compared with the developed countries. For example, looking at the figures in the lower right corners of Tables 11.2 and 11.3, we see that while an LDC university student costs 87.9

Table 11.2 Ratios of Total Costs by Educational Level per Student Year

	Relative cost	
Groups of countries	Secondary/primary	Higher/primary
United States, Great Britain, New Zealand	6.6	17.6
Malaysia, Ghana, South Korea, Kenya, Uganda, Nigeria, India	11.9	87.9

SOURCE: George Psacharopoulos, *The Returns to Education: An International Comparison* (Amsterdam: Elsevier, 1972), Table 8.2.

Table 11.3 Ratios of Average Annual Earnings of Labor by Educational Level

Groups of countries	Relative earnings	
	Secondary/primary	*Higher/primary*
United States, Canada, Great Britain	1.4	2.4
Malaysia, Ghana, South Korea,		
Kenya, Uganda, Nigeria, India	2.4	6.4

SOURCE: George Psacharopoulos, *The Returns to Education: An International Comparison* (Amsterdam: Elsevier, 1972), Table 8.4.

times as much as a primary pupil to educate for one year, the university student on the average earns only 6.4 times as much as the typical primary pupil—a very high (and often artificial) differential, but not as high as the cost differential. To the extent that average relative earnings reflect average relative productivity, the wide disparity between relative earnings and relative costs of higher versus primary education implies that in the past LDC governments may have unwisely invested too much in higher education. These funds might have been more productively invested in primary school expansion. This does not necessarily imply that future relative cost/benefit ratios will continue to favor primary school expansion; much depends on the relative employment prospects of the various educational groups. Moreover, although most empirical studies in the 1970s revealed that the returns to investment in education were the highest at the primary level regardless of the number of students,[4] recent research by Behrman and Birdsall casts considerable doubt on this widely held belief.[5] Their studies indicate that it is the "quality" of education (i.e., the quality of teaching, facilities, and curricula) and not its quantity alone (years of schooling) that best explains differential earnings and productivity. The implication is that governments should spend more to upgrade existing schools and less to expand the number of school places—that is, they should "deepen" the investment in human capital rather than extend it to more people. Unfortunately, this raises serious equity questions—a topic we will examine shortly.

BASIC PROBLEMS OF PRIMARY AND SECONDARY EDUCATION[6]

Inertia and Inefficiency

While the foregoing statistics provide a useful summary of public enrollments, dropouts, literacy rates, costs per student, and returns to education, there are other underlying but less quantifiable problems of education in the Third World—problems that are sometimes serious in industrialized nations as well. These are broadly referred to as the *inefficiencies* and *inertia of educational systems.*

One might start with the outdated content and dubious quality of education at all levels. As stated by a former deputy director-general of UNESCO:

> *The learning techniques . . . remain the same: the rote method, the technique of cramming, and, once the examination menace is passed, of forget-*

*ting all these useless impedimenta. The examination system is not an evalua-
tion of a student's personality and intellectual equipment, his powers of
thinking for himself, reflection, and reasoning. It is a challenge to resourceful
deception and display of superficial cleverness. . . . Looked at as a business
enterprise, the school and college present a woebegone spectacle. We find in
education antediluvian technology which would not survive for an instant in
any other economic sector. The teaching methods and learning techniques
. . . are rusty, cranky and antiquated.*

Deficiencies of learning methods and curricula are closely related to a lack of
competence and motivation on the part of most teachers, who are usually
underpaid and without incentive or opportunity to upgrade and update
their own training. The situation is hardly better among educational administrators.

Poor Management and Distorted Incentives

Indeed, problems seem most acute and difficult to remedy in the realm of
educational management—its direction, organization, and programming.
Here are the immediate causes of perpetuating old and dysfunctional patterns. Rigidity persists along with a lack of requisite information of the
society's needs, conditions, and developmental possibilities, and a lack of
practically oriented research, experimentation, and evaluation.

These problems of education arise in part because socially perceived
needs within the educational system vastly exceed available funds and
other resources. But they also result from demands, pricing, and financial
and nonfinancial incentives in the society at large, *outside* the educational
system. What society and individuals want of education are often impossible dreams, demands frequently out of line with priorities of national development, indeed, often running counter to those priorities.

These demands sometimes also take the form of political interference in
the educational system and distortion of its governing policies. Thus political pressures intrude at all levels in education, forcing the system to respond, and yet may have little relationship to primary goals of national
development or to real changing needs in the society as a whole.

Maladjustment to Social Needs at the Primary Level

Nowhere is the maladjustment of the educational system to needs of national development more evident than in rural primary schools. Primary
education receives the lion's share of Third World expenditures. More than
50% of all educational expenditure and almost 10% of governmental recurrent expenditure is allocated to primary education. Primary education received approximately 3.8% of the total GNP of LDCs in the 1970s, over $43
billion annually.

Given the tremendous importance of primary education for national
development and the distinctive economic, social, and cultural conditions
of less developed nations, one must seriously question the advisability and
utility of a system that for all practical purposes is no different in structure
and content from its counterpart in the advanced nations.

The basic problems of primary education, especially in the rural areas, and the reasons why it is often out of tune with the real needs of poor societies can best be summarized as follows:

1. Over 70% of the children in LDCs live and attend school in rural areas.
2. Over 80% of these children are likely to spend their lives earning a living either directly from the land or from unskilled paid employment in rural areas. Yet primary schools spend little time giving these students the knowledge, skills, and ideas necessary to function efficiently in their rural environment (e.g., farming practices and management, hygiene, nutrition, community development).
3. Primary schools typically attempt to prepare students for secondary school, with training in literacy, basic arithmetic, and foreign languages receiving highest priority. The training, moreover, usually consists of recitation, repetition, and drill learning rather than thinking and problem solving.
4. In those developed nations in which the vast majority of primary school entrants proceed to secondary school, which in turn tends to concentrate on college preparatory education, the heavy emphasis on literacy, arithmetic, and foreign languages is less questionable. But it has been estimated that it takes approximately 5 years (depending on age of entry) for a child to achieve literacy and even longer to master arithmetic and foreign languages (even if languages were really relevant).
5. The problem with this approach to primary and secondary education (i.e., structuring the primary school curriculum solely as a preparation for secondary school) in the LDCs is that

    a. For a variety of economic and social reasons, over 15% of the children who enter primary school will drop out after the first year, with an additional 10% dropping out the following year.

    b. Approximately 50% of those who enter the first class of primary school are unlikely to complete four years.

    c. Less than 10% of those who enter primary school are likely to succeed in reaching secondary school, even though 25−30% of the original entrants might complete the primary cycle.

    d. Of those who do get to secondary school, less than 60% are likely to complete the course (the ratio is much lower in Africa) and only about 20% will proceed to a university.

    e. For those who do make it through secondary school but do not continue on, the probability of finding a job in the modern sector (toward which their secondary education has been oriented) gets lower with each passing year.

Clearly something is seriously wrong with a primary and secondary educational system modeled on its counterpart in economically advanced societies and transferred to an environment to which it has little if any relevance (we deal with the problems of university education in the next section). But documenting these problems is not the same thing as offering solutions. What is urgently needed are detailed studies and well-conceived experiments to answer such critical questions as the following.[7]

1. At what age should a child who is going to have only a few years of primary education enter school?
2. Should primary education in a rural community in a developing country be full-time or part-time?
3. Assuming that some type of formal education is desirable, do literacy and basic arithmetic skills constitute the highest-priority areas of instruction for children destined to spend their lives in rural areas?
4. If the medium of instruction in higher and secondary education is a language other than the mother tongue, is it therefore necessary to teach this language in primary school?

5. Given that for financial reasons it is not possible to lengthen the training of teachers (salaries are usually directly related to length of training), can the training given to teachers be changed and the curriculum and inspection system altered so that the teacher becomes more effective?

6. If children are given certain ideas that they forget because they have no possibility of practicing them, are they more or less likely to accept and practice these ideas again when they are reintroduced later in adult life?

7. Have the children who drop out of primary school after one, two, or three years gained much, if anything? If not, can a curriculum be designed so that they would benefit more?

8. Are the highest priority areas of instruction the same for (a) those children proceeding to secondary education, (b) those children getting paid employment in the modern sector, and (c) those children remaining in the rural areas? If not, is it possible to structure the system in such a way as to both provide some equality of opportunity and fulfill their differing requirements?

9. Related to (8), is it possible to design a reasonably just and incorruptible selection procedure (for entrance into the next level) that does not overinfluence what is taught in the schools?

10. Should the school and community be integrated? Should adult and child education be integrated? Should mass education (or community development) be designed to solve particular developmental problems? If so, how?

These and other questions of great significance to the nation-building aspirations of Third World countries need to be answered if their primary (and secondary) educational systems are to make maximum contributions to development.

PROBLEMS OF HIGHER EDUCATION

President Julius Nyerere of Tanzania perhaps best summed up the role of universities in developing societies when he said:

> The University in a developing society must put the emphasis of its work on subjects of immediate moment to the nation in which it exists, and it must be committed to the people of that nation and their humanistic goals. . . . We in poor societies can only justify expenditure on a University—of any type—if it promotes real development of our people. . . . The role of a University in a developing nation is to contribute; to give ideas, manpower, and service for the furtherance of human equality, human dignity and human development.[8]

Higher education in the LDCs is a very much smaller world than that of primary and secondary levels. Students in higher education make up less than 5% of the total, and teachers less than 8%. Although there are a considerable variety of institutions in higher education (e.g., colleges and professional schools), the university is generally identified as the most important and apex institution. Yet Third World universities have been found by many observers to be as maladjusted and out of step with the real needs of development as the educational institutions in lower levels. Many of the problems basic to primary and secondary education already discussed recur in more or less aggravated form in universities.

The basic causes of university defects have been examined in what is now a substantial literature and are generally agreed on. Most Third World universities were modeled in structure and function on universities in the industrialized societies. Such modeling has continued to the present. Over the last 20 years many national programs of university development have resulted in (even where it was not the primary intention) additions and changes in LDCs that resemble practices established in the United States, France, Great Britain, and other developed countries. By long and powerful tradition the universities of the Western world are structured by professional disciplines, as they have been since the medieval period. This structure of departments (disciplines) and their groupings (faculties) was exported on a large scale to universities in the LDCs. Little thought or effort was given to questions of how this mode of academic organization would serve existing Third World conditions and problems. "Excellence" continued to be measured in terms of externally formulated international academic standards rather than contributions to national development. But the pressures of expanding enrollments, tight budgets, and, most important, student demands for relevant and meaningful curricula have recently caused many Third World university leaders to rethink their role and mission and to begin to heed the advice of thoughtful observers like President Nyerere of Tanzania.[9]

Factors Affecting the Ability to Learn: Some Causes and Consequences

Recent evidence from a wide range of countries, both developed and less developed, has convincingly demonstrated that early factors in the life of a child—the health and feeding habits of mothers during pregnancy, the child's own health and nutritional status during his or her first few years of life, the family's income and living conditions, etc.—can determine whether or not the child will perform well in school and in later life.[10] Figure 11.1 portrays the influence of these early factors (individual, family, and nonfamily environment) not only on school performance ("later factors") but also on individual capacities for behavioral change and the private and social benefits derived from such change, mainly in the area of employment.

The figure shows, for example, that early malnutrition and disease can adversely affect a child's ability to read, write, perform arithmetic operations, and think clearly and logically in school ("cognitive" abilities). They also can adversely affect one's chances of obtaining and/or holding a job (employment status) and lower productivity and general performance in that job. Thus family and child health are important determinants of both school performance and the physical and mental ability of an individual to function effectively in later life.

Children from poor families with low levels of living are therefore often placed at a competitive disadvantage vis-à-vis the economically better-off child in school activities. For example, most studies of school performance reveal that the four most important factors in determining a child's capacity to learn are:

1. *Family environment*, including income levels, parents' education, housing conditions, number of children in household

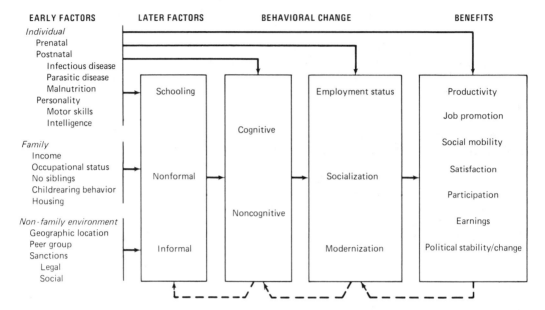

Figure 11.1.   The learning system: Causes, consequences, and interactions. *Source:* John Simmons, "The Investment in Education for Developing Countries: National Strategy Options" (Washington, D.C.:IBRD, 1976), p. 196. Reprinted by permission of The World Bank and Oxford University Press.

2. *Peer-group interactions*: the type of children with whom an individual child associates
3. *Personality*: the child's inherited intelligence and abilities
4. *Early nutrition and health*

If a child enters school deficient in all four of the above factors, as many very poor children do, the educational process may have little effect on his capacity for self-improvement and economic advancement. In developing countries he is very likely to be among the 50% of primary school students who drop out before completing 4 years. Equality of educational opportunity—a social goal professed by all nations—can thus have little meaning in societies where children come from very unequal backgrounds.

THE ECONOMICS OF EDUCATION AND EMPLOYMENT

Much of the literature and public discussion about education and economic development in general, and education and employment in particular, revolves around two fundamental economic processes: (a) the interaction between economically motivated *demands* and politically responsive *supplies* in determining how many school places are provided, who gets access to these places, and what kind of instruction they receive; and (b) the important distinction between "social" versus "private" *benefits* and *costs* of different levels of education, and the implications of these differentials for educational investment strategy.

Educational Supply and Demand: The Relationship between Employment Opportunities and Educational Demands[11]

The amount of schooling received by an individual, although affected by many nonmarket factors, can be regarded as largely determined by demand and supply, just as any other commodity or service. However, since most education is publicly provided in less developed countries, the determinants of demand turn out to be much more important than the determinants of supply. On the demand side the two principal influences on the amount of schooling desired are (a) a more educated student's prospects of earning considerably more income through future modern sector employment (i.e, his or his family's "private benefits" of education), and (b) the educational costs, both direct and indirect, which a student and/or his family must bear. The demand for education is thus in reality a "derived demand" for high-wage employment opportunities in the modern sector. This is because access to such jobs is largely determined by an individual's education. Most people (especially the poor) in less developed nations do not demand education for its intrinsic noneconomic benefits but simply because it is the only means of securing modern sector employment. These derived benefits must in turn be weighed against the costs of education.

On the supply side, the quantity of school places at the primary, secondary, and university levels is determined largely by political processes, often unrelated to economic criteria. Given mounting political pressure throughout the Third World for greater numbers of school places, we can for convenience assume that the public supply of these places is fixed by the level of government educational expenditures. These in turn are influenced by the level of aggregate private demand for education.

Since it is the demand for education that largely determines the supply (within the limits of government financial feasibility), let us look more closely at the economic (employment-oriented) determinants of this derived demand.

The *demand* for an education sufficient to qualify an individual for entry into modern sector jobs appears to be related to or determined by the combined influence of the following four variables:

The wage and/or income differential. This is the wage differential between jobs in the modern sector and those outside it (family farming, rural and urban self-employment, etc.), which for simplicity we can designate as the traditional sector. Entry into modern sector jobs depends initially on the level of completed education, whereas income-earning opportunities in the traditional sector have no fixed educational requirements. The greater the modern-sector/traditional-sector income differential, the greater will be the demand for education, Thus, *our first relationship states that the demand for education is positively related to the modern–traditional sector wage differential.* Since we know from empirical studies that these differentials can be considerable in developing nations, we might expect the demand for education to be relatively high.

The probability of success in finding modern sector employment. An individual who successfully completes the necessary schooling for entry into the modern sector labor market has a higher probability of getting that well-paid urban job than someone who does not. Clearly, if urban unemployment rates among the educated are growing and/or if the supply of, say, secondary school graduates continually exceeds the number of new job openings for which a secondary graduate can qualify, then we need to modify the "actual" wage differential and instead speak once again about an "expected" income differential (see Chapter 9). Since the probability of success is inversely related to the unemployment rate—that is, the more people with appropriate qualifications who seek a particular job, the lower will be the probability that any one of them will be successful—we can argue that the demand for education through, say, the secondary level will be *inversely* related to the current unemployment rate among secondary school graduates.[12]

The direct private costs of education. We refer here to the current out-of-pocket expenses of financing a child's education. These expenses include school fees, books, clothing, and related costs. We would expect that *the demand for education would be inversely related to these direct costs*—that is, the higher the school fees and associated costs, the lower would be the private demand for education, everything else being equal.

The indirect or "opportunity costs" of education. An investment in a child's education involves more than just the direct, out-of-pocket costs of that education, especially when the child reaches the age at which he can make a productive contribution to family income. At this point, for each year the child continues his education he in effect foregoes the money income he could expect to earn or the output he could produce for the family farm. This "opportunity cost" of education must also be included as a variable affecting its demand. One would expect the relationship between opportunity costs and demand to be *inverse*—that is, *the greater are the opportunity costs, the lower will be the demand for education.*

Although several other important variables, many of which are non-economic (e.g., cultural traditions, social status, education of parents, and size of family), certainly influence the demand for education, we believe that by concentrating on the four variables described above, important insights can be gained into the relationship between the demand for education and the supply of employment opportunities.

To give an example, suppose we have a situation in an LDC where the following conditions prevail:

1. The modern–traditional or urban–rural wage gap is of the magnitude of, say, 100% for secondary versus primary school graduates.
2. The rate of increase in modern sector employment opportunities for primary school dropouts is slower than the rate at which such individuals enter the labor force. The same may be true at the secondary level and even the university level in countries such as India, Mexico, Egypt, Pakistan, and more recently, Ghana, Nigeria, and Kenya.
3. Employers, faced with an excess of applicants, tend to select by level of education. They will choose candidates with secondary rather than primary education even though satisfactory job performance may require no more than a primary education.
4. Governments, supported by the political pressure of the educated, tend to bind the going wage to the level of educational attainment of jobholders rather than to the minimum educational qualification required for the job.
5. School fees at the primary level are often nominal or even nonexistent. They tend to rise sharply at the secondary level and then decline again at the university level as the state bears a larger proportion of the college student's costs.

Under these conditions, which conform closely to the realities of the employment and education situation in many developing nations, we would expect the demand for education to be substantial. This is because the anticipated "private" *benefits* of more schooling would be large compared to the alternative of little or no schooling, while the direct and indirect private educational *costs* are relatively low. And the demand spirals upward over time. As job opportunities for the uneducated diminish, individuals must safeguard their position by acquiring a complete primary education. This may suffice for a while, but the internal dynamics of the employment demand–supply process eventually lead to a situation in which job prospects for those with only primary education begin to decline. This in turn creates a growing demand for secondary education. But the demand for primary education must increase concurrently, as some who were previously content with no education are now being squeezed out of the labor market.

The irony is that *the more unprofitable a given level of education becomes as a terminal point, the more demand for it increases as an intermediate stage or precondition to the next level of education!* This puts great pressure on governments to expand educational facilities at *all* levels to meet the growing demand. If they cannot respond fast enough, the people may do so on their own, as evidenced, for example, by the "Harambee" school self-help movement in Kenya, where community-sponsored secondary schools were built throughout the country with the knowledge that their maintenance would be taken over later by the government.

The upshot of all this is the chronic tendency for developing nations to expand their educational facilities at a rate that is extremely difficult to justify either socially or financially in terms of optimal resource allocation. Each worsening of the employment situation calls forth an increased demand for (and supply of) more formal education at *all* levels. Initially it is primarily the uneducated who are found among the ranks of the unemployed. However, over time there is an inexorable tendency for the average educational level of the unemployed to rise as the supply of school graduates continues to exceed the demand for middle- and high-level manpower. The better educated must, after varying periods of unemployment during which aspirations are scaled downward, take jobs requiring lower levels of education. The diploma and degree thus become basic requirements for employment; they are no longer an entrée into a high-paid job, much less are they the education they were intended to signify.

Governments and private employers in many LDCs tend to strengthen this trend by continuously upgrading formal educational entry requirements for jobs previously filled by those less educated. Excess educational qualification becomes formalized and may resist downward adjustment. Moreover, to the extent that trade unions succeed in binding going wages to the educational attainments of jobholders, the going wage for each job will tend to rise (even though worker productivity in that job has not significantly increased). Existing distortions in wage differentials will be magnified, thus stimulating the demand for education even further.

As a result of this "educational displacement phenomenon," those who for some reason (mostly their poverty) are unable to continue their education will fall by the wayside as unemployed school dropouts. At the same time, the more affluent continue to overqualify themselves through more years of education. In the extreme case, one gets a situation like that of contemporary India, Pakistan, and Bangladesh, where the higher education system is in effect an "absorber of last resort" for the great numbers of educated unemployed.[13] This is a terribly expensive form of unemployment compensation. Moreover, since people cannot remain students until they retire, these great masses will eventually have to emerge from behind the walls of academia into a world of tight labor markets. The result will be a more visible unemployment among those who are both highly educated and highly vocal. For example, a recent study in Bangladesh revealed that the unemployment rate among university graduates was 47%.[14]

Finally, it should be pointed out that many individuals tend to resist what they see as a downgrading of their job qualifications. Consequently, even though on the demand-for-labor side employers will attempt to substitute the more educated for the less educated for a given job, on the supply side there will be many job seekers whose expectations exceed the emerging realities of the labor market. They might prefer to remain unemployed for some time rather than accept a job that they feel is beneath them. It follows that as a result of these "frictional" effects and "lags" in adjustment on the supply side, unemployment will exist at all levels of education even though it is concentrated at lower levels and, in general, is inversely related to educational attainment.

Social versus Private Benefits and Costs

The inexorable attraction of ever higher levels of education is even more costly than this simple picture suggests. Typically in developing countries, the social cost of education (i.e., the opportunity cost to society as a whole resulting from the need to finance costly educational expansion at higher levels when these limited funds might be more productively used in other sectors of the economy) increases rapidly as students climb the educational ladder. The private costs (those borne by the student himself) increase more slowly or, indeed, may decline.

This widening gap between social and private costs provides an even greater stimulus to the demand for higher education than it does for education at lower levels. Educational demand, therefore, becomes increasingly exaggerated at the higher (postsecondary) levels. But educational opportunities can be accommodated to these distorted demands only at full social cost. As demands are generated progressively through the system, the social cost of accommodation grows much more rapidly than the places provided. More and more resources, therefore, may be misallocated to educational expansion in terms of social costs, and the potential for creating new jobs will consequently diminish for lack of public financial resources.

Figure 11.2 provides an illustration of this divergence between private versus social benefits and costs. It also demonstrates how this divergence can lead to a misallocation of resources when private interests supersede social investment criteria. In Figure 11.2a expected private returns and actual private costs are plotted against years of completed schooling. As a student completes more and more years of schooling his expected private returns grow at a much faster rate than his private costs for reasons ex-

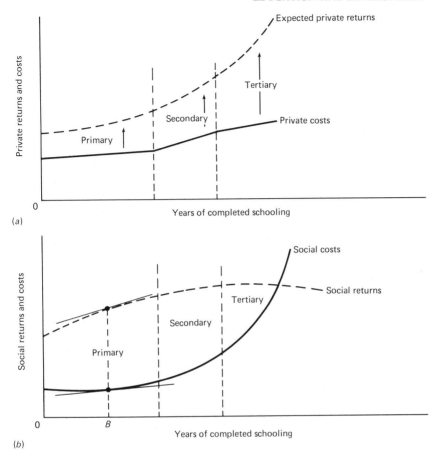

Figure 11.2.   Private versus social benefits and costs of education: An illustration.

plained earlier. In order to maximize the difference between expected benefits and costs (and thereby the private rate of return to investment in education), the optimal strategy for a student would be to secure as much schooling as possible.

  Consider now Figure 11.2b, where social returns and social costs are
plotted against years of schooling. The social benefits curve rises sharply at
first, reflecting the improved levels of productivity of, say, small farmers and
the self-employed that result from receipt of a "basic" education and the
attainment of literacy, arithmetic skills, and elementary vocational skills.
Thereafter, the marginal social benefit of additional years of schooling
increases but at a decreasing rate—thus the declining slope of the social
returns curve. On the other hand, the social cost curve shows a slow rate of
growth for early years of schooling (basic education) and then a much more
rapid growth for higher levels of education. This rapid increase in the
marginal social costs of postprimary education is the result both of the much
more expensive capital and recurrent costs of higher education (i.e., build-

ings and equipment) and, more important, of the fact that much postprimary education in developing countries is heavily subsidized.

It follows from Figure 11.2b that the *optimal* strategy from a social viewpoint (i.e., the one that maximizes the net social rate of return to educational investment) would be one that focuses on providing all students with at least 0B years of schooling. Beyond 0B years marginal social costs exceed marginal social benefits, so that additional educational investment in new, higher-level school places will yield a negative social rate of return. Moreover, in light of the recent empirical results of the Behrman–Birdsall study (see Note 5), the optimal social investment strategy may be to upgrade the quality of existing primary schools rather than to expand their quantity. This quality–quantity tradeoff would be represented in the figure by an upward shift of the social return curve in Diagram (b).

Figure 11.2, therefore, illustrates the inherent conflict between optimal private and social investment strategies—a conflict that will continue to exist as long as private and social valuations of investment in education continue to diverge as students climb the educational ladder.

To a large degree, therefore, the problem of divergent social versus private benefits and costs has been artificially created by inappropriate public and private policies with regard to wage differentials, educational selectivity, and the pricing of educational services. As a result, private perceptions of the value of education exceed its social value, which must take account of rising unemployment. As long as artificial and nonmarket incentives in the form of disproportionate expected benefits and subsidized costs continue to exist and place a premium on the number of years one spends "getting an education," the individual will decide that it is in his best private interests to pursue a lengthy formal education process even though he may be aware that modern sector jobs are becoming more scarce and unemployment rates are rising. Unless these various price signals are made to conform more closely to social realities, the misallocation of national resources (in this case too much expenditure on formal education) will persist and possibly increase.

What is needed, therefore, is a properly functioning reward- and cost-structure that develops and allocates human resources in accordance with requirements and opportunities in various segments of the economy. Where this is absent (i.e., where very high wage premiums are paid to workers in the modern urban sector and scarce jobs allocated on the basis of ever increasing educational credentials) two obvious misallocations of human resources are likely to occur. First, with the output of the educational system greatly in excess of what the economy can absorb, many students will emerge seeking jobs for which they may be educationally qualified but which have been preempted by others with even more education. They become temporarily unemployed for as long as it takes for their aspirations and status requirements, partly perhaps instilled in them by the educational system itself, to adjust to the stinging realities of unemployment in the modern sector. Second, those who adjust their sights downward and secure modern sector employment normally have to take jobs for which they are overeducated in terms of the number of years spent in school. Those who fail to get modern sector jobs at all swell the ranks of the permanently unemployed or become self-employed in the traditional sector. They are thus denied the opportunity to contribute productively to the society that invested so heavily in their education. This combination of the overpaid and, in many cases, overeducated employed and the impoverished and unproductive educated unemployed reflects a serious misallocation of scarce national resources. The resources allocated to the expansion of the educational system might alternatively have been spent on, say, needed rural public works projects. Such investment would provide emergency employment opportunities for recent graduates as well as for those with less education.

Policies to Curtail Artificially Induced Educational Demands: Convergent Benefits and Costs

The imbalance between educational demands and productive job opportunities is not likely to be rectified by the manipulation of the supply of school places, as popular political pressures usually prevent substantial supply adjustments. Rather, pressures from the growing army of unemployed must build until policy attention is turned to the more fundamental issues of tempering demand to more realistic proportions and generating more urban and rural employment opportunities. Related to these issues are several policy recommendations.

1. *Making the beneficiary (as opposed to his family or society as a whole) bear a larger and rising proportion of his educational costs as he proceeds through the system (with appropriate subsidies for the able poor at low levels of education and, through loan programs, also at higher levels) to temper the demand for education*

There are three principles in this policy recommendation. First, the share of educational costs borne privately should be substantially larger than they typically are in many developing countries. This would reduce the demand for education beyond literacy. Second, the rate of educational subsidy should decline as an individual advances in the educational system. As a result, the private demand for education would be curtailed more at high levels where it is socially most expensive and where most of the overeducation in terms of educational requirements for jobs takes place. A policy of declining subsidies would also respond to the valid criticism that current programs involving rising subsidies are antiegalitarian and in fact represent a subsidy to the rich by the poor. Third, the private share of educational costs should, insofar as possible, fall on the beneficiary, not on his or her family or friends. It is the beneficiary's future earnings that will be increased, although the extended family is likely to share in the benefits. Ideally, the beneficiary should pay for his education out of those future earnings. This suggests, of course, that private educational costs should be financed directly out of a student's own resources or indirectly through loans repaid either by financial levies against his future income or by social contributions of his expertise, such as national service in rural areas. Such arrangements seem especially desirable and feasible for postsecondary education. Below that level the burden of private costs would probably continue to fall on the family and would necessitate a system of subsidizing the able poor.

2. *Reducing income differentials between the modern and traditional sectors and within the modern sector to ensure a more realistic appraisal of the prospective benefits of education*

It would carry us too far from the field of education to consider means in detail here (but see the policy recommendations for promoting rural development in Chapter 10 and for reducing internal migration in Chapter 9). We note only that these means are much more extensive than direct, sharp, and unrealistic cuts in modern sector money wages. They include more time-consuming processes of holding the line on average and minimum wages in the modern sector while rural productivity and prices are adjusted upward.

3. *Ensuring that minimum job specifications do not overvalue education*

Students should not be encouraged to seek levels of education that overqualify them for the jobs they can realistically expect to obtain. It is essential for that purpose that the economic system should not exaggerate educational prerequisites to employment. Governments can take direct action on this matter by eliminating allocation of jobs within the civil service where a large share of modern sector employment is to be found solely on the basis of accumulated school certificates.

4. *Ensuring that wages are related to jobs and not to educational attainments*

If the other policies are effective, this becomes essentially an interim measure. So long as overeducation is increasing and those emerging from the system must accept jobs that realistically require progressively lower educational qualifications, the tendency, particularly in teaching and the civil service, to tie salaries to levels of education simply increases rates of overpayment. This eventually induces even more students to follow the same privately profitable but socially costly path.

5. *Increasing the supply of urban and rural job opportunities*

As was already suggested in previous chapters, governments should also

a. *Reduce factor-price distortions to the extent that these enter into employment decisions in both the public and private sectors*
b. *Give more careful consideration to improving rural infrastructure and to the possible location of new modern sector activities in areas where wages have not yet reached the distorted levels typical of established urban centers*
c. *Allocate a larger share of public budgets to productive employment-creating activities and less to educational expansion than has been the pattern in the last decade*

Item (c) is not meant to imply that funds spent on education do not also create employment: they do. Rather, the point is simply that some of the funds so spent in the past might have been more usefully allocated to other, more productive, labor-intensive activities, including the provision of complementary resources for the productive employment of the already educated. Education beyond literacy should compete for funds on these social benefit/cost criteria, not on the notion that it is a privileged activity exempt from such social and economic considerations.

Having looked at the economics of education and employment, we can now examine some of the broader interrelationships between education, society, and development.

EDUCATION, SOCIETY, AND DEVELOPMENT: SOME ISSUES

One cannot discuss the relationship between education and development without explicitly linking the structure of the educational system to the economic and social character of the Third World society in which it is contained. Educational systems more often than not reflect the essential nature of that society. For example, if the society is very inegalitarian in economic and social structure, the educational system will probably reflect that bias in terms of who is able to proceed through the system. At the same time education *can* influence the future shape and direction of society in a number of ways. Thus the linkage between education and development is a two-way process. By reflecting the socioeconomic structures of the societies in which they function (whether egalitarian or not), educational systems tend to perpetuate, reinforce, and reproduce those economic and social structures. On the other hand, educational reform, whether introduced from within or outside the system, has the great potential for inducing corresponding social and economic reform in the nation as a whole.

With these general observations in mind, let us look at six specific economic components of the development question—growth, inequality and poverty, population and fertility, internal migration, rural development, and external migration—to see in what way they influence or are influenced by most LDC educational systems. Such an examination will demonstrate the important two-way relationship that exists between education and development. It should also provide us with an even broader understanding of the development problems and issues that have been discussed in previous chapters.

Education and Economic Growth

For many years the proposition that educational expansion promoted and in some cases even determined the rate of overall GNP growth remained unquestioned. The logic seemed fairly straightforward. Third World nations were very deficient in their supply of semiskilled and skilled manpower. Without such manpower, which it was assumed could be created only through the formal educational system, development leadership in both the public and private sectors would be woefully lacking.

Impressive statistics and numerous quantitative studies of the sources of economic growth in the West were paraded out to demonstrate that it was not the growth of physical capital but rather of human capital (the "residual" in econometric production function estimates) that was the principal source of economic progress in the developed nations.[15] Clearly, in the newly independent nations of Africa and Asia, there was an immediate need to build up the human as well as physical capital infrastructure in order to provide indigenous leadership for the major tasks of development. Rapid quantitative expansion of enrollments therefore appeared justified in light of the substantial manpower scarcities of the 1950s and 1960s. And, although it is extremely difficult to document statistically, it seems clear that the expansion of educational opportunities at all levels has probably contributed to *aggregate economic growth* by (a) creating a more productive labor force and endowing it with increased knowledge and skills; (b) providing widespread employment and income-earning opportunities for teachers, school and construction workers, textbook and paper printers, school uniform manufacturers, etc; (c) creating a class of educated leaders to fill vacancies left by departing expatriates or otherwise vacant positions in governmental services, public corporations, private businesses, and professions; and (d) providing the kind of training and education that would promote literacy and basic skills while encouraging "modern" attitudes on the part of diverse segments of the population. Even if alternative investments in the economy could have generated greater growth, this would not detract from the important contributions, noneconomic as well as economic, education can make and has made to promoting aggregate economic growth. That an educated and skilled labor force is a necessary condition of sustained economic growth cannot be denied.

On the other hand, any evaluation of the role of education in the process of economic development should go beyond the analysis of a single statistic of aggregate growth. One must also consider the *structure* and *pattern* of that economic growth and its *distribution implications*—who benefits.

Education, Inequality, and Poverty

Until recently, most of the work on the economics of education in both developed and developing nations focused on the linkages between education, labor productivity, and output growth. This is not surprising since, as we have seen, the principal objective of development during the 1950s and 1960s was the maximization of aggregate rates of output growth. As a result, the impact of education on the distribution of income and the elimination of absolute poverty was largely neglected. Recent studies, however, have demonstrated that contrary to what might have been assumed, *the educational systems of many developing nations act to increase rather than to decrease income inequalities.*[16]

The basic reason for this perverse effect of formal education on income distribution is the positive correlation between a person's level of education and his level of lifetime earnings. This correlation holds especially for those who are able to complete secondary and university education where income differentials over workers who have only completed part or all of their primary education can be on the order of 300–800%. Since levels of earned income are so clearly dependent on years of completed schooling, it follows that large income inequalities will be reinforced if students from middle-and upper-income brackets are represented disproportionately in secondary and university enrollments. In short, if for financial and/or other reasons the poor are effectively denied access to secondary and higher educational opportunities, then the educational system can actually perpetuate and even increase inequality in Third World nations.

Educational economist John Simmons, for example, gives the following sketch of how the poor are beginning to regard education:

> Schooling, the poor quickly learn, in most countries, is an escape from poverty for only a few. The poor are the first to drop out because they need to work, the first to be pushed out because they fall asleep in class as one result of malnourishment, and the first to fail their French or English tests because upper income children have had better opportunities at home. The hope brought to village parents by the construction of the primary school soon fades. Enough schooling to secure a steady, even menial job for their son, let alone for their daughter, seems just beyond their grasp. Before . . . any schooling would have done to achieve their aspiration. Now a primary school certificate is needed, and some are saying that even students with some secondary schooling cannot get a steady job; and they could never afford to send their son away to town for secondary schooling.[17]

There are two fundamental economic reasons why one might suspect that many LDC educational systems are inherently inegalitarian, in the sense that poor students have less chance of completing any given educational cycle than more affluent students. First, the private *costs* of primary education (especially in view of the "opportunity cost" of a child's labor to poor families) are higher for poor students than for more affluent students. Second, the expected *benefits* of primary education are lower for poor students. Together, the higher costs and lower expected benefits of education mean that a poor family's "rate of return" from investment in a child's education is lower than it is for other families. The poor are, therefore, more likely to drop out during early years of schooling. Let's examine in slightly more detail the reason why costs might be relatively higher and benefits relatively lower for a poor child.

First, the higher opportunity cost of labor to poor families means that even if the first few years of education are free, they are not without cost to the family. Children of primary school age typically are needed to work on family farms—often at the same time they are required to be at school. If a child cannot work because he is at school, the family will either suffer a loss of valuable subsistence output or be required to hire paid labor to replace the absent child. In either case there is a real cost to a poor family of having an able-bodied child attend school when there is productive work to be done on the farm—a cost not related to tuition and of much less significance to higher-income families, many of whom may live in urban areas where child work is not needed.

As a result of these higher opportunity costs, school attendance and therefore school performance tends to be much lower for children of poor families than for those from relatively higher income backgrounds. Thus, in spite of the existence of free and universal primary education in many LDCs, children of the poor, especially in rural areas, are seldom able to proceed beyond the first few years of their education. Their relatively poor school performance may have nothing to do with a lack of cognitive abilities. On the contrary, it may merely reflect their disadvantaged economic circumstances.

This financial process of eliminating the relatively poor during their first few years of schooling is often compounded by the substantial tuition charged at the secondary level. In many developing countries annual tuition is roughly equivalent to the per capita national income. The cost of education therefore becomes prohibitive to lower-income families. This in effect amounts to a system of educational advancement and selection based not on any criteria of merit but strictly on family income levels. It thus perpetuates concentration of income within certain population groups and means that "earned income" will accrue primarily to those who already possess the bulk of "unearned" income and wealth—those whose assets already place them in the upper deciles of the personal income distribution scale.

The inegalitarian nature of many Third World educational systems is compounded even further at the university level where the government may pay the full cost of tuition and fees as well as provide university students with income grants in the form of stipends. Since most university students already come from upper-income brackets (and were so selected at the secondary level), highly subsidized university education utilizing public funds often amounts to a subsidy or transfer payment from the poor to the wealthy—in the name of "free" higher education![18]

On the benefit side, the poor are also at a disadvantage vis-à-vis the rest of the population. Even if they are able to complete their primary education, the poor typically have more difficulty competing for rural and urban jobs because they lack the range of contacts and influences that others have. In other words, for any given level of completed education (except perhaps university education), the poor student will tend to be less likely to be selected for a job requiring that educational certification than the more affluent student. Even in agriculture one could argue that although education may raise farm labor productivity, the benefits of this will accrue disproportionately to those farm families who own their land and also have the complementary financial resources to modernize their agricultural techniques (i.e., the well-to-do, large-scale farmer). In the extreme case of landless rural laborers, the greatest proportion of the benefits of their limited education and higher productivity may accrue largely to the rich landlord on whose farm they work.

It follows that in Third World countries characterized by highly unequal distributions of personal income, sizable secondary school tuition, and subsidized higher education, the educational system, especially at the secondary and higher levels, probably operates to *increase* inequality and perpetuate poverty. It should be stressed, however, that this outcome is not the result of the educational system per se but of the institutional and social structure within which that system must function. Specifically, as long as wage differentials between workers of different educational attainments are kept artificially wide in spite of rising levels of unemployment, as long as access to jobs is based almost exclusively on educational credentials irrespective of the relationship between years of schooling and job performance, and as long as family income serves as the basic criterion of who is able to proceed up the educational ladder to highly paid jobs, then publicly supported educational systems will merely serve to reproduce the inegalitarian social and economic structure that, at least in theory, they were devised to combat. *Equality of educational opportunity can have little meaning if financial assets and income-earning opportunities are very unequally distributed.*

Finally, we should note that even if all of the above cost and benefit distributions in favor of the rich were removed (e.g., by taxing higher incomes at higher rates, subsidizing the education of the poor, broadening employment opportunities for all, making the rich bear the full costs of their education) so as to make progress in the educational system strictly a function of merit and school performance, the poor would nevertheless *still* be at a competitive disadvantage. As we saw earlier in the chapter, a childhood characterized by poor nutrition and a congested and illiterate home environment has negative effects on ability and functioning.

We are therefore compelled to conclude that as in the case of the population problem where family-planning programs are most effective in the context of an economic motivation for smaller families based on improved levels of living, the problems of inequality and poverty depend ultimately on the direct measures aimed at eliminating them and only partially on indirect measures such as universal education. As long as the institutional, social, and economic structures of Third World nations cater primarily to the needs and desires of upper-income groups, an educational system that at least in principle is open to all classes, tribes, and castes and that is considered socially progressive, a matter of national pride, and an instrument of egalitarianism, can in reality merely provide short-term cover for the further widening of the gap between rich and poor. But with rising unemployment, greater inequality, and the chronic persistence of absolute poverty, the political cover provided by thinly disguised inegalitarian systems of Third World education becomes ever more difficult to maintain. Ironically, it is often the middle- and upper-class students themselves, especially at the university level, who are in the vanguard of economic and social reform. In recent years student-led movements have motivated economic and social reforms in a number of Third World countries, including Thailand, Ethiopia, Sri Lanka, Colombia, Pakistan, and the Philippines.

Education, Internal Migration, and Fertility

Education seems to be an important factor influencing both rural–urban migration and levels of fertility. The relationship between education and migration, however, appears to be more powerful than that between education and fertility. Moreover, existing empirical evidence reveals that education influences labor mobility even more directly (i.e., through its impact on higher income expectations) than fertility.

Numerous studies of migration in diverse countries have documented the positive relationship between the educational attainment of an individual and his or her propensity to migrate from rural to urban areas. Basically, individuals with higher levels of education face wider urban–rural real income differentials and higher probabilities of obtaining modern sector jobs than those with lower levels of education (recall from Chapter 9 how income differentials and job probabilities interact to determine migration patterns). The probability variable in particular accounts for the growing proportion of the more educated rural migrants in the face of rising levels of urban unemployment among the less educated.[19]

With regard to the education and fertility relationship, the evidence is less clear. While most studies reveal an inverse relationship between the education of women and their size of family, particularly at lower levels of education, the mechanism through which education per se influences decisions regarding family size is still subject to considerable speculation.

Assuming that lower levels of urban unemployment (especially among the educated) and lower levels of fertility are important policy objectives for Third World governments, the basic issue is whether the continued rapid quantitative expansion of the formal educational system (and the resource allocation decisions implicit therein) will ameliorate or exacerbate the twin problems of accelerating internal migration and rapid population growth. With respect to this issue both theory and evidence seem once again to indicate that given limited government resources, the further excessive quantitative expansion of school places beyond perhaps basic education is both undesirable and unwise. There are two main reasons for this conclusion.

First, as we discovered earlier in the chapter, any rapid expansion of the formal primary system creates inexorable pressures on the demand side for the expansion of secondary and tertiary school places. The net result is the widespread phenomenon of excessive expansion of school places from the standpoint of real resource needs and the associated dilemma of rising levels of rural–urban migration and urban unemployment among a cadre of increasingly more educated and more politically vocal migrants.

Second, if, as many have argued, the education of women does affect their fertility behavior, primarily through the mechanism of raising the opportunity cost of their time in child-rearing activities (see Chapter 7), then it follows that unless sufficient employment opportunities for women (as well as for men) can be created, the reliance on educational expansion as a policy instrument for lowering fertility will be weak if not totally ineffective.

Education and Rural Development

In Chapter 10 we argued that if national development is to become a reality in Third World nations, there needs to be a better balance between rural and urban development. Since most of the priority projects of the past few decades focused on the modernization and development of the urban sector, much more emphasis needs to be placed in future years on expanding economic and social opportunities in rural areas. While agricultural development represents the main component of any successful rural development program simply because 70% of Third World rural populations are engaged directly or indirectly in agricultural activities, rural development nevertheless must be viewed in a broader perspective.

First and foremost, it needs to be viewed in the context of far-reaching transformations of economic and social structures, institutions, relationships, and processes in rural areas. The goals of rural development cannot simply be restricted to agricultural and economic growth. Rather, they must be viewed in terms of a balanced economic and social development with emphasis on the *equitable distribution*, as well as the rapid generation, of the benefits of higher levels of living. Among these broader goals, therefore, are the creation of more productive employment opportunities both on and off the farm; more equitable access to arable land; more equitable distribution of rural income; more widely distributed improvements in health, nutrition, and housing; and, finally, a broadened access to both formal (in-school) and nonformal (out-of-school) education, for adults as well as children, of a sort that will have *direct relevance* to the needs and aspirations of rural dwellers.

How do present Third World systems of education fit into this holistic view of the meaning of rural development? Basically, not very well. As we saw earlier in the chapter, the formal primary school system in most LDCs is with minor modifications a direct transplant of the system in developed countries. The overriding goal is to prepare all children to pass standard qualifying examinations for secondary schools; hence the curricula have a very strong urban bias. The priority needs of the greatest proportion of students—those who will live and work in rural areas—are given minimal attention. Major groups with important rural training needs such as out-of-school children and youth, women, and small subsistence farmers are largely neglected by organized educational programs, both formal and nonformal. As a result, much of the education in the rural communities of developing nations contributes little toward improving levels of agricultural productivity or toward assisting the student to function more effectively in the rural environment.

What, then, might be the real and lasting educational needs for rural development? Philip H. Coombs, a noted educational economist, has provided one very appealing typology.[20] He groups these educational needs for both young people and adults, males and females, into four main categories:

1. *General or basic education* (literacy, arithmetic, an elementary understanding of science and one's environment, etc.)—what most primary and secondary schools now seek to achieve
2. *Family improvement education*—designed primarily to impart knowledge, skills, and attitudes useful for improving the quality of family life and including such subjects as health and nutrition, homemaking and child care, home repairs and improvements, and family planning
3. *Community improvement education*—designed to strengthen local and national institutions and processes through instruction in such matters as local and national government, cooperatives, and community projects
4. *Occupational education*—designed to develop particular knowledge and skills associated with various economic activities that are useful in making a living

For the most part only Category 1—general education—has been emphasized in developing countries. But the learning needs of the three principal occupational subgroups of rural areas—farmers and farm workers, persons engaged in nonfarm rural enterprises, and rural general personnel—are likely in each case to fit quite poorly with most formal educational curricula. Table 11.4 shows how these learning needs vary among the three groups. Effective and well-designed educational programs catering to *each* of these three diverse occupational groups are needed if education is to make its essential contribution to rural development.

Education and International Migration: Intellectual Dependence and the Brain Drain

In addition to the transfer of production and consumption technology (i.e., production processes and consumer tastes), a major aspect of the international transfer of institutional technology lies in the area of transplanted

Table 11.4 Illustrative Rural Occupational Groups and Their Learning Needs

Groups	Types of learning needs (at varying levels of sophistication and specialization)

A. *Persons directly engaged in agriculture*
  1. Commercial farmers
  2. Small subsistence and semi-subsistence farm families
  3. Landless farm workers
	Farm planning and management, rational decision making, recordkeeping, cost and revenue computations, use of credit
	Application of new inputs, varieties, improved farm practices
	Storage, processing, food preservation
	Supplementary skills for farm maintenance and improvement, and sideline jobs for extra income
	Knowledge of government services, policies, programs, targets
	Knowledge and skills for family improvement (e.g., health, nutrition, home economics, child care, family planning)
	Civic skills (e.g., knowledge of how cooperatives, local government, national government function)

B. *Persons engaged in off-farm commercial activities*
  1. Retailers and wholesalers of farm supplies and equipment, goods and and other items
  2. Suppliers of repair and maintenance services
  3. Processors, storers, and shippers of agricultural commodities
  4. Suppliers of banking and credit services
  5. Construction and other artisans
  6. Suppliers of general transport services
  7. Small manufacturers
	New and improved technical skills applicable to particular goods and services
	
	Quality control
	Technical knowledge of goods handled sufficient to advise customers on their use, maintenance, etc.
	Management skills (business planning; recordkeeping and cost accounting; procurement and inventory control; market analysis and sales methods; customer and employee relations; knowledge of government services, regulations, taxes; use of credit)

C. *General services personnel: rural administrators, planners, technical experts*
  1. General public administrators, broad-gauged analysts, and planners at subnational levels
  2. Managers, planners, technicians, and trainers for specific public services (e.g., agriculture, transport, irrigation, health, small industry, education, family services, local government)
  3. Managers of cooperatives and other farmer associations
  4. Managers and other personnel of credit services
	General skills for administration, planning, implementation, information flows, promotional activities
	Technical and management skills applying to particular specialties
	Leadership skills for generating community enthusiasm and collective action, staff team work, and and support from higher echelongs

SOURCE: Philip H. Coombs and Manzoor Ahmed, *Attacking Rural Poverty: How Nonformal   Education Can Help* (Baltimore: Johns Hopkins University Press, 1974), p. 17.

formal educational systems. And just as foreign techniques of production may be ill suited to the factor endowments and output priorities of developing nations, so too the formal educational systems of the highly industrialized, highly urbanized, and technologically sophisticated nations of the West may be, and usually are, ill suited to the human resource needs of agrarian societies attempting to modernize. The inherently dysfunctional nature of such systems of formal education for Third World rural areas has been discussed in earlier sections of this chapter.

But in addition to rich-country dominance in the international development and transfer of physical and intellectual technology, there is also the problem of the international migration of high-level educated manpower—the so-called brain drain—from poor to rich countries. This is particularly true in the case of scientists, engineers, academics, and doctors, many thousands of whom have been trained in home-country institutions at considerable social cost only to reap the benefits from and contribute to the further economic growth of the already affluent nations. Table 11.5 reveals the annual magnitude of the professional and technical brain drain from the developing nations to North America and the United Kingdom for the period 1962–1973. Note particularly the rapid jump in immigration to the United States following the liberalization of immigration laws in 1966.

The international brain drain deserves mention not only because of its effects on the rate and structure of LDC economic growth but also because of its impact on the style and approach of Third World educational systems. The brain drain, broadly construed, has not merely reduced the supply of vital professional people available within developing countries; perhaps

Table 11.5 Gross Immigration of Professional and Technical Personnel from Less Developed Countries into the United States, Canada, and the United Kingdom, 1962–1973

Year	United States	Canada	United Kingdom	3-country sum
1962	9,024	1,381	—	—
1963	11,029	1,525	4,600	17,154
1964	11,418	1,873	—	—
1965	11,001	3,707	3,230	17,938
1966	13,986	5,548	—	—
1967	23,361	7,897	2,900	34,158
1968	28,511	6,930	2,420	37,861
1969	27,536	7,585	1,720	36,841
1970	33,796	6,118	1,000	40,914
1971	38,647	5,184	1,270	45,101
1972	39,106	5,360	377	44,843
1973	31,939	—	—	—

SOURCE: Edwin P. Reubens, "Professional immigration into developed countries from less developed countries," in J. N. Bhagwati (ed.), *The Brain Drain in Taxation* (Amsterdam: North Holland, 1976), Table 1, p. 220.

even more seriously, it has diverted the attention of those scientists, doctors, architects, engineers, and academics who remain from important local problems and goals. These include the development of appropriate technology; the promotion of low-cost preventive health care; the construction of low-cost housing, hospitals, schools, and other service facilities; the design and building of functional yet inexpensive labor-intensive roads, bridges, and machinery; the development of relevant university teaching materials such as appropriate introductory economics texts; and the promotion of problem-oriented research on vital domestic development issues. Such needs often go neglected as, dominated by rich-country ideas as to what represents true professional excellence, those highly educated and highly skilled Third World professionals who do not physically migrate to the developed nations nevertheless migrate "intellectually" in terms of the orientation of their activities. This "internal" brain drain is much more serious than the external one.

For example, one constantly finds developing nations with numerous doctors specializing in heart diseases while preventive tropical medicine is considered to be a second-rate specialty. Architects are concerned with the design of national monuments and modern public buildings, while low-cost housing, schools, and clinics remain an area of remote concern. Engineers and scientists concentrate on the newest and most modern electronic equipment while simple machine tools, hand- or animal-operated farm equipment, basic sanitation and water-purifying systems, and labor-intensive mechanical processes are relegated to the attention of "foreign experts." Finally, some academic economists teach and do research on totally irrelevant, sophisticated mathematical models of nonexistent competitive economies, while problems of poverty, unemployment, rural development, and education are considered less intellectually interesting. In all these diverse professional activities, performance criteria are based not on contributions to national development but rather on praise from the international community (i.e., professional mentors in the developed nations). Thus, the acceptance of an LDC scholar's publication in international professional journals or the receipt of an invitation to attend a professional meeting in London, Paris, New York, or Moscow is often deemed more important than finding a solution to a local technological, agricultural, medical, or economic problem.

This international dominance of professional attitudes and orientations in developing nations (especially in former colonial countries) for a while tended to permeate the whole educational and intellectual establishment, with obvious antidevelopmental effects. While difficult to quantify in terms of rates of economic growth and levels of poverty, the combined brain drain and outward-looking orientation of many LDC professionals has no doubt been an important factor contributing to the perpetuation of conditions of underdevelopment in Africa, Asia, and Latin America. Recent student and faculty calls for more relevant curricula, teaching materials, and research activities, however, attest to the emergence of a new spirit of nationalism and collective self-reliance, which appears to be gathering momentum among Third World intellectuals. If a good university is to be more than "just a collection of books," as the philosopher Thomas Carlyle once remarked, Third World universities and professional schools have a vital role to play in making higher education more tuned to the real needs of social and economic development.

SUMMARY AND CONCLUSIONS: MAJOR EDUCATIONAL POLICY OPTIONS[21]

Developing nations are confronted with two basic alternatives in their policy approaches to problems of education. They can continue to expand formal systems quantitatively, with perhaps some minor modifications in curricula, teaching methods, and examinations, while retaining the same institutional labor market structures and educational costing policies. Or they can attempt to reform the overall educational system by modifying the conditions of demand for and the supply of educational opportunities and by reorienting curricula in accordance with the real resource needs of the nation. Our evidence leads to the conclusion that the first alternative can only exacerbate the problems of unemployment, poverty, inequality, rural stagnation, and international intellectual dominance that now define the conditions of underdevelopment in much of Africa, Asia, and Latin America and that, therefore, the second alternative needs to be pursued.

Since educational systems largely reflect and reproduce rather than alter the economic and social structures of the societies in which they exist, any program or set of policies designed to make education more relevant for development needs must operate simultaneously on two levels:

1. Modifying the economic and social signals and incentives *outside* the educational system that largely determine the magnitude, structure, and orientation of the aggregate private demand for education and consequently the political response in the form of the public supply of school places
2. Modifying the *internal* effectiveness and equity of educational systems by appropriate changes in course content (especially for rural areas), structures of public versus private financing, methods of selection and promotion, and procedures for occupational certification by educational level

Only by policies designed simultaneously to achieve these two objectives can the real positive links between education and development be successfully forged. Let us conclude, therefore, with a brief review of what these external and internal policies might specifically encompass.

Policies Largely External to Educational Systems

Adjusting Imbalances, Signals, and Incentives

Policies that tend to remedy major economic imbalances and incentive distortions (e.g., in income and wage differentials) and alleviate social and political constraints on upward mobility can have the multiple beneficial effect of increasing job opportunities, modifying the accelerated rate of rural–urban migration, and facilitating development-related modifications of educational systems.

Modifying Job Rationing by Educational Certification

In order to break the vicious circle in which overstated job specifications make overeducation necessary for employment, policies are needed that will induce or require public and private employers to seek realistic qualifications even though the task of job rationing may be made somewhat more difficult as a result. Basic to this procedure would be the elimination of school certificates for many of the jobs, especially in the public sector (janitors, messengers, file clerks, etc.), which tends to set the pattern for the private sector.

Curbing the Brain Drain

Controlling or taxing the international migration of indigenously trained high-level professional manpower is a very sensitive area. It can potentially infringe on the basic human right and freedom to choose the nature and location of one's work. In a repressive regime, such a restrictive policy can be morally repugnant. On the other hand, when a nation invests scarce public financial resources in the education and training of its people only then to forego the social returns on that investment as a result of international migration, it seems both economically and morally justifiable to seek either to temporarily restrict that movement in the national interest, or better, to tax if possible the overseas earnings of professional migrants and reinvest these revenues in programs of national development. Such a tax on overseas earnings would act as a financial disincentive to migrate. Its implementation, however, would require the cooperation and assistance of the governments of countries to which these professionals migrate.[22]

Policies Internal to Educational Systems

Educational Budgets

Where politically feasible, educational budgets should grow more slowly than in the past to permit more revenue to be used for the creation of rural and urban employment opportunities. Moreover, a larger share of educational budgets should be allocated to the development of primary as opposed to secondary and higher education, in order to promote self-education and rural work-related learning experiences in later life.

Subsidies

Subsidies for the higher levels of education should be reduced as a means of overcoming distortions in the aggregate private demand for education. Policies should be promoted by which the beneficiary of education (as opposed to his family or society as a whole) would bear a larger proportion of his educational costs as he proceeds through the system. This should be done either directly, through loan repayments, or by service in rural areas. At the same time low-income groups should be provided with sufficient subsidies to permit them to overcome the sizable private costs (including opportunity costs) of schooling.

Primary School Curricula in Relation to Rural Needs

In order to maximize the productivity of rural human resources, primary school curricula as well as nonformal educational opportunities for school dropouts and adults need to be directed more toward the occupational requirements of rural inhabitants whether in small-farm agriculture, non-farm artisan and entrepreneurial activities, or public and commercial services. Such curricula and task-related reorientations of rural learning systems, however, will not be effective in eliciting popular support unless *rural economic opportunities* are created through which small farmers, artisans, and entrepreneurs can take advantage of their vocational knowledge and training. Without these incentives, people will justifiably view such formal and nonformal occupational training programs with considerable skepticism. They would probably rather pursue the formal school certificate and take their chances in the urban job lottery.

Quotas

To compensate for the inequality effects of most existing formal school systems some form of quotas may be required to ensure that the proportion of low-income students at secondary and higher educational levels at least bears some relationship to their proportion in the overall population. Under present systems "indirect" quotas by income status often determine which students proceed through the educational system. Replacing this de facto quota system with an alternative that ensures that capable low-income students will be able to improve their own and their family's well-being by overcoming the financial barriers to educational advancement would go a long way to making educational systems true vehicles of economic and social equality. The nature of such quota systems will obviously vary from country to country. But there is no a priori basis for assuming that such a quota-by-income-level system will not be more efficient and socially productive for both growth and equity than the present system, which tends to perpetuate poverty and inequality while having a dubious impact on the overall rate of economic growth.

NOTES

1. Frederick H. Harbison, *Human Resources as the Wealth of Nations* (New York: Oxford University Press, 1973), p. 3.
2. For an additional analysis and profile of education, see World Bank, "Human development issues and policies: Education," Reading 23 in *The Struggle for Economic Development*.
3. George Psacharopoulos, *The Returns to Education: An International Comparison* (Amsterdam: Elsevier, 1972).
4. For a review of the empirical studies of the 1970s, see George Psacharopoulos, "Returns to education: An updated international comparison," *Comparative Education* 17 (June 1981), and Christopher Colclough, "The impact of primary schooling on economic development: A review of the evidence," *World Development* 10 (April 1982).
5. Jere Behrman and Nancy Birdsall, "The quality of schooling: Quantity alone is misleading," *American Economic Review* 73, no. 5 (December 1983).
6. A penetrating critique of the experience of education in Third World nations is contained in John Simmons, "Education for development, reconsidered," Reading 24 in *The Struggle for Economic Development*.
7. Nicholas Bennett, *Primary Education in Rural Communities: An Investment in Ignorance*, International Institute for Educational Planning, Paris, 1972 (mimeo), pp. 5–6.
8. Julius Nyerere, *The University's Role in the Development of New Countries*, paper presented at the World University Service Assembly, Dar es Salaam, Tanzania, June 27, 1966.

9. See, for example, Kenneth W. Thompson, *Education in the Nation's Service: Experiments in Higher Education for Development*, prepared by International Council for Educational Development, New York, May 1975.

10. For a review of the evidence for both developed and less developed nations, see J. Simmons and L. Alexander, *The Determinants of School Achievement: Education Production Function Analysis* (Washington, D.C.; World Bank, 1974).

11. Much of the material in this section is drawn from the author's joint paper with E. O. Edwards, "Educational demand and supply in the context of growing unemployment in less developed countries," *World Development* 1, nos. 3 and 4 (1973).

12. In fact, since most expectations for the future tend to be based on a "static" picture of the employment situation that now prevails, we might anticipate that when the employment situation is worsening individuals tend to overestimate their expected incomes and demand even more education than is justified even in terms of "correct" private calculations of benefits and costs.

13. For a penetrating analysis of the Indian educational/employment problem, see Marc Blaug *et al., Causes of Graduate Unemployment in India* (Harmondsworth, England:Penguin, 1967).

14. R. Islam, "Graduate unemployment in Bangladesh: A preliminary analysis," *Bangladesh Development Studies*, Autumn 1980, pp. 47–74.

15. See, for example, Edward F. Denison, *The Sources of Economic Growth in the United States* (New York: National Bureau of Economic Research, 1962), and Robert Solow, "Technical change and the aggregate production function," *Review of Economics and Statistics*, August 1957.

16. See, for example, Jagdish Bhagwati, "Education, class structure and income equality," *World Development* 1, no. 5 (1973).

17. John Simmons, "Education, poverty and development," *World Bank Staff Working Papers* No. 188 (1974):32.

18. For some evidence of the regressive nature of educational subsidies in Latin America, see Jean-Pierre Jallade, *Public Expenditures on Education and Income Distribution in Colombia* (Baltimore: Johns Hopkins University Press, 1974); "Basic education and income inequality in Brazil: The long-term view," *World Bank Staff Working Papers* No. 268 (June 1977); and especially, "Financing education for income distribution," Reading 25 in *The Struggle for Economic Development*.

19. For evidence of this in the case of Tanzania, see H. N. Barnum and R. H. Sabot, *Migration, Education and Urban Surplus Labor,* OECD Development Center Employment Series Monograph, October 1975 (mimeo).

20. Philip H. Coombs and Manzoor Ahmed, *Attacking Rural Poverty: How Nonformal Education Can Help* (Baltimore: Johns Hopkins University Press, 1974), p. 15.

21. As in other chapters, the policies put forward here are designed primarily to stimulate group discussion and individual analysis. Although I believe they are sensible policies with a solid economic rationale, they should not be viewed as absolute and/or immutable, let alone unarguable.

22. For an analysis of the problem, see Jagdish Bhagwati and William Dellalfar, "The brain drain and income taxation," *World Development* 1, nos. 1 and 2 (1973): 94–101; see also the entire September 1975 issue of the *Journal of Development Economics*, which is devoted to the subject of the international brain drain.

CONCEPTS FOR REVIEW

Human resources

Schooling

Formal educational system

"Nonformal" education

Manpower planning

Universal education

Enrollment ratios

Private versus social benefits
   of education

Private versus social costs
   of education

Economic signals and
   incentives

Overeducation

Dropout (or wastage) rates
Literacy
Cognitive abilities
Derived demand
Educational rates of
    return
Opportunity costs of
    education
Educational certification
Basic education
Family improvement education
International brain drain
Sociopolitical constraints
    on educational mobility
Educational job displacement
    phenomenon

Job rationing by education
On-the-job training
High-level manpower
Equal educational opportunity
Early childhood environmental effects
    on ability to learn
Modern sector or urban bias
    of educational systems
Internal effectiveness of
    educational systems
Community improvement education
Occupational education
Internal brain drain
Educational subsidies
Quota systems

QUESTIONS FOR DISCUSSION

1. What reasons would you give for the rather sizable school dropout rates in Third World countries? What might be done to lower these rates?

2. What are the differences between formal and nonformal education? Give some examples of each.

3. It is often asserted that Third World educational systems especially in rural areas are "dysfunctional"—that is, they are not suited to the real social and economic needs of development. Do you agree or disagree with this statement? Explain your reasoning.

4. How would you explain the fact that relative "costs of" and "returns to" higher education are so much higher in LDCs than in developed countries?

5. What is the supposed rationale for subsidizing higher education in many Third World countries? Do you think that it is a legitimate rationale from an economic viewpoint? Explain.

6. Early childhood environmental factors are said to be important determinants of school performance. What are some of these factors, how important do you think they are, and what might be done to ensure that these factors are not negative?

7. What do we mean by "the economics of education"? To what extent do you think educational planning and policy decisions ought to be guided by economic considerations? Explain, giving hypothetical or actual examples.

8. What is meant by the statement "the demand for education is a 'derived demand' for high-paying modern sector job opportunities"? Many educational specialists claim that families and children in LDCs demand education not so much as an investment good but as a consumption good. What do you think is the meaning of this statement and what do you think is the relative importance of the consumption demand for education among your student friends?

9. What are the linkages between educational systems, labor markets, and employment determination in many Third World countries? Describe the process of educational job displacement.

10. Distinguish carefully between private and social benefits and costs of education. What economic factors give rise to the wide divergence between private and social benefit/cost valuations in most developing countries? Should governments attempt through their educational and economic policies to narrow the gap between private and social valuations? Explain.

11. Describe and comment on each of the following education−development relationships:
    a. Education and economic growth: does education promote growth? How?
    b. Education, inequality, and poverty: do educational systems typical of most LDCs tend to reduce, exacerbate, or have no effect on inequality and poverty? Explain with specific reference to a country with which you are familiar.

    c. Education and migration: does education stimulate rural–urban migration? Why?

    d. Education and fertility: does the education of women tend to reduce their fertility? Why and how?

    e. Education and rural development: do most LDC formal educational systems contribute substantially to the promotion of rural development? Explain.

    f. Education and the brain drain: what factors cause the international migration of high-level educated manpower from LDC to developed countries? What do we mean by the internal brain drain? Explain, giving examples.

12. Governments can influence the character, quality, and content of their educational systems by manipulating important economic and noneconomic factors or variables both outside of and within educational systems. What are some of these external and internal factors and how can government policies make education more relevant to the real meaning of development?

FURTHER READINGS

For an informative, general approach to the study of education and human resource development, see Frederick H. Harbison, *Human Resources as the Wealth of Nations* (New York: Oxford University Press, 1973).

Excellent surveys of current economic issues relating education to development can be found in John Simmons, "Education for development, reconsidered," *World Development* 7 (1979):1005–1016, and M. Blaug, *An Introduction to the Economics of Education* (Harmondsworth, England: Penguin, 1970).

A good review of the 1970s empirical research on the economic returns to investment (both private and social) in education can be found in George Psacharopoulos, "Returns to education: An updated international comparison," *Comparative Education* 17 (June 1981):221–241, while an alternative view focusing on the quality rather than quantity of education is contained in Jere Behrman and Nancy Birdsall, "The quality of schooling: Quantity alone is misleading," *American Economic Review* 73, no. 5 (December 1983): 928–946.

For a broad analysis of how education can promote rural development, see Philip H. Coombs and Manzoor Ahmed, *Attacking Rural Poverty: How Nonformal Education Can Help* (Baltimore: Johns Hopkins University Press, 1974).

A challenging and critical view of the role of education in society can be found in Ivan Illich, *Deschooling Society* (New York: Harper & Row, 1970), and also in Ronald Dore, *The Diploma Disease* (Berkeley and Los Angeles: University of California Press, 1976).

A good summary of the issues involved in the question of education and inequality can be obtained from Jagdish Bhagwati, "Education, class structure and income equality," *World Development* 1, no. 5 (1973).

Finally, a multidisciplinary approach to education and development well worth reading can be found in F. Champion Ward (ed.), *Education and Development Reconsidered* (New York: Praeger, 1974).

Additional readings can be found on pp. 629–630.

III

PROBLEMS AND POLICIES

INTERNATIONAL

12

TRADE THEORY AND
DEVELOPMENT EXPERIENCE

The opening of a foreign trade ... sometimes works a sort of industrial revolution in a country whose resources were previously underdeveloped.
John Stuart Mill, 1846

For unto everyone that hath shall be given, and he shall have abundance; but from him that hath not shall be taken away, even that which he hath.
Matthew 25:29

THE IMPORTANCE OF INTERNATIONAL TRADE AND FINANCE

International trade has often played a crucial though not necessarily a benign role in the historical development of the Third World. Throughout Africa, Asia, the Middle East, and Latin America, primary product exports have traditionally accounted for a sizable proportion of individual gross national products. In some of the smaller countries anywhere from 25 to 40% of the monetary GNP is derived from the overseas sale of agricultural commodities such as coffee, tea, cotton, cocoa, and sugar. In the special circumstances of the oil-producing nations in the Persian Gulf, the sale of unrefined and refined petroleum products to countries throughout the world accounts for over 70% of their national incomes. But, unlike the oil-producing states, most developing countries must depend on nonmineral primary product exports for the vast majority of their foreign exchange earnings. Since the markets for these exports are often very unstable, primary product export dependence carries with it a degree of risk and uncertainty that few nations desire.

In addition to their export dependence, many developing countries rely, generally to an even greater extent, on the importation of raw materials, machinery, capital goods, intermediate producer goods, and consumer products to fuel their industrial expansion and satisfy the rising consumption aspirations of their people. For most non-petroleum-rich developing nations, import demands have increasingly exceeded the capacity to generate sufficient revenues from the sale of exports. This has led to chronic deficits on their balance of payments position vis-à-vis the rest of the world. While such deficits on the "current account" (i.e., an excess of import *payments* over export *receipts* for goods and services) were often more than compensated for by a surplus on the "capital account" of their balance of payments table (i.e., a receipt of foreign private and public lending and investment in excess of repayment of principal and interest on former loans and investments), in recent years the debt burden of repaying earlier international loans and investments has become increasingly acute. In a number of LDCs severe deficits on current and capital accounts have therefore led to a rapid depletion of their international monetary reserves and a slowdown in economic growth.

In the 1980s, this combination of rising trade deficits, growing foreign debts, and diminished international reserves led to the widespread adoption of fiscal and monetary austerity measures (often at the instigation of the IMF) which may have further exacerbated the slowdown in economic growth and the worsening of the poverty and unemployment problems throughout the developing world. The precise meaning of these various concepts of international economics will be explained later in this chapter and in the next. Here the point is merely that a chronic excess of foreign expenditures over receipts (which may have nothing to do with an LDC's inability to handle its financial affairs, but may rather be related to its vulnerability to global economic disturbances) can significantly retard development efforts. It can also greatly limit a poor nation's ability to determine and pursue its most desirable economic strategies.

But international trade and finance must be understood in a much broader perspective than simply the intercountry flow of commodities and financial resources. By opening their economies and societies to world trade and commerce and by looking outward to the rest of the world, Third World countries invite not only the international transfer of goods, services, and financial resources, but also the developmental or antidevelopmental influences of the transfer of production technologies, consumption patterns, institutional and organizational arrangements, educational, health and social systems, and the more general values, ideals, and life-styles of the developed nations of the world, both capitalist and socialist. The impact of such technological, economic, social, and cultural transfers on the character of the development process can be either benign or malevolent. Much will depend on the nature of the political, social, and institutional structure of the recipient country and its development priorities. Whether it is best for LDCs to look outward as the free traders and cultural internationalists advocate, or to look inward as the protectionists and cultural nationalists propose, or to be simultaneously and strategically outward- *and* inward-looking in their international economic policies cannot be stated a priori. The individual developing nations need to appraise their present and prospective situations in the world community realistically in the light of their specific development objectives. Only thus can they judge how much to expose themselves, if at all, to the obvious benefits and the many dangers of international commerce.

Unfortunately, many small and very poor countries (and these constitute well over half of all Third World nations) may have little choice about whether to "opt out" or not. As we shall see, however, a potentially promising strategy, especially for these smaller LDCs, may be to look outward but in a different direction (toward cooperation with other LDCs) and inward toward each other as members of a group of nations trying to integrate their economies and coordinate their joint development strategies in an effort to achieve collective self-reliance.

The study of foreign trade and international finance is among the oldest and most controversial branches of the discipline of economics. It dates back to the sixteenth century and Europe's mercantilist passion for Spanish gold. It flowered in the eighteenth and nineteenth centuries as modern economic growth was fueled and propelled by the "engine" of international trade. The greatest minds in economics—Adam Smith, David Ricardo, and John Stuart Mill—provided the basic concepts and insights that endure to this day. A deep and abiding concern with global international relations flourishes even more today, not only because of the still bitter controversies between those who advocate more trade and those who advocate less, especially in the context of development, but also because modern transport and communication are rapidly shrinking the world to the point where some even refer to it as a "global village." It is for these and the other reasons mentioned above that we now turn to this important and still controversial area of economic analyses and policy.

FIVE BASIC QUESTIONS ABOUT TRADE AND DEVELOPMENT

In order to give the discussion contemporary relevance, our objective in this chapter is to focus on the traditional theories of international trade in the context of five basic themes or questions of particular importance to developing nations.

1. How does international trade affect the rate, structure, and character of LDC economic growth? This is the traditional "trade-as-an-engine-of-growth" controversy but set in terms of contemporary development aspirations.
2. How does trade alter the distribution of income and wealth within a country and among different countries or groups of countries? Is trade a force for international and domestic equality or inequality? In other words, how are the gains and losses distributed and who benefits at whose expense (for every "winner" must there be at least one or, more likely, many "losers")?
3. Under what conditions can trade help LDCs achieve their development objectives?
4. Can LDCs by their own actions determine how much they trade?
5. In the light of past experience and prospective judgment, should LDCs adopt an outward-looking (freer trade, expanded flows of capital and human resources, ideas and technology, etc.) or an inward-looking (protectionism in the interest of self-reliance) policy, or should they pursue some combination of both, for example, in the form of regional economic cooperation? What are the arguments for and against these alternative trade strategies for development?

Clearly, the answers or suggested answers to these five questions will not be uniform throughout the diverse economies of the Third World. The whole economic basis for international trade rests on the fact that *countries do differ* in their resource endowments, their economic and social institutions, and their capacities for growth and development. Developing countries are no exception to this rule. Some are very populous yet deficient in natural resources and human skills. Others are sparsely populated yet endowed with abundant mineral and raw material resources. Still others—the majority—are small and economically weak, having at present neither the human nor the material resources on which to base a sustained and largely self-sufficient strategy of economic and social development. Yet, with the notable exception of the now very wealthy oil nations of the Middle East and a few other countries rich in internationally demanded mineral resources, most developing nations face similar issues and choices in their international relations with the developed countries and with each other. Consequently, while an effort will be made here to place generalizations about LDC trade prospects and policy alternatives in the context of a broad typology of Third World nations, the goal of being comprehensive in coverage will necessitate a number of sweeping generalizations, many of which may not hold for a particular country at a particular time. On balance, however, the benefits of this broad Third World perspective seem clearly to outweigh the costs of having to make some analytical and policy generalizations.

Accordingly, we begin with a statistical summary of recent Third World trade performance and patterns. There follows a simplified presentation of the classical and more recent theories of international trade and its effect on efficiency, equity, stability, and growth (four basic economic concepts related to the central questions outlined above). We then move to an extensive critique of "free trade" theories in the light of both historical experience and the contemporary conditions and strategies of economic development. In succeeding chapters, some alternative trade and commercial policies for development are surveyed and the controversies surrounding each summarized.

THE IMPORTANCE OF TRADE FOR DEVELOPMENT: A STATISTICAL REVIEW

Exports, Imports, and Current Account Balances

The export of commodities, of which primary products (food, food products, raw materials, minerals, and fossil fuels) constitute over three-quarters of the total, provides by far the most important source of foreign exchange earnings for the developing world. We see from Table 12.1, for example, that over the period from 1971 to 1981 receipts from commodity exports increased from 66% to 76% of the total balance of payments receipts of all developing countries (see line 20). In 1981 they were almost five times as large as the value of loans and direct investments received by these countries. In other words, over the 1971–1981 period the sale of commodities in foreign markets provided steadily greater amounts of foreign exchange than the combined value of "bilateral" grants and loans (those provided by one government to another), "multilateral" grants and loans (those from a variety of countries channeled through international organizations like the World Bank, the IMF, and the various regional development banks), private (bank) loans, and foreign investments.

Table 12.1 Major Components of the Balance of Payments of Third World Nations as a Whole, 1971, 1975, 1981 (billions of dollars)

	1971	**1975**	**1981**
Goods, services and private transfers			
1. Exports of goods (FOB)	60.87	208.24	529.55
2. Imports of goods (FOB)	−59.25	−181.73	−473.73
3. Trade balance = (1) + (2)	1.62	26.51	55.82
4. Receipts from services	14.60	43.97	139.64
5. Payments to services	−28.18	−75.03	−231.82
6. Private transfers (net)	0.43	1.52	2.75
7. Balance = (3) + (4) + (5) + (6)	−11.53	−3.03	−33.61
8. Government transfers (net)	2.29	1.56	4.32
Capital account			
9. Loans received by government	8.32	18.19	35.17
10. Other loans received	6.66	20.91	67.79
11. Loan repayments abroad	−6.80	−16.10	−45.10
12. Direct investment	2.86	8.63	17.92
13. Other long-term capital	0.73	−15.39	−31.78
14. Total long-term capital (net)			
= (9) + (10) + (11) + (12) + (13)	11.77	16.24	43.99
15. Short-term capital (net)	0.95	0.35	−9.30
16. Errors and omissions	.33	−5.15	−14.59
17. Overall balance = (7) + (8) + (14)			
+ (15) + (16)	3.81	9.97	−9.20
18. SDR allocations and gold monetization	0.74	0.05	2.25
19. Changes in reserves = −(17) − (18)	−4.55	−10.02	6.95
20. Exports as % of total receipts			
(lines 1 + 4 + 6 + 8 + 14 + 15 + 16 + 18)	65.8%	77.9%	75.9%

SOURCE: UNCTAD, *Handbook of International Trade and Development Statistics 1983*, Table 5.1.

Table 12.1 conceals the fact that for most LDCs the value of commodity exports over this period did not expand as fast as commodity imports. This is because the table includes the export earnings of major oil-producing countries. In 1981, for example, exports from developing countries amounted to $530 billion—27.8% of total world exports. However, the OPEC countries alone accounted for over half ($276 billion) of this amount. In fact, OPEC's share of total world exports more than doubled between 1970 and 1981, going from 6.7% to 14.1%. As a result, and as shown in Figure 12.1, OPEC's excess of export earnings over import expenditures—its current account surplus—rose dramatically from slightly over $3 billion in 1973 to a high of $111 billion in 1980 before plummeting to a deficit of $16 billion in 1982–1983 as oil prices retreated in the face of a world recession and efforts to conserve energy on the part of oil importers. By contrast, the aggregate current account *deficit* of the non-oil-exporting developing countries rose from an annual level of $14 billion in 1973 to a high of $109 billion in 1981

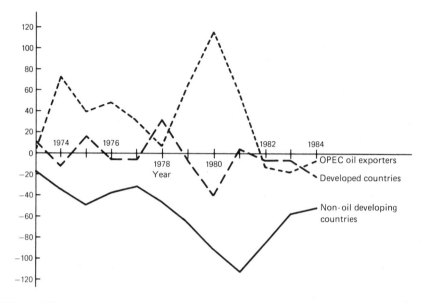

Figure 12.1.   Current account balances by groups of countries, 1973–1984 (billions of dollars). *Sources:* International Monetary Fund, *World Economic Outlook, 1984,* Table 25, and *International Financial Statistics,* various issues.

before finally settling at the $50 billion level in 1984. This increased trade deficit alone far exceeded the *total* annual flow of private foreign investments and public development assistance to *all* developing nations over the same period! Export and current account prospects for the non-oil primary producers of the Third World remain rather bleak for the rest of the 1980s.

Importance of Exports to Different Developing Nations

While overall Third World figures for export growth rates and OPEC shares of total world exports are important indicators of patterns of trade for the group as a whole (see Figure 12.2), the varying importance of exports and imports to the economic well-being of individual nations is masked by these aggregate statistics. In order, therefore, to provide a capsule picture on the relative importance of commodity export earnings to various developing nations of different sizes and in different regions, Table 12.2 has been compiled. For purposes of comparison, several key developed countries are included at the bottom of the table.

We see that large countries like Brazil and India tend to be less dependent on foreign trade in terms of national income than relatively small countries like those in tropical Africa and Central America. As a group, however, less developed nations are more dependent on foreign trade in terms of its share in national income than are the very highly developed countries. This is shown clearly in the cases of the United States and the USSR, whose exports amount to 7.0 and 5.9% of their respective GDPs.

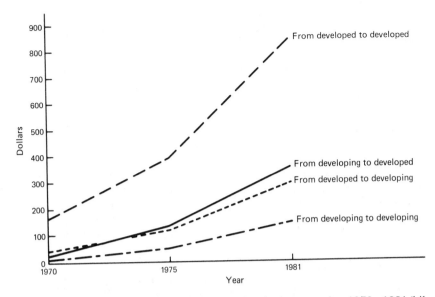

Figure 12.2. Exports from developed and developing countries, 1970–1981 (billions of dollars). *Source:* ODC, *U.S. Foreign Policy and the Third World, Agenda 1983* (New York: Praeger, 1983), p. 246.

Table 12.2 Export Earnings as a Percentage of GDP in Selected Third World Countries, 1982.

Country	Percentage of GDP
Togo	26.7
Kenya	18.4
India	5.6
Sri Lanka	23.0
Zaire	10.6
Brazil	7.5
Mexico	12.3
Nicaragua	13.8
Philippines	12.6
Nigeria	27.2
United States	7.0
USSR	5.9
Japan	13.4

SOURCE: *World Development Report 1984*, Annex Tables 9, 3. Reprinted by permission of Oxford University Press.

The Composition of Trade

Another critical dimension of trade in the Third World is the commodity composition of exports and imports. Although the past two decades have seen considerable expansion in exports of manufactured goods (from 23 to 42% of the total value of all non-OPEC LDC exports between 1960 and 1983), this progress has been largely concentrated in four East Asian nations (South Korea, Taiwan, Hong Kong, and Singapore), which together account for more than 60% of total developing country manufactured exports. In the rest of the Third World, primary products, the traditional mainstay, remain the predominant export. This can be seen from Table 12.3, which shows that LDCs still depend heavily on their exports of primary products while the developed nations export primarily manufactured goods. In spite of the preponderance of manufactured exports, however, the United States and Canada still dominate world exports of the principal cereals such as wheat, corn, and rice. We discuss the economic and political implications of this North American dominance of world food exports in Chapter 17.

We have an important clue here as to why the export performance of the majority of LDCs has been relatively weak compared with the export performance of rich countries. It relates to the concept of elasticity of demand. Most statistical studies of world demand patterns for different commodity groups reveal that in the case of primary products the "income elasticity of demand" is relatively low—that is, the percentage increase in quantity demanded will rise by less than the percentage increase in national income. On the other hand, for fuels, certain raw materials, and manufactured goods, the income elasticity is relatively high. For example, it has been estimated that a 1% increase in developed country incomes will normally raise their import of foodstuffs by 0.6%, agricultural raw materials such as rubber and vegetable oils by 0.5%, petroleum products and other fuels by 2.4%, and manufacturers by about 1.9%. Consequently, when incomes rise in rich countries their demand for food, food products, and raw materials from the Third World nations goes up relatively slowly whereas their demand for manufactures, the production of which is dominated by the developed countries, goes up very rapidly.

Finally, the concentration, especially in Africa, of export production on relatively few major noncereal primary commodities such as cocoa, tea, sugar, and coffee renders certain LDCs very vulnerable to market fluctuations in the prices of specific products. Nearly half the Third World nations earn over 50% of their export receipts from a single primary commodity, such as coffee, cocoa, or bananas. And about three-quarters of the Third World nations earn 60% or more of their export receipts from no more than three primary products. Significant price variations, therefore, for these commodities can render development strategies highly uncertain. It is for this reason that international commodity agreements (such as those for coffee, cocoa, and sugar) among primary producing nations exporting the same commodity have come into being in recent years.

The Terms of Trade

The question of changing relative price levels for different commodities brings us to another important quantitative dimension of the trade problems

Table 12.3 Composition of World Exports and Imports by Groups of Countries, 1980 (%)

	Developed economies	Developing economies	Centrally planned economies	World
	Exports			
Primary products	23.8	79.1	41.8	40.9
Food, beverages, and tobacco	10.3	10.2	8.2	10.1
Crude materials (excluding fuels); oils and fats	6.6	7.1	7.8	6.9
Mineral fuels and related materials	6.9	61.8	25.8	23.9
Manufactured products	74.6	20.1	52.2	57.4
Miscellaneous	1.6	0.8	5.7	1.7
Total	100.0	100.0	100.0	100.0
	Imports			
Primary products	43.6	34.3	36.5	40.9
Food, beverages, and tobacco	9.3	10.7	15.5	10.1
Crude materials (excluding fuels); oils and fats	7.3	5.0	8.9	6.9
Mineral fuels and related materials	27.0	18.6	12.2	23.9
Manufactured products	55.2	63.0	61.5	57.4
Miscellaneous	1.2	2.6	2.0	1.7
Total	100.0	100.0	100.0	100.0

SOURCE: Based on data from United Nations, *Monthly Bulletin of Statistics* 36, no. 5 (May 1982), Special Table C.

historically faced by Third World nations. The total value of export earnings depends not only on the *volume* of these exports sold abroad but also on the *price* paid for them. If export prices decline, a greater volume of exports will have to be sold merely to keep total earnings constant. Similarly, on the import side, the total foreign exchange expended depends on both the quantity and price of imports.

Clearly, if the price of a country's exports is falling *relative* to the prices of the products it imports, it will have to sell that much more of its export product and enlist more of its scarce productive resources merely to secure the same level of imported goods that it purchased in previous years. In other words, the real or social opportunity costs of a unit of imports will rise for a country when its export prices decline relative to its import prices.

Economists have a special name for the relationship or ratio between the price of a typical unit of exports and the price of a typical unit of imports. This relationship is called the *commodity terms of trade* and it is expressed as P_x/P_m where P_x and P_m represent export and import price indexes calculated on the same base period (e.g., 1975 = 100). The terms of trade are said to "deteriorate" for a country if P_x/P_m falls, that is, if export prices decline relative to import prices, even though both may rise. Historically, the prices of primary commodities have declined relative to manufactured goods. As a result, the terms of trade have on the average tended to worsen over time for the non-oil-exporting developing countries while showing a relative improvement for the developed countries. Figure 12.3 shows the rapid and continuous deterioration of the terms of trade of non-oil developing countries between 1977 and 1982 before rising slightly in 1983 and 1984. In fact, during the early 1980s, the terms of trade for these nations fell to their lowest level in 25 years, reflecting a precipitous decline in the prices of their commodity exports relative to the prices of their imports (both manufactured goods and oil). The LDCs therefore had to sell greater quantities of their primary products (the international demand for which, as we have seen, is relatively income inelastic) in order to purchase a given quantity of manufactured and fuel imports. One estimate has placed the extra costs of deteriorating terms of trade for the LDCs at over $2.5 billion per year during the last decade. By contrast, using 1975 = 100 as an index, oil-exporting nations realized an extraordinary improvement in their terms of trade from an average of 98 in 1965 to 594 in 1981.

A good deal of the argument against primary product export expansion and in favor of diversification into manufactured exports for developing

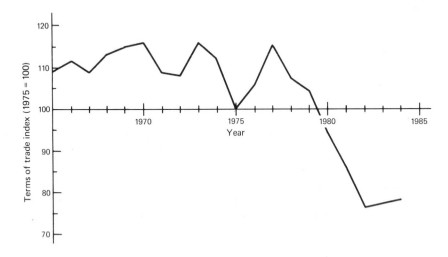

Figure 12.3. Terms of trade of non-oil developing countries (1975 = 100). *Source:* International Monetary Fund, *International Financial Statistics: Supplement on Trade Statistics*, 1982, pp. 158–159; United Nations, *World Economic Survey 1983*, ST/ESA/131, Table II-3; and International Monetary Fund, "World Economic Outlook," *Occasional Paper #27*, 1984, Table 10.

countries during the 1950s and 1960s was based on the secular deterioration of the non-oil commodity terms of trade. But since past commodity price trends are no indication of what future prices will be (witness the dramatic rise and then fall in world food grain, raw material, and other primary product prices during the 1973−1977 and the 1979−1983 periods) and since the international economic vulnerability of developing nations is not confined to adverse movements in commodity terms of trade, it is important to understand both the broader theory and the practice of international economics. We will therefore first review the traditional theory of international trade and then look at the factors that determine the actual trade patterns and performances of developing nations.

THE TRADITIONAL THEORY OF INTERNATIONAL TRADE

Specialization and the Principle of Comparative Advantage: The Classical Labor−Cost Model

The phenomenon of transactions and exchange is a basic component of human activity throughout the world. Even in the most remote villages of Africa, people regularly meet in the village market to exchange goods, sometimes for money, but mostly for other goods through simple barter transactions. A transaction is an exchange of two things—something is given up in return for something else. In an African village, women may barter food such as cassava for cloth or simple jewelry for clay pots. Implicit in all transactions is a "price." For example, if 20 cassavas are traded for a meter of bark cloth, the implicit price (or "terms of trade") of the bark cloth is 20 cassavas. If 20 cassavas can also be exchanged for one small clay pot, it follows that clay pots and pieces of bark cloth can be exchanged on a one-to-one basis. A price system is already in the making.

Why do people trade? Basically, because it is profitable to do so. Different people possess different abilities and resources and may want to consume goods in different proportions. Diverse preferences as well as varied physical and financial endowments open up the possibility of profitable trade. People usually find it profitable to trade the things they possess in large quantities (i.e., relative to their tastes or needs) in return for things they want more urgently. Since it is virtually impossible for each individual or family to provide itself with all the consumption requirements of even the simplest life, they usually find it profitable to engage in those activities for which they are best suited or have a "comparative advantage" in terms of their natural abilities and/or resource endowments. They can then exchange any surplus of these home-produced commodities for products that others may be relatively more suited to produce. The phenomenon of specialization based on comparative advantage arises, therefore, to some extent in even the most primitive of subsistence economies.

These same principles of specialization and comparative advantage have long been applied by economists to the exchange of goods between individual nations. In answer to the question of what determines which goods are traded and why some countries produce some things while others produce different things, economists since the time of Adam Smith have sought the answer in terms of *international differences in costs of produc-*

tion and prices of different products. Countries, like people, specialize in a limited range of production activities because it is to their advantage to do so. They specialize in those activities where the gains from specialization are likely to be the largest.

But why, in the case of international trade, should costs differ from country to country? For example, how can Germany produce cameras, electrical appliances, and automobiles cheaper than Kenya and exchange these manufactured goods for Kenya's relatively cheaper agricultural produce (fruits, vegetables, coffee, and tea)? Again, the answer is to be found in international differences in the structure of costs and prices. Some things (basically manufactured goods) are relatively cheaper to produce in Germany and can profitably be exported to other countries like Kenya; other things (e.g., agricultural goods) can be produced in Kenya at a lower relative cost and are therefore imported into Germany in exchange for its manufactures.

The concept of *relative* cost and price differences is basic to the theory of international trade. The principle of comparative advantage, as it is called, asserts that a country will specialize in the export of those products it can produce at the lowest *relative* cost. Germany may be able to produce cameras and cars as well as fruits and vegetables at lower *absolute* unit costs than Kenya, but since the commodity cost differences between countries are greater for the manufactured goods than for agricultural products, it will be to Germany's advantage to specialize in the production of manufactured goods and exchange them for Kenya's agricultural produce. Thus, while Germany may have an absolute cost advantage in both commodities, its comparative cost advantage lies in manufactured goods. Conversely, Kenya may be at an absolute disadvantage vis-à-vis Germany in both manufacturing and agriculture in that its absolute unit costs of production are higher for both types of products. It can nevertheless still engage in profitable trade because it has a comparative advantage in agricultural specialization (or, alternatively, because its absolute disadvantage is less in agriculture). It is this phenomenon of differences in comparative advantage that gives rise to profitable trade even among the most unequal trading partners.

Perhaps the best way to demonstrate the theoretical advantages of trade is to consider what would happen to a nation's production and consumption levels in its absence. Let us for simplicity and convenience divide the world into two groups: the Third World and the rest of the world. For the moment think of "Third World" as a single country. Suppose Third World is endowed with 100 units of labor. It is capable of producing two types of goods, agricultural and manufactured goods. A unit of manufacturing output requires 5 units of labor while a unit of agricultural output may require only 1 labor unit. If these input–output relationships (i.e., 5 labor input units per unit of manufacturing output and 1 labor input unit per unit of agricultural output) are *fixed* by the prevailing technology, then if the entire labor supply were in manufacturing production, a total of 20 units could be produced. Alternatively, if all Third World labor were to engage in agriculture, a total of 100 units of output could be produced. Finally, if Third World wished to produce some of each of these two categories of goods, it could do so by transferring labor from one sector to the other in a *constant proportion* of 5 to 1; that is, for every additional unit of manufacturing output desired 5 units of labor and, therefore, 5 units of agricultural output will have to be sacrificed. In other words, if Third World were producing 100 units of agricultural output by applying all its labor to this sector and if it wanted to produce 10 units of manufactured goods, it would have to reduce its food output by 50 units (50 laborers). It therefore has the choice of producing the following options: 20 manufacturing and 0 agriculture, 0 manufacturing and 100 agriculture, or 10 manufacturing and 50 agriculture. In fact, it could theoretically produce any number of combinations along its "production-possibility" line *BPA* in Figure 12.4. Note that in this simple labor-cost model the production-possibility line is straight because labor is the only variable factor of production and it is used in *fixed proportions* (constant quantities) for each unit of output. We revert to the typical bow-shaped production-possibility curve in the next section.

Line *BPA* therefore represents *both* the production and the consumption possibilities of Third World. That is, if there are no unemployed resources Third World's people could produce and consume any combination of manufactured and agricultural goods represented by Line *BPA*. Moreover, the relative costs and prices of agriculture in terms of manufactured goods are reflected in the slope of Line *BPA*, where the slope is measured by the vertical distance 0*B* divided by the horizontal distance 0*A* or, simply, 0*B*/0*A*. This price ratio P_a/P_m is thus equal to 1:5 (or 20/100 = 0*B*/0*A*). A unit of manufactured goods costs five times as much as a unit of agricultural output because it requires five times as much labor and labor is the only scarce factor of production. In other words, in order to produce 5 more units of agricultural output, 1 unit of manufactured output will *always* have to be sacrificed. The actual production and consumption point in Third World's closed economy will be determined by domestic demand or consumer preference patterns which, as we learned in Chapter 5, are greatly influenced by the domestic distribution of income. Let's assume that Point *P* represents this final combination. Thus 10 units of manufactured goods and 50 units of food are being produced and consumed in Third World's closed economy.

Now let us open up the possibility of trade by introducing another country which we shall call "Rest of the World." For simplicity, assume that

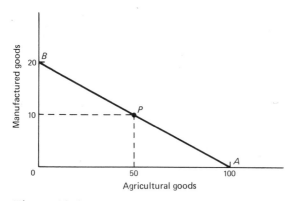

Figure 12.4. Third World's production-possibility frontier.

in Rest of the World everything is the same as in Third World, including the same availability of 100 labor units. The only difference is that instead of requiring 5 units of labor as in Third World to produce 1 unit of manufactured output, Rest of World requires only 2 labor input units. Rest of World is thus a more efficient (lower-cost) producer of manufactured goods than is Third World. Assume agriculture requires the same 1 labor input per unit of output as in Third World. Both "countries," therefore, are equally efficient in food production (i.e., they have the same real labor costs per unit of output). If Rest of World's labor resources are fully employed, it is capable of producing 50 units of manufacturing output and no agriculture, or 100 units of agricultural output and no manufacturing, or any combination between these two extremes with a 2-to-1 tradeoff. Its production and consumption possibilities are shown by Line $B'P'A'$ in Figure 12.5.

Note once again that the slope of this production-possibility line will depict the relative costs and prices of Rest of World's agriculture in terms of its manufactured goods (P_a/P_m). This slope will be equal to ½—that is, $O'B'/O'A' = ½$. For each unit of manufacturing output sacrificed, 2 units of agricultural output can be produced. Assume that Rest of World's domestic demand structure results in Point P' being the effective production and consumption combination, so that 50 units of food and 25 manufactured goods are produced and consumed.

Now if we allow Third World to trade with Rest of World, their differing cost and price structures create the possibility of profitable exchange for both. Even though Rest of World is just as efficient as Third World in agriculture (i.e., both require 1 unit of labor per unit of output), it is much more efficient in manufacturing, where it requires only two-fifths as much labor to produce a unit of output. Rest of World, therefore, has a comparative advantage and should specialize in the production of manufactured goods. Conversely, even though Third World does not have an absolute productivity and cost advantage in either commodity vis-à-vis Rest of World, it does have a comparative advantage in agricultural production. It should therefore specialize in food production and export the excess over its domestic consumption requirements in exchange for Rest of World's manufactured goods.

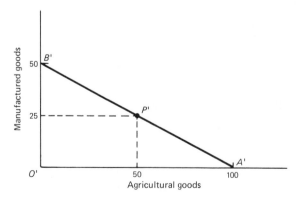

Figure 12.5.   Rest of World's production-possibility frontier.

The opportunity for free trade between Third World and Rest of World will in theory create one worldwide market for goods with a single common price ratio. This world price ratio $(\overline{P}_a/\overline{P}_m)$ will depend on relative demand conditions in both regions for both commodities. It will have to settle somewhere between the two extremes of 1:5 and 1:2 in Third World and Rest of World in order for profitable trade to occur for both. Suppose it settled at 1:4—that is, 1 unit of manufactured goods trades for 4 units of agriculture, or is 4 times as expensive as a unit of agriculture, in "world" commodity markets. Third World, therefore, could *completely specialize* in food production by producing 100 units. At the international price of 1 to 4, it could then exchange, say, 50 units of its food for 12.5 units of Rest of World's manufactured goods. Third World's final (after trade) consumption combination, therefore, would be 50 units of food and 12.5 units of manufactured goods. This combination is shown by Point C in Figure 12.6a.

Similarly, Rest of World could specialize completely in the production of manufactures by producing 50 units of manufactured goods and trading

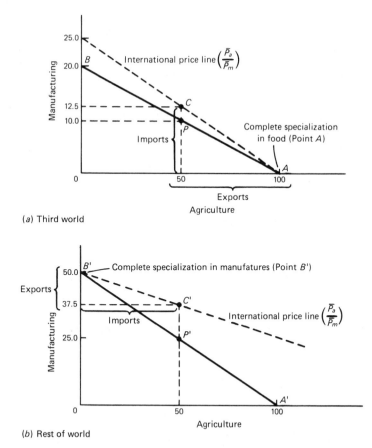

(a) Third world

(b) Rest of world

Figure 12.6.   The theoretical benefits of free trade between the Third World and the Rest of World.

12.5 of these to Third World in return for 50 units of food products. Its consumption combination, therefore, would be 37.5 units of manufactured goods and 50 units of agricultural goods, as shown by Point C' in Figure 12.6b.

Figure 12.6 can now be used to show the two major theoretical benefits of free trade. The first is that *trade enables all countries to escape from the confines of their resource endowments and consume commodities in combinations that lie outside their production-possibility frontiers.* This is clearly shown in both (a) and (b). By specializing in food production and engaging in trade, Third World is able to consume the same amount of food as before trade (i.e., 50 units) but 25% more manufactured goods (i.e., 12.5 compared with 10). It is therefore clearly better off as a nation in terms of the total availability of goods. How these goods are distributed and who benefits is another question, and one which we take up later. Similarly, Rest of World by specializing completely in the production of manufactured goods and trading these at international prices with Third World is able to consume the same quantity of food as before (50 units) but 50% more of its own manufactured goods (37.5 compared with 25). It clearly is also better off. Note also that both countries could have wound up consuming more of *both* commodities if they so desired. Thus, the important conclusion is drawn that *free international trade will benefit all nations of the world,* even though the benefits may be disproportionately distributed depending on world demand conditions and cost differences for different commodities in different countries.

The second major implication of the classical theory of international trade is that *free trade will maximize global output* by permitting every country to specialize in what it does best, that is, by concentrating on the production of those goods in which it has a comparative advantage. We see from Figure 12.6 that without trade total world production and consumption of food and manufactured goods would equal 100 and 35 units respectively (Point P + Point P'). As a result of specialization and trade, total world output of food stayed the same while world manufacturing output increased by over 40%, from 35 to 50 units. Clearly, using other labor input coefficients we could demonstrate that specialization and trade can lead to world output increases for *all* traded commodities. Finally, note that commodity trade is balanced in the sense that the value of exports equals the value of imports in both regions. This is an important assumption of classical trade theory.

Relative Factor Endowments and International Specialization: The Neoclassical Model

The two-country, two-product classical theory of free trade just presented is a static model based strictly on a one-variable-factor (labor cost), complete specialization approach to demonstrating the gains from trade. This nineteenth-century free trade model primarily associated with David Ricardo and John Stuart Mill was modified and refined in the twentieth century by two Swedish economists, Eli Hecksher and Bertil Ohlin, to take into account differences in factor supplies (mainly land, labor, and capital) on international specialization. The Hecksher–Ohlin neoclassical (i.e., variable proportions) factor-endowment approach also enables one to describe analytically the impact of economic growth on trade patterns and the impact of trade on the structure of national economies and on the differential returns or payments to various factors of production.

Unlike the classical labor-cost model, however, where trade arises because of fixed but differing labor productivities for different commodities in different countries, the factor endowment model assumes away inherent differences in relative labor productivity by postulating that *all countries have access to the same technological possibilities for all commodities.* If domestic factor prices were the same, all countries would use identical methods of production and therefore have the same relative domestic product price ratios and factor productivities. The basis for trade arises, therefore, not because of inherent technological differences in labor productivity for different commodities between different countries but because *countries are endowed with different factor supplies.* Given different factor supplies, relative factor prices will differ (e.g., labor will be relatively cheap in labor-abundant countries) and so too will domestic commodity price ratios and factor combinations. Countries with cheap labor will have a relative cost and price advantage over countries with relatively expensive labor in those commodities which make abundant use of labor (e.g., primary products). They should therefore focus on the production of these labor-intensive products and export the surplus in return for imports of capital-intensive goods.

On the other hand, countries well endowed with capital will have a relative cost and price advantage in the production of manufactured goods, which tend to require relatively large inputs of capital compared with labor. They can thus benefit from specialization in and export of capital-intensive manufactures in return for imports of labor-intensive products from labor-abundant countries. Trade therefore serves as a vehicle for a nation to capitalize on its abundant resources through more intensive production and export of those commodities that require large inputs of those resources, while relieving its factor shortage through the importation of commodities that utilize large amounts of its relatively scarce resources.

To summarize, the factor-endowment theory is based on two crucial propositions:

1. *Different products require productive factors in different relative proportions.* For example, agricultural products generally require relatively greater proportions of labor per unit of capital than manufactured goods which require more machine time (capital) per worker than most primary products. The proportions in which factors are actually used to produce different goods will depend on their relative prices. But, no matter what factor prices may be, the factor-endowment model assumes that certain products will always be relatively more capital-intensive while others will be relatively more labor-intensive. These relative factor intensities will be no different in India than in the United States; primary products will be the relatively labor-intensive commodities compared with secondary manufactured goods in both India and the United States.

2. *Countries have different endowments of factors of production.* Some countries, like the United States, have large amounts of capital per worker and are thus designated as "capital-abundant" countries. Others, like India, Egypt, or Colombia, have little capital and much labor and are thus designated as "labor-abundant" countries. In general, developed countries are relatively capital abundant (one could also add that they are well endowed with skilled labor) while, for the most part, Third World countries are labor abundant.

The factor-endowment theory goes on to argue that capital-abundant countries will tend to specialize in such products as automobiles, aircraft, sophisticated electronic communication goods, and computers, which utilize capital intensively in their technology of production. They will export some of these capital-intensive products in exchange for those labor- or land-intensive products like food, raw materials, and minerals which can best be produced by those countries that are relatively well endowed with labor and/or land.

This theory, which played a predominant role in the early literature on trade and development, encouraged Third World countries to focus on their labor- and land-intensive primary product exports. It was argued that by trading these primary commodities for the manufactured goods that developed countries were "best suited" to produce, Third World nations could best realize the enormous potential benefits to be had from free trade with the richer nations of the world. This free trade doctrine also served the political interests of colonizing nations searching for raw materials to feed their industrial expansion and for market outlets for their manufactured goods.

The mechanism through which the benefits of trade are transmitted across national boundaries under the factor-endowment approach is analogous to that of the classical labor-cost approach. However, in the factor-endowment case with the possibility of differing factor combinations for producing different commodities, nations are assumed to be operating initially at some point on their concave (or increasing opportunity cost) production-possibility frontier determined by domestic demand conditions. Point A on Third World production-possibility frontier $P-P$ in Figure 12.7a provides an example. With full employment of all resources and under perfectly competitive assumptions, Third World will be producing and consuming at Point A where the relative price ratio, P_a/P_m, will be given the slope of the dotted line ($[P_a/P_m]T$) at Point A.[1] Similarly, Rest of World may be producing and consuming at Point A' in Figure 12.7a, with a domestic price ratio ($[P_a/P_m]R$) that differs (i.e., agricultural goods are relatively more costly or, conversely, manufactured goods relatively cheaper) from that of Third World. Note that with a closed economy both countries will be producing both commodities. However, Third World, being poorer, will produce a greater proportion of food products in its (smaller) total output.

The relative differences in costs of production and prices at Points A and A' (i.e., their different slopes) gives rise once again to the possibilities of profitable trade. As in the previous labor-cost model, the international free trade price ratio ($\bar{P}_a/\bar{P}_m$) will settle somewhere between $(P_a/P_m)T$ and $(P_a/P_m)R$, the domestic price ratios of Third World and Rest of World respectively. The lines $\bar{P}_a/\bar{P}_m$ in Figure 12.7(a) and (b) denote the common world price ratio. For Third World, this steeper slope of $\bar{P}_a/\bar{P}_m$ means that it can get more manufactured goods for a unit of agriculture than in the absence of trade; that is, the world price of agricultural goods in terms of manufactures is higher than Third World's domestic price ratio. It will therefore reallocate resources away from its costly capital-intensive manufacturing sector and specialize more on labor-intensive agricultural production. Under perfectly competitive assumptions it will produce at Point B on its production frontier, where its relative production (opportunity) costs are

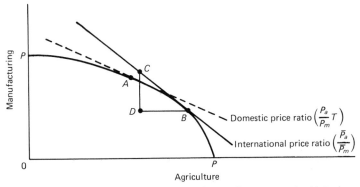

(a) Third world (without trade, production and consumption occurs at A; with trade, production is at B, consumption at C; exports = BD; imports = DC)

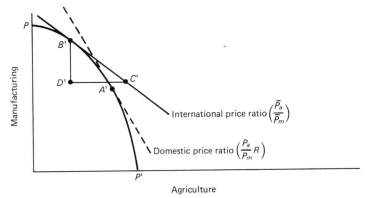

(b) Rest of world (without trade, production and consumption occurs at A'; with trade, production is at B', consumption at C'; exports = $B'D'$; imports = $D'C'$)

Figure 12.7.   Trade with variable factor proportions and different factor endowments.

just equal to relative world prices. It can then trade along $\bar{P}_a/\bar{P}_m$, the prevailing international price line, exporting BD agricultural products in return for DC manufactured imports and arrive at a final consumption point C with more of *both* goods than before trade. To give a numerical example, suppose the free trade international price ratio, $\bar{P}_a/\bar{P}_m$, were 2:1. In other words, a unit of agricultural goods sells at a price twice that of a unit of manufactured goods. This means that for every unit of agriculture Third World exports to Rest of World, it can import 2 units of manufactured goods. The slope of the international price line graphically portrays this trading ratio or terms of trade. Therefore, if Third World exports BD agriculture (e.g., 30 units), it will receive DC manufactures (60 units) in return.

Similarly, for Rest of World the new international price ratio means more agricultural products in exchange for manufactured goods than at domestic prices. Graphically, the international price ratio has a lesser slope than Rest of World's domestic price ratio (see Figure 12.7b). Rest of World will therefore reallocate its abundant capital resources in order to produce more manufactured goods and less agriculture, as at Point B' where its relative domestic production costs are just equal to relative world prices. It can then trade $B'D'$ ($= DC$) of these manufactures for $D'C'$ ($= BD$) of Third World's agricultural products. Rest of World can therefore also move outside the confines of its production frontier and end up consuming at a point like C' in Figure 12.7b. Trade is balanced: the value of exports equals the value of imports for both regions. Moreover, it has resulted in increased consumption of *both* goods for *both* regions, as shown by a comparison between free trade points C and C' and no-trade points A and A' in Figure 12.7.

The principal conclusions from the factor-endowment model of free trade are therefore the same as those of the labor-cost model: all countries gain and world output is increased. However, in addition to these two basic conclusions there are several others. First, due to increasing opportunity costs associated with resource shifting among commodities with different factor intensities of production, *complete specialization will not occur* as in the simple labor-cost model. Countries will tend to specialize in those products which utilize their abundant resources intensively. They will compensate for their scarce resources by importing those products which utilize these scarce resources most intensively. But rising domestic costs and, therefore, prices in excess of world prices will prevent complete specialization from occurring.

Second, given identical technologies of production throughout the world, the equalization of domestic product price ratios with the international free trade price ratio *will tend to equalize factor prices across trading countries.* Wage rates, for example, will rise in labor-abundant Third World as a result of the more intensive use of human resources in the production of additional agricultural output. On the other hand, the price of scarce capital will decline due to the diminished production of manufactured goods which are heavy users of capital. In Rest of World, the price of its abundant capital will rise relative to its scarce labor as more emphasis is placed on the production of capital-intensive manufactured goods and less on labor-intensive agriculture.

The factor-endowment, variable-factor-proportions theory, therefore, makes the important prediction that *international real wage rates and capital costs will gradually tend toward equalization.*[2] This is also one of its greatest defects since we know that in the real world just the opposite is happening: international income inequalities are increasing with each passing year. We shall see below how the restrictive and unreal assumptions of both the labor-cost and factor-endowment theories can often lead to erroneous conclusions about the actual structure of world trade and the distribution of its benefits.

Third, within countries the factor-endowment theory of trade predicts that the *economic return to owners of the abundant resources will rise in relation to owners of scarce resources* as the abundant factor is more intensively utilized. In Third World countries this in general would mean a rise in the share of national income going to labor. In the absence of trade, labor's share might be smaller. Thus *trade tends to promote more equality in domestic income distributions.*

Finally, by enabling countries to move outside their production-possibility frontiers and secure capital as well as consumption goods from other parts of the world, *trade is assumed to stimulate, or be an engine of, economic growth*. It also enables a nation to obtain those domestically expensive raw materials and other products (as well as knowledge, ideas, new technologies, etc.) with which it is relatively less well endowed at lower world market prices. It can thus create the conditions for a more broadly based and self-sustaining growth of a nation's industrial output.

Trade Theory and Development: The Traditional Arguments

We are now in a position to summarize the economic results of traditional trade theories. The "classical" labor-cost and the "neoclassical" factor-endowment theories of international trade provide the following theoretical answers to our five basic questions about trade and development.

1. *Trade is an important stimulator of economic growth.* It enlarges a country's consumption capacities, increases world output, and provides access to scarce resources and worldwide markets for products without which poor countries would be unable to grow.
2. *Trade tends to promote greater international and domestic equality* by equalizing factor prices, raising real incomes of trading countries, and making efficient use of each nation's and the world's resource endowments (e.g., raising relative wages in labor-abundant countries and lowering them in labor-scarce countries).
3. *Trade helps countries to achieve development* by promoting and rewarding those sectors of the economy where individual countries possess a comparative advantage whether in terms of labor efficiency or factor endowments.
4. In a world of free trade, *international prices and costs of production determine how much a country should trade* in order to maximize its national welfare. Countries should follow the dictates of the principle of comparative advantage and not try to interfere with the free workings of the market.
5. Finally, in order to promote growth and development, an *outward-looking international policy is required*. In all cases, self-reliance based on partial or complete isolation is asserted to be economically inferior to participation in a world of free unlimited trade.

SOME CRITICISMS OF TRADITIONAL FREE TRADE THEORIES IN THE CONTEXT OF THIRD WORLD EXPERIENCE

The labor-cost and factor-endowment theories of international trade are both based on a number of explicit and implicit assumptions that in many ways are grossly contrary to the reality of international economic relations in the 1980s. These theories therefore often lead to conclusions foreign to both the historical and contemporary trade experience of many developing nations. This is not to deny the potential benefits of a world of free trade, but rather to recognize that free trade exists mostly in the diagrams and models of economists, whereas the real world is beset by all varieties of national protection and international noncompetitive pricing policies.

What are the major and crucial assumptions of the traditional theories of international trade, and how are these assumptions violated in the real world? What are the implications for the trade and financial prospects of developing nations when a more realistic assessment of the actual mechanism of international economic and political relations is made?

There are six basic assumptions of the classical and neoclassical trade models.

1. All productive resources are fixed in quantity and constant in quality across nations. They are fully employed and there is no international mobility of productive factors.
2. The technology of production is fixed (classical model) or similar and freely available to all nations (factor-endowment model). Moreover, the spread of such technology works to the benefit of all. Consumer tastes are also fixed and independent of the influence of producers (i.e., international consumer sovereignty prevails).
3. Within nations, factors of production are perfectly mobile between different production activities and the economy as a whole is characterized by the existence of perfect competition. There are no risks and uncertainties.
4. The national government plays no role in international economic relations, so that trade is strictly carried out among many atomistic and anonymous producers seeking to minimize costs and maximize profits. International prices are therefore set by the forces of supply and demand.
5. Trade is balanced for each country at any point in time and all economies are readily able to adjust to changes in the international prices with a minimum of dislocation.
6. The gains from trade that accrue to any country benefit the nationals of that country.

We can now take a critical look at each of these assumptions in the context of the contemporary position of Third World countries in the international economic system.

Fixed Resources, Full Employment, and the International Immobility of Capital and Skilled Labor

Trade and Resource Growth

This initial assumption about the static nature of international exchange—that resources are fixed, fully utilized, and internationally immobile—is central to the whole traditional theory of trade and finance. In reality, the world economy is characterized by rapid change and factors of production are fixed neither in quantity nor quality. Not only do capital accumulation and human resource development take place all the time, but trade has always been and will continue to be one of the main *determinants* of the *unequal growth* of productive resources in different nations. This is especially true with respect to those resources most crucial to growth and development, such as physical capital, entrepreneurial abilities, scientific capacities, the ability to carry out technological research and development, and the upgrading of technical skills in the labor force.

It follows, therefore, that relative factor endowments and comparative costs are *not* given but are in a state of constant change. Moreover, they are often determined by, rather than themselves determining, the nature and character of international specialization. In the context of unequal trade between rich and poor nations, this means that *any initial state of unequal resource endowments will tend to be reinforced and exacerbated by the very trade that these differing resource endowments were supposed to justify.* Specifically, if rich nations as a result of historical forces are relatively well endowed with the vital resources of capital, entrepreneurial ability, and skilled labor, their continued specialization in products and processes that intensively utilize these resources will create the necessary conditions and economic incentives for their further growth. On the other hand, Third World countries, endowed with abundant supplies of unskilled labor, by specializing in products that intensively utilize unskilled labor, and whose world demand prospects and terms of trade may be very unfavorable, often find themselves locked into a stagnant situation that perpetuates their "comparative advantage" in unskilled, unproductive activities. This in turn will inhibit the domestic growth of needed capital, entrepreneurship, and technical skills.

A cumulative process is therefore set in motion in which trade exacerbates already unequal trading relationships, distributes the benefits largely to those who already "have," and perpetuates the physical and human resource underdevelopment that characterizes Third World nations. No country likes to think of itself specializing in unskilled labor activities while letting foreigners reap the rewards of higher skills, technology, and capital. By pursuing the theoretical dictates of their factor endowments, however, less developed countries may lock themselves into a domestic economic structure that reinforces such relatively poor endowments and is inimical to their long-run development aspirations. Some countries, like the Asian "gang of four" (Taiwan, South Korea, Singapore, and Hong Kong), may succeed in transforming their economies through international trade from unskilled-labor to skilled-labor to capital-intensive production. However, for the vast majority of poor nations, the possibilities of trade stimulating similar structural economic changes are remote at best.

Unemployment, Resource Underutilization, and the Vent-for-Surplus Theory of Trade

The assumption of full employment in traditional trade models, like that of the standard perfectly competitive equilibrium model of microeconomic theory, violates the reality of unemployment and underemployment in developing nations. Two conclusions could be drawn from the recognition of widespread unemployment in the Third World. The first is that underutilized human resources create the opportunity to expand productive capacity and GNP at little or no real cost by producing for export markets products that are not demanded locally. This is known as the *vent-for-surplus* theory of international trade. First formulated by Adam Smith, it has been expounded more recently in the context of developing nations by the Burmese economist Hla Myint.

According to this theory, the opening of world markets to remote agrarian societies creates opportunities not to reallocate fully employed resources as in the traditional models but, rather, to make use of formerly *underemployed* land and labor resources to produce greater output for export to foreign markets. The colonial system of plantation agriculture as well as the commercialization of small-scale subsistence agriculture were made possible, according to this view, by the availability of unemployed and underemployed human resources. In terms of our production-possibility analyses, the vent-for-surplus argument can be represented by a shift in production from Point V to Point B in Figure 12.8 with trade enlarging final domestic consumption from Point V to C.

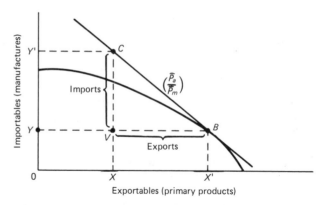

Figure 12.8. The "vent-for-surplus" theory of trade in LDCs.

We see that before trade, the resources of this closed Third World economy were grossly underutilized. Production was occurring at Point V, well within the confines of the production-possibility frontier, and $0X$ primary products and $0Y$ manufactures were being produced and consumed. The opening up of the nation to foreign markets (probably as a result of colonization) provides the economic impetus to utilize these idle resources (mostly excess land and labor) and expand primary product exportable production from $0X$ to $0X'$ at Point B on the production frontier. Given the international price ratio $(\overline{P}_a/\overline{P}_m)$, $X-X'$ (equal to VB) primary products can now be exported in exchange for $Y-Y'$ (equal to VC) manufactures, with the result that the final consumption point, C, is attained with the same primary products $(0X)$ being consumed as before but with $Y'-Y$ more imported manufactures now available.

The vent-for-surplus argument does provide a more realistic analytical scenario of the historical trading experience of many LDCs than do either the classical or neoclassical models. However, in the short run the beneficiaries of this process were often colonial and expatriate entrepreneurs rather than LDC nationals. And in the long run the heavy structural orientation of the LDC economy toward primary product exports in many cases created an export "enclave" situation and thus inhibited needed structural transformation in the direction of a more diversified and self-reliant economy.

The second conclusion that one may draw from the recognition of widespread unemployment in the Third World is that a major way to create substantial local job opportunities is to protect domestic industries (both manufacturing and agriculture) against low-cost foreign competition. This protection is accomplished through the erection of various trade barriers such as tariffs or quotas. Although we discuss the pros and cons of commercial policy in the next chapter, the point is that those LDCs that place priority on employment creation may wish to pursue a short-run protectionist policy in order to build up local rural and urban industries to absorb their surplus labor.

International Factor Mobility and Multinational Corporations

The third component of the crucial first assumption of traditional trade theory—the international immobility of productive factors—is, after the assumption of perfect competition, the most unrealistic of all premises of classical and neoclassical trade theory. Capital and skilled labor have always moved between nations. The nineteenth-century growth experience of Western nations can largely be explained in terms of the impact of international capital movements. Perhaps the most significant development in international economic relations during the past two decades has been the spectacular rise in power and influence of the giant multinational corporations. These international carriers of capital, technology, and skilled labor with their diverse productive operations throughout the Third World greatly complicate the simple theory of international trade, especially as regards the distribution of its benefits. Companies like IBM, Ford Motor, Exxon, Philips, Hitachi, British Petroleum, Renault, Volkswagen, and Coca-Cola have so internationalized their production process that calculations of the distribution of the benefits of international production between foreigners and nationals becomes exceedingly difficult. We return to this important issue in Chapter 14, where we examine the pros and cons of private foreign investment. For the present, let us recognize that enormous international movements of capital and skills play a crucial role in international economic relations. To assume away their existence and their impact on the economies and economic structures of developing nations, as in the classical and factor-endowment theories of trade, is to blind ourselves to one of the major realities of the contemporary world economy.

Fixed, Freely Available Technology and Consumer Sovereignty

Just as capital resources are rapidly growing and being dispersed to maximize the returns of their owners throughout the world, so too is rapid technological change (mostly in the West) profoundly affecting world trading relationships. One of the most obvious examples of the impact of developed country technological change on Third World export earnings is the development of synthetic substitutes for many traditional primary products. Over the past 20 years, synthetic substitutes for such diverse commodities as rubber, wool, cotton, sisal, jute, hides, and skins have been manufactured in increasing quantities. The Third World's market shares of these natural products in all cases has fallen steadily. For example, between 1950 and 1980 the share of the natural rubber in total world rubber consumption fell from 62 to 28%, while cotton's share of total fiber consumption dropped from 41 to 29%. Technological substitution, together with the low income and price elasticities of demand for primary products and the rise of agricultural protection in the markets of developed nations, goes a long way toward explaining why uncritical adherence to the theoretical dictates of "comparative advantage" can be a risky and often unrewarding venture for many LDCs.

The assumption of fixed worldwide consumer tastes and preferences dictating production patterns to market-responsive atomistic producers is another fiction of trade theory. Not only are capital and production technologies disseminated throughout the world by means of the multinational corporations often aided and abetted by their home governments, but consumption technologies (i.e., consumer preferences and tastes) are often created and reinforced by the advertising campaigns of the powerful financial giants who dominate local markets. By creating demands for imported goods, market-dominating international enterprises can manufacture the conditions for their own further aggrandizement. For example, it has been estimated that in many developing nations over 90% of all advertising is financed by foreign firms selling in the local market. As pointed out earlier, contemporary consumers are rarely "sovereign" about anything, let alone about what and how much major corporations are going to produce.

Internal Factor Mobility and Perfect Competition

The traditional theory of trade assumes that nations are readily able to adjust their economic structures to the changing dictates of world prices and markets. Movements along production-possibility frontiers involving the reallocation of resources from one industry to another may be easy to make on paper. But they are extremely difficult to achieve in practice. This is especially true in Third World nations where production structures are often very rigid and factor movements largely restricted. The most obvious example of this is plantation and small-farm commercial agriculture. In economies that have gradually become heavily dependent on a few primary product exports, the whole economic and social infrastructure (roads, railways, communications, power locations, credit and marketing arrangements, etc.) may be geared to facilitate the movement of goods from production locations to shipping and storage depots for transfer to foreign markets. Over time cumulative investments of capital may have been sunk into these economic and infrastructure facilities and they cannot easily be transferred to those Third World manufacturing activities located elsewhere. Thus, the more dependent nations become on a few primary product exports, the more inflexible their economic structures become and the more vulnerable they are to the unpredictabilities of international markets. It may take many years to transform an underdeveloped economy from an almost exclusively primary product, export-oriented reliance to a more diversified, multisector structure.

In short, the internal processes of adjustment and resource reallocation necessary to capitalize on changing world economic conditions are much more difficult for the less diversified economies of the Third World to realize than for their rich counterparts in the northern hemisphere. And yet, curiously enough, those LDCs that can expand their capacities to produce low-cost, labor-intensive manufactured goods for export in industries such as textiles, shoes, sporting goods, handbags, processed foodstuffs, wigs, and rugs often find these exports blocked by tariff and nontariff barriers erected by developed countries to restrict the entry of such low-cost goods into their home markets. The reason usually given is that this low-cost foreign competition will create unemployment among the higher-cost domestic industries of the developed country and that the problems of internal economic adjustment are too serious to permit such unfettered foreign competition! Thus, the internal factor mobility assumption turns out to have limited applicability—whether because of real or imagined rationales—in even the most diversified economies of the developed nations.

We need not dwell on the limitations of the perfectly competitive model here since this issue was discussed in Chapter 1. Nevertheless, it is essential to point out two major limitations of the application of this model to the theory of international trade. First, by assuming either fixed or diminishing returns to scale (i.e., fixed or increasing production costs as output is expanded), the labor-cost and factor-endowment theories of trade neglect one of the most important phenomena in international economic relations. This is the pervasive and income-widening effect of increasing returns to scale and, therefore, decreasing costs of production. Decreasing production costs mean simply that large existing firms are able to underprice smaller or new firms and thus exert monopolistic control over world markets. Far from being a rare exception, as the defenders of free trade would like to suggest, *economies of scale (increasing returns and decreasing costs) are a pervasive factor in determining trade patterns*—and not least in the area of agriculture, where huge agribusiness enterprises in developed countries are able to underprice the lower-productivity family farm in Third World countries. Economies of large-scale production lead to monopolistic and oligopolistic control of world supply conditions (just as they do in domestic markets) for a wide range of products. Moreover, this process of market domination and control is largely irreversible—poor-country industries, once behind, simply cannot compete with the giant corporations.

Monopolistic and oligopolistic market control of internationally traded commodities means that large individual corporations are able to manipulate world prices and supplies (and often demands as well) in their own private interests. *Instead of competition, one finds joint producer activities and oligopolistic bargaining among giant buyers and sellers as the most pervasive price and quantity determining force in the international economy.* But from the perspective of developing nations trying to diversify their economies and promote industrial exports in particular, the widespread phenomenon of increasing returns (decreasing costs) to large-scale production in addition to the noneconomic power of large multinational corporations (i.e., their political influence with many governments) means that those who were first to industrialize (the rich nations) are able to take advantage of these economies of scale and perpetuate their dominant position in world markets. It is simply another case of the rich getting richer by holding all the economic and political cards.

The second major limitation of the perfectly competitive assumption of trade models is its exclusion of *risk* and *uncertainty* in international trading arrangements. Even if one were to accept all the unreal assumptions of the traditional trade model as applied to the LDCs, it may still not be in their long-run interest to invest heavily in primary product export promotion given the historical instability of world markets for primary commodities in comparison to manufactured goods. As was already pointed out, concentration on one or two vital primary exports can play havoc with LDC development plans when foreign exchange earnings are largely unpredictable from one year to the next. Thus, following the dictates of static comparative advantage even in the unreal world of traditional trade theory may not be the best policy from the perspective of long-run development strategy.

The Absence of National Governments in Trading Relations

In domestic economies, the coexistence of rich and poor regions, of rapidly growing and stagnating industries, and of the persistent disproportionate regional distribution of the benefits of economic growth can all, at least in theory, be counteracted and ameliorated by the *intervention of the state.* Thus, cumulative processes for inequality within nation-states by which "growth poles" may enrich themselves at the expense of the regions left behind can be modified by government legislation, taxes, transfer payments, subsidies, social services, regional development programs, and so forth. But since there is no effective international government to modify and counter the natural tendency of the rich nations to grow often at the trading expense of the poor, the highly uneven gains from trade can easily become self-sustaining. This result is then reinforced by the uneven power of national governments to promote and protect the interests of their own countries. The spectacular export successes of Japan and, more recently, South Korea and Taiwan were in no small way aided and abetted by government planning and promotion of favored export industries.

By focusing on the atomistic behavior of competitive firms in the context of different commodities being produced in anonymous countries, standard trade theory has ignored the crucial role governments play in international economic affairs. Governments possess many instruments of commercial policy, such as tariffs, import quotas, and export subsidies, to manipulate their trade position vis-à-vis the rest of the world. Moreover, when developed-nation governments pursue restrictive economic policies designed to deal with purely domestic issues like inflation or unemployment, these policies can have profound negative effects on the economies of poor nations.

The reverse, however, is not true. Third World domestic economic policies generally have little impact on the economies of rich nations. Moreover, governments of developed countries often join to promote their shared interests through coordinated trade and other economic ventures. While these governments may not intend for such activities to promote their own welfare at the expense of the welfare of poor countries, this is often the result. Increasingly, however, poor nations are themselves recognizing the benefits of coordinating activities and are attempting to present a united front in international negotiations, especially in the area of scarce natural resources and raw materials where some do have considerable leverage.

Our point, therefore, is quite simple. Traditional trade theories neglect the crucial role national governments can and do play in the international economic arena. Governments often serve to reinforce the unequal distribution of resources and gains from trade resulting from differences in size and economic power. Rich-country governments can influence world economic affairs by their domestic and international policies. They can resist countervailing economic pressures from weaker nations and can act collusively and often in conjunction with their powerful multinational corporations to manipulate the terms and conditions of international trade to their own national interests. There is no superagency or world government to protect and promote the interests of the weaker parties (i.e., the LDCs) in such international affairs. Trade theory makes no mention of these powerful governmental forces. Its prescriptions are therefore greatly weakened by this neglect.

Balanced Trade and International Price Adjustments

The theory of international trade, like other perfectly competitive "general equilibrium" models in economics, is not only a full-employment model but also one in which flexible domestic and international product and resource prices always adjust instantaneously to conditions of supply and demand. In particular, the terms of trade (international commodity price ratios) adjust to equate supply and demand for a country's exportable and importable products so that trade is always balanced; that is, the value of exports (quantity times price) is always equal to the value of imports. With balanced commodity trade and no international capital movements, balance of payments problems never arise in the pure theory of trade.

But the realities of the world economy in the 1980s, especially in the period following the rapid increase in international oil prices in the 1970s, are such that balance of payments deficits and the consequent depletion of foreign reserves (or the need to borrow foreign funds to cover commodity deficits) are a major cause of concern for all nations, rich and poor.

For the non-oil-producing poor nations in particular, a combination of declining terms of trade and sluggish international demands for their export products has meant chronic commodity trade deficits. The gradual drying up of bilateral and multilateral foreign assistance and the growing concern of LDCs with the social costs of private foreign investment (see Chapter 14) have meant that severe balance of payments problems necessitate further departures from relatively free trade. In addition to coping with chronic balance of payments deficits and rising foreign debt burdens, developing nations faced a new and even more serious economic threat in the early 1980s—a world recession accompanied by high interest rates and persistent local inflation. All in all, gross imperfections in the international economy and the prevalence of nonmarket-determined commodity pricing systems make the "automatic adjustment" mechanism of traditional trade theory appear rather far-fetched.

Country Trade Gains Accrue to Country Nationals

The sixth and final major assumption of traditional trade theory, that country trade gains accrue to country nationals, is more implicit than the other five. It is rarely spelled out, nor need it be if one accepts the assumption that factors are internationally immobile. But given the gross unreality of that assumption, we need to examine the implicit notion, rarely challenged, that if developing countries do benefit from trade, it is the people of these countries who reap the benefits. The issue thus revolves around the question of who owns the land, the capital, and the skills that are rewarded as a result of trade. Are they nationals or are they foreigners? If both, in what proportions are the gains distributed?

We know, for example, that in the "enclave" Third World economies, like those with substantial foreign-owned mining and plantation operations, foreigners pay very low rents for the rights to use land, bring in their own foreign capital and skilled labor, hire local unskilled workers at subsistence wages, and in general, have a minimal effect on the rest of the economy even though they may generate significant export revenues. Although such visible enclaves are gradually disappearing in the Third World, they are often being replaced by more subtle forms of foreign domination (i.e., the economic penetrations of multinational corporations). The distinction, therefore, between gross domestic product (GDP), which is a measure of the value of output generated within defined geographic boundaries, and gross national product (GNP), which measures the income actually earned by nationals of that country, becomes extremely important. To the extent that the export sector, or for that matter any sector of the economy, is foreign owned and operated, GDP will be that much higher than GNP and few of the benefits of trade will actually accrue to LDC nationals. It is even possible for the value of exports to be greater than GNP; that is, foreign export earnings may exceed the total value of domestically accrued income.

Our point here is an important one. With the proliferation of multinational corporations and the international ownership of the means of production in a wide range of countries, aggregate statistics for LDC export earnings may mask the fact that LDC nationals, especially those in lower income brackets, may not benefit at all from these exports. The major gains from trade may instead accrue to nonnationals who often repatriate large proportions of these earnings. The trade that is being carried out may look like trade between rich and poor nations. But in reality such trade is being conducted between rich nations and *other nationals of rich nations* operating in Third World countries! Until recently the activities of most mining and plantation operations had this characteristic. More important, much of the recent import-substituting, export-oriented manufacturing activities in poor countries may merely be masking the fact that many of the benefits are still being reaped by foreign enterprises. In short, LDC export performances can be deceptive unless we analyze the character and structure of export earnings by ascertaining who owns or controls the factors of production that are rewarded as a result of export expansion.

SOME CONCLUSIONS: TRADE AND ECONOMIC DEVELOPMENT, THE LIMITS OF THEORY

We can now attempt to provide some preliminary general answers to the five questions posed at the beginning of the chapter. Again, we must stress that our conclusions are highly general and set in the context of the diversity of developing nations. Many will not be valid for specific nations at any given point in time. But on the whole these conclusions do appear to represent the consensus of current economic thinking, especially among Third World economists, on the relationship between trade and development, as the latter term has been defined throughout this book.

First, with regard to the rate, structure, and character of economic growth, our conclusion is that *trade can be an important stimulus to rapid economic growth*. This has been amply demonstrated by the successful experiences of countries like Brazil, Taiwan, and South Korea and of OPEC and other oil exporters like Mexico. Access to the markets of developed nations (an important "if" for those Third World nations bent on export promotion) can provide an important stimulus for the greater utilization of idle human and capital resources. Expanded foreign exchange earnings through improved export performance also provide the wherewithal by which LDCs can augment their scarce physical and financial resources. In short, where opportunities for profitable exchange arise, foreign trade can provide an important stimulus to aggregate economic growth along the lines suggested by the traditional theory.

But, as we have seen in earlier chapters, rapid growth of national output may have little impact on development. An export-oriented strategy of growth, particularly when a large proportion of export earnings accrue to foreigners, may not only bias the structure of the economy in the wrong directions (by not catering to the real needs of local people) but may also reinforce the internal and external dualistic and inegalitarian character of that growth. Therefore, the fact that trade may promote expanded export earnings, even increase output levels, does not mean that it is a desirable strategy for economic and social development. It all depends on the nature of the export sector, the distribution of its benefits, and its linkages with the rest of the economy.

As for the distributional effects of trade, we can state almost without reservation that *the principal benefits of world trade have accrued disproportionately to rich nations and within poor nations disproportionately to both foreign residents and wealthy nationals.* This should not be construed as an indictment of the inherent nature of trade. Rather, it reflects the highly inegalitarian institutional, social, and economic ordering of the global system, in which a few powerful nations and their multinational corporations control vast amounts of world resources. The conclusion of traditional trade theory that free trade will tend to equalize incomes is no more than a theoretical construct. *Trade, like education, tends to reinforce existing inequalities.* But it has the added defect of being conducted at the international level where the absence of a "supranational" state eliminates the possibility, which at least exists in theory at the national level, of redistributing the gains or investing them to promote development in disadvantaged regions. Factors such as the widespread existence of increasing returns, the highly unequal international distribution of economic assets and power, the growing influence of large multinational corporations, the often blatant collusion among a few powerful governments and their giant corporations, and the combined ability of both to manipulate international prices, levels of production, and patterns of demand—all these factors, assumed not to exist in the traditional theory of trade, are crucial. Together, they lead us to the general conclusion that *Third World countries have in the past benefited disproportionately less from their economic dealings with developed nations and many may have in fact even suffered absolutely from this association.*

It should be apparent by now that the answer to the third question—the question of the conditions under which trade can help LDCs to achieve their development aspirations—is to be found largely in the ability of developing nations (probably as a group) to extract favorable trade concessions from the developed nations, especially in the form of the latter's elimination of barriers to LDC exports of labor-intensive manufactured goods. (We discuss the economic effects of tariffs in the next chapter.) Second, the extent to which LDC exports can efficiently utilize scarce capital resources while making maximum use of abundant but presently underutilized labor supplies will determine the degree to which export earnings benefit the ordinary citizen. Here linkages between export earnings and other sectors of the economy are crucial. For example, small-farm agricultural export earnings will expand the demand for domestically produced simple household goods while export earnings from capital-intensive manufacturing industries are more likely to find their way back to rich nations in payment for luxury imports. Finally, much will depend on how well LDCs can influence and control the activities of private foreign enterprises. Their ability to deal effectively with multinational corporations in guaranteeing a fair share of the benefits to local citizens is extremely important.

The answer to the fourth question—whether LDCs can determine how much they trade—can only be speculative. *For most small and poor countries, the option of not trading at all, by closing their borders to the rest of the world, is not very feasible.* Not only do they lack the resources and market size to be self-sufficient but their very survival, especially in the area of food production, often depends on their ability to secure foreign goods and resources. Some 32 of the least developed countries face annual threats of severe famine for which international assistance is not a choice but a necessity.

And even for the bulk of developing nations, the international economic system, however unequal and biased against their long-run development interests, still offers the only real source of scarce capital and needed technological knowledge. The conditions under which such resources are obtained will greatly influence the character of the development process. As we show in the next chapter, the long-run benefits from trade among Third World countries themselves through the creation of regional trading blocs similar to the European Economic Community (EEC) may offer better prospects for a balanced and diversified development strategy than the current almost exclusive reliance on the very unequal trading relations that they individually engage in with the developed nations. Finally, for the few countries rich in mineral resources and raw materials, especially those that have been able to establish an effective international bargaining stance against the large corporations that purchase their exports (e.g., the members of OPEC), trade has been and continues to be a vital source of development finance.

The fifth question—whether on balance it is best for Third World countries to look outward toward the rest of the world or more inward toward their own capacities for development—turns out not to be an either-or question at all. The consensus among most development economists, especially those from the Third World, leans in the direction of a greater degree of collective self-reliance.[3] Their basic argument goes like this: Trade in the past has not been a great help to many developing nations and it has been positively harmful to some. Given the present imbalance in international power and wealth, pursuit of so-called free trade policies and a more equitable distribution of the benefits of trade will more than likely be subverted by the wealthy to further their own private or national interests. Therefore, LDCs have to be very selective in their economic relations with the developed countries. They need to guard against entering into agreements and joint production ventures over which they are likely to relinquish control. While not shutting themselves off from trade with the rest of the world, developing countries should seek ways to expand their share of world trade and extend their economic ties with one another. For example, by pooling their resources, small countries can overcome the limits of their small individual markets and their serious resource constraints while retaining an important degree of autonomy in pursuing their individual development aspirations. While it may not be possible for most LDCs to be self-reliant on an individual country basis, some form of trade and economic cooperation among equals is probably preferable to continued exposure to the dominating international power of rich nations and their potent multinational corporations.

There is thus a growing consensus of opinion that a "new international economic order" needs to be established in which developing countries can begin to reap the benefits of international trade which they have long been denied. Early in 1975 a joint resolution among 150 Third World and developed countries (with only the United States casting a negative vote) was passed in Lima, Peru, setting as a target a 25% share of world manufacturing output for the LDCs by the year 2000 as opposed to the 8% now being produced. Moreover, there is now widespread belief that Third World countries should begin to look *both* outward and inward—outward toward new forms of economic cooperation and trade with one another and inward to a greater degree of collective self-reliance through the intelligent economic use of their own joint resources, both human and physical. The on-again, off-again experiment in cooperation among the five Andean nations in South America (Bolivia, Chile, Colombia, Ecuador, and Peru) is a real-world manifestation of this outward—inward search for collective self-reliance (in the next chapter we deal in detail with the various arguments for and against economic integration among developing countries). It remains to be seen whether political factors will continue to inhibit such forms of economic cooperation, as they have in the past for regional groupings like the Latin American Free Trade Association and the East African Community, or whether the powerful economic logic of such cooperation will transcend and overcome political obstacles.

If politics can be transcended, it seems clear that increased economic cooperation among diverse Third World nations at roughly equal stages of development offers a viable and real alternative to their present pursuit of separate and very unequal trade relationships with the rest of the world. Thus, it may still be possible for LDCs to capture some of the real potential gains from specialization and trade (among themselves) while minimizing the "backwash" effects of a contemporary world economy and trading system dominated by a small group of rich nations and their powerful multinational corporations.

NOTES

1. Recall that the slope of a line tangent to any point on the concave production-possibility frontier will show the opportunity or real costs of reducing the output of one commodity in order to produce more of the other at that point on the curve. In a world of perfect competition these relative costs would also equal relative market prices. Therefore, the slope of the dotted line tangent to Point *A* also shows relative

commodity prices. The steeper the slope, the higher would be the price of "*a*" relative to "*m*." As we move from left to right (e.g., from Point *A* to Point *B* in Figure 12.7*a*), the slope of the tangent line becomes progressively steeper, indicating the increasing opportunity costs of producing more food. Similarly a right-to-left movement along the production frontier (from *B* to *A*) would represent increasing opportunity costs of producing more manufactured goods in terms of foregone food output.

2. The classic article on factor-price equalization is that of Paul A. Samuelson, "International trade and equalization of factor prices," *Economic Journal*, June 1948, pp. 163–184.

3. See, for example, the Santiago Declaration of Third World economists, April 1973, and the Communiqué of the Third World Forum, Karachi, 1975.

CONCEPTS FOR REVIEW

Export dependence	Labor theory of value
Intermediate producer goods	Resource endowments
Primary products	Factor-endowment trade theory
Commodity composition of trade	Labor- versus capital-abundant nations
Export concentration	Factor-price equalization
Commodity terms of trade	Factor mobility
Comparative advantage	Vent-for-surplus theory
Absolute advantage	of trade
Barter transactions	Synthetic commodity substitutes
Specialization	Monopolistic and oligopolistic
Foreign exchange earnings	market control
Commercial policy	Collusion
Foreign reserves	Increasing returns and decreasing
Closed versus open economy	costs
Domestic versus international price	Growth poles
ratios	Balanced trade
Free trade	Enclave economies
Gains from trade	Collective self-reliance

QUESTIONS FOR DISCUSSION

1. The effects of international trade on a country's development are often related to four basic economic concepts: efficiency, growth, equity, and stability. Briefly explain what is meant by each of these concepts as they relate to the theory of international trade.

2. Compare and contrast the classical labor-cost theory of comparative advantage with the neoclassical factor-endowment theory of international trade. Be sure to include an analysis of both assumptions and conclusions.

3. Briefly summarize the major conclusions of the traditional theory of free trade with regard to its theoretical effects on world and domestic efficiency, world and domestic economic growth, world and domestic income distribution, and the pattern of world production and consumption.

4. Proponents of free trade, primarily developed country economists, argue that the liberalization of trading relationships between rich and poor countries (i.e., the removal of tariff and nontariff barriers) would work toward the long-run benefit of *all* countries. Under what conditions might the removal of all tariffs and other impediments to trade work to the best advantage of Third World countries? Explain.

5. What factors—economic, political, and/or historical—do you think will determine whether or not a particular Third World nation is more or less dependent on international exchange? Explain your answer, giving a few specific examples of different LDCs.

6. Explain some of the reasons why the non-oil-producing countries of the Third World seem to have benefited relatively less than the developed nations over the past 25 years from their participation in international trade.

7. Traditional free trade theories are based on six crucial assumptions, which may or may not be valid for Third World nations (or for developed nations for that matter). What are these crucial assumptions and how might they be violated in the real world of international trade?

8. Traditional free trade theory is basically a *static* theory of international exchange leading to certain conclusions about the benefits likely to accrue to all participants. What *dynamic* elements in real-world economies will tend to negate the widespread distribution of the benefits of free trade? Explain this dynamic process.

9. Third World critics of international trade sometimes claim that present trading relationships between developed and underdeveloped countries can be a source of "anti-development" for the latter and merely serve to perpetuate their weak and dependent status. Explain their argument. Do you tend to agree or disagree and why?

FURTHER READINGS

For an explication of the traditional classical and neoclassical theories of free trade, see Peter Kenen, *International Economics*, 2d ed. (Englewood Cliffs, N.J.: Prentice-Hall, 1967), or Gerald M. Meier, *The International Economics of Development: Theory and Policy* (New York: Harper & Row, 1968), Chapter 2.

A more comprehensive and slightly advanced survey of trade theory can be found in J. Bhagwati, "The pure theory of international trade: A survey, " *Economic Journal*, March 1964, pp. 1–84, while an excellent overall review and critique of alternative models of trade and development is provided by Sheila Smith and John Toye, "Three stories about trade and poor economies," *Journal of Development Studies* (1979), Reading 26 in *The Struggle for Economic Development*.

For a critique of the traditional theory of trade as applied to underdeveloped nations, see H. Myint, "The classical theory of international trade and underdeveloped countries," *Economic Journal* 68 (1968); H. Kitamura, "Capital accumulation and the theory of international trade," *Malayan Economic Review* 3, no. 1 (1968); G. Myrdal, *The Challenge of World Poverty* (New York: Pantheon, 1970), Chapter 9; H. Myint, "International trade and the developing countries," in P.A. Samuelson (ed.), *International Economic Relations* (London: Macmillan, 1969); T. Balogh, "Fact and fancy in international economic relations, Part I," *World Development* 1, nos. 1 and 2 (1973); special issue on Trade and Poor Economies, *Journal of Development Studies* 15, no. 3 (April 1979); and James Riedel, "Trade as an engine of growth in developing countries: A reappraisal," *World Bank Staff Working Papers* No. 555 (1983).

Additional readings can be found on pp. 630–631.

13

THE BALANCE OF PAYMENTS AND COMMERCIAL POLICIES

What the Third World must ask of the international order is protection of its legitimate interests in the trade field, not trade concessions.
Santiago Resolution of Third World Social Scientists,
April 1973

Developed countries should take effective steps . . . for the reduction or removal . . . of nontariff barriers affecting the products of export interest to developing countries.
Resolution on Development and International Cooperation,
UN Special Seventh Session, 1975

EXTENDING OUR ANALYSIS TO COMMERCIAL AND FINANCIAL POLICIES

In the previous chapter we examined the scope and limitations of the traditional theory of international trade as applied to the contemporary position of less developed nations in the world economy. Our focus was primarily on international commodity trade in theory and practice and its likely effects on Third World growth, efficiency, equity, and stability in comparison to the developed world. In this chapter and the next we extend this analysis in two ways. First, in this chapter, we examine the range of LDC commercial and financial policies—for example, import tariffs, physical quotas, export promotion versus import substitution, exchange rate adjustments, international commodity agreements, and economic integration— within the broad framework of outward- versus inward-looking strategies of development. In Chapter 14 we go beyond simple commodity trade to examine the international flow of financial resources. Traditionally this flow has been almost exclusively a "North–South" phenomenon (i.e., financial resources have been transferred from the developed to the less developed countries). However, the need to "recycle" the vast new OPEC oil wealth during the 1970s opened up new possibilities for intra-Third World resource transfers—possibilities to be examined in the next chapter.

The flow of financial resources has two main components: the flow of *private foreign investments* and other resources, primarily via the carrier of the modern multinational corporation, and the flow of *public* resources in the form of bilateral and multilateral *foreign aid*. From the standpoint of both components, we will review some alternative Third World policy approaches toward financial dealings with the developed world. But first let us look more closely at the nature of a country's balance of payments and some of the issues surrounding various trade strategies for industrialization and development.

THE BALANCE OF PAYMENTS

The extension of our analysis beyond simple commodity trade into the area of the international flow of financial resources permits us to examine the *balance of payments* position of Third World nations vis-à-vis the rest of the world. A balance of payments table is designed to summarize a nation's transactions with the outside world; for example, Table 12.1 showed changes over time in "inflows" and "outflows" of international funds for all developing countries. A more analytically convenient way to present such a table is to divide it into three components. The *current account* component portrays the flow of goods and services in the form of exports and imports for a country during a given year. It allows us to analyze the impact of various commercial policies on commodity trade. The *capital account* shows the volume of private foreign investment (including loans from private international banks) and public grants and loans from individual nations and multilateral agencies such as the IMF and the World Bank. It permits us to examine the relative importance of international flows of financial resources in augmenting a nation's domestic savings. Finally, the *cash account* shows how cash balances (foreign reserves) and short-term claims have changed in response to current and capital account transactions. The cash account is thus the balancing item that is lowered (i.e., a net outflow of foreign exchange) whenever total disbursements on the current and capital accounts exceed total receipts. In practice, the dividing line between the capital and cash accounts is arbitrarily set so that claims and debts maturing in more than a year (or those that have no fixed maturity date as in the case of grants) are listed in the capital account. All other short-term financial claims and debts—those that mature in one year or less—are normally included in the cash account.

A balance of payments table for a hypothetical developing country is shown in Table 13.1. We see that there is a net negative balance of $15 million on current account. Commodity imports (primarily manufactured consumer, intermediate, and capital goods) plus payments to foreign shipping firms exceed commodity exports (primarily agricultural and raw material products) by these $15 million. On the capital account we see that there is a net inflow of $7 million of private foreign investments (both from multinational corporations which build factories in the LDC and from pri-

Table 13.1 A Hypothetical Balance of Payments Table
for a Developing Nation

Item		
A. *Current account*		
Commodity exports		+35
Primary products	25	
Manufactured goods	10	
Commodity imports		−45
Primary products	10	
Manufactured goods	35	
Services (e.g., shipping costs)		− 5
Balance on current account		−15
B. *Capital account*		
Private foreign investment (net)		+ 7
Government and multilateral flows (net)		+ 3
Loans	+ 5	
Grants	+ 1	
Debt repayments	− 3	
Private transfer payments (net)		− 1
Balance on capital account		+ 9
Balance on current and capital accounts		− 6
C. *Cash account*		
Net decrease in official monetary reserves		+ 6
Balance on cash account		+ 6

vate banks which make short-term loans to help refinance rising debt burdens). There is also a net positive $3 million inflow of public loans and grants in the form of foreign aid and multilateral agency assistance. Note that the gross inflow of $6 million in public loans and grants is partially offset by a $3 million capital outflow representing amortization and interest payments on former loans. For an increasing number of Third World nations, however, these figures are reversed. In fact, the outflow to repay accumulated debts may greatly exceed the inflow of *both* public aid and new refinancing bank loans. And in relation to export earnings, in 1982 the "debt service burden" (i.e., the proportion of export earnings that must be used to repay interest and amortization on former loans) reached 24% (compared with 14% in 1974). For some countries it was as high as 125%. The actual outstanding debt, moreover, rose in 1984 to over 145% of total export earnings! Figure 13.1 shows changes in debt and debt service from 1973 to 1984. If forced to repay all these loans, many poor countries may soon on balance actually be transferring financial resources to rich nations. We shall discuss the origins and nature of the staggering Third World debt problem further in Chapter 17 when we explore some of the major issues confronting developing countries in the 1980s.

Returning to Table 13.1, we see that private transfer payments of $1

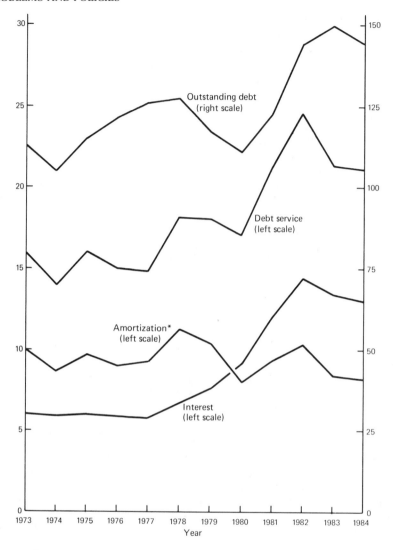

Figure 13.1.   Non-oil developing countries: Debt and debt service, 1973 – 1984 (as a percentage of exports of goods and services). *Source:* Based on data from International Monetary Fund, "World Economic Outlook," *Occasional Paper #27*, Washington, D.C. (1984), Tables 36, 38; * = on long-term debt only.

million—monetary outflows to private individuals such as friends and relatives living overseas—bring the capital accounts into a net positive balance of $9 million. This means that the combined net balance on current and capital accounts is a negative $6 million This amount represents the balance of payments deficit of our hypothetical LDC. If the balance on current and capital accounts were positive it would be called a balance of payments surplus.

FINANCING PAYMENTS DEFICITS: THE INTERNATIONAL MONETARY SYSTEM AND SPECIAL DRAWING RIGHTS

In order to finance this $6 million negative balance on combined current and capital accounts, our hypothetical country will have to draw down on its Central Bank holdings of official monetary reserves. Such reserves consist of gold and a few major foreign currencies (usually the traditionally "strong" currencies like U.S. dollars and British pounds sterling but more recently German marks or Swiss francs as well) and Special Drawing Rights (see below) to the tune of $6 million or its equivalent. International reserves serve for countries the same purpose that bank accounts serve for individuals. They can be drawn on to pay bills and debts; they are increased with deposits representing export sales and capital inflows; and they can be used as collateral to borrow additional reserves.

We see, therefore, that the balance on current account *plus* the balance on capital account must be offset by the balance on cash account. This is shown by the net *decrease* of $6 million in official monetary reserves. If the country is very poor, it is likely to have a very limited stock of these official monetary reserves. This overall balance of payments deficit of $6 million, therefore, may pose severe strains on the economy and greatly inhibit the country's ability to continue importing needed capital and consumer goods. In the least developed nations of the world, which have to import food to feed a hungry population and which possess very limited stocks of monetary reserves, such payments deficits may spell disaster for many millions of people.

Faced with existing or projected balance of payments deficits on combined current and capital accounts, developing nations have a variety of policy options. First, they can seek to improve the balance on current account by promoting export expansion and/or limiting imports. In the former case, there is the further choice of concentrating on primary or secondary product export expansion. In the latter case, policies of import substitution (i.e., the protection and stimulus of domestic industries to replace previously imported manufactured goods in the local market) and/or selective physical quotas or bans on the importation of specific consumer goods may be tried. Alternatively, countries can seek to achieve both objectives simultaneously by altering their official foreign exchange rates through a currency devaluation which lowers export prices and increases import prices. We will examine the controversy over export promotion, import substitution, and exchange rate adjustments in the next section.

A second alternative, though often not exclusive of the first, is for developing countries to try to improve the balance on their capital account by encouraging more private foreign investment and seeking more public foreign assistance. But neither private foreign investment nor a major proportion of foreign aid comes in the form of gifts (i.e., outright grants). The receipt of loan assistance implies the necessity of future repayments of principal and interest. Directly productive foreign investments in, say, building local factories entail the potential repatriation of sizable proportions of the profits of the foreign-owned enterprise. Moreover, as shown in the next chapter, the encouragement of private foreign investment has broader development implications than the mere transfer of financial and/or physical capital resources.

Finally, Third World nations can seek to modify the detrimental impact of chronic balance of payments deficits by expanding their stocks of official monetary reserves. One way of doing this is through the acquisition of a greater share of a new international "paper gold" known as Special Drawing Rights (SDRs). Traditionally, under the workings of the international monetary system, countries with deficits in their balance of payments were required to pay for these deficits by drawing down on their official reserves of the two principal international monetary assets, gold and U.S. dollars. But, with the phenomenal growth in the volume and value of world trade, a new kind of international asset was needed to supplement the limited stock of gold and dollars. Consequently, in 1970 the IMF was given the authority to create $10 billion of these Special Drawing Rights. These new international assets perform many of the functions of gold and dollars in settling balance of payments accounts. They are valued on the basis of a basket of currencies (i.e., a weighted average of the value of different currencies) and constitute claims on the IMF. They thus may be exchanged for convertible currencies to settle international official transactions. By 1980 the total value of SDRs actually allocated was in excess of $18 billion, of which $3.6 billion was earmarked for the non-oil-exporting less developed nations. Eventually, the IMF would like to see all international financial settlements conducted in SDRs, with gold and dollars dropped as official mediums of exchange.

A major issue of great concern to developing countries, therefore, is the distribution of the benefits of SDRs. The present formula for distributing SDRs gives 75% of the total to the 25 industrial nations. This leaves only 25% to be distributed among the 90 or so Third World countries that participate in the international monetary system. Dissatisfied with this situation, these countries are now as a group exerting pressure on the developed nations to agree to the creation of supplementary Special Drawing Rights that would be allocated in preferential amounts and/or preferential terms to developing nations. The issue of these supplementary SDRs could have greatly helped solve the short-run financial crisis faced by most Third World nations, particularly the 40 or so least developed, as a result of the rapid rise in international oil and food prices in the 1970s.[1]

More generally, Third World nations are acting together to seek a greater voice in the shaping and control of a reformed international monetary system. Before 1972, less developed nations had virtually no role and no voting power in the monetary system. It was run by a so-called Committee of Ten, which consisted of 10 rich nations whose decisions rarely took into account the plight of the vast majority of the world's peoples. More recently, this committee was increased on a permanent basis to the new IMF Committee of Twenty which includes some developing nations. It is thus to be hoped that future reforms of the international monetary system will increasingly reflect the needs and desires of these nations. In any event, they now have a forum in which to express their views and air their grievances. Most important, if Third World nations can present a unified stance, they now possess the voting power to veto any monetary reform they believe is not in their best economic interests.

Having summarized some basic balance of payments concepts and issues as they relate to both commodity trade and international flows of financial resources we can now turn to the question of alternative trade policies for development.

TRADE STRATEGIES FOR DEVELOPMENT: TO LOOK OUTWARD OR INWARD, OR OUTWARD AND INWARD?

A convenient and instructive way to approach the complex issues of appropriate trade policies for development is to set these specific policies in the context of a broader LDC strategy of looking outward or looking inward.[2] In the words of Professor Streeten, outward-looking policies "encourage not only free trade but also the free movement of capital, workers, enterprises and students, . . . the multinational enterprise, and an open system of communications." On the other hand, inward-looking policies stress the need for LDCs to evolve their own styles of development and to be the masters of their own fate. This means policies to encourage indigenous "learning by doing" in manufacturing and the development of indigenous technologies appropriate to a country's resource endowments. According to proponents of inward-looking trade policies, greater self-reliance can be accomplished only if "you restrict trade, the movement of people and communications, and if you keep out the multinational enterprise, with its wrong products and wrong want-stimulation and hence its wrong technology."[3]

Within these two broad philosophical approaches to development, one can conveniently analyze specific commodity trade policies by applying the following fourfold categorization:

1. *Primary outward-looking policies* (encouragement of agricultural and raw material exports)
2. *Secondary outward-looking policies* (promotion of manufactured exports)
3. *Primary inward-looking policies* (mainly agricultural self-sufficiency)
4. *Secondary inward-looking policies* (manufactured commodity self-sufficiency through import substitution)

Keeping this typology in mind, let us look at three broad areas of commercial and financial policy and then examine the important question of economic integration. These areas are export promotion, import substitution, and exchange rate adjustment.

Export Promotion: Looking Outward and Seeing Trade Barriers

The promotion of LDC exports, either primary or secondary, has long been considered a major ingredient in any viable long-run development strategy. The colonial territories of Africa and Asia with their foreign-owned mines and plantations were classic examples of primary outward-looking regions. It was partly in reaction to this enclave economic structure and partly as a consequence of the industrialization bias of the 1950s and 1960s that newly independent states as well as older LDCs put great emphasis on the production of manufactured goods initially for the home market (secondary inward) and then for export (secondary outward). Let us, therefore, look briefly at the scope and limitations of LDC export expansion, first with respect to primary products and then with respect to manufactured exports.

Primary Commodity Export Expansion

As we discovered in the previous chapter, the Third World still relies on primary products for over 70% of its export earnings. With the notable exception of petroleum exports and a few needed minerals, primary product exports have grown more slowly than total world trade. Moreover, the LDC share of these exports has been falling over the past two decades. Since food, food products, and raw materials make up almost 40% of all LDC exports and, for the vast majority of Third World nations, constitute their principal source of foreign exchange earnings, we need to examine the factors affecting the demand for and supply of primary product exports.

On the demand side there appear to be at least five factors working against the rapid expansion of Third World primary product, and especially agricultural, exports to the developed nations (their major markets). First, the per capita income elasticities of demand for agricultural foodstuffs and raw materials are relatively low compared with those for fuels, certain minerals, and manufactures. For example, the income elasticities of demand for sugar, cocoa, tea, coffee, and bananas have all been estimated at less than one, with most in the range of 0.3–0.5.[4] This means that only a sustained high rate of per capita income growth in the developed countries can lead to even modest export expansion of these particular commodities from the LDCs. Such high growth rates prevailed in the 1960s but were not matched in the 1970s or early 1980s. Second, developed-country population growth rates are now at or near the replacement level so that little expansion can be expected from this source. Third, the price elasticity of demand for most nonfuel primary commodities appears to be relatively low, although the data on this point are far from convincing. When relative agricultural prices are falling, as they have during most of the last two decades and especially during the "free fall" period of 1981–1982, such low elasticities mean less total revenue for agricultural exporting nations. But when commodity prices are rapidly rising, as they did for, say, sugar during the 1973–1974 period, exporters, like the 19 or so LDCs that together supply 80% of world sugar exports, stand to gain substantial short-run revenues. Coffee exporting nations enjoyed a similar experience in the late 1970s.

A device that is widely used to modify the tendency for primary product prices to decline relative to other traded goods is that of establishing *international commodity agreements*. The primary purposes of such agreements are to set overall output levels, to stabilize world prices, and to assign quota shares to various producing nations for such items as coffee, tea, copper, lead, and sugar. Commodity agreements can also provide greater protection to individual exporting nations against excessive competition and the overexpansion of world production. Such overexpansion of supply tends to drive down prices and curtail the growth of earnings for all countries. In short, commodity agreements are intended to guarantee participating nations a relatively fixed share of world export earnings and a more stable world price for their commodity. It is for this reason that at its fourth world conference held in Nairobi in May 1976 the UN Committee on Trade and Development (UNCTAD) advocated the establishment of an $11 billion common fund to finance "buffer stocks" to support the prices of some 19 primary commodities (including sugar, coffee, tea, bauxite, jute, cotton, tin, and vegetable oil) produced by various Third World nations in order to stabilize export earnings. Unfortunately for LDC exporters, there has been little progress on the UNCTAD proposal.

The fourth and fifth factors working against the long-run expansion of LDC primary product export earnings—the development of synthetic substitutes and the growth of agricultural protection in the developed countries—are perhaps the most important. Synthetic substitutes for commodities like cotton, rubber, sisal, jute, hide, and skins act both as a brake against higher commodity prices and as a direct source of competition in world export markets. As we saw in the previous chapter, the synthetic share of world market export earnings has steadily risen over time while the share of natural products has fallen. In the case of agricultural protection, which usually takes the form of tariffs, quotas, and nontariff barriers such as sanitary laws regulating food and fiber imports, the effects can be devastating to Third World export earnings. The common agricultural policy of the European Economic Community, for example, is much more discriminatory against LDC food exports than the policies that had formerly prevailed in the individual EEC nations.

On the supply side, a number of factors also work against the rapid expansion of primary product export earnings. The most important is the structural rigidity of many Third World rural production systems. We discussed rigidities such as limited resources, poor climate, bad soils, antiquated rural institutional, social, and economic structures, and non-productive patterns of land tenure in Chapter 10. Whatever the international demand situation for particular commodities (and these will certainly differ from commodity to commodity), little export expansion can be expected when rural economic and social structures militate against positive supply responses from peasant farmers who are averse to risk. Furthermore, in those developing nations with markedly dualistic farming structures (i.e., large corporate capital-intensive farms existing side by side with thousands of fragmented, low-productivity peasant holdings), any growth in export earnings is likely to be distributed very unevenly among the rural population.

We may conclude, therefore, that the successful promotion of primary product exports cannot occur unless there is a reorganization of rural social and economic structures along the lines suggested in Chapter 10 to raise total agricultural productivity and distribute the benefits more widely. The primary objective of any Third World rural development strategy must be to provide sufficient food to feed the indigenous people *first* and only then be concerned about export expansion. But having accomplished this most difficult internal development task, LDCs may be able to realize the potential benefits of their comparative advantage in world primary commodity markets only if they can (a) *cooperate* with one another; (b) be *assisted* by developed nations in formulating and carrying out international commodity agreements; and (c) secure *greater access* to developed country markets. Unfortunately, given the structure of world demands for primary products, the threat of local food shortages and thus the desire for agricultural self-sufficiency, the inevitability of the development of further synthetic substitutes, and the unlikelihood of lower levels of agricultural protection among developed nations, the real scope for primary product export expansion in individual LDCs seems limited.

Nevertheless, such primary product export pessimism should be no cause for a retreat from emphasis on rural development. The rapid expansion of local food production is or should be a major component of any national development strategy whether or not a country seeks to export its surplus food to the rest of the world. Moreover, for some commodities, such as food grains, timber products, fish, meat, and certain fruits and vegetables, world demand is better suited for rapid export expansion, since both income and price elasticities are relatively high. In the final analysis, then, one cannot really talk about primary product export expansion without reference to particular commodities and specific countries. Unfortunately, such a specific commodity and country analysis is beyond the scope of this book.[5]

Expanding Exports of Manufactured Goods

The expansion of Third World manufactured exports has been given great stimulus by the spectacular export performances of countries like South Korea, Singapore, Hong Kong, Taiwan, and Brazil during the 1960s and 1970s.[6] For example, Taiwan's total exports grew at an annual rate of over 20%, while exports from South Korea grew even faster. In both cases, this export growth was led by manufactured goods, which contributed almost 75% of both nations' foreign exchange earnings. For the Third World as a whole, manufactured exports grew from 6% of total merchandise exports in 1950 to 42% by 1980 (recall, however, that South Korea, Taiwan, Singapore, and Hong Kong account for over 60% of all LDC manufactured exports). Despite this growth, the LDC share of total world trade in manufactures has remained relatively unchanged at under 10% during the past two decades.

The demand problems facing LDC export expansion of manufactured goods, though different in basic economic content from those facing primary products, are nonetheless similar in practice. Thus, although income and price elasticities of international demand for manufactured goods in the aggregate are higher than for primary commodities, they afford little relief to many developing nations bent on expanding their exports. This is largely because of the growing protection in developed nations against the manufactured exports of LDCs—which is in part the direct result of the successful penetration of low-cost labor-intensive manufactures from countries like Taiwan, Hong Kong, and Korea during the 1960s and 1970s. The Canadian economist Gerald Helleiner makes the point well when he observes:

> *Of fundamental importance to the issue of Third World manufacturing export prospects are the barriers which are erected by the developed countries to restrict entry of these products to their own markets. Tariffs, quotas and other barriers in the markets of the rich constitute a major impediment to large-scale industrial exports. The tariff structures of the rich nations are such as to offer the greatest degree of effective protection to their producers in the very industries in which poor countries are most likely to be competitive—light industries relatively intensive in the use of unskilled labour such as textiles, footwear, rugs, sporting goods, handbags, processed foodstuffs, etc. This is precisely because of these industries' inability freely to compete, unskilled labour-intensity putting them at a comparative disadvantage within the context of their relatively high wage economies.[7]*

The growth of unemployment in developed countries, especially in traditional industries such as textiles where almost 40% of Third World manufactured exports are concentrated, makes the prospects for lower trade barriers on LDC light manufactures seem rather remote. Moreover, as more and more developing countries attempt to emulate the spectacular manufactured export performance of a few, the competition for access to the narrowing developed country markets is likely to lead to many unforeseen difficulties and disappointments.[8] As in the case of agricultural production, however, this uncertain export outlook should be no cause for curtailing the needed expansion of manufacturing production to serve local LDC markets. Moreover, as we will argue below, there is great scope for mutually beneficial trade in manufactures among Third World countries themselves within the context of the gradual economic integration of their national economies. Too much emphasis has been placed on the analysis of trade prospects of individual LDCs with the developed nations (North–South trade) and not enough on the prospects for mutually beneficial trade with one another (South–South trade).

Import Substitution: Looking Inward but Still Paying Outward

The Industrialization Strategy and Results

Over the past two decades developing countries, in the context of declining world markets for their primary products, growing balance of payments deficits on current account, and a general belief in the magic of industrialization, turned to what has come to be known as an "import substitution" strategy of industrial development. Import substitution entails an attempt to replace commodities that are being imported, usually manufactured goods, with domestic sources of production and supply. The typical strategy is first to erect tariff barriers or quotas on the importation of certain commodities, then to try to set up a local industry to produce these goods—items such as radios, bicycles, or household electrical appliances. Typically, this involves cooperation with foreign companies, which are encouraged to set up their plants behind the wall of tariff protection and given all kinds of tax and investment incentives. While initial costs of production may be higher than former import prices, the economic rationale put forward for the establishment of import-substituting manufacturing operations is either that the industry will eventually be able to reap the benefits of large-scale production and lower costs (the so-called infant industry argument for tariff protection) or that the balance of payments will be improved as fewer consumer goods are imported. Often a combination of both arguments is advanced. Eventually, it is hoped, the infant industry will grow up and be able to compete in world markets. It will then be able to generate net foreign exchange earnings once it has lowered its average costs of production.

Most observers agree that the import-substituting strategy of industrialization in a large number of developing countries, especially those in Latin America, has for the most part been unsuccessful.[9] Specifically, there have been four undesirable outcomes. First, the main beneficiaries of the import substitution process have been the foreign firms that were able to locate behind tariff walls and take advantage of liberal tax and investment incentives. After deducting interest, profits, royalty and management fees, most of which are remitted abroad, the little that may be left over usually accrues to the wealthy local industrialists with whom foreign manufacturers cooperate and who provide their political and economic cover.

Second, most import substitution has been made possible by the heavy and often government-subsidized importation of capital goods and intermediate products by foreign and domestic companies. In the case of foreign companies, much of this is purchased from parent and sister companies abroad. There are two immediate results. First, capital-intensive industries are set up, usually catering to the consumption habits of the rich while having a minimal employment effect. Second, far from improving the LDCs' balance of payments situation, indiscriminate import substitution often worsens it by increasing the need for imported capital-good inputs and intermediate products while, as we have just seen, a good part of the profits is remitted abroad in the form of private transfer payments.

A third detrimental effect of many import substitution strategies has been their impact on traditional primary product exports. In order to encourage local manufacturing through the importation of cheap capital and intermediate goods, foreign exchange rates (i.e., the rate at which the Central Bank of a nation is prepared to purchase foreign currencies) are often artificially "overvalued." This has the effect of raising the price of exports and lowering the price of imports in terms of the local currency. For example, if the "appropriate" or free market exchange rate between Pakistani rupees and U.S. dollars was 20 to 1 but the official exchange rate was 10 to 1, an item that cost $10 in the U.S. could be imported into Pakistan for 100 rupees (excluding transport costs and other service charges). If the free market exchange rate prevailed (i.e., the exchange rate determined by the supply and demand for Pakistani rupees in terms of dollars), that item would cost 200 rupees. Thus, by overvaluing their exchange rate, LDC governments are able effectively to lower the domestic currency price of their imports. At the same time, their export prices are increased—for example, at an exchange rate of 10 to 1, U.S. importers would have to pay 10 cents for every 1-rupee item rather than the 5 cents they would pay if the hypothetical free market ratio of 20 to 1 were in effect. Table 13.2 provides rough estimates of the extent of currency overvaluation in nine developing countries during major periods of import substitution.

The net effect of overvaluing exchange rates in the context of import substitution policies is to encourage capital-intensive production methods still further (since the price of imported capital goods is artificially lowered) and penalize the traditional primary product export sector by artificially raising the price of exports in terms of foreign currencies. This overvaluation, then, causes local farmers to be less competitive in world markets. In terms of its income distribution effects, the outcome of such government policies may be to penalize the small farmer and the self-employed while improving the profits of the owners of capital, both foreign and domestic. *Industrial protection thus has the effect of taxing agricultural goods in the home market as well as discouraging agricultural exports.* Import substitution policies in practice have often worsened the local distribution of income by favoring the urban sector and the higher-income groups while discriminating against the rural sector and the lower income groups.

Fourth, and finally, import substitution, which may have been con-

Table 13.2 Official and Estimated Free Market Exchange Rates

			Units of national currency per US $		
Country	Year	**Domestic currency units**	*Official rate*	*Degree of overvaluation (%)*	*Implied free market exchange rate*
Argentina	1958	Pesos	18.0	100	36.0
Brazil	1966	Cruzeiros	2,220.0	50	3,330.0
Chile	1961	Pesos	1.053	68	1.769
Colombia	1968	Pesos	15.89	22	19.39
Malaya	1965	Dollars (M)	3.06	4	3.18
Mexico	1960	Pesos	12.49	15	14.36
	1960	Pesos	12.49	9	13.61
Pakistan	1963–1964	Rupees	4.799	50	7.199
Philippines	1965	Pesos	3.90	20	4.68
	1965	Pesos	3.90	15	4.49
Taiwan	1965	$NT	40.10	20	48.12

SOURCE: Derek Healey, "Development policy: New thinking about an interpretation," *Journal of Economic Literature* 10, no. 3 (1972):781. Reprinted by permission of the author and the American Economic Association.

ceived with the idea of stimulating self-sustained industrialization by creating "forward" and "backward" linkages with the rest of the economy, has in practice often inhibited that industrialization. By increasing the costs of inputs to potentially forward-linked industries (those that purchase the output of the protected firm as inputs or intermediate products in their own productive process, e.g., a printer's purchase of paper from a locally protected paper mill) and by purchasing their own inputs from overseas sources of supply rather than through backward linkages to domestic suppliers, inefficient import substituting firms may in fact block the hoped-for process of self-reliant integrated industrialization.

A consideration of patterns of import substitution leads to conclusions such as those of Professor Helleiner, whose views seem to reflect a consensus among development economists:

> It is difficult to find any rationale for the pattern of import substituting industrialization which has, whether consciously or not, actually been promoted. It has given undue emphasis to consumer goods in most countries; it has given insufficient attention to potential long-run comparative advantages, i.e. resource endowments and learning possibilities; and it has employed alien and unsuitable, i.e. capital-intensive, technologies to an extraordinary and unnecessary degree. If a selective approach to import substitution is to be pursued at all, and there is a strong case to be made for a more generalized approach, the selection actually employed in recent years has left a great deal to be desired. The consequence has too frequently been the creation of an inefficient industrial sector operating far below capacity, and creating very little employment, very little foreign exchange saving, and little prospect of further productivity growth. The object of policy must now be gradually to bring incentive structures and thus the relative efficiencies of various industrial activities into some sort of balance, thereby encouraging

domestic manufacture of intermediate and capital goods at the expense of importable consumer goods and the development eventually of manufacture for export.[10]

Tariff Structures and Effective Protection

Since import substitution programs are based on the protection of local industries against competing imports primarily through the use of tariffs and physical quotas, we need to analyze the role and limitations of these commercial policy instruments in developing nations. Governments impose tariffs and physical quotas on imports for a variety of reasons. For example, tariff barriers may be erected in order to raise public revenue. In fact, given administrative and political difficulties of collecting local income taxes, fixed percentage taxes on imports (*ad valorem* tariffs) collected at a relatively few ports or border posts often constitute one of the cheapest and most efficient forms of raising government revenue. In many LDCs, these foreign trade taxes are thus a central feature of the overall fiscal system. On the other hand, physical quotas on imports like automobiles and other "luxury" consumer goods, while more difficult to administer and more subject to delay, inefficiency, and corruption (e.g., with regard to the granting of import licenses), provide an effective means of restricting the entry of particularly troublesome commodities. Tariffs, too, may serve to restrict the importation of nonnecessity products (usually expensive consumer goods). By restricting imports, both quotas and tariffs can improve the balance of payments. And like overvaluing the official rate of foreign exchange, tariffs may be used to improve a nation's terms of trade. However, in a small country unable to influence world prices of its exports or imports (in other words, most LDCs) this terms of trade argument for tariffs (or devaluation) has little validity. Finally, as we have just seen, tariffs may form an integral component of an import substitution policy of industrialization.

Whatever the means used to restrict imports, such restriction always protects domestic firms from competition with producers from other countries. To measure the degree of protection we need to ask by how much do these restrictions cause the domestic prices of imports to exceed what their prices would be if there were no protection. There are two basic measures of protection: (*a*) the nominal rate of protection and (*b*) the effective rate of protection.

The *nominal rate of protection* shows the extent, in percentages, to which the domestic price of imported goods exceeds what their price would be in the absence of protection. Thus the nominal (*ad valorem*) tariff rate (*t*) refers to the final prices of commodities and can be defined simply as

$$t = \left| \frac{p' - p}{p} \right| \tag{1}$$

where p' and p are the unit prices of industry's output with and without tariffs respectively.

For example, if the domestic price (p') of an imported automobile is $5,000 whereas the CIF (cost plus insurance and freight) price (p) when the automobile arrives at the port of entry is $4,000, then the nominal rate of tariff protection (*t*) would be 25%.

On the other hand, the *effective rate of protection* shows the percentage by which the *value added* at a particular stage of processing in a domestic industry can exceed what it would be without protection. In other words, it shows by what percentage the sum of wages, interest, profits, and depreciation allowances payable by local firms can, as a result of protection, exceed what this sum would be if these same firms had to face unrestricted competition (i.e., no tariff protection) from foreign producers.[11] The effective rate (g) can therefore be defined as

$$g = \frac{v' - v}{v} \tag{2}$$

where v' and v are *value added* per unit of output with and without protection, respectively. A more precise formula is

$$g_j = \frac{(t_j - \sum_i a_{ij} t_i)}{(1 - \sum_i a_{ij})} \tag{2a}$$

where t_j is the nominal tariff on final product of industry j, t_i is the rate of tariff on intermediate input i, and a_{ij} is the free trade value of intermediate input i per unit value of final product of industry j.

The important difference between nominal and effective rates of protection can be illustrated by means of an example.[12] Consider a nation without tariffs in which automobiles are produced and sold at the international or world price of $10,000. The value added by labor in the final assembly process is assumed to be $2,000 while the total value of the remaining inputs is $8,000. Assume for simplicity that the prices of these nonlabor inputs are equal to their world prices. Suppose that a nominal tariff of 10% is now imposed on imported automobiles, which raises the domestic price of motor cars to $11,000 but leaves the prices of all the other importable, intermediate inputs unchanged. The domestic process of automobile production can now spend $3,000 per unit of output on labor inputs as contrasted with $2,000 per unit before the tariff. The theory of effective protection, therefore, implies that under these conditions the nominal tariff of 10% on the final product (automobiles) has resulted in an "effective" rate of protection of 50% for the local assembly process in terms of its value added per unit of output. (It follows, therefore, that for any given nominal tariff rate, the effective rate is greater the smaller the value added of the process; i.e., $g = t[1/1 - a]$ where t is the nominal rate on final product and a is the proportionate value of the importable inputs in a free market where these inputs are assumed to enter the country duty free.)

Most economists argue that the effective rate is the more useful concept (although the nominal or *ad valorem* rate is simpler to measure) for ascertaining the degree of protection and encouragement afforded by a given country's tariff structure to its local manufacturers. This is because effective rates of protection show the *net* effect on a firm or industry of restrictions on the imports of *both* its outputs and inputs. For most countries, both developing and developed, the effective rate normally exceeds the nominal rate, sometimes by as much as 200%. For example, Little, Scitovsky, and Scott found that average levels of effective protection exceeded 200% for India and Pakistan during the early 1960s, 100% for Argentina and Brazil, 50% for the Philippines, 33% for Taiwan, and 25% for Mexico.[13]

Among the many implications of analyzing effective as opposed to nominal tariff structures with regard to developing countries, two stand out as particularly noteworthy:

1. Most developing countries, as we have seen, have pursued import-substituting programs of industrialization with emphasis on the local production of final consumer goods for which a ready market was presumed to exist. Moreover, final good production is generally less technically sophisticated than intermediate, capital goods production. The expectation was that in time rising demand and economies of scale in finished good production would create strong backward linkages leading to the creation of domestic intermediate goods industries. The record of performance, as we have also seen, has been disappointing for most developing countries. Part of the reason for this lack of success has been that developing country tariff structures have afforded exceedingly high rates of effective protection to final goods industries while intermediate and capital goods have received considerably less effective protection. The net result is an attraction of scarce resources away from intermediate goods production and toward the often inefficient production of highly protected final consumer goods. Backward linkages do not develop, intermediate good import costs rise and, perhaps most important from a long-run view, the development of an indigenous capital goods industry focusing on efficient, low-cost, labor-intensive techniques is severely impeded.

2. Even though nominal rates of protection in developed countries on imports from the developing countries may seem relatively low, rates of effective protection can be quite substantial. Raw materials are usually imported duty free while processed products such as roasted and powdered coffee, copra oil, and cocoa butter appear to have low nominal tariffs. The theory of effective protection suggests that in combination with zero tariffs on imported raw materials, low nominal tariffs on processed products can represent substantially higher rates of effective protection. For example, if a tariff of 10% is levied on processed copra oil whereas copra itself can be imported duty free, then if the value added in making oil from copra is 5% of the total value of copra oil, the *process* is actually being protected at 200%! This greatly inhibits the development of food and other raw material processing industries in developing nations and ultimately cuts back on their potential earnings of foreign exchange.

Effective rates of protection against potentially lucrative foreign-exchange-earning exportable goods from the Third World can be considerably higher than nominal rates in the developed countries. For example, the effective rate on thread and yarn, textile fabrics, clothing, wood products, leather, and rubber goods averaged more than twice the nominal rate on these same items in the United States, United Kingdom, and EEC countries during the 1960s.[14] In the EEC, effective rates on coconut oil were over 10 times the nominal rate (150% compared with 15%) while those on processed soybean were 16 times the nominal rate (160 as opposed to 10%).

To sum up, the standard argument for tariff protection in developing countries has four major components:

1. Duties on trade are the major source of government revenue in most LDCs, since they are a relatively easy form of taxation to impose and even easier to collect.

2. Import restrictions represent an obvious response to chronic balance of payments problems.
3. Protection against imports is one of the most appropriate means for fostering industrial self-reliance and overcoming the pervasive state of economic dependence in which most Third World countries find themselves.
4. Finally, by pursuing policies of import restriction, developing countries can gain greater control over their economic destinies while encouraging foreign businessmen to invest in local import-substituting industries, generating high profits and thus the potential for greater saving and future growth. They can also obtain imported equipment at relatively favorable prices and reserve an already established domestic market for local or locally controlled producers.

Although the above arguments can sound convincing and some protective policies have proven highly beneficial to the developing world, as we discovered in the previous section, many have failed to bring about their desired results. Protection *does* have an important role to play in the development of the Third World—for both economic and noneconomic reasons—but it is a tool of economic policy that needs to be employed selectively and wisely, not a panacea to be applied indiscriminately and without reference to both short- and long-term ramifications.

Foreign Exchange Rates, Exchange Controls, and the Devaluation Decision

In the section on import substitution, we briefly discussed the question of foreign currency exchange rates. Remember that a country's official exchange rate is the rate at which its Central Bank is prepared to transact exchanges of its local currency for other currencies in approved foreign exchange markets. Official exchange rates are usually quoted in terms of U.S. dollars—so many pesos, cruzeiros, pounds, shillings, rupees, Bhat, etc., per dollar. For example, the official exchange rate of Egyptian pounds for U.S. dollars in 1983 was approximately 0.7 per dollar while the Indian rupee was officially valued at approximately 10 rupees per dollar. If an Egyptian manufacturer wished to import fabrics from an Indian textile exporter at, say, a cost of 10,000 rupees, he would need 700 pounds to make the purchase. However, since almost all foreign exchange transactions are conducted in U.S. dollars, the Egyptian importer would need to purchase $1,000 worth of foreign exchange from the Central Bank of Egypt for his 700 pounds and then transmit these dollars through official channels to the Indian exporter.

Official foreign exchange rates are not necessarily set at or near the economic "equilibrium" price for foreign exchange—that is, the rate at which the domestic demand for a foreign currency such as dollars would just equal its supply in the absence of governmental regulation or intervention. In fact, as we saw in Table 13.2, the currencies of most Third World countries are usually overvalued by the exchange rate. Whenever the official price of foreign exchange is established at a level which, in the absence of any governmental restrictions or controls, would result in an excess of local demand over the available supply of foreign exchange, the domestic currency in question is said to be overvalued.

The economic results of pursuing an international policy of currency overvaluation were succinctly summarized in the following extract from the 1968 *Economic Survey of Asia and the Far East*:

> *All exporters (who predominantly sold agricultural goods) were required to surrender foreign exchange earnings at the official rate of exchange. This clearly constituted a tax on the agricultural sector of the economy. At the official rate of exchange there existed a large unsatisfied demand for imports. Thus a strict rationing of the entitlement to import through licensing had to be made. The overvalued rate of exchange and the consequent unsatisfied demand for imports naturally meant domestic prices for imports substantially above international prices. This price differential was not absorbed by the government through license fees for import surcharges, but was allowed to be converted into monopoly profit for the license holder, and served as a major source of investible funds in the private sector. The excess demand generated by the strict quantitative control of imports further opened up high profit opportunities for investors in import substituting industries.*[15]

In such situations of excess demand, LDC Central Banks have three basic policy options in order to maintain the official rate of exchange. First, they can attempt to accommodate this excess demand by running down their reserves of foreign exchange and/or by borrowing additional foreign exchange abroad and thereby incurring further debts. Second, they can attempt to curtail the excess demand for foreign exchange by pursuing commercial policies and tax measures designed to lessen the demand for imports (e.g., tariffs, physical quotas, licensing). Third, and finally, they can regulate and intervene in the foreign exchange market by rationing the limited supply of available foreign exchange to preferred customers. Such a rationing device is more commonly known as "exchange control." It is a policy in wide use throughout the Third World and is probably the major financial mechanism for preserving the level of foreign exchange reserves at the prevailing official exchange rate.

The mechanism and operation of exchange control can be illustrated diagrammatically with the aid of Figure 13.2. Under free market conditions the equilibrium price of foreign exchange would be P_e with a total of 0M units of foreign exchange demanded and supplied. If, however, the government maintains an artificially low price of foreign exchange (i.e., an overvaluation of its domestic currency) at P_a, then the supply of foreign exchange will amount to only 0M′ units since exports are overpriced. But at price P_a, the demand for foreign exchange will be 0M″ units, with the result that there is an "excess demand" equal to M′M″ units. Some mechanism, therefore, will have to be devised to ration the available supply of 0M′. If the government were to auction this supply, importers would be willing to pay a price of P_b for the foreign exchange. In such a case the government would make a profit of P_aP_b per unit. Typically, however, such open auctions are not carried out and limited supplies of foreign exchange are allocated through some administrative quota or licensing device. Opportunities for corruption, evasion, and the emergence of "black markets" are thus made possible since importers are willing to pay as much as P_b per unit of foreign exchange.

Why have most Third World governments opted for an overvalued official exchange rate? Basically, as we have seen, they have done so as part of widespread programs of rapid industrialization and import substitution.

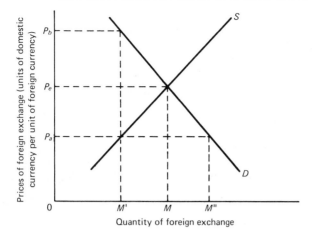

Figure 13.2. The free market and controlled rate of foreign exchange.

Overvalued exchange rates reduce the domestic currency price of imports below that which would exist in a free market for foreign exchange (i.e., by the forces of supply and demand). Cheaper imports, especially capital and intermediate producer goods, are needed to fuel the industrialization process. But overvalued exchange rates also lower the domestic currency price of imported consumer goods, especially expensive luxury products. Third World nations wishing to limit such unnecessary and costly imports often need, therefore, to establish import controls (mostly physical quotas) or to set up a dual exchange rate system—one rate, usually highly overvalued, to be applied to capital and intermediate good imports and the other, much lower, for luxury consumption good imports. Such dual exchange rate systems make the domestic price of imported luxury goods very high while maintaining the artificially low and thus subsidized price of producer good imports. Needless to say, dual exchange rate systems, like exchange controls and import licenses, present serious problems of administration and promote corruption and evasion.

On the other hand, overvalued currencies reduce the returns to local exporters and to those import-competing industries which are not protected by heavy tariffs or physical quotas. Exporters receive less domestic currency for their products than would be forthcoming if the free market exchange rate prevailed. Moreover, in the absence of export subsidies to reduce the foreign currency price of an LDC's exports, exporters, mostly farmers, become less competitive in world markets since the price of their produce has been artificially elevated by the overvalued exchange rate. In the case of import-competing but unprotected local industries, the overvalued rate artificially lowers the domestic currency price of foreign imports of the same product (e.g., radios, tires, bicycles, household utensils).

In the absence, therefore, of effective government intervention and regulation of the foreign exchange dealings of its nationals, overvalued exchange rates have a tendency to exacerbate balance of payments problems simply because they cheapen imports while making exports more costly. As we mentioned in our discussion of the balance of payments, chronic payments deficits resulting primarily from current account transactions (i.e, exports and imports) can possibly be ameliorated by a currency devaluation. Simply defined, a country's currency is "devalued" or, more strictly, "depreciated" when the official rate at which its Central Bank is prepared to exchange the local currency for dollars is increased. For example, a devaluation of the Egyptian pound and the Indian rupee would occur if their official exchange rates of approximately 0.7 pounds and 10 rupees to the dollar were changed to, say, 2 pounds and 20 rupees per dollar. Following these devaluations U.S. importers of Egyptian and Indian goods would pay fewer dollars to obtain the same products. On the other hand, U.S. exports to Egypt and India would become more expensive (i.e., require more pounds and/or rupees to purchase) than before. In short, by lowering the *foreign* currency price of its exports (and thereby hopefully generating more foreign demand) while raising the *domestic* currency price of its imports (and, thereby, lowering domestic demand) Third World nations that devalue their currency hope to improve their trade balance vis-à-vis the rest of the world.

An alternative to a currency devaluation would be to allow foreign exchange rates to fluctuate freely in accordance with changing conditions of international demand and supply. Freely fluctuating or flexible exchange rates in the past were not thought to be desirable, especially in Third World nations heavily dependent on exports and imports, because they are extremely unpredictable, subject to wide and uncontrollable fluctuations, and susceptible to foreign and domestic currency speculation. Such unpredictable fluctuations can wreak havoc with both short- and long-range development plans. Nevertheless, during the world balance of payments and debt crises of 1982–1983, a number of Third World countries, including Mexico, Argentina, Chile, and the Philippines, were forced to let their exchange rates float freely in order to correct sizable payments imbalances and to prevent continued capital flight.

The present international system of floating exchange rates, formally legalized at the 1976 Jamaica IMF meeting, represents a compromise between a fixed (artificially "pegged") and a fully flexible exchange rate system. Under this "managed" floating system major international currencies are permitted to fluctuate freely, but erratic swings are limited through Central Bank intervention. Most developing countries, however, have decided to continue to peg their currencies to those of developed countries. Some, like Kenya, have gone further and decided to tie their currencies to the movements of a weighted index of the world's major currencies rather than to tie them to a particular currency, like the U.S. dollar or the British pound sterling.

One final point that should be made about Third World currency devaluations, particularly in the light of previous chapter discussions, concerns their probable effect on domestic prices. Devaluation has the immediate effect of raising prices of imported goods in terms of the local currency. Imported shirts, shoes, radios, records, foodstuffs, bicycles, etc. that formerly cost x rupees now cost x + y rupees, depending on the magnitude of the devaluation. If, as a result of these higher prices, domestic workers seek to preserve the real value of their purchasing power, they are likely to initiate increased wage and salary demands. Such increases, if granted, will raise production costs and tend to push local prices up even higher. A wage–price spiral of domestic inflation is thereby set in motion. In fact, a vicious circle of devaluation—domestic wage and price increases, higher export prices, and worsened balance of trade—could result. Thus, the devaluation decision could simply exacerbate the external balance of payments problem while generating galloping inflation domestically. The experience of many Latin American nations, in particular, with such chronic and uncontrollable inflation has made them reluctant users of the tool of currency devaluation despite IMF pressures and Western protestations.

As for the distributional effects of a devaluation, it is clear that by altering the domestic price and returns of "tradeable" goods (exports and imports) and creating incentives for the production of exports as opposed to domestic goods, devaluation will benefit certain groups at the expense of others. In general, urban wage earners, those with fixed incomes, the unemployed, and those small farmers and rural and urban small-scale producers and suppliers of services who do not participate in the export sector stand to be financially hurt by the domestic inflation that typically follows a devaluation. On the other hand, large exporters (usually large landowners and foreign-owned corporations) as well as the more medium-sized local businesses engaged in foreign trade stand to benefit the most. While we cannot categorically assert that devaluation tends to worsen income distribution, we may conclude that the more that ownership of and control over the export sector is concentrated in private as opposed to public hands, the greater is the liklihood that devaluation will have an adverse effect on income distribution. For this reason, among others, international commercial and financial problems (e.g., chronic balance of payments deficits) cannot be divorced from domestic problems (e.g., poverty and inequality) in Third World nations. Policy responses to alleviate one problem can either improve or worsen others. This interaction between problems and policies will be discussed at length in Chapter 16.

Conclusions: Trade Policies and Development

In the final analysis, it is not a developing country's inward- or outward-looking stance vis-à-vis the rest of the world that will determine whether or not it develops along the lines described in Chapter 3 and in many other parts of this book. Inward-looking, protectionist policies such as tariffs, quotas, and exchange rate adjustments do not necessarily guarantee more jobs, higher incomes that are more equitably distributed, adequate nutrition and health, clean water, and relevant education any more than do outward-looking, noninterventionist policies. Even though most development economists would agree with the conclusion reached by Anne Krueger and her colleagues in their exhaustive study of the impact of trade policies on LDC growth in the 1960s and 1970s—namely, that policies of export promotion appear to have contributed more to GNP growth than import substitution (see Note 6)—it does not follow that similar results will occur in the 1980s and 1990s. Moreover, in terms of our broadened definition of development, even the results of the past two decades are ambiguous. Much depends on the structure of both the domestic LDC economy and the world economy. In fact, as Professor Streeten so skillfully pointed out when summarizing a Cambridge University conference on trade and development:

> *A curious paradox came out of the discussion [of the effects of trade on LDC inequalities]. It seemed that both inward-looking, import-substituting, protectionist, interventionist policies and outward-looking, market-orientated, non-interventionist policies tend to increase market imperfections and monopolies and reduce the demand for labour-intensive processes, the latter because the market rewards most those factors that are relatively scarce (capital, management, professional skills) and penalizes those in abundant supply and because the market strengthens the ability to accumulate of those who have against those who have not. But though it is paradoxical that both a protectionist "distorted" system of prices, interest rates, wages and exchange rates and a market-determined one should increase inequalities, there is no contradiction. It is plausible that within a certain social and political framework, both export-orientated market policies and import-substitution-orientated, interventionist, "distorting" policies should aggravate inequalities, though one set may do this somewhat more than the other. Perhaps economists have been barking up the wrong tree when disputing which set of price policies contributes more to equality. In an inegalitarian power structure, both make for inequality; in an egalitarian power structure, both may make for equality.*[16]

The reader will do well to reflect on these observations before reaching any final judgment about trade policies for development, especially within the context of the poverty and inequality issue.

ECONOMIC INTEGRATION: THE POTENTIAL BENEFITS OF LOOKING BOTH OUTWARD AND INWARD

Some Basic Concepts

One significant variant of the free trade doctrine that can have relevance for many developing countries involves economic integration. Economic integration occurs whenever a group of nations in the same region, preferably of relatively equal size and at equal stages of development, join together to form an economic union by raising a common tariff wall against the products of nonmember countries while freeing internal trade among members. In the terminology of integration literature, nations that levy common external tariffs while freeing internal trade are said to have formed a *customs union*. If external tariffs against outside countries differ among member nations while internal trade is free, the nations are said to have formed a *free trade area*. Finally, a *common market* possesses all the attributes of a customs union (i.e., common external tariffs and free internal trade) plus the free movement of labor and capital among the partner states.

The theory of customs unions and economic integration is associated primarily with the work of Professor Jacob Viner of Princeton University in the 1940s. The traditional core of this theory, which focuses on the static resource and production reallocation effects within highly integrated and flexible industrialized nations, is of limited value to contemporary developing nations intent on building up their industrial base. Yet many concepts of the theory of integration provide valid criteria on which to evaluate the probable short-run success or failure of economic cooperation among Third World countries.

The basic economic rationale for the gradual integration of less developed economies is a long-term dynamic one: integration provides the opportunity for industries that *have not yet been established* as well as for those that have to take advantage of the *economies of large-scale production* made possible by expanded markets. Integration therefore needs to be viewed as a mechanism to encourage a rational division of labor among a group of countries, each of which is too small to benefit from such a division by itself. In the absence of integration, each separate country may not provide a sufficiently large domestic market to enable local industries to lower their production costs through economies of scale. In such cases, import-substituting industrialization will typically result, as we have seen, in the establishment of high-cost, inefficient local industries. Moreover, in the absence of integration, the same industry (e.g., textiles or shoes) may be set up in two or more adjoining small nations. Each will be operating at less than optimal capacity but will be protected against the imports of the other by high tariff or quota barriers. Not only does such duplication result in wasted scarce resources, it also means that consumers are forced to pay a higher price for the product than if the market were large enough for high-volume, low-cost production to take place at a single location.

This leads to a second dynamic rationale for LDC economic integration. By removing barriers to trade among member states, the possibility of *coordinated industrial planning* is created, especially in those industries where economies of scale are likely to exist. Examples include fertilizer and petrochemical plants, heavy industry like iron and steel, capital goods and machine tool industries, and small farm mechanical equipment. But the coordinated planning of industrial expansion that enables all member states to accelerate their rates of industrial growth by assigning given industries to different members takes the partners that much closer to full economic and, eventually, political union. Problems of sovereignty and national self-interest impinge at this stage. To date they have overwhelmed the economic logic of a close and coordinated union. However, as Third World nations, especially small ones, continue to experience the futility of either development in isolation (i.e., autarchy) or full participation in the highly unequal world economy, it is likely that interest will increase in the coming decades in the long-run benefits of some form of economic (and perhaps political) cooperation.

In addition to these two long-term dynamic arguments for integration, there also exist the standard textbook *static* evaluative criteria known as "trade creation" and "trade diversion." Trade creation is said to occur when common external barriers and internal free trade lead to a shift in production from high- to low-cost member states. For example, before integration both Country A and Country B may produce textiles for their respective local markets. Country A may be a lower-cost producer, but its exports to Country B are blocked by the latter's high tariffs. If A and B form a customs union by eliminating all barriers to internal trade, Country A's more efficient low-cost textile industry will service both markets. Trade will have been created in the sense that the removal of barriers has led to a shift in Country B's consumption from its own relatively high-cost textiles to the lower-cost textiles of Country A.

Similarly, trade diversion is said to occur when the erection of external tariff barriers causes production and consumption of one or more member states to shift from lower-cost nonmember sources of supply (e.g., a developed country) to higher-cost member producers. Trade diversion is normally considered undesirable since both the world and member states are perceived to be worse off as a result of the diversion of production from more efficient foreign suppliers to the less efficient domestic industries of member states. But this static argument against economic integration ignores two basic facts. First, because of potential economies of scale, the creation of local jobs, and the circular flow of income within the integrated region, static trade diversion may turn out to be dynamic trade creation. This is simply a variant of the standard "infant industry" argument for protection, but with the more likely possibility that the infant will grow up as a result of the larger market in which it now operates. Second, if in the absence of integration, each member state were to protect its local import-substituting industry against all lower-cost foreign suppliers, the common external tariff of member states would cause no more trade diversion than would have happened anyway. But, as we just saw, if there are scale economies, the possibility of dynamic trade creation can emerge. Hence we conclude that static concepts like trade creation and trade diversion are useful. However, it is important that they be analyzed in the dynamic context of growth and development and based on the realities of current commercial policies of developing nations, rather than in the theoretical vacuum of traditional free trade models.

Third World Regional Integration in Practice: Some Case Studies[17]

Having outlined some basic concepts of economic integration, we can now formulate a set of specific questions to use in evaluating various recent integration schemes in the Third World. These questions are the following:

1. Has integration stimulated a more rapid growth rate of internal trade among member states?
2. Has the growth of internal trade had the character of "trade creation" or "trade diversion" (bearing in mind some of the previously discussed limitations of these concepts)?
3. How has integration affected the trade of individual member countries?
4. What effect has integration had on the aggregate economic growth rates of member countries?
5. What have been the main obstacles hindering integration?

We can draw primarily on Dr. Pazos's study to provide preliminary answers to these questions on the basis of the integration experiences of developing countries in Latin America, the Caribbean, and Africa. Seven regional groups of varying size, economic structure, and levels of development have entered into arrangements to integrate their economies—some more closely than others—since 1960. They are:

1. The *Latin American Free Trade Association* (LAFTA), formed in 1960 and consisting of 11 Latin American countries (see Table 13.3)

2. The *Central American Common Market* (CACM), also formed in 1960 and composed of 5 Central American nations (Costa Rica, El Salvador, Guatemala, Honduras, and Nicaragua) until it was disbanded following political differences in the 1970s

3. The *Andean Group*, formed in 1969 and consisting of Bolivia, Chile (since withdrawn), Ecuador, Colombia, and Peru

4. The *Caribbean Free Trade Area* (CARIFTA), formed in 1968 and consisting of 12 Caribbean nations (in July 1973 the Caribbean Free Trade Area was converted into a full-fledged Caribbean Community)

5. The *Central African Customs and Economic Union* (CACEU), formed in 1964 and comprising Cameroon, Central African Republic, Congo, and Gabon

6. The *East African Community* (EAC), which was in existence from colonial times until the mid 1970s and consisted of Kenya, Uganda, and Tanzania

7. The recently formed (1975) *Economic Community of West African States* (ECOWAS) consisting of 15 countries—9 French-, 5 English-, and 1 Portuguese-speaking—with a total population of 124 million and an area of 6.5 million square km

Table 13.3 summarizes the expansion of trade among member states of the six integration groups between 1960 and 1970. It can be seen that in two of the four "older groups", the CACM and the CACEU, internal trade grew at a phenomenal annual rate of 28.8 and 23.2% respectively during most of the 1960s. The other two older groups, LAFTA and EAC, showed only moderate rates of growth of between 7 and 8% annually. But it is important to note that in both cases this internal growth rate was significantly higher than the growth rate of total trade for each. This can be seen by the rise in internal trade as a percentage of total trade between 1960 and 1970 for both groups, from 8.5 to 10.6% for LAFTA and from 14.6 to 17.3% for EAC. The relatively slow growth of intratrade within LAFTA and EAC can be attributed largely to the emergence of new forms of protective restriction in the 1960s designed to permit the weaker partners to catch up slowly with the stronger ones.

Both the Andean Group and the CARIFTA, formed in the late 1960s, showed big jumps in their internal trade in 1969. In the 1970s intracountry trade growth slowed considerably as disagreements and numerous minor and major political disputes hampered further consolidation efforts. Nevertheless, the rapid pace at which trade started to expand in both CARIFTA and the Andean Group testifies to the economic capacity of Third World nations to conduct mutually beneficial exchange with each other. Finally, the fact that the bulk of the increase in intratrade among the various integration groups was concentrated in the manufacturing sector (e.g., in CACM, 74% of all intratrade was in manufacturing categories) shows that industrial growth can be greatly strengthened by economic cooperation among various LDCs. Instead of trying to compete with one another for access to heavily protected manufactured good markets of developed countries, Third World nations may stand a better long-run chance to diversify their economies successfully by trading with one another behind the protective barrier of a common tariff.

With regard to the complex and in some cases irrelevant question of trade creation and trade diversion, Dr. Pazos's analysis reveals evidence of the existence of both. But, on the whole, he concludes with respect to CACM (the most carefully analyzed group) that "integration has created competition among the producers of the five countries and has probably promoted industrial specialization by types of products, thus permitting larger pro-

Table 13.3 Intratrade of Integration Groups, 1960–1970

Integration group	Value of exports to area ($ million)				Share of exports to the area in total exports (%)				Annual growth rate of exports to the area (%)		
	1960	1968	1969	1970	1960	1968	1969	1970	1960–1968	1969	1970
Latin America											
LAFTA*	564	999	1,206	1,254	8.5	10.7	11.7	10.6	7.4	20.7	3.9
Andean Group†	40	60	84	109	2.5	2.2	2.9	3.3	5.2	40.0	29.8
CACM‡	33	247	250	286	7.5	26.0	25.7	26.1	28.8	1.2	14.4
Caribbean											
CARIFTA**	27	52	66	—	5.0	5.9	7.2	—	8.6	26.9	—
Africa											
CACEU††	3	16	21	—	1.7	4.0	4.6	—	23.2	31.2	—
EAC‡‡	63	116	122	142	14.6	17.1	16.8	17.3	7.9	5.2	16.4

*Latin American Free Trade Association: Argentina, Bolivia, Brazil, Chile, Colombia, Ecuador, Mexico, Paraguay, Peru, Uruguay, Venezuela.
†Andean Group: Bolivia, Chile, Colombia, Ecuador, Peru.
‡Central American Common Market: Costa Rica, El Salvador, Guatemala, Honduras, Nicaragua.
**Caribbean Free Trade Area: Barbados, Guyana, Jamaica, Trinidad and Tobago, Antigua, British Honduras, Dominica, Grenada, Montserrat, St Kitts-Nevis-Anguilla, St Lucia, St Vincent.
†† Central African Customs and Economic Union: Cameroon, Central African Republic, Congo, Gabon.
‡‡ East African Community: Kenya, Uganda, United Republic of Tanzania.

SOURCE: Felipe Pazos, "Regional integration of trade among less developed countries," *World Development* 7 (1973):2, Table 1.

duction scales and lower costs."[18] Thus trade creation does seem to have pervaded the CACM prior to its political dismantling.

Regarding the benefits of integration in terms of growth rates of member-country exports, their GNPs, and their intracountry trade balances which often are not uniformly distributed, especially when there is a dominant country in the group (as in the case of Kenya in EAC), all participants of CACM appear to have benefited from an expansion of exports and also to have received considerable net benefits in terms of national output and employment rates of growth.[19]

Dr. Pazos concludes his analysis of the economic effects of integration with regard to the CACM with the observation:

> The experience of Central America shows that, under appropriate circumstances, the elimination of restrictions on the mutual trade of a group of developing countries brings about considerable expansion in their commercial interchange, fuller use of industrial capacity, specialization of production, economies of scale, increased industrialization and faster economic growth, without any rise in the number of industrial failures or in the amount of unemployment.[20]

In spite of the impressive economic record achieved by the Central American Common Market while it operated and the early favorable results of the Andean and CACEU experiences, there still remain major stumbling blocks, some real, others psychological and especially political, in the path of a more widespread Third World movement toward economic integration. The major problems relate to differences in levels of development among prospective members of regional groups and the consequent expectation among the lesser developed countries that a uniform trade liberalization policy would disproportionately benefit the more developed countries at their expense. In order for an integration scheme to be successful, it must not penalize any members while assuring that the distribution of the benefits of cooperation are reasonably equitable. If there are severe imbalances among member countries at the outset (as in the case of Kenya vis-à-vis its two East African neighbors), the tendency for unequal gains from trade to emerge and for the income gap between rich and poor members to widen will be reinforced. Such unequal benefit distribution is entirely analogous to that between rich and poor nations described in our critique of traditional free trade theory.

However, in the case of regional integration, it is at least possible to redistribute the gains from trade or, through coordinated policy planning, to plan for the more rapid industrial development of weaker members to enable them to catch up. Redistribution was attempted in the EAC (Kenya provided direct financial transfers to the other two members in the early 1960s) with mixed success. Problems stemmed largely from the fact that EAC member states were still able to pursue their own separate and often conflicting industrial development strategies. Moreover, there was no really effective supranational agency to enforce compliance with the provisions of the integration scheme.

Conclusions

We may conclude, therefore, that Third World countries at relatively equal stages of industrial development, with similar market sizes, and with a strong interest in coordinating and rationalizing their joint industrial growth patterns stand to benefit most from the combined inward/outward-looking trade policies represented by economic integration. In particular, regional groupings of small nations like those of Central America and Central and West Africa can create the economic conditions (mainly in the form of larger internal markets) for accelerating their joint development efforts. Such groupings can also promote long-run development by enabling nations to block certain forms of trade with the more powerful developed nations and perhaps also to restrict or prohibit the deep penetration of multinational corporations into their industrial sectors. In any event, integration is crucial;[21] without cooperation and integration, the prospects for sustained economic progress are bleak.

But, while such an integration strategy may seem economically logical and persuasive on paper (and in fact be the only long-run solution to the economic problems of small nations), in practice it requires a degree of statesmanship and a regional rather than nationalistic orientation that is often lacking in many countries. The unfortunate demise of both the Central American Common Market and the East African Community in the 1970s demonstrates how political and ideological conflict can more than offset the economic logic of regional cooperation. Nevertheless, as time goes on, if developing nations continue to see their individual destinies as more closely tied to those of their neighbors, and if the pursuit of greater collective self-reliance and self-sufficiency gathers momentum, it is quite possible that the pressures for some form of economic and political integration will gradually overcome the forces of separation and continued dependency.

TRADE POLICIES OF DEVELOPED COUNTRIES: THE NEED FOR REFORM

We have seen that a major obstacle to LDC export expansion, whether in the area of primary products or manufactures, has been the various trade barriers erected by developed nations against the principal commodity exports of developing countries. In the absence of economic integration or even in support of that effort, the prospects for future LDC trade and foreign exchange expansion depend largely on the domestic and international economic policies of developed nations. While internal structural and economic reform may be essential to economic and social progress, an improvement in the competitive position of those industries where LDCs do have a dynamic comparative advantage will be of little benefit either to them or the world as a whole so long as their access to major world markets is restricted by rich country commercial policies.

Four major areas where a developed country's economic and commercial policies stand out as the most important from the perspective of future Third World foreign exchange earnings are

1. Tariff and nontariff barriers to LDC exports
2. Developed country export incentives

3. Adjustment assistance for displaced workers in developed country industries hurt by freer access of labor-intensive, low-cost LDC exports
4. The general impact of rich-country domestic economic policies on developing economies

Rich-Nation Tariff and Nontariff Trade Barriers

The present tariff and nontariff barriers (e.g., excise taxes, quotas, sanitary regulations) imposed by rich nations on the commodity exports of poor ones represent the most significant obstacle to the expansion of the latter's export-earning capacities. Moreover, as we have seen, many of these tariffs increase with the degree of product processing; that is, they are higher for processed foodstuffs compared with basic foodstuffs (e.g., groundnut oil compared with groundnuts) or for shirts as opposed to raw cotton. These high effective tariffs inhibit LDCs from developing and diversifying their own secondary export industries and thus act to restrain their industrial expansion.

The overall effect of developed country tariffs, quotas, and nontariff barriers (e.g., sanitary laws for meat imports that are more stringent than domestic regulations) is to lower the effective price received by LDCs for their exports (i.e., worsen their terms of trade), reduce the quantity exported, and diminish foreign exchange earnings. Although the burdens developed country tariffs impose on LDC primary and secondary product exports vary from commodity to commodity, the net impact of trade barriers on all products is to reduce Third World foreign exchange earnings by many billions of dollars. In the absence of widespread reductions in these trade barriers (they actually increased between 1978 and 1984) and the establishment of special preferences for LDC primary product exports, there can be little optimism about the possibility of accelerating Third World export earnings through trade with the developed nations.

Export Incentives of Developed Countries

In addition to restricting the imports of products from the Third World, many developed countries provide generous financial incentives for their own export industries in the form of public subsidies and tax rebates. The Japanese government has made the greatest use of this policy, working closely in support of its private export industries. Although LDC governments also provide export incentives, their limited fiscal capacity prevents them from effectively counteracting the impact of export subsidies in rich countries. The overall effect of this public support of private industries is to make rich-country industries more "competitive" in world markets and to delay the time when Third World industries are able to compete effectively. It is simply another instance of the ability of the wealthy to stay on top.

The Problem of Adjustment Assistance

One of the major obstacles to the lowering of tariff barriers of rich countries against the manufactured exports of poorer nations is the political pressure exerted by those traditional light manufacturing industries which find their products underpriced by low-cost, labor-intensive foreign goods.[22] Not only can this cause economic disruption for these higher-cost domestic industries; it can also lead to a loss of employment for their workers. In classical trade theory the answer to this dilemma would be simple: merely shift these rich-country workers with their complementary resources to those other more capital-intensive industries where a comparative advantage still exists. Everybody will be better off as a result.

Unfortunately, even in the most industrialized and economically integrated societies of the world, the process of adjustment is not so simple. More important, the political power of many of these older industries is such that whenever they feel threatened by low-cost foreign imports, they are able to muster enough support effectively to block competition from the LDCs. Such activities make a mockery of pious statements about the benefits of free trade.

Unless some scheme of adjustment assistance is established by which the governments of developed nations financially assist industries and their workers in the transition to alternative and more profitable activities, trade barriers against competitive Third World exports will continue to be raised. Many such schemes have been proposed. To date, none has been really effective in persuading threatened industries and industrial workers to forego their private interests in the interest of maximum world welfare. This is not surprising. In fact, the typical response of developed country governments has been to subsidize new investment in threatened industries to keep them afloat. Nevertheless, continuous efforts must be made to search for an acceptable program of adjustment assistance which will not unduly penalize displaced workers who often come from the lower income brackets. Without the introduction of such programs in developed nations, the world market for Third World manufactured exports will always remain highly restricted both for new entrants and for the growth of existing suppliers.

Domestic Economic Policies

While it is beyond the scope of this chapter to examine the myriad ways in which the economic welfare of many export-oriented poor nations is tied to the domestic fiscal and monetary policies of rich nations, the importance of this linkage must not be overlooked. The major factor determining the level and growth of Third World export earnings (and this was clearly confirmed by their relatively good performance in the 1960s and their sharp decline during the recessions of the 1970s and early 1980s) has been the ability of rich nations to sustain high rates of economic growth without inflation. Even a low income elasticity of demand for LDC exports can be compensated for by a high rate of income growth in a developed country. It follows that under present international economic relationships, Third World export performance is directly related to the growth and price stability of developed country economies.

But just as the poor are often said to be "the last to be hired and the first to be fired," so too when international economic disruptions occur, the world's poor nations feel the effects much sooner and more substantially than do the rich nations. The worldwide inflationary spiral of the 1970s caused by a combination of Keynesian-type excess aggregate "demand pull" and natural resource, especially petroleum, "cost push" factors provides a classic example of this phenomenon. Faced with rampant inflation at home, developed countries were able to call on traditional macroeconomic policies designed to restrict aggregate demand (e.g., lower government expenditure, higher taxes, higher interest rates, a slower-growing money supply) while attempting to control wage and price rises. When rapid inflation is accompanied by growing balance of payments deficits and rising domestic unemployment as in the 1970s, these "deflationary" domestic fiscal and monetary policies tend to be reinforced by specific government actions to curtail imports and control the outflow of foreign exchange. Those hit the hardest by these belt-tightening measures are usually the weakest, most vulnerable, and most dependent nations of the world—the 40 or so least developed countries. While they are not the intended victims of such domestic economic policies, the fact remains that they are the main victims.

Clearly, one cannot blame the developed nations for first looking after their own domestic economic interests. Nevertheless, it would not appear too unreasonable to ask them to try to ease the burden of their spending cutbacks on the poorest nations by giving the exports of these nations some form of preferential treatment. But the lesson is clear. As long as developing nations, either individually or as a group, whether willingly or unwillingly, permit their economies to be linked too closely to the economic policies of rich nations, they will remain its chief, though innocent, victims in times of stress while in times of prosperity their rewards will be minimal. Even more disturbing is the loss of their capacity to control their own economic and social destinies.

The lessons of the past 15 years thus revealed to Third World nations, as no economic model could have, their need to make every effort to reduce their individual and joint economic vulnerabilities. One method of achieving this goal is to pursue policies of greater collective self-reliance within the context of mutual economic cooperation and a more cautious attitude toward the further penetration of their economies by products, technologies, and corporations from rich countries. While not denying their interdependence with developed nations and their need for growing developed country export markets, many developing countries now realize that in the absence of major reforms of the international economic order, a concentrated effort at reducing their current international economic dependence and vulnerability is an essential ingredient in any successful long-run development strategy.

NOTES

1. An important step in this direction was taken at a meeting of the IMF held in Jamaica in January 1976. At that meeting the IMF agreed to increase SDR quotas for non-oil-exporting LDCs by 50%, thus adding about $1 billion to their reserves. It also agreed to set up a special fund based on the sale of gold to help the developing world balance its deficit payments. In addition, the meeting legalized the IMF's present system of floating exchange rates. Two valuable readings on the origin and nature of SDRs and their unique importance to developing countries are W.O. Habermeier, "The SDR as an international unit of account," *Finance and Develop-*

ment 16, no. 1 (March 1979), and Graham Bird, "The benefits of Special Drawing Rights for less developed countries," *World Development* 7 (1979):281–290.

2. For excellent discussions of inward vs. outward development policies, see P.P. Streeten, "Trade strategies for development: Some themes for the seventies," *World Development* 1, no. 6 (1973):1–10, and Donald B. Keesing, "Trade policy for developing countries," *World Bank Staff Working Papers* No. 53 (1979), reprinted as Reading 28 in *The Struggle for Economic Development*.

3. Streeten, "Trade strategies," p. 2.

4. See A. Maizels, *Exports and Economic Growth of Developing Countries* (London: Cambridge University Press, 1968).

5. However, see Maizels, *Exports and Economic Growth*, for such an analysis.

6. For a comprehensive empirical analysis extolling the growth-inducing benefits of manufactured export promotion based on the 1960s and 1970s experience, see Anne O. Krueger, *Trade and Employment in Developing Countries, Vol. 3: Synthesis and Conclusions* (Chicago: University of Chicago Press for the National Bureau of Economic Research, 1983).

7. Gerald K. Helleiner, *International Trade and Economic Development* (Harmondsworth, England: Penguin, 1972), pp. 69–70.

8. For an interesting and provocative counterargument to the shift in development thinking toward greater emphasis on export promotion in imitation of Taiwan and South Korea, see Paul Streeten, "A cool look at outward-looking industrialization and trade strategies," *PIDE Tidings*, Pakistan Institute of Development Economics, November–December 1982.

9. For one of the most comprehensive analyses and critiques of import substitution policies in developing countries, see I. Little, T. Scitovsky, and M. Scott, *Industry and Trade in Some Developing Countries* (London: Oxford University Press, 1970).

10. Helleiner, *International Trade*, p. 105. See also Werner Baer, "Import substitution and industrialization in Latin America: Experiences and interpretations," reprinted as Reading 27 in *The Struggle for Economic Development*.

11. I. Little, T. Scitovsky, and M. Scott, *Industry and Trade in Some Developing Countries: A Comparative Study* (London: Oxford University Press, 1970), p. 39.

12. Herbert G. Grubel, "Effective tariff protection: A nonspecialist introduction to the theory, policy implications and controversies," in H. Grubel and H. Johnson (eds.), *Effective Tariff Protection* (Geneva: GATT, 1971), p. 2.

13. Little, Scitovsky, and Scott, *Industry and Trade*, p. 4.

14. Bela Balassa, "Tariff protection in industrial countries: An evaluation," *Journal of Political Economy* (October 1965), pp. 580 and 588.

15. UNECAFE, *Economy Survey of Asia and the Far East 1968* (Bangkok, 1969), p. 67.

16. Streeten, "Trade strategies," pp. 3–4.

17. For a useful summary of Third World regional integration experiences, see Felipe Pazos, "Regional integration of trade among less developed countries," *World Development* 1, no. 7 (1973):1–12; David Morawetz, *The Andean Group: A Case Study in Economic Integration among Developing Countries* (Cambridge, Mass.: MIT Press, 1974); and Peter Robson, *Integration, Development and Equity: Economic Integration in West Africa* (London: Allen and Unwin, 1983).

18. Pazos, "Regional integration," p. 4.

19. *Ibid.*, pp. 6–9.

20. *Ibid.*, p. 9.

21. For a recent empirically based argument for expanded trade among developing countries as a stimulant to long-term growth and development, see Yves Sabolo, "Trade between developing countries, technology transfers and employment," *International Labor Review* 122, no. 5 (September–October 1983).

22. More recently, as newly industrializing Third World countries (NICs) like Brazil, Mexico, and South Korea expanded their exports of capital-intensive manufactured products such as steel, developed nations, like the United States in 1984, sought and received increased protection from lower cost steel imports.

CONCEPTS FOR REVIEW

Balance of payments	Free trade area
Current account	Common market
Balance of payments surplus vs. deficit	Trade creation
Trade surplus versus trade deficit	Trade diversion
Capital account	Export promotion
Cash account	Import substitution
Commercial policies	Tariffs
Autarchy	Quotas
Adjustment assistance	Nontariff trade barriers
Export incentives	Infant industry
Outward- versus inward-looking	Export duty or subsidy
development policies	Official exchange rate
Special drawing rights	Dual exchange rate
International commodity agreements	Devaluation, depreciation
Nominal and effective rates of protection	Floating exchange rates
Exchange control	"Overvalued" exchange rate
Economic integration	Forward and backward industrial
Customs union	linkages

QUESTIONS FOR DISCUSSION

1. Draw up a balance of payments table similar in format to Table 13.1 but using the most recent available data from a Third World country. Explain the significance or nonsignificance of the various entries in the current and capital accounts. What happened to the level of this country's foreign reserves during the year in question?
2. Explain the distinction between primary and secondary inward- and outward-looking development policies.
3. Briefly summarize the range of commercial policies available to Third World countries and explain why some of these policies might be adopted.
4. What are the possibilities, advantages, and disadvantages of "export promotion" in Third World nations with reference to specific types of commodities (e.g., primary food products, raw materials, fuels, minerals, manufactured goods)?
5. Most less developed countries in Latin America, Africa, and Asia have pursued policies of import substitution as major components of their development strategies. Explain the theoretical and practical arguments in support of import substitution policies. What have been some of the weaknesses of these policies in practice and why have the results often not lived up to expectations? Explain.
6. Explain some of the arguments in support of the use of tariffs, quotas, and other trade barriers in developing countries.
7. What are the basic static and dynamic arguments for economic integration in less developed countries? Briefly describe the various forms economic integration can take (e.g., customs union, free trade areas). What are the major obstacles to effective economic integration in Third World regions?
8. How do the trade policies of developed countries affect the ability of less developed countries to benefit from greater participation in the world economy? How do "non-trade" domestic economic policies of rich nations affect the export earnings of Third World countries? What is meant by "adjustment assistance" and why is it so important to the future of Third World manufactured export prospects? Explain.

FURTHER READINGS

Four of the best general sources of information on trade policies and strategies for development are Gerald K. Helleiner, *International Trade and Economic Development* (Harmondsworth, England: Penguin, 1972); Paul Streeten, "Trade strategies for development: Some themes for the seventies," *World Development* 1, no. 6 (1973):1–10; Donald B. Keesing, "Trade policy for developing countries," *World Bank Staff Working Papers* No. 53 (1979), reprinted as Reading 28 in *The Struggle for Economic Develop-*

ment; and Anne O. Krueger, *Trade and Employment in Developing Countries, Volume 3: Synthesis and Conclusions* (Chicago: University of Chicago Press for the National Bureau of Economic Research, 1983). See also P.K. Ghosh (ed.), *International Trade and Third World Development* (Westport, Conn.: Greenwood, 1984) for a useful collection of readings and statistics.

The following are more specialized readings on the topics covered in this chapter: R.L. Allen, "Integration in less developed areas," *Kyklos* 14, fasc. 3 (1961):315–336; B. Balassa, "The impact of industrial countries' tariff structure on their imports of manufactures from less developed areas," *Economica* 34, no. 136 (1967):372–383; B. Balassa, "Trade policies in developing countries," *American Economic Review* 61, no. 2 (1971): 178–187; H. Bruton, "The import-substitution strategy of economic development: A survey," *Pakistan Development Review* 10, no. 2 (1970):123–146; C. Cooper and B. Massell, "Toward a general theory of customs unions for developing countries," *Journal of Political Economy* 73, no. 5 (1965):461–474; I. Little, T. Scitovsky, and M. Scott, *Industry and Trade in Some Developing Countries: A Comparative Study* (London: Oxford University Press, 1970); D. Morawetz, *The Andean Group: A Case Study in Economic Integration among Developing Countries* (Cambridge, Mass.: MIT Press, 1974); and P.K. Ghosh (ed.), *Economic Integration and Third World Development* (Westport, Conn.: Greenwood, 1984).

Additional readings can be found on pp. 631–633.

14

FOREIGN INVESTMENT AND AID: OLD CONTROVERSIES AND NEW OPPORTUNITIES

What the Third World must ask of the international order is . . . a genuine transfer of real resources, not the present "aid" charade.
Santiago Resolution, April 1973

Two decades of experience with international economic cooperation have convinced many leaders in the developing countries that basic changes in their economies and social systems are more important than quantitative increases in external resource transfers.
Communiqué of Third World Social Scientists, March 1974

THE INTERNATIONAL FLOW OF FINANCIAL RESOURCES

In Chapter 13 we learned that a country's international financial situation as reflected in its balance of payments and its level of monetary reserves depends not only on its current account balance (its commodity trade) but also on its balance on capital account (its net inflow or outflow of private and public financial resources). Since almost all non-oil-exporting developing nations incur deficits on their current account balance, a continuous net inflow of foreign financial resources represents an important ingredient in their long-run development strategies.

The international flow of financial resources takes two main forms: *private foreign investment*, mostly foreign direct investment by large multinational corporations with headquarters in the developed nations and flows of financial capital by private international banks whose lending activities accelerated greatly during the late 1970s, and *public development assistance* (foreign aid), both from individual national governments and multinational donor agencies. In this chapter we examine the nature, significance, and controversy over private direct foreign investment and foreign aid in the context of the changing world economy. Although our principal emphasis is on the traditional "North—South" flow of development finance (i.e., from developed to less developed nations), we shall also look briefly at OPEC aid. The emergence of wealthy Arab oil nations in the 1970s with their vast surplus of "petrodollars" seemed at first to open up important new possibilities for intra—Third World development assistance. Unfortunately, a combination of mounting political conflicts among member states and unexpected balance of payments deficits due to falling oil prices led to a reversal of OPEC's aid growth in the early 1980s. We explore the declining significance of OPEC's aid at the end of the chapter.

PRIVATE FOREIGN INVESTMENT AND THE MULTINATIONAL CORPORATION

Few developments have played as critical a role in the extraordinary growth of international trade and capital flows during the past two decades as the rise of the multinational corporation (MNC). These huge business firms from North America, Europe, and Japan present a unique opportunity and a host of serious problems for the many developing countries in which they conduct their business.

The growth of private foreign investment in the Third World has been extremely rapid. It has risen from an annual rate of $2.4 billion in 1962 to over $11 billion by 1981. Multinationals based in the United States provided almost half of the total flow during the 1970s, with the United Kingdom, Japan, and West Germany making up most of the balance. Major recipients were concentrated among the higher-income LDCs such as Brazil, Mexico, Argentina, Indonesia, and Hong Kong, although the country spread of MNC investments widened considerably during the last decade. But direct foreign investment involves much more than the simple transfer of capital or the establishment of a local factory in a developing nation. Multinationals carry with them technologies of production, tastes and styles of living, managerial services, and diverse business practices including cooperative arrangements, marketing restrictions, advertising, and the phenomenon of "transfer pricing," to be discussed shortly. They engage in a range of activities, many of which have little to do with the development aspirations of the countries in which they operate. But before analyzing some of the arguments for and against private foreign investment in general and multinational corporations in particular, let us examine the character of these enterprises.[1]

MULTINATIONAL CORPORATIONS: SIZE, PATTERNS, and TRENDS

Two central characteristics of multinational corporations are their large size and the fact that their worldwide operations and activities tend to be centrally controlled by parent companies. Many MNCs have annual sales volumes in excess of the entire GNPs of the developing nations in which they operate. Table 14.1 shows, for example, that in 1980 the 3 largest multinationals (Exxon, Royal Dutch/Shell, and Mobil) had a gross sales

Table 14.1   Ranking of Countries and Multinational Corporations According to Size of
Annual Product, 1980

Rank	Economic entity	Product ($ billion)	Rank	Economic entity	Product ($ billion)
1	United States	2,639.1	32	Venezuela	58.4
2	USSR	1,208.0	33	*General Motors*	57.7
3	Japan	1,053.9	34	South Korea	56.9
4	West Germany	758.5	35	Yugoslavia	56.6
5	France	601.5	36	Norway	52.2
6	United Kingdom	476.9	37	*Texaco*	51.2
7	Italy	359.2	38	Rumania	50.9
8	China	267.8	39	*British Petroleum*	48.1
9	Brazil	255.1	40	Finland	46.3
10	Canada	243.8	41	*Standard Oil of California*	40.5
11	Spain	195.7	42	Greece	39.9
12	Netherlands	155.7	43	Bulgaria	37.3
13	India	153.3	44	*ENI*	37.2
14	Australia	147.1	45	*Ford Motor*	37.1
15	Poland	139.6	46	Colombia	32.5
16	Mexico	137.6	47	Thailand	31.6
17	East Germany	121.3	48	*Gulf Oil*	28.4
18	Sweden	114.3	49	*Standard Oil (Indiana)*	27.8
19	*Exxon*	110.4	50	*IBM*	26.2
20	Belgium	109.6	51	*General Electric*	25.5
21	Switzerland	101.4	52	Pakistan	25.5
22	Czechoslovakia	89.0	53	*Atlantic Richfield*	24.5
23	*Royal Dutch/Shell*	77.3	54	*Fiat*	24.2
24	Nigeria	73.5	55	*Unilever (GBR)*	24.1
25	Argentina	71.8	56	*Compagnie Française des Petroles*	23.9
26	South Africa	71.6	57	*ITT*	23.8
27	Austria	70.6	58	*VEBA*	23.1
28	Indonesia	66.3	59	Portugal	22.4
29	*Mobil Oil*	63.7	60	Hungary	20.6
30	Turkey	61.6	61	*Petroles de Venezuela*	19.7
31	Denmark	61.5	62	All other developing countries: less than	19.7

SOURCE: Gross national product figures from the *World Bank Atlas* (Washington, D.C.: World Bank, 1983). Corporate sales figures from United Nations, Department of Economic and Social Affairs, *Transnational Corporations in World Development: Third Survey* (New York: United Nations, 1983) Annex Table II.31; and *World Development Report 1980*.

value greater than the GNPs of all but 7 developing nations (China, Brazil, India, Mexico, Nigeria, Argentina, and Indonesia). By 1983 the 20 largest MNCs had annual sales volumes in excess of $20 billion, while more than 200 others had sales in excess of $12 billion. As the table shows the largest U.S. multinationals, like Exxon, Mobil, General Motors, and Texaco, each sold over $50 billion worth of their products in 1980, and Standard Oil of

Indiana and Ford each had annual sales well in excess of $35 billion. The combined sales of these 6 MNCs alone exceeded the GNPs of many *developed* nations including Australia, Canada, Belgium, Sweden, and Switzerland. In fact, the largest multinational, Exxon, had total revenues in 1980 in excess of $110 billion, thus by itself surpassing the entire gross national products of countries like Norway, Belgium, and Switzerland!

Such enormous size confers great economic (and sometimes political) power on MNCs vis-à-vis the countries in which they operate. This power is greatly strengthened by their predominantly "oligopolistic" market positions; that is, by the fact that they tend to operate in product markets dominated by a few sellers and buyers. This situation gives them the ability to manipulate prices and profits, to collude with other firms in determining areas of control, and in general to restrict the entry of potential competition by means of their dominating influences over new technologies, special skills, and, through product differentiation and advertising, consumer tastes.

The largest MNCs have many foreign branches and overseas affiliates. Nearly 200 have subsidiaries in 20 or more countries. Of the 10 largest MNCs, 8 are based in the United States, and U.S. firms exercise control over about 30% of all foreign affiliates. British, German, French, and U.S. firms together control over 75% of all MNC affiliates. Latest estimates put the book value of total MNC foreign investment in excess of $220 billion, with over 80% of that total owned by firms in these four countries and Japan. Of this total, approximately one-third is located in developing countries. But, given their small size, the LDCs feel the presence of multinational corporations more acutely than do the developed countries.

Historically, multinational corporations, especially those operating in developing nations, focused on extractive and primary industries, mainly petroleum, nonfuel minerals, and plantation activities where a few "agribusiness" MNCs became involved in export-oriented agriculture and local food processing. Recently, however, manufacturing interests have occupied an increasing share of MNC production activities. At present, manufacturing accounts for almost 28% of the estimated stock of foreign direct investment in LDCs while petroleum and mining represent 40 and 9% respectively. And the overall importance of MNCs in the economies of Third World nations, especially in the manufacturing and service sectors, is rapidly growing. In the 1970s, MNC private direct investments represented about 16% of the total flow of resources to LDCs. Moreover, this flow increased at an annual average rate of 9% during the 1960s and 1970s. Thus, the stock of foreign private investment increased faster than the GNPs of most poor countries during the past two decades.

Given this brief sketch of the size and importance of multinational corporations, we can now discuss some of the arguments for and against their activities in the context of the development aspirations of Third World nations.

Private Foreign Investment: Some Pros and Cons for Development

Few areas in the economics of development arouse so much controversy and are subject to such varying interpretations as the issue of the benefits and costs of private foreign investment. If, however, we look closely at this controversy, we will find that the disagreement is not so much about the influence of MNCs on traditional economic aggregates such as GNP, investment, savings, and manufacturing growth rates (though these disagreements do indeed exist) as about the fundamental economic and social meaning of development as it relates to the diverse activities of MNCs. In other words, the controversy over the role and impact of foreign private investment in Third World economies often has as its underlying, though usually unstated, basis a fundamental disagreement about the nature, style, and character of a desirable development process. The basic arguments for and against the developmental impact of private foreign investment in the context of the type of development it tends to foster can be summarized as follows.

Traditional Economic Arguments in Support of Private Investment: Filling Gaps

The pro-foreign-investment arguments grow largely out of the traditional neoclassical analysis of the determinants of economic growth. Foreign private investment (as well as foreign aid) is typically seen as a way of filling in gaps between the domestically available supplies of savings, foreign exchange, government revenue, and skills and the planned level of these resources necessary to achieve development targets. For a simple example of the "savings–investment gap" analysis, recall that the basic Harrod–Domar growth model postulates a direct relationship between a country's rate of savings, s, and its rate of output growth, g, via the equation $g = s/k$ where k is the national capital–output ratio. If the planned rate of national output growth, g, is targeted at 7% annually and the capital–output ratio is 3, then the needed rate of annual saving is 21% (since $s = g \times k$). If the saving that can be domestically mobilized amounts to only, say, 16% of GNP, then a "savings gap" equal to 5% can be said to exist. If the nation can fill this gap with foreign financial resources (either private or public), it will better be able to achieve its target rate of growth.

Therefore, the first and most often cited contribution of private foreign investment to national development (i.e., when this development is defined in terms of GNP growth rates—an important implicit conceptual assumption) is its role in filling the resource gap between targeted or desired investment and locally mobilized savings.

A second contribution, analogous to the first, is its contribution to filling the gap between targeted foreign exchange requirements and those derived from net export earnings plus net public foreign aid. This is the so-called foreign exchange or trade gap. ("Two-gap" models are discussed more fully in the context of foreign aid later in the chapter.) An inflow of private foreign capital can not only alleviate part or all of the deficit on the balance of payments current account but it can also function to remove that deficit over time *if* the foreign-owned enterprise can generate a net positive flow of export earnings. Unfortunately, as we discovered in the case of import substitution, the overall effect of permitting MNCs to establish subsidiaries behind protective tariff and quota walls is often a net *worsening* of both the current and capital account balances. Such deficits usually result both from the importation of capital equipment and intermediate products (normally from an overseas affiliate and often at inflated prices) and the outflow of foreign exchange in the form of repatriated profits, management fees, royalty payments, and interest on private loans.

The third gap said to be filled by foreign investment is the gap between targeted governmental tax revenues and locally raised taxes. By taxing MNC profits and participating financially in their local operations, LDC governments are thought to be better able to mobilize public financial resources for development projects.

Fourth and finally there is the gap in management, entrepreneurship, technology, and skill presumed to be partially or wholly filled by the local operations of private foreign firms. Multinationals not only provide financial resources and new factories to poor countries, they also supply a "package" of needed resources including management experience, entrepreneurial abilities, and technological skills which can then be transferred to their local counterparts by means of training programs and the process of "learning by doing." Moreover, according to this argument, MNCs can educate local managers about how to establish contacts with overseas banks, locate alternative sources of supply, diversify market outlets, and, in general, become better acquainted with international marketing practices. Finally, MNCs bring with them the most sophisticated technological knowledge about production processes while transferring modern machinery and equipment to capital-poor Third World countries. Such transfers of knowledge, skills, and technology are assumed to be both desirable and productive for the recipient nations.

Arguments against Private Foreign Investment: Widening Gaps

There are two basic arguments against private foreign investment in general and the activities of MNCs in particular—the strictly economic and the more philosophical or ideological.

On the economic side, the four gap-filling pro-foreign-investment positions outlined above are countered by the following arguments:

1. Although MNCs provide capital, they may lower domestic savings and investment rates by stifling competition through exclusive production agreements with host governments, failing to reinvest much of their profits, generating domestic incomes for those groups with lower savings propensities, inhibiting the expansion of indigenous firms that might supply them with intermediate products by instead importing these goods from overseas affiliates, and imposing high interest costs on capital borrowed by host governments.
2. Although the initial impact of MNC investment is to improve the foreign exchange position of the recipient nation, its long-run impact may be to reduce foreign exchange earnings on both current and capital accounts. The current account may deteriorate as a result of substantial importation of intermediate products and capital goods while the capital account may worsen because of the overseas repatriation of profits, interest, royalties, management fees, etc.
3. While MNCs do contribute to public revenue in the form of corporate taxes, their contribution is considerably less than it should be as a result of liberal tax concessions, excessive investment allowances, disguised public subsidies, and tariff protection provided by the host government.
4. The management, entrepreneurial skills, technology, and overseas contacts provided by MNCs may have little impact on developing local sources of these scarce skills and resources and may in fact inhibit their development by stifling the growth of indigenous entrepreneurship as a result of the MNCs' dominance of local markets.

But the really significant criticism of MNCs is usually conducted on more fundamental levels than those briefly outlined above. In particular, Third World countries have commonly raised the following objections:[2]

1. Their impact on development is very uneven, and in many situations MNC activities reinforce dualistic economic structures and exacerbate income inequalities. They tend to promote the interests of the small number of well-paid modern sector workers against the interests of the rest by widening wage differentials. They divert resources away from needed food production to the manufacture of sophisticated products catering primarily to the demands of local elites. And they tend to worsen the imbalance between rural and urban economic opportunities by locating primarily in urban areas and contributing to the accelerated flow of rural–urban migration.

2. Multinationals typically produce inappropriate products (those demanded by a small rich minority of the local population), stimulate inappropriate consumption patterns through advertising and their monopolistic market power, and do this all with inappropriate (capital-intensive) technologies of production. This is perhaps the major area of criticism of MNCs.

3. As a result of (1) and (2), local resources tend to be allocated for socially undesirable projects. This in turn tends to aggravate the already sizable inequality between rich and poor and the serious imbalance between urban and rural economic opportunities.

4. Multinationals use their economic power to influence government policies in directions unfavorable to development. They are able to extract sizable economic and political concessions from competing LDC governments in the form of excessive protection, tax rebates, investment allowances, and the cheap provision of factory sites and essential social services. As a result, the private profits of MNCs may exceed social benefits. In some cases, these social returns to host countries may even be negative! Alternatively, a MNC can avoid much local taxation by artificially inflating the price it pays for intermediate products purchased from overseas affiliates so as to lower its stated local profits. This phenomenon, known as "transfer pricing," is a major practice of MNCs and one over which host governments can exert little control so long as corporate tax rates differ from one country to the next.

5. Multinationals may damage host economies by suppressing domestic entrepreneurship and using their superior knowledge, worldwide contacts, advertising skills, and range of essential support services to drive out local competitors and inhibit the emergence of small-scale local enterprises.

6. Finally, at the political level, the fear is often expressed that powerful multinational corporations can gain control over local assets and jobs and can then exert considerable influence on political decisions at all levels. In extreme cases, they may even, either directly by payoffs to corrupt public officials at the highest levels or indirectly by contributions to "friendly" political parties, subvert the very political process of host nations (e.g., the ITT experience in Chile).

Reconciling the Pros and Cons

While the above lists provide a range of conflicting arguments, the real debate ultimately centers on different ideological and value judgments about the nature and meaning of economic development and the principal sources from which it springs. The advocates of private foreign investment tend to be "free market, private enterprise, laissez-faire" proponents who firmly believe in the efficacy and beneficence of the free market mechanism, where this is usually defined as a hands-off policy on the part of host governments. As we have seen, however, the actual operations of MNCs tend to be monopolistic and oligopolistic. Price setting is achieved more as a result of international bargaining and collusion than as a natural outgrowth of free market supply and demand.

Those who argue against the activities of MNCs are often motivated more by a sense of the importance of national control over domestic economic activities and the minimization of dominance/dependence relationships between powerful MNCs and Third World governments. They see these giant corporations not as needed agents of economic change but more as vehicles of antidevelopment. Multinationals, they argue, reinforce dualistic economic structures and exacerbate domestic inequalities with their wrong products and inappropriate technologies. Some opponents, therefore, call for the outright confiscation (without compensation) or the nationalization (with some compensation) of foreign-owned enterprises.[3] Others advocate a more stringent regulation of foreign investments, a tougher bargaining stance on the part of host governments, a willingness on the part of LDCs to "shop around" for better deals, the adoption of performance standards and requirements, increased domestic ownership and control, and finally, a greater coordination of LDC strategies with respect to terms and conditions of foreign investment. One example of such coordinated strategies was the decision by the Andean Group in Latin America to require foreign investors to reduce their ownership in local enterprises to minority shares over a 15-year period. Tanzania adopted a similar policy of securing a controlling share of foreign enterprises, in line with its Arusha Declaration of 1967 on socialism and self-reliance. As might be expected, the annual flow of private foreign investment declined as a result of both of these more stringent conditions.

In view of the strong anti-MNC sentiment being aired in the capitals of many Third World nations (as, indeed, in the developed countries as well) and the "demonstration effect" of the power of OPEC nations to gain increasing control over foreign oil companies, it appears that the phenomenal growth of MNC influence in less developed countries during the past three decades may not be matched in the 1980s. The arguments both for and against private foreign investment have a certain empirical validity while reflecting important differences in value judgments. Perhaps the only really valid conclusion is that private foreign investment can be an important stimulus to economic and social development so long as the interests of MNCs and host country governments coincide (assuming, of course, that they don't coincide along the lines of dualistic development and widening inequalities). As long as MNCs see their role in terms of global output or profit maximization with little interest in the long-run domestic impact of their activities, the accusations of the anti-private-investment school of thought will gain increasing Third World acceptance. Perhaps there can be no real congruence of interest between the profit maximizing objectives of MNCs and the development priorities of LDC governments. On the other hand, a strengthening of the relative bargaining powers of host country governments through their coordinated activities, while probably reducing the overall magnitude and growth of private foreign investment, may make that investment better fit the long-run development needs and priorities of poor nations. Alternatively, it might be useful to explore some form of domestic and international guarantees of minimal rates of return financed, for example, by donor agency and local government contributions. Such guarantees would provide the necessary risk reduction to induce MNCs to adopt a longer-run perspective with particular emphasis on adapting their existing technologies of production to the resource needs of developing nations. The net social benefit of this tradeoff between quantity and relevance would probably have a positive impact on national development. Whatever the outcome, it certainly will be interesting and instructive to see what happens to the magnitude, direction, and nature of private foreign investment and the role of MNCs during the last half of the 1980s.

FOREIGN AID: THE DEVELOPMENT ASSISTANCE DEBATE

Conceptual and Measurement Problems

In addition to export earnings and private foreign direct and financial investment, the final major source of Third World foreign exchange is public bilateral and multilateral development assistance, known also as foreign aid.

In principle, all real resource transfers from one country to another (mostly from developed to less developed nations but increasingly in the 1970s from OPEC to other Third World countries) should be included in the definition of foreign aid. Even this simple definition, however, raises a number of problems:[4]

1. Many resource transfers can take disguised forms such as the granting of preferential tariffs by developed countries to Third World exports of manufactured goods. This permits LDCs to sell their industrial products in developed country markets at higher prices than would otherwise be possible. There is consequently a net gain for LDCs and a net loss for developed countries which amounts to a real resource transfer to the LDCs. Such implicit capital transfers, or "disguised flows," should be counted in quantifying foreign aid flows. Normally, however, they are not.
2. On the other hand, we should not include *all* transfers of capital to LDCs, particularly the capital flows of private foreign investors. For a number of years aid was calculated as the sum of official and private capital flows, although now these two items are listed separately (see Table 14.2). Private flows represent normal commercial transactions, are prompted by commercial considerations of profits and rates of return, and therefore should not be viewed as aid any more than LDC exports to developed countries should be viewed as aid to the LDCs. Commercial flows of private capital are *not* a form of foreign assistance, even though they may benefit the developing country in which they take place.

Economists have defined foreign aid, therefore, as any flow of capital to LDCs that meets two criteria: (a) its objective should be noncommercial from the point of view of the donor; and (b) it should be characterized by "concessional" terms, that is, the interest rate and repayment period for borrowed capital should be "softer" (less stringent) than commercial terms.[5] Even this definition can sometimes be inappropriate since it could include military aid, which is both noncommercial and concessional. Normally, however, military aid is excluded from international measurements of foreign aid flows. The concept of foreign aid that is now widely used and accepted, therefore, is one that encompasses all official grants and concessional loans, in currency or in kind, that are broadly aimed at transferring resources from developed to less developed nations (and, more recently, from OPEC to other Third World countries) on development and/or income

Table 14.2 Net Flow of Resources from Development Assistance Committee* Countries to Developing Countries and Multilateral Institutions,† 1965–1967, 1970, 1975, 1980, 1981 ($ millions)

	1965–1967 Average	1970	1975	1980	1981
Official	*6,533.1*	*7,929.2*	*16,608.7*	*32,536.1*	*32,242.6*
Official Development Assistance (ODA)	6,118.0	6,790.5	13,585.1	27,264.3	25,635.2
Bilateral	5,642.6	5,666.7	9,815.3	18,108.0	18,282.7
Grants and grantlike contributions	3,656.2	3,309.2	6,268.0	14,123.5	13,184.3
Development lending and capital	1,986.3	2,357.4	3,547.1	3,984.5	5,098.4
Contributions to multilateral institutions	475.4	1,123.8	3,769.6	9,156.3	7,352.5
Grants	240.8	551.7	2,028.7	4,159.1	4,031.1
Capital subscription payments	223.7	540.6	1,731.6	4,959.1	3,289.3
Concessional lending	10.9	31.5	9.3	38.1	32.1
Other official flows	415.1	1,138.7	3,023.6	5,271.7	6,607.4
Private, at market terms	*4,134.8*	*6,875.1*	*22,427.6*	*40,430.0*	*53,779.7*
Private investment and lending	3,174.0	4,733.2	18,285.6	28,940.5	43,186.6
Private export credits	960.8	2,141.9	4,141.9	11,489.5	10,593.1
Grants by private voluntary agencies	*n/a*	*857.5*	*1,341.8*	*2,386.3*	*2,017.6*
Total	*10,667.9*	*15,661.8*	*40,378.1*	*75,352.4*	*88,039.8*
(as % of GNP)	0.74	0.78	1.05	1.04	1.21

*A specialized committee of developed countries that monitors development assistance levels and policies. Consists of Australia, Austria, Belgium, Canada, Denmark, Finland, France, the Federal Republic of Germany, Italy, Japan, the Netherlands, New Zealand, Norway, Sweden, Switzerland, the United Kingdom, and the United States (see Table 14.3).

†International development banks like the World Bank and regional development banks like those in Africa, Asia, and Latin America as well as U.N. organizations like the United Nations Development Program (UNDP) and the United Nations Fund for Population Activities (UNFPA).

SOURCE: Based on data from Report by the Chairman of the Development Assistance Committee, *Development Co-operation, 1982 Review* (Paris: OECD, 1982), pp. 204–206.

distributional grounds. Unfortunately, there often is a thin line separating purely "developmental" grants and loans from those ultimately motivated by security and/or commercial interests.

The money volume of "official development assistance," which includes bilateral grants, loans, and technical assistance as well as multilateral flows, has grown from about an annual rate of $4.6 billion in 1960 to $28 billion in 1982. However, in terms of the percentage of developed country GNPs allocated to official development assistance, there has been a steady decline from 0.51% in 1960 to 0.3% in 1983.[6] The United States is still the major supplier of public aid to Third World nations, but its proportion of total development assistance has declined from 59% in 1960 to approximately 24% in 1983. Tables 14.2 and 14.3 provide recent data on the flow of public and private funds from the developed market economies to the developing world, while Table 14.4 provides information on official assistance from the USSR, Eastern Europe, and China from 1970 to 1976. Finally, Table 14.5 shows the flow of development assistance from international donor organizations to developing countries from 1970 to 1981.

But just as there are conceptual problems associated with the definition of foreign aid, so too there are measurement and conceptual problems in the calculation of actual development assistance flows. In particular, three major problems arise in measuring aid:

First, one cannot simply add together the dollar values of grants and loans since each has a different significance to both aid-giving and aid-receiving countries. Loans must be repaid and, therefore, "cost" the donor and "benefit" the recipient less than the "nominal" value of the loan itself. Conceptually, one should deflate or discount the dollar value of interest-bearing loans before adding them to the value of outright grants.

Second, aid can be "tied" either by *source* (i.e., loans and/or grants have to be spent on the purchase of donor country goods or services) or by *project* (funds can only be used for a specific project—e.g., a road or a steel mill). In either case the real value of the aid is reduced because the specified source is likely to be an expensive supplier or the project is not of the highest priority (otherwise, there would be no need to tie the aid). Additionally, aid may be tied to the importation of capital-intensive equipment, which may impose an additional real resource cost—in the form of higher unemployment—on the recipient nation. Or the project itself may require purchase of new machinery and equipment from monopolistic suppliers while existing productive equipment in the same industry is being operated at very low levels of capacity.

Finally, we always need to distinguish between the "nominal" and "real" value of foreign assistance, especially during periods of rapid inflation. Aid flows are usually calculated at nominal levels and tend to show a steady rise over time. However, when deflated for rising prices, the actual real volume of aid from most donor countries has declined substantially during the last decade. For example, during the period 1960–1980 the nominal outflow of foreign aid from the United States increased by 66% while the real value actually declined by over 24%.

Quite apart from these measurement difficulties, quoting statistics on the volume, direction, and trends in development assistance is of little relevance without an understanding of the ultimate objectives of foreign aid

Table 14.3 Official Development Assistance from Development Assistance Committee Countries as a Percentage of GNP, 1960, 1970, 1976–1983

	1960	1970	1976	1977	1978	1979	1980	1981	1982	1983*
Australia	.37	.59	.42	.42	.55	.53	.48	.41	.57	.49
Austria	—	.07	.12	.22	.27	.19	.23	.48	.54	.23
Belgium	.88	.46	.51	.46	.55	.57	.50	.59	.59	.59
Canada	.19	.41	.46	.50	.52	.48	.43	.43	.42	.47
Denmark	.09	.38	.56	.60	.75	.77	.74	.73	.77	.73
France	1.35	.66	.62	.60	.57	.60	.64	.73	.74	.76
Germany	.31	.32	.31	.33	.37	.45	.44	.47	.48	.48
Italy	.22	.16	.13	.10	.14	.08	.17	.19	.24	.24
Japan	.24	.23	.20	.21	.23	.27	.32	.28	.29	.33
Netherlands	.31	.61	.82	.86	.82	.98	1.03	1.08	1.08	.91
New Zealand	—	.23	.41	.39	.34	.33	.33	.29	.28	.28
Norway	.11	.32	.70	.83	.90	.93	.85	.82	1.01	1.10
Portugal	1.45	.67	—	—	—	—	—	—	—	—
Sweden	.05	.38	.82	.99	.90	.97	.79	.83	1.02	.88
Switzerland	.04	.15	.19	.19	.20	.21	.24	.24	.25	.31
United Kingdom	.56	.41	.38	.45	.46	.52	.35	.44	.38	.36
United States	.53	.32	.25	.25	.27	.20	.27	.20	.27	.24
DAC Totals										
ODA ($ billion) nominal prices	4.6	7.0	14.6	15.7	20.0	22.8	27.3	25.6	28.0	27.5
ODA as % of GNP	.51	.34	.34	.33	.35	.35	.38	.35	.39	.37
ODA ($ billion) constant 1980 prices	16.4	18.2	21.8	21.9	24.1	24.9	27.3	25.8	28.4	27.4
GNP ($ trillion) nominal prices	.9	2.0	4.2	4.7	5.7	6.5	7.2	7.3	7.2	7.5
ODA deflator	.28	.38	.68	.72	.83	.92	1.00	.99	.98	1.01

*Estimated.

Source: *World Development Report, 1984,* Annex Table 18.

Table 14.4   Economic Aid from USSR, Eastern Europe, and China
to Developing Countries: Gross Commitments, 1970–1981 ($ millions)

	1970	**1972**	**1975**	**1981**
Donors				
USSR	194	581	1,299	2,096
Eastern Europe	188	655	422	640
People's Republic of China	709	499	273	n/a
Total	1,091	1,735	1,994	2,736
Recipients				
Africa	589	419	444	n/a
Asia	395	940	1,308	n/a
Middle East	—	—	25	n/a
Latin America	107	331	217	n/a
Total	1,091	1,690	1,994	—

SOURCE: U.S. Department of State, Bureau of Intelligence and Research, "Communist states and developing countries: Aid and trade in 1973," Research Study INR RS-20 (October 1974). Based on data from U.S. Central Intelligence Agency, *Communist Aid to the Less Developed Countries of the Free World, 1976,* Docket No. ER77-10296 (August 1977), and *International Policy Report* 11, no. 1 (April 1976). Published by the Institute for International Policy, Washington, D.C., and OECD as *Development Cooperation: 1982 Review,* p. 162.

and its role and/or limitations in promoting economic and social development. But this presents difficulties. For the actual definition of aid and the meaning and motives attached to it may vary from donor country to donor country and from one multilateral development assistance agency to another. More important, there are likely to be fundamental differences in attitudes and motivations between donor and recipient countries. "Aid" is thus a complex and confusing term, especially when it is used to cover a variety of resource transfers from one country to another. Many of these, as we have seen, may be military and/or political in nature and have nothing to do with assisting economic development.

Because foreign aid is seen differently by donor and recipient countries, we must first analyze the giving and receiving process from these two often contradictory viewpoints. One of the major criticisms of the literature on foreign aid is that it has concentrated almost exclusively on the motives and objectives of donor countries while devoting little attention to why LDCs accept aid and what they believe it will accomplish. After examining the aid question from both perspectives, we will summarize the conflicting views of the effects of traditional aid relationships over the past two decades, look at the aid role of OPEC oil nations, and conclude the chapter with an analysis of how development assistance can be made more effective.

Why Donors Give Aid

Donor countries give aid primarily because it is in their political, strategic, and/or economic self-interest to do so. While some development assistance

Table 14.5 Net Flow of Resources from Multilateral Institutions to Developing Countries, 1970, 1976, 1980, and 1981 ($ millions)

	Concessional				Total			
	1970	**1976**	**1980**	**1981**	**1970**	**1976**	**1980**	**1981**
World Bank group	163	1,326	1,650	2,006	671	3,050	4,816	5,609
International Development Association (IDA)	163	1,310	1,543	1,918	163	1,310	1,543	1,918
United Nations	498	1,252	2,487	n/a	498	1,252	2,487	n/a
Regional banks	225	369	614	n/a	326	936	1,619	n/a
Inter-American Development Bank (IDB)	224	282	326	438	308	567	893	1,081
Asian Development Bank	1	62	149	n/a	16	294	477	n/a
African Development Bank	—	11	96	91	2	55	193	161
Caribbean Development Bank	—	14	43	n/a	—	20	56	n/a
European communities (EC)	210	501	1,013	1,440	221	559	1,270	1,681
OPEC and Arab institutions	—	419	294	415	—	419	422	680
Total	1,096	3,867	6,058	n/a	1,716	6,216	10,614	n/a

SOURCE: Report by the Chairman of the Development Assistance Committee, *Development Co-operation, 1982 Review* (Paris: OECD, 1982).

may be motivated by moral and humanitarian desires to assist the less fortunate (e.g., emergency food relief programs), there is no historical evidence to suggest that over longer periods of time donor nations assist others without expecting some corresponding benefits (political, economic, military, etc.) in return. We can therefore characterize the foreign aid motivations of donor nations into two broad, but often interrelated, categories: political and economic.

Political Motivations

Political motivations have been by far the most important for aid-granting nations, especially for the major donor country, the United States. The United States has viewed foreign aid from its beginnings in the late 1940s under the Marshall Plan, which aimed at reconstructing the war-torn economies of Western Europe, as a means of containing the international spread of Communism. When the balance of cold war interests shifted from Europe to the Third World in the mid-1950s, the policy of containment embodied in the U.S. aid program dictated a shift in emphasis toward political, economic, and military support for "friendly" less developed nations, especially those considered geographically strategic. Most aid programs to developing countries were therefore oriented more toward purchasing their security and propping up their sometimes shaky regimes than promoting long-term social and economic development. The successive shifts in emphasis from South Asia to Southeast Asia, to Latin America, to the Middle East, and back to Southeast Asia during the 1950s and 1960s, and then toward Africa and the Persian Gulf in the late 1970s and the Caribbean and Central America in the 1980s reflect changes in U.S. strategic and political interests more than changing evaluations of economic need.

Even the Alliance for Progress, inaugurated in the early 1960s with such fanfare and noble rhetoric about promoting Latin American economic development, was in reality formulated primarily as a direct response to the rise of Fidel Castro in Cuba and the perceived threat of Communist takeovers in other Latin American countries. As soon as the security issue lost its urgency and other more pressing problems came to the fore (the war in Vietnam, the growing dollar crisis, the rise in U.S. domestic violence, etc.), the Alliance for Progress stagnated and began to fizzle out. Our point is simply that where aid is seen primarily as a means of furthering donor country interests, the flow of funds tends to vary in accordance with the donor's political assessment of changing international situations and not the relative need of different potential recipients.

The experience of other major Western donor countries like Great Britain and France has been similar to that of the United States. Although exceptions can be cited (e.g., Sweden, Norway, perhaps Canada), by and large these Western donor countries have utilized foreign aid as a political lever to prop up or underpin "friendly" political regimes in Third World countries, regimes whose continued existence they perceived as being in their "national security" interests. Most socialist aid, especially that of the Soviet Union, grew out of essentially the same political and strategic motivations, although its form and content may have been somewhat different. Soviet aid programs to Cuba, Angola, and Syria provide obvious examples.

Economic Motivations: Two-Gap Models and Other Criteria

Within the broad context of political and strategic priorities, foreign aid programs of the developed nations have had a strong economic rationale. In fact, while the political motivation may have been of paramount importance, the economic rationale was at least given greater lip service as the overriding motivation for assistance.

The principal economic arguments advanced in support of foreign aid are as follows:

Foreign Exchange Constraints. External finance (both loans and grants) can play a critical role in supplementing domestic resources in order to relieve savings or foreign exchange bottlenecks. This is the familiar "two-gap" analysis of foreign assistance mentioned briefly in the previous section on private investment.[7]

The basic argument of the two-gap model is that most developing countries are faced either with a shortage of domestic savings to match investment opportunities or a shortage of foreign exchange to finance needed imports of capital and intermediate goods. Most two-gap models assume that the savings (domestic real resources) and foreign exchange gaps are unequal in magnitude and that they are mutually independent; that is, there is no substitutability between savings and foreign exchange. (This assumption is obviously unreal but it greatly facilitates the mathematical analysis.)

The implication that follows is that one of the two gaps will be "binding" or "dominant" for any LDC at a given point in time. If, for example, the savings gap is dominant, this would indicate that the country is operating at full employment and is not using all of its foreign exchange earnings. It may have enough foreign exchange to purchase additional capital goods from abroad, but there is not enough excess domestic labor or other productive resources to carry out additional investment projects. The importation of such capital goods would only redirect domestic resources from other activities and probably lead to inflation. As a result, "excess" foreign exchange, including foreign aid, might be spent on the importation of luxury consumption goods. Such a country is said to have a shortage of "productive resources" which, from a different viewpoint, can be regarded as a shortage in saving. An outstanding example of "savings gap" nations would be the Arab oil states during the 1970s. Note, however, that the savings gap analysis overlooks the possibility that excess foreign exchange *can* be used to purchase productive resources—for example, Saudi Arabia and Kuwait used their surplus petrodollars to pay for hired labor from non-oil-exporting countries in the region and overseas. Savings gap countries therefore do not need foreign aid.

Most developing countries, however, are assumed to fall into the second category where the foreign exchange gap is binding. These countries have excess productive resources (mostly labor) and all available foreign exchange is being used for imports. The existence of complementary domestic resources would permit them to undertake new investment projects if they had the external finance to import new capital goods and associated technical assistance. Foreign aid can therefore play a critical role in overcoming the foreign exchange constraint and raising the real rate of economic growth.

Algebraically, the simple two-gap model can be formulated as follows:

1. *The savings constraint or gap.* Starting with the identity that capital inflows (i.e., the difference between imports and exports) add to investible resources (i.e., domestic savings), the savings–investment restriction can be written as

$$I \leqslant F + sY \tag{1}$$

where F is the amount of capital inflows. If F plus sY exceeds I and the economy is at full capacity, a savings gap is said to exist.

2. *The foreign exchange constraint or gap.* If LDC investment has a marginal import share m_1 (typically ranging from 30 to 60% in most LDCs) and the marginal propensity to import out of a unit of GNP (usually around 10–15%) is given by the parameter m_2 then the foreign exchange constraint or gap can be written as

$$m_1 I + m_2 Y - E \leqslant F \tag{2}$$

where E is the exogenous level of exports.

The term F enters both inequality constraints and becomes the critical factor in the analysis. If F, E, and Y are initially assigned an exogenous current value, only one of the above two inequalities will prove binding; that is, investment (and therefore the output growth rate) will be constrained to a lower level by one of the inequalities. Countries can therefore be classified according to whether the savings or foreign exchange constraint is binding. More important from the viewpoint of foreign aid analysis is the observation that the impact of increased capital inflows will be greater where the foreign exchange gap—Equation (2)—rather than the savings gap—Equation (1)—is binding. But this does not imply that savings gap countries do not need foreign aid! Two-gap models simply provide a crude methodology for determining the relative need and ability of different LDCs to use foreign aid effectively.

The problem is that such gap forecasts are very mechanistic and are themselves constrained by the necessity of fixing import parameters and assigning exogenous values to exports and net capital inflows. In the case of exports, this is particularly constricting since a liberalization of trade relations between the developed and the developing world would contribute more toward relieving foreign exchange gaps than foreign aid. Although E and F are substitutable in Equation (2), they can have quite different indirect effects, especially in the case where F represents interest-bearing loans that need to be repaid. Thus, the alteration of import and export parameters through both LDC and developed country government policy can in reality determine whether the savings or foreign exchange constraint is restricting the further growth of national output (or, in fact, whether neither is binding).

Growth and Savings. External assistance also is assumed to facilitate and accelerate the process of development by generating additional domestic savings as a result of the higher growth rates which it is presumed to induce. Eventually, it is hoped, the need for concessional aid will disappear as local resources become sufficient to give the development process a self-sustaining character.

Technical Assistance. Financial assistance needs to be supplemented by "technical assistance" in the form of high-level manpower transfers to assure that aid funds are most efficiently utilized to generate economic growth. This "manpower"-gap-filling process is thus analogous to the financial-gap-filling process mentioned earlier.

Absorptive Capacity. Finally, the amount of aid should be determined by the recipient country's "absorptive capacity," a euphemism for its ability to use aid funds wisely and productively (often, the way donors want them to be used). Typically, the donor countries decide which LDCs are to receive aid, how much, in what form (i.e., loans or grants, financial and/or technical assistance), for what purposes, and under what conditions on the basis of their (i.e., the developed countries') assessment of LDC absorptive capacities. But the total amount of aid rarely has anything to do with Third World absorptive capacities; typically, foreign aid is a residual and low-priority element in donor-country expenditure. In most instances, the recipient countries have had little say in the matter.

Economic Motivations and Self-Interest

The above arguments on behalf of foreign aid as a crucial ingredient for LDC development should not mask the fact that even at the strictly economic level, definite benefits accrue to donor countries as a result of their aid programs. The increasing tendency toward providing loans instead of outright grants (interest-bearing loans now constitute over 70% of all aid compared to less than 40% in earlier periods) and toward tying aid to the exports of donor countries has saddled many LDCs with substantial debt repayment burdens. It has also increased their import costs often by as much as 40%. These extra import costs arise because aid tied to donor country exports limits the receiving nation's freedom to shop around for low-cost and suitable capital and intermediate goods. Tied aid in this sense is clearly a "second best" option to untied aid (and perhaps also to freer trade through a reduction of developed country import barriers). As one former U.S. aid official candidly put it:

> The biggest single misconception about the foreign aid program is that we send money abroad. We don't. Foreign aid consists of American equipment, raw materials, expert services, and food—all provided for specific development projects which we ourselves review and approve. . . . Ninety-three percent of AID funds are spent directly in the United States to pay for these things. Just last year some 4,000 American firms in 50 states received $1.3 billion in AID funds for products supplied as part of the foreign aid program.[8]

Similarly, a former British minister of overseas development once noted that "about two-thirds of our aid is spent on goods and services from Britain . . . trade follows aid. We equip a factory overseas and later on we get orders for spare parts and replacements . . . [aid] is in our long-term interest."[9]

Why LDC Recipients Accept Aid

The reasons why Third World nations, at least until recently, have been very eager to accept aid, even in its most stringent and restrictive forms, have been given much less attention than the reasons why donors provide aid. This omission is puzzling in view of the many instances where both parties may have conflicting rather than congruent motives and interests. Basically, one can identify three reasons—one major and two minor—why LDCs have sought foreign aid.

The major reason is clearly economic in concept and practice. Third World countries have often tended to accept uncritically the proposition, typically advanced by developed country economists, taught in all university development courses, and supported by reference to "success" cases like Taiwan, Israel, and South Korea to the exclusion of many more "failures," that aid is a crucial and essential ingredient in the development process. It supplements scarce domestic resources; it helps to transform the economy structurally; and it contributes to the achievement of LDC takeoffs into self-sustaining economic growth. Thus, the economic rationale for aid in LDCs is based largely on their acceptance of the donor's perceptions of what they, the poor countries, require to promote their economic development.

Conflicts generally arise, therefore, not out of any disagreement about the role of aid but over its amount and conditions. Naturally, LDCs would like to have more aid in the form of outright grants or long-term low-cost loans with a minimum of strings attached. This means the abolition of tying aid to donor exports and the granting of greater latitude to recipient countries to decide for themselves what is in their best long-run development interests.

The two minor though still important motivations for LDCs to seek aid are political and moral. In some countries aid is seen by both donor and recipient as providing greater political leverage to the existing leadership to suppress opposition and maintain itself in power. In such instances, assistance takes the form not only of financial resource transfers but military and internal security reinforcement as well. While South Vietnam represents the most dramatic illustration of this "aid" phenomenon in the 1960s, as do perhaps Iran in the 1970s and El Salvador in the 1980s, many other Third World nations also have this political motivation. The problem is that once aid is accepted, the ability of recipient governments to extricate themselves from implied political and/or economic obligations to donors and prevent donor governments from interfering in their internal affairs can be greatly diminished.

Finally, we come to the moral motivation. Whether on grounds of basic humanitarian responsibilities of the rich toward the welfare of the poor or because of a belief that the rich nations owe the poor "conscience money" for past exploitation, many proponents of foreign aid in both developed and developing countries believe that rich nations have an obligation to support the economic and social development of the Third World. They then go on to link this moral obligation with the need for greater LDC autonomy with respect to the allocation and use of aid funds.

The Effects of Aid

The issue of the economic effects of aid, like that of the effects of private foreign investment, is fraught with disagreements. On one side are the "economic traditionalists," who argue that aid has indeed helped to promote growth and structural transformation in many LDCs.[10] On the other side are those who argue that aid does not promote faster growth but may in fact retard it by substituting for, rather than supplementing, domestic savings and investment and by exacerbating LDC balance of payments deficits as a result of rising debt repayment obligations and the linking of aid to donor country exports.

Aid is further criticized for focusing on and stimulating the growth of the modern sector, thereby increasing the gap in living standards between the rich and the poor in Third World countries. Some would even assert that foreign aid has been a positive force for antidevelopment in the sense that it both retards growth through reduced savings and worsens income inequalities.[11] Rather than relieving economic bottlenecks and filling gaps, aid, and for that matter private foreign investment, not only widens existing savings and foreign exchange resource gaps but may even create new ones (e.g., urban-rural or modern sector–traditional sector gaps).

Quite apart from these criticisms, the 1970s witnessed, on the donor side, a growing disenchantment with foreign aid, as domestic issues like inflation, unemployment, and balance of payments problems gained increasing priority over international cold war politics. During this period, one often heard the expression "aid weariness" used to describe the attitudes of developed countries toward foreign assistance. Taxpayers became more concerned with domestic economic problems especially as they increasingly realized that their tax moneys allocated to foreign aid often were benefiting the small elite groups in LDCs who in many cases were richer than the taxpayers. Given the declining real value of Western aid programs, hope arose among the LDCs that the vast new oil wealth generated by the OPEC trade surpluses in the 1970s might help to compensate for lost revenues. Let's see what actually happened.

The Rise and Decline of OPEC's Development Assistance

Following the first oil shock in 1973, OPEC emerged as a major source of Official Development Assistance (ODA) to developing countries, providing some compensation for the severe setbacks suffered as a result of the twelvefold increase in world oil prices. In fact, so impressive was the growth of OPEC aid, mushrooming as it did from $704 million in 1972 to $9.1 billion in 1980 (see Table 14.6), that many developing countries hoped OPEC's surplus oil revenues would become an important source of funding for their development plans throughout the 1980s. Unfortunately, their optimism was shortlived as a world oil glut and political problems in the Middle East appeared after 1980, causing OPEC's economic power, along with its aid programs, to decline.

The decline in aid was rapid, from $9.1 billion in 1980 to $7.8 billion in 1981. In real terms, the amount of aid disbursed in 1981 was the lowest since 1973. As a percentage of the OPEC members' collective GNP, aid declined from 1.74% in 1980 to 1.46% in 1981 (see Table 14.7). Moreover, OPEC's share of the total aid disbursed to developing countries dropped from 23.7% in 1980 to 21.8% in 1981, considerably lower than its almost 30% share in 1975.

The disappearance of huge OPEC surpluses following the world oil glut was the primary reason for the fall in OPEC aid. As the demand for oil in industrial countries had fallen and the supply from non-OPEC sources had increased, oil prices fell and OPEC's share of the world oil market plummeted from 60% in 1980 to less than 30% in 1983. As a result, OPEC's current account surplus, which had been the major source of its aid programs, diminished from its peak of $115 billion in 1980 to $20 billion in 1982. In 1983, OPEC fortunes worsened further as it registered a deficit of $30 billion. In particular, Saudi Arabia, which accounted for 74% of total OPEC aid, experienced a deficit of approximately $18 billion in 1983.

The other reason for the decline in OPEC aid has been the political instability in Iran and Iraq, both large aid donors in the 1970s. Following the political upheaval in 1979, Iran's aid program collapsed; by 1981, Iran had become a net recipient of aid. With the onset of the Iran−Iraqi war in 1981, Iraq's aid plunged nearly $700 million.

Aggravating the problem of declining OPEC aid has been the continuing concentration of aid to countries with religious and political ties to OPEC members. The Gulf states—Saudi Arabia, Kuwait, Qatar, and the United

Table 14.6 Foreign Aid by OPEC Members, 1970–1981: Net Disbursements ($ millions)

	1970	1971	1972	1973	1974	1975	1976	1977	1978	1979	1980	1981
Gulf states												
Kuwait	148	108	153	356	631	946	532	1309	991	477	645	685
Qatar	—	—	—	94	185	338	195	194	109	280	284	175
Saudi Arabia	173	214	366	1118	2153	2756	3033	3138	5507	4674	5944	5798
United Arab Emirates	—	50	74	289	510	1046	1021	1060	891	967	906	799
Total	321	372	593	1857	3479	5086	4781	5701	7498	6398	7779	7457
Other Arab donors												
Algeria	—	—	—	25	47	41	54	47	44	272	65	65
Iraq	4	8	11	11	423	215	231	61	173	847	829	143
Libya	68	64	69	215	147	259	94	113	146	105	282	105
Total	72	72	80	251	617	515	379	221	363	1224	1176	313
Non-Arab donors												
Iran	4	3	3	2	408	593	753	221	278	25	7	−150
Nigeria	—	—	—	5	15	14	83	64	38	30	42	149
Venezuela	1	5	28	18	60	31	108	56	115	109	125	67
Total	5	8	31	25	483	638	944	341	431	164	174	66
Overall total	398	452	704	2133	4579	6239	6104	6263	8292	7786	9129	7836
Total in 1981 constant prices	1026	1097	1537	4158	8076	9540	9056	8603	9895	8239	8855	7836

SOURCE: Report by the Chairman of the Development Assistance Committee, *Development Co-operation, 1982 Review* (Paris: OECD, 1982), p. 242.

Table 14.7 Foreign Aid by OPEC Members, 1970–1981: Net disbursements as Percentage of GNP

	1970	1971	1972	1973	1974	1975	1976	1977	1978	1979	1980	1981
Gulf states												
Kuwait	6.21	3.45	4.39	8.62	5.33	7.40	3.64	8.20	5.64	1.79	2.04	1.98
Qatar	n.a.	n.a.	n.a.	15.62	9.26	15.59	7.95	7.76	3.75	6.03	4.25	2.64
Saudi Arabia	5.60	5.04	6.57	14.80	9.32	7.76	6.47	5.33	8.45	6.12	5.09	4.77
United Arab Emirates	n.a.	(3.82)	(4.62)	12.67	7.04	11.69	8.88	7.27	6.27	5.09	3.38	2.88
Total	5.86	4.28	5.57	12.76	7.78	8.56	6.33	6.20	7.51	5.05	4.28	3.92
Other Arab donors												
Algeria	n.a.	n.a.	n.a.	0.28	0.37	0.27	0.33	0.24	0.18	0.89	0.17	0.16
Iraq	0.13	0.23	0.27	0.21	3.98	1.63	1.44	0.33	0.76	2.53	2.13	(0.37)
Libya	2.01	1.60	1.49	3.33	1.26	2.29	0.63	0.63	0.85	0.45	0.92	0.37
Total	1.10	0.97	0.94	1.21	1.76	1.31	0.80	0.39	0.56	1.40	1.08	0.29
Non-Arab donors												
Iran	0.03	0.03	0.02	0.01	0.87	1.13	1.16	0.29	(0.37)	(0.03)	(0.01)	–
Nigeria	n.a.	n.a.	n.a.	0.03	0.05	0.04	0.19	0.13	0.07	0.04	0.05	0.17
Venezuela	0.01	0.04	0.21	0.11	0.23	0.11	0.34	0.15	0.29	0.22	0.21	0.10
Total	0.02	0.02	0.06	0.04	0.48	0.55	0.68	0.21	0.25	0.08	0.07	0.03
Overall total	1.18	1.10	1.43	2.25	2.53	2.92	2.32	2.03	2.46	1.88	(1.74)	(1.46)

Note: GNP figures were supplied by the World Bank, except figures in parentheses, which are OECD estimates.

Source: Report by the Chairman of the Development Assistance Committee, *Development Co-operation, 1982 Review* (Paris: OECD, 1982), p. 243.

Arab Emirates (UAE)—which now account for about 95% of all OPEC aid, have disbursed the bulk of their aid bilaterally to a few select countries. Since the bilateral component has traditionally weighed heavily in the total amount of OPEC aid, accounting for over 88% of the total OPEC aid disbursed in 1981, most of OPEC's aid has been concentrated in a handful of Arab countries. During the 1970s, Egypt, Syria, Jordan, and Pakistan monopolized OPEC's aid. More recently, the concentration of aid has shifted somewhat, with Syria, Jordan, Oman, Lebanon, Turkey, Yemen, and Morocco absorbing about a third of all OPEC bilateral assistance. Aid to Egypt, which amounted to 42% of the OPEC total in 1975, fell to zero in 1980 following Egypt's suspension from membership in the Arab League in early 1979. Prior to this suspension, OPEC aid to Egypt covered more than 80% of both the government's budget deficit and the current account deficit. United States aid to Egypt after 1979, however, rose to fill much of this revenue gap.

Regionally, the areas hardest hit by OPEC oil shocks have received little bilateral aid, with the entire continents of Africa and South America receiving only 11% and .02% of total OPEC bilateral aid respectively. In the case of Africa, three quarters of this assistance is concentrated in Arab North Africa. In view of the concentration of OPEC aid, therefore, it appears that few countries have received the amounts of aid corresponding to their relative poverty and needs. This is indicated by Table 14.8, which shows the distribution of OPEC Arab aid.

In short, given the above distributional limitations and with experts predicting a further decline in OPEC's economic power, the prospects for substantial OPEC aid in the 1980s seem bleak. For developing countries, the decline in OPEC assistance may be exacerbated by a further tightening of credit from Western banks which had previously made loans out of the vast OPEC revenue surpluses during the 1970s. As a result, despite the easing of their import burden through lower oil prices, many developing countries in the Middle East, South Asia, and North Africa are disheartened rather than elated by the decline of OPEC. For the rest of the non-oil-producing Third World, however, the stabilization of international energy prices in the 1980s is on balance a welcome occurrence even though OPEC's potential as a source of foreign assistance has all but vanished for the time being.

Table 14.8 Estimated Geographic Distribution of Bilateral Concessional Assistance from Arab OPEC members, 1975–1981 (%)

	1975	1976	1977	1978	1979	1980	1981	Total 1975–1981
Arab countries	81.2	62.3	70.3	73.0	84.2	78.1	83.6	78.4
Africa	2.8	1.6	1.7	5.0	2.6	5.2	7.7	3.6
Asia	15.6	31.6	26.7	12.7	5.3	11.0	1.0	12.1
Europe	0.3	0.3	—	—	0.5	4.5	2.7	1.1
Unspecified	0.1	4.2	1.3	9.2	7.4	1.2	5.0	4.8
	100.0	100.0	100.0	100.0	100.0	100.0	100.0	100.0

SOURCE: Zubair Iqbal, "Arab concessional assistance, 1975–81," *Finance and Development*, June 1983, p. 33.

CONCLUSIONS: TOWARD A NEW VIEW OF FOREIGN AID

The combination of "aid disillusionment" on the part of many Third World recipients and "aid weariness" among some traditional developed country donors does not augur well for the continuation of past relationships. But it can be argued that this is desirable rather than disheartening. Dissatisfaction on both sides creates the possibility for new arrangements characterized by greater congruence of interest and motivation on the part of donor and recipient. A lower total volume of aid from the developed nations that is, however, geared more to the real development needs of recipients and permits them greater flexibility and autonomy in meeting their development priorities would on balance represent a positive step. The change in emphasis from industrial growth to basic needs and rural development on the part of USAID in the late 1970s provided a case in point. The rising proportion of development assistance funds now being channeled through multilateral assistance agencies like the World Bank, whose political motives are presumably less narrowly defined compared with those of individual donor countries, is also a welcome development. It tends to minimize one of the major criticisms of past foreign aid practices, that is, the linking of economic aid to political conditions.

More aid is better than less aid for some of the reasons outlined earlier. But from the viewpoint of LDC recipients, whatever the source and volume of aid, the more it takes the form of outright grants and concessional loans, the less it is tied to donor exports, the more autonomy is permitted in its allocation and the more it is supplemented by the reduction of donor country tariff and nontariff trade barriers against Third World exports, the greater will be the development impact of this foreign assistance.[12] In fact, many argue that better opportunities for profitable trade with the industrial nations are much more vital to Third World economic growth than quantitative increases in development assistance. Although it may seem wishful thinking to imagine that rich countries (both capitalist and socialist) will move in the direction of such real development-oriented trade and aid policies that at first glance appear to be against their economic self-interests, on closer examination this viewpoint may not be so far-fetched after all.

As the realities of global interdependence slowly penetrate the political perceptions of developed nation governments, and perhaps eventually their populaces as well, it may begin to dawn on them that their real long-run economic and political interests in fact lie with the achievement of broad-based development in Third World nations. Eliminating poverty, minimizing inequality, and in general raising levels of living for the masses of LDC peoples may just turn out to be in the most fundamental "self-interest" of developed nations, not because of any humanitarian ideals (though one would hope that these are present) but simply because in the long run there can be no two futures for mankind, one for the very rich, the other for the very poor, without the proliferation of global conflict. Enlightened self-interest, therefore, may be the only peg on which to build the hope for a "new international economic order," one in which both foreign assistance and private investment can begin to make a real and lasting contribution to Third World development.

NOTES

1. For a comprehensive review of the nature and pattern of MNC investments in the Third World during the 1970s, see United Nations Center on Transnational Corporations, *Transnational Corporations in World Development: Third Survey* (New York: United Nations, 1983), Chapter 2. See also "Multinational Corporations in World Development," Reading 29 in *The Struggle for Economic Development* and P.K. Ghosh (ed.), *Multi-National Corporations and Third World Development* (Westport, Conn.: Greenwood, 1984).

2. P.P. Streeten, "The multinational enterprise and the theory of development policy," *World Development* 1, no. 10 (1973).

3. The question of whether or not "nationalized" foreign enterprises or confiscated domestic private property (e.g., large but unproductive land holdings) should be compensated and, if so, at what amount is typically a political issue. In general, however, such compensation should depend on (a) the manner in which the enterprise or property was acquired, (b) the historical and replacement costs of the assets confiscated, (c) the nature and record of the enterprise's relations with the government and people of the confiscating country prior to confiscation, and (d) the financial benefits and economic returns that have already been reaped prior to confiscation. Compensation should be based on a careful evaluation of these four factors, with (a) and (c) providing the political criteria and (b) and (d) the economic criteria for the decision. For an early economic defense of policies of confiscation and nationalization of foreign-owned property in Third World countries, see Martin Bronfenbrenner, "The appeal of confiscation in economic development," *Economic Development and Cultural Change*, April 1955, pp. 201–208.

4. Jagdish N. Bhagwati, "Amount and sharing of aid," in *Assisting Countries: Problems of Debt, Burden-Sharing, Jobs and Trade* (New York: Praeger, 1972), pp. 72–73.

5. *Ibid*, p. 73.

6. Even these figures can be very misleading and exaggerate the actual "aid" (i.e., concessional) component of development assistance. For a harsh critique of how "official development assistance" statistics can be very misleading or downright false, see G. Myrdal, *The Challenge of World Poverty* (New York: Pantheon, 1970), p. 10.

7. See H.B. Chenery and A.M. Strout, "Foreign assistance and economic development," *American Economic Review*, September 1966, pp. 680–733.

8. William S. Gaud, "Foreign aid: What it is; how it works; why we provide it," *Department of State Bulletin* 59, no. 1537 (1968).

9. Statement by Earl Grinstead, reported in *Overseas Development*, November 1968, p. 9. In a similar vein one of the staunchest defenders of the role of foreign aid in the development process, economist Hollis Chenery, admitted that "in the most general sense, the main objective of foreign assistance, as of many other tools of foreign policy, is to produce the kind of political and economic environment in the world in which the United States can best pursue its own social goals." ("Objectives and criteria of foreign assistance," in G. Ranis [ed.], *The U.S. and the Development Economies* [New York: Norton, 1964], p. 88.)

10. See, for example, H.B. Chenery and N.G. Carter, "Foreign assistance and development performance," *American Economic Review* 63, no. 2 (1973):459–468.

11. See, for example, Keith Griffin and J.L. Enos, "Foreign assistance: Objectives and consequences," *Economic Development and Cultural Change*, April 1970, pp. 313–327.

12. For a recent discussion of the importance of increased foreign assistance see Brandt Commission, "Development finance: Current needs," Reading 30 in *The Struggle for Economic Development*. A useful set of readings can be found in P.K. Ghosh (ed.), *Foreign Aid and Third World Development* (Westport, Conn.: Greenwood, 1984).

CONCEPTS FOR REVIEW

Private foreign investment	"Strong" currencies
Foreign aid	Savings–investment gap
Grants versus loans	Foreign exchange gap
Foreign monetary reserves	"Tied" aid
Multinational donor agencies	Absorptive capacity
Bilateral donor agencies	Learning by doing
Debt burden	Multinational corporations
Two-gap models	Transfer pricing
"Soft" loans	"Inappropriate" products
Private transfer payments	Technical assistance
	Aid weariness

QUESTIONS FOR DISCUSSION

1. The emergence of giant multinational corporations over the past two decades is said to have altered the very nature of international economic activity. In what ways do these MNCs affect the structure and pattern of trading relationships between the developed and underdeveloped world?

2. Summarize the arguments for and against the role and impact of private foreign investment in less developed countries. What strategies might LDCs adopt to make private foreign investment fit their development aspirations better without destroying all incentives for foreign investors?

3. How important is foreign aid for the economies of the Third World in relation to their other sources of foreign exchange receipts? Explain the various forms development assistance can take and distinguish between bilateral and multilateral assistance. Which do you think is more desirable and why?

4. What is meant by "tied aid"? Both capitalist and socialist nations have increasingly shifted from grants to loans and from untied to tied loans and grants during the past decade. What are the major disadvantages of tied aid especially when this aid comes in the form of interest-bearing loans?

5. Under what conditions and terms do you think LDCs should seek and accept foreign aid in the future? If aid cannot be obtained on such terms, do you think LDCs should accept whatever they can get? Explain your answer.

FURTHER READINGS

For an economic analysis of private foreign investment and the role and influence of multinational corporations, see Sanjaya Lall, "Less developed countries and private foreign direct investment: A review article," *World Development* 2, nos. 4 and 5 (1974); Gustav Ranis, "The multinational corporation as an instrument of development," *Discussion Paper No. 123*, Yale Economic Growth Center, September 1974; Paul Streeten, "The multinational enterprise and the theory of development policy," *World Development* 1, no. 10 (1973); and United Nations, *Transnational Corporations in World Development: Third Survey* (New York: United Nations, 1983).

For an account of the power and inside workings of multinationals whose decisions shape the lives of all peoples and often transcend national and international laws, see R.J. Barnet and R.E. Müller, *Global Reach: The Power of Multinational Corporations* (New York: Simon and Schuster, 1975).

On the question of the benefits and costs of foreign aid, see Lester B. Pearson (chairman), *Partners in Development: Report of the Commission on International Development* (New York: Praeger, 1969), Chapters 1, 6, 7, 8, 9, and 11; Gunnar Myrdal, *The Challenge of World Poverty* (New York: Pantheon, 1970), Chapters 10 and 11; J.N. Bhagwati and R.S. Eckaus (eds.), *Foreign Aid* (Harmondsworth, England: Penguin, 1970); Charles R. Frank, Jr., "Debt and terms of aid," in *Assisting Developing Countries*, ODC Studies (New York: Praeger, 1972), pp. 3–66; Jagdish N. Bhagwati, "Amount and sharing of aid," in *Assisting Developing Countries*, ODC Studies (New York: Praeger, 1972), pp. 69– 128; George C. Abbot, "Two concepts of foreign aid," *World Development* 1, no. 9 (1973); and Brandt Commission, *North–South: A Program for Survival* (Cambridge, Mass.: MIT Press, 1980).

Finally, a good review and analysis of OPEC aid programs to developing countries can be found in Maurice J. Williams, "The aid programs of the OPEC countries," *Foreign Affairs* 54, no. 2 (1976):308–324, and in Zubair Iqbal, "Arab concessional assistance, 1975–81," *Finance and Development* (June 1983).

Additional readings can be found on pp. 633–635.

IV

POSSIBILITIES AND PROSPECTS

15

DEVELOPMENT PLANNING: THEORY AND PRACTICE

Planning is the exercise of intelligence to deal with facts and situations as they are and find a way to solve problems.

Jawaharlal Nehru

If we could first know where we are, and whither we are tending, we could better judge what to do, and how to do it.

Abraham Lincoln

THE PLANNING MYSTIQUE

In the decades since the Second World War, the pursuit of economic development has been crystallized by the almost universal acceptance of development planning as the surest and most direct route to economic progress. Until recently, few in the Third World would have questioned the advisability or desirability of formulating and implementing a national development plan. Planning has become a way of life in government ministries, and every 5 years or so the latest development plan is paraded out with the greatest fanfare.

But why, until recently, has there been such an aura and mystique about development planning and such universal faith in its obvious utility? Basically, because centralized national planning was widely believed to offer the essential and perhaps the only institutional and organizational mechanism for overcoming the major obstacles to development and for ensuring a sustained high rate of economic growth. In some cases central economic planning even became regarded as a kind of open sesame that would allow Third World nations to pass rapidly through the barrier dividing their pitiably low standard of living from the prosperity of their former rulers. But in order to catch up, poor nations were persuaded and became convinced that they required a comprehensive national plan. The planning record, unfortunately, has not lived up to its advance billing, and there now exists a growing skepticism about the planning mystique.

In this chapter we examine the role and limitations of development planning as practiced in Third World nations both in its own right and within the broader framework of national economic policy formulation. We start with a brief review of the nature of development planning and a summary of general planning issues. After examining the main arguments for and against the role of planning in underdeveloped societies and reviewing different models of economy-wide planning and project appraisal, we conclude with an analysis of the recent history of LDC planning. Appendix 15.1 then reviews the current (1980s) debate about the pros and cons of free markets versus planning in contemporary Third World nations. In Chapter 16 we take up the broader questions of the role and limitations of economic policy for development and examine some of the positive and negative factors (both economic and noneconomic) associated with substantial state intervention in economic activities.

THE NATURE OF DEVELOPMENT PLANNING[1]

Basic Concepts

Economic planning may be described as a deliberate governmental attempt to coordinate economic decision making over the long run and to influence, direct, and in some cases even control the level and growth of a nation's principal economic variables (income, consumption, employment, investment, saving, exports, imports, etc.) in order to achieve a predetermined set of development objectives. An *economic plan* is simply a specific set of quantitative economic targets to be reached in a given period of time. Economic plans may be either comprehensive or partial. A *comprehensive plan* sets its targets to cover all major aspects of the national economy. A *partial plan* covers only a part of the national economy—industry, agriculture, the public sector, the foreign sector, and so forth. Finally, the *planning process* itself can be described as an exercise in which a government first chooses social objectives, then sets various targets, and finally organizes a framework for implementing, coordinating, and monitoring a development plan.

In 1951, in one of its first publications dealing with developing countries, the UN Department of Economic Affairs distinguished *four types of planning,* each of which has been used in one form or another by most LDCs:

> *First, . . . it [planning] refers only to the making of a program of public expenditure, extending over from one to say ten years. Second, it refers sometimes to the setting of production targets, whether for private or for public enterprises, in terms of the input of manpower, of capital, or of other scarce resources, or use in terms of output. Thirdly, the word may be used to describe a statement which sets targets for the economy as a whole, purporting to allocate all scarce resources among the various branches of the economy. And fourthly, the word is sometimes used to describe the means*

which the government uses to try to enforce upon private enterprise the targets which have been previously determined.[2]

Proponents of economic planning for developing countries argue that the uncontrolled market economy can, and often does, subject these nations to economic stagnation, fluctuating prices, and low levels of employment. In particular, they claim that the market economy is not geared to the principal operational task of poor countries: mobilizing limited resources in a way that will bring about the structural change necessary to stimulate a sustained and balanced growth of the entire economy. Planning has come to be accepted, therefore, as an essential and pivotal means of guiding and accelerating economic growth in almost all Third World countries.

Planning in Mixed Developing Economies

Most development plans are formulated and carried out within the framework of the "mixed" economies of the Third World. These economies are characterized by the existence of an institutional setting in which some of the productive resources are privately owned and operated and some are controlled by the public sector. The actual proportionate division of public and private ownership varies from country to country, and neither the private nor the public sector can really be considered in isolation from the other. However, unlike market economies where only a small degree of public ownership usually exists, LDC mixed economies are distinguished by a substantial amount of government ownership and control. The private sector typically comprises four distinct forms of individual ownership:

1. The traditional subsistence sector, consisting of small-scale private farms and handicraft shops selling a part of their products to local markets
2. Small-scale individual or family-owned commercial business and service activities
3. Medium-sized commercial enterprises in agriculture, industry, trade, and transport owned and operated by local entrepreneurs
4. Large jointly owned or completely foreign-owned manufacturing enterprises, mining companies, and plantations, primarily catering to foreign markets but sometimes with substantial local sales (the capital for such enterprises usually comes from abroad and a good proportion of the profits tends to be transferred overseas)

In the context of such an institutional setting, we can identify two principal components of development planning in mixed economies:

1. The government's deliberate utilization of domestic saving and foreign finance to carry out public investment projects and to mobilize and channel scarce resources into areas that can be expected to make the greatest contribution toward the realization of long-term economic objectives (e.g., the construction of railways, schools, hydroelectric projects, and other components of "economic infrastructure," as well as the creation of import-substituting industries)
2. Governmental economic policy (e.g., taxation, industrial licensing, the setting of tariffs and the manipulation of quotas, wages, interest rates, and prices) to stimulate, direct, and in some cases even control private economic activity in order to ensure a harmonious relationship between the desires of private businessmen and the social objectives of the central government

The compromise nature of this situation between the extremes of market inducement and collectivist control is readily evident from the above simplified characterization of planning in mixed-market economies.

THE RATIONALE FOR PLANNING IN DEVELOPING ECONOMIES

The widespread acceptance of planning as a development tool rests on a number of fundamental economic and institutional arguments. Of these we can single out four as the most often put forward.

The Market-Failure Argument

Markets in LDCs are permeated by imperfections of structure and operation. Commodity and factor markets are often badly organized and the existence of "distorted prices" often means that producers and consumers are responding to economic signals and incentives that are a poor reflection of the "real" cost to society of these goods, services, and resources. It is therefore argued that governments have an important role to play in integrating markets and modifying prices. Moreover, the "failure" of the market correctly to price factors of production is further assumed to lead to gross disparities between social and private valuations of alternative investment projects (see below). In the absence of governmental interference, therefore, the market is said to lead to a misallocation of present and future resources or, at least, to an allocation that may not be in the best long-run social interests. This market-failure argument is perhaps the most often quoted reason for the expanded role of government in underdeveloped countries.

A clear statement of this viewpoint was presented in a 1965 report of a UN conference on planning, which asserted:

> It is an integral task of planning to achieve the best possible use of scarce resources for economic development. . . . The need for using appropriate criteria for selecting projects arose because of the failure of the market mechanism to provide a proper guideline. In less-developed economies, market prices of such factors of production as labour, capital and foreign exchange deviated substantially from their social opportunity costs and were not, therefore, a correct measure of the relative scarcity or abundance of the factor in question.[3]

A 1970 publication of the United Nations Industrial Development Organization (UNIDO) provided the following explicit market-failure rationale for planning in LDCs:

> Governments can not, and should not, take a merely passive role in the process of industrial expansion. Planning has become an essential and integral part of industrial development programmes, for market forces, by themselves, cannot overcome the deepseated structural rigidities in the economies of developing countries. . . . Today the need for some degree of economic planning is universally recognised. It is, of course, an integral part of the economy of the Soviet Union and the other centrally planned countries. . . . In developing countries, planning is more feasible and more desirable than in developed market economies. The greater feasibility is a result of the

smaller number of variables that must be taken into consideration, and the greater desirability stems from the fact that the automatic mechanisms for co-ordination of individual actions function less satisfactorily in developing than in developed economies. Planning in developing countries is made necessary by, inter alia, the inadequacies of the market as a mechanism to ensure that individual decisions will optimize economic performance in terms of society's preferences and economic goals. . . . The inadequacy of the market mechanism as a means of allocating resources for industrial development sometimes results from government policy itself or because the theoretical assumptions (particularly with respect to the mobility of the factors of production) do not apply to the actual economic situation. Even more importantly, the market mechanism cannot properly allow for the external effects of investment.[4]

The Resource Mobilization and Allocation Argument

Third World economies cannot afford to waste their limited financial and skilled manpower resources on unproductive ventures. Investment projects must be chosen not solely on the basis of a partial productivity analysis dictated by individual industrial capital/output ratios but also in the context of an overall development program that takes account of external economies, indirect repercussions, and long-term objectives. Skilled manpower must be utilized where its contribution will be most widely felt. Economic planning is assumed to help modify the restraining influence of limited resources by recognizing the existence of particular constraints and by choosing and coordinating investment projects so as to channel these scarce factors into their most productive outlets. In contrast, it is argued, competitive markets will tend to generate less investment, to direct that investment into socially low-priority areas (e.g., consumption goods for the rich), and to disregard the extra benefits to be derived from a planned and coordinated long-term investment program.

The Attitudinal or Psychological Argument

It is often assumed that a detailed statement of national economic and social objectives in the form of a specific development plan can have an important attitudinal or psychological impact on a diverse and often fragmented population. It may succeed in rallying the people behind the government in a national campaign to eliminate poverty, ignorance, and disease. By mobilizing popular support and cutting across class, caste, racial, religious, or tribal factions with the plea to all citizens to work together toward building the nation, it is argued that an enlightened central government, through its economic plan, can best provide the needed incentives to overcome the inhibiting and often divisive forces of sectionalism and traditionalism in a common quest for widespread material and social progress.

The Foreign Aid Argument

The formulation of detailed development plans with specific sectoral output targets and carefully designed investment projects has often been a necessary condition for the receipt of bilateral and multilateral foreign aid. In fact, some cynics would argue that the real reason why LDCs construct development plans is to secure more foreign aid. With a "shopping list" of projects, Third World governments are better equipped to solicit foreign assistance and persuade donors that their money will be used as an essential ingredient in a well-conceived and internally consistent plan of action. To a certain extent this process is a charade, motivated by developed country desires for sophisticated and detailed project descriptions within the framework of a comprehensive development plan.

THE PLANNING PROCESS: SOME BASIC MODELS

Characteristics of the Planning Process

Despite a great diversity of development plans and planning techniques, certain basic characteristics of "comprehensive" planning are common to most developing countries. Killick has listed the following six characteristics as representative:

1. Starting from the political views and goals of the government, planning attempts to *define policy objectives*, especially as they relate to the future development of the economy.
2. A development plan sets out a *strategy* by means of which it is intended to achieve these objectives, which are normally translated into specific targets.
3. The plan attempts to present a *centrally coordinated, internally consistent set of principles and policies*, chosen as the optimal means of implementing the strategy and achieving the targets and intended to be used as a framework to guide subsequent day-to-day decisions.
4. It *comprehends the whole economy* (hence it is "comprehensive," in contrast to "colonial" or "public sector" planning).
5. In order to secure optimality and consistency, the comprehensive plan employs a more-or-less *formalized macroeconomic model* (which, however, will often remain unpublished), and this is employed to project the intended future performance of the economy.
6. A development plan typically covers a period of, say, 5 years and finds physical expression as a *medium-term plan document*, which may, however, incorporate a longer-term perspective plan and be supplemented by annual plans.[5]

Although the formulation of a comprehensive plan is the goal of most poor countries, it is sometimes necessary to base such plans on a more partial sectoral analysis. In very poor countries with limited data and minimal industrial diversification, partial plans may be the most that can be accomplished. In general, however, the ideal planning process can be broadly conceived as consisting of three basic stages, each of which is associated with a particular type of planning model.

Planning in Stages: Three Basic Models

Most development plans are based initially on some more-or-less formalized macroeconomic model. Such economy-wide planning models can conveniently be divided into two basic categories: (a) *aggregate growth models*, involving macroeconomic estimates of planned or required changes in principal economic variables; and (b) *multisector input−output models*, which ascertain (among other things) the production, resource, employment, and foreign exchange implications of a given set of final demand targets within an internally consistent framework of interindustry product flows. Finally, the third and probably most important component of plan formulation is the detailed selection of specific investment projects within each sector through the technique of *project appraisal and social cost–benefit analysis*. These three "stages" of planning—aggregate, sectoral, and project—provide the main intellectual tools of the planning authority.

Aggregate Growth Models: Projecting Macro Variables

The first and most elementary planning model used in almost every developing country is the aggregate growth model. It deals with the entire economy in terms of a limited set of those macroeconomic variables deemed most critical to the determination of levels and growth rates of national output: savings, investment, capital stocks, exports, imports, foreign assistance, etc. Aggregate growth models provide a convenient method for forecasting output (and perhaps also employment) growth over a 3–5-year period. Almost all such models represent some variant of the basic Harrod–Domar model described in Chapter 3.

Recall that the Harrod–Domar model views limited savings as the major constraint on aggregate economic growth. Given targeted GNP growth rates and a national capital/output ratio, the Harrod–Domar model can be used to specify the amount of domestic saving necessary to generate such growth. In most cases, this necessary amount of domestic saving is not likely to be realized on the basis of existing savings functions, and so the basic policy problem of how to generate additional domestic savings and/or foreign assistance comes into play. For planning purposes, the Harrod–Domar model is usually formulated as follows:[6]

We start with the assumption that the ratio of total output to reproducible capital is constant so that

$$K(t) = kY(t) \tag{1}$$

where $K(t)$ is capital stock at time t, $Y(t)$ is total output (GNP) at time t, and k is the average (equal to the marginal) capital–output ratio. We assume next that a constant share (s) of output (Y) is always saved (S), so that

$$I(t) = K(t + 1) - K(t) + \delta K(t) = sY = S(t) \tag{2}$$

where $I(t)$ is gross investment at the time t and δ is the fraction of the capital stock depreciated in each period. Now if g is the targeted rate of growth of output such that

$$g = [Y(t + 1) - Y(t)]/Y(t) = \Delta Y(t)/Y(t) \tag{3}$$

then capital must be growing at the same rate since from Equation (1) we know that

$$\Delta K/K = k \, \Delta Y/K = \frac{k \, \Delta Y/Y}{K/Y} = \Delta Y/Y$$

Using Equation (2), we therefore arrive once again at the basic Harrod–Domar growth formula (although this time with a capital depreciation parameter):

$$g = \frac{sY - \delta K}{K} = \frac{s}{k} - \delta \tag{3a}$$

Finally, since output growth can also be expressed as the sum of labor force growth (n) and the rate of growth of labor productivity (p), Equation (3a) can be rewritten for planning purposes as

$$n + p = \frac{s}{k} - \delta \tag{4}$$

Given an expected rate of labor force and productivity growth (labor force growth can be calculated from readily available demographic information while productivity growth estimates are usually based either on extrapolations of past trends or on an assumed constant rate of increase), Equation (4) can then be used to estimate whether domestic savings will be sufficient to provide an adequate number of new employment opportunities to a growing labor force. One way of doing this is to disaggregate the overall savings function (S = sY) into at least two component sources of saving: normally, the propensity to save out of wage income, W, and profit income, π.

Thus, we define

$$W + \pi = Y$$

and

$$s_\pi \pi + s_w W = I \tag{5}$$

where s_π and s_w are the savings propensities from π and W respectively. By manipulating Equation (3a) and substituting (5) into it, we arrive at a modified Harrod–Domar growth equation:

$$k(g + \delta) = (s_\pi - s_w)(\pi/Y) + s_w \tag{6}$$

which can then serve as a formula for ascertaining the adequacy of current saving out of profit and wage income. For example, if a 4% growth rate is desired and if $\delta = 0.03$, $k = 3.0$, and $(\pi/Y) = 0.5$, then Equation (6) reduces to $0.42 = s_\pi + s_w$.[7] If savings out of capital income amount to 25%, then wage earners must save at a 17% rate to achieve the targeted rate of growth. In the absence of such a savings rate out of labor income, the government could pursue a variety of policies to raise domestic saving and/or seek foreign assistance.

In countries where inadequate foreign exchange reserves are believed to be the principal constraint on economic growth, the aggregate growth model typically employed is some variant of the two-gap model described in Chapter 14. (Two-gap models are simply Harrod−Domar models generalized to take foreign trade problems into account.) In either case, aggregate growth models can provide only a rough first approximation of the general directions an economy might take. As such, they rarely constitute the operational development plan. Perhaps more important, the simplicity and relatively low cost in terms of data collection of using aggregate growth models can often blind one to their very real limitations, especially when application is carried out in a much too mechanical fashion. Average capital/output ratios are notoriously difficult to estimate and may bear little relation to marginal capital/output ratios, while savings rates can be highly unstable. The operational plan requires a more disaggregated multisector model of economic activity like the well-known input−output approach.

Input−Output Models and Sectoral Projections: The Basic Idea

A much more sophisticated approach to development planning is to utilize some variant of the *interindustry or input−output model*, in which the activities of the major industrial sectors of the economy are interrelated with one another by means of a set of simultaneous algebraic equations expressing the specific production processes or technologies of each industry. All industries are viewed both as producers of *outputs* and users of *inputs* from other industries. For example, the agricultural sector is both a producer of output (e.g., wheat) and a user of inputs from, say, the manufacturing sector (e.g., machinery, fertilizer). Thus, direct and indirect repercussions of planned changes in the demand for the products of any one industry on output, employment, and imports of all other industries can be traced throughout the entire economy in an intricate web of economic interdependence. Given the planned output targets for each sector of the economy, the interindustry model can be used to determine intermediate material, import, labor, and capital requirements with the result that a comprehensive economic plan with mutually consistent production levels and resource requirements can, in theory, be constructed.

Interindustry models range from simple input−output models, usually consisting of from 10 to 30 sectors in the developing economies and from 30 to 400 sectors in advanced economies, to the more complicated "linear-programming" or "activity-analysis" models where checks of feasibility (i.e., what is possible given certain resource constraints) and optimality (what is best among different alternatives) are also built into the model. But the distinguishing characteristic of the interindustry or input−output approach is the attempt to formulate an internally consistent, comprehensive development plan for the entire economy.

An Illustration.[8] Table 15.1 provides a numerical example of a hypothetical input−output system. For simplicity, we assume the existence of only five sectors: agriculture (Sector 1), extractive industry (Sector 2), manufacturing (Sector 3), power (Sector 4), and transportation (Sector 5). Actual tables can range in size from 20 to 400 sectors, with most developing countries at the lower end of the spectrum.

Note that each sector appears twice; as a producer of outputs (Rows 1−5) and as a user of inputs (Columns 1−5). Each row shows how each industry disposed of its output. For example, the first row shows (in the last

Table 15.1 Hypothetical Input–Output Table

Producing sector (outputs) ↓ / Using sector inputs →	Intermediate use						Final use (demand)					
	Agriculture	Extractive industry	Manufacturing	Power	Transportation	Total intermediate demand	Household consumption	Government — Investment	Government — Noninvestment expenditure	Exports	Total final demand	Total output
Agriculture	$15(x_{11})$	$0(x_{12})$	$20(x_{13})$	$0(x_{14})$	$10(x_{15})$	$45 \; \sum_{j=1}^{5} x_{1j}$	35	10	5	30	$80(Y_1)$	$125(X_1)$
Extractive industry	$0(x_{21})$	$0(x_{22})$	$0(x_{23})$	$0(x_{24})$	$0(x_{25})$	$0 \; \sum_{j=1}^{5} x_{2j}$	0	10	0	30	$40(Y_2)$	$40(X_2)$
Manufacturing	$10(x_{31})$	$0(x_{32})$	$25(x_{33})$	$15(x_{34})$	$5(x_{35})$	$55 \; \sum_{j=1}^{5} x_{3j}$	15	20	5	5	$45(Y_3)$	$100(X_3)$
Power	$5(x_{41})$	$15(x_{42})$	$15(x_{43})$	$0(x_{44})$	$15(x_{45})$	$50 \; \sum_{j=1}^{5} x_{4j}$	5	10	10	0	$25(Y_4)$	$75(X_4)$
Transportation	$5(x_{51})$	$10(x_{52})$	$15(x_{53})$	$0(x_{54})$	$5(x_{55})$	$35 \; \sum_{j=1}^{5} x_{5j}$	5	8	2	0	$15(Y_5)$	$50(X_5)$
Total purchases	35	25	75	15	35	185	60	52	22	65	205	
Imports	$15(m_1)$	$0(m_2)$	$10(m_3)$	$30(m_4)$	$5(m_5)$	$60(M_r)$	5	5	0	0	(10)	60(70)
Government (taxes)	20	5	3	7	2	37	(35)	(0)	(0)	(20)	(55)	37(92)
Households (labor)	$40(L_1)$	$5(L_2)$	$6(L_3)$	$5(L_4)$	$2(L_5)$	$58(L_T)$	1	0	12	0	13	71
Capital (C)	$5(C_1)$	$3(C_2)$	$5(C_3)$	$12(C_4)$	$4(C_5)$	$29(C_T)$	0	0	0	0	0	29
Natural resources (N)	$10(N_1)$	$2(N_2)$	$1(N_3)$	$6(N_4)$	$2(N_5)$	$21(N_T)$	0	0	0	0	0	21
Value added	75	15	30	30	10	145	1	0	12	0	13	158
Total inputs	125	40	100	75	50	390	66	63	34	65	218	608

SOURCE: M.P. Todaro, *Development Planning: Models and Methods* (Nairobi: Oxford University Press, 1971), p. 18.

column) that the agricultural sector produced a total output of 125 units (for the present disregard all algebraic symbols in the parentheses), and that of these 15 were used by agriculture itself as inputs (e.g., seeds), 20 by manufacturing (e.g., coffee or tea for processing), and 10 by transportation (e.g., as food served on passenger railways). The total intermediate use of agricultural products (i.e., use for further production) is 45 units. To this figure must be added the quantity of agricultural goods demanded by final users. In Table 15.1 this consists of the consumption of 35 units by households, total government expenditure of 15 units, and exports to foreign countries of 30 units. The sum of total intermediate and total final demand yields a gross output for agricultural production of 125 units. Similarly, we see that the extractive sector produces a total output of 40 units. None of this output is sold on an interindustry basis to other sectors; the government purchases 10 units, and 30 units are exported. The disposition of the total outputs of the other three sectors can be read from the table in the same manner.

The role of the agricultural sector as a purchaser of inputs is shown by Column 1. Reading down this column we see that in order to produce its total output of 125 units, agriculture had to use 15 units of its own output (e.g., using a portion of maize or bean output for replanting), 10 units of manufacturing output (e.g., fertilizers, insecticides), 5 units of power (e.g., to operate rotating water sprays and other electrical equipment), and 5 units of transportation's product (e.g., for transporting perishable goods to local markets or to the coast for export). Thus, the total domestic interindustry purchases of intermediate material goods and services by agriculture were 35 units. The remaining 90 units of total inputs purchased by agriculture consisted of the importation of 15 units of foreign goods and the creation of 75 units of *value added* in the form of payments of 20 units to the government as taxes, 40 units to households as wages, 5 units for the use of capital, and 10 units for the use of land. Thus the value of the total output of agriculture is equal to the total value of all inputs purchased (i.e., 125 units). This same procedure can be followed in analyzing the input–output structure of each and every sector of the economy.

The crucial assumption of input–output analysis—that is, the one that makes the system operationally effective—is the assumption that a *single-process production function* exists in every industry. Actually, this assumption has two closely related but distinct parts. The first is the assumption of *constant returns to scale*. The second, and by far the more controversial, is the corresponding assumption that *no substitution among inputs* is possible in the production of any good or service. An alternative way of stating this is that since there is only one process or method of production in each industry, the level of output uniquely determines the level of each input required. Technically we may say that the production process is characterized by *constant* "technical coefficients of production," that is, each *additional* unit of new output is produced by an unchanging proportional combination of material inputs from the other sectors. For example, in Table 15.1 we see that in order to produce its 100 units of output, the manufacturing sector had to purchase 20 units of agricultural output for its intermediate input needs. Dividing 20 by 100 we find that our proportionality assumption indicates that for every unit of manufacturing output, 0.20 units of agricultural products will *always* be required as inputs so long as the production process of the manufacturing sector remains unchanged by the prevailing technology. Similarly, for every unit of its output produced, the manufacturing sector requires 0.25 units of its own goods (25/100 = 0.25), 0.15 units of power (15/100 = 0.15), and 15 units of transportation (15/100 = 0.15) as material inputs. These technical coefficients of production for manufacturing were obtained by dividing each element in Column 3 of the interindustry transactions matrix by the total output of the manufacturing sector, 100.

By letting a_{ij} represent the number of units of the ith product (say, manufacturing, where $i = 1, 2, \ldots, n$ and designates the *row* in which the industry is located) necessary to produce *one unit* of output of the jth sector (say, transportation, where j also equals any number from 1 to n and designates the *column* location of that particular industry within the transactions matrix), we can derive a 5 × 5 matrix of "technical coefficients of production." For example, a_{13} would designate the coefficient located in the 1st row and 3rd column of the derived technical matrix. It would represent the number of units of the 1st industry (agriculture) required by the 3rd sector (manufacturing) in order to produce a unit of its own (i.e., manufacturing) output. As was noted above, a_{13} in our example would be equal to 20/100, or 0.20.

The calculation of all a_{ij}'s is a relatively straightforward task. Simply divide the number located in the ith row and jth column of the original interindustry transactions matrix by the total output of industry j. Each column of the new matrix comprises the input coefficients of one particular sector, j. It represents the single-process *production function* of that industry. Thus, the entire A matrix, as the matrix of technical coefficients is often designated (see Table 15.2), summarizes the production processes of the entire economy in the form of goods that flow into and out of each industry. Algebraically,

$$a_{ij} = \frac{x_{ij}}{X_j} \quad \begin{matrix} i = 1, 2, \ldots, n \\ j = 1, 2, \ldots, n \end{matrix} \tag{7}$$

where x_{ij} represents the number of units of goods i used by industry j—that is, the figure in the ith row and jth column of the transactions matrix; and X_j equals the *total output* of industry j shown by the last figure in the jth row of the input-output table.

The matrix of technical coefficients of production for any input-output table with n sectors would consist of $n \times n$ elements. For a table with only 5 sectors, as in our example, the 25 technical coefficients of the matrix would be arranged symbolically as shown in Table 15.2.

Using Equation (7) to calculate the a_{ij}'s for our hypothetical 5-sector input–output table, we arrive at the A matrix shown in Table 15.3.

Thus, for example, we see that the amount of manufactured goods required to produce a unit of agricultural output, a_{31}, is 0.08; the amount of power necessary to produce a unit of output of the extractive industry, a_{42}, is 0.375; the amount of transportation needed to produce a unit of power output, a_{54}, is 0; and the necessary agricultural *input* required to produce a

Table 15.2 A 5 × 5 "*A*" Matrix of Technical Coefficients

	Sector 1	Sector 2	Sector 3	Sector 4	Sector 5
Sector 1	a_{11}	a_{12}	a_{13}	a_{14}	a_{15}
Sector 2	a_{21}	a_{22}	a_{23}	a_{24}	a_{25}
Sector 3	a_{31}	a_{32}	a_{33}	a_{34}	a_{35}
Sector 4	a_{41}	a_{42}	a_{43}	a_{44}	a_{45}
Sector 5	a_{51}	a_{52}	a_{53}	a_{54}	a_{55}

Table 15.3 The "*A*" Matrix of Technical Coefficients for Our Hypothetical 5-Sector Economy

	Agriculture	Extractive Industry	Manufacturing	Power	Transportation
Agriculture	15/125 = 0.12	0/40 = 0.00	20/100 = 0.20	0/75 = 0.00	10/50 = 0.20
Extractive Industry	0/125 = 0.00	0/40 = 0.00	0/100 = 0.00	0/75 = 0.00	0/50 = 0.00
Manufacturing	10/125 = 0.08	0/40 = 0.00	25/100 = 0.25	15/75 = 0.20	5/50 = 0.10
Power	5/125 = 0.04	15/40 = 0.375	15/100 = 0.15	0/75 = 0.00	15/50 = 0.30
Transportation	5/125 = 0.04	10/40 = 0.25	15/100 = 0.15	0/75 = 0.00	5/50 = 0.10

unit of agricultural *output*, a_{11}, is 0.12. Since these coefficients are assumed to be *constant* over time, the input–output table can be utilized to measure the *direct* and the *indirect* effects on the entire economy of any sectoral change in total output or final demand. This can be demonstrated most easily by expressing the input–output system as a set of simultaneous algebraic equations.

The Mathematical Input–Output Model. The mathematics of input–output analysis consists of two basic sets of equations. First, there is a set of accounting equations, one for each producing sector of the economy. The first of these equations states that the total output of Sector 1 is equal to the sum of the separate amounts sold by Sector 1 to the other industries plus the amount produced to satisfy final demands. The second equation says the same thing for Sector 2, and so on for all n industries. In terms of the input–output table, these equations state that for any sector, total output is equal to the sum of all the entries in that sector's row in the table. Thus, an implicit assumption of input–output analysis common to all general equilibrium models is that in all sectors the entire product produced is consumed either by other industries as intermediate inputs or by final demanders. In short, supply always equals demand. Symbolically, this first set of equations can be expressed as follows (to facilitate a comprehension of the relationships involved in the mathematical input–output model, the student should refer back to the symbols contained in the parentheses in Table 15.1). Let

X_i measure the annual rate of total output (in constant value units) of industry *i*;

x_{ij} represent the amount of the product of industry i absorbed annually as an intermediate input by industry j; and

Y_i equal the amount of the same product i produced to satisfy "final demand."

The overall input−output accounting balance for the entire economy comprising n separate industries or sectors can be described in terms of n linear equations:

$$\sum_{j=1}^{n} x_{ij} + Y_i = X_i \tag{8}$$

$$\text{where}\quad i = 1, 2, \ldots, n$$

Each equation states that in all sectors the entire product produced (X_i) is consumed either by the other industries ($\sum_{j=1}^{n} x_{ij}$) or by final demanders (Y_i). For example, in Table 15.1 we have five accounting equations. The one for Industry 3, manufacturing, would read as follows:

$$x_{31} + x_{32} + x_{33} + x_{34} + x_{35} + Y_3 = X_3$$

or, substituting the appropriate numerical figures,

$$10 + 0 + 25 + 15 + 5 + 45 = 100$$

The second and more important set of equations central to input−output analysis is another set of n equations, one for each industry, describing the input−output structure of each industry in terms of a derived set of a_{ij} technical coefficients of production. Thus, the commodity flows, x_{ij}, included in the first balance equations are subject to the following set of structural relationships:

$$x_{ij} = a_{ij}X_j \qquad \begin{array}{l} i = 1, 2, \ldots, n \\ j = 1, 2, \ldots, n \end{array} \tag{9}$$

Since a_{ij} has already been defined as being equal to x_{ij}/X_i, System (9) is merely another way of expressing this definition of proportionality, that is,

$$a_{ij} = \frac{x_{ij}}{X_j} \Rightarrow x_{ij} = a_{ij}X_j \tag{9a}$$

Substituting for x_{ij} from Equation 9 into Equation 8 and transposing terms, we obtain the basic input−output system of equations:

$$X_i - \sum_{j=1}^{n} a_{ij}X_j = Y_i \tag{10}$$

In terms of our hypothetical economy, System (10) would consist of five linear equations that could be written symbolically and numerically as follows:

Symbolic representation

$$X_1 - a_{11}X_1 - a_{12}X_2 - a_{13}X_3 - a_{14}X_4 - a_{15}X_5 = Y_1$$
$$X_2 - a_{21}X_1 - a_{22}X_2 - a_{23}X_3 - a_{24}X_4 - a_{25}X_5 = Y_2$$
$$X_3 - a_{31}X_1 - a_{32}X_2 - a_{33}X_3 - a_{34}X_4 - a_{35}X_5 = Y_3$$
$$X_4 - a_{41}X_1 - a_{42}X_2 - a_{43}X_3 - a_{44}X_4 - a_{45}X_5 = Y_4$$
$$X_5 - a_{51}X_1 - a_{52}X_2 - a_{53}X_3 - a_{54}X_4 - a_{55}X_5 = Y_5$$

Numerical representation

$$125 - 0.12\,(125) - 0.000\,(40) - 0.20\,(100) - 0.00\,(75) - 0.20\,(50) = 80$$
$$40 - 0.00\,(125) - 0.000\,(40) - 0.00\,(100) - 0.00\,(75) - 0.00\,(50) = 40$$
$$100 - 0.08\,(125) - 0.000\,(40) - 0.25\,(100) - 0.20\,(75) - 0.10\,(50) = 45$$
$$75 - 0.04\,(125) - 0.375\,(40) - 0.15\,(100) - 0.00\,(75) - 0.30\,(50) = 25$$
$$50 - 0.04\,(125) - 0.250\,(40) - 0.15\,(100) - 0.00\,(75) - 0.10\,(50) = 15$$

For convenience we can rewrite System (10) in terms of matrix and vector notations as follows. (Students who are unfamiliar with elementary matrix algebra may wish to consult any of a number of introductory texts on mathematics for economists. However, the following presentation should be self-explanatory.)

$$\bar{X} - [A] \cdot \bar{X} = \bar{Y} \qquad \textbf{(11)}$$

where $\quad \bar{X}$ represents a *column vector* of total outputs consisting of n elements (in our example $n = 5$), each of which numerically represents the total output of one of the n industries; [A] is an nxn square matrix of technical coefficients (Table 15.2) and $\bar{Y}$ is a column vector of total final demands.

Thus, if the economy were divided into 30 sectors ($n = 30$), System (11) would be a convenient way of avoiding the tedious task of writing out a set of 30 simultaneous linear equations.

We can now premultiply both sides of Equation (11) by the "identity" or "unit" matrix, denoted [I], to obtain the following expression:

$$[I] \cdot \bar{X} - [A] \cdot \bar{X} = \bar{Y} \qquad \textbf{(12)}$$

Note that the "identity" matrix is merely a square matrix in which all the diagonal elements reading from left to right have a value of 1 while all other elements are equal to 0. Thus, a 3×3 identity matrix would be

$$[I] = \begin{vmatrix} 1 & 0 & 0 \\ 0 & 1 & 0 \\ 0 & 0 & 1 \end{vmatrix}$$

The operation of the identity matrix in matrix algebra has the same effect as the operation of the number 1 in simple algebraic equations; that is, multiplication leaves the value of all elements in the system unchanged.

Thus, if a column vector (e.g., $\bar{X}$) is premultiplied by an identity matrix $[I]$, we obtain the same column vector with unchanged values. For example:

$$\begin{vmatrix} 1 & 0 & 0 \\ 0 & 1 & 0 \\ 0 & 0 & 1 \end{vmatrix} \times \begin{vmatrix} 2 \\ 1 \\ 4 \end{vmatrix} = \begin{vmatrix} (1\cdot2)+(0\cdot1)+(0\cdot4) \\ (0\cdot2)+(1\cdot1)+(0\cdot4) \\ (0\cdot2)+(0\cdot1)+(1\cdot4) \end{vmatrix} = \begin{vmatrix} 2 \\ 1 \\ 4 \end{vmatrix}$$

or, symbolically, $[I] \cdot \bar{X}$.

Factoring out the $\bar{X}$ column vectors on the left side of Equation (12), we derive a very familiar expression of input–output mathematics, namely:

$$(I - A) \cdot \bar{X} = \bar{Y} \tag{13}$$

The $(I - A)$ matrix, often called the "Leontief matrix" in honor of the father of input–output analysis, is obtained mathematically by subtracting each element of the A matrix from its counterpart in the I matrix.

We come now to the crucial mathematical manipulation of the input–output model, the one that gives the system its predictive and planning potentialities. Given a matrix of a_{ij} technical coefficients of production (assumed to be constant and independent of the volume of output) and a column vector of final demands $(Y_1, Y_2, \ldots, Y_n)$, System (13) can be solved for all values of total output $(X_1, X_2, \ldots, X_n)$ simply by dividing both sides of (13) by the Leontief matrix, $(I - A)$, to obtain the following expression:

$$X = \frac{\bar{Y}}{(I - A)}$$

or,

$$\bar{X} = (I - A)^{-1} \bar{Y} \tag{14}$$

This operation with matrices is analogous to the technique of division in elementary algebra. For example, in elementary algebra if we had the equation $(1 - a)x = y$ and we wished to solve for x in terms of a and y, we would divide through by $(1 - a)$, which is equivalent to multiplying y by the reciprocal of $(1 - a)$; that is,

$$x = \frac{y}{(1 - a)} = (1 - a)^{-1}y$$

The expression $(1 - A)^{-1}$ is called the "inverted" Leontief matrix and is commonly designated by the block letter R; that is, System (14) may be written as

$$\bar{X} = [R] \cdot \bar{Y} \tag{14a}$$

By inserting any given, predicted, or planned final demand, $Y_{j_{j=1,\dots,n}}$ into the right-hand side of each equation of System (14a), we can determine the corresponding level of output, $X_{i_{i=1,2,\dots,n}}$, of commodity i that will be produced as a result of this level of demand. Similarly, and more important, System (14a) can be used to measure the probable effects of any change in final demands on the total output of all sectors of the economy. To measure the effects of these changes we merely rewrite (14a) as

$$\Delta X_i = \sum_{j=1}^{n} r_{ij} \Delta Y_{j_{j=1,2,\dots,n}} \tag{14b}$$

where the symbol Δ stands for "the change in" final demand, ΔY, or "the change in" total output, ΔX. (Note that each of the constants, r_{ij}, is a function of all the a_{ij}'s and if the production process of any one sector is altered due to technological advancement, better management, etc., more than one r_{ij} [in all probability quite a few of r_{ij}'s] will be affected. Consequently the assumption that the technical coefficients are constant in the short run is vital to the applicability of the input–output model.)

For example, if the final demands for the products of the manufacturing industry, Sector 3 in Table 15.1, were expected to increase or were planned to increase by, say, 10 units, we could determine how much additional total output would have to be produced in all 5 sectors by using the equations in System (14b). Thus, if we are given $\Delta Y_3 = +10$ and we wish to determine ΔX_1, ΔX_2, ΔX_3, ΔX_4 and ΔX_5, the procedure would be as follows:[9]

$$\Delta X_1 = 1.19(\Delta Y_1)+0.11(\Delta Y_2)+0.40(\Delta Y_3)+0.08(\Delta Y_4)+0.34(\Delta Y_5)$$
$$\Delta X_2 = 0.00(\Delta Y_1)+1.00(\Delta Y_2)+0.00(\Delta Y_3)+0.00(\Delta Y_4)+0.00(\Delta Y_5)$$
$$\Delta X_3 = 0.16(\Delta Y_1)+0.19(\Delta Y_2)+1.55(\Delta Y_3)+0.30(\Delta Y_4)+0.30(\Delta Y_5)$$
$$\Delta X_4 = 0.10(\Delta Y_1)+0.50(\Delta Y_2)+0.32(\Delta Y_3)+1.06(\Delta Y_4)+0.41(\Delta Y_5)$$
$$\Delta X_5 = 0.08(\Delta Y_1)+0.31(\Delta Y_2)+0.27(\Delta Y_3)+0.05(\Delta Y_4)+1.18(\Delta Y_5)$$

Since $\Delta Y_1 = \Delta Y_2 = \Delta Y_4 = \Delta Y_5 = 0$ in our simple example, we can eliminate the 1st, 2nd, 4th, and 5th terms on the right-hand side of the above five equations and arrive at our answer more directly. Thus,

$$\Delta X_1 = 0.40\ \Delta Y_3 = 0.40(10) = \quad 4.0$$
$$\Delta X_2 = 0.00\ \Delta Y_3 = 0.00(10) = \quad 0.0$$
$$\Delta X_3 = 1.55\ \Delta Y_3 = 1.55(10) = 15.5$$
$$\Delta X_4 = 0.32\ \Delta Y_3 = 0.32(10) = \quad 3.2$$
$$\Delta X_5 = 0.27\ \Delta Y_3 = 0.27(10) = \quad 2.7$$

As a result of an increase in total final demand for manufactured products of 10 units, total output of agriculture (X_1) will rise by 4.0 units, output of the extractive industry (X_2) will remain unchanged, and the total outputs of the manufacturing (X_3), power (X_4), and transportation (X_5) sectors will rise by 15.5, 3.2, and 2.7 units respectively. Since each sector must purchase inputs from other sectors in order to produce more units of its own outputs, we see that the total *direct* and *indirect* effects of an initial increase in final demand will reverberate throughout the entire economy in a vast maze of economic interdependences until the combined increase in total output of all sectors of the economy is many times the magnitude of the initial stimulus. In short, if we are given, anticipate, or plan any change in final demands for any good or combination of goods, the input–output equations of System (14b) would portray the full direct and indirect impact of this change on all sectors of the economy.[10]

Criticisms and Conclusions. The usefulness of the input–output model as a tool of development planning ultimately depends on the reliability of the *A* matrix of technical coefficients. For most applications of the model, these coefficients are assumed to be constant, thus implying no technical change in sectoral production processes. Moreover, the coefficients are usually derived from actual interindustry transactions at least 3–5 years *prior* to their use in the planning exercise. One of the major objectives of planning is to transform a developing economy's industrial structure and to improve the production process in a number of industries. The use of unadjusted preplan technical coefficients would thus be inappropriate. Some account, therefore, must be taken of planned or projected changes in these input coefficients through periodic revisions of the technical coefficients matrix.

The assumption of a single production process in each sector as well as the aggregation of different-size firms into a single industry further limits the practical application of input–output planning techniques. This is particularly true with regard to employment projections, where choice of technique and size of firm can be critical in determining whether a given increase in output will have a major or a minor effect on job creation. The problem of choice of techniques and alternative labor coefficients can be handled theoretically by using linear and nonlinear programming or activity-analysis models, but in actual practice such models require a degree of information well beyond that which is available in most LDCs.[11]

Finally, input–output projection models are clearly of greater use to countries with a sizable industrial base, a relatively large flow of interindustry transactions, and a reliable system of data collection. While this limits the immediate application of the model to only a few of the more industrially advanced Third World countries, those others in the early stages of industrial growth and structural transformation may wish to construct simple input–output tables of, say, only 10–20 sectors, if for no other reason than to initiate a system of data collection and sectoral accounts that may yield high planning payoffs in the future.

Project Appraisal and Social Cost–Benefit Analysis

Although most planning agencies in developing countries employ a variant of the basic Harrod–Domar growth model, and some work with simplified input–output sectoral models, the vast majority of day-to-day operational decisions with regard to the allocation of limited public investment funds are based on a microeconomic technique of analysis known as "project appraisal." The intellectual as well as the operational linkage among these three major planning techniques, however, should not be overlooked. Macro growth models set the broad strategy; input–output analysis assures an internally consistent set of sectoral targets; and project appraisal is designed to assure the efficient planning of individual projects within each sector. The degree to which these three stages of planning interact will determine to a large extent the success of the planning exercise.

Basic Concepts and Methodology.[12] The methodology of project appraisal rests on the theory and practice of "social" cost–benefit analysis. The basic idea of cost–benefit analysis is simple: in order to decide on the worth of projects involving public expenditure (or, indeed, in which public policy can play a crucial role), it is necessary to weigh up the advantages (benefits) and the disadvantages (costs) to *society as a whole*. The need for social cost–benefit analysis arises because the normal yardstick of "commercial profitability" that guides the investment decisions of private investors may not be an appropriate guide for public investment decisions. Private investors are interested in maximizing private profits and therefore normally take into account only those variables that affect net profit: receipts and expenditures. Both receipts and expenditures are valued at prevailing market prices for inputs and outputs.

The point of departure for social cost–benefit analysis is that it does not accept that actual receipts are a true measure of social benefits nor actual expenditures a true measure of social costs. In other words, where social costs and benefits diverge from private costs and benefits, investment decisions based entirely on the criterion of commercial profitability may lead to a set of "wrong" decisions from the point of view of social welfare, which should be the government's major concern. Although social valuations may differ significantly from private valuations, the practice of cost–benefit analysis is based on the assumption that these divergences can be adjusted for by public policy so that the difference between social benefit and cost will properly reflect "social profitability" just as the difference between actual receipts and expenditures measures the private profitability of an investment.

Thus, we can define social profit in any period as the difference between social benefits and social costs where these are measured both directly (the real costs of inputs and the real value of outputs) and indirectly (e.g., employment effects, distributional effects). The calculation of the social profitability of an investment then involves a three-step process:[13]

1. We must first specify the objective function to be maximized—normally "net" social benefit—with some measure of how different benefits (e.g., per capita consumption, income distribution) are to be calculated and what the tradeoff between them might be.

2. In order to arrive at calculations of net social benefit, we need some social measures of the unit values of all project inputs and outputs. Such social measures are often called "accounting" or "shadow" prices of inputs and outputs to distinguish them from actual market prices (see below).[14] In general, the greater the divergence between shadow and market prices, the greater the need for social cost–benefit analysis in arriving at public investment decision rules.

3. Finally, we need some decision criterion to reduce the stream of projected social benefit and cost flows to an index, the value of which can then be used to select or reject a project or to rank it relative to alternative projects.

Let us briefly examine each of these steps of project appraisal.

Setting Objectives. The social worth of a project must be evaluated in light of national economic and social objectives. As we have seen, the setting of such objectives is the first and most important stage in the formulation of a development plan. Although all plans are designed to maximize social welfare in one form or another, it is essential that the main measures of social welfare be specified and quantified as carefully as possible. Given the difficulty of attaching numerical values to such objectives as national cohesion, self-reliance, political stability, modernization, and more generally, "quality of life," economic planners typically measure the social worth of a project in terms of the degree to which it contributes to the net flow of future goods and services in the economy, that is, by its impact on future levels of consumption.

Recently, a second major criterion, the project's impact on income distribution, has also received increased attention. Rather than focusing on the simple quantitative increase in consumption generated by a particular investment, planners are now also asking how the particular project will benefit different income groups, particularly the low-income classes. If preference is to be given to raising the consumption standards of low-income groups, then the social worth of a project needs to be calculated as a weighted sum of the distribution of its benefits, where additional consumption by low-income groups may receive a disproportionately high weight in the social welfare objective function. (The attentive reader will note that this procedure is analogous to that of constructing a poverty-weighted index of economic growth, discussed in Chapter 5.)

Computing Shadow Prices and Social Discount Rates. The core of social cost–benefit analysis is the calculation and/or estimation of the prices to be used in determining the true value of benefits and the real magnitude of costs. There are many reasons for believing that in developing countries market prices of outputs and inputs do not give a true reflection of social benefits and costs. Five such reasons, in particular, are often cited.

Inflation and currency overvaluation. Many developing countries are beset by rampant inflation, with a resulting proliferation of price controls. Such prices do not typically reflect the real opportunity cost to society of producing these goods and services. Moreover, in almost all countries, the government manages the price of foreign exchange. With inflation and unaltered foreign exchange rates, the domestic currency becomes overvalued (see Chapter 13) so that (a) import prices underestimate the real cost to the country of purchasing foreign products and (b) export prices (again in local currency terms) understate the real benefit accruing to the country from a given volume of exports. In short, the official price of foreign exchange in most LDCs does not provide a true reflection of the social costs and benefits of importing and exporting. As a result, public investment decisions based on this price will tend to be biased against export industries and in favor of import substitutions.

Wage rates, capital costs, and unemployment. Almost all developing countries exhibit factor-price distortions resulting in wage rates exceeding the social opportunity cost (or shadow price) of labor and interest rates understating the social opportunity cost of capital. This leads, as we discovered in Chapter 7, to the widespread phenomenon of unemployment and underemployment and the excessive capital-intensity of industrial production technologies. If governments were to use unadjusted market prices for labor and capital in calculating the costs of alternative public investment projects, they would grossly underestimate the real costs of capital-intensive projects and tend to promote these at the expense of the socially less costly labor-intensive projects. Moreover, if the social welfare objective function places a premium on improved income distribution, the choice of capital-intensive projects would not only underestimate costs but would also contribute marginally less to improved social welfare than the alternative labor-intensive project.

Tariffs, quotas, and import substitution. As we saw in Chapter 13, the existence of high levels of nominal and effective tariff protection in combination with import quotas and overvalued exchange rates discriminates against the agricultural sector and in favor of the import-substituting manufacturing sector. In addition to reflecting incorrectly the real terms of trade between agriculture and industry, such distorted domestic product prices tend once again to favor upper-income groups (urban manufacturers and modern sector workers) disproportionately in relation to society's lower-income groups (rural farmers as well as the urban and rural self-employed).

Savings deficiency. Given the substantial pressures for providing higher immediate consumption levels to the masses of undernourished and poorly clothed people, the level and rate of domestic savings in most developing countries is often thought to be suboptimal. Although the public understandably places a high premium on present compared with future consumption and thus does little saving, it is up to the government to adopt a longer-term perspective and consider the value of higher levels of present saving on accelerating future income and consumption. According to this argument, governments should use a discount rate that is *lower* than the market rate of interest in order to promote projects that have a longer payoff period and generate a higher stream of investible surpluses in the future. In short, governments should place a premium on projects that generate savings (i.e., by placing a higher shadow price on saving) as opposed to those that merely generate consumption[15] in order to maximize consumption at some future, unspecified period.[16]

The social rate of discount. In our discussion of the shadow price of savings, we mentioned the need for governments to choose appropriate discount rates in calculating the worth of project benefits and costs that occur over time. The "social rate of discount" (also sometimes referred to as "social time preference") is essentially a "price" of time—that is, it is the rate planners use to calculate the net present value of a time stream of project benefits and costs, where the net present value (NPV) is calculated as

$$\text{NPV} = \sum_t \frac{B_t - C_t}{(1 + r)^t} \tag{15}$$

where B_t is the expected benefit of the project at time t, C_t is the expected cost (both evaluated using shadow prices), and r is the government's social rate of discount. Social discount rates may differ from market rates of interest (normally used by private investors to calculate the profitability of investments) depending on the subjective evaluation that planners place on future net benefits: the higher the future benefits and costs are valued in the government's planning scheme, the lower will be the social rate of discount.

In view of the above five forces leading to considerable product, factor, and money price distortions, as well as considerations of external economies and diseconomies of production and consumption (by definition, factors *not* taken into account in private investment decisions), it has been widely argued and generally agreed that a strong case can be made for concluding that a project's *actual* anticipated receipts and expenditures often do *not* provide an accurate measure of its social worth. It is primarily for this reason that the tools of social cost–benefit analysis for project appraisal are now considered essential to an efficient process of project selection in developing countries.

Choosing Projects: Some Decision Criteria. Having computed relevant shadow prices (either from an economy-wide programming model or, more likely, by intelligent adjustments of individual market prices), projected a time stream of expected benefits and costs (including indirect or external effects), and selected an appropriate social discount rate, planners are now in a position to choose from among a set of alternative investment projects those thought to be most desirable. They therefore need to adopt a decision criterion to be followed. Normally, economists advocate using the Net Present Value (NPV) rule in choosing investment projects; that is, projects should be accepted or rejected according to whether their net present values are positive or negative. (Note the similarity between this project appraisal decision rule and our theory of rural–urban migration of Chapter 9.) As we have seen, however, net present value calculations are very sensitive to the choice of a social discount rate. An alternative approach is to calculate the discount rate that gives the project an NPV of zero, compare this "internal rate of return" with either a predetermined social discount rate or the market rate of interest, and choose those projects where internal rates exceed the predetermined or market rate. This approach is widely used in evaluating educational investments.

Since most developing countries face substantial capital constraints, the choice of investment projects will normally also involve a *ranking* of all those projects that satisfy the NPV rule. Projects are ranked in descending order of their net present values (more precisely, by their benefit/cost ratios which are arrived at by dividing NPV by the constraint on total capital cost, K, that is, an NPV/K ratio is calculated for each project). The project or set of projects (some investments should be considered as a "package" of projects) with the highest NPV/K ratio is chosen first, then the next highest and so on down the line until all available capital investment funds have been exhausted.

Conclusions: Planning Models and Plan Consistency

The process of formulating a comprehensive, detailed development plan is obviously a more complicated process than that described by our three-stage approach. It involves a constant dialogue and feedback mechanism between national leaders who set priorities, planners, statisticians, research workers, and departmental or ministry officials. Internal rivalries and conflicting objectives (not to mention political pressure from powerful vested-interest groups) are always to be reckoned with. Nevertheless, the preceding presentation should at least serve to provide students with a "feel" for the mechanics of planning and to demonstrate the ways in which aggregate, input–output, and project planning models can be interrelated and used to formulate an internally consistent and comprehensive development plan.

IMPORTANT CONSIDERATIONS IN CHOOSING PARTICULAR PLANNING MODELS

There are a number of different economic models and planning approaches from which a developing nation can choose. The preceding section reviewed three of the most well-known and widely used models. A country about to draw up a development plan will have to decide which method, or combination of methods, is most suitable to its own special circumstances, needs, and objectives. The ultimate choice is not simply a matter of drawing any plan out of a hat or hastily taking that approach which seems to have been most successful in some other country. Rather, an intelligent and informed choice will depend on the answers to a number of important questions that must be specifically analyzed before reaching a final decision. Some of the more relevant considerations are the following.

Stage of Development

The choice of a particular plan or strategy obviously depends on the current level of a country's economic development. If the economy is still characterized by small-scale subsistence agriculture, a limited monetary sector, and little or no interindustry relations, then detailed quantitative economy-wide planning can have only limited applicability. It would probably be more appropriate to concentrate on individual "social overhead" public investment projects aimed at creating the necessary conditions for economic transformation. Some general idea of possible overall rates of growth of GDP and its major components as well as considerations of population growth and, in the case of most small economies, possibilities of import substitution and export expansion loom more important at this early stage. Two- or three-gap models to identify constraints and bottlenecks in combination with public project appraisal in a few major sectors would probably be most appropriate at this stage. In the later stages, the likely path of development is often more clearly discernible, and greater detail in planning methods may become more feasible.

Institutional Structure

Another important consideration concerns the institutional structure of the economy and the relative roles envisaged for the public and private sectors in the development process. Where the private sector is not very influential and is expected to play a relatively passive role, the public sector will ordinarily be expected to take up the slack and provide the initial stimulus and continued overall direction. Accordingly, more attention will be devoted to public investment projects and sources of government finance. However, if the private sector is considerably more active, the plan is more likely to concentrate on the creation of favorable conditions in which private economic activity is free to flourish in a manner that contributes to the social good. One of the factors involved in this public–private consideration is that of the general attitude and willingness of the private sector to cooperate with the central government in promoting national development. Where conflict exists between public and private interests, the task of development planning is made that much more difficult.

Availability and Quality of Statistical Information

The availability of reliable statistical information represents a third and obviously critical influence on the choice of particular planning approaches. Where existing data are poor and unreliable, the possibility of employing sophisticated mathematical programming models will be greatly diminished. However, while the complete absence of certain statistical information may preclude the use of particular models, economic planners are sometimes advised to resort to educated guesses or to the adaptation of empirical information from economies in similar circumstances rather than forego completely a particularly useful approach merely for lack of full statistical data.

Resource Constraints

The character of the development plan is often greatly influenced by the particular resource constraints or bottlenecks present in the economy. The nature and character of resource constraints are often related to the stage of a country's economic development. However, in general, domestic savings and foreign exchange scarcity usually have been regarded as the principal bottlenecks limiting rapid economic progress. If capital constitutes the crucial constraint, every care must be taken to ensure its most effective and productive utilization (e.g., through the intelligent application of social cost–benefit analysis). When depleted foreign exchange reserves emerge as the operative constraint, export promotion and/or some form of import control in conjunction, perhaps, with increased inflows of foreign aid will assume increased importance in the plan. Other possible economic bottlenecks that might appear during the development process include limited supplies of skilled labor and managerial expertise, inadequate transport facilities, and limited government finance.

Priorities and Objectives

Finally, the specific long-run social and economic goals and objectives the less developed nation deems most important must provide the conceptual basis for the entire plan. Those economic goals most commonly mentioned include the following:

1. Rapid increase in per capita income
2. High level of employment
3. Relatively stable price level
4. Reduction of poverty and income inequalities
5. Favorable balance of payments situation
6. Diversified and self-reliant economy

While each of the above objectives may be desirable in itself, serious conflicts may easily arise if all are pursued with equal intensity. Therefore, it often becomes necessary to determine, in the light of existing social, economic, and institutional conditions and constraints, the specific objective, or combination of objectives, that should receive special priority in the development plan. The remaining targets might then constitute some form of associated "side conditions," or secondary priorities to be realized as far as possible in the course of seeking fulfillment of the first priority objectives.

This completes our review of the nature of development planning and the role of planning models. Let us now look at some of the limitations and shortcomings of planning in practice.

THE CRISIS IN PLANNING: PROBLEMS OF IMPLEMENTATION AND PLAN FAILURES

After more than two decades, the results of development planning in Third World countries have been generally disappointing. In his exhaustive study of the development planning experience in some 55 countries, Albert Waterston concluded that:

> *an examination of postwar planning history reveals that there have been many more failures than successes in the implementation of development plans. By far the great majority of countries have failed to realize even modest income and output targets in their plans except for short periods. What is even more disturbing, the situation seems to be worsening instead of improving as countries continue to plan.[17]*

In a similar vein, Derek Healey in a review article on development policy over the postwar decades concluded that the results of planned development have been "sadly disillusioning for those who believed that planning was the only way."[18] The widespread rejection of central planning based on poor performance has had a number of practical outcomes, the most important of which is the adoption in a growing number of LDCs of a more free market-oriented economic system and a return to fashion of free market economics among some Western development economists (see Appendix 15.1 for some examples).

What went wrong? Why has the early euphoria about planning gradually been transformed into disillusionment and dejection? We can identify two interrelated sets of answers—one dealing with the gap between the theoretical economic benefits and the practical results of development planning and the other associated with more fundamental defects in the planning process, especially as it relates to administrative capacities, political will, and plan implementation.

Theory versus Planning Practice

The principal economic arguments for planning briefly outlined earlier in this chapter—market failure, divergences between private and social valuations, resource mobilization, investment coordination, etc.—have often turned out to be weakly supported by the actual planning experience. Commenting on this planning failure, Killick has noted that *it is doubtful whether plans have generated more useful signals for the future than would otherwise have been forthcoming; governments have rarely, in practice, reconciled private and social valuations except in a piecemeal manner; because they have seldom become operational documents, plans have probably had only limited impact in mobilizing resources and in coordinating economic policies.[19]*

To take the specific case of the market-failure argument and the presumed role of governments in reconciling the divergence between private and social valuations of benefits and costs, the experience of government policy in many LDCs has been one of often *exacerbating* rather than reconciling these divergences. We touched on these issues in several of the problem-focused chapters, but to illustrate the point, let us look again at four crucial areas where private and social valuations tend to diverge and where the impact of government policy has often tended to increase rather than reduce these divergences.

Factor Prices, Choice of Technique, and Employment Creation

A presumed conflict between two major planning objectives—rapid industrial growth and expanded employment opportunities—has typically resulted in the neglect of employment creation in the interest of industrial growth. As we saw in Chapter 8, there need be no such conflict if government policies were more geared to adjusting factor-price signals to the real resource scarcities of developing societies. But, in fact, these private price signals have increasingly diverged from their implicit social valuations partially as a result of public policies that have raised the level of wages above labor's shadow price or scarcity value by various devices such as minimum wage legislation, tying wages to educational attainment, and structuring rates of remuneration at higher levels on the basis of comparable "international" salary scales. Similarly, we saw how investment depreciation and tax allowances, overvalued exchange rates, low effective rates of protection, quotas, and credit rationing at low interest rates all served to lower the private cost of capital far below its scarcity or social cost.

The net effect of these factor-price distortions has been to encourage private and public enterprises to adopt more capital-intensive production methods than would exist if public policy attempted to "get the prices right." In short, private valuations of benefits and costs often dictate more capital-intensive methods of production while true social valuations would point to more labor-intensive technologies. This divergence between private and social valuation is, as we have seen, one of the major reasons for the slow growth of employment opportunities. Within the mystique of development planning, the more powerful mystique of forced industrialization has remained a high priority for many years. Contrary to the expectations of its most vocal advocates, planning has had a far from salutary effect on efficient resource allocation in most developing countries.[20] Planning advocates would probably claim that their arguments still hold. The problem has been "bad" planning and not the mere fact of planning.

Rural–Urban Imbalances and Migration

A second major area of divergence between private and social valuations where, until recently, LDC economic policy appears to have been counterproductive to social concerns relates to the widespread phenomenon of rural–urban migration. As we discovered in Chapter 9, government policies that are strongly biased in favor of urban development, as revealed by the existence of sizable urban–rural income differentials and disparities in locational economic opportunities, have stimulated an excessive outflow of rural migrants in search of limited but highly paid urban jobs. With growing urban unemployment and stagnating agriculture, the continued heavy influx of rural migrants represents a net social loss to society in the context both of lost agricultural output and higher social costs of their urban accommodation. However, from the private viewpoint of the typical migrant, the existence of urban unemployment and thus a less than unitary probability of finding an urban job is more than compensated for by high urban–rural wage differentials. The "expected" urban wage still exceeds rural incomes. It is therefore "privately" rational in terms of discounted expected benefits and costs for rural dwellers to continue migrating to the cities despite high and rising levels of urban unemployment. However, a social benefit–cost analysis would probably indicate that such continued migration is undesirable.

Again, the heavy urban industrialization bias of most LDC development plans in the 1950s and 1960s, combined with relative rural and agricultural neglect, created the conditions and the distorted price signals and economic incentives that have contributed to the urban employment crisis. Rather than narrowing the gap between private and social valuations, the planning experience seems to have widened them and thus to have exacerbated the misallocation of human resources in many Third World countries.

The Demand for Education and the Employment Problem

In Chapter 11, we discovered how economic signals and incentives in many LDCs have served to exaggerate the private valuations of the returns to education to a point where the private demand for ever more years of schooling is greatly in excess of the social payoff. The tendency to ration scarce high-paying employment opportunities by level of completed education and the policy of most LDC governments to subsidize the private costs of education, especially at the higher levels, have together led to a situation in which the social returns to investment in further quantitative educational expansion seem hardly justified in comparison with alternative investment opportunities (e.g., the creation of productive employment projects). But, as long as private benefit/cost valuations show high returns and in the absence of effective policies like those suggested in Chapter 11 to alter these signals to accord with social valuations, LDC governments will continue to face extraordinary public pressure to expand school places at all levels.

As a result of these socially incorrect pricing policies, even greater proportions of future government recurrent expenditures will have to be earmarked for educational expansion. As noted, the problem with such outlays is not only that they represent an investment in idle human resources, but also that the government's financial ability to undertake other public projects will be reduced correspondingly. Educational planning appears, therefore, to have contributed little to reconciling divergences between social and private valuations of investment in schooling.

The Structure of the Economy

As a final example of the way in which planning and development policy have often contributed to the maintenance or exaggeration of socially incorrect signals and incentives, consider the emphasis on rapid industrialization through import substitution. We saw in Chapter 13 how a wide range of external and internal pricing policies, including special tax concessions to foreign investors, overvalued foreign exchanges, higher effective tariff rates designed to lower the cost of capital and intermediate goods imports, quotas, subsidized interest rates and credit rationing to new industries plus a whole array of bureaucratic industrial licensing procedures, have all served to provide an artificial stimulus to import-substituting industrial expansion. But we also learned that for the most part the experience of import substitution, especially in Latin America, has failed to meet planned expectations in terms of the eventual realization of low-cost efficient production by local industries. Moreover, the heavy emphasis on urban industrial growth and the concomitant attempt through an economic policy of distorted signals and incentives to reward private industrial activity have greatly contributed to the stagnation of the agricultural sector.

To take a single case, overvalued exchange rates designed to lower import prices of intermediate goods also raise export prices in terms of foreign currencies. If the nation and the vast majority of its rural people must rely on primary product export earnings, such exchange rate policies designed to stimulate industrialization can make agricultural exports less competitive and be a drain on agricultural expansion. Similarly, most other policies designed to stimulate industrial growth tend to work against the interests of the rural sector. The net result of this relative rural neglect in most development plans, especially during the first two decades of planning, has been the phenomenon of agricultural stagnation and rural poverty described in Chapter 10.

Reasons for Plan Failures

In view of the preceding examples, we may conclude that the gap between the theoretical economic benefits of planning and its practical results in most Third World countries has been quite large. The gap between public rhetoric and economic reality has been even greater. While supposedly concerned with eliminating poverty, reducing inequality, and lowering unemployment, many LDC planning policies have in fact unwittingly contributed to their perpetuation. Some of the major explanations for this have to do with the failures of the planning process itself; these failures, in turn, arise out of certain specific problems.[21]

Deficiencies in Plans and Their Implementation

Plans are often overambitious. They try to accomplish too many objectives at once without consideration of how some of the objectives are competing or even conflicting. They are often grandiose in design but vague on specific policies for achieving stated objectives. Finally, the gap between plan formulation and implementation is often enormous (i.e., many plans, for reasons to be discussed below, are never implemented).

Insufficient and Unreliable Data

The economic wisdom of a development plan depends to a great extent on the quality and reliability of the statistical data on which it is based. When these data are weak, unreliable, or simply nonexistent, as in many poor countries, the accuracy and internal consistency of economy-wide quantitative plans are greatly diminished. And when these unreliable data are compounded by an inadequate supply of qualified economists, statisticians, and other planning personnel (as is also the situation in most poor nations) the attempt to formulate and carry out a comprehensive and detailed development plan is likely to be frustrated at all levels. In such situations, it can be both foolish and a waste of scarce high-level human resources to engage in an extensive planning exercise.

Unanticipated Economic Disturbances, External and Internal

Since most LDCs are "open economies" with a considerable dependence on the vicissitudes of international trade, aid, and private foreign investment, it becomes exceedingly difficult for them to engage in even short-term forecasting, let alone long-range planning. The oil price increases of 1974 and 1979 obviously caused havoc in most LDC development plans. But the energy crisis was only an extreme case of a general tendency for economic factors over which most LDC governments have little control to determine the success or failure of their development policies. Given such vulnerability to external factors, LDC governments need to retain a maximum flexibility in their economic plans and be ready to make needed adjustments as the occasion arises. In the long run, however, a policy of greater self-reliance and less external dependence provides an obvious although often difficult answer to this dilemma. As was pointed out in Chapter 13, economic integration offers an attractive alternative to both strictly outward- and inward-looking development policies.

Institutional Weaknesses

Much has been written about the institutional weaknesses of the planning processes of most developing countries. These include, among others, the separation of the planning agency from the day-to-day decision-making machinery of government; the failure of planners, administrators, and political leaders to engage in a continuous dialogue and internal communication about goals and strategies; and the international transfer of institutional planning practices and organizational arrangements that may be inappropriate to local conditions.

In addition, there has been much concern about incompetent and unqualified civil servants; cumbersome bureaucratic procedures; excessive caution and resistance to innovation and change; interministerial personal and departmental rivalries (e.g., finance ministries and planning agencies are often conflicting rather than cooperative forces in LDC governments); lack of commitment to national goals as opposed to regional, departmental, or simply private objectives on the part of political leaders and government bureaucrats; and, finally, in accordance with this lack of national as opposed to personal interest, the political and bureaucratic corruption that is pervasive in many Third World governments.

While it is beyond the scope of this chapter to deal further with these substantial institutional weaknesses, one should not underestimate their importance in holding back the structural and institutional reforms needed to accelerate economic and social development. They are critical factors, in addition to the three previously mentioned, in explaining the widespread failures of contemporary development planning.

Lack of Political Will

The ultimate cause of LDC planning failures is not simply lack of economic potential nor even inadequate administrative capacity. Rather, poor plan performance and the growing gap between plan formulation and implementation is also attributable to a lack of commitment and "political will" on the part of many Third World leaders and high-level decision makers. Waterston summarizes his analysis of the development planning experience thus:

> The available evidence makes it clear that in countries with development plans, lack of adequate government support for the plans is the prime reason why most are never carried out. Conversely, the cardinal lesson that emerges from the planning experience of developing countries is that the sustained commitment of a politically stable government is the sine qua non for development. Where a country's political leadership makes development a central concern, the people can also be interested through a judicious use of economic incentives. And, although it is never easy to reform administrative and institutional inefficiency, commitment by political leaders is a necessary condition for reform; without it, reform is impossible.[22]

One might add, parenthetically, that such a political "will to develop" on the part of national leaders (assuming that by "development" we mean eliminating poverty, inequality, and unemployment as well as promoting aggregate per capita GNP growth) will require an unusual ability to take a long-term view and to elevate national social interests above factional class, caste, or tribal interests. It will also necessitate the cooperation of the economic elites, who may correctly see their privileged positions challenged by such a development posture. Thus, a political will to develop entails much more than high-minded purposes and noble rhetoric. It requires an unusual ability and a great deal of political courage to challenge powerful elites and vested interest groups and to persuade them that such development is in the long-run interests of *all* citizens. In the absence of their support, whether freely offered or coerced, a will to develop on the part of politicians is likely to meet with staunch resistance, continuous frustration, and growing internal conflict.

NOTES

1. For a more detailed discussion of planning and planning models see M. P. Todaro, *Development Planning: Models and Methods* (Nairobi: Oxford University Press, 1971).
2. UN Department of Economic Affairs, *Measures for the Economic Development of Underdeveloped Countries* (New York: UNDEA, 1951), p. 63.

3. United Nations, *Planning the External Sector: Techniques, Problems and Policies* (New York: United Nations, 1965), p. 12.

4. R. Helfgoth and S. Schiavo-Campo, "An introduction to development planning," *UNIDO Industrializaton & Productivity Bulletin* No. 16 (1970):11. See Appendix 15.1, however, for some recent counterarguments.

5. T. Killick, "The possibilities of development planning," *Oxford Economic Papers*, July 1976, reprinted as Reading 31 in *The Struggle for Economic Development*.

6. Lance Taylor, "Theoretical foundations and technical implications," in Charles R. Blitzer *et al.* (eds.), *Economy-Wide Models and Development Planning* (London: Oxford University Press, 1975), pp. 37−42.

7. *Ibid.*, p. 39.

8. The following illustration, as well as material in the subsequent subsection, is based on Todaro, *Development Planning*, Chapter 2, pp. 17−37.

9. The numerical coefficients 1.19, 0.11, 0.40, etc. are the actual elements of the 5×5 R matrix using the figures in our hypothetical table. For the derivation of these coefficients see Todaro, *ibid.*, pp. 30−31.

10. The precise meaning of direct and indirect impacts can be explained by means of a simple example. Suppose the final demand for automobiles dropped by 10%. The direct impact of this change would naturally be a 10% drop in the production of cars. However, since car manufacturers use steel, rubber, cloth, etc., in producing their cars, they would demand less of these inputs and the *initial* indirect effect of this 10% reduction in car output would be a reduction in the steel, rubber, cloth, and other interindustry outputs used as inputs in car production. Finally, with their outputs also curtailed, the steel, rubber, and cloth industries will in turn demand less inputs from other industries. This "iterative" process of second-, third-, and fourth-round effects of the initial stimulus will continue until practically all sectors of the economy whose output is in any way connected with car production have been affected. Thus, the total effect will be substantially greater than the initial *direct* impact of reduced auto demand.

11. For an introductory discussion of the use of economy-wide programming models, see Todaro, *Development Planning*, Chapter 5.

12. For a good introduction to cost-benefit analysis stressing linkages with economic theory, see A. K. Dasgupta and D. W. Pearce, *Cost-Benefit Analysis: Theory and Practice* (London: Macmillan, 1972).

13. A. K. Dasgupta, *Economic Theory and the Developing Countries* (London: Macmillan, 1974), Chapter 9.

14. For those familiar with the techniques of linear programming, shadow prices are merely the solution values of the "dual" to a linear-programming output or profit maximization problem. See Todaro, *Development Planning*, Chapter 5.

15. Note the implicit change in the objective function from consumption maximization to savings maximization.

16. This approach is advocated by I. M. D. Little and J. A. Mirrlees in their book, *Project Appraisal and Planning in Developing Countries* (New York: Basic Books, 1974).

17. Albert Waterston, *Development Planning: Lessons of Experience* (Baltimore: Johns Hopkins University Press, 1965), p. 293.

18. Derek T. Healey, "Development policy: New thinking about an interpretation," *Journal of Economic Literature* 10, no. 3 (1973):761.

19. Killick, "Possibilities of development planning," pp. 3−4.

20. For an extensive analysis of how public policy and the proliferation of controls has tended to exacerbate development problems in seven major developing countries, see I. M. D. Little, T. Scitovsky, and M. Scott, *Industry and Trade in Some Developing Countries: A Comparative Study* (London: Oxford University Press, 1970).

21. Killick, "Possibilities of development planning," p. 4

22. Waterston, *Development Planning*, p. 367.

CONCEPTS FOR REVIEW

Economic planning
Economic plan
Comprehensive versus partial plans
Inducement versus control in
  planning
Centralized versus decentralized
  planning
Development planning
Economic infrastructure
Market failure
Cost–benefit analysis
Shadow price
Input–output analysis
Technical coefficient of production
Leontief matrix
Final demands
Policy objectives
Plan targets

Internal plan consistency
Short-, medium- and long-term
  planning
Aggregate, sectoral, and interindustry
  planning models
Project appraisal
"Stage of development" in
  relation to choice of planning
  technique
Social rate of discount
Net present value
External economies and
  diseconomies
Internal rate of return
Plan implementation
"Incorrect" signals and incentives
External economic disturbances
"Political will"

QUESTIONS FOR DISCUSSION

1. Why do you think so many Third World countries were persuaded of the necessity of development planning? Were the reasons strictly economic? Comment.
2. Explain and comment on some of the major arguments or rationales, both economic and noneconomic, for planning in Third World economies.
3. Planning is said to be more than just the formulation of quantitative economic targets. It is often described as a "process." What is meant by the planning process and what are some of its basic characteristics?
4. Compare and contrast three basic types of planning models: aggregate growth models, input–output analysis, and project appraisal. What do you think are some of the strengths and weaknesses of these models from the standpoint of planning in developing nations?
5. "A developing country should choose the most sophisticated quantitative planning model when drawing up a comprehensive plan." Comment on this statement, being sure to include in your answer a discussion of the types of considerations relevant to choosing a particular planning model.
6. There is much talk today of a crisis in Third World planning. Many have even claimed that development planning has for the most part been a failure. List and explain some of the major reasons for plan failures. Which reasons do you think are the most important? Explain.

FURTHER READINGS

On the nature and role of development planning, see Jan Tinbergen, *Development Planning* (London: Weidenfeld and Nicolson, 1967); Michael P. Todaro, *Development Planning: Models and Methods* (Nairobi: Oxford University Press, 1971); Hollis Chenery (ed.), *Studies in Development Planning* (Cambridge, Mass.: Harvard University Press, 1971); and P. K. Ghosh (ed.), *Development Policy and Planning: A Third World Perspective* (Westport, Conn.: Greenwood, 1984).

For a more advanced treatment of the use of mathematical models in development planning, see C. R. Blitzer, P. B. Clark, and L. Taylor (eds.), *Economy-Wide Models and Development Planning* (London: Oxford University Press, 1975).

An informative and thoughtful study of the methodology and use of cost–benefit analysis for project appraisal in developing countries can be found in I. M. D. Little and J. A. Mirrlees, *Project Appraisal and Planning for Developing Countries* (New York: Basic Books, 1974).

Finally, for a review of the planning experience of Third World countries during the past decades as well as a critique of the "planning mystique," see Albert Waterston, *Development Planning: Lessons of Experience* (Baltimore: Johns Hopkins University Press, 1965); Mike Faber and Dudley Seers (eds.), *The Crisis in Planning* (2 vols.) (London: Chatto & Windus, 1972), especially the article by Seers on "The prevalence of pseudo-planning"; and Tony Killick, "The possibilities of development planning," *Oxford Economic Papers*, July 1976, reprinted as Reading 31 in *The Struggle for Economic Development*.

Additional readings can be found on pp. 635–636.

APPENDIX 15.1

MARKETS VERSUS PLANNING

THE NEW DEBATE OF THE EIGHTIES

As a result of the disenchantment with central planning, a growing number of (mostly Western) economists, some finance ministers in developing countries, and the heads of the major international development organizations have begun in recent years to advocate the increased use of the market mechanism as a key instrument for promoting greater efficiency and more rapid economic growth. President Ronald Reagan of the United States became famous (or "infamous," depending on one's point of view) for his reference to the "magic of the marketplace" in his 1981 speech at Cancun, Mexico. Several Third World countries had already instituted major economic reforms in the direction of the "free market" in the hope that the "invisible foot" would provide a more powerful kick toward economic growth and development than the "visible hand" of central planning. If the decade of the seventies could be described as a period of increased public sector activity in the pursuit of more equitable development, the early eighties witnessed the reemergence of free market economics as part of the ever-changing development orthodoxy.

Among the early converts were some of the Latin American countries including Uruguay (1974), Chile (1973), and Argentina (1976), although presumably their right-wing governments needed little "enlightenment." More recently, others have joined the "free market" bandwagon, ranging from the traditionally more market-oriented countries such as Kenya, Peru, the Philippines, and the Ivory Coast to the more socialist-inclined countries such as Sri Lanka, Jamaica, and Turkey. As part of their domestic "market liberalization" programs, these countries have sought to reduce the role of the public sector, encourage greater private sector activity, and eliminate "distortions" in interest rates, wages, and the prices of consumer goods. The intent of such changes is to lubricate the wheels of the market mechanism. In addition, these countries have sought to improve their "comparative advantage" in the international economy by lowering exchange rates, promoting export industries, and eliminating protection of domestic industries. Even a few of the socialist countries are experimenting with the use of the market mechanism in some sectors of their economies. In China's rural sector, there has been a substantial privatization of agricultural production, with plots of land being allocated to individual families rather than to a collective. Moreover, the government has been experimenting with profit incentives for farmers by reducing state grain taxes and raising the prices for many agricultural commodities. In 1984, China also began to free up urban markets. In Hungary, the government has divided state firms into smaller units to promote competition, linked domestic and international prices more closely, and tied wages to productivity in an effort to eliminate price distortions.

Among the international organizations preaching the virtues of the free market are the IMF and the World Bank. The IMF is increasingly requiring substantial market liberalization programs and policies to improve comparative advantage as conditions for countries to gain access to its higher credit windows. The World Bank is carefully scrutinizing its project lending to ensure that the projects proposed could not otherwise be undertaken by the private sector. Furthermore, it is emphasizing joint ventures between governments and private enterprise.

What are the reasons behind all of this sudden "market madness"? In part, it has been fostered by the Southeast Asian "success stories," notably by South Korea and Taiwan, which relied extensively on private enterprise, particularly in the *later* stages of development. However, for the most part it has arisen from the growing dissatisfaction with government intervention in general and central planning in particular. Many attribute the poor rates of growth, massive inflation, and balance of payments problems experienced by numerous developing countries during the seventies to the rising burden of public spending, excessive price distortions, and inward-looking trade policies.

In most developing countries, the public sector has grown dramatically over the past two decades, now accounting for 15–25% of the GDP and some 50–60% of *total* investment. However, associated with the rise of the public sector, there has been a considerable amount of inefficiency and waste. The returns to public investment, in terms of GDP growth, declined nearly 25% between 1960 and 1980. Much of this diminishing return has resulted from poor investment decisions, delays in construction, low capacity utilization, and poor maintenance of public projects. Given these problems, many of the "free marketeers" are suggesting that a greater role for private enterprise in undertaking projects could lead to more efficient utilization of resources.

With regard to price distortions, the World Bank in its 1983 *World Development Report* found that price distortions slowed GDP growth in many developing countries. It estimated that countries with highly distorted prices during the seventies experienced growth rates 2% lower than the average for developing countries. Moreover, it found that credit allocations and subsidized interest rates resulted in a bias toward capital-intensive industries; minimum wage requirements reduced the demand for labor; and subsidized prices for consumer goods, especially for food, frequently discouraged producers and thereby created widespread shortages. As a result, many are calling for the elimination of government-induced distortions in interest rates, wages, and the prices of consumer goods, in the hope that the market mechanism will operate more smoothly and produce a more efficient allocation of resources. This in turn will lead to the use of more labor-intensive technology, generate more employment, eliminate scarcities, and improve economic growth. Few heed the neoclassical warning that eliminating only a few distortions will not necessarily lead to an improvement in welfare. They seem instead to be arguing for a "second best" position, in which a little public intervention to deal with market-failure problems is better than widespread intervention which leads to an even worse situation.

On the international scene, many have blamed the balance of payments ills of developing countries on their failure to exploit their comparative advantage. They claim that overvalued exchange rates and excessive protection of domestic industries have resulted in a lack of competitiveness on the international markets. Thus, they argue that by allowing flexible exchange rates, reducing trade restrictions, and promoting exports of goods that use the relatively abundant factor in their production, developing countries may be able to capture more of the gains from trade.

What has been the impact of this "free marketization" by some developing countries? The early results, as might be expected, show both failures and successes. Chile managed initially during the 1970s to raise its rate of growth and to reduce inflation. However, few of these limited benefits "trickled down" to the lower classes. On the negative side, unemployment rose sharply, foreign debt problems became onerous and the distribution of income continued to worsen. In addition, investment levels were low, many private enterprises began to falter, and in the industrial and financial sectors powerful conglomerates emerged, gaining considerable economic and political influence. Thus, in his comprehensive review of the free market, monetarist experiment in Chile, Ricardo F. French-Davis writing in 1983 concluded that "the balance of the [economic] results were clearly negative during the 1973–81 period: output stagnated, the concentration of wealth was spectacular, and savings and investment rates fell significantly."[1] Turkey was successful in dealing with its debt crisis, achieving rapid growth in exports, and reducing inflation; however, it experienced only modest growth in private investment and employment.

Sri Lanka has been one of the most successful in terms of an overall improvement in its economy as a result of market reforms. It managed to double its annual growth rate (from 2.9% in 1970–1976 to 6.2% in 1977–1982), halve its unemployment rate (from 26% to 13%), and raise both public and private investment. The government has taken steps to ensure that the benefits of the liberalization program "trickle down" to the majority of the population by promoting widespread private ownership and enterprise throughout the economy, maintaining assistance programs for low-income families, and providing free education and health services. China has also seen some improvement in its rural sector as a result of its new emphasis on private activities in its agricultural policies. The annual growth rate of agricultural output has doubled and the per capita income of peasants has tripled over the past five years (see Appendix 10.1).

It is too early to come to any final conclusions about the impact of these "free market" reforms on long-term economic growth and development. The question which naturally arises is that of the extent to which Third World countries can rely on the market mechanism, as opposed to central planning and widespread public intervention, to foster their development. Obviously, the answer will depend on the particular circumstances in individual countries. However, in many Third World nations there are a number of factors that may limit the extent to which heavy reliance on market forces is possible. In general, countries will not be able to rely on the market mechanism to the extent that the industrial countries did during their early stages of development. There are several reasons for this conclusion, some of which were mentioned at the beginning of this chapter.

Perhaps the most important reason is that in most developing countries markets are characterized by widespread *imperfections*. One such imperfection not mentioned earlier is the *lack of information* and the *presence of uncertainty* that most individual producers and consumers face. Thus in many developing countries producers are often unsure about the size of local markets, the presence of other producers, and the availability of inputs both domestic and imported. Consumers may be unsure about the quality and availability of products and their substitutes. Moreover, in contrast to their counterparts in developed countries, Third World producers and consumers usually lack the tools to ferret out this information since little is done by way of marketing. Under such circumstances, profit- and utility-maximizing behavior may be based on the wrong information and hence not lead to an efficient allocation of resources. The government may attempt to provide this information, but this is obviously too costly on a large scale, or it may decide to intervene in the market by guiding producers and consumers.

A second imperfection in the market is the *lack of effective (not to mention "perfect") competition*. In most developing countries, the existence of imperfect competition is widespread, particularly in the industrial sector where heavy concentrations of monopoly power are usually found. This situation results from the economies of scale which often characterize modern industries coupled with the relatively small market for manufactured goods which limits the number of firms that can compete. The result is an inefficient allocation of resources, with output lower and prices higher than under perfect competition and a subsequent transfer of wealth from the consumer to the producer (as happened, for example, in Chile in the late 1970s). The government must, therefore, often intervene to limit monopoly power by regulating the size of firms, by controlling price, or by assuming ownership.

A third major imperfection in Third World markets is the presence of substantial *externalities*. Many goods may have a high social value that is not reflected in their market price. Since such goods—including, for example, education and health services—must be provided at a price below their cost or even free, the private sector has no incentive to produce them. Thus, the government must often be responsible for providing these goods, in order to ensure a minimum of welfare. In view of the rapid population growth and mass poverty that characterize many developing countries, it is likely that public sector activity in this area will continue to expand.

The above arguments have shown how the market mechanism can fail in the presence of the widespread imperfections that characterize many developing countries. This does not mean that countries should not rely more on the market to allocate their products and resources. No Third World central planning agency is capable of regulating the vast array of different goods and services. Rather, it means that governments must seek to determine in which areas the market can most efficiently operate and in which areas the government itself can achieve the best results given its own limited human resources.

Even if the market operated relatively efficiently in allocating current resources, however, governments still have to contend with allocating resources over time. *Capital formation* is a fundamental requirement for economic development. Private savings are very low in the early stages of development, and hence through their fiscal and monetary policies, governments usually must play a major role in accumulating capital (see Chapter 16). Investment in infrastructure, particularly during the early stages of development, is of crucial importance as it sets the framework for subsequent investment by both the private and public sector. Furthermore, even in the later stages of development, the private sector may not be able to generate the massive funds required to establish certain industries, despite their long-run profitability. The government may also need to create certain "linkages" that will permit the private sector to flourish in the future. Lastly, the government must often assist in the creation of human capital through educating and training the labor force, so that labor productivity will increase.

Another major concern in the debate over markets versus planning relates to *income distribution*. While the market mechanism may result in a more efficient allocation of resources, it can also produce a distribution of income that is highly unequal. Most developing countries, as we have seen, have a very skewed pattern of income distribution. Excessive reliance on the market mechanism will not improve that distribution. In fact, it may tend to exacerbate the problem since wealthy individuals with their monopoly of "dollar votes" determine the allocation of resources and, hence, income. This provides a strong social welfare case for government intervention.

Finally, it is important to remember that economic development is a process of structural change. The market may be efficient in allocating resources at the margin, allowing certain industries to emerge and others to fail, but may be ineffective in producing large discontinuous changes in the economic structure, changes that may be crucial to the country's long-term development. The government may therefore have to intervene in sectors crucial to the country's development to ensure that they change over time and flourish.

In summary, there are degrees to which different developing countries will be able to rely on the market mechanism to foster economic development. It would appear that those countries still in the early stages of development will have to continue to rely more on planning in the public sector, since their markets are generally underdeveloped, capital formation is low, income distribution is highly skewed, and they face enormous structural changes in the future. Countries in the later stages of development, such as some of those newly industrializing countries (NICs) in Latin America or Southeast Asia have conditions that allow a greater reliance on private markets and competitive prices. But they must always remain wary of the pitfalls of relying solely on the private sector to allocate resources and distribute income in the pursuit of long-term development objectives.

NOTES

1.   Ricardo F. French-Davis, "The monetarist experiment in Chile: A critical survey, "*World Development* 11, no. 11, (November 1983):905.

16

MONETARY AND FISCAL POLICY: THE ROLE AND LIMITATIONS OF THE STATE

There are extremely powerful structural factors in Latin America which lead to inflation and against which traditional monetary policy is powerless.
Raul Prebish, Director General of the Latin American Institute for Economic and Social Planning, United Nations, Santiago, Chile

The taxation potential in underdeveloped countries is rarely fully exploited . . . no more than one-fifth or possibly one-tenth of what is due [is collected].

N. Kaldor, Cambridge University

AN ECLECTIC VIEW OF DEVELOPMENT POLICY

Although development planning is the most visible aspect of public economic policy in Third World nations, the actual day-to-day policy decisions of LDC governments are typically unplanned and often ad hoc responses to emerging and unforeseen economic crises. Within the broad framework of development objectives, a country's various macroeconomic policies and public investment projects tend to have less internal consistency and economic rationality than many textbook planning models would lead us to believe. The very real physical, human, and administrative resource limitations of most developing countries are sufficient to prevent comprehensive planning from being more than a paper exercise—albeit one that can yield important insights into the functioning of an economy and the identification of its principal growth constraints.

In this chapter we provide a broader yet more eclectic view of economic policy in developing countries by taking a critical look at two traditional aspects of government activity in mixed-market economies: monetary and fiscal policy. We then examine the interdependence between development problems and development policies. We conclude the chapter by discussing the role and limitations of public sector activities in the context of administrative constraints and the special circumstances of state-owned enterprises in developing nations. Appendix 16.1 then examines the debate over the impact of public military expenditures on economic development.

SOME COMPONENTS OF MACROECONOMIC POLICY IN DEVELOPING COUNTRIES

A fruitful way to examine the economic impact of public policies in developing countries is to pick specific development problems and analyze how policies have affected them in the past and in what ways such policies might be improved in the future. Our discussion throughout Parts II and III followed this problem-oriented approach. We saw that major development problems such as poverty, inequality, population growth, unemployment, migration, education, rural development, and foreign trade and finance are all affected by and affect government policies. In many cases, policies designed to ameliorate one problem only serve to worsen another. But, by and large, the interdependence between problems and policies is of a complementary rather than a conflicting nature. For example, measures to eliminate poverty and reduce inequality will probably be consistent with stimulating rural development, curtailing rural–urban migration, and counteracting the incentives to have large families. Conversely, measures to promote rural development, to improve educational access, to create urban and rural job opportunities, and to expand foreign exchange earnings are likely to help reduce poverty and lessen inequality.

We will return to this theme of the interdependence between problems and policies in a people-oriented development strategy later in the chapter when we attempt to summarize the analysis of preceding chapters. For the present we will examine the main components of LDC economic policy by utilizing the traditional textbook division between "monetary" and "fiscal" policies.[1] But rather than merely running through a "shopping list" of different public policies, we will focus on how LDC monetary and fiscal policy can promote or retard a broad-based strategy of economic and social development.

Monetary and Financial Policies: The Limitations of Traditional Macro Instruments

In developed nations, monetary and financial policy plays a major direct and indirect role in governmental efforts designed to expand economic activity in times of unemployment and surplus capacity and to contract that activity in times of excess demand and inflation. Basically, monetary policy works on two principal economic variables—the aggregate supply of money in circulation and the level of interest rates. The supply of money (basically currency plus commercial bank demand deposits) is thought to be directly related to the level of economic activity in the sense that a greater money supply induces expanded economic activity by enabling people to purchase more goods and services. This in essence is the so-called monetarist theory of economic activity. Its advocates argue that by controlling the growth of money supplies, governments of developed countries can regulate their nations' economic activity and control inflation.

On the other side of the monetary issue are the so-called Keynesian economists, who argue that an expanded supply of money in circulation increases the availability of loanable funds. A supply of loanable funds in excess of demand leads to lower interest rates. Since private investment is assumed to be inversely related to prevailing interest rates, businessmen will expand their investments as interest rates fall and credit becomes more available. More investment in turn raises aggregate demand, leading to a higher level of economic activity (i.e., more employment and a higher GNP). Similarly, in times of excess aggregate demand and inflation, governments pursue "restrictive" monetary policies designed to curtail the expansion of aggregate demand by reducing the growth of the national money supply, lowering the supply of loanable funds, raising interest rates, and thereby inducing a lower level of investment and, hopefully, less inflation.

Although this description of monetary policy in developed countries grossly simplifies a complex process, it does point out two important aspects that developing countries lack. First, the ability of developed country governments to expand and contract their money supplies and to raise and lower the costs of borrowing in the private sector (i.e., through direct and indirect manipulation of interest rates) is made possible by the existence of highly organized, economically independent, and efficiently functioning money and credit markets. Financial resources are continuously flowing in and out of savings banks, commercial banks, and other nationally controlled public and private "financial intermediaries" with a minimum of interference. Moreover, interest rates are regulated both by administrative credit controls and by market forces of supply and demand so that there tends to be a consistency and relative uniformity of rates in different sectors of the economy and in all regions of the country.

By contrast, markets and financial institutions in most developing countries are highly *unorganized*, often externally *dependent*, and spatially *fragmented*.[2] Many LDC commercial banks are merely overseas branches of major private banking institutions in developed countries. Their orientation therefore, like that of multinational corporations, may be more toward external and less toward internal monetary situations. The ability of Third World governments to regulate the national supply of money is further constrained by the openness of their economies and by the fact that the accumulation of foreign currency earnings is a significant but highly variable source of their domestic financial resources. Most important, the commercial banking system of most LDCs restricts its activities almost exclusively to rationing scarce loanable funds to "credit-worthy" medium- and large-scale enterprises in the modern manufacturing sector. Small farmers and indigenous small-scale entrepreneurs and traders in the manufacturing and service sectors must normally seek finance elsewhere—usually through local moneylenders and loan sharks who charge exorbitant rates of interest.

Thus, most developing countries operate under a dual monetary system—a small and largely externally controlled or influenced *organized* money market catering to the financial requirements of a special group of middle- and upper-class foreign and local businesses in the modern industrial sector, and a large but amorphous *unorganized*, uncontrolled, and often usurious money market to which most low-income individuals are obliged to turn in times of financial need. This is just another manifestation of the dual structure of many LDC economies and their tendency, whether intentional or not, to serve the needs of wealthy elites while neglecting the requirements of the relatively poor.

The second major limitation of standard (Western) monetary theory and policy when applied to the structural and institutional realities of most Third World nations is the assumption of a direct linkage between lower interest rates, higher investment, and expanded output. In Third World nations, investment decisions are rarely sensitive to interest rate movements. Moreover, as we will shortly discover, a number of larger and more industrially advanced countries in Latin America (e.g., Brazil and Argentina) have followed a policy of inflationary-financed industrial growth, in which expansionary monetary policy in conjunction with budgetary deficits has resulted in negative real interest rates (i.e, inflation rates exceeding interest levels), high profits, expanded investment, and a relatively high rate of industrial output growth. But, as we discussed in Chapter 8, there may be severe structural supply constraints (i.e., low elasticities of supply) inhibiting the expansion of output even when the demand for it increases.

These constraints include poor management, the absence of essential (usually imported) intermediate products, bureaucratic rigidities, licensing restrictions, and, in general, an overall lack of interdependence within the industrial sector. Whatever the reasons, structural supply rigidities mean that any increase in the demand for goods and services will not be matched by increases in supply. Instead, the excess demand (in this case, for investment goods) will merely bid up prices and lead to or worsen inflation. In some Latin American nations, this "structural" inflation has been a chronic problem made even worse on the cost side by the upward spiral of wages as workers attempt to protect their real income levels through indexing wage increases to price rises.

Despite some of the above limitations, however, traditional Central Banks and newly formed Development Banks do play an increasingly important role in the monetary policies of developing nations. Let us look at each of these institutions in turn.

The Role of Central Banks

Role in Developed Nations

In developed nations, Central Banks conduct a wide range of banking, regulatory, and supervisory functions. They have substantial public responsibilities and a broad array of executive powers. Their major activities can be grouped into five general functions:[3]

1. *Currency issue and management of foreign reserves.* Central Banks print money, distribute notes and coins, intervene in foreign exchange markets to regulate the national currency's rate of exchange with other currencies, and manage foreign asset reserves to maintain the external value of the national currency.

2. *The role of banker to the government.* Central Banks provide bank deposit and borrowing facilities to the government while simultaneously acting as the government's fiscal agent and underwriter.

3. *The role of banker to domestic commercial banks.* Central Banks also provide bank deposit and borrowing facilities to commercial banks and act as a lender of last resort to financially troubled commercial banks.

4. *The regulation of domestic financial institutions.* Central Banks ensure that commercial banks and other financial institutions conduct their business prudently and in accord with relevant laws and regulations. They also monitor reserve ratio requirements and supervise the conduct of local and regional banks.

5. *The operation of monetary and credit policy.* Finally, Central Banks attempt to manipulate monetary and credit policy instruments (e.g., the domestic money supply, the discount rate, the foreign exchange rate, commercial bank reserve ratio requirements, etc.) in order to achieve major macroeconomic objectives such as controlling inflation, promoting investment, or regulating international currency movements.

Role in Developing Nations

Central Banks are capable of effectively carrying out their wide range of administrative and regulatory functions in developed nations primarily because these countries have a highly integrated, complex economy, a sophisticated and mature financial system, and a highly educated, well-trained, and well-informed population. In developing countries, the situation is quite different. As we have seen in previous chapters, Third World economies may be dominated by a narrow range of exports accompanied by a much larger diversity of imports, the relative prices of which (i.e., the terms of trade) are likely to be beyond local control. Their financial systems are likely to be rudimentary and characterized by (a) foreign-owned commercial banks that mostly finance domestic and export industries, (b) an informal and often usurious credit network serving the bulk of the rural economy, (c) a central banking institution that may have been inherited from colonial rulers and which operates largely as a currency board,[4] (d) an unskilled and inexperienced work force unfamiliar with the many complexities of domestic and international finance, and (e) a degree of political influence and control by the central government not usually found in more developed nations.

Under such circumstances, the most that a Central Bank can hope to accomplish is to instill a sense of confidence among local citizens and foreign trading partners in the credibility of the local currency and in the prudence and responsibility of the domestic financial system. Given the substantial differences in economic structure and financial sophistication between most rich and poor nations, Central Banks in Third World countries simply do not possess the flexibility and the independence to undertake the range of monetary macroeconomic and regulatory functions performed by their developed country counterparts. What, then, can they do? And are there alternatives to a full-fledged Central Bank for the many small, export-oriented developing countries?

Alternatives to Central Banks

Collyns has suggested four alternatives to the standard Central Bank.[5] First, a *transitional central banking institution* can be formed as an intermediate step between a currency board and a Central Bank with the government exerting a strong influence on its financial activities. The range of such activities, however, is checked by statutory limitations on the monetary authority's discretionary powers. British colonies such as Fiji, Belize, Maldives, and Bhutan provide the most common examples of transitional central banks. Second, a *supranational central bank* may be created to undertake central banking activities for a group of smaller countries participating in a monetary union, perhaps also as part of a customs union (see Chapter 14). Three examples of such monetary unions with regional central banks include the West African Monetary Union (franc zone), the Central African Monetary Area (also franc related), and the East Caribbean Currency Authority. Third, a *currency enclave* might be established between an LDC central banking institution and a monetary authority of a larger trading partner, usually but not necessarily the former colonial power. Such an arrangement provides a certain degree of stability to the LDC currency, but the dominating influence of the partner with its own economic priorities renders the enclave almost as dependent as a colony. Examples include Liberia and Panama, which are tied to the U.S. dollar although there is no formal support agreement with the U.S. government. Finally, in an *open economy central banking institution*, where both commodity and international capital flows represent significant components of national economic activity, the monetary environment is likely to be subject to the dominating influence of world commodity and financial markets. As a result, the central banking institution will be engaged primarily in the regulation and promotion of a stable and respected financial system. Examples of such institutions include Singapore, Hong Kong, Kuwait, Saudi Arabia, and the United Arab Emirates. Table 16.1 summarizes the major features of these four categories of Central Bank alternatives as well as those of the currency board and the Central Bank.

In the final analysis, however, it is not so much the organizational structure of the central banking institution nor even its degree of political autonomy that matters. Rather, it is the extent to which such an institution is capable of financing and promoting domestic economic development, through its commercial and development banking system, in an international economic and financial environment characterized by various degrees of dominance and dependence. Commercial banks in Third World countries need to take a much more activist role in promoting new industries and financing existing ones than is usual for banks in developed nations. They need to be sources of venture capital as well as repositories of the commercial knowledge and business skills that are typically in such short supply domestically. It is because of their failure to do this that new financial institutions, known as Development Banks, have emerged over the past two decades in a wide variety of Third World countries.

The Emergence of Development Banking

Development Banks are specialized public and private financial institutions that supply medium- and long-term funds for the creation and/or expansion of industrial enterprises. They have arisen in many Third World nations because the existing banks usually focus on either relatively short-term lending for commercial purposes (commercial and savings banks) or, in the

Table 16.1 The Range of Central Banking Institutions

Institution	Currency issue	Banker to government	Banker to commercial banks	Regulation of financial institutions	Operation of monetary policy	Promotion of financial development
Full-fledged Central Bank	3*	3	3	3	3G	1
Supranational Central Bank	3E	2E	2	2	2E	2
Open economy central banking institution	3C	2C	2	3	1	3
Transitional central banking institution	3CG	2C	2	1	2G	3
Currency enclave central banking institution	1,2CE	2CE	2	1	1	3
Currency board	3C	1	1	1	1	1

Key: 1 = limited involvement; 2 = substantial involvement; 3 = full involvement. C = considerable constitutional restrictions; E = considerable external influence; G = considerable government influence.

SOURCE: Charles Collyns, "Alternatives to the Central Bank in the developing world," *International Monetary Fund, Occasional Paper No. 20* (July 1983), p. 22.

case of Central Banks, the control and regulation of the aggregate supply of money. Moreover, existing commercial banks set loan conditions that often are inappropriate for establishing new enterprises or for financing large-scale projects. Their funds more often are allocated to "safe" borrowers (i.e., established industries, many of which are foreign owned or run by well-known local families). True "venture capital" for new industries rarely finds approval.

In order to facilitate industrial growth in economies characterized by a scarcity of financial capital, Development Banks have sought to raise capital, initially focusing on two major sources: (a) bilateral and multilateral loans from national aid agencies like the U.S. Agency for International Development (USAID) and from international donor agencies like the World Bank, and (b) loans from their own governments. However, in addition to raising capital, Development Banks have had to develop specialized skills in the field of industrial project appraisal. In many cases their activities go far beyond the traditional banker's role of lending money to credit-worthy customers. The activities of Development Banks often encompass direct entrepreneurial, managerial, and promotional involvement in the enterprises they finance—including government-owned and -operated industrial corporations. Development Banks are thus playing an increasingly important role in the industrialization process of many LDCs.

Although Development Banks are a relatively new phenomenon in the Third World, their growth and spread has been substantial. In the mid-1940s there were no more than 10 to 12 such institutions; by the end of the 1970s, their numbers had increased into the hundreds, and their financial resources had ballooned into billions of dollars. Moreover, although the initial sources of capital were agencies like the World Bank, bilateral aid agencies, and local governments (e.g., the Industrial Credit and Investment Corporation of India was established in 1954 with a 30-year interest-free advance of 75 million rupees from the Indian government), the growth of Development Bank finance has increasingly been facilitated by capital from private investors, both institutional and individual, foreign and local. Almost 20% of the share capital of these banks was foreign owned in 1980 with the remaining 80% derived from local investors.

In spite of their impressive growth and their increasing importance for Third World industrial expansion, Development Banks have come under mounting criticism for their excessive concentration on large-scale loans. Some privately owned finance companies (also categorized as Development Banks) refuse to consider loans of less that $20,000–50,000. They argue that smaller loans do not justify the time and effort involved in their appraisal. As a result, these finance companies almost totally remove themselves from the area of aid to small enterprises, even though such aid is of major importance to the achievement of broadly based economic development in most countries and often may constitute the bulk of assistance needed in the private sector. Small-scale entrepreneurs, often lacking technical, purchasing, marketing, organizational, and accounting skills, as well as access to bank credit, are thus forced to seek funds in the exploitive unorganized money markets. Unless these small-enterprise financial and technical needs can begin to be served, the long-run impact of Development Banks, public as well as private, will be confined mainly to assisting a relatively few private corporations and parastatal enterprises to consolidate their combined economic power even further.

We may conclude, therefore, that in spite of the growth of Development Banks in almost every Third World nation, there remains a need for the establishment of new types of savings institutions and financial intermediaries. Such institutions should not only mobilize domestic savings from small as well as large savers but, more important, should begin to channel these financial resources to those small entrepreneurs, both on the farm and in the marginal or "informal" sector of urban areas, who have until now been almost totally excluded from access to needed credit at reasonable rates of interest.[6]

Fiscal Policy for Development

Taxation: Direct and Indirect

In the absence of well-organized and locally controlled money markets, most developing countries have had to rely primarily on fiscal measures to mobilize domestic resources. The principal instruments of such public resource mobilization have been government tax policies. Typically, "direct" taxes—those levied on private individuals, corporations, and property—make up from 20 to 40% of total tax revenue for most LDCs and range from 2 to 5% of their GNPs (see Table 16.2). It is "indirect" taxes such as import and export duties, as well as "excise" taxes (i.e., purchase, sales, and turnover taxes), that comprise the major source of fiscal revenue. Table 16.2 shows the tax structure and revenue sources of 22 selected LDCs.

Traditionally, taxation in developing countries has had two purposes. First, tax concessions and similar fiscal incentives have been thought of as a means of stimulating private enterprise. Such concessions and incentives have typically been offered to foreign private investors to induce them to locate their enterprises in the less developed country. Such tax incentives may indeed increase the inflow of private foreign resources, but as we discovered in Chapter 14, the overall benefits of such "special treatment" of foreign firms is by no means self-evident.

Table 16.2 The Tax Structure and Revenue Sources of Selected Developing Nations

Country	Direct taxes			Indirect taxes		
	Personal and corporate	Property	Total direct	Foreign (import and export duties)	Domestic (excise taxes)	Total indirect
Ethiopia	15.6	8.3	23.9	33.3	42.8	76.1
India	19.8	9.3	29.1	17.8	53.1	70.9
Somalia	7.2	1.1	8.3	58.1	33.6	91.7
Indonesia	28.8	2.1	30.9	43.3	25.8	69.1
Congo	14.1	0.1	14.2	62.0	23.8	85.8
Kenya	42.6	0.7	43.3	34.2	22.5	56.7
Pakistan	15.7	5.7	21.4	24.2	54.3	78.5
South Korea	33.8	8.3	42.1	16.2	41.0	57.2
Sri Lanka	20.7	2.9	23.6	47.6	28.4	76.0
Thailand	13.6	2.1	15.7	41.5	42.8	84.3
Egypt	20.4	8.2	28.6	21.8	31.3	53.1
Philippines	23.9	8.2	32.1	21.4	43.4	64.8
Morocco	29.7	5.5	35.2	19.9	42.4	62.3
Tunisia	29.7	3.8	33.5	13.3	52.0	65.3
Paraguay	11.7	5.8	17.5	50.8	29.0	79.8
Ecuador	11.5	9.9	21.4	56.7	21.6	78.3
Brazil	11.4	1.4	12.8	3.5	70.1	73.6
Honduras	27.2	2.0	29.2	38.4	32.4	70.8
Ghana	23.2	2.7	25.9	49.1	25.0	74.1
Guatemala	12.4	5.6	18.0	32.5	49.4	81.9
Costa Rica	23.1	6.3	29.4	34.2	36.4	70.6
Chile	35.3	6.4	41.7	12.2	45.9	58.1

SOURCE: Montek Ahluwalia, "The scope for policy intervention," in H. Chenery, J. Duloy, and R. Jolly (eds.), *Redistribution with Growth: An Approach to Policy* (Washington, D.C.: IBRD, 1973), Table I. Reprinted by permission of The World Bank and Oxford University Press.

The second purpose of taxation—the mobilization of resources to finance public expenditures—is by far the more important. Whatever the prevailing political or economic ideology of the less developed country, its economic and social progress largely depends on its government's ability to generate sufficient revenues to finance an expanding program of essential, nonrevenue yielding public services such as health, education, transport, communications, and other components of the economic and social infrastructure. In addition, most Third World governments are directly involved in the economic activities of their nations through their ownership and control of public corporations and state trading agencies. Direct and indirect tax levies enable the government to finance the capital and recurrent expenditures of these public enterprises, many of which often operate at a loss.

In general, the taxation potential of a country depends on the following five factors:

1. The level of per capita real income
2. The degree of inequality in the distribution of that income
3. The industrial structure of the economy and the importance of different types of economic activity (e.g., the importance of foreign trade, the significance of the modern sector, the extent of foreign participation in private enterprises, the degree to which the agricultural sector is commercialized as opposed to subsistence oriented)
4. The social, political, and institutional setting and the relative power of different groups (e.g., landlords as opposed to manufacturers, trade unions, village or district community organizations)
5. The administrative competence, honesty, and integrity of the tax-gathering branches of government

We now examine the principal sources of public tax revenues—direct and indirect—in the context of this fivefold classification of tax potential. We can then consider how the tax system might be used either to redistribute incomes or simply to expand government economic activity.

PERSONAL INCOME AND PROPERTY TAXES. Personal income taxes yield much less revenue as a proportion of GNP in the less developed as compared with the more developed nations. In the latter, the income tax structure is said to be "progressive," that is, people with higher incomes theoretically pay a larger percentage of that income in taxes. In practice, however, the average level of taxation in countries like the United States does not vary much between middle- and upper-income groups. This is because of the many tax loopholes available to wealthy individuals. In developing countries, a combination of more exemptions, lower rates on smaller incomes, and a general administrative weakness in collecting income taxes means that less than 3% of Third World populations pay income tax. This figure compares with 60–80% of the populations of developed nations who pay some form of income tax.

It would be administratively too costly and economically regressive to attempt to collect substantial income taxes from the poor, but the fact remains that most LDC governments have not been persistent enough in collecting taxes from the very wealthy. Since it is the highest-income groups that offer the greatest potential yield to the tax collector, the large income inequalities prevailing in most Third World countries mean that there is great scope for expanding income tax revenues. Moreover, in those countries where the ownership of property is heavily concentrated and therefore represents the major determinant of unequal incomes (e.g., most of Asia and Latin America), property taxes can be an efficient and administratively simple mechanism both for generating public revenues and for correcting gross inequalities in income distribution. But as can be seen from Table 16.2, in none of the 22 countries listed does the property tax constitute more than 10% of total public revenues. Moreover, in spite of much public rhetoric about reducing income inequalities, the share of property taxes as well as overall direct taxation has remained roughly the same for the majority of Third World countries over the past two decades. Clearly, this phenomenon cannot be attributed to government tax-collecting inefficiencies as much as to the political and economic power and influence of the large landowning classes in many Asian and Latin American countries. The "political will" to carry out development plans must therefore include the political will to extract public revenue from the most accessible sources to finance development projects. Where the former is absent, so too will be the latter.

CORPORATE INCOME TAXES.   Taxes on corporate profits, of both domestically and foreign-owned companies, amount to less than 2% of GDP in most developing countries, compared with more than 6% in most developed nations. The main reasons that these taxes generate such limited revenue in Third World countries is that there is relatively less corporate activity in the overall economy and that LDC governments tend to offer all sorts of tax incentives and concessions to manufacturing and commercial enterprises. Typically, new enterprises are offered long periods (sometimes up to 15 years) of tax exemption and thereafter take advantage of generous investment depreciation allowances, special tax write-offs, and other measures to lessen their tax burden.

In the case of multinational foreign enterprises, the ability of LDC governments to collect substantial taxes is often frustrated. These locally run enterprises are able to "shift" profits to partner companies in those countries offering the lowest levels of taxation through transfer pricing (discussed in Chapter 14). When local subsidiaries of multinational corporations buy from or sell to partner companies in other countries, the prices in such transactions are merely internal accounting prices of the overall corporation; it makes no difference to the calculation of total corporate profits what price one subsidiary charges another since the cost of one will be offset by the income of the other. For example, in high-tax countries, MNC exports to branches in low-tax countries can be invoiced at artificially low prices. This practice reduces corporate profits in the high-tax country and raises them in the low-tax one. The latter is often referred to as a "tax haven." Thus, by means of transfer pricing, multinational corporations are able to shift their profits from one place to another in order to lower their overall tax assessment while leaving their total profits unchanged. As long as such tax havens exist, this profit-shifting practice greatly limits the ability of individual LDCs to increase public revenues by raising taxes on foreign corporations.

INDIRECT TAXES ON COMMODITIES.   The largest single source of public revenue in developing countries is the taxation of commodities in the form of import, export, and excise duties (see Table 16.2). These taxes which individuals and corporations pay indirectly through their purchase of commodities are relatively easy to assess and collect. This is especially true in the case of foreign-traded commodities, which must pass through a limited number of frontier ports and are usually handled by a few wholesalers. The ease of collecting such taxes is one reason why countries with extensive foreign trade typically collect a greater proportion of public revenues in the form of import and export duties than do those countries with limited external trade. For example, in open economies with up to 40% of their GNPs derived from foreign trade an average import duty of 25% will yield a tax revenue equivalent of 10% of GNP. By contrast, in countries like India and Brazil with only about 7% of their GNPs derived from exports, the same tariff rate would yield only 2% of GNP in equivalent tax revenues.

Although we discussed import and export duties in the context of LDC trade policies in Chapter 14, one further point about these taxes, often overlooked, needs to be mentioned. It is that import and export duties, in addition to representing the major sources of public revenue in many LDCs, can also be an efficient substitute for the corporate income tax. To the extent that importers are unable to pass on to local consumers the full costs of the tax, an import duty can serve as a proxy tax on the profits of the importer (often a foreign company) and only partially a tax on the local consumer. Similarly, an export duty can be an effective way of taxing the profits of producing companies, including those locally based multinational firms that practice transfer pricing. But export duties designed to generate revenue should not be raised to the point of discouraging local producers from expanding their export production.

In selecting commodities to be taxed, whether in the form of duties on imports and exports or excise taxes on local commodities, certain general economic and administrative principles need to be followed to minimize the cost of securing "maximum" revenue. First, the commodity should be imported or produced by a relatively small number of licensed firms so that evasion can be controlled. Second, the price elasticity of demand for the commodity should be low so that total demand is not choked by the rise in consumer prices that results from the tax. Third, the commodity should have a high income elasticity of demand so that as incomes rise more tax revenue will be collected. Fourth, for equity purposes it is best to tax those commodities like cars, refrigerators, imported fancy foods, and household appliances, which are consumed largely by the upper-income groups, while foregoing taxation on items of mass consumption like basic foods, simple clothing, and household utensils even though these may satisfy the first three criteria set forth above.

PROBLEMS OF TAX ADMINISTRATION. In the final analysis, a developing nation's ability to collect taxes for public expenditure programs and to use the tax system as a basis for modifying the distribution of personal incomes will depend not only on the enactment of appropriate tax legislation but, more importantly, on the efficiency and integrity of the tax authorities who must implement these laws. As Professor Kaldor noted over two decades ago:

> *In many underdeveloped countries the low revenue yield of taxation can only be attributed to the fact that the tax provisions are not properly enforced, either on account of the inability of the administration to cope with them, or*

on account of straightforward corruption. No system of tax laws, however carefully conceived, is proof against collusion between the tax administrators and the taxpayers; an efficient administration consisting of persons of high integrity is usually the most important requirement for obtaining maximum revenue, and exploiting fully the taxation potential of a country.[7]

Thus, the ability of Third World governments to expand their "tax nets" to cover the higher-income groups and minimize tax evasion by local and foreign individuals and corporations will largely determine the efficiency of the tax system in achieving its dual function of generating sufficient public revenues to finance expanding development programs and transferring income from upper- to lower-income groups in order to reduce poverty and income inequality. Much will depend, once again, on the political will to enact and enforce such progressive tax programs.

FISCAL POLICY TO CONTROL INFLATION.   The spiraling inflation that spread like wildfire throughout the world in the 1970s affected every nation in Africa, Asia, and Latin America. In the developed countries, inflation rates of 12–25% per annum were the highest recorded in many decades. The economic and political stability of countries like Great Britain and Italy were threatened more by this inflation than by any other event since the Second World War. But the problem was even worse in the developing countries, where the average rate of inflation was in excess of 30% per annum between 1974 and 1980. Although global inflationary forces subsided during the economic slowdown of the early 1980s, Figure 16.1 shows that in the non-oil developing countries, inflation, as measured by the consumer price index, continued to accelerate at an even greater pace than during the 1970s.

Economists have variously attributed the inflation of the 1970s to two major factors—the upward demand-pull of prices as a result of a previous decade of expansionary fiscal and monetary policy (and in the United States, the heavy expenditures on the war in Vietnam), and the upward cost-push of raw material and commodity prices resulting from the unprecedented 1200% rise in oil prices and the worldwide failure of agricultural production to keep pace with rising demand.[8] Given these traditional economic factors of demand-pull and cost-push inflation, psychological factors also entered the picture as workers' expectations of continuing price rises and of a further erosion of their real incomes caused them to press for ever higher wage increases. These spiraling wage increases exerted additional upward pressure on production costs leading to even higher consumer prices. Thus, inflation has a way of becoming self-generating and extremely difficult to stop. A number of Latin American nations (e.g., Argentina and Brazil) were aware of this fact long before the global inflation of the 1970s and, in fact, continue to struggle with it in the 1980s.

Faced with rising prices and higher levels of unemployment (a combination of forces unprecedented in modern Western economic history and which contradicted traditional macroeconomic theories that postulated an inverse relationship between inflation and unemployment), most developed countries, as we have seen, pursued a combination of economic policies. These included (a) slowing monetary growth and raising interest rates; (b) curtailing the growth of government current and capital expenditure; (c) raising taxes, especially for middle- and upper-income groups; (d) establish-

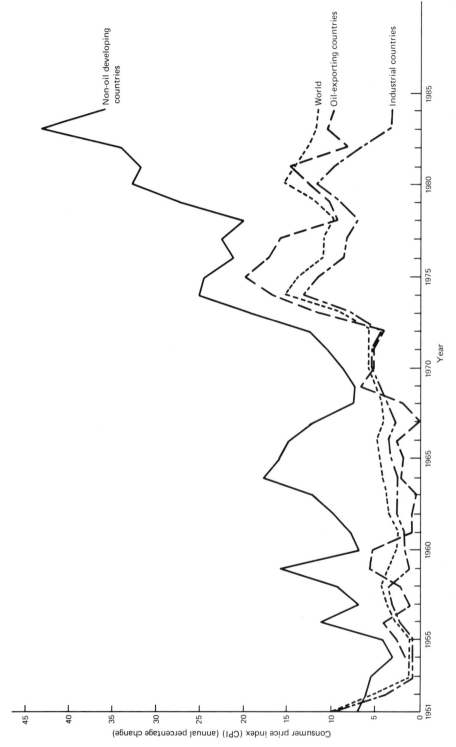

Figure 16.1. Trends in inflation, 1951–1984. *Sources*: International Monetary Fund, *Finance and Development*, September 1983, p. 48; and International Monetary Fund, *World Economic Outlook* (1984), Tables 3 and 7.

ing wage and price guidelines through legislative controls in an effort to curtail the upward movement of costs and prices; and (e) manipulating foreign exchange rates in general and attempting to cut back specifically on oil imports in an effort to reduce payments deficits and prevent the further erosion of their foreign exchange positions. While such restrictive monetary, fiscal, and commercial policies may have imposed severe economic hardships on their poorest families, developed country governments at least possessed the economic tools to cope with the unique inflationary forces of the 1970s.

But what about the less developed countries? Can their domestic monetary and fiscal policies also act as an effective brake on the inflation they too experienced with even more severe economic dislocations and hardships than the developed countries? Or must they resign themselves to minor efforts to modify their domestic rates of inflation while essentially standing on the sidelines as the developed countries do battle against inflation? This second rhetorical question better described the position of most contemporary developing nations in the 1970s and 1980s.

Unlike the inflationary experience of a number of Latin American countries in the 1960s—an experience that largely grew out of deficit-financed expansionary domestic demand policies (see below) combined with production supply inelasticities—the inflation of the 1970s was for most LDCs largely *external in origin*. Being much more dependent than developed countries on the importation of oil, certain capital goods, other raw materials, intermediate products, and consumer goods over whose prices they have virtually no control, the non-oil-exporting Third World nations found themselves with equally high or higher rates of inflation but without many of the economic policy tools with which to combat this price spiral. Most LDCs had therefore to content themselves with policies to control the importation of certain nonnecessity goods, to stimulate and promote greater exports to compensate for the increased cost of imports, to seek special international foreign exchange credits, to ration limited credit from both domestic and foreign sources to essential industrial uses, to hold the line on wage increases while attempting to expand the tax net, and to seek ways to control the rising prices of imported foodstuffs and basic subsistence commodities consumed by the urban and rural poor, often by means of costly government food subsidy programs.

While the above components of antiinflationary LDC economic policy can help to modify the impact of rising prices, especially for those income groups who can least afford it, they are nevertheless insufficient to control domestic inflation. Third World dependence on the world economy in general and on developed country domestic and international economic policies in particular (not to mention the policies of their oil-producing OPEC neighbors) was never more dramatically illustrated than by the inflation and resource-squeeze crises of the 1970s. The most lasting impact of this experience was probably the realization by many LDCs of the real need for increased cooperation among themselves in the pursuit of a greater degree of national or regional self-reliance. In the final analysis, therefore, the achievement of some form of individual or collective economic independence provides one of the only real vehicles for LDCs to control inflation by purely domestic measures.

Inflationary-Financed Industrial Growth: Scope and Limitations

Even before the worldwide inflationary spiral of the 1970s, many developing nations had come to accept rapid price increases as an inevitable and sometimes even necessary way of life. Because of the inadequacy of savings and the difficulty of directing them into productive investments, a number of developing country governments, most notably Brazil and Argentina, have intentionally sought to raise the level of investment and to create modern industries by running chronic budgetary deficits financed by expanded bank credit. This discriminatory, inflationary financing of chosen sectors of the economy is based on the rationale that deficit-financed inflation itself can lead to increased investment. Three reasons are normally given. First, rising relative prices in certain sectors of the economy mean greater profits and a higher return on private investments. This stimulates firms to expand their capacity. Second, the rapid expansion of bank credit in combination with a ceiling on nominal interest rates and rising output prices means that favored investors can often borrow funds at negative real rates of interest. If their industries are also highly protected against foreign competition, a rapid (but socially costly) rate of industrial expansion can be achieved. Finally, inflation was thought to provide an indirect mechanism of transferring real income from nonsavers (i.e., low-income workers and small rural and urban enterprises) to a saving group (wealthy local and foreign industrialists) assumed to reinvest their excess profits and incomes in productive industrial projects. The expectation is that this will maintain a higher level of investment and growth. Regarding this final point, however, Little, Scitovsky, and Scott concluded in their study of seven developing nations (including Brazil and Argentina) that "there is no evidence anywhere of inflation having increased the flow of saving."[9]

In his study of the Brazilian experience, Huddle also has shown that the policy of providing credit for certain industries through the use of inflationary finance during the past two decades has involved some substantial social costs.[10] First, the gains of such growth are very unevenly distributed. Large firms, having privileged access to subsidized finance, become dominant in production even though they may be less efficient than their small- or medium-sized competitors. Second, capital-intensive industries and firms expand at the expense of labor-intensive ones, thus exacerbating the problems of unemployment and surplus labor. Third, deficit-financed inflation can lead to an undesirable pattern of demand which reinforces this tendency toward large-scale, capital-intensive enterprises by channeling finance and, as a result, factor incomes to those groups in society whose consumption patterns are oriented toward domestic capital-intensive and/ or import-intensive "luxury" products. Such policies can therefore reinforce the dualistic nature of developing economies. Fourth, inflation tends to reduce the level of voluntary savings as individuals attempt to protect their real incomes by further bidding up prices of consumer durables, while the pattern of investment can be distorted as funds are used to produce luxury housing, purchase real estate, and build up inventories as a hedge against further inflation. Capacity to resist depreciation becomes the overriding criterion for investment instead of social productivity. Finally, inflation ultimately has a tendency to feed on itself and become self-reinforcing as budget deficits, wage pressures, and occasional devaluations all contribute to a chronic upward spiral of domestic prices. This has been the experience of a number of Latin American countries. Although higher aggregate growth rates may continue to be achieved, rising unemployment and a worsening distribution of income make such growth inimical to development.

We can conclude, therefore, that although inflationary financing may, under certain conditions, succeed in generating high rates of industrial expansion, in the process if often reinforces dualistic tendencies within developing countries, increases levels of unemployment, and worsens the distribution of personal incomes. Today, few economists would seriously contend that chronic budgetary deficits financed by expanding bank credit and rising prices can be a significant factor in promoting Third World development.

THE INTERRELATIONSHIP BETWEEN PROBLEMS AND POLICIES

It was convenient for instructional purposes throughout Parts II and III to isolate major development problems and then to identify an appropriate range of corresponding fiscal, monetary, and other public policy alternatives. As already stressed, however, in reality all these problems and many of the policy responses are highly interrelated. Problems of Third World poverty and inequality cannot be separated from problems of rapid population growth, rising urban unemployment, stagnating agriculture, and unequal and inappropriate educational systems. Similarly, problems of excessive rural−urban migration and rising urban unemployment cannot be analyzed in isolation from problems of mass rural poverty, highly unequal land tenure arrangements, rapid population growth, and the elitist, urban-oriented structure of most formal systems of education. One could go on indefinitely demonstrating the many ways in which development problems and policies are linked in an intricate web of cause and effect.

For illustrative purposes, however, and by way of summarizing much of what has been said in Parts II and III, we look again at five critical development problems analyzed separately in earlier chapters along with some of their major policy implications. Table 16.3 provides a brief summary of the major domestic policy options suggested for coping with the problems of poverty and inequality, population growth, urban unemployment, rural underdevelopment, and inappropriate educational structures.

It may be seen that for the most part policies designed to deal with one problem often contribute to the solution of one or more of the others. Thus, for example, policies designed to eliminate poverty, such as land reform, asset redistribution, taxes and subsidies, the provision of rural social services, and the creation of widespread job opportunities, are also policies that should help to curtail rapid population growth, reduce rural−urban migration, and promote agricultural progress and rural development. Similarly, policies designed to promote rural development, such as institutional reforms to aid the small farmer, rural public works programs, the provision of rural social services and economic infrastructure, and the restructuring of rural educational systems and training programs, also contribute to the

Table 16.3 The Interrelationship between Problems and Policies: An Illustration

Problem	Policy instruments and/or objectives
1. Poverty and inequality	Asset redistribution (mainly from growth). Land reform. Provision of rural social services. Poverty-focused investments (target groups). Tax and subsidy policies (including direct "transfer payments"). Job creation—urban and rural. Improved educational access.
2. Excessive population growth	Eradicate poverty (see 1 above). Provide family planning services. Monetary incentives and disincentives. Education and job opportunities for women. Improved maternal and child nutrition and health.
3. Urban unemployment	Reducing migration by eliminating artificial urban-rural incentive and economic opportunity imbalances. "Getting factor prices right." Choosing and/or developing appropriate labor-intensive technologies. Poverty-focused rural investments. Modifying urban incentive effects of inappropriate education systems. Slowing population growth (see 2 above).
4. Agricultural stagnation and rural underdevelopment	Rural institutional reforms (land tenure, small-farmer access to credit, information, biological and chemical farm inputs, crop insurance, new seeds). Improved rural education, health delivery, sanitation, water supplies, and other social services. Specialized rural training programs. Rural public works. Export promotion.
5. Inappropriate and unequal education	Modifying educational demands by re-orientation of economic signals and incentives toward rural sector. Improved access through system of loans, subsidies, and tuition according to ability to pay. Minimizing excessive credentialization. Promoting nonformal, out-of-school lifetime education. Reorienting curricula along functional lines.

alleviation of urban unemployment (e.g., through lowering the incentives to migrate), the reduction of rural fertility levels, and the amelioration of living conditions where 80% of Third World poverty is located. Finally, policies designed to make education more relevant for development (e.g., by giving it a more functional and rural-oriented structure or by improving access for lower-income groups) can be a major force in promoting rural development, reducing urban unemployment, lowering population growth rates (especially as more women are educated), and providing realistic income-earning opportunities for children of low-income families.

Note that in Table 16.3 we have left out the whole range of international issues and policies dealing with problems of trade, aid, and foreign investment. This was done for convenience of exposition. Clearly, policies designed to minimize the harmful effects of trade, aid, and foreign investment while maximizing their beneficial potentialities will have a direct and indirect impact on the five major problem areas depicted in the table. Finally, Table 16.4 looks at the policy–problem nexus from the opposite perspective of Table 16.3, namely by listing the 23 basic "instruments" of economic policy under four broad headings and showing their typical uses in developing countries.

PUBLIC ADMINISTRATION: THE SCARCEST RESOURCE[11]

Throughout this chapter, and in previous ones, we have tended in our policy discussions to gloss over one of the most critical shortages in the development process. This is the very real and often binding constraint on economic progress that arises out of the shortage of public (and private) administrative capability. Many observers would argue that the lack of such managerial and administrative capability is the single scarcest public resource in the developing world. The problem is not only a lack of training or experience. It also arises out of the political instability of numerous Third World nations. When power is constantly changing hands, considerations of efficiency and public welfare are likely to be subordinated to political loyalty. Moreover, the larger the group of officials affected by a change of power, the more difficult it will be to maintain any continuity in the formulation and execution of policy.

Public administration is unlikely to function efficiently when the rule of law is in question, when there is public disorder, or when there is little consensus on fundamental issues. Acute conditions of class, tribal, or religious conflict within a society will usually be reflected in the management and operation of government departments and public agencies. In a highly traditional society, where kinship ties are strong and such concepts as statehood and public service have not yet taken firm root, there is little place for a merit system. Similarly, where the dominant values are religious or transcendental, traditional incentives to perform in the wider public interest may not have much appeal.

Many LDC governments may also have civil service goals other than performance: to break up traditional elites, to "nationalize" the civil service, to conform to ideological correctness, to reflect or favor an ethnic ratio, to include or exclude minorities. Most governments also are organized in the traditional hierarchical form. But some have experimented with negative

Table 16.4 Chief Instruments of Economic Policy and Their Use

Policy instruments	Typical uses
1. *Fiscal policy*	
(a) Direct taxes on income and profits	To reduce income inequalities; to regulate aggregate demand.
(b) Import duties	Protection of domestic producers.
(c) Other indirect taxes (purchase, sales, and turnover taxes)	To discourage luxury consumption.
(d) Social security levies	To finance pensions; compulsory saving.
(e) Transfer payments (unemployment, sickness, and retirement benefits; subsidies)	To reduce income inequalities and poverty.
(f) Government current expenditures	Provision of services (justice, education, agricultural extension, family planning).
(g) Government capital expenditures	Provision of infrastructure (roads, communications, water).
(h) The budgetary balance (extent of government borrowing)	To adjust the balance between aggregate domestic demand and supply.
2. *Financial and Monetary Policy*	
(a) Promotion/support of financial intermediaries	To improve credit and saving facilities.
(b) Variation of interest rates	To regulate the macroeconomic
(c) Credit controls	balance of the economy.
3. *Direct Controls*	
(a) Exchange controls	To protect the balance of payments.
(b) The exchange rate	
(c) Price and rent controls	To counter inflation.
(d) Wage controls	To set minimum standards; to prevent inflationary wage increases; to encourage employment creation.
(e) Immigration quotas	To promote training of indigenous personnel.
(f) Industrial licensing	To achieve a planned pattern of industrialization.
4. *Miscellaneous*	
(a) Exhortation for voluntary action	'Buy local goods', 'work harder', 'pay your taxes'.
(b) Creation of parastatal organizations	Marketing boards; provision of public utilities; research institutions; agricultural production boards.
(c) Nationalization	To promote economic independence.
(d) Investment incentives (tax holidays, accelerated depreciation)	To encourage investment, especially from abroad.
(e) Other legislative provisions	Company and anti-monopoly legislation; patent laws; land reform.
(f) Requests for official foreign aid	To encourage investment and protect balance of payments.

SOURCE: Tony Killick, *Policy Economics* (London: Heinemann, 1981), p. 38.

hierarchy (from bottom to top), ad hocracy (temporary arrangements), and polyarchy (cooperation with outside organizations)—this last being attempted particularly when some special form of expertise is involved.

Virtually all LDC bureaucracies are hopelessly overstaffed at the bottom and hopelessly understaffed at the top. There is a chronic and desperate shortage of skilled competent managers capable of independent decision making. The greater the number of parastatal organizations set up—the more state-owned enterprises and nationalized industries, quasi-governmental bodies, development corporations, training institutions—the thinner this layer of managers is spread.

In the case of nationalized industries most experiments have been economically disastrous and have resulted in all kinds of strains within the central civil service. Personnel systems within the public service are usually not adequate for the increased management complexities of an industrial enterprise. So parallel personnel systems have been set up, multiplying the public service systems, draining skills, leading to disparities in terms and conditions of service, and resulting in manpower shortages and morale problems. Political considerations often affect the ability to recruit competent managers with special technical skills. In short, nationalization in many instances has often added to the financial burden of the government budget.

But whatever the organizational and political problems of public administration, the sheer difficulty of efficiently managing complex modern economic systems is often cited when referring to critical public policy issues in the Third World. A striking example of the administration problem is provided by the case of the Tazara railroad through Tanzania and Zambia.

The Tazara railway, giving Zambia access to the sea at Dar es Salaam, the capital of Tanzania, was built in less than 5 years by the Chinese and was formally opened in July 1976. In October 1978 President Kaunda of Zambia announced that, effective immediately, and in spite of UN sanctions, OAU pressures, and the civil war in Zimbabwe-Rhodesia, he was reopening Zambia's border with Rhodesia and resuming the interrupted rail link with the South. The reason: massive administrative breakdowns had so impaired the functioning of the railway that it was threatening to strangle the entire Zambian economy.

In early 1978 the EEC had granted Zambia $8 million for fertilizer desperately needed by its ailing agricultural sector. The first consignments from the United States were unloaded at Dar es Salaam, where the railway was unable to handle them and they were left in the open to rot. As the pileup increased, Tanzania was reported to have increased storage and demurrage charges by 1000%. Zambia then ordered the fertilizer rerouted through Beira, Mozambique, whence it went by rail to the town of Moatize, and then by road through Malawi and Zambia. After 60,000 tons had been transported, it became clear that Mozambique's railways and Zambia's transporters, already short of fuel and spare parts, could not cope. Shippers refused to take the remaining 90,000 tons to Dar es Salaam because of the congestion there. Zambia then suggested it go to Maputo, Mozambique, from which it could be carried by South African Railways through South Africa via Pretoria and Mafeking to Francistown, where an armada of small Zambian truckers would carry it across the Kazungulu ferry. But the Dunkirk did not materialize. By the end of September, Zambia had spent an extra $25,000 in transport costs, Maputo and Francistown were drowning in fertilizer, only some 2,000 tons had arrived in Zambia, and the plowing season had begun.

In addition, some 100,000 tons of Zambian copper was either awaiting transportation or trapped somewhere on the line. Further stockpiles at the mines reached 70,000 tons by early October, causing cash shortages to the copper companies, which do not get paid until the copper is on the high seas. Production was hampered by shortages of spare parts and lubricating oil, which were held up elsewhere.

In 4 years' time, Tanzania and Zambia would have to start repaying their $400 million debt to China. About a hundred Chinese specialists were brought back to try and restore the line to working order; they saw little chance of its paying its way unless its administration was completely overhauled. More than half the locomotives were under repair. A quarter of the 2,100 freight cars were off the line at any one time. The accounts department wasn't getting the bills out, and the railway was owed millions of dollars. Without huge spending on new equipment and training programs there was little possibility of Tazara handling even a fraction of its capacity; even the massive spending would not necessarily guarantee results.

This is a dramatic example of an administrative shortfall in one sector—unanticipated in any feasibility study or economic blue print—whose effects were felt not only in other sectors of the Zambian economy but also in neighboring states. It serves to illustrate the crucial importance of the administrative component in economic development planning—not only in relation to the particular project under consideration but also in relation to the functioning of the entire public and private economic system.

STATE-OWNED ENTERPRISES

Associated with the problems of public administration in developing countries have been the widespread activities of state-owned enterprises (SOEs), public corporations owned and operated by the government. In recent years there has been a rapid growth in the number and size of these state-owned enterprises in developing countries. In addition to their traditionally dominant presence in utilities (gas, water, and electricity), transportation (railroads, airlines, and buses), and communications (telephone, telegraph, and postal services), SOEs are now emerging in such key sectors as large-scale manufacturing, construction, finance, services, natural resources, and agriculture. In some cases, they may even dominate these sectors, particularly in the areas of natural resources and manufacturing. For example, in Senegal, Tanzania, Bangladesh, Burma, India, Mexico, and Nicaragua, SOEs produced more than 75% of the annual output in natural resources. In Syria, Tunisia, Egypt, and Ethiopia, SOEs accounted for 60% or more of the value-added in manufacturing.[12]

Overall, it is clear that SOEs are playing a major role in the economies of developing nations, contributing an average of 7–15% of their GDPs. In some cases, their contribution is considerably higher; for example, they produce 20–30% of the domestic output in Senegal, Guinea, Tunisia, and Venezuela and almost 40% of the output in Ghana and Zambia. In addition,

SOEs account for a substantial amount of investment in developing countries, yielding at least a quarter of the total capital formation and in a few cases considerably more.

While contributing to domestic output and capital formation, SOEs are also absorbing substantial amounts of resources and, in many cases, are imposing a heavy fiscal burden on governments. For example, a study of 27 developing countries in 1976–1979 revealed that the net budgetary payments to nonfinancial SOEs averaged more than 3% of GDP. Current spending alone represented 1.4% of GDP. And SOEs were found to be major borrowers of foreign exchange, accounting for 28% of all Third World Eurocurrency borrowing in 1980. They also absorb a large part of domestic credit, particularly in small countries; in Benin, Guinea, Mali, and Senegal, for example, over 40% of domestic credit was absorbed by SOEs.

Given the growing importance of state-owned enterprises in the economies of developing countries and their increasing demands on scarce resources, it is important to understand the reasons for their creation, the causes underlying their increasing demands on resources, and the measures that might be undertaken to improve their efficiency and to help them meet their economic and social objectives.

Some of the reasons for the creation of SOEs have been suggested in Appendix 15.1. One such reason is the persistence of monopoly power in many Third World countries. Direct government control may be required to ensure prices are not set above the costs of producing the output. Moreover, as was also mentioned, certain goods that have a high social benefit are usually provided at a price below their costs or even free; hence, the private sector has no incentive to produce such goods, and the government must be responsible for their provision.

The second rationale for the creation of SOEs is *capital formation*, which, as already suggested, is particularly strong at the early stages of development, when private savings are very low. Investment in infrastructure at this point is crucial to lay the groundwork for further investment. And SOEs remain important at later stages in those industries that require massive funds.

The *lack of private incentive* to engage in promising economic activities because of factors such as uncertainty about the size of local markets, unreliable sources of supply, and the absence of technology and skilled labor is a third major motivation for creating public enterprises. Third World governments may also seek to expand *employment* and facilitate *training* of their labor force through engaging in public production. They may desire to increase export earnings by creating *export industries*, particularly those that might otherwise be unable to compete. For reasons of *income distribution*, the government may seek to locate enterprises in certain sectors, particularly in backward economic areas where there is no private incentive for creating such economic activity.

Other reasons for the creation of SOEs include the desire of some Third World governments to gain national control over *strategic sectors* of the economy such as defense, or over *foreign owned enterprises* (MNCs) whose interests may not coincide with those of the country, or over *key sectors* for planning purposes. Government involvement may also come about as a result of recent independence or of bankruptcy in a major private industry. Finally, *ideological motivations* may be a factor in the creation of state-owned enterprises.

Despite these many valid reasons for their existence, in recent years SOEs have come under increasing attack for wasting resources. As already mentioned, SOEs make significant demands on government resources, as well as on domestic and foreign credit. In many cases, the level of these demands is related to low profitability and inefficiency. Although it is difficult to generalize across countries, available data from the World Bank for state-owned enterprises in 24 developing countries in 1977 revealed only a small operating surplus.[13] And once factors such as interest payments, subsidized input prices, and taxes and accumulated arrears were taken into account, SOEs in many of these countries showed a large deficit. Turkish enterprises averaged net losses equivalent to 3% of GDP during 1977–1979. Mexican SOEs showed a net loss of 1.2% of GDP in 1980. Moreover a 1983 study of SOEs in four African countries (Ghana, Senegal, Tanzania, and Zambia) also revealed a generally poor performance. Most SOEs in these countries failed to show a profit. Operating on a deficit, they proved to be a massive drain on government resources. There was also evidence that labor and capital productivity were generally lower than in the private sector. These African SOEs were also found to be less successful in generating employment as a result of their bias toward capital intensiveness.[14]

There are several factors that contribute to the overall poor performance of SOEs in terms of profitability and efficiency. Perhaps the most important is that SOEs differ from private firms in that they are expected to pursue both commercial and social goals. Providing goods at prices below costs in an effort to subsidize the public, or hiring extra workers to meet national employment objectives inevitably reduces profitability. Another factor adversely affecting the profitability and efficiency of SOEs is the overcentralization of their decision making, which allows little flexibility for managers in the everyday operation of the firm. An additional problem is the bureaucratization of management; many decision makers are not accountable for their performance and little incentive is provided for improved decision making. Finally, despite the abundant labor supply and the employment mandate, access to capital at subsidized interest rates has often encouraged unnecessary capital intensiveness as in the cases of the four African nations cited above.

For the most part, however, the problems which have plagued many Third World public corporations are not beyond solution. Clarifying objectives and perhaps attaching weights to social goals may prove SOEs to be socially desirable, even if not commercially profitable. Decentralizing decision making to allow for more flexibility and providing better incentives for managers could increase production efficiency, while providing capital at its market rate may eliminate the bias toward capital intensiveness. The Chinese government took important steps in this direction when it gave greater autonomy to and increased competition among its million urban SOEs in late 1984. In short, public corporations can play an important role in economic development as long as the "political will" is there to minimize abuse of power and the "economic will" is there to correct socially unnecessary price and market distortions.

DEVELOPMENT POLICY AND THE ROLE AND LIMITATIONS OF THE STATE: CONCLUDING OBSERVATIONS

Keeping the public administration and state-owned enterprises issues in mind, we may now conclude this chapter with some further generalizations on the actual formulation of economic policy in the Third World and speculate about the future role and limitations of the state in the mixed-market economies characteristic of most countries of Asia, Africa, and Latin America.[15]

In view of the record of the past two decades, most development economists would now probably agree that their early and almost mystical belief in the efficacy and benefits of central planning has not been validated by Third World experience.[16] Moreover, as mentioned earlier, economic policies have more often than not tended to be ad hoc responses to recurring and often unexpected crises rather than the playing out of a grand economic design for development. We should never forget that political leaders and decision makers are human beings like the rest of us with all the usual human idiosyncrasies, foibles, and weaknesses. Except in very unusual cases, they will tend to take a parochial (class, caste, tribal, religious, ethnic, regional, etc.) rather than national point of view. In democracies, politicians will respond first to their political constituencies and the vested interest groups within their home areas. In more autocratic forms of government, whether military dictatorship or strict one-party rule, political leaders will still have a natural tendency to respond to those groups to whom they owe their power or on whom their continued power depends. We must always bear in mind that economic policies are ultimately made not by economists or planners but by politicians, who may well be more interested in "muddling through" each emerging crisis and staying in power than in instituting major social and economic reforms. But this situation may change, if only because, as many now believe, the coming years will see a development crisis that simply may not be resolvable without widespread economic and social reform.

We therefore need to be pragmatic about the role and limitations of economic policies in developing nations. On the one hand, we should avoid the tendency to assume that political leaders and decision makers place the "national interest" above their own private interests, or base their policies on some notion of social welfare as opposed to the private welfare of those groups to whom they are primarily indebted. On the other hand, we should equally avoid the cynical view that the social interest, and especially the interest of the poor, the weak, and the inarticulate, will never be considered short of revolution. Social and political revolutions are notorious vehicles by which one elite replaces another while the welfare of the poor remains largely unaffected (China and Cuba being probably the most notable exceptions). It appears more reasonable, therefore, to base our discussion of the role and limitations of the state on the proposition that most Third World governments are beset by conflicting forces, some elitist, others egalitarian, and that their economic policies will be largely a reflection of the relative strength of these competing forces. Although narrow elitist interests have tended to prevail in the past, the groundswell for a more egalitarian development process has now reached the point where politicians and planners can no longer ignore it or camouflage it behind noble but empty rhetoric.

Whatever one's ideological preconceptions about the proper role of government, there can be no denying that over the past two decades governments in developing countries have increasingly claimed responsibility for the management and direction of their economies. It has been said that in many countries, especially in Africa, if the government does not induce development, then it probably will not happen at all. If nothing else, governments in these countries are the most important users of trained manpower. How they deploy these limited human resources thus becomes a crucial issue for the success or failure of the development effort. In short, how governments are structured and how they manage development has been vitally important and will become even more so in the future.

In classical economics the role of government was conceived simply in terms of maintaining law and order, collecting taxes, and generally providing a minimum of social services. With the Keynesian revolution, the economic role of government was greatly expanded. Governments were assigned prime responsibility within a market economy for stabilizing overall economic activity by means of countercyclical monetary and fiscal policies with the objective of maintaining full employment without inflation. At the same time that the Keynesian revolution in Western economic thought was occurring, the Soviet Union was demonstrating to the world the power of central planning to mobilize resources and accelerate industrial growth.

As indigenous leadership replaced colonial leadership in Third World nations, these two models of the role of the state were at hand. Impressed by the Soviet planning performance yet inheriting a free enterprise structure and philosophy from colonial days, most LDCs adopted the system of a mixed market combined with planning, with, as we have seen, a relatively heavy emphasis on central coordination and public sector participation in all aspects of economic activity. Given the rising concern with questions of poverty and inequality, however, the role of the state today has increased to an even greater extent despite the consensus that planning has not worked the magic that some believed it would and that many public corporations are inefficient users of valuable financial and human resources.

Thus there seems to be general agreement today among economists that LDC governments should not necessarily do less, but that they should do what they are now doing better than in the past. Most would agree that the machinery of many Third World governments has become too cumbersome. There are too many ministries often with competing interests, too many public corporations, and too many boards of one kind or another. Governments are criticized for being too centralized and too urban-oriented in both staff and outlook. Civil servants and other trained personnel are often poorly utilized, badly motivated, and in most respects less productive than they should be. There is too much corruption and too little inventiveness and innovation. Bureaucratic red tape and ossified procedures and processes sap originality and flexibility. In short, contemporary LDC governments are criticized for being not too different from almost any other government around the world!

But, whether one likes it or not, Third World governments must inevitably assume a more active responsibility for the future well-being of their countries than the governments of the more developed nations. As their primary tasks of nation-building (in the newly independent countries) and generating rapid economic growth (in all LDCs) are gradually supplemented by preoccupations with problems of poverty, unemployment, and inequality, Third World governments are forging a new role, one that will require innovation and change on a scale that has rarely occurred in the past. Central to this new role will be institutional and structural reform in the fields of land tenure, taxation, asset ownership and distribution, educational and health delivery systems, credit rationing, labor market relations, pricing policies, the organization and orientation of technological research and experimentation, the organization of state trading corporations and public sector enterprises, and the very machinery of government and planning itself.

Whether or not such a transition from a purely growth-oriented development strategy to one also emphasizing the elimination of poverty and the reduction of inequality will require major political transformations, as some have suggested,[17] or whether the existing leadership can respond to the new environment of development by initiating and carrying out fundamental institutional reforms remains open to debate. But whatever the nature of the response, one can certainly predict that the public sector, whether centralized or decentralized, whether jointly with private enterprise or on its own, will in the coming decades continue to claim increasing responsibility for the "commanding heights" of most Third World economies. It is hoped, therefore, that LDC governments have learned much from their experiences of the past two decades and that future successes will more than compensate for any past inadequacies.

NOTES

1. In reality, LDC governments have at least *four* major "policy instruments" at their disposal (see Table 16.4): fiscal policy; monetary and financial policy; legislative controls (e.g., on foreign exchange, prices, wages, industrial licensing, immigration); and miscellaneous policy interventions including creation of parastatal organizations (e.g., marketing boards, public utilities, research institutions), nationalization, exhortation for voluntary action, requests for foreign aid, antimonopoly laws, and land reform. In this chapter we focus only on the first two. The other instruments have been dealt with elsewhere.

2. One of the earliest and best descriptions of the unorganized and fragmented nature of money markets in developing countries can be found in U Tun Wai, "Interest rates outside the organized money markets," *IMF Staff Papers*, November 1957.

3. Charles Collyns, "Alternatives to the Central Bank in the developing world," *International Monetary Fund, Occasional Paper No. 20* (July 1983), p. 2. Much of the discussion that follows is based on this informative report.

4. Currency boards were common in the British colonial nations of Africa and Asia prior to independence. They typically issued domestic currency for foreign exchange and offered limited banking facilities to commercial banks. They could not create new money, conduct monetary policy, give policy advice or supervise the banking system. They simply acted as agents for the colonial banks and were charged with the responsibility of maintaining a fixed parity with the colonial power's currency.

5. Collyns, "Alternatives to the Central Bank," p. 21.

6. For one suggested approach to this problem, see C. Loganathan, "A new deal in development banking," *Development Digest*, October 1972, pp. 25–36.

7. N. Kaldor, "Taxation for economic development," *Journal of Modern African Studies* 1, no. 1 (1963).

8. For a provocative analysis from a Marxist perspective of U.S. macro policy during the 1960s and how it contributed to the inflation and international instability of the 1970s, see J.R. Crotty and L.A. Rapping, "The 1975 Report of the President's Council of Economic Advisors: A radical critique," *American Economic Review*, December 1975.

9. I. M. D. Little, T. Scitovsky, and M. Scott, *Industry and Trade in Some Developing Countries: A Comparative Study* (London: Oxford University Press, 1970), p. 77.

10. Donald L. Huddle, "Inflationary financing, industrial expansion and the gains from development in Brazil," *Program of Development Studies, Rice University, Paper No. 60* (Winter 1975).

11. I am grateful to a former graduate student, Diana Boernstein, for assistance in preparing this section.

12. See World Bank, *World Development Report 1983* (New York: Oxford University Press, 1983), Figures 5.4 and 5.5.

13. *Ibid.*, Chapter 8.

14. Tony Killick, "The role of the public sector in the industrialization of African developing countries," *Industry and Development* 7 (1983): 57–88.

15. Although, spurred by the early Chinese experience and the growing pressures of egalitarian reforms, some Third World countries may turn to greater public ownership and control over domestic resources in the coming decades, it is fair to assume that the vast majority will remain "mixed" in overall economic structure.

16. See, for example, Little, Scitovsky, and Scott, *Industry and Trade*, Chapter 9; and Derek Healey, "Development policy: New thinking about an interpretation," *Journal of Economic Literature* 10, no. 3 (1972): 792–794.

17. See, for example, A. Shourie, "Growth, poverty and inequality," *Foreign Affairs* 51, no. 2 (1973).

CONCEPTS FOR REVIEW

Monetary and fiscal policies

Inflation: cost-push, demand-pull, and structural

Restrictive versus expansionary monetary policy

Financial intermediary

"Organized" money markets

Deficit-financed inflationary growth

"Unorganized" money markets

Central Bank

Development Banks

Direct versus indirect taxes

Progressive versus regressive taxation

Tax loopholes

State-owned enterprises

Expansionary fiscal policies

Contractionary fiscal policies

Recession

Currency board

QUESTIONS FOR DISCUSSION

1. The current debate on the role and limitations of development planning in mixed Third World economies turns on the age-old economic question of how much economic activity should be guided by market forces and how much state intervention there should be. Where do you stand in this debate concerning planning versus the market? Explain the reasoning behind your answer.

2. Keynesian-type macro *monetary* and *fiscal* policies have proved to be effective instruments of government economic policy in developed nations but their relevance and effectiveness in most Third World economies is greatly limited. Comment on this statement, being sure to include in your discussion a description of various monetary and fiscal policies.

3. What is meant by the terms "inflation" and "recession"? Is it possible for an economy to experience an inflation and a recession simultaneously? If so, can you explain how this could come about and give some recent examples? If not, explain why.

4. Distinguish between "demand-pull," "cost-push," and "structural" inflation. Is it possible to have them all occurring simultaneously? Explain.

5. What policy alternatives (both fiscal and monetary) do Third World governments possess in coping with the worldwide inflation like that which occurred during the 1970s? Is it possible for most LDCs to control this type of inflation completely or must they attempt to contain its excesses while relying ultimately on the effectiveness of developed nation antiinflationary policies? Explain your answer.

6. Summarize the arguments for and against the establishment of state-owned enterprises (SOEs) in developing nations. Do you think that SOEs should or should not be discouraged? Explain.

FURTHER READINGS

On fiscal and monetary policy for Third World nations, see W. Arthur Lewis, *Development Planning: The Essentials of Economic Policy* (New York: Harper & Row, 1966); Derek T. Healey, "Development policy: New thinking about an interpretation," *Journal of Economic Literature* 10, no. 3 (1972): 792–794; R. I. McKinnon, *Money and Capital in Economic Development* (Washington, D.C.: Brookings Institution, 1973); E. S. Nassef, *Monetary Policy in Developing Countries* (Rotterdam, The Netherlands: Rotterdam University Press, 1972); C. Loganathan, *Development Savings Banks and the Third World* (New York: Praeger, 1973); J. H. Adler, "Fiscal policy in a developing country," in K. Berrill (ed.), *Economic Development with Special Reference to East Asia* (New York: St. Martin's Press, 1965); R. J. Chelliah, "Trends in taxation in developing countries," *IMF Staff Papers*, July 1971; Richard M. Bird and Oliver Oldman (eds.), *Readings on Taxation in Developing Countries*, rev. ed. (Baltimore: Johns Hopkins University Press, 1970); J. Toye (ed.), *Taxation and Economic Development* (London: Frank Cass, 1979); and Richarde Goode, *Government Finance in Developing Countries* (Washington, D.C.: The Brookings Institution, 1984).

An excellent introduction to the economics and politics of public policy in developing nations can be found in Tony Killick's *Policy Economics: A Text for Developing Countries* (London: Heinemann, 1981). For a review and critique of the role of the state in development activities, see World Bank, *World Development Report 1983* (New York: Oxford University Press, 1983), Part II, pp. 41–127.

Additional readings can be found on pp. 636–638.

APPENDIX 16.1

MILITARY EXPENDITURES AND ECONOMIC DEVELOPMENT

One government-related activity not discussed in the chapter but of growing importance in many Third World economies is that of mounting military expenditures. Since the early 1970s, military expenditures by developing countries have been rising very rapidly despite a world recession, soaring food and oil prices, declining growth in export earnings, and skyrocketing foreign debts. Military spending in the Third World has tripled over the past decade, with countries in the Middle East and North Africa averaging annual increases of 22% (see Table A16.1). In 1980, total military expenditures by developing countries amounted to $142.4 billion, accounting for 22% of world military expenditures. Moreover, many of the world's poorest nations have been regularly allocating 5–10% of their GNP to military purposes compared to the average of 5.4% allocated by the industrial nations (see Table A16.2). Overall, as shown in Table A16.3, developing countries spent more in 1979 in per capita terms on the military ($34 per capita) than on either education ($27 per capita) or health ($11 per capita). By contrast developed countries spent the greatest share on public education ($428 per capita, compared to $345 on the military and $320 on the health sector).

Not only is military spending on the rise but there has also been a shift in its composition, away from paying armies and toward the procurement of sophisticated weaponry. Imports of weapons by developing countries rose dramatically during the 1970s, increasing from $5.6 billion in 1970 to $16.1 billion in 1979, and the rate of growth of arms imports appears to be accelerating in the 1980s. Developing countries are now importing 75% of the world's arms, with countries in the Middle East and North Africa emerging as leading arms importers. A few developing countries have emerged as arms exporters, including Brazil, India, Taiwan, Singapore, and South Korea, although 80% of all arms exports are still supplied by the United States, the Soviet Union, and a few European countries.

Apart from its political implications, the recent military expansion in the Third World has stirred debate over the economic impact of military expenditures on developing countries, where resources are scarce and the opportunity costs of military spending may therefore be high. Arguments and empirical evidence have been presented in support of a positive net effect on economic growth and development; most recent studies, however, indicate that military spending has had more of an adverse effect.

Supporters of military spending argue that such expenditures have a

Table A16.1 World Military Expenditures, 1971 and 1980

	1971			1980		
	$ billion current	*$ billion constant*	*% of world*	*$ billion current*	*$ billion constant*	*% of world*
NATO countries	120.5	206.1	44.1	253.4	229.8	38.6
Warsaw Pact countries	97.4	166.6	35.6	241.1	218.9	36.8
Developed countries	226.0	386.5	82.7	514.3	466.3	78.3
United States	74.9	128.1	27.4	144.0	130.5	21.9
USSR	82.4	140.9	30.1	207.4	188.0	31.6
Other	68.7	117.5	25.1	162.9	147.8	24.8
Developing countries	47.3	80.9	17.3	142.4	129.1	21.7
China	21.5	36.8	7.9	47.0	42.6	7.2
Middle East/North Africa[*]	7.7	13.2	2.8	48.1	43.5	7.3
Latin America	3.6	6.2	1.3	10.4	9.4	1.6
Other	14.5	24.7	5.3	36.9	33.6	5.6
World total	**273.3**	**467.4**	**100.0**	**656.7**	**595.4**	**100.0**

[*]Middle East: Bahrain, Cyprus, Iran, Iraq, Israel, Jordan, Kuwait, Lebanon, Oman, Qatar, Saudi Arabia, Syria, United Arab Emirates, Yemen Arab Republic, and People's Republic of Yemen. North Africa: Algeria, Egypt, Libya, Mauritania, Morocco, Sudan, Tunisia.

NOTE: All constant dollar figures in 1979 dollars. Percentage figures are based on constant dollar military expenditures.

SOURCE: Overseas Development Council, *U.S. Foreign Policy and the Third World, Agenda 1983* (New York: Praeger, 1983), p. 261.

positive impact on economic growth as a result of the relatively large *benefits* of (a) increased aggregate demand generated by military spending; (b) the creation of employment and training opportunities; and (c) the construction of basic infrastructure. It is argued that the opportunity *costs* of military spending are relatively smaller because (a) the resources devoted to military consumption might otherwise go to private consumption or "social investment," such as housing, medical care, or education, which contribute little to future economic growth. Furthermore, it is argued that military spending has a relatively smaller opportunity cost because (b) the resources used for military purposes might not otherwise be available for public use since such resources are often available only through foreign military aid and loans.

The major empirical work in support of this view is the 1978 study conducted by Benoit, which found a positive correlation between military expenditure and economic growth for 44 developing countries over the period 1950–1965. The study concluded that countries with a heavy defense burden had the most rapid rates of growth, while those with the lowest defense burdens tended to have the lowest growth rates.

Critics dispute the purported large benefits of military expenditures. First, it is unlikely that military spending will significantly increase domestic demand due to its high import content. Instead, much of the military demand, which takes the form of demand for military equipment, will be diverted to

Table A16.2 Relative Military Expenditures of 136 Countries, 1980

Per capita GNP under $400	Per capita GNP $400–$999	Per capita GNP $1,000–$3,499	Per capita GNP $3,500 and up
Military expenditures more than 10% of GNP			
Vietnam, 10.6%	Yemen (PDR), 12.8%	Syria, 18.1%	Israel, 29.1%
	Yemen (YAR), 11.2%	Jordan, 12.0%	Oman, 24.6%
			Soviet Union, 14.6%
			Saudi Arabia, 14.4%
			Bulgaria, 12.4%
Military expenditures 5–10% of GNP			
Ethiopia, 9.7%	Zimbabwe, 8.4%	Korea, Dem., 8.2%	Qatar, 8.4%
China, 8.5%	Morocco, 6.1%	Iraq, 8.0%	United Arab
Guinea-Bissau, 6.4%	Egypt, 6.0%	Taiwan, 6.5%	Emirates, 6.4%
Somalia, 6.2%	Cuba, 5.6%	Korea, Rep., 6.2%	Germany (GDR), 5.7%
Chad, 5.0%		Iran, 6.1%	Singapore, 5.7%
Tanzania, 5.0%		Peru, 5.7%	United States, 5.5%
Pakistan, 5.0%			Greece, 5.4%
			Poland, 5.4%
			United Kingdom, 5.1%
Military expenditures 2–4.9% of GNP			
Madagascar, 4.1%	Congo, 4.1%	Malaysia, 4.8%	Czechoslovakia, 4.9%
Burma, 3.8%	Guyana, 3.9%	Yugoslavia, 4.8%	Hungary, 4.4%
Kenya, 3.8%	Zambia, 3.8%	Turkey, 4.5%	Kuwait, 4.2%
Cape Verde, 3.4%	Botswana, 3.5%	Romania, 4.4%	France, 4.0%
Mozambique, 3.1%	Thailand, 3.2%	Portugal, 3.7%	Belgium, 3.4%
Upper Volta, 3.1%	Indonesia, 2.8%	South Africa, 3.2%	Germany (FRG), 3.3%
Zaire, 3.1%	Nicaragua, 2.7%	Argentina, 2.4%	Netherlands, 3.2%
Sudan, 3.0%	Nigeria, 2.6%	Chile, 2.4%	Sweden, 3.1%
India, 2.8%	Senegal, 2.6%	Algeria, 2.2%	Norway, 3.0%
Burundi, 2.6%	El Salvador, 2.5%		Denmark, 2.5%
Mali, 2.5%	Swaziland, 2.5%		Italy, 2.4%
Togo, 2.4%	Philippines, 2.4%		Australia, 2.3%
Benin, 2.2%	Bolivia, 2.0%		Switzerland, 2.0%
Rwanda, 2.0%			
Military expenditures 1–1.9% of GNP			
Central African	Honduras, 1.9%	Ecuador, 1.8%	Bahrain, 1.9%
Republic, 1.8%	Cameroon, 1.5%	Cyprus, 1.6%	Canada, 1.9%
Malawi, 1.8%	Liberia, 1.5%	Uruguay, 1.6%	New Zealand, 1.9%
Uganda, 1.8%	Mauritania, 1.5%	Dominican Rep., 1.5%	Ireland, 1.8%
Afghanistan, 1.7%	São Tomé &	Tunisia, 1.4%	Finland, 1.7%
Bangladesh, 1.4%	Principe, 1.3%	Ivory Coast, 1.2%	Libya, 1.7%
Haiti, 1.4%	Papua New Guinea, 1.3%	Paraguay, 1.2%	Spain, 1.7%
Sierra Leone, 1.1%		Colombia, 1.1%	Austria, 1.2%
Niger, 1.0%		Mauritius, 1.0%	Venezuela, 1.2%
			Luxembourg, 1.0%
Military expenditures less than 1% of GNP			
Nepal, 0.9%	Lesotho, 0.0%	Brazil, 0.9%	Japan, 0.9%
Sri Lanka, 0.7%		Fiji, 0.9%	Gabon, 0.4%
Ghana, 0.0%		Guatemala, 0.8%	Trinidad &
Gambia, 0.0%		Jamaica, 0.8%	Tobago, 0.3%
		Panama, 0.8%	Iceland, 0.0%
		Malta, 0.4%	
		Mexico, 0.4%	
		Barbados, 0.3%	
		Costa Rica, 0.0%	

NOTE: In 1980, world military expenditures totaled $656.7 billion. On average, the developed countries spent 5.4% of their GNP on military expenditures, and developing countries spent 5.1% of their GNP.

SOURCE: Overseas Development Council, *U.S. Foreign Policy and The Third World, Agenda 1983* (New York: Praeger, 1983), p. 261.

Table A16.3 Military Expenditures and Education and Health Expenditures, 1979[a]

Countries	Total military expenditures ($ millions)	Per capita military expenditures $	Rank	Per capita public education expenditures $	Rank	Rank in literacy	Per capita public health expenditures $	Rank	Rank in life expectancy
USSR	183,000	433	9	210	29	1	91	34	46
United States	122,279	543	8	676	9	1	383	12	7
People's Republic of China	44,500	32	72	16	105	65	7	88	57
West Germany	24,776	404	12	566	11	1	676	5	19
France	22,439	424	10	560	12	1	654	6	11
United Kingdom	19,169	342	17	360	21	1	343	16	11
Saudi Arabia	13,831	1,837	2	521	14	128	123	29	96
Japan	9,557	83	45	508	16	1	378	13	1
Poland	8,707	111	35	112	41	1	127	27	27
Italy	7,784	136	29	259	25	27	262	21	11
East Germany	7,190	235	22	249	26	1	251	22	19
Czechoslovakia	5,396	148	28	161	32	1	151	24	33
Netherlands	5,037	359	15	850	4	1	691	4	4
Israel	4,814	1,464	3	389	19	40	191	23	19
Iran	4,489	119	33	111	42	89	35	51	86
India	4,155	6	117	6	121	96	2	121	91
Canada	4,120	174	26	715	8	22	460	9	7
Belgium	3,631	368	14	668	10	1	454	10	19
Romania	3,628	64	54	106	45	22	82	37	33
Sweden	3,387	408	11	1,164	2	1	924	1	1
South Korea	3,385	86	44	52	71	32	3	112	59
Spain	3,272	95	41	110	43	32	151	24	11
Turkey	3,155	57	59	48	74	75	11	73	68
Yugoslavia	2,963	97	40	122	39	44	127	27	33
Australia	2,836	213	23	505	17	1	350	15	7
Iraq	2,671	211	24	84	53	101	21	61	80
Argentina	2,641	55	63	75	57	32	10	77	33
Bulgaria	2,547	106	39	134	37	30	39	74	19
Greece	2,424	257	20	103	46	42	122	30	11
South Africa	2,205	27	74	81	55	69	8	84	71
Hungary	2,138	95	41	167	31	1	110	32	33
Taiwan	2,105	120	31	66	65	44	48	46	27
Switzerland	2,053	324	18	789	6	1	625	7	4
Egypt	1,984	46	66	19	94	84	7	88	80
Nigeria	1,860	27	74	34	78	108	5	95	102
Indonesia	1,784	12	96	6	121	69	4	105	96
Brazil	1,647	14	90	64	66	62	29	53	59
Syria	1,577	238	21	69	62	81	5	95	64
Denmark	1,518	297	19	789	6	1	823	2	7
Norway	1,453	357	16	857	3	1	721	3	4

[a]Countries are listed according to level of total military expenditures in 1979. Ranks are among 141 countries; rank order number is repeated if more than one country has the same level of expenditure.

NOTE: In 1979, world military expenditures of $578.4 billion were slightly more than the total amount of $545.9 billion spent by governments on education and 1.5 times the $373.5 billion spent by governments on medical care and other health services. In developing countries as a whole, more public revenue was devoted to military programs ($133.3 billion) than to education and health care combined ($126.5 billion).

SOURCE: Overseas Development Council, *U.S. Foreign Policy and The Third World, Agenda 1983* (New York: Praeger, 1983), p. 265.

suppliers abroad. In some of the poorer nations, even military demand for "civilian type" goods such as uniforms, boots, and simple construction materials must be met with imported supplies. The remaining demand generated by workers in the defense sector with relatively higher incomes may divert resources from industries producing wage goods to those producing imported luxury items. Second, the benefits of employment creation and training may be considerably smaller than was thought. With the trend toward procurement of weapons rather than paying armies, employment creation for a given military outlay is rapidly diminishing. Furthermore, if increased military spending is compensated for by a reduction in public or private investment, overall employment is likely to fall. In addition, it is debatable that the military sector provides training for the labor force. With its increasingly technical and sophisticated activities, it generates a demand for workers who are already skilled and may in fact divert scarce technicians, engineers, and other skilled workers from local industry. Furthermore, it is not clear that the training of military personnel makes valuable additions to the labor force since skills acquired in the military are not easily transferable to the civilian sector. As to the last supposed benefit, the creation of a basic infrastructure to meet the needs of the military is less justifiable, on the grounds of long-term economic growth and employment generation, than the creation of an infrastructure to meet public and private sector needs.

Critics are equally skeptical of the purported relatively lower opportunity costs of military spending. First, it is not convincing that the opportunity costs of diverting revenues that could otherwise be spent on health, education, or generally improving people's lives are low because such expenditures contribute little to future economic growth. The argument ignores the effects of investment in human capital which provides a foundation for long-term economic growth. Furthermore, it implicitly assumes that investment in the military sector provides a basis for generating future growth through increasing productive capacity. This has not been substantiated empirically. Second, the argument that resources used in the military sector have a low opportunity cost because they would not otherwise be available is no longer valid, given the decline in foreign aid in recent years and its concentration in a few select countries. Most developing countries must now rely on indigenous resources to support the military. With output constrained by scarce resources, increases in military spending can occur only at the high opportunity cost of lower capital formation or reduced civilian consumption. Magnifying the costs of reduced investment and private consumption is the recent trend toward arms imports that require substantial amounts of scarce foreign exchange. When such imports are financed by export earnings, they compete with investment that might be used to increase a country's capacity to earn foreign exchange in the future. With most countries facing deteriorating terms of trade, the use of foreign exchange for arms will have a high opportunity cost. When financed by external loans, arms imports also add to the rising burden of the external debt, which may force countries to eventually pursue fiscal and monetary policies that reduce private consumption and investment, and, hence, diminish economic growth.

In summary, the purported benefits of military spending seem considerably smaller and, in fact, may become very costly in cases where (a) military demand is diverted to foreign suppliers or results in a shift away from the production of wage goods, or (b) where an increase in military expenditure is compensated by a decrease in public spending, causing a reduction of employment, or (c) where military demand diverts scarce skilled workers from other industries, or (d) where it fails to create appropriate infrastructure. The costs of military spending are likely to be high in terms of reduced levels of human capital formation and private investment and, hence, lower long-term economic growth.

Recent empirical work supports this view that military spending has had a negative effect on economic growth. For example, a 1983 article by Lim examined the relationship between defense spending and economic growth for 54 developing countries over a more recent period than the earlier Benoit study (1965–1973) and reached the opposite conclusion, namely, that there is a negative correlation between military spending and economic growth rates in developing countries. Similar results were obtained by Faine, Annez, and Taylor in a 1984 study of 69 countries. It has been suggested that the earlier Benoit study's findings that military spending and economic growth have a positive correlation could be spurious because high military spending was correlated with high foreign aid during the period examined. With the decline in foreign aid in the 1970s and 1980s, it is argued, the relationship between military expenditure and economic growth has been reversed. Whatever the reasons, it is now clear that high military expenditures are draining Third World economies of scarce resources needed to finance long-term development efforts.

FURTHER READINGS

Readings on defense and development include Shaja Nawaz, "Economic impact of defense," *Finance and Development* 20 (March 1983); Emile Benoit, "Growth and defense in developing countries," *Economic Development and Cultural Change* 25, no. 2 (January 1978); David Lim, "Another look at growth and defense in less developed countries," *Economic Development and Cultural Change* 31, no. 2 (1983); Olof Palme, "Military spending: The economic and social consequences," *Challenge*, September–October 1982; Mary Kaldor, "The military in development," *World Development* 4, no. 6 (1976); Overseas Development Council, *U.S. Foreign Policy and the Third World: Agenda 1983* (New York: Praeger, 1983), Annex F; P. K. Ghosh (ed.), *Disarmament and Development: A Global Perspective* (Westport, Conn.: Greenwood, 1984); and Riccardo Faine, Patricia Annez, and Lance Taylor, "Defense spending, economic structure, and growth: Evidence among countries and over time," *Economic Development and Cultural Change* 32, no. 3 (April 1984), 487–498.

17

GLOBAL ECONOMIC ISSUES
IN THE 1980s

ENERGY, FOOD, DEBT, AND THE INTERNATIONAL ORDER

I believe that with all the dislocations that we are now experiencing there also exists an extraordinary opportunity to form for the first time in history a truly global society, carried by the principle of interdependence.
Henry Kissinger, former U.S. Secretary of State

More than ever before it is necessary for the world community to take a global approach to the world's resources and to the structure and operation of international economic relationships.
Statement by Third World social scientists,
Santiago

GLOBAL INTERDEPENDENCE

We live in an increasingly interdependent world, and perhaps some day we will live in a "world without borders," to borrow from the title of a provocative book of the 1970s.[1] For Third World countries, dependence on rich nations is and has always been a stark fact of their economic lives. It is the principal reason for their heightened interest in promoting greater individual and collective self-reliance. At the same time, the developed world, which once prided itself on its apparent economic self-sufficiency, has come to realize that in an age of increasingly scarce natural and mineral resources and burgeoning Third World debts, it is becoming ever more economically dependent on the developing world. In the case of the United

537

States, for example, Third World nations supply 80% of its fuel imports, as well as 26% of its imports of industrial supplies, 25% of its imports of capital goods, and 53% of its imports of consumer goods.

However, rich-nation dependence does not center solely on the need for energy and raw material supplies, or on the ability of key nations like Brazil, Mexico, and Argentina to repay earlier loans. It is also manifested in the growing importance of Third World nations as markets for export products. In the case of U.S. trade, exports to developing countries increased at a 15% annual rate between 1975 and 1981 and grew faster than U.S. exports to any other group of countries. By the early 1980s over 41% of all U.S. exports went to developing nations. One out of every six jobs in the U.S. manufacturing sector was directly dependent on exports to Third World markets. Of the 20 largest U.S. trading partners, 11 were developing nations, and together these 11 nations accounted for more than 26% of all U.S. trade and 22% of all U.S. exports (see Tables 17.1 and 17.2). When Third World economies

Table 17.1 Twenty Largest U.S. Trading Partners, 1981 ($ billions)

	Total transactions	Exports	Imports
Canada	86.0	39.6	46.4
Japan	59.4	21.8	37.6
Mexico	31.6	17.8	13.8
United Kingdom	25.2	12.4	12.8
Saudi Arabia	21.7	7.3	14.4
West Germany	21.7	10.3	11.4
France	13.2	7.3	5.9
Taiwan	12.3	4.3	8.0
Venezuela	11.0	5.4	5.6
Netherlands	11.0	8.6	2.4
Nigeria	10.7	1.5	9.2
Italy	10.6	5.4	5.2
South Korea	10.2	5.1	5.1
Brazil	8.3	3.8	4.5
Belgium-Luxembourg	8.1	5.8	2.3
Hong Kong	8.0	2.6	5.4
Australia	7.7	5.2	2.5
Indonesia	7.3	1.3	6.0
Libya	6.1	0.8	5.3
Algeria	5.7	0.7	5.0
Total, 20 countries	375.8	167.0	208.8
Total, 11 developing countries	132.9	50.6	82.3
Total U.S. trade	495.0	233.7	261.3
11 developing countries as % of total U.S. trade	26.8	21.7	31.5

NOTE: All figures are FAS (free alongside ship) transaction values.

SOURCE: Overseas Development Council, *U.S. Foreign Policy and the Third World, Agenda 1983* (New York: Praeger, 1983), p. 180.

Table 17.2 Ten Largest Developing Country Markets for U.S. Exports

	1975		1981		1975–1981
	U.S. exports ($ billion)	Share of U.S. exports to developing countries (%)	U.S. exports ($ billion)	Share of U.S. exports to developing countries (%)	Average annual growth in U.S. exports (%)[a]
Mexico	5.1	12.5	17.8	31.8	23.2
Saudi Arabia	1.5	3.7	7.3	13.1	30.2
Venezuela	2.2	5.4	5.4	9.7	16.1
South Korea	1.8	4.4	5.1	9.1	19.0
Taiwan	1.7	4.2	4.3	7.7	16.7
Brazil	3.1	7.6	3.8	6.8	3.4
China	0.3	0.7	3.6	6.4	51.3
Singapore	1.0	2.4	3.0	5.4	20.0
South Africa	1.3	3.2	2.9	5.2	14.3
Hong Kong	0.8	2.0	2.6	4.7	21.7
Total, 10 countries	18.8	46.0	55.9	56.1	19.9
Other developing countries	22.1	54.0	43.7	43.9	12.0
Total U.S. Exports	107.6		233.7		13.8
Developing countries	40.9		96.2		15.3
(as % of total exports)		38.0		41.2	
Developed countries	66.2		136.6		12.8
(as % of total exports)		62.0		58.4	

[a]Compound annual rates of change.

NOTE: Countries are ranked according to 1981 percentage share of U.S. exports to developing countries. Data include developing centrally planned economies. Total U.S. export figures include trade with unidentified countries. Figures are FAS (free alongside ship) transaction values.

SOURCE: Overseas Development Council, *U.S. Foreign Policy and the Third World, Agenda 1983* (New York: Praeger, 1983), p. 179.

stagnate, industrial economies feel the effects in terms of diminished exports and lost jobs. For example, during the 1981–1982 recession, sales to non-oil developing nations fell by over $24 billion. In the United States, the Commerce Department has estimated that each $1 billion in exports sustains approximately 25,200 American jobs. By that yardstick, declining U.S. exports to Latin American alone accounted for a loss of nearly 400,000 American jobs in 1982 and 1983. For the first time in recent history, therefore, the economic progress of developing countries has a direct and indirect impact on the economic performance of industrialized nations, and this "reverse economic dependence" will continue to grow in the 1980s.[2]

   In our concluding chapter we examine some of the major manifestations of this emerging global interdependence by focusing on four key issues that are likely to dominate Third World (as well as First World) economic prospects in the latter half of the 1980s: (a) energy and resource balances,

(b) the global food–population equation, (c) the crisis of Third World debt, and (d) demands for a restructuring of the international economic order. We close the chapter with a few final observations on the future of the world economy in an age of increasing interdependence.

ENERGY AND RAW MATERIALS

Energy and the World Economy

If anyone ever doubted that energy and energy supplies (e.g., oil, coal, natural gas, and hydroelectric power) were the foundations of modern industrial economies, the "energy shocks" of the 1970s dramatically proved the point. The developed nations, which make up less than one-quarter of the world's population, consume annually almost 85% of world energy production. But the non-oil-producing Third World countries also rely heavily on oil to fuel their growing industrial and agricultural economies. The massive and unprecedented 400% price increase announced by members of the Organization of Petroleum Exporting Countries in 1974 resulted in enormous additions to their total export revenues, which rose from some $14.5 billion in 1972 to over $110 billion in 1974. Admittedly, a vast proportion of these revenues was derived from the principal oil-importing developed nations like West Germany, France, Italy, Japan, and the United States. But the oil import bill of non-OPEC developing countries—about 90 of them—rose from $4 billion in 1973 to over $15 billion in 1974, an increase of more than $10 billion, or 250%. That increase in the cost of imports alone amounted to more than the total value of all official foreign aid provided to these countries by the developed world. The continued upward spiral in petroleum prices in 1979 further aggravated the balance of payments and inflationary problems of developed and developing nations, with the latter again feeling the impact more severely than the former. For example, the 1979 price increases added $10 billion to the import bills of the oil-importing developing nations and lowered their aggregate growth rates by over 20%.

The oil price explosion, regardless of what its eventual outcome may be, clearly demonstrated the following points about the world economy of the 1970s and 1980s:

1. Almost all the developed countries are net importers of oil, and as such are ultimately dependent on the pricing policies of an organized group of Third World nations. Japan, for example, depends on imports for 99% of its petroleum needs; Western Europe imports 96% of its requirement. The oil price explosion shook these economies in a way that no other single event in the previous 30 years had done. For example, Figure 17.1 shows the strong inverse relation between increases in OPEC's benchmark price for crude oil and real GNP growth rates of the seven major industrial countries. For the foreseeable future, therefore, the oil-exporting countries remain in positions of great importance despite the recession and decline in oil prices during the early 1980s and the gradual erosion of OPEC's dominance as a result of the expansion of oil production in Mexico, Alaska, the North Sea, and other areas. The six Middle East nations, which account for little more than 1% of world population, still control almost half of the world's known reserves of petroleum and a far greater share of total exportable reserves.

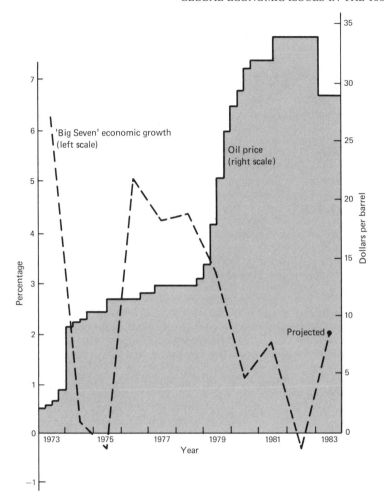

Figure 17.1. The relationship between oil prices and the growth rates of seven major industrial countries—United States, Canada, Japan, Great Britain, Italy, West Germany, and France (price of Saudi Arabian Light, OPEC's benchmark oil price, in dollars per barrel and the aggregate annual change in real gross national product of the seven major industrial countries, in percentages). *Source:* Organization of Economic Cooperation and Development, as reported in the *New York Times,* September 23, 1983.

2. The non oil-exporting LDCs are even more vulnerable to rapid increases in the price of fuels than are the developed nations. For illustrative purposes, however, we can distinguish among four groups of Third World countries according to their vulnerability to rapid energy cost increases. The first group consists of countries like Colombia, Bolivia, and Peru which are self-sufficient in oil and are therefore not directly affected. For the second group, including Malaysia, Morocco, and Chile, the effects of the increases were mitigated in the 1970s by a gradual rise in the prices of their own scarce exportable raw materials. A third category consists of nations like South Korea,

Hong Kong, Taiwan, and Singapore. These countries are all closely integrated into the world economy, primarily through their import of raw and intermediate materials for processing into manufactured goods. The energy component of their imports is large, but they are able to pass on most of their extra energy and raw material costs in the form of higher prices to buyers of their manufactured export products. Moreover, the dynamism of their economies is such that they have relatively good access to export credits and foreign financial support.

The fourth and last category of nations consists of those 40 or so Third World countries that are extremely vulnerable to rapid world price increases for petroleum and other products. Included among these countries are most of those in sub-Saharan Africa, South Asia (Pakistan, Thailand, and Bangladesh), Central America, and a few others such as Uruguay, Jamaica, and the Philippines. Together they contain almost 50% of the population of Third World countries (excluding China). For these countries, the economic consequences of rising resource and commodity prices are overwhelmingly adverse. They are the poorest countries, with the lowest anticipated economic growth rates and the most limited margin for economic maneuvering. Having large accumulated debt burdens and limited foreign-exchange-earning capacities, they are unlikely to have any access to short-term credit. This is the most dependent and vulnerable group of all.

3. The *direct* dependence of *both* developed nations and less developed nations on energy imports is compounded in the case of the latter by the indirect effects of their economic dependence and vulnerability to the economic policies of the former. These indirect effects are related to the ability of rich countries to adjust their economies to the altered international circumstances. For example, in their efforts to combat the negative effects of higher import prices for energy and raw materials and the general inflationary trends of the 1970s, rich countries were able to cut back on nonessential imports, foreign travel, and foreign assistance. These and related deflationary and restrictive policies exacerbated an already difficult foreign exchange position for the least developed nations.

4. Finally, one of the most disturbing legacies of the oil shocks of the 1970s and the resulting spiral of inflation and then recession is the enormous debt of developing countries. Much of the debt was incurred to finance the import needs of an ambitious industrialization program. By 1983 the debt problems became so severe and worrisome to *both* developed country lenders and Third World debtors that the financial stability of the international economic system—not to mention the development hopes of poor nations—became seriously endangered (see discussion below). In this context, any further shocks to the financial system, such as another large oil price jump or a persistence of very high real interest rates, could wreak havoc with the economies of both rich and poor nations.

Raw Materials and Mineral Resources

No nation or continent is endowed with *all* the raw materials essential for the functioning of a modern industrial economy. As these materials become increasingly scarce, their very uneven distribution throughout the world could thrust previously weak nations into positions of considerable economic power, much as occurred with the oil-producing states. World mineral interdependence and, especially, the growing raw material dependence of rich nations on poor ones, is a new and vital component of the growing economic interdependence of all nations. Raw material interdependence in particular has two main aspects.

First, the consumption of nearly all essential minerals, both metallic and nonmetallic, is rapidly rising. Those countries of North America and especially Western Europe that industrialized earliest have almost depleted many of their indigenous supplies of basic raw materials. According to Lester Brown,

> the rich countries, particularly the United States, Japan, and those of Western Europe, with their steadily rising consumption of minerals required to support their affluence, are becoming increasingly dependent on the poor countries with their largely unexploited mineral reserves. In Western Europe, consumption of eleven basic industrial raw materials—bauxite, copper, lead, phosphate, zinc, chrome ore, manganese ore, magnesium, nickel, tungsten and tin—exceeds production. In the case of copper, phosphates, tin, nickel, manganese ore and chrome ore, nearly all needs must now be met from imports.[3]

Table 17.3 shows the degree to which the United States, the countries of the European Economic Community, and Japan are dependent on imports for their consumption of many critical industrial raw materials. We note that the United States, for example, has to import over 80% of its aluminum, chromium, cobalt, manganese, rubber, and tin. By 1990 iron, lead, and tungsten will probably be added to the list, bringing it to a total of nine of the thirteen basic industrial raw materials. By the year 2000 the United States will more than likely be dependent primarily on foreign sources of supply for all its basic industrial raw materials with the probable exception of phosphate. Its total imports of energy fuels and minerals, which cost $8 billion in 1970, is projected to increase to almost $64 billion by the turn of the century. As competition for dwindling reserves of high-grade minerals

Table 17.3 United States, EEC, and Japanese Import Dependence on Selected Industrial Raw Materials (net imports as percentage of consumption)

	United States	EEC	Japan
Aluminum*	84	75	100
Chromium	91	98	98
Cobalt	98	98	98
Copper	+	98	90
Iron*	29	55	99
Lead	11	85	73
Manganese	98	99	88
Natural rubber	100	100	100
Nickel	72	100	100
Phosphates	+	100	100
Tin	84	93	97
Tungsten	55	100	100
Zinc	61	70	53

*Ore and metal.
+ Net exporter.

SOURCE: Based on data from *International Economic Report of the President*, transmitted to Congress, January 1977 (Washington, D.C.: Government Printing Office, 1977), p. 187.

becomes more intense in the coming decades, the United States and other industrialized countries will feel increasingly vulnerable to external forces beyond their control. Conversely, supplier nations, mostly in the Third World, will experience a rise in their international bargaining power, especially if organizations like OPEC are formed for other scarce minerals.

The second aspect of raw material interdependence, therefore, is the fact that known reserves of a number of minerals are highly concentrated in a few, mostly Third World, locations around the globe. For example, four less developed countries (Chile, Peru, Zambia, and Zaire) supply much of the world's exports of copper. Three others (Bolivia, Malaysia, and Thailand) supply over 70% of all tin traded in international markets. Mexico, Brazil, and China account for almost 80% of the world's traded supply of graphite. Jamaica and Guinea supply almost 60% of the bauxite while Mexico and Brazil supply almost all of U.S. imports of strontium and columbium respectively. The importance of LDCs as suppliers of these and other essential minerals to the United States (and, even more so, to other developed countries) is indicated by Table 17.4.

Growing resource scarcities therefore promise to modify current international economic and political relationships among nations with the likely elevation of the relative influence and power of certain Third World countries in the international hierarchy. Whatever the ultimate outcome, however, it can no longer be said that international dependence runs only from poor countries to rich countries.

WORLD FOOD SHORTAGES

The 1970s and early 1980s also witnessed the transition from a previous era of commercial food surpluses to one of global shortages, rising prices, and growing national concern, especially among the least developed countries. Although catastrophic droughts in much of Africa in 1973/74 and again in 1983/84 as well as in parts of South Asia exacerbated the short-term seriousness of the world food problem, the long-term trend is itself ominous. The excess of total world production over world consumption has been narrowing steadily. Food prices in the 1980s are likely to remain much higher than they were during the previous decade, and one continent, North America, is emerging as the only source of exportable world grain supplies. Almost half of the world's population will continue to be overwhelmingly dependent on North American grain surpluses. For example, despite improved harvests in the late 1970s, the world's developing countries still had to import 56 million metric tons of cereal in 1981, almost all of which came from North America. This compares with average imports of only 13.8 metric tons in 1969–1971 (see Table 17.6). Estimates by the International Food Policy Research Institute in Washington, D.C., show that LDCs as a group will probably have food deficits averaging anywhere from 95 to 100 million metric tons in the late 1980s. Moreover, rising prices of petroleum and fertilizer, major imports of most poor countries, in combination with severe recessions and mounting debt service burdens have greatly depleted the foreign exchange funds that would ordinarily be used to buy food from these large grain suppliers.

Although high food prices and periodic grain shortages represent at most an inconvenience to the affluent in both rich and poor nations, to the very poor they may mean the difference between life and death. For the approximately 700 million people in 32 Third World countries who already survive on the margin of nutritional subsistence or who spend 80% of their incomes on food, there are no second chances when prices double, or a crop fails, or the rains don't come. Moreover, when global food reserve stocks are low (they had fallen from 26% of annual world grain consumption in 1961 to less than 7% by 1980), the capacity of developed nations to respond collectively with food aid to emergency areas of drought, floods, or crop failures is severely diminished. This was dramatically illustrated by the general failure of the World Food Conference held in Rome in 1974 to come up with more than token transfers of food grains to starving nations. Table 17.5 shows how rapidly world grain reserves fell between 1960 and 1980; Table 17.6 shows that developing nations have had to increase their net grain imports by more than 500% over the past two decades while North America has more than tripled its exports. Third World dependence on North American grain supplies has therefore increased dramatically during a period when domestic food production should have been given top priority in development policies.

What are the principal factors behind the dramatic alteration of the world food situation? We can identify several in particular. On the demand side, we have the combined effects of rising population and affluence. On the supply side, there are the four critical resource constraints of land, water, energy, and fertilizer as manifested in (a) the limited scope for expanding areas of cultivation; (b) the growing shortage of water for agricultural production; and (c) rising energy costs slowing down the growth of high-energy and fertilizer-intensive agriculture. Together, rapidly rising demand and slowly growing supply are pushing up the international prices of vital foods. Let's look briefly at the determinants of world food demand and supply.[4]

Determinants of Food Demand: Population and Affluence

In the 1960s the world food problem was perceived primarily as a race against time between rising numbers of people in Third World countries and total food supplies. The race always seemed to remain fairly close, but there was a general optimism that new breakthroughs in the technology of food production—the so-called Green Revolution—would ultimately declare food the winner. In the long run population growth would have to be reduced. But for the immediate future it appeared that famine and starvation were an unlikely occurrence.

What these watchers of the race between food and population failed to realize and what the 1970s vividly revealed was the fact that, in addition to Third World population growth, rising affluence in the developed nations was becoming a major factor in the annual increases in food demands. While population growth remains the dominant source of expanding food demand (e.g., with world population growing at approximately 1.7% per year, maintaining current levels of world per capita consumption will require a doubling of food production every 40 or so years), rising income levels account for an ever-increasing proportion of this demand. For example, in terms of

Table 17.4 U.S. Imports of Selected Metals and Minerals, 1981 (percentages of total imports)

	Imports from developing countries	Imports from developed countries	Import reliance[a]	Principal suppliers with percentage of U.S. imports supplied by each
Strontium[b]	100.0	—	100	Mexico, 99
Tin[c]	97.3	2.7	80	Malaysia, 44; Bolivia, 17; Thailand, 20; Indonesia, 10
Columbium	91.7	8.3	100	Brazil, 84; Nigeria, 7; Canada, 8
Graphite	88.6	11.4	100	Mexico, 57; China, 10; Brazil, 10
Chromium	83.9	16.1	90	South Africa, 34; Yugoslavia, 8; Zimbabwe, 9
Antimony	83.9	16.1	51	Bolivia, 35; France, 9; China, 12
Bauxite[b]	82.0	18.0	94	Jamaica, 36; Australia, 18; Guinea, 22
Petroleum	85.3	14.7	31	Saudi Arabia, 25; Mexico, 11; Nigeria, 14; United Kingdom, 8
Manganese[b]	76.2	23.8	98	South Africa, 33; France, 17; Australia, 17; Gabon, 12
Tungsten[b]	70.7	29.3	53	Canada, 26; China, 18; Bolivia, 25; Thailand, 9

				Major foreign sources, 1978–81 (%)
Platinum group metals	63.2	36.8	85	South Africa, 57; United Kingdom, 11; USSR, 13
Cobalt	45.0	55.0	91	Zaire, 27; Norway, 10; Canada, 12
Copper[b]	50.9	49.1	14	Canada, 28; Japan, 20; Peru, 10; Chile, 23; Zambia, 12
Silver[b]	49.1	50.4	7	Canada, 39; Mexico, 19; Peru, 23
Nickel	31.9	68.1	72	Canada, 38; Philippines, 5; Norway, 11
Iron ore[b]	30.8	69.2	28	Canada, 69; Brazil, 8; Venezuela, 14
Vanadium	23.1	76.9	42	Canada, 26; South Africa, 18; West Germany, 20
Zinc[b]	19.4	80.6	60	Canada, 66; Australia, 6; Peru, 7; Mexico, 6

[a]Import reliance = net import reliance as a percentage of apparent consumption. (Net import reliance = imports − exports, + adjustments for government and industry stock changes. Apparent consumption = U.S. primary and secondary production [i.e., from scrap and waste] + net import reliance.)
[b]1980 figures.
[c]1979 figures.

SOURCE: Overseas Development Council, *U.S. Foreign Policy and the Third World, Agenda 1983* (New York: Praeger, 1983), p. 185.

Table 17.5 Indicators of World Food Security, 1960–1980

	Reserve grains of stock (million metric tons)	Grain equivalent of idled U.S. cropland (million metric tons)	Total world reserves (million metric tons)	Reserves as days of annual grain consumption
1960	168	68	236	103
1963	157	70	227	94
1966	167	53	220	82
1967	189	60	249	89
1968	220	74	298	103
1969	206	71	277	92
1970	166	48	214	69
1971	183	65	248	78
1972	142	35	177	54
1973	147	3	150	44
1974	131	3	134	40
1975	138	3	141	42
1976	194	1	195	55
1977	191	24	215	59
1978	226	24	251	65
1979	191	15	206	51
1980	151	0	151	40

SOURCE: Overseas Development Council, *U.S. Foreign Policy and the Third World, Agenda 1980* (p. 178) and *U.S. Foreign Policy and the Third World, Agenda 1982* (p. 188).

the demand for basic food grains (wheat, corn, and rice), which dominate world consumption patterns, people in the less developed nations consume approximately 181 kg per person per year. Nearly all of this is consumed *directly* as bread, maizemeal, and rice to meet minimum energy requirements. On the other hand, the average North American consumes over 450 kg per year. But out of this total, only 65 kg is consumed directly in the form of bread, pastry, and breakfast cereals. The remaining 385 kg per capita is consumed *indirectly* in the form of meat, milk, and eggs; that is, 385 kg of cereal grains per capita are used to feed livestock and poultry, the products of which are then consumed by the North American public.

The agricultural resources (mainly land, water, energy, and fertilizer) required to produce this output for an average North American are often five to seven times that expended for his Asian or African counterpart. Moreover, as per capita incomes rise, a significant share of this additional income is spent on high-quality beef and poultry, which in turn means greater indirect consumption of feed grains and soybeans, much of which will have to be imported. This only exacerbates an already tight world food market and can mean less direct consumption for the poorest in Third World nations.

Table 17.6 World Net Grain Trade, by Groups of Countries and Regions (million metric tons)

	1960/61– 1962/63 Average	1969/70– 1971/72 Average	1980/81 Average
Developed market economies	*18.0*	*29.1*	*122.6*
North America	42.4	54.2	137.2
Western Europe	−25.8	−21.5	−3.9
Australia and New Zealand	6.7	10.8	13.2
Japan	−5.3	−14.4	−23.9
Centrally planned economies	*−3.2*	*−5.9*	*−60.9*
People's Republic of China	−3.9	−3.1	−14.2
USSR and Eastern Europe	0.7	−2.8	−46.7
Developing countries	*−10.2*	*−13.8*	*−56.1*
Africa and Middle East	−5.8	−8.7	−32.7
Asia	−6.5	−10.4	−12.6
Latin America	2.1	5.3	−10.8
Other	*−0.9*	*−2.2*	*−6.6*
Total world exports	*n/a*	*105.4*	*211.7*

NOTE: The world grains that are traded include wheat and wheat flour, milled rice, and coarse grains (corn, barley, rye, oats, and sorghum).

SOURCE: Based on data from U.S. Department of Agriculture, Economic Research Service, *World Agricultural Situation*, Publication No. WAS-14 (October 1977):32; U.S. Department of Agriculture, Foreign Agricultural Service, "World situation and outlook for grains," June 1982; and Overseas Development Council, *U.S. Foreign Policy and the Third World, Agenda 1983* (New York: Praeger, 1983), p. 235.

Constraints on Supply: Land, Water, Energy, and Fertilizers

As noted, there are four critical factors of modern agricultural production that are serious resource constraints on its expansion: land, water, energy, and fertilizer. The principal mechanisms for expanding world food supplies fall into two basic categories:

1. Increasing the total amount of land under cultivation
2. Raising yields on existing arable land through the more intensive use of water, energy, and fertilizer

Both cases represent increases in agricultural *inputs* that should lead to higher *outputs* in accordance with the basic economic theory of production. But, in the contemporary world, the possibilities of increasing these production inputs are restricted by the following factors.

Land Expansion. Historically, enlarging the area of cultivation has been the traditional approach to expanding agricultual production. But the potential for further expansion of farm acreage is limited today by the growing competition for land use by industrial development, urbanization, new town development, and transportation.

Fresh Water Expansion. Water was once thought to be a "free" good, that is, it was thought to be present in such plentiful supplies that one person's use of it would not limit its availability to another. But it is far from free for modern agriculture. In fact, it is a scarce and critical input. In many regions of the world, particularly in Africa, the availability of sufficient water could turn unproductive land into a productive resource. The principal way of achieving this is through irrigation projects made possible by the damming up of natural waterways. But most of the world's rivers that are suitable for damming and irrigation have already been developed. Any future efforts to expand fresh water supplies for agriculture will require alternative techniques such as river diversion (but this creates serious problems when a river flows between more than one country), desalting ocean water, or cloud-seeding to create and manipulate rainfall in dry agricultural areas. Unfortunately, the outlook for these efforts is, at present, not very promising.

Energy Expansion. An alternative means of intensifying agricultural production on existing land is that of applying greater energy inputs through the use of mechanized farm equipment such as tractors, seeders, reapers, and combines. However, as we have seen, the sharp increases in world oil prices make such efforts extremely costly. In fact, high energy prices are more than likely to hold down total food production, especially in energy-intensive areas like North America and the Soviet Union, unless food prices rise equally fast.

Fertilizer Expansion. In addition to land, fresh water, and energy, supplies of fertilizer are becoming increasingly more costly as a result of substantially higher prices for phosphate and potash and alternative uses for the petroleum inputs into fertilizer production. The process of manufacturing chemical fertilizers requires large amounts of costly energy inputs. In the face of these rising costs and the enormous expansion of world demand for fertilizer, it is likely that future prices will continue to rise. In 1974, for example, fertilizer prices almost quadrupled. Third World countries had to pay many hundreds of millions of dollars more for their fertilizer imports than in previous years. Worse still, many nations could not even obtain adequate supplies at any price. Included among these nations were the very populous and food-scarce countries of South and Southeast Asia (e.g., Pakistan, Bangladesh, and the Philippines). A continuation of high prices and limited supplies of chemical fertilizer means lower per capita outputs and increased food import needs for these nations over the coming years. Unfortunately, this increase in basic food needs usually occurs at times when world food prices are also high and global grain reserves are at dangerously low levels.

It should be evident from the preceding description of the prospects for world food demand and supply that many of the least developed Third World countries are likely to become even more dependent on food imports from the developed regions, mainly the United States but also Canada and the Soviet Union. With world demand outpacing supply, rising prices and/ or falling incomes will mean greater burdens on the very poor. Worse still, shortages of vital agricultural resource inputs such as energy and fertilizer will probably lead to some form of world food "rationing." With the United States controlling three-quarters of exportable world grain supplies, the use of food as a new and deadly weapon of "political blackmail" against hungry Third World nations becomes a distinct and frightening possibility.[5]

It becomes all the more urgent, therefore, for such populous, food-short nations as Bangladesh, Pakistan, Indonesia, and much of sub-Saharan Africa as well as parts of Latin America to intensify their efforts to expand food production through the promotion of labor-intensive and energy-saving small- and medium-scale commercial farm development. This is where the greatest and least costly output potential lies. We discussed and reviewed the possible nature of such labor-intensive agricultural and rural development strategies in Chapter 10.

THE GLOBAL DEBT CRISIS

Origins and Prospects

The accumulation of external debt is a common phenomenon of Third World countries at the stage of economic development where the supply of domestic savings is low, current account payments deficits are high, and imports of capital are needed to augment domestic resources. Prior to the early 1970s, the external debt of developing countries was relatively small and primarily an official phenomenon, the majority of creditors being foreign governments and international financial institutions such as the IMF, the World Bank, and regional development banks. Most loans were on concessional terms and were extended for purposes of implementing development projects and expanding imports of capital goods. More recently, commercial banks began playing a large role in international lending, issuing general purpose loans to provide balance of payments support and expansion of export sectors.

While foreign borrowing can be highly beneficial, providing the resources necessary to promote economic growth and development, it has its costs. In recent years, these costs seem to have outweighed the benefits for many developing nations. The main cost associated with the accumulation of a large external debt is "debt servicing." Debt servicing is the payment of amortization (i.e., the liquidation of the principal) and accumulated interest; it is a contractually fixed charge on domestic real income and savings. As the size of the debt grows or as interest rates rise, debt service charges increase. Debt service payments must be made with foreign exchange. In other words, debt service obligations can be met only through export earnings, curtailed imports, and/or further external borrowing. Under normal circumstances, most of a country's debt service obligations are met by its export earnings. However, should the composition of imports change or should interest rates rise significantly, causing a ballooning of debt service payments, or should export earnings diminish, debt servicing difficulties are likely to arise.

In the 12-year period between 1971 and 1983, the total external debt of developing nations grew from $90 billion to $817 billion, an increase of over 900% (see Table 17.7). Debt service payments increased by over 1000% and were in excess of $131 billion by the end of 1982 (see Table 17.8). During 1981, 9 LDCs sought debt relief from the IMF, the largest number to do so since the inception of IMF multilateral debt relief exercises. In addition, by the end of 1983, more than 25 countries were in arrears, in the process of rescheduling, or had already rescheduled portions of their enormous bank debt.

The seeds of the 1980s debt crisis were sown in the 1974–1979 period, when there was a virtual explosion in international lending, precipitated by the first major OPEC oil price increase. By 1974, developing countries had begun playing a larger role in the world economy, having averaged growth rates of 6.6% in 1967–1973. The newly industrializing countries, particularly those like Mexico, Brazil, Venezuela, and Argentina in Latin America, had growth rates well above the developing countries' average. To meet their growth needs, many countries had begun importing heavily, especially capital goods, oil, and food. Following outward-looking development strategies, they expanded their exports aggressively. In the face of high oil prices and a world recession, in which the growth rates of the industrialized countries fell from an average of 5.2% in 1967–1973 to an average of 2.7% for the rest of the decade, many developing countries sought to sustain their high growth rates through increased borrowing. While lending from official sources increased significantly, particularly nonconcessional lending, it was insufficient to meet the growth needs of the middle-income and newly industrializing developing countries. Furthermore, countries with an excess of imports over lagging exports were reluctant to approach official sources, such as the IMF, that might submit them to painful policy adjustments (see below). Thus the middle-income and newly industrializing developing countries turned to commercial banks and other private lenders, which began issuing general purpose loans to provide balance of payments support. Commercial banks, holding the bulk of the OPEC surplus (which had jumped from $7 billion in 1973 to $68 billion in 1974 and ultimately peaked at $115 billion in 1980) and facing a low demand for capital from the slower growing industrialized countries, aggressively competed with one another in lending to developing countries on comparatively permissive and favorable terms.

As a result of all these factors, the total external debt of developing countries more than doubled from $180 billion in 1975 to $406 billion in 1979, increasing over 20% annually. More significantly, an increasing portion of the debt was now on nonconcessional terms involving shorter maturities and market rates of interest, often at variable rates. In 1971, about 40% of the total external debt was on nonconcessional terms. This increased to 68% by 1975, and by 1979 over 77% of the debt was on harder terms. Although the increase in nonconcessional lending by official institutions was partly responsible for this rising proportion, the more than tripling of lending by private capital markets played the major role. Together, the large increase in the size of debt and the larger proportion scheduled on harder terms were responsible for the tripling of debt service payments, which rose from $25 billion in 1975 to $75 billion in 1979. Tables 17.7 and 17.8 sum-

Table 17.7 Total Debt Disbursed at Year-End 1971–1983 and Debt Service During 1982 of Developing Countries, by Terms of Lending and Income Group

Income group	Total debt ($ billion)	Percentage share of total			
		Official development assistance (ODA)	Nonconcessionary Multilateral	Total export credits	Private markets
1. Low-income countries					
1971	18	74	6	18	2
1975	40	73	4	16	7
1980	86	67	6	21	6
1982	110	69	5	20	6
1982 debt service	11.5	24	6	49	21
2. Middle-income countries					
1971	25	45	8	33	14
1975	40	33	10	29	29
1980	107	25	10	28	38
1982	144	24	10	27	39
1982 debt service	23.5	11	9	37	43
3. Newly industrializing countries					
1971	32	16	6	40	38
1975	72	9	7	24	60
1980	192	4	6	24	65
1982	266	3	6	24	67
1982 debt service	63.3	1	3	24	72
Total non-OPEC					
1971	75	41	6	33	20
1975	152	32	7	23	38
1980	385	24	7	24	44
1982	520	23	7	24	46
1982 debt service	98.3	6	5	30	39
1983	668	n/a	n/a	n/a	n/a
4. OPEC					
1971	15	21	10	54	15
1975	28	29	4	42	25
1980	79	13	4	46	37
1982	79	13	4	47	37
1982 debt service	33.0	2	2	56	40
1983	149	n/a	n/a	n/a	n/a
Total LDCs					
1971	90	37	7	36	20
1975	180	32	6	26	36
1980	465	22	7	28	43
1982	626	21	7	28	44
1982 debt service	131.3	5	4	36	55
1983	817	n/a	n/a	n/a	n/a

SOURCE: Organization for Economic Cooperation and Development, *Debt Survey* (Paris: OECD, 1982), Table 9; and IMF, "World Economic Outlook," *Occasional Paper #27* (1984), Table 35.

Table 17.8 Total Annual Debt Service of Developing Countries during 1971–1982, by Source and Terms of Lending (in $ billion)

Source and terms of lending	1971	1975	1976	1977	1978	1979	1980	1981	1982
Development Assistance Committee countries and capital markets	9.2	22.0	27.1	36.3	51.7	66.5	75.8	95.9	115.2
ODA (Official Development Assistance)	1.4	1.8	1.9	2.0	2.3	2.6	2.8	2.9	3.4
Total export credits	5.1	10.7	12.4	16.5	20.5	25.6	29.6	35.5	44.8
Capital markets[a]	2.7	9.5	12.8	17.8	28.8	38.3	43.4	57.5	67.0
of which: bank loans	n.a.	8.1	10.6	14.4	24.6	33.1	38.1	49.6	56.0
Multilateral organizations	0.9	1.7	2.0	2.6	3.3	3.8	4.8	5.6	6.7
of which: concessional	0.2	0.6	0.6	0.7	0.8	0.7	0.9	1.0	1.2
USSR and Eastern bloc countries	0.6	0.8	0.9	1.1	1.4	1.7	1.8	2.1	2.5
OPEC	x	0.2	0.2	0.6	1.0	1.3	1.9	2.4	3.0
Other LDCs	0.1	0.4	0.5	0.5	0.6	0.8	1.0	1.3	1.9
Unspecified and adjustments	0.2	0.7	1.0	0.9	1.0	1.5	1.7	2.0	2.0
Total debt service	*11.0*	*25.8*	*31.9*	*42.1*	*59.0*	*75.6*	*86.9*	*109.3*	*131.3*
Of which: interest	3.3	9.3	10.5	12.9	17.6	26.0	37.2	48.5	60.1
amortization	7.7	16.5	21.4	29.2	41.4	49.6	49.7	60.8	71.2
Of which: nonconcessional	9.3	22.7	28.6	38.2	54.6	71.1	81.5	103.2	124.4
concessional	1.7	3.1	3.3	3.9	4.4	4.5	5.4	6.1	6.9

[a]Bank loans (other than export credits), bonds, and other private lending.

SOURCE: Organization for Economic Cooperation and Development, *Debt Survey* (Paris: OECD, 1982), Table 2.

marize the statistical evolution of the debt and debt service problems of developing nations between 1971 and 1983.

Yet despite the huge increases in debt-servicing obligations, the ability of most developing countries to meet their debt service payments remained largely unimpaired. This was primarily a function of the international economic climate that prevailed during the late 1970s. Specifically, a combination of declining real oil prices as a result of inflation, low or negative real interest rates, and increased export earnings narrowed current account deficits toward the end of the decade and enabled developing countries to sustain relatively high growth rates, averaging 5.2% during 1973–1979, through massive borrowing.

In sum, the surge in international lending following the first oil shock was largely a success during 1974–1979. In the presence of a congenial economic atmosphere, it permitted developing countries to maintain relatively high rates of growth with little debt-servicing difficulty. It also facilitated the recycling of a huge surplus from oil exporters to oil importers through the lending activities of private international banks, and it helped to dampen the recession in industrialized countries by providing for increased export demand on the part of Third World countries.

Unfortunately, this success was shortlived, and in fact, the surge in international lending that occurred during 1974–1979 had laid the groundwork for all the problems that were to come. The second oil shock, which occurred in 1979, brought about a complete reversal of the economic conditions conducive to the success of international lending in the previous period. Now, developing countries faced an abrupt increase in oil prices which added to oil import bills and affected industrial goods imports. There was also a huge increase in interest rates caused by the industrialized countries' economic stabilization policies and a decrease in Third World export earnings resulting from a combination of slowed growth in the more developed nations and a precipitous decline of over 20% in primary commodity export prices. Moreover, developing countries inherited from the previous period a huge debt and debt service obligation, which was made even more onerous by burgeoning interest rates and more precarious as a result of the bunching of short-term maturities.

Faced with this critical situation, Third World countries had two policy options. They could either curtail imports and impose restrictive fiscal and monetary measures, impeding growth and development objectives, or they could finance their widening current account deficits through more external borrowing. Unable, and sometimes unwilling, to adopt the first option as a means of solving the balance of payments crisis, many countries were forced in 1981 and 1982 to rely on the second option, borrowing even more heavily. As a result, massive debts and debt service obligations accumulated, so that by 1983 countries like Brazil, Mexico, Argentina, the Philippines, and Chile faced severe difficulties in paying even the interest on their debts out of export earnings (see Table 17.9). Now, however, they could no longer borrow funds in the world's private capital markets without first asking IMF assistance and facing up to the IMF stabilization program, the conditions of which were tantamount to the first policy option.

Table 17.9 Interest Payments on External Debt in Relation
to Export Earnings of Major Debtor Countries, 1983

Country	Total external debt ($ billion)	Estimated export earnings ($ billion)	Share of export earnings to pay interest (%)[a]
Brazil	93.5	17.5	64
Mexico	86.6	22.2	47
South Korea	40.3	19.4	25
Argentina	38.5	9.2	50
Venezuela	31.5	12.9	29
Indonesia	28.8	16.8	21
Poland	27.0	10.2	31
Turkey	23.6	5.2	54
Philippines	22.7	5.7	47
Yugoslavia	20.0	10.3	23
Chile	18.7	4.1	54
Thailand	13.5	8.4	19
Peru	12.5	3.7	41
Malaysia	11.3	12.4	11
Taiwan	8.5	27.5	4
Ecuador	7.1	2.1	38

[a]Assumes interest rate of 12%; total debt service, including principal repayment, is of course much larger.

SOURCE: Lester R. Brown et al., *State of the World 1984* (New York: Norton, 1984), Table 1–7.

IMF Stabilization Policies

One course of action that has been increasingly but often reluctantly used by countries facing serious balance of payments and private foreign debt problems is to renegotiate loans with private international banks in an effort to either stretch out the payment period for principal and interest or obtain additional finance on more favorable terms. Typically, however, such debtor countries must deal with the IMF before a consortium of international banks will agree to refinance or defer existing loan schedules. Relying on the IMF to impose its usual medicine of tough "stabilization policies" before it first agrees to lend LDCs funds in excess of their legal IMF quotas, the private banks perceive negotiations with the IMF as a sign that borrowing countries are making serious efforts to reduce payments deficits and earn the foreign exchange needed to repay earlier loans. There are four basic components to the typical IMF stabilization program:[6]

1. Abolition or liberalization of foreign exchange and import controls
2. Devaluation of the official exchange rate
3. A stringent, domestic antiinflation program consisting of (a) control of bank credit to raise interest rates and reserve requirements; (b) control of the government deficit through curbs on spending, especially in the areas of social services for the poor and staple food subsidies, along with increases in taxes and in public enterprise prices;

(c) control of wage increases, in particular assuring that such increases are at rates less than the inflation rate (i.e., abolishing wage indexing); and (d) dismantling of various forms of price controls
4. Greater hospitality to foreign investment and a general opening up of the economy to international commerce

In 1982–1983, for example, numerous debtor countries with greatly depleted foreign reserves, including Mexico, Brazil, Argentina, and the Philippines, had to turn to the IMF to secure additional foreign exchange. In order to do this, they were required to adopt some or all of the above stabilization policies. Such policies are politically very unpopular since they strike at the heart of development efforts by disproportionately hurting the lower- and middle-income groups. Moreover, since they are being imposed by an international agency that is perceived by many, especially those of the dependency school, to be merely an arm of the rich capitalist nations, stabilization policies are often viewed by debtor countries as measures primarily designed to maintain the poverty and dependency of Third World nations while preserving the global market structure for the industrialized nations. For example, in an extensive dependency critique of the IMF and its stabilization programs, Cheryl Payer has argued that the IMF functions within a First-World-dominated global trading system "as the chosen instrument for imposing imperialist financial discipline upon poor countries," and thus creates a form of "international peonage" or debt slavery, in which the balance of payments problems of LDCs are not resolved but rather perpetuated. Payer argues further that the IMF encourages LDCs to incur additional debt from international financial institutions while it "blackmails" (i.e., through threats of loan rejection) them into antidevelopmental stabilization programs. This added debt burden thus becomes a source of future balance of payments problems, so that a vicious cycle sets in—one in which Third World debtor nations have to run faster merely to stay in place.[7]

A less radical perspective sees the IMF neither as a developmental nor as an antidevelopmental institution, but simply as an institution carrying out its original although somewhat outdated mandate to hold the global capitalist market together through the pursuit of orthodox short-term countercyclical economic policies. Its primary goal is the maintenance of an international exchange system designed to promote monetary cooperation, expand international trade, encourage exchange rate stability and, most important, assist countries to deal with *short-run* balance of payments problems through the provision of scarce foreign exchange resources. Unfortunately, in a highly unequal trading world, the balance of payments problems of many Third World nations may be structural and *long-term* in nature with the result that short-term stabilization policies may easily lead to long-run development crises. In the absence of a major restructuring of the international economic order (see next section), the adoption of orthodox Western economic policies in pursuit of orthodox balance of payments objectives may in fact jeopardize the very system that the IMF seeks to preserve. While its motives are probably not the sinister ones ascribed to it by Payer and other dependency theorists, the IMF's policies of severe financial repression of debtor countries tend to inflict a harsh and often unnecessary economic burden on nations that in many cases can ill afford it. Greater flexibility and a willingness to modify its prescribed medicine to fit the varied illnesses of its patients (many of which may have resulted from too much contact and exposure to developed nations!) would appear to be a more logical, humane, and, in the long-run, more developmental course of action for the IMF.

Conclusions

The debt problem has thus become truly a worldwide problem with serious economic implications for both developed and less developed countries. In fact, the debt crises of the 1980s called into question the very existence, stability, and viability of the international financial system. Fears were voiced that if one or two of the major debtor countries (Brazil, Mexico, or Argentina) were to default or if a group of debtor nations were to jointly repudiate their debts by forming a "debtor's cartel," the economies of Western nations might be seriously affected. Emergency meetings between international bankers and government officials of both developed nations and LDC debtors were convened in the financial capitals of the world. Rumors of imminent default led currency speculators to purchase dollars, driving up the dollar's market value well beyond its "shadow" value and adding even further to the dollar-denominated debt burdens of developing nations.

All in all, the debt crisis has underlined the tremendous interdependence and political fragility of the international economic and financial system. It has also demonstrated that not only were Third World economies terribly vulnerable to 1 or 2 percentage-point increases in U.S. interest rates but, perhaps more significantly, developed countries could indeed be harmed by the economic failures and/or public policies of key developing nations.

While many developing countries can be held at least partially responsible for the massive accumulation of debt, the adverse economic conditions that face them are often outside of their control. In fact, this adverse economic climate was, in part, precipitated by the industrialized countries' own economic stabilization policies, which led to soaring interest rates, worldwide economic recession, and the resulting decrease in demand for developing country exports. Cline has estimated, for example, that almost 85% ($401 billion) of the total increase ($480 billion) in the external debt of the non-oil LDCs between 1973 and 1982 can be attributed to four factors outside of their control: OPEC oil price increases, the rise in dollar interest rates in 1981–1982, the decline in Third World export volume as a result of the worldwide recession, and the dramatic fall in commodity prices and the consequent worsening of their terms of trade.[8]

Thus, the burden of the global debt crisis must be shared by all. Several developing countries may have to undergo a period of difficult adjustment. At the same time, industrialized countries will have to relax restrictive monetary policies and encourage imports. International organizations, primarily the IMF and World Bank, will need to provide sufficient financial liquidity until the economic climate changes and developing countries can make the necessary adjustments. And perhaps most important of all from a long-run perspective is the need to gradually restructure the entire international economic and financial system—a topic with which we conclude this final chapter on the growing global interdependence of the world economy.

THE NEW INTERNATIONAL ECONOMIC ORDER (NIEO)

Evidence of Present Inequities

The 1970s were also marked by a major challenge by Third World nations against an international economic order that they believed to be strongly stacked against their economic interest. Although we have identified and analyzed the fundamental areas of contention in our chapters on international trade, private investment, and foreign assistance, it is useful to reiterate the impressive and growing evidence that demonstrates how poor nations are being disadvantaged by existing global market structures.[9]

First, there is the substantial imbalance in the distribution of international monetary reserves. Although Third World nations contained over 70% of the world's population, they received less than 4% of the international reserves of $131 billion during the first half of the 1970s. Since rich nations control the creation and distribution of these reserves (e.g., through their own monetary expansion and through their effective control over actions of the IMF), they have the power to manipulate these international financial assets to their own benefit.

Second, rich nations benefit disproportionately in the distribution of the value added to the products traded between themselves and the poor nations. Unlike the developed countries, Third World nations receive back only a small fraction of the final price obtained from international purchases of their products. The reason is simple: LDCs are often too weak and powerless to exercise any substantial control over the processing, shipping, and marketing of their primary products. Often they themselves must purchase back at substantially marked-up prices the final products processed from their own raw materials.

Third, in order to protect and perpetuate profits and jobs in uncompetitive and declining sectors of their economies, rich nations typically resort to tariff and nontariff protection of inefficient domestic industries while restricting immigration to maintain high wages. Thus, their rhetoric in support of the "free" working of the international market mechanism belies the reality of their market management and control. Third World countries contend, therefore, that any genuine competitive successes they may realize from international trade become nullified by the restrictive commercial policies of increasingly protectionist industrial nations.

Fourth, most of the contracts, leases, and concessions that the multinational corporations have negotiated in the past with the developing countries have unfairly benefited the MNC at the expense of the host country. Thus LDC host governments contend that because of royalty payments, tax concessions, transfer pricing, capital allowances, and so forth, they receive only a small fraction of the benefits derived from the exploitation of their own natural resources by the MNCs.

Fifth, and finally, when it comes to critical economic decisions affecting the workings of the world economy, Third World nations have only a pro forma participation in the decision-making process. Their advice is rarely solicited by the industrial powers in key decisions relating to the future of the world economy. More importantly, although they represent a large majority of the world's population, developing countries have less than one-third of the total votes in such key international economic institutions as the World Bank and the IMF. Their numerical majority in the UN General Assembly carries no influence on international economic decisions.

Given this background of international inequities in economic power and influence, Third World nations launched a major drive in the 1970s to try to reshape the world economic order to better serve their own interests. As is not uncommon in social and political movements, the rhetoric used was often unnecessarily inflammatory, and many charges and allegations were patently unfounded. Nonetheless, many charges were based on the facts we have discussed, and it is informative to trace the new international economic order (NIEO) movement and to highlight some of its key provisions.

Origins and Content of the NIEO

Although its origins can be traced back to the 1950s and early 1960s to the "center–periphery" analysis of Raul Prebisch and other Latin American *dependencia* economists, the NIEO movement received its first formal political endorsement at the sixth Special Session of the UN General Assembly in 1974. In this session, convened in the immediate aftermath of the petroleum crisis, the General Assembly concluded its deliberations by committing itself

> to work urgently for the establishment of a new international economic order based on equity, sovereign equality, common interest and cooperation among all states, irrespective of their economic and social systems, which shall correct inequalities and redress existing injustices, make it possible to eliminate the widening gap between the developed and the developing countries and ensure steadily accelerating economic and social development and peace and justice for present and future generations.

In the years following its announcement, this Program of Action on the Establishment of a NIEO became one of the most publicized issues of international politics and economics. The movement did not come suddenly into being, however; it had its roots in the international social and political climate of the post-World War II era. The liquidation of colonies and the concomitant rise of a host of new Third World nations was hailed as the inevitable march toward global democracy. But political colonization ended only to be replaced in many countries by de facto economic colonization.

To this day, non-oil-exporting LDCs account for less than one-fifth of the world's trade; and that figure decreases every year. Three-fourths of their exports are bound for the developed markets, often the former colonial power. Four-fifths of all export earnings are generated by about a dozen commodities, excluding oil. The developing countries account for less than 7% of world industrial production and are particularly vulnerable to fluctuations in commodity pricing, inflation, and recession. This, it is argued, is the heritage of the colonial venture.

The effects of colonialism are also felt in financing. Foreign investment, often by a single capital-rich country and typically controlled by a foreign-based multinational corporation, is seen as an absolute necessity for rapid growth. But it can severely limit any sense of autonomy or freedom of choice. Developing countries are also dependent on foreign sources for technology in nearly all fields; about 98% of the world's research and development capability is located in the developed world alone, as are 94% of all patents.

The pattern of colonial dependent development—economic, political, and social—could not be set aside by fiat. The historical process that gave the majority of the world's population equal status in the realm of states left them in a position of economic dependence. The newly granted sovereignty triggered a "revolution of rising expectations." Governments, desiring rapid social and economic change, established ambitious plans for national development. Most followed the pattern set by the industrialized West and reviewed earlier in this book.

A series of programs and targets in the early 1960s created a mood of optimism. The launching of the first UN Development Decade, the Alliance for Progress in 1961, and the Yaunde Convention in 1963 all fired expectations. By the late 1960s, however, enthusiasm waned as the unintended side effects of rapid economic growth became evident—uncontrolled growth of cities, neglect of rural areas, and increasing social stratification, among others. Outward-looking policies predicated on the benefits of free international trade failed as the nature of the primary commodity markets in relation to manufactured goods could not sustain the flow of foreign capital necessary for development projects. Inward-looking policies of import substitution also failed, largely because of inefficiencies of production, reliance on foreign capital investment, and lack of intermediate goods.

The second UN Development Decade of the 1970s therefore incorporated a more sober assessment of development prospects, but even these revised expectations were falling short. Then came the sudden and unexpected rise in Third World economic power in the wake of OPEC's 1973 oil embargo and subsequent pricing policies. These actions conclusively demonstrated that the world economy was truly a world (i.e., an interdependent) economy. It was in this light that the NIEO was created, and Third World countries attempted to utilize their newly found economic leverage to demand a new structure of international economic relations and a new set of rules affecting trade, industrialization, transfer of technology, and foreign assistance.

Four main points of the Program for Action deserve special attention (the complete NIEO agenda is presented in Appendix 17.1):

1. Renegotiating the debts of developing countries
2. Redefining the terms of trade and assuring greater access to developed country markets
3. Reforming the IMF and its decision-making process
4. Attaining UN official development assistance targets

Renegotiating the Debts of Developing Countries. At the heart of most developing countries' plans for rapid economic progress is the need for a continuous flow and stable stock of foreign currency. By far the most serious drain on these stocks is the ever-increasing debt burden discussed in the preceding section. The Program for Action calls for urgent action to "mitigate adverse consequences for the current and future development of developing countries arising from the external burden of debt contracted on hard terms." It further demands "debt renegotiation . . . with a view to concluding agreements on debt cancellation, moratorium, rescheduling or interest subsidization."

The major concern is to halt the drain on foreign currency that debt repayment aggravates, often to the point where a large percentage of foreign exchange earnings goes solely to the repayment of past debt, thereby crippling current development projects. It was hoped that debt renegotiation would enable a developing country to continue debt-servicing payments and so restore its position in international financial markets. On becoming a "better risk," a developing country would then be better able to attract needed foreign private capital. One suggested method of reservicing was for the IMF to act as an international facility to "finance part of the financial requirements of countries' deficits."

Redefining the Terms of Trade and Access to Markets. The main purpose of reforms related to trade and market access would be to secure a stable if not increasing amount of foreign currency. Faced with deteriorating terms of trade, the non-oil-exporting developing nations sought to stabilize their financial situation in several ways:

1. Through *indexation*, the tying of primary commodity prices to those of manufactured goods. This policy would arrest the tendency of primary commodities to lose ground to imported manufactured goods, thus stabilizing the real price of LDC exports.
2. Through the *creation of a Common Fund* to help stabilize commodity price fluctuations of such products as tin, rubber, sugar, and cocoa, partly by establishing *buffer stockpiles*. In June 1980 agreement was reached with industrialized countries to establish a Common Fund Under the Integrated Program for Commodities, as it is formally known. The accord, reached under the auspices of UNCTAD, provided $750 million (Third World countries had initially demanded $6 billion) to aid individual groupings of commodity-producing and -consuming nations in their efforts to stabilize markets and promote trade in primary products.
3. Through *preferential treatment* of LDC exports by a nonreciprocal lowering of tariff barriers by the developed West and Soviet bloc nations, as well as reforms concerning nontariff programs, duties, and restrictive import regulations, particularly those concerning processed goods.

With these reforms, the developing nations argued, they would be better able to compete with the developed countries and to expand and diversify their export capacities. Expansion and diversification would in turn allow for more rapid and continuous growth.

REFORM OF THE IMF. Developing nations, like the end of a whip, are affected in the extreme by fluctuations in the developed economies on which their development programs ultimately depend. The NIEO seeks a way to assure the stable and continuous flow of development assistance from the IMF, whose major contributors are the OECD nations, and hence a source of protection from the deteriorating effects of inflation and recession in the West.

In addition, the NIEO proposes a restructuring of the decision-making process within the IMF to give a greater voice to the developing world when critical decisions are to be made.

ATTAINING UN OFFICIAL DEVELOPMENT AID TARGETS. Set out in the objectives of the NIEO is the goal that each economically advanced nation should progressively increase its development assistance to 0.7% of its GNP. In principle, this aid is to be untied and provided on a long-term and continuous basis. Several mechanisms have been put forward, including the sale of gold held by the IMF and a development tax in developed countries. Major emphasis is on stable, concessional (i.e., grant or very soft) untied flows.

By 1981 only the Netherlands, Sweden, Norway, Denmark, and France met the 0.7% GNP target. The United States, Japan, Switzerland, Finland, and Italy each contributed less than 0.3% of their GNP, with the United States (at 0.20) ranked 16th among the 17 major aid-giving nations in terms of the proportion of GNP allocated to development assistance. The average of all DAC countries was only 0.35% of total GNP.

Observations on the NIEO

The program of the NIEO is not a doctrine nor is it necessarily a document of confrontation. Rather, it is a proposal, a series of demands subject to negotiation. As with all documents (the Magna Carta and the U.S. Constitution come immediately to mind), its true importance is not in its content but in how that content is used. The meanings and rhetoric, with which the Program for Action overflows, can be changed, bent, or "interpreted." As of this writing, progress on the establishing of a new international economic order has been extremely limited and the so-called North–South dialogue is largely silenced. In fact, many would claim that in the 1980s the old economic order was replaced not by a new order but by a new disorder. Declining commodity prices, worldwide recession, and rising unemployment simultaneously weakened the will of industrialized Western nations to be generous, while creating widening cracks in Third World solidarity. But the NIEO did and may still provide a rallying point, acting as a symbol of unity of purpose among the Third World nations in their increasing efforts for recognition by, and often their struggle with, the industrialized West.

SUMMARY AND CONCLUDING REMARKS

Our discussion in this final chapter has touched on many of the economic and noneconomic manifestations of the growing interdependence of nations. We have seen that whereas two decades ago this interdependence was perceived primarily in terms of the dependence of poor nations on rich ones, today developed countries have discovered that in a world of growing mineral and raw material scarcities, declining Third World export markets, and burgeoning LDC debt problems, their future economic well-being will depend increasingly on the international economic policies of many Third World countries. Let there be no misunderstanding, however. The poor nations are now and will remain considerably more vulnerable to the economic events and policies of rich nations than vice versa. But their international economic power is undoubtedly on the rise.

The events of the 1970s and 1980s have underlined that the world is in the midst of a fundamental and profound economic transformation. For decades, the developed nations experienced continuous economic progress based on ever-expanding industrial production and rising exports to one another and to the less developed countries. Raw material inputs were cheap and in plentiful supply. It was a buyer's market; sellers (mostly LDCs) had to compete vigorously with one another to find markets for their abundant raw materials. More simply, supply increases continuously exceeded demand expansion.

But during the 1970s, for the first time since the Great Depression, there was a worldwide seller's market for many goods, in which more buyers had to compete with one another to obtain limited supplies. The list of scarce items went beyond oil, food, and fertilizer to include, for example, timber, minerals, and other raw materials. Although a severe global recession, declining commodity prices, and the need to expand exports to pay for mounting debts combined to shift the global balance once again in the early 1980s to a situtation of abundant commodity supplies and a corresponding buyer's market, many economists forecast a return to resource scarcities in the late 1980s and 1990s as the world economy resumes its expansionary momentum. What will happen to countries, both rich and poor, in such a situation of renewed scarcity?

One thing is clear. Any new era of scarcity is bound to alter international economic relations. It may even lead to a major revision of the international economic system as first demanded by Third World nations in the form of the controversial Program of Action on the Establishment of a New International Economic Order. Those countries rich in minerals and basic raw materials, both rich and poor, will discover in the former case a greater and in the latter case a new economic power. Countries without such natural resource supplies, especially those in the Third World, will find their already economically vulnerable position even weaker. As scarcities become more pronounced, so will the threat of "economic warfare" among nations—that is, the possibility that individual resource-rich countries may use their resources as a way to make exorbitant demands of economically desperate resource-poor nations.

Our point here is that the question of how limited supplies of scarce resources, such as energy and certain raw materials, and commodities such as food grains are "rationed" and who gets "access" to these supplies is likely to assume increasing economic and political importance in future years. The outcome will probably be determined by *both* economic and noneconomic considerations. Over the last decade, the world has witnessed a rapid international shift, especially for the developed countries, from the basic question of how to get *access* to foreign markets (both developed and Third World) where finished products could be *sold*, to the very different question of how to get *access* to markets (both less developed and developed) where raw materials could be *purchased*.

With this shifting world economic situation, the names and numbers of players as well as the rules of the international power game were rapidly changed. No longer was it simply a competitive or cooperative game among a select group of rich countries vying for poor country markets to sell their expensive manufactures in return for cheap primary products and natural resources. Resource-rich Third World nations are likely to have a much greater impact on the future functioning and status of the world economy. Whether or not they act as spokesmen for the larger issues of Third World development on behalf of their less fortunate compatriots remains to be seen.

The crucial question, however, is whether this new economic interdependence among all nations, both developed and underdeveloped, will lead to greater cooperation or greater conflict. As a result of the oil and resource scarcities of the seventies and the debt crises of the eighties the more developed countries have begun to realize that the economic futures of both groups of nations are intimately linked. No longer can rich nations totally dominate the established international economic order without inviting harmful repercussions. Cooperation becomes essential. On the other hand, the potential for economic conflict will probably become even more pronounced if resource-rich Third World countries once again attempt to overexploit their strengths. Such a strategy may merely invite heavy retaliation from the still more powerful rich nations who, as we have seen, could even use food as a counterweapon against the Third World's raw materials. In the final analysis, the only feasible outcome of this growing international interdependence is one in which everyone either wins or loses. In the interdependent world of the last decades of the twentieth century, there cannot in an ultimate sense be simultaneous winners and losers. Global development can never again be a zero-sum game!

With each passing year, therefore, rich and poor nations alike share an increasingly common destiny. The world community must begin to realize that a new international economic order is not only possible, it is essential. Such a new order should be based on the fundamental principle that each nation's and each individual's development is intimately bound to the development of every other nation and every other individual. The future of all mankind is linked more closely today than ever before. All indications are that it will become even more so in the coming decades. Let us hope, therefore, that reason and good sense will prevail so that the First, Second, and Third Worlds can truly become part of One World—forged together by a common economic destiny and guided by the humane principles of peace, brotherhood, and mutual respect.

NOTES

1. Lester Brown, *World without Borders* (New York: Random House, 1972).
2. For documentation of this reverse dependency phenomenon, see John W. Sewell, "Can the North prosper without growth and progress in the South?" in M. McLaughlin *et al.* (eds.), *The United States and World Development: Agenda 1979*, (New York: Praeger, 1979), Chapter 2, reprinted as Reading 34 in *The Struggle for Economic Development*.
3. Brown, *World without Borders*, p. 193.
4. For a more comprehensive discussion of these determinants, see Lester Brown and Erik P. Eckholm, "Food: Growing global insecurity," in Overseas Development Council, *Agenda for Action, 1974* (New York: Praeger, 1974), Chapter 4.
5. In fact, a 1974 report of the U.S. Central Intelligence Agency entitled *Potential Implications of Trends in World Population, Food Production and Climate* specifical-

ly addresses itself to the possibility of using food as a political lever to influence the policies of needy nations.

6. For a review and discussion of Third World stabilization programs from a developed country perspective, see W. R. Cline and S. Weintraub (eds.), *Economic Stabilization in Developing Countries* (Washington, D.C.: Brookings Institution, 1981).

7. Cheryl Payer, *The debt trap: The IMF and the Third World* (New York: Monthly Review, 1974), pp. 1–49.

8. William R. Cline, *International Debt and the Stability of the World Economy* (Washington, D.C.: Institute for International Economics, 1983).

9. Mahbub ul Haq, "A view from the South: The second phase of the North–South dialogue," in McLaughlin et al., *Agenda 1979*, Chapter 4, pp. 116–117, reprinted as Reading 33 in *The Struggle for Economic Development*.

CONCEPTS FOR REVIEW

Debt servicing	Buffer stockpiles
Stabilization policies	Indexation
Debt rescheduling	Common fund
Economic interdependence	Debtor's cartel
Grain reserves	New international economic order

QUESTIONS FOR DISCUSSION

1. The 1970s ushered in an era in which, for the first time, developed nations began to recognize their growing dependence on and vulnerability to the policies of certain Third World groups of nations. Briefly describe this new source of developed country dependence.

2. The actions of OPEC in 1973–1974 dramatically demonstrated that coordinated action by Third World nations in the area of physical resource control could substantially benefit a diverse group of LDCs. Do you think the future will bring greater cooperation among Third World nations in the area of international collective bargaining? What are some of the major obstacles?

3. Another event in 1974 was the first World Food Conference, held in Rome, which brought all nations together to discuss the "world food crisis." Do you believe that there is such a global food crisis? If so, what are its origins and prospects?

4. How are the world food and energy crises interrelated? What is meant by global food reserves? Who controls these reserves and what position might Third World nations adopt with regard to assuring access to these reserves? Explain your answer.

5. "In an era of growing mineral and raw material resource scarcities, problems of nonprice *rationing* and *access* assume increasing importance while traditional allocations by the international pricing mechanism become relatively less important." Explain the meaning of and comment on this statement.

6. Describe the economic origins of the Third World debt crisis of the 1980s. To what extent are these debts the fault of LDCs and to what extent did developed country policies contribute?

7. What are economic stabilization programs and how are they designed to relieve balance of payments problems? What are the economic and social costs of such programs?

8. Can the growing objective of greater self-reliance in Third World nations be reconciled with the tendency toward greater global economic and noneconomic interdependence? Explain your answer.

FURTHER READINGS

In addition to newspapers and magazines, which in almost every issue carry some piece on energy, food, and/or the debt problem, a good, nontechnical discussion of global interdependence can be found in Lester R. Brown, *World without Borders* (New York: Random House, 1972), and Barbara Ward, *Progress for a Small Planet* (New York: Norton, 1979).

For an analysis of the world food and energy crises as these affect Third World nations, see James P. Grant, "Energy shock and the development prospect," in Overseas Development Council, *Agenda for Action, 1974* (New York: Praeger, 1974), Lester R. Brown and Erik P. Eckholm, "Food: Growing global insecurity," in the same volume, and P.K. Ghosh (ed.), *Energy Policy and Third World Development* (Westport, Conn.: Greenwood, 1984).

Much has been written recently on the origin and nature of Third World debt problems. One of the better empirical and analytical studies is the OECD's *Debt Survey* (Paris: Office for Economic Cooperation and Development, 1982). See also W. Cline and S. Weintraub (eds.), *Economic Stabilization in Developing Countries* (Washington, D.C.: Brookings Institution, 1981); Sidney Dell, "Stabilization: The political economy of over-kill," in C. K. Wilber (ed.), *The Political Economy of Development and Underdevelopment* (New York: Random House, 1984), pp. 146−161; and C. Payer, *The Debt Trap: The IMF and the Third World* (New York: Monthly Review, 1974).

Among the good books on the new international economic order, the following are most noteworthy: J. Bhagwati, *The New International Economic Order* (Cambridge, Mass.: MIT Press, 1976); J. Singh, *The New International Economic Order* (New York: Praeger, 1977); E. Lazslo *et al.*, *The Objectives of the New International Economic Order* (New York: Pergamon, 1978); and M. McLaughlin *et al.*, *The United States and World Development: Agenda 1979* (New York: Praeger, 1979), especially Chapters 2 and 4 by John Sewell and Mahbub ul Haq, which are reprinted as the last two readings of *The Struggle for Economic Development*.

Finally, for statements by Third World social scientists on many of these issues, see "Self-reliance and international reform," *World Development* 2, no. 6 (1974):52−55, and a recently published volume of readings, P.K. Ghosh (ed.), *New International Economic Order: A Third World Perspective* (Westport, Conn.: Greenwood, 1984).

Additional readings can be found on pp. 638−640.

APPENDIX 17.1

TWENTY-FIVE KEY OBJECTIVES OF THE NIEO[1]

Listed below, by way of summary, are 25 explicit objectives of the NIEO as contained in various UN documents and resolutions. For convenience they are grouped into four major categories: (a) issues of aid and assistance, (b) issues of international trade, (c) issues of industrialization and technology, and (d) social issues.

ISSUES OF AID AND ASSISTANCE

1. *Attaining UN official development assistance targets.* Each economically advanced country is to progressively increase its development assistance aid to a minimum of 0.7% of its GNP. In principle, the aid is to be untied and provided on a long-term and continuous basis.

2. *Providing technical assistance for development and eliminating the brain drain.* The Declaration of the Establishment of an NIEO reiterates the principle of increased developmental assistance "free from any political or military considerations." The Program for Action adds that "the international community should continue and expand . . . the operational and instruction oriented technical assistance programmes, including vocational training and management development of national personnel." In regard to the issue of the brain drain the program urges national and international policies to avoid this "reverse transfer of technology."

3. *Renegotiating debts of developing countries.* The program calls for the renegotiating of international debt with the result being agreements on debt cancellation, moratoriums, the rescheduling of debt to "soft" terms over a longer period of time, or interest subsidization, in order that the LDCs might "mitigate [the] adverse consequences for the current and future development of developing countries arising from the external burden of debt contracted on hard terms."

4. *Undertaking special measures to assist landlocked, least developed, and island developing countries.* Special attention is to be paid to countries in these categories and their special needs addressed. Specific proposals include preferential treatment to imports of goods produced by least developed countries, removal of tariff barriers, choosing appropriate technologies on favorable terms, and establishing financial and advisory services.

5. *Using funds from disarmament for development.* Progress toward general and complete disarmament should release substantial additional resources, which should be used for the development needs of developing countries.

INTERNATIONAL TRADE ISSUES

6. *Improving terms and conditions of trade: tariff and nontariff barriers.* Stated simply, the NIEO goal is improved access to world markets. There are a

multitude of suggested mechanisms—the removal of tariff barriers, an end to restrictive business practices and monopolies, setting up a system of preferential tariffs to encourage the export of agricultural primary commodities (processed and semiprocessed), etc. The object is to increase the developing countries' ability to earn foreign exchange to pay for imports and to service their foreign debt.

7. *Adopting an integrated approach to commodities: buffer stocks, producers' associations, indexation.* Again, the object is stabilization. The nature of the primary commodity export industry under present market conditions does not allow sustained, predictable growth; hence the call for an integrated program for commodities. It is hoped that by establishing buffer stocks the historical instability of primary commodities could be controlled by manipulating their supply. Producers' associations, similar to OPEC, would strengthen the bargaining position of the producing nations and improve export income. By indexation, or the tying of LDC export prices to the price of imports to assure an equitable relationship, the eroding terms of trade could be halted.

8. *Developing an international food program.* The three major features of this issue are

    (a) Increased production via expanded cultivation utilizing more inputs such as irrigation, fertilizer, and pesticides; the arrest of desertification and salinization; and improved storage

    (b) Developing countries should be assured of the ability to import the necessary quantity of food without undue strain on their foreign currency reserves

    (c) Food security: there should be a world food-grain reserve

9. *Economic policies of developed countries to facilitate diversification and expansion of LDC export potential.* This proposal reiterates the NIEO demand for greater access to developed markets via the lowering of tariff barriers, a generalized system of preferences, and the use of adjustment assistance to aid in diversification of export products.

10. *Improving and intensifying trade relations between countries having different social and economic conditions.* This is directed specifically toward the USSR and the Eastern bloc nations asking—as in (9)—for greater access to their markets on a nonreciprocal, nondiscriminatory basis.

11. *Strengthening economic and technical cooperation among developing countries.* This issue specifically addresses the need for cooperation among LDCs via economic integration at the regional and subregional levels. Suggestions include preferential treatment for imports from other LDCs; cooperation in the fields of finance, credit, and monetary relations; and the establishment of cooperation in the fields of industry, technology, transport, and communication.

12. *Reforming the IMF.* This issue originally arose as a result of the disorder in the international monetary system and in particular the problems with the world's principle reserve currency, the U.S. dollar, in the 1970s. This demand seeks to secure a stable flow of development assistance through the use of SDRs and to maintain "the real value of the currency reserves . . . by preventing their erosion from inflation and exchange rate depreciation."

13. *Participation by LDCs in IMF decision making.* This issue simply calls for "more effective participation by developing countries . . . in the decision-making process . . . of the IMF."

14. *Increasing transfers of resources through the World Bank and the IMF.* The goal of this demand is "to make additional capital available to the poorest countries on highly concessional terms" through the organs of the World Bank and the IMF.

ISSUES OF INDUSTRIALIZATION AND TECHNOLOGY

15. *Negotiating a redeployment of industrial productive capacity to developing countries.* This issue proposes a shifting of the industrial capacity of developed countries to the Third World. It specifically mentions (a) industries having a high labor content, (b) industries requiring natural resources (e.g., shipyards, petrochemical plants, and steel mills), and (c) industries processing locally available raw materials.

16. *Establishing mechanisms for the transfer of technology.* Access to modern technology is essential if LDCs are to reach their development objectives. Recognizing this, the NIEO calls for greater access to technologies via (a) a review of international patents, (b) facilitating access to patented and non-patented technology, (c) expanded assistance to developing countries for research and development programs, and (d) control over the import of technology.

17. *Regulating and supervising the activities of transnational enterprises (MNCs) and eliminating restrictive business practices.* The NIEO proposed an international code of conduct for transnational corporations (a) to prevent interference in the internal affairs of the countries where they operate; (b) to eliminate restrictive business practices and conform to the national development plan and objectives; (c) to bring about assistance, transfer of technology, and management skills to developing countries on equitable terms; (d) to regulate the repatriation of profits accruing from their operation; and (e) to promote reinvestment of their profits in developing countries.

18. *Improving the competitiveness of natural resources and their waste.* The NIEO calls for "improving the competitiveness of natural materials facing competition from synthetic substitutes." To bring this about, the program requests that "in cases where natural resources can satisfy the requirements of the market, new investment for the expansion of the capacity to produce synthetic materials should not be made." It also requests that "all states . . . put an end to the waste of natural resources, including food products."

19. *Providing equitable access to resources of the seabed and the ocean floor.* Stating that the oceans and seabeds are the "common heritage of mankind," the NIEO calls for equitable distribution of the benefits derived from exploration and calls for an international treaty to this effect.

SOCIAL ISSUES

20. *Achieving a more equitable distribution of income and raising the level of employment.* The benefits of industrialization should be distributed equitably among all sectors of the population. Capital-intensive technology should be limited to special uses and not interfere with rising levels of employment. Fiscal, monetary, and trade policy should be promoted with a view toward enhancing the level of employment and economic growth.

21. *Providing health services, education, higher cultural standards and qualifications for the work force, and assuring the well-being of children and the integration of women in development.* The concepts of social development and social well-being appear in conjunction with the proclamation of an NIEO. As social well-being is so closely connected with economic well-being, it is only natural that it be included in the objectives of the NIEO.

22. *Assure the economic sovereignty of states.* This is directed at the pervasive condition of dependency throughout the Third World. It calls for sovereignty over natural resources and the right to control their exploitation, including the right to nationalize.

23. *Compensation for adverse effects on the resources of states due to foreign occupation, colonial domination, or apartheid.* This demand calls for restitu-

tion for the exploitation and depletion of natural resources under the above conditions.

24. *Establishing a system of consultations to promote industrial development.* The aim of this goal is to minimize adverse effects of disposals of production surpluses or reserves and to redeploy these to aid global, regional, or sectoral industrial development.

25. *Restructuring the economic and social sections of the UN.*

NOTES

1. For an extensive discussion including relevant official documents for each of the 25 NIEO objectives listed in this appendix, see Ervin Laszlo *et al.*, *The Objectives of the New International Economic Order* (New York: Pergamon, 1978).

GLOSSARY

The following glossary of terms is designed to cover most of the major concepts and organizations discussed in the text. Note that the *italicized* words that appear in any definition are themselves defined elsewhere in the glossary.

absolute (cost) advantage   if Country A can produce more of a commodity with the same amount of real *resources* than Country B (i.e., at a lower absolute *unit cost*), Country A is said to have absolute cost advantage over Country B. See also *comparative advantage*.

absolute poverty   a situation where a population or section of a population is able to meet only its bare *subsistence* essentials of food, clothing, and shelter in order to maintain minimum *levels of living*. See also *international poverty line* and *subsistence economy*.

absorptive capacity   the ability of a country to effectively "absorb" foreign private or public financial assistance (i.e., to use the funds in a productive manner).

adjustment assistance   public financial assistance provided to workers and industries hurt by imports of lower-priced foreign goods. Such assistance allows them to "adjust" to a new occupation during a transitional period.

"advanced" capitalism   an *economic system* characterized by private ownership but with a major role played by the *public sector*. Most developed *market economies* like those in North America, Western Europe, Japan, and Australia are examples of advanced capitalism.

African Development Bank   a regional bank, established in 1963, to assist independent African countries through the provision of *loans* and *technical assistance*.

AID   see *USAID*.

age structure (of population)   the age composition of a given population. For example, in LDCs the age structure of the population is typified by a large portion of population under 15 years old, a slightly smaller proportion aged between 15 and 45 years, and a very small proportion above 45 years old.

aggregate consumer demand   that part of the total demand (*aggregate demand*) for goods and services in the economy attributed to the demands of households for consumer goods and services within a specific period, usually one year. See also *consumption*.

aggregate demand   a measure of the real purchasing power of the community. Commonly referred to as the total effective demand or total expenditure, it normally comprises private *consumption* (C), private and public *investment* (I), government expenditure (G), plus net exports (X − M).

agrarian system   the pattern of land distribution, ownership, and management, also the social and *institutional* structure of the agrarian economy. Many Latin American and Asian agrarian systems are characterized by concentrations of large tracts of land in the ownership of a few powerful *landlords. Rural development* in many LDCs may require extensive reforms of the existing agrarian system.

agricultural extension services   services offered to farmers usually by the government in the form of transmitting information, new ideas, methods, and advice about, for instance, the use of fertilizers, control of pests and weeds, appropriate machinery, soil conservation methods, simple accounting, etc., in a bid to stimulate high *farm yields*.

agricultural labor productivity   the level of agricultural output per unit of labor input, usually measured as output per man-hour or man-year. It is very low in LDCs compared to developed countries. See also *labor productivity* and *farm yields*.

agricultural mechanization   the extensive use of machinery in farm production activities thereby reducing the amount of labor input necessary to produce a given level of output. See also *labor-saving technological progress*.

agricultural sector   comprises agriculture, forestry, hunting, and fishing.

Andean Group   a common market formed by Bolivia, Colombia, Ecuador, Peru, and Venezuela in an effort to promote *economic integration*, coordinate industrial development, regulate foreign investment, and maintain a *common external tariff* among the member countries.

"appropriate" technology   a technology that is appropriate for existing factor endowments. For example, a technology employing a higher proportion of labor relative to other factors in a labor-abundant economy is usually more appropriate than one that uses smaller labor proportions relative to other factors. See also *factor price distortion, principle of economy,* and *neoclassical price-incentive model*.

Arab Bank for Economic Development in Africa   a development bank established in 1975 by Arab countries to assist non-Arab African countries through the provisions of loans and *technical assistance*.

Asian Development Bank (ADB)   a regional development bank whose major objective is to assist the development of Asian nations through the provision of *loans* and *technical assistance*.

asset ownership   the ownership of land, *physical capital* (factories, buildings, machinery, etc.), *human capital,* and financial resources which generate income for owners. The distribution of asset ownership is a major determinant of the distribution of personal income in any nonsocialist society. See also *income distribution*.

autarchy   a *closed economy* that attempts to be completely *self-reliant*.

average cost   the total cost of production of a commodity incurred by a producer during a period divided by the number of units of output produced in that period. See also *unit cost*.

average propensity to consume (APC)   the proportion of total income spent on *consumption*; derived by dividing total consumption, C, by total income, Y—i.e., APC = C/Y. See also *marginal propensity to consume*.

average propensity to save (APS) the proportion of total income, Y, that is set aside as *savings*, S—i.e., APS $= S/Y$. See also *marginal propensity to save* and *savings ratio*.

balance of payments (table) a summary statement of a nation's financial transactions with the outside world. See also *current account, capital account,* and *cash account*.

balanced trade a situation where the value of a country's exports and the value of its imports of visible items are equal.

barter transactions the trading of goods directly for other goods in economies not fully monetized.

basic needs a term used by the *ILO* to describe the basic goods and services (food, shelter, clothing, sanitation, education, etc.) necessary for a minimum standard of living.

basic science and **technological innovation** (relationship between) basic science refers to a systematic scientific and objective investigation aimed at bringing into existence "new" knowledge or tools, while technological innovation has to do with the application of *inventions* of basic science (such as the new tools or knowledge) to perform tasks in a more efficient way.

"big push" theory of development theory stating that all that LDCs require to "take off" into a period of self-sustaining *economic growth* is a massive investment program designed to promote rapid *industrialization* and the building up of *economic infrastructure*.

bilateral assistance (aid) see *foreign aid*.

birthrate, crude number of children born alive each year, per thousand population (e.g., a crude birthrate of 20 per 1,000 is the same as a 2% increase). See also *general fertility rate* and *death rate*.

black market a situation in which there is illegal selling of goods at prices above a legal maximum set by the government. It occurs due to relative *scarcity* of the goods concerned and the existence of an excess demand for them at the established price. See also *rationing* and *exchange control*.

bottlenecks sectors in the economy where the development process leads to a more rapid expansion of demand than supply in the goods or factor markets.

brain drain the emigration of highly educated and skilled professional and technical manpower from the developing to the developed countries.

buffer stocks stocks of commodities held by countries or international organizations to moderate the commodities' price fluctuations.

CACM: Central American Common Market an economic union formed in 1960 and disbanded in the 1970s. It consisted of five Central American nations: Costa Rica, El Salvador, Guatemala, Honduras, and Nicaragua.

calorie requirement (daily per capita) refers to the calories needed to sustain the population at normal levels of activity and health, taking account of its age and sex distributions, average body weights, and physical environment.

calorie supply (daily per capita) calculated by dividing the calorie equivalent of the available food supplies in a country by its total population.

capital see *physical capital* and *human capital*.

capital account   that portion of a country's *balance of payments* table that shows the volume of *private foreign investment* and public *grants* and *loans* that flow into and out of a country over a given period, usually 1 year. See also *current account* and *cash account*.

capital accumulation   increasing a country's stock of real *capital* (i.e., net investment in fixed assets). To increase the production of capital goods necessitates a reduction in the production of consumer goods. "Economic" development largely depends on the rate of *capital accumulation*.

capital-intensive technique   a more capital-using process of production; that is, one using a higher proportion of capital relative to other *factors of production* such as labor or land per unit output.

capital/output ratio   a ratio that shows the units of *capital* required to produce a unit of output over a given period of time. See *Harrod–Domar equation*.

capital-saving technological progress   arises as a result of some *invention* or *innovation* that facilitates achievement of higher output levels using the same quantity of capital inputs.

capital stock   total amount of physical goods existing at a particular time period which have been produced for use in the production of other goods (including services).

capitalism   see *pure market capitalism* and *advanced capitalism*.

cartel   an organization of producers agreeing to limit the output of their product in an effort to raise prices and profits.

cash account   the "balancing" portion of a country's *balance of payments* table showing how cash balances (*foreign reserves*) and short-term financial claims have changed in response to *current* and *capital account* transactions.

cash crops   crops produced entirely for the market (e.g., coffee, tea, cocoa, cotton, rubber, pyrethrum, jute, wheat).

casual employment   employment on an ad hoc basis without regular hours or a wage contract; constitutes employment in the *informal sector*.

centralized planning   the determination by the state of what shall be produced and how *factors of production* shall be allocated among different uses. Central planning is done at the "center" and then dictated to various sections in the economy.

ceterus paribus   a Latin expression widely used in economics meaning "all else being equal"—i.e., all other variables are held constant.

"character" of economic growth   the distributive implications of the process of *economic growth*; for example, participation in the growth process, asset ownership, etc. In other words, how that *economic growth* is achieved and who benefits.

child death rate   the number of deaths among children 1−4 years of age per 1,000 children of that age in a given year.

Chinese People's commune   a multipurpose political, administrative, and organizational unit covering the full range of economic, social, and administrative activities in a rural community. The people's agricultural communes were the basis of *rural development* in China during the 1960s and early 1970s. Communal ownership included all the rural land, all means of agricultural production, and commune-owned industries.

closed economy   an economy in which there are no foreign trade transactions or any other form of economic contacts with the rest of the world. See also *autarchy* and *"inward-looking" developing policies.*

cognitive skills the ability to perceive and understand abstract concepts and think logically, to have knowledge and/or be aware of a range of relevant information.

collectivism an economic system in which the means of production are owned by collective agencies, such as the government or community, and not by private individuals or business firms.

collusion an agreement among sellers of a commodity (or commodities) to set a common price and/or share their commodity market.

"command" socialism a type of *economic system* where all *resources* are state owned and their allocation and degree of utilization are determined by the centralized decisions of planning authorities rather than by a *price system.* The USSR is the most outstanding example of a command socialist economy.

commercial bank a financial institution that provides a wide range of services, including accepting deposits and making *loans* for commercial purposes.

commercial policy policy encompassing instruments of "trade protection" employed by countries to foster industrial promotion, export diversification, employment creation, and other desired development-oriented strategies. They include *tariffs, physical quotas*, and *subsidies.*

common external tariff tariff imposed by members of a *customs union, common market,* or *economic community* on imports from nonmembers.

common fund *UNCTAD's* proposed *buffer stock*, incorporating at least 10 core commodities.

common market a form of *economic integration* in which there is free internal trade, a common *tariff,* plus the free movement of labor and capital among partner states. The *EEC (European Economic Community)* provides an example. See also *customs union* and *free trade area.*

commune a cooperative farm or other collectively organized unit.

comparative advantage a country has a comparative advantage over another if in producing a commodity it can do so at a relatively lower *opportunity cost* in terms of the foregone alternative commodities that could be produced. Taking two countries, A and B, each producing two commodities, X and Y, Country A is also said to have comparative advantage in the production of X if its *absolute advantage* margin is greater or its absolute disadvantage is less in X than in Y.

complementary resources *factors of production* that are necessarily used along with others to produce a given output or to accomplish a specific task; e.g., man-hours of farm labor are complementary to a hectare of land in the production of maize; machinery and equipment are complementary to labor in the construction of a road.

comprador a local labor recruiter or purchasing agent employed by a foreign firm.

comprehensive plans those *economic plans* that set their targets to cover all the major sectors of the national economy.

concessional loan credit extended in terms that are more favorable to the borrower than are available on the money markets.

conditionality   usually refers to the requirement imposed by the *IMF* that a borrowing country undertake fiscal, monetary, and international commercial reforms as a condition to receiving a loan for *balance of payments* difficulties.

constraints   see *economic constraint.*

consumer sovereignty   the notion central to *Western economic theory* that consumers determine what and how much shall be produced in an economy. The free play of the *price system* and *market mechanism* is then assumed to equilibrate consumer demand with producer supply of that commodity.

consumption   that part of total *national income* devoted to expenditure on *final goods* and *services* by individual consumers during a given period of time, typically 1 year. Total private consumption is assumed to be directly related to the level of aggregate personal income.

consumption diseconomies   problems (costs) that occur to individuals or society as a whole as a result of the unpopular consumption habits of another individual. Examples include alcoholism, poor individual hygiene, drug addiction.

consumption economies   advantages (benefits) that accrue to individuals or society as a whole as a result of increases in the consumption of certain types of goods or services by other individuals (e.g., education, health care).

consumption-possibility line   in international *free trade* theory a locus of points showing the highest possible consumption combinations that can be attained as a result of trade. Graphically, the *consumption-possibility line* is represented by the international price line at its tangency to the domestic *production-possibility* curve of a country.

cost–benefit analysis   a basic tool of economic analysis in which the actual and potential *costs* (both *private* and *social*) of various economic decisions are weighed against actual and potential *private* and *social benefits*. Those decisions or projects yielding the highest benefit/cost ratio are usually thought to be most desirable. See also *project appraisal.*

cost-push inflation   *inflation* that results primarily from the upward pressure of production costs, usually because of rising raw material prices (e.g., oil) or excessive wage increases resulting from trade union pressures. See also *demand-pull* and *structural inflation.*

creditor nation   nation with a *balance of payments* surplus.

curative medicine   medical care that focuses on curing rather than preventing disease. Requires extensive availability of hospitals and clinics. See also *preventive medicine.*

current account   that portion of a *balance of payments* table which portrays the market value of a country's "visible" (e.g., commodity trade) and "invisible" (e.g., shipping services) exports and imports with the rest of the world. See also *capital account* and *cash account.*

current account balance   the difference between (*a*) exports of goods and services plus inflows of unrequited official and private transfers, and (*b*) imports of goods and services plus unrequited transfers to the rest of the world. Excluded from this figure are all interest payments on external public and publicly guaranteed debt.

customs union   a form of *economic integration* in which two or more nations agree to free all internal trade while levying a common external *tariff* on all nonmember countries. See also *common market* and *free trade area*.

death rate, crude   yearly number of deaths per 1,000 population—e.g., an annual crude death rate of 15 per 1,000 or 1.5% of the population. See also *birthrate* and *infant mortality*.

debt outstanding (external public)   the amount of public and publicly guaranteed loans that has been disbursed, net of canceled loan commitments and repayments of principal.

debt renegotiation   changing the terms of existing loans, usually by extending repayment dates without increases in nominal interest rates.

debt service   the sum of interest payments and repayments of principal on external public and publicly guaranteed debt.

debtor nation   nation with a *balance of payments* deficit.

decentralized planning   regionalized or sectoral planning as opposed to planning at the center. See *centralized planning*.

decile   a 10% proportion of any numerical quantity; e.g., a population divided into deciles would be one which was divided into 10 equal numerical groups. See also *quintile*.

decreasing costs   if *increasing returns* exist then a given proportionate change in output will require a smaller proportionate change in quantities of factor inputs thus implying a fall in cost per unit of output. In short, a fall in *average costs* of production as output expands.

deficit expenditure   amount by which planned government expenditure exceeds realized tax revenues. *Deficit expenditure* is normally financed by borrowed funds and its major object is to stimulate economic activity by increasing *aggregate demand*.

demand curve   graphical representation of the quantities of a commodity or resource that would be bought over a range of prices at a particular time, when all other prices and incomes are held constant. When demand curves of all consumers in the market are aggregated a "market demand" curve is derived showing the total amount of the good that consumers are willing to purchase at each price.

demand-pull inflation   *inflation* that arises because of the existence of excess Keynesian *aggregate demand*, i.e., when total effective demand exceeds the productive capacity (aggregate supply) of the economy.

demographic transition   the phasing-out process of *population growth rates* from a virtually stagnant growth stage characterized by high *birth* and *death rates*, through a rapid growth stage with high birthrates and low death rates, to a stable, low growth stage in which both birth and death rates are low.

demonstration effects   the effects of transfers of alien ways of life upon nationals of a country. Such effects are mainly cultural and attitudinal in nature, e.g., *consumption* habits, modes of dressing, patterns of education, leisure and recreation.

dependence   a corollary of *dominance*; a situation where the LDCs have to rely on developed country domestic and international *economic policy* to stimulate their own *economic growth*. *Dependence* can also mean that the LDCs adopt developed country education systems, technology, economic and political systems, attitudes, *consumption* patterns, dress, etc.

dependency burden   that proportion of the total population of a country falling in the ages of $0-15$ and $64+$, which is considered economically unproductive and therefore not counted in the labor force. In many LDCs the population under the age of 15 accounts for almost as much as half of the total population, thus posing a burden to the generally small productive labor force and to the government which has to allocate *resources* on such things as education, public health, housing for the *consumption* of people who don't contribute to production.

devaluation   a lowering of the "official" *exchange rate* between one country's currency and those of the rest of the world.

development   the process of improving the quality of all human lives. Three equally important aspects of development are: (*a*) raising people's living levels, i.e., their incomes and *consumption* levels of food, medical services, education, etc., through "relevant" *economic growth processes*; (*b*) creating conditions conducive to the growth of people's *self-esteem* through the establishment of social, political, and *economic systems* and *institutions* which promote human dignity and respect; and (*c*) increasing people's *freedom to choose* by enlarging the range of their choice variables, e.g., increasing varieties of consumer goods and services.

Development Banks   specialized public and private *financial intermediaries* providing medium- and long-term credit for development projects.

development plan   the documentation by a government planning agency of the current national economic conditions, proposed public expenditures, likely developments in the *private sector*, a macroeconomic projection of the economy, and a review of government policies. Many LDCs publish 5-year *development plans* to announce their economic objectives to their citizens and others.

diminishing returns   the principle that if one *factor of production* is fixed and constant additions of other factors are combined with it, the *marginal productivity* of *variable factors* will eventually decline. The major assumptions of this principle are that at least one factor is fixed, units of the variable factor are identical, and there exists no *technical progress*. For example, if a fixed land area is combined with constant additions of labor using simple tools to produce coffee, output will initially increase, but as more and more labor units are added, average output per man-hour/year declines as do marginal additions to total product. See also *"surplus" labor*.

disguised underemployment   a situation in which available work tasks are split among *resources* (typically labor) such that they all seem fully employed, but in reality much of their time is spent in unproductive activities.

disposable income   the income that is available to households for spending and saving after personal income taxes have been deducted.

division of labor   allocation of tasks among the workers such that each one engages in tasks that he performs most efficiently. *Division of labor* promotes worker specialization and thereby raises overall *labor productivity*. It has its historical origins in Adam Smith's *Wealth of Nations*.

dominance   in international affairs, a situation in which the developed countries have much greater power than the less developed countries in decisions affecting important international economic issues, e.g., the prices of agricultural commodities and raw materials in world markets. See also *vulnerability* and *dependence*.

doubling time (of population)   period that a given population size takes to increase itself by its present size. Doubling time is approximated by dividing any numerical growth rate into 70—e.g., a population growing at 2% per year will double in size approximately every 35 years.

dual price system   government-operated pricing mechanism whereby producers of, say, a staple crop are paid a different price from the one consumers (mostly urban consumers) are charged. In short, any two-price system, one for sellers and the other for buyers.

dualism   the coexistence in one place of two situations or phenomena (one desirable and the other one not) which are mutually exclusive to different groups of a society; e.g., extreme poverty and affluence, modern and traditional economic sectors, growth and stagnation, university education among a few and mass illiteracy.

EAC: East African Community   an integrated economic grouping of the three East African countries—Kenya, Uganda, and Tanzania—established by the Treaty of East African Cooperation of 1967, but eventually dismantled in the mid-1970s. Cooperation took the form of joint administration of a number of common public services (railways, airways, ocean and lake transport, research) and a *customs union* which involved internal *free trade* and a common external *tariff* on imports.

ECA: Economic Commission for Africa   a regional branch of the *United Nations* system located in Addis Ababa, Ethiopia, and devoted to the analysis of economic developments and trends in African nations. Statistical bulletins and technical analyses of economic trends in individual countries and groups of countries in various regions of Africa are regularly published. See also *ECLA* and *ECAFE*.

ECAFE: Economic Commission for Asia and the Far East   a regional branch of the *United Nations* system located in Bangkok, Thailand, and devoted to the technical and statistical analysis of economic developments and trends in the diverse countries of Asia and the Far East. See also *ECA* and *ECLA*.

ECLA: Economic Commission for Latin America   a regional branch of the *United Nations* system located in Santiago, Chile, and devoted to the regular publication of technical and statistical analyses of economic trends in Latin America as a whole and in individual Latin American nations. See also *ECA* and *ECAFE*.

economic community   economic union of countries seeking to coordinate fiscal and monetary policies as a step toward a common currency. This takes place in addition to maintaining a *common external tariff* and similar commercial policies and to removing restrictions on trade within the community.

economic constraint   a barrier to the attainment of a set target (e.g., *economic growth*) in a particular period of time. For example, physical *capital* has long been thought of as the major constraint on *economic growth* in LDCs.

economic disincentives (for fertility reduction)   economic disadvantages (costs) and risks of having small families, e.g., parents' insecurity during their old age (no children or too few children to care for them), shortages of parents' farm labor supply.

economic good   any commodity or service which yields "utility" to an individual or community and which must be paid for in money terms in a monetary economy, or "in kind" in a nonmonetary economy.

economic growth   the steady process by which the productive capacity of the economy is increased over time to bring about rising levels of *national income*. Rapid *economic growth* has been a major preoccupation of economists, planners, and politicians in LDCs in the last two or three decades because it has been thought to be a major precondition determining *levels of living*. Emphasis is now shifting to problems of *income inequality, poverty,* and *unemployment.*

economic incentives (for fertility reduction)   economic motivations aimed at encouraging parents to limit their families to a specified size. Such economic incentives include free or subsidized education for children of families within the specified family size, free or subsidized medical treatment for small families, and high wages for mothers with few children.

economic infrastructure   the underlying amount of *capital accumulation* embodied in roads, railways, waterways, airways, and other forms of transportation and communication plus water supplies, financial institutions, electricity, and public services such as health and education. The level of infrastructural development in a country is a crucial factor determining the pace and diversity of economic development.

economic integration   the merging to various degrees of the economies and economic policies of two or more countries in a given region. See also *common market, customs union, free trade area, trade creation,* and *trade diversion.*

economic plan   a written document containing government policy decisions on how *resources* shall be allocated among different uses in order to attain a targeted rate of *economic growth* over a certain period of time. See *economic planning, centralized planning, planning model,* and *plan implementation.*

economic planning   a deliberate and conscious attempt by the state to formulate decisions on how the *factors of production* shall be allocated among different uses or industries, thereby determining how much of total *goods* and *services* shall be produced in the ensuing period(s). See also *economic plan* and *centralized planning.*

economic policy   statement of objectives and the methods of achieving these objectives (*policy instruments*) by government, political party, business concern, etc. Some examples of government economic objectives are maintaining *full employment*, achieving a high rate of *economic growth*, reducing *income* and regional development *inequalities*, maintaining price stability. *Policy instruments* include fiscal policy, monetary and financial policy, and legislative controls (e.g., price and wage control, rent control).

economic principles   basic concepts of economic theory that provide the tools of economic analysis. Examples of economic principles are the *principle of substitution*, the *principle of economy*, the *principle of diminishing returns*, the concept of *scarcity.*

economizing spirit   the act of minimizing the real *resource* costs of producing any level of output. In general, allocating scarce *resources* with great care. See also the *optimization principle.*

economic system   the organizational and institutional structure of an economy including the nature of *resource* ownership and control (i.e., private versus public). Major economic systems include *subsistence economy, pure market capitalism, advanced capitalism, market socialism, command socialism,* and the *"mixed" systems* that characterize most LDCs.

economic variable   a measure of economic activity such as income, consumption, and price that can take on different quantitative values. Variables are classified either as "dependent" or "independent" in accordance with the economic model being used.

economies of scale   these are economies of growth resulting from expansion of the scale of productive capacity of a firm or industry leading to increases in its output and decreases in its cost of production per unit of output.

economy, principle of   see *principle of economy.*

ECOWAS: Economic Community of West African States   an economic community, formed in 1975, of 15 West African countries—9 French, 5 English, and 1 Portuguese—with a total population of over 125 million and a land area of 6.5 million square miles. It is the largest example of *economic integration* in Africa and includes such countries as Nigeria, Ghana, Upper Volta, Senegal, Niger, and Chad.

educational certification   the phenomenon by which particular jobs require specified levels of education. Applicants must produce "certificates" of such completed schooling in the *formal educational system.*

EEC: European Economic Community   a European economic federation (*common market*) established under the Treaty of Rome in 1957 with a view of abolishing interstate *tariffs* within the federation in order to increase trade volume (and hence GDP) of member states. The current membership of EEC includes West Germany, Luxembourg, Great Britain, Italy, Denmark, Austria, Belgium, Switzerland, France, and the Netherlands.

efficiency, allocative   producing the maximum output possible, given quantities of inputs and using cost-minimizing techniques of production.

efficiency, economic   producing the maximum-valued output possible, using cost-minimizing techniques of production and considering effective market demand.

efficiency, technical   producing the maximum output possible, given quantities of inputs and existing technology, without regard to effective market demand.

elasticity of demand   see *price elasticity of demand* and *income elasticity of demand.*

elasticity of factor substitution   a measure of the degree of "substitutability" between *factors of production* in any given *production process* when relative factor prices change.

employment gap   (a) *deflationary:* amount by which employment at equilibrium national output falls short of employment that would obtain at capacity output; (b) *inflationary:* amount by which prices at equilibrium national output exceeds those which would obtain at capacity or *potential output* level. The employment gap is a major Keynesian concept but one that has limited relevance for many LDCs.

enclave economies   those economies found among LDCs in which there exist small pockets of economically developed regions (often due to the presence of colonial or foreign firms engaged in plantation and mining activities) with the rest of the larger outlying areas experiencing very little progress. See also *dualism*.

energy consumption per dollar of GDP   refers to the ratio of total energy consumption to GDP in constant dollars. This indicator shows the intensity of energy use in the economy.

equilibrium price   the price at which the quantity demanded of a good is exactly equal to the quantity supplied. It is often referred to as the price at which the market clears itself. See also *price system*.

equilibrium wage rate   the wage rate that equates the demand for and supply of labor—i.e., the wage at which all the people who want to work at that wage are able to find jobs and also at which the employers are able to find all the workers they desire to employ. In other words, it is the wage rate that clears the labor market.

Eurodollars   dollar deposits of European banks in American ones, or dollar deposits in European banks, which the European banks may use as reserves for dollar loans.

exchange control   a governmental policy designed to restrict the outflow of domestic currency and prevent a worsened *balance of payments* position by controlling the amount of *foreign exchange* that can be obtained or held by domestic citizens. Often results from *overvalued exchange rates*.

exchange rate   the rate at which central banks will exchange one country's currency for another (i.e., the "official" rate). See also *overvalued exchange rate* and *devaluation*.

exports (of goods and nonfactor services)   represent the value of all goods and nonfactor services sold to the rest of the world; they include merchandise, freight, insurance, travel, and other nonfactor services. The value of factor services (such as investment receipts and worker's remittances from abroad) is excluded from this measure. See also *merchandise exports and imports*.

export dependence   a situation in which a country relies heavily on exports as the major source of finance needed for carrying out development activities. This is the situation of many LDCs which must export *primary products* to earn valuable *foreign exchange*.

export incentives   public *subsidies*, tax rebates, and other kinds of financial and nonfinancial measures designed to promote a greater level of economic activity in export industries.

export promotion   purposeful governmental efforts to expand the volume of a country's exports through *export incentives* and other means in order to generate more *foreign exchange* and improve the *current account* of its *balance of payments*.

external diseconomies of production   these are the increased costs that a single firm or a group of firms faces in increasing its output beyond a certain level, because of problems for which the firm or the group of firms concerned is not responsible. Such diseconomies include increases in clearing costs due to pollution of other firms and transport delays due to too many vehicles on the road.

external economies of production   increases in output (or decreases in costs) of an individual firm over a certain range of production and plant scale due to production advantages it derives from the expansion activities of other firms—e.g., its use of new equipment that has been invented by an outside group of growing firms. See also *internal economies of production*.

factors of production   *resources* or *inputs* required to produce a *good* or service. Basic categories of *factors of production* are land, labor, and *capital*.

factor-endowment trade theory   the neoclassical model of *free trade* which postulates that countries will tend to specialize in the production of those commodities which make use of their abundant *factors of production* (land, labor, *capital*, etc.). They can then export the surplus in return for imports of the products produced by factors with which they are relatively less endowed. The basis for trade arises because of differences in relative factor prices and thus domestic price ratios as a result of differences in factor supplies. See also *comparative advantage*.

factor mobility   the unrestricted transference or free voluntary movement of factors of production among different uses and geographic locations.

factor-price distortions   situations in which *factors of production* are paid prices that do not reflect their true *scarcity* values (i.e., their competitive market prices) because of institutional arrangements which tamper with the free working of market forces of supply and demand. In many LDCs the prices paid for *capital* and *intermediate producer goods* are artificially low because of special capital depreciation allowance, tax rebates, investment subsidies, etc., while labor is paid a wage above its competitive market value partly because of trade union and political pressures. *Factor-price distortions* can lead to the use of "inappropriate" techniques of production. See also *neoclassical price-incentive model* and *appropriate technology*.

factor-price equalization   in *factor-endowment theory of free trade* the proposition that because countries trade at a common international price ratio, factor prices among trading partners will tend to be equalized given the assumption of identical technological possibilities for all commodities across countries. The prices of the more abundantly utilized *resources* will tend to rise while those of the relatively scarce factors fall. Over time, international factor payments will tend toward equality, e.g., real wage rates for labor will be the same in Britain or Botswana.

"false paradigm" model of underdevelopment   the proposition that *Third World* countries have failed to develop because their development strategies (usually given to them by Western economists) have been based on an "incorrect" model of development, one that overstressed *capital accumulation* without giving due consideration to needed social and *institutional* change.

family-planning programs   public programs designed to help parents to plan and regulate their family size in accordance with their ability to support a family. The program usually includes supply of contraceptives to adult population, education on the use of birth control devices, mass media propaganda on benefits derived from smaller families, and pre- and post-natal health care for mothers.

FAO: Food and Agricultural Organization   a department of *United Nations* based in Rome, Italy, whose major concern is to expand world food production in order to meet food intake requirements of the growing world population. FAO researches into modern methods of increasing *farm yields* and educates farmers on their use. It also works in collaboration with such bodies as the World Food Council and the Overseas Food Organization.

farm yields   a quantitative measure of the productivity of a given unit of farm land in producing a particular commodity—usually measured in terms of output per hectare (e.g., so many kilos of rice per hectare).

farmer cooperatives   associations of farmers mainly engaged in cash crop production to enable them to reap the benefits of *economies of scale*. Large tracts of farm land are jointly owned and operated by the cooperative with profits being shared in accordance with a prearranged pattern of distribution (not necessarily equal for all farm families).

fertility rate, general   yearly number of children born alive per 1,000 women within the childbearing age bracket (normally between the ages of 15 and 49 years). See also *crude birthrate*.

fertility rate (total)   the number of children that would be born to a woman if she were to live to the end of her childbearing years and bear children at each age in accordance with the prevailing age-specific fertility rates.

final goods   commodities that are *consumed* to satisfy wants rather than passed on to further stages of production. Whenever a *final good* is not *consumed* but is used as an *input* instead, it becomes an *intermediate good*.

financial intermediary   any financial institution, public or private, that serves to channel loanable funds from savers to borrowers. Examples include commercial banks, savings banks, *development banks*, finance companies.

First World   the now economically advanced *capitalist* countries of Western Europe, North America, Australia, New Zealand, and Japan. These were the first countries to experience sustained and long-term *economic growth*.

fixed exchange rate   the exchange value of a national currency is fixed in relation to another (usually the U.S. dollar), not free to fluctuate on the international money market.

fixed inputs   *inputs* that do not vary as output varies. A hectare of land for example is a *fixed input* on a small family farm because it can be used to produce different quantities of, say, maize output without its size changing. See also *variable inputs*.

fixed input coefficients   a phenomenon in the economics of production in which any level of output requires a fixed ratio of *factor* inputs—e.g., 3 units of labor are always required to produce 10 units of output so that in order to produce 50 units of output, 15 units of labor will be required. The labor (input) coefficient (L/Q) in this case would be 0.3 ($= \frac{3}{10}$).

flexible exchange rate   the exchange value of a national currency is free to move up and down in response to shifts in demand and supply arising from international trading.

flexible institutions   *institutions* that are self-responsive or can be made to respond to changing *development* requirements; e.g., a system of land tenure that can adjust itself or be adjusted to allow for a more equitable redistribution of land. See also *rigid institutions*.

flexible wages   wages that adjust upward or downward depending on the directions of forces of demand for and supply of labor; e.g., if the demand for labor increases (decreases) or its supply decreases (increases), *ceterus paribus*, wages will increase (decrease).

foreign aid   the international transfer of public funds in the form of *loans* or *grants* either directly from one government to another (*bilateral assistance*) or indirectly through the vehicle of a *multilateral assistance* agency like the *IBRD (World Bank)*. See also *tied aid* and *private foreign investment*.

foreign exchange   claims on a country by another held in the form of currency of that country. Foreign exchange system enables one currency to be exchanged for (or be converted into) another, thus facilitating trade between countries. See also *exchange rate* and *foreign reserves*.

foreign reserves   the total value (usually expressed in dollars) of all gold, dollars, and *Special Drawing Rights (SDRs)* held by a country as both a reserve and a fund from which international payments can be made.

"formal" educational system   the organized and accredited school system with licensed teachers, standard curricula, regular academic years, and recognized certification. Encompasses primary, secondary, and tertiary educational institutions. See also *nonformal education*.

free market   see *pure market capitalism, price system*, and *market mechanism*.

free trade   trade in which goods can be imported and exported without any barriers in the form of *tariffs, physical quotas*, or any other kind of restriction.

free trade area   a form of *economic integration* in which there exists free internal trade among member countries but each member is free to levy different external tariffs against nonmember nations. See also *customs union, common market*, and *LAFTA*.

freedom to choose (of a society)   a situation in which a society has at its disposal a variety of alternatives from which to satisfy its wants. See also *development*.

full employment   (*a*) a situation where everyone who wants to work at the prevailing wage rate is able to get a job or, alternatively, (*b*) a situation whereby some job seekers cannot get employment at the going wage rate but *open unemployment* has been reduced to a desired level (e.g., 2 percent).

functional distribution of income   the distribution of income to *factors of production* without regard to the ownership of the factors. See *factor shares* and *marginal productivity*.

gains from trade   the increase in output and consumption resulting from specialization in production and *free trade* with other economic units including persons, regions, or countries.

GATT: General Agreement on Tariffs and Trade   an international body set up in 1947 to probe into the ways and means of reducing tariffs on internationally traded goods and services. Between 1947 and 1962 GATT held about seven conferences but met only with moderate success. Its major success was achieved in 1967 during the "Kennedy Round" of talks when tariffs on primary commodities were drastically slashed.

GDP deflator (*inflation rate*)   calculated by dividing, for each year of period in question, the value of GDP in current market prices by the value of GDP in constant market prices, both in national currencies.

Gini coefficients   an aggregate numerical measure of *income inequality* ranging from zero (perfect equality) to one (perfect inequality). It is graphically measured by dividing the area between the perfect equality line and the *Lorenz curve* by the total area lying to the right of the equality line in a Lorenz diagram. The higher the value of the coefficient, the higher the *inequality of income distribution*; and the lower it is, the more equitable the *distribution of income.* See also *Lorenz curve* and *"skewed" distribution of income.*

goods   see *economic goods*; also *final goods.*

grants   an outright *transfer payment* usually from one government to another (*foreign aid*), i.e., a gift of money or *technical assistance* which does not have to be repaid. See also *loans* and *tied aid.*

Green Revolution   the revolution in grain production associated with the scientific discovery of new hybrid seed varieties of wheat, rice, and corn which have resulted in high *farm yields* in many LDCs.

gross domestic investment   consists of the outlays for additions to the fixed assets of both the private and public sectors plus the net value of inventory changes. See also *investment.*

gross domestic product (GDP)   measures the total final outputs of goods and services produced by the country's economy—i.e., within the country's territory by residents and nonresidents, regardless of its allocation between domestic and foreign claims. See also *gross national product.*

Group of 77   a loose coalition of over 100 countries, predominantly developing ones, originally formed by 77 countries at the *United Nations Conference on Trade and Development (UNCTAD)* in 1964, to express and further their collective interests in the world economic system.

Group of 10   the *IMF*'s 10 largest members.

gross domestic savings   shows the amount of gross domestic investment financed from domestic output. It is calculated as the difference between gross domestic investment and the deficit on current account of goods and nonfactor services (excluding net current transfers). It comprises both public and private savings. See also *savings.*

gross national product (GNP)   measures the total domestic and foreign output claimed by residents of a country. It comprises *gross domestic product* plus factor incomes accruing to residents from abroad, less the income earned in the domestic economy accruing to persons abroad. See also *national income* and *national expenditure.*

growth   see *economic growth.*

"growth poles"   regions that are more economically and socially advanced than others around them—e.g., urban centers vis-à-vis rural areas in LDCs. Large-scale economic activity tends to cluster around such "growth poles" due to economies of agglomeration—i.e., lower costs of locating an industry in an area where much *economic infrastructure* has been built up.

"hard" loan   see *loans.*

Harrod–Domar equation   this is a functional economic relationship in which the *growth rate of gross domestic product (g)* depends directly on the *national savings rate (s)* and inversely on the national *capital/output ratio (k)* so that it is written as $g = s/k$. The equation takes its name from a synthesis of analyses of growth process by two economists (Sir Roy Harrod of Britain and E.V. Domar of the United States).

hidden momentum (of population growth)   a dynamic latent process of population increase that continues even after a fall in *birthrates* because of a large youthful population that widens the population's parent base. Fewer children per couple in the succeeding few generations will not mean a smaller or stable population size because at the same time there will be a much larger number of childbearing couples. Thus a given population will not stabilize until after two or so generations.

hidden unemployment a situation in which labor is fully employed but is unproductive either because the workers are incapacitated, sick, uneducated, hungry, unmotivated, or are using unsuitable tools in their tasks. See also *underemployment* and *disguised underemployment*.

hybrid seeds seeds produced by cross-breeding plants or crops of different species through scientific research. See also *Green Revolution*.

human capital productive *investments* embodied in human persons. These include skills, abilities, ideals, health, etc., that result from expenditures on education, on-the-job training programs, and medical care. See also *physical capital*.

IBRD: International Bank for Reconstruction and Development (World Bank) an international financial institution forming part of the *United Nations* and based in Washington, D.C. One of its main objectives is to provide "development funds" to the needy *Third World* nations (especially the poorest countries) in the form of *interest*-bearing *loans* and *technical assistance*. The *World Bank* operates with funds borrowed primarily from rich nations but increasingly from *OPEC* countries as well. See also *IDA*.

IDA: International Development Association an international body set up in 1960 to assist the *World Bank (IBRD)* in its efforts to promote economic development of the underdeveloped countries by providing additional *capital* on a low *interest* basis (i.e., through *"soft" loans*) especially to the poorest of the poor developing countries.

IFC: International Finance Corporation an international financial institution that was set up in 1956 to supplement the efforts of the *World Bank* in providing development *capital* to private enterprises (mainly industrial) of the underdeveloped countries.

ILO: International Labor Organization one of the *United Nations* functional organizations based in Geneva whose central task is to look into problems of world manpower supply, its training, utilization, domestic and international distribution, etc. Its aim in this endeavor is to increase "world output" through maximum utilization of available human *resources* and thus improve *levels of living* for people.

IMF: International Monetary Fund an autonomous international financial institution that originated from the Bretton Woods Conference of 1944. Its main purpose is to regulate the international monetary exchange system which also originated from that conference but has since been modified. In particular, one of the central tasks of the IMF is to control fluctuations in *exchange rates* of world currencies in a bid to alleviate severe *balance of payments* problems.

imperfect competition a market situation or structure in which producers have some degree of control over the price of their product. Examples include *monopoly* and *oligopoly*. See also *perfect competition*.

imperfect market a market where the theoretical assumptions of *perfect competition* are violated by the existence of, for example, a small number of buyers and sellers, barriers to entry, nonhomogeneity of products, and imperfect information. The three imperfect markets commonly analyzed in economic theory are *monopoly, oligopoly,* and monopolistic competition.

import substitution   a deliberate effort to replace major imports by promoting the emergence and expansion of domestic industries such as textiles, shoes, household appliances. Requires the imposition of protective *tariffs* and physical *quotas* to get the new industry started. See also *infant industry.*

income distribution   see *functional distribution of income* and *size distribution of income.*

income effect   the implicit change in *real income* resulting from the effects of a change in a commodity's price on the quantity demanded.

income elasticity of demand   the responsiveness of the quantity demanded of a commodity to changes in the consumer's income, measured by the proportionate change in quantity divided by the proportionate change in income.

income gap   the gap between the incomes accruing to the bottom poor and the top rich sectors of a population. The wider the gap the greater the inequality in the *income distribution.* Also used to refer to the gap between *income per capita* levels in rich and poor nations.

income "in kind"   a household's or firm's income in the form of goods or services instead of in the form of money. Payments in a *barter* and *subsistence economy* are mainly made "in kind."

income inequality   the existence of disproportionate distribution of total *national income* among households whereby the share going to rich persons in a country is far greater than that going to the poorer persons (a situation common to most LDCs). This is largely due to differences in the amount of income derived from ownership of property and to a lesser extent the result of differences in earned income. Inequality of personal incomes can be reduced by steeply *progressive income* and *wealth taxes.* See also *Gini coefficient* and *Lorenz curve.*

income per capita   total *GNP* of a country divided by the total population. Per capita income is often used as an economic indicator of the *levels of living* and *development.* It, however, can be a "biased" index because it takes no account of *income distribution* and the ownership of the *assets* which are employed to generate part of that income.

increasing opportunity cost   in a state of *full employment* the shifting away of increasing amounts of productive *resources* from the production of one commodity (e.g., automobiles) to another (e.g., food) involves an *opportunity cost.* The *opportunity cost* of producing a given increase in automobiles is the amount of food production foregone. As more and more cars are produced at the expense of food there will be increasing opportunity costs of additional auto production. This gives rise to the phenomenon of the ("concave") *production-possibility curve* in economic theory.

increasing returns   a disproportionate increase in output which results from a change in the scale of production. In traditional economic theory, increasing returns (and thus decreasing costs) will occur until a certain output level has been reached and thereafter *diminishing returns* (increasing costs) are assumed to set in. Some industries (e.g., utilities, transportation) are characterized by increasing returns over a wide range of output. This leads to *monopoly* situations. See also *economies of scale.*

incremental capital/output ratio (ICOR)   the amount of capital needed to raise output by one unit.

indirect taxes   taxes levied on goods purchased by the consumer (and exported by the producer) for which the taxpayer's liability varies in proportion to the quantity of particular goods purchased or sold. Examples of indirect taxes are customs duties (*tariffs*), excise duties, sales taxes, and export duties. The indirectness of such taxes arises because the consumer or producer can avoid paying them by not consuming or producing the taxed goods. They are a major source of tax revenue for most LDCs as they are easier to administer and collect than *direct taxes* (e.g., income and property taxes).

industrialization   the process of building up a country's capacity to "process" raw materials and to manufacture goods for consumption or further production—e.g., setting up firms and acquiring plant and equipment (including *human capital*) to process agricultural products and extracted raw materials or to make manufactures such as radios, cars, canned foods, plows, clothes.

infant industry   a term given to a newly established industry usually set up behind the protection of a *tariff* barrier as part of a policy of *import substitution*. Once the industry is no longer an "infant," the protective tariffs are supposed to disappear but they often do not.

infant mortality   the deaths among children between birth and 1 year of age. The infant mortality rate measures the number of these deaths per 1,000 live births.

inferior good   a good whose demand falls as consumer incomes rise. The *income elasticity of demand* of an inferior good is thus negative.

inflation   a period of above-normal general price increases as reflected, for example, in the consumer and wholesale price indexes. More generally, the phenomenon of rising prices. See also *cost-push, demand-pull*, and *structural inflation*.

informal sector   that part of the urban economy of LDCs characterized by small competitive individual or family firms, petty retail trade and services, *labor-intensive* methods of doing things, low *levels of living*, poor working conditions, high *birthrates*, low levels of health and education, etc. It often provides a major source of urban employment and economic activity.

infrastructure   see *economic infrastructure*.

innovation   the application of *inventions* of new production processes and methods to production activities as well as the introduction of new products. Innovations may also include the introduction of new social and institutional methods of organization and management commensurate with modern ways of conducting economic activities. See *inventions* and *modernization ideals*.

inputs   goods and services—e.g., raw materials, man-hours of labor—used in the process of production. See also *factors of production* and *resources*.

institutions   norms, rules of conduct, and generally accepted ways of doing things. *Social institutions* refer to well-defined and formal organizations of society that govern the way that society operates—e.g., class system, private versus communal ownership, educational system—while *political institutions* refer to the systems that govern the operations of the government of a particular society—e.g., formal power structures, political parties, mechanism of getting into power.

integrated rural development   the broad spectrum of rural development, which includes small-farmer agricultural progress; improvement of *levels of living* (incomes, employment, education, health and nutrition, housing, and other social services) for the rural people; reductions in the inequality in the distribution of rural incomes and in urban – rural imbalances in incomes and economic opportunities; and the capacity of the rural sector to sustain and accelerate the pace of these improvements over time.

integration   see *economic integration*.

Inter-American Development Bank   a regional development bank, established in 1959 by the Organization of American States, offering loans for project development and export financing.

interdependence   interrelationship between *economic* and *noneconomic variables*. Also, in international affairs, the situation in which one nation's welfare depends to varying degrees on the decisions and policies of another nation and vice versa. See also *dependence, dominance,* and *vulnerability*.

interest   the payment (or price) for the use of borrowed funds. See also *interest rate, social discount rate, time preference*.

interest rate   the amount that a borrower must pay a lender over and above the total amount borrowed expressed as a percentage of the total amount of funds borrowed—e.g., if a man borrowed 100 rupees for 1 year at the end of which he had to repay 110 rupees, the *interest rate* would be 10% per annum.

intermediate producer goods   goods that are used as *inputs* into further levels of production, for example, leather in shoe manufacture, iron ore in steel production. See also *final goods*.

intermediate technology   a technology that is halfway between the highly capital-intensive technologies of the developed countries and the primitive, indigenous techniques of the developing countries, usually relying on the use of local materials and skills. See *appropriate technology*.

internal economies (diseconomies) of production   these are the advantages (lower costs) in the case of economies or the *constraints* (additional costs) in the case of diseconomies to a single firm as its scale of production expands. They include decreasing or increasing administrative costs, improved or worsened coordination problems, shortages of appropriate manpower skills. See also *external economies* and *diseconomies of production*.

international poverty line   an arbitrary international *real income* measure, usually expressed in constant dollars (e.g., $200), used as a basis for estimating the proportion of the world's population that exists at bare levels of *subsistence*—i.e., those whose incomes fall below this poverty line.

invention   the discovery of something new, for example, a new product (e.g., *hybrid corn*) or a new production process (e.g., a cheaper and more efficient way of producing synthetic rubber). See also *innovation*.

investment   that part of *national income* or *expenditure* devoted to the production of *capital goods* over a given period of time. "Gross" investment refers to the total expenditure on new *capital goods*, while "net" investment refers to the additional *capital goods* produced in excess of those that wear out and need to be replaced.

"investment" in children   the process by which parents raise the "quality" and hence the "earning capacity" of children by providing them with an education in expectation of future returns. In this sense, children in poor societies are viewed as *capital goods* and a source of old-age security. See also *human resources*.

invisible hand this term has its origin in Adam Smith's famous book *Wealth of Nations* written in 1776. It argues that the unbridled pursuit of individual self-interest automatically contributes to the maximization of the social interest. See also *laissez faire, perfect competition*, and *pure market capitalism*.

inward-looking development policies policies that stress economic *self-reliance* on the part of LDCs, including the development of indigenous *"appropriate" technology*, the imposition of substantial protective *tariffs* and nontariff trade barriers in order to promote *import substitution*, and the general discouragement of private *foreign investment*. See also *autarchy* and *outward-looking development policies*.

Keynesian economies that branch of *Western macroeconomic theory* focusing on the determination of aggregate income and employment in a *market economy* based on *"advanced" capitalism*. Named after its originator, Lord John Maynard Keynes, the famous British economist of the 1930s.

Keynesian model model developed by Lord John Maynard Keynes in the early 1930s to explain the cause of economic depression and hence the unemployment of that period. The model states that unemployment is caused by insufficient *aggregate demand* (AD) and it can be eliminated by, say, government expenditure that would raise AD and activate idle and/or underutilized resources and thus create jobs.

Kuznets curve a relationship between a country's income per capita and its equality of income distribution, in which as per capita incomes increase, the distribution of income at first worsens and later improves from very low levels. Named after Nobel Laureate Simon Kuznets who first statistically identified this relationship for developed nations.

labor force describes economically active persons, including the armed forces and the unemployed, but excluding housewives, students, and economically inactive groups.

labor-intensive technique method of production that uses proportionately more labor relative to other *factors of production*. See also *capital-intensive technique*.

labor- or capital-augmenting technological progress *technological progress* that raises the productivity of an existing quantity of labor (or capital), e.g., labor by general education, on-the-job training programs, etc., and capital by *innovation* and new *inventions*. See also *labor-saving technological progress*.

labor productivity the level of output per unit of labor input, usually measured as output per man-hour or man-year.

labor-saving technological progress associated with the achievement of higher output using an unchanged quantity of labor inputs as a result of some *invention* (e.g., the computer) or *innovation* (such as assembly-line production).

labor theory of value in classical international trade theory, the proposition that relative commodity prices depend on relative amounts of labor used to produce those commodities. Much of Marxist economics is based on the labor theory of value.

LAFTA: Latin American Free Trade Association   an economic federation of 11 Latin American states formed in 1960 and within which all commodities are traded free of tariff. Each member state, however, may charge tariffs and legislate other trade restrictions on goods entering it from countries that are not members of the federation. The primary purpose of LAFTA is to encourage trade creation in the economically integrated area; its current membership includes Brazil, Argentina, Chile, and Venezuela.

laissez faire   an expression often used to represent the notion of free enterprise, market capitalism. See also *perfect competition* and *pure market capitalism.*

land reform   deliberate attempt to reorganize and transform existing *agrarian systems* with the intention of improving the distribution of agricultural incomes and thus fostering *rural development.* Among its many forms, *land reform* may entail provision of secured tenure rights to the individual farmer; transfer of land ownership away from small classes of powerful landowners to tenants who actually till the land; appropriation of land estates for establishing small new settlement farms; instituting land improvements and irrigation schemes, etc.

landlord   a proprietor of a freehold interest in land with rights to lease out to tenants in return for some form of payment for the use of the land.

latifundios   very large land holdings found in the Latin American *agrarian system*, capable of providing employment for over 12 people each, owned by a small number of *landlords*, and comprising a large proportion of total agricultural land. See also *minifundios.*

laws (versus *tendencies*)   a law is a universal truth—it holds in all situations and its validity is independent of the social and/or political context in which it is observed (e.g., in the physical sciences, the law of gravity holds whether an experiment is conducted in North America, the USSR, China, Botswana, or Brazil). On the other hand, *tendencies* (as in economics) are only inclinations of behavior or phenomena that may occur under similar conditions but are not always true in different social contexts.

levels of living   the extent to which a person, a family, or group of people can satisfy their material and spiritual wants. If they are able to afford only a minimum quantity of food, shelter, and clothing their levels of living are said to be very low. On the other hand, if they do enjoy a greater variety of food, shelter, clothing, and other things, such as good health, education, leisure, then clearly they are enjoying relatively high levels of living. See *development.*

life expectancy at birth   indicates the number of years newborn children would live if subject to the *mortality* risks prevailing for the cross-section of population at the time of their birth. See also *birthrate.*

life sustenance   those basic goods and services like food, clothing, and shelter that are necessary to sustain an average human being at the bare minimal *level of living.*

literacy   the ability to read and write. Literacy rates are often used as one of the many social and economic indicators of the state of development within a country.

literacy rate   percentage of population aged 15 and over able to read and write.

loans   the transfer of funds from one economic entity to another (e.g., government to government, individual to individual, bank to individual) which must be repaid with *interest* over a prescribed period of time. "Hard" loans refer to those given at "market" rates of interest whereas "soft" loans are given at "concessionary" or low rates of interest. See also *grants*.

Lorenz curve   a graph depicting the variance of the *size distribution of income* from perfect equality. See also *Gini coefficient*.

low-income countries   countries with a per capita income in 1980 under $600; essentially the least-developed countries including Bangladesh, India, certain countries of sub-Saharan Africa, Indonesia, and Vietnam.

luxury goods   goods whose demand is generated in large part by the higher-income groups within a country. Luxuries are regarded as suitable objects of taxation from the social point of view (in order to improve income distribution) as they are not considered necessary for life maintenance. Examples of luxuries in a less developed economy are very expensive motorcars, imported expensive clothing, cosmetics, jewelry, television sets.

"macro" population–development relationship   a general cause-and-effect relationship between the development process and population growth. Development causes population growth rates to slow down and stabilize by providing *economic incentives* that motivate people to have smaller families. Population growth (in the absence of a population problem) in turn affects development in many ways; e.g., it increases *aggregate demand* that stimulates increases in national output, provides more people for national defense.

macroeconomics   that branch of economics which considers the relationships among broad economic aggregates such as *national income*, total volumes of *saving, investment, consumption* expenditure, employment, *money supply*, etc. It is also concerned with determinants of the magnitudes of these aggregates and their rates of change through time. See also *Keynesian economics*.

malnutrition   a state of ill-health resulting from an inadequate or improper diet—usually measured in terms of average daily protein consumption.

Malthusian population trap   an inevitable population level envisaged by Thomas Malthus (1766–1834) at which population increase was bound to stop because after that level life-sustaining resources, which increase at an arithmetic rate, would be insufficient to support human population, which increases at a geometric rate. Consequently, people would die of starvation, disease, wars, etc. The Malthusian population trap therefore represents that population size that can just be supported by the available resources.

manpower planning   the long-range planning of skilled and semiskilled manpower requirements and the attempt to gear educational priorities and investments in accordance with these future *human resource* needs.

marginal cost   the addition to total cost incurred by the producer as a result of varying output by one more unit.

marginal product   the increase in total output resulting from the use of one additional unit of a variable *factor of production*.

marginal propensity to consume (MPC)   the change in consumption, C, divided by the change in income, Y, that brought it about, i.e., MPC $= \Delta C/\Delta Y$.

marginal propensity to save (MPS)   the change of saving, S, that results from a given change in income, Y, that is, the ratio of change in saving to the change in income so that MPS $= \Delta S/\Delta Y$ or dS/dY in calculus. By definition MPC + MPS = 1. See *marginal propensity to consume (MPC)*.

marginal utility   the satisfaction derived by consuming one additional or one less unit of a good. A consumer's marginal utility is said to be maximized if his marginal utility per last unit of expenditure on that good is equal to marginal utilities of all other goods available to him, divided by their respective prices.

market economy   a free private enterprise governed by a *price system* and *market mechanism*. See also *perfect competition* and *pure capitalism*.

market failure   a phenomenon that results from the existence of market imperfections (e.g., monopoly power, factor immobility, lack of knowledge) which weaken the functioning of a free market economy—i.e., it "fails" to realize its theoretical beneficial results. Market failure often provides the justification for government interference with the working of the free market.

market mechanism   the system whereby *prices* of commodities or services freely rise or fall when the buyer's demand for them rises or falls or the seller's supply of them decreases or increases. See *price system*.

market socialism   economic system in which all resources are owned by the state but their allocation in the economy is done primarily by a *market price system*. See also *"command" socialism*.

mass production   large-scale production of goods or services achieved primarily through automation, specialization, and the *division of labor*.

merchandise exports and imports   covers all international changes in ownership of merchandise passing across the customs borders of the compiling countries. Exports are valued FOB (free on board). Imports are valued CIF (cost, insurance, and freight).

microeconomics   that branch of economics concerned with individual decision units—firms and households—and the way in which their decisions interact to determine relative prices of goods and factors of production and how much of these will be bought and sold. The market is the central concept in microeconomics. See also *price system* and *traditional economics*.

microeconomic theory of fertility   an extension of the theory of economic behavior of individual firms and households to the family formation decisions of individual couples. The central proposition of this theory is that family formation has costs and benefits and thus the size of families formed will depend on these costs and benefits. If the costs of family formation are high (low) relative to its benefits, the rates at which couples will decide to bring forth children will decline (increase). See also *"opportunity cost" of a woman's time, (general) fertility rate, (crude) birthrate, economic incentives* and *disincentives of fertility reduction*.

microfundios   very small landholdings in Latin American *agrarian system*, which are further divisions of *minifundios* as a result of growing populations on crowded areas of poor land; e.g., in Guatemala microfundios yield an average income that is less than one-third of that provided by the *minifundios*.

middle-income countries   developing countries with a per capita income in 1980 exceeding $600 but less than $3,500; includes many countries in Latin America, some in Southeast Asia (the Philippines, Thailand, and Malaysia), and a few in sub-Saharan Africa (Ivory Coast, Liberia, and Nigeria).

minifundios   landholdings in the Latin American *agrarian system* considered too small to provide adequate employment for a single family. They are too small to provide the workers with a *level of living* much above the bare survival minimum. Holders of minifundios are often required to provide unpaid seasonal labor to *latifundios* and to seek outside low-paid employment to supplement their meager incomes. See also *latifundios* and *microfundios*.

mixed commercial farming   the first step in the transition from *subsistence* to *specialized farming*. This evolutionary stage is characterized by the production of both staple crops and cash crops and, in addition, simple animal husbandry.

"mixed" systems   *economic systems* that are a mixture of both *capitalist* and *socialist* economies. "Mixed" economic systems characterize most developing countries. Their essential feature is the coexistence of substantial private and public activity within a single economy. See also *market socialism* and *advanced capitalism*.

model   an analytical framework used to portray functional relationships among economic factors.

modernization ideals   ideals often regarded as necessary for sustained economic growth. They include *rationality, economic planning*, social and economic equalization, and improved *institutions* and attitudes.

money income   the income accruing to a household or firm expressed in terms of some monetary unit, e.g., 1,000 rupees or pesos per year.

money supply   sum total of currency in circulation plus commercial bank demand deposits (M_1) plus sometimes savings bank time deposits (M_2).

moneylender   in Asia, a person who lends money at higher than market rates of *interest* to peasant farmers to meet their needs for seeds, fertilizers, and other inputs. Activities of moneylenders are often unscrupulous and can help to accentuate landlessness among the rural poor.

monopolistic market control   a situation in which the output of an industry is controlled by a single producer (or seller) or by a group of producers who make joint decisions.

monopoly   a market situation in which a product which does not have close substitutes is being produced and sold by a single seller. See also *perfect competition* and *oligopoly*.

multilateral assistance agency   see *foreign aid*.

multinational corporation (MNC)   an international or transnational corporation with headquarters in one country but branch offices in a wide range of both developed and developing countries. Examples include General Motors, Coca-Cola, Firestone, Philips, Renault, British Petroleum, Exxon, ITT.

national expenditure   total expenditure on *final goods* and services in an economy over a given time period. National expenditure (E) includes consumption expenditure (C), investment expenditure (I), government expenditure (G), and expenditure on exports by foreigners (X), less expenditure on imports by domestic residents (M). Thus $E = C + I + G + X - M$.

national income   total monetary value of all *final goods* and services produced in an economy over some period of time, usually a year. See also *gross national product (GNP)* and *national expenditure*.

necessary condition   a condition that must be present, although need not be in itself sufficient, for an event to occur. For example, *capital* formation is a necessary condition for sustained *economic growth* (i.e., before growth in output can occur, there must be tools to produce it). But for this growth to be continued, social, *institutional*, and attitudinal changes must also occur.

necessity goods   life-sustaining items (e.g., food, shelter, protection, medical care). See also *luxury goods*.

neoclassical economics   see *traditional (Western) economics*.

neoclassical price-incentive model   model whose main proposition is that if market prices are to influence economic activities in the right direction, they must be adjusted to remove *factor-price distortions* by means of subsidies, taxes, etc., so that factor prices may reflect the true *opportunity cost* of resources being used. See also *"appropriate" technology*.

neocolonial model of underdevelopment   model whose main proposition is that underdevelopment exists in *Third World* countries because of exploitative economic, political, and cultural policies of developed nations toward less developed countries, e.g., inappropriate transfers of technology, unequal trading relationships, misdirected assistance programs.

net reproduction rate (NRR)   indicates the number of daughters that a newborn girl will bear during her lifetime, assuming fixed age-specific *fertility rates* and a fixed set of *mortality rates*. An NRR of 1 indicates that fertility is at replacement level.

newly industrialized countries   group of countries at a relatively advanced level of economic development with a substantial and dynamic industrial sector and with close links to the international trade, finance, and investment system (Argentina, Brazil, Greece, Hong Kong, South Korea, Mexico, Portugal, Singapore, Spain, Taiwan, and Yugoslavia).

noneconomic variables   elements of interest to economists in their work but which are not given a monetary value or expressed in numerals because of their intangible nature. Examples of these include beliefs, values, attitudes, norms, and power structure. Sometimes *noneconomic variables* are more important than the quantifiable economic variables in promoting development.

"nonformal" education   basically, any "out of school" program that provides basic skills and training to individuals. Examples include adult education, on-the-job training programs, agricultural and other extension services. See also *"formal" education system*.

nonrenewable resources   natural resources whose quantity is fixed in supply and cannot be replaced. Examples include petroleum, iron ore, coal, and other minerals. See also *renewable resources*.

"nontariff" trade barrier   barriers to *free trade* that take forms other than *tariffs* such as *quotas*, sanitary requirements for imported meats and dairy products.

normal and superior goods   goods whose purchased quantities increase as the incomes of consumers increase. Such goods have a positive *income elasticity of demand*. See also *inferior goods*.

normative economics   the notion that economics must concern itself with what "ought to be." Thus, it is argued that economics and economic analysis always involve *value judgments*, whether explicit or implicit, on the part of the analyst or observer. See *positive economics*.

OECD: Organization for Economic Cooperation and Development an organization of 20 countries from the Western world including all of those in Europe and North America. Its major objective is to assist the economic growth of its member nations by promoting cooperation and technical analysis of national and international economic trends.

official development assistance (ODA)   consists of net disbursements of *loans* or *grants* made at concessional financial terms by official agencies of the members of the Development Assistance Committee of the *Organization for Economic Cooperation and Development (OECD)* and members of the *Organization of Petroleum Exporting Countries (OPEC)* with the objective of promoting economic development and welfare.

oligopolistic market control   exists when a market structure has a small number of rival but not necessarily competing firms dominating the industry. Thus, all recognize the fact that they are interdependent and can maximize their individual advantages through explicit (cartel) or implicit (collusion) joint actions.

oligopoly   a market situation whereby there are a few sellers and many buyers of similar but differentiated products. *OPEC* provides a good example of international oligopoly. See also *imperfect competition*.

OPEC: Organization of Petroleum Exporting Countries   an organization consisting of the 13 major oil-exporting countries of the Third World which act as a "cartel" or *oligopoly* to promote their joint national interests. Members include Saudi Arabia, Nigeria, Algeria, Venezuela, Libya, Kuwait, United Arab Emirates, Iran, Iraq, Ecuador, Qatar, Gabon, and Indonesia.

open economy   an economy that engages in foreign trade and has financial and nonfinancial contacts with the rest of the world, e.g., in areas such as education, culture, technology. See also *closed economy* and *outward-looking development policies*.

open unemployment   includes both voluntary and involuntary unemployment. Voluntarily unemployed persons are those unwilling to accept jobs for which they could qualify, probably because they have means of support other than employment. Involuntary unemployment is a situation in which job seekers are willing to work but there are no jobs available for them. Open unemployment is most conspicuous in the cities of less developed countries. See also *underemployment, surplus labor*, and *disguised unemployment*.

opportunity cost   in production, the real value of resources used in the most desirable alternative—e.g., the opportunity cost of producing an extra unit of manufactured good is the output of, say, food that must be foregone as a result of transferring resources from agricultural to manufacturing activities; in consumption, the amount of one commodity that must be foregone in order to consume more of another. See also *increasing opportunity cost*.

"opportunity cost" of a woman's time   real or monetary wages or *profits* that a woman sacrifices by deciding to stay home and bear children instead of working for a wage or engaging in profit-making self-employment activities. The higher the opportunity cost of a woman's time involved in bearing children, the more unwilling she will be to have more children—at least in terms of the *microeconomic theory of fertility*.

optimization, principle of   a principle which states that in order to minimize costs in production or maximize "satisfaction" in *consumption*, scarce *resources* should be used in the economically most "efficient" manner while *goods* and *services* should be consumed so that the last unit of expenditure yields the same marginal utility for all individuals. See also the *principle of economy, appropriate technology, economic efficiency*.

"organized" money market   the formal banking system in which loanable funds are channeled through recognized and licensed *financial intermediaries*. See also *"unorganized" money market*.

output-employment lag   a phenomenon in which employment growth lags substantially behind output growth—normally, when output grows at a rate of three to four times that of employment as it has in most modern sectors of developing nations.

outward-looking development policies   policies that encourage *free trade*, the free movement of capital, workers, enterprises and students, a welcome to *multinational corporations*, and an open system of communications. See also *open economy*.

"overvalued" exchange rate   an *exchange rate* that is "officially" set at a level higher than its real or "shadow" value—i.e., 7 Kenya shillings per dollar instead of, say, 10 shillings per dollar. Overvalued rates cheapen the real cost of imports while raising the real cost of exports. They often lead to a need for *exchange control*.

"package" of policies   a set of multidimensional economic and social policies aimed, for example, at removing inequalities and improving living standards for the masses. In short, a set of different but mutually reinforcing policies designed to achieve a single or multiple objective.

paradigm   implicit assumptions from which theories evolve; a model or framework of analysis.

partial plans   plans that cover only a part of the national economy (e.g., agriculture, industry, tourism).

per capita food production   total food production divided by the total population.

per capita food production index   shows the average annual quantity of food produced per capita as a percentage of the average annual amount produced.

per capita income   see *income per capita*.

perfect competition   a market situation characterized by the existence of (a) very many buyers and sellers of (b) homogeneous goods or services with (c) perfect knowledge and (d) free entry so that no single buyer or seller can influence the price of the good or service. See also *price system, laissez faire, traditional (Western) economics*, and *pure market capitalism*.

personal income   the amount of *money income* received by households over a given period of time. Note that some incomes are earned (as a result of rendering productive services) but not currently received (e.g., undistributed profits and contributions for social insurance), while some incomes received by the household sector are not earned through current productive activity (e.g., *transfer payments*). Personal income is derived by adding to *national income* the various incomes received by the households but not earned, and subtracting those that are earned but not received.

physical capital   tangible investment goods (e.g., plant and equipment, machinery, building). See also *human capital*.

plan   see *economic plan* and *development plan*.

plan implementation   the practical carrying out of the objectives set forth in the *development plan*. Some of the difficulties encountered in attempting to attain plan targets result from insufficient availability of economic resources (physical and financial capital, skilled manpower, etc.), insufficient foreign aid, the effects of inflation, and, most importantly, lack of *political will*.

planning model   a mathematical model (e.g., an input−output or "macro" planning model) designed to stimulate quantitatively the major features of the economic structure of a particular country. Planning models provide the analytical and quantitative basis for most national and regional *development plans*. See also *economic plan* and *plan implementation*.

policy   see *economic policy*.

policy instruments   see *economic policy*.

political economy   the attempt to merge economic analysis with practical politics—i.e., to view economic activity in its political context. Much of "classical" economics was *political economy* and today "political economy" is increasingly being recognized as necessary for any realistic examination of development problems.

political will   a determined, deliberate, purposeful, independent decision on or choice of a course of action by persons in political authority, such as elimination of inequality, poverty, and unemployment through various reforms of social, economic, and institutional structures. Lack of political will is often said to be one of the main obstacles to development and the main reason for the failure of many *development plans*. See *plan implementation*.

population density   the number of inhabitants per unit area of land (e.g., per square mile).

population increase (rate of)   rate at which a given population grows over a period of time, say, one year. Part of this rate, that which results entirely from increases in the number of births, is called the *rate of natural increase of population*, to distinguish it from the rate resulting from, say, immigration.

positive economics   the notion that economics should be concerned with "what is," was, or will be. Positive economics addresses questions such as what government policies will generate faster GNP growth; what government policies will reduce unemployment, inflation, inequality, etc. Answers to these questions are supposedly based on facts or empirical observation. See also *normative economics*.

potential output   the aggregate capacity output of a nation—i.e., maximum quantity of goods and services that can be produced with available resources and a given state of technology.

poverty   see *absolute poverty*.

poverty line   see *international poverty line*.

present consumption   expenditure on goods and services that satisfy short-term wants—e.g. expenditures on food and entertainment. "Future consumption" refers to expenditures on consumer items that yield want-satisfying benefits over a long time period, normally beyond a year, such as expenditure on cars, residential houses, furniture. See also *consumption.*

present value   the discounted value at the present time of a sum of money to be received in the future.

preventive medicine   medical care that focuses on the prevention of sickness and disease through immunology and health education. See also *curative medicine.*

price   monetary or real value of a resource, commodity, or service. The role of prices in a *market economy* is to *ration* or allocate resources in accordance with supply and demand; additionally, relative prices should reflect the relative scarcity values of different resources, goods, or services. See *price system.*

price controls   setting of maximum or minimum prices by the government.

price elasticity of demand   the responsiveness of the quantity of a good demanded to change in its price, expressed as the percentage change in quantity demanded divided by the percentage change in price.

price elasticity of supply   the responsiveness of the quantity of a commodity supplied to change in its price, expressed as the proportionate change in quantity supplied divided by the proportionate change in price.

price system   the mechanism by which scarce resources, goods, and services are allocated by the free upward or downward movements of prices in accordance with the dictates of supply and demand in a *market economy*. See also *perfect competition* and *pure market capitalism.*

primary industrial sector   that part of the economy which specializes in the production of agricultural products and the extraction of raw materials. Major industries in this sector include mining, agriculture, forestry, and fishing.

primary products   products derived from all extractive occupations—farming, lumbering, fishing, mining, and quarrying—namely, foodstuffs and raw materials.

principles   see *economic principles.*

principle of economy   the proposition in *perfect competition* that for a given level of *resources* (inputs), producers will tend to minimize costs for a given level of output or maximize output for a given cost. The need to "economize" arises because resources are "scarce" and are therefore not free.

private benefits   gains that accrue to a single individual—e.g., profits received by an individual firm. See also *social benefits.*

private costs   the direct monetary outlays or costs of an individual economic unit; e.g., the private costs of a firm are the direct outlays on *fixed* and *variable inputs* of production.

private consumption   consists of the market value of all goods and services purchased or received as *income in kind*, by households and nonprofit institutions. Includes imputed rent for owner-occupied dwellings.

private foreign investment   the investment of private foreign funds in the economy of a developing nation, usually in the form of *import-substituting* industries by *multinational corporations (MNCs)*. See also *foreign aid.*

private sector   that part of an economy whose activities are under the control and direction of nongovernmental economic units such as households or firms. Each economic unit owns its own *resources* and uses them mainly to maximize its own well-being.

production function   a technological or engineering relationship between the quantity of a good produced and the quantity of *inputs* required to produce it.

productivity gap   the difference between per capita product, say, of the agricultural population (i.e., *agricultural labor productivity*), in LDCs versus developed countries. It has tended to be wide because of differences in the application of technological and biological improvements.

production process   see *production technique.*

production-possibility curve   a curve on a graph indicating alternative combinations of two commodities or categories of commodities (e.g., agricultural and manufactured goods) that can be produced when all the available *factors of production* are efficiently employed. Given available resources and technology, the $P-P$ curve sets the boundary between which combination is attainable and which is unobtainable. See also *opportunity cost* and *production function.*

production technique   method of combining *inputs* to produce required output. A production technique is said to be *appropriate* ("best") if it produces a given output with the least cost (thus being economically efficient) or with the least possible quantity of real resources (technically efficient). A technique may be *labor intensive* or *capital intensive.*

profit   the difference between the market value of output and the market value of *inputs* that were employed to produce that output. Alternatively, a firm's or farm's profits can be defined as the difference between total revenue and total cost.

profit maximization   making as large as possible the profits of a firm or farm. Producers often desire to find the level of output which results in maximum profits, at least according to a fundamental assumption of *Western economic theory.*

progressive income tax   a tax whose rate increases with increasing personal incomes—i.e., where the proportion of personal income paid by a rich person in taxes is higher than that paid by a poorer person. A progressive tax structure therefore tends to improve *income distribution.* See also *regressive tax.*

project appraisal   the quantitative analysis of the relative desirability (profitability) of investing a given sum of public and/or private funds in alternative projects—e.g., building a steel mill or a textile factory. *Cost—benefit analysis* provides the major analytical tool of project appraisal.

public consumption (general government consumption)   includes all current expenditures for purchases of goods and services by all levels of government. Includes capital expenditure on national defense and security.

public good   a commodity or service which if supplied to one person can be made available to others at no extra cost.

public sector   that portion of an economy whose activities (economic and noneconomic) are under the control and direction of the state. The state owns all resources in this sector and uses them to achieve whatever goals it may have—e.g., to promote the economic welfare of the ruling elite or to maximize the well-being of society as a whole. See also *private sector.*

pure market capitalism   *economic system* in which all resources are privately owned and their allocation is done exclusively by a *price system*. See also *perfect competition, market economy, invisible hand*, and *laissez faire*.

quintile   a 20% proportion of any numerical quantity; e.g., a population divided into quintiles would be one which was divided into five equal numerical groups. See also *decile*.

quota   a physical limitation on the quantity of any item that can be imported into a country, e.g., so many automobiles per year.

rate of natural increase (of population)   see *population increase* (rate of).

"rational" choice   a choice commensurate with logical reasoning. In economic theory it is often assumed that everyone behaves rationally in his economic activities. See, for example, the *principle of economy, profit maximization, optimization*, and *rationality*.

rationality   one of the foundations (with regard to people's behavior) on which *traditional* or *Western economic theory* is built. An economically "rational" person is one who will always attempt to maximize satisfaction or profits, or minimize costs. The notion of rationality as one of the modernization ideals means the replacement of age-old traditional practices by modern methods of "objective" thinking and logical reasoning in production, distribution, and consumption. See also *rational choice, principles of economy, optimization*, and *profit maximization*.

rationing   a system of distribution employed to restrict the quantities of goods and services that consumers or producers can purchase or be allocated freely. It arises because of excess demand and inflexible prices. *Rationing* can be by coupons, points, or simply administrative decisions with regard to commodities, by academic credentialization with regard to job allocation, by industrial licenses with regard to capital good imports, etc. See also *black market*.

real income   the income that a household or firm receives in terms of the real goods and services it can purchase. Alternatively, it is simply *money income* adjusted by some price index.

recession   a period of slack general economic activity as reflected in rising unemployment and excess productive capacity in a broad spectrum of industries.

redistribution policies   policies geared to reducing inequality of incomes and expanding economic opportunities in order to promote *development*. Examples include *progressive tax* policies, provision of services financed out of such taxation to benefit persons in the lower-income groups, rural development policies giving emphasis to raising *levels of living* for the rural poor through *land reform*, and other forms of *asset* and wealth redistribution.

regressive tax   if the ratio of taxes to income as income increases tends to decrease, the tax is called "regressive"; i.e., relatively poor people will pay a larger proportion of their income in taxes than will relatively rich people. A regressive tax therefore tends to worsen *income distribution*. See also *progressive tax*.

renewable resources natural resources which can be replaced so that the total supply is not fixed for all time as in the case of *nonrenewable resources*. Examples include timber and other forest products.

rent in the context of macroeconomics, the share of *national income* going to the owners of the productive resource, land (i.e., landlords). In everyday usage, the price paid for rental property (e.g., buildings and housing). In the theory of microeconomics it is a short form for "economic rent"—i.e., the payment to a *factor* over and above its highest *opportunity cost*.

replacement fertility level of *fertility* at which childbearing women have just enough daughters to "replace" themselves in the population. This keeps the existing population size constant through an infinite number of succeeding generations. See also general *fertility rate* and *birthrate*.

research and development (R & D) a scientific investigation with a view toward improving the existing quality of human life, products, profits, *factors of production*, or just plain knowledge. There are two categories of R & D: (*a*) "basic" R & D (without a specific commercial objective) and (*b*) "applied" R & D (with a commercial objective).

reserves (gross international) the sum of a country's holdings of gold. *Special Drawing Rights (SDRs)*, the reserve position of the *IMF* members in the Fund, and holdings of *foreign exchange* under the control of monetary authorities.

resource balance the difference between exports and imports of goods and nonfactor services.

resource endowment a nation's supply of *factors of production*. Normally such endowments are supplied by nature (e.g., mineral deposits, raw materials, timber forests, labor). See also *factor-endowment trade theory*.

resources, physical and human *factors of production* used to produce goods and services to satisfy wants. Land and capital are frequently referred to as *physical resources* and labor as the *human resource*. See also *fixed* and *variable inputs*.

rigid institutions *institutions* designed in such a way that they cannot be adjusted or adjust themselves to accommodate *development* requirements; e.g., a social system—typically a clan unit—that has conservative values which render it resistant to *modernization ideals* is often referred to as a rigid institution.

risk a situation in which the probability of obtaining some outcome of an event is not precisely known; i.e., known probabilities cannot be precisely assigned to these outcomes but their general level can be inferred. In everyday usage a risky situation is one in which one of the outcomes involves some loss to the decision maker (e.g., changes of demand, weather, and tastes). See also *uncertainty*.

rural development see *integrated rural development*.

rural support systems systems that need to be created to stimulate the productivity of both small- and large-scale agricultural farms. These include making more effective and efficient the rural *institutions* directly connected with production, e.g., banks, *moneylenders*, public credit agencies, seed and fertilizer distributors; and provision of services such as technical and educational *extension services*, storage and marketing facilities, rural transport and feeder roads, and water.

savings   that portion of *disposable income* not spent on *consumption* by households plus profits retained by firms. Savings are normally assumed to be positively related to the level of income (personal or national).

savings ratio   savings expressed as a proportion of *disposable income* over some period of time. It shows the fraction of *national income* saved over any period. The savings ratio is sometimes used synonymously with the *average propensity to save*. See also *Harrod–Domar equation*.

"scale-neutral" technological progress   *technological progress* that can lead to the achievement of higher output levels irrespective of the size (scale) of the firm or farm—i.e., that is equally applicable to small- and large-scale production processes. An often-cited example is the hybrid seeds of the *Green Revolution* which theoretically can increase yields on both small and large farms (if *complementary resources* such as fertilizer, irrigation, and pesticides are available).

scarcity   in economics, the term referring to a situation which arises when there is less of something (e.g., an *economic good, service*, or *resource*) than people would like to have if it were free. The quantity of goods and services are scarce relative to people's desire for them because the economy's resources used in their production are themselves scarce. Scarcity therefore gives rise to the need for efficient allocation of resources among alternative competing uses through, for example, the free *market mechanism* in capitalist economies or through a centralized *command system* in planned economies.

scatter diagram   a two-dimensional graph on which numerical values of statistically observed variables are plotted in pairs, one measured on the horizontal axis and the other on the vertical axis.

Second World   the now economically advanced *socialist* countries. Major Second World countries include the Soviet Union and other Soviet-type economies of Eastern Europe such as Poland, Czechoslovakia, and Yugoslavia. See also *First World* and *Third World*.

secondary industrial sector   the manufacturing portion of the economy that uses raw materials and *intermediate products* to produce *final goods* or other intermediate products. Industries such as motor assembly, textiles, and building and construction are part of this sector.

self-esteem (of a society)   feeling of "human worthiness" that a society enjoys when its *social, political*, and *economic systems* and *institutions* promote human respect, dignity, integrity, self-determination, etc. See *development*.

self-reliance   reliance on one's own capabilities, judgment, resources, and skills in a bid to enhance political, economic, social, cultural, attitudinal, and moral independence. Countries may also desire to be self-reliant in particular aspects such as food production, manpower, and skills. Increasingly, the term "collective self-reliance" is being used in *Third World* forums.

services   comprises economic activity other than industry and primary goods production.

shadow price   price that reflects the true *opportunity cost* of a resource.

sharecropper   in the *agrarian systems* of LDCs the tenant peasant farmer whose crop produce has to be shared with the *landlord*. The *landlord* usually appropriates a large share of the tenant's total crop production.

shifting cultivation   peasant agricultural practice in Africa in which land is tilled by a family or community for cropping until such time that it has been exhausted of fertility. Thereafter the family or community moves to a new area of land, leaving the former to regain fertility until eventually it can be cultivated once again.

size distribution of income   the distribution of income according to size class of persons, e.g., the share of total income accruing to, say the poorest 40% of a population or the richest 10%, without regard to the sources of that income (e.g., whether it comes from wages, interest, rent, or profits). See also *functional distribution of income, Lorenz curve* and *Gini coefficient.*

"skewed" distribution of income   skewness is a lack of symmetry in a "frequency distribution." If income is perfectly distributed such a distribution is said to be symmetrical. A skewed distribution of income is one diverging from perfect equality. Highly skewed distribution of income occurs in situations where the rich persons, say the top 20% of the total population, receive more than half of the total *national income.* See also *Lorenz curve* and *Gini coefficient.*

small farmer   a farmer owning a small family-based plot of land on which he grows subsistence crops and perhaps one or two cash crops, relying almost exclusively on family labor.

small-scale industry   an industry whose firms or farms operate with small-sized plants, low employment, and hence small output capacity. *Economies of scale* do not normally exist for such firms or farms but they often tend to utilize their limited *physical, human*, and financial *capital* more efficiently than many large-sized firms or farms.

social benefits   gains or benefits that accrue or are available to the society as a whole rather than solely to a private individual—e.g., the protection and security provided by the police or the armed forces, the *external economies* afforded by an effective health delivery system, and the widespread benefits of a literate population. See *private benefits.*

social cost   the cost to society as a whole of an economic decision, whether private or public. Where there exist *external diseconomies* of production (e.g., pollution) or consumption (alcoholism), *social costs* will normally exceed *private costs* and decisions based solely on private calculations will lead to a misallocation of resources.

social discount rate   the rate at which the society "discounts" potential future *social benefits* to find out whether such benefits are worth their present *social cost.* The rate used in this discounting procedure is usually the social opportunity cost of the funds committed.

social science   that branch of study that concerns itself with human society, its behavior, activities, and growth (e.g., sociology, history, philosophy, political science, economics).

social system   term used to refer to the *organizational* and *institutional* structure of the society including its *value premises*, attitudes, power structures, and traditions. Major social systems include political set-ups, religions, and clans.

socialism   see *command socialism* and *market socialism.*

"soft" loan   see *loans.*

Special Drawing Rights (SDRs)   a new form of international financial asset—often referred to as "paper gold"—created by the *International Monetary Fund (IMF)* in 1970 and designed to supplement gold and dollars in settling international *balance of payments* accounts. At present 75% of the total SDR issue is distributed to 25 industrial nations while only 25% is distributed among the more than 100 developing countries that participate in the international monetary system.

specialization   a situation in which *resources* are concentrated in the production of a relatively few commodities rather than being used for a wider range of commodities. See also *comparative advantage* and *division of labor*.

specialized farming   the final and most advanced stage of the evolution of agricultural production in which farm output is produced wholly for the market. It is most prevalent in advanced industrial countries. High farm yields are ensured by a high degree of *capital formation, technological progress*, and scientific *research and development*. See also *subsistence farming* and *commercial farming*.

spread effects   impact felt beyond the initial place of action. Sometimes referred to as "echo effects." The spread effects, for example, of increasing medical services are a reduction in death rates, a rise in *life expectancy* at birth, a healthy and productive labor force, etc.

stabilization policies   a coordinated set of mostly restrictive fiscal and monetary policies aimed at reducing *inflation*, cutting budget deficits, and improving the *balance of payments*. See *conditionality* and *IMF*.

"stages of growth" model of development   this theory of development is associated with the American economic historian W.W. Rostow. According to Rostow, in achieving development, a country inevitably passes through the following stages: (*a*) traditional and stagnant low per capita stage; (*b*) transitional stage (in which the "preconditions for growth" are laid down); (*c*) the "takeoff" stage (beginning of *economic growth* process); (*d*) industrialized, mass production and consumption stage (*development* stage).

staple food   a leading or main food consumed by a large section of a country's population (e.g., maize meal in Kenya, Zambia, and Tanzania; rice in Southeast Asian countries; yams in West Africa; mandioca in Brazil).

stationary population   one in which age- and sex-specific *mortality rates* have remained unchanged over a long period and, simultaneously, age-specific *fertility rates* have remained at replacement level (*NRR* = 1). In such a population, the birthrate will be constant and equal to the death rate, the age structure will be constant, and the growth rate will be zero.

structural inflation   *inflation* that arises as a result of supply inelasticities and structural rigidities (e.g., inefficient marketing and distribution systems) in the industrial sectors of the economy. A form of *demand-pull inflation*, but can exist with considerable excess capacity and unemployment.

structural theory of underdevelopment   hypothesis that underdevelopment in *Third World* countries is due to underutilization of *resources* arising from structural and/or *institutional* factors that have their origins in both domestic and international *dualistic* situations. Development, therefore, requires more than just accelerated *capital* formation as espoused in the *"stages of growth"* and *"false paradigm"* models of development.

structural transformation   the process of transforming the basic industrial structure of an economy so that the contribution to *national income* by the manufacturing sector increasingly becomes higher than that by the agricultural sector. More generally, an alteration in the industrial composition of any economy. See *primary, secondary*, and *tertiary industrial sectors*.

subsidy a payment by the government to producers or distributors in an industry to prevent the decline of that industry (e.g., as a result of continuous unprofitable operations) or an increase in the prices of its products, or simply to encourage it to hire more labor (as in the case of a wage subsidy). Examples of subsidies are export subsidies to encourage the sale of exports, subsidies on some foodstuffs to keep down the cost of living especially in urban areas, farm subsidies to encourage expansion of farm production and achieve *self-reliance* in food production.

subsistence economy an economy in which production is mainly for own consumption and the standard of living yields no more than the basic necessities of life—food, shelter, and clothing. See also *subsistence farming*.

subsistence farming farming in which crop production, stock rearing, etc., is mainly for "own consumption" and is characterized by low productivity, *risk*, and *uncertainty*. See also *subsistence economy*.

sufficient condition a condition which when present causes an event to occur; e.g., being a university student may be a sufficient condition to get a loan under university education loan schemes. See also *necessary condition*.

supply curve a positively sloped curve relating the quantity of a commodity supplied to its price.

"surplus" labor the excess supply of labor over and above the quantity demanded at the going "free" market wage rate. In Arthur Lewis' two-sector model of economic development, surplus labor refers to that portion of the rural labor force whose *marginal productivity* is zero or negative. See also *underemployment*.

synthetic commodity substitutes commodities that are artificially produced but of like nature with and substitutes for the natural commodities (e.g., those involving rubber, cotton, wool, camphor, pyrethrum). Producers of raw materials, mainly LDCs, are becoming more and more vulnerable to competition from synthetics from industrialized countries as a result of the latter's more advanced state of scientific and technical progress.

tariff (ad valorem) a fixed percentage tax (e.g., 30%) on the value of an imported commodity levied at the point of entry into the importing country.

technical assistance *foreign aid* (either *bilateral* or *multilateral*) that takes the form of the transfer of expert personnel, technicians, scientists, educators, economic advisers, consultants, etc., rather than a simple transfer of funds.

technological progress increased application of new scientific knowledge in form of *inventions* and *innovations* with regard to *capital*, both *physical* and *human*. Such progress has been a major factor in stimulating the long-term *economic growth* of contemporary developed countries. See also *labor-augmenting, labor-saving, capital-augmenting,* and *scale-neutral technological progress*.

tenant farmer one who farms on land held by a *landlord* and therefore lacks secure ownership rights and has to pay for the use of that land, e.g., by surrendering part of his output to the owner of the land. Examples are found in the Latin American and Asian *agrarian systems*. See also *sharecropper*.

terms of trade (commodity) the ratio of a country's average export price to its average import price. A country's *terms of trade* are said to improve when this ratio increases and to worsen when it decreases, i.e., when import prices rise at a relatively faster rate than export prices (the experience of most LDCs over the past two decades).

tertiary sector   the services and commerce portion of an economy. Examples of services include repair and maintenance of *capital goods*, haircuts, public administration, medical care, transport and communications, teaching. See also *primary* and *secondary sectors*.

Third World   the present 143 or so developing countries of Asia, Africa, the Middle East, and Latin America. These countries are mainly characterized by low *levels of living*, high rates of *population growth*, low levels of *per capita income*, and general economic and technological *dependence* on *First* and *Second World* economies.

Third World or "development" economics   the economics of the less developed nations of Africa, Asia, and Latin America, which addresses itself mainly to problems of *economic growth*, poverty, unemployment, and inequality.

tied aid   *foreign aid* in the form of *bilateral loans* or *grants* that require the recipient country to use the funds to purchase goods and/or services from the donor country—thus the aid is said to be "tied" to purchases from the assisting country.

total factor productivity   total monetary value of all units of output per unit of each and every *factor of production* in an economy. It is a measure of the average productivity of all factors employed in an economy.

trade (as an engine of growth)   *free trade* has often been described as an "engine of growth" because it encourages countries to *specialize* in activities in which they have *comparative advantages* thereby increasing their respective production efficiencies and hence their total outputs of *goods* and *services*.

trade creation   a situation in the theory of *customs unions* that occurs when, following the formation of the union, there is a shift in the geographic location of production from higher-cost to lower-cost member states. See also *trade diversion*.

trade diversion   occurs when the formation of a *customs union* causes the locus of production of formerly imported goods to shift from a lower-cost nonmember state to a higher-cost member nation. See also *trade creation*.

tradeoff   the necessity of sacrificing ("trading off") something in order to get more of something else—e.g., sacrificing *consumption* now for *consumption* later by devoting some present *resources* to *investment*. See also *opportunity cost*.

traditional (Western) economics   the economics of capitalist market economies characterized by *consumer sovereignty*, *profit maximization*, *private enterprise*, and *perfect competition*. The major focus is on the efficient allocation of scarce resources (see *economic efficiency*) through the *price system* and the forces of supply and demand. See also *microeconomics, macroeconomics, Keynesian economics, laissez faire, invisible hand*, and *market economy*.

transfer payment   any payment from one economic entity to another that takes the form of a "gift"—i.e., it is not for a service rendered and it need not be repaid. Examples include unemployment insurance, food stamps, welfare payments, *subsidies*, bilateral *grants*.

transfer pricing   an accounting procedure usually designed to lower total taxes paid by *multinational corporations (MNCs)* in which intracorporate sales and purchases of goods and services are artificially invoiced so that profits accrue to those branch offices located in low-tax countries ("tax havens") while offices in high-tax countries show little or no taxable profits.

"trickle down" theory of development   the notion that *development* is purely an "economic" phenomenon in which rapid gains from the overall growth of *GNP* and *per capita income* would automatically bring benefits (i.e., "trickle down") to the masses in the form of jobs and other economic opportunities. The main preoccupation is therefore to get the growth job done while problems of *poverty, unemployment,* and *income distribution* are perceived to be of secondary importance.

UN: United Nations   a global organization set up at the end of the Second World War with the basic aim of cultivating international cooperation and hence ensuring that any conflicts or misunderstanding between or among countries would be resolved by peaceful means. At present the UN has a membership of over 160 countries drawn from both the developed and less developed nations.

uncertainty   a situation in which the probability of obtaining the outcome(s) of an event is not known. There is thus a plurality of possible outcomes to which no objective probability can be attached. See also *risk*.

UNCTAD: United Nations Conference on Trade and Development   a body of the *United Nations* whose primary objective is to promote *international trade* and commerce with a principal focus on trade and *balance of payments* problems of developing nations. Its first Secretary General was Raul Prebisch of Latin America.

underdevelopment   an economic situation in which there are persistent low *levels of living* in conjunction with the following characteristics: absolute poverty, low *per capita incomes*, low rates of *economic growth*, low *consumption* levels, poor health services, high *death rates*, high *birthrates*, *vulnerability* to and *dependence* on foreign economies, and *limited freedom to choose* between variables that satisfy human wants. See also *development*.

underemployment   a situation in which persons are working less, either daily, weekly, monthly, or seasonally, than they would like to work. See also *open unemployment* and *surplus labor*.

underutilization of labor   operation of labor force at levels below their capacity or potential output. See also *open unemployment, underemployment, disguised underemployment, voluntary unemployment*.

UNESCO: United Nations Educational, Scientific and Cultural Organization   a major organ of the *United Nations* system charged with the responsibility of promoting "international understanding" by (a) spreading ideas or knowledge through the educational process; (b) encouraging multiracial coexistence through reconciliation of cultural values of different societies; and (c) sponsoring educational, cultural, and scientific exchange programs that make it possible for educators, artists, writers, and scientists from a wide variety of countries and cultures to meet and exchange ideas and knowledge.

UNDP: United Nations Development Program   a body of the *United Nations* family whose major function is to promote *development* in *Third*

World countries. Major development-oriented projects financed and carried out by UNDP include the initiation of nutrition, health, and education programs and the building up of agricultural, industrial, and transport infrastructure.

unit cost   the average total cost per unit of output of any *economic good* or service.

unlimited supplies of labor   infinite elasticity of labor at a given wage rate as postulated in Lewis' model.

"unorganized" money market   the informal and often usurious credit system that exists in most developing countries (especially in rural areas) where low-income farms and firms with little collateral are forced to borrow from moneylenders and loansharks at exorbitant rates of interest. See also *"organized" money market*.

urbanization   economic and demographic growth process of the urban centers.

USAID: United States Agency for International Development   a *bilateral assistance agency* of the U.S. government whose primary objective is to assist *Third World* countries in their *development* efforts as part of U.S. foreign policy. The "economic" assistance given by USAID normally takes the form of educational *grants*, special-interest *loans*, and *technical assistance*. However, much of AID's activity consists of "noneconomic" (mostly military) assistance to "friendly" LDC governments.

variable   see *economic variables*.

variable inputs   *inputs* or *resources* whose required use in a *production function* will vary with changes in the level of output. For example, in the production of shoes, labor is usually a variable *input* because as more shoes are produced, more labor must be used. See also *fixed inputs*.

values and value premises   principles, standards, or qualities considered worthwhile or desirable. A value judgment is one based on or reflecting one's personal or class beliefs. See also *normative economics*.

"vent for surplus" theory of trade   states that the opening up of world markets to developing countries through international trade provides them with the opportunity to take advantage of formerly underutilized land and labor resources to produce larger *primary product* outputs, the surplus of which can be exported to foreign markets. Such economies will usually be operating at a point somewhere inside their *production-possibility frontiers* so that trade permits an outward shift of such a production point.

vested interest (groups)   group of persons that have acquired rights or powers in any sphere of activities within a nation or in international affairs which they often struggle to guard and maintain. Examples of powerful vested interest groups in developing countries include *landlords*, political elites, and wealthy private local and foreign investors.

vicious circle   a self-reinforcing situation in which there are factors that tend to perpetuate a certain undesirable phenomenon—e.g., low incomes in poor countries lead to low consumption which then leads to poor health and low labor productivity and eventually to the persistence of poverty.

BIBLIOGRAPHY

The books and articles in this bibliography are intended to supplement those already identified in the Further Readings at the end of each chapter. They are organized to coincide with the various topics covered in each chapter of the text and to include works published through 1984. Students interested in an even more detailed bibliography (e.g., for term papers) may wish to consult a very useful source book listing other publications in the 1960s and 1970s: J. P. Powelson, *A Select Bibliography on Economic Development: With Annotations* (Boulder, Colo.: Westview Press, 1979).

Chapter 1   Economics, Institutions, and Development Studies

1. Social Aspects of Development

Adelman, Irma, and Morris, Cynthia Taft. *Society, Politics and Economic Development: A Quantitative Approach.* Baltimore: Johns Hopkins University Press, 1967.

Goldschmidt, Walter. "Toward an anthropological approach to economic development." *Human Organization* 41, no. 1 (1982):80–82.

Goldthorpe, J. E. *The Sociology of the Third World: Disparity and Involvement.* New York: Cambridge University Press, 1975.

Hardiman, Margaret, and Midgley, James. *The Social Dimensions of Development: Social Policy and Planning in the Third World.* New York: Wiley, 1982.

Hoben, Allan. "Anthropologists and development." *Annual Review of Anthropology* 11 (1982):349–375.

MacPherson, Stewart. *Social Policy in the Third World: The Social Dilemmas of Underdevelopment.* Totowa, N.J.: Littlefield Adams, 1982.

Chapter 2   Diverse Structures and Common Characteristics of Developing Nations

1. Africa

Acharya, Shankar. "Perspectives and problems of development in sub-Saharan Africa." *World Development* 9, no. 2 (1981):109–148.

Adams, J. "The economic development of African pastoral societies: A model." *Kyklos* 28, no. 4 (1975).

Duignan, Peter, and Gann, Lewis H., eds. *Colonialism in Africa 1870–1960, vol.*

4: The Economics of Colonialism. New York: Cambridge University Press, 1975.

Harris, Richard, ed. *The Political Economy of Africa.* Cambridge, Mass.: Schenkman, 1975.

Institute of Social Studies. "Future of nomads in Africa." *Development and Change* 13, no. 2 (1982).

International Monetary Fund. *Surveys of African Countries.* 7 volumes. *Vol. 1: Cameroon, Central African Republic, Chad, Congo, Brazzaville, Gabon* (1968). *Vol. 2: Kenya, Tanzania, Uganda, Somalia* (1969). *Vol. 3: Benin, Ivory Coast, Mauritania, Niger, Senegal, Togo, Upper Volta* (1970). *Vol. 4: Zaire, Malagasy Republic, Malawi, Mauritius, Zambia* (1973). *Vol. 5: Botswana, Lesotho, Swaziland, Burundi, Equatorial Guinea, Rwanda* (1973). *Vol. 6: Gambia, Ghana, Liberia, Nigeria, Sierra Leone* (1975). *Vol. 7: Algeria, Mali, Morocco, Tunisia* (1977). Washington, D.C.: International Monetary Fund, 1968–1977.

Kamarck, Andrew M. *The Economics of African Development,* rev. ed. Foreword by Pierre Moussa. New York: Praeger, 1971.

Kamarck, Andrew M. *The Tropics and Economic Development: A Provocative Inquiry into the Poverty of Nations.* Baltimore and London: Johns Hopkins University Press for the World Bank, 1976.

Markovitz, Irving Leonard. *Power and Class in Africa.* New York: Prentice-Hall, 1977.

Robson, P., and Lury, D. A. *The Economics of Africa.* Evanston, Ill.: Northwestern University Press, 1969.

Seidman, Ann. *Planning for Development in Sub-Saharan Africa.* Praeger Special Studies in International Economics and Development. New York: Praeger, 1974.

Selwyn, Percy, ed. "Southern Africa: The political economy of inequality," *IDS Bulletin* 11, no. 4 (1980).

van deWalle, Etienne. "Trends and prospects of population in tropical Africa." *The Annals* 432 (July 1977):1–11.

2. Asia

Asian Development Bank. *Rural Asia: Challenge and Opportunity.* New York: Praeger, 1978.

Crane, Donald K. *The ASEAN States: Coping with Dependence.* New York: Praeger, 1983.

Ho, Alfred K. *Developing the Economy of the People's Republic of China.* New York: Praeger, 1982.

Maxwell, Neville, ed. *China's Road to Development,* 2d ed. Oxford: Pergamon, 1979.

Myrdal, Gunnar. *Asian Drama: An Inquiry into the Poverty of Nations.* 3 vols. New York: Pantheon, 1968.

Parker, Guy J.; Golay, Frank H.; and Enloe, Cynthia H. *Diversity and Development in Southeast Asia: The Coming Decade.* New York: McGraw-Hill, 1977.

Wawn, Brian. *The Economies of the ASEAN Countries: Indonesia, Malaysia, Philippines, Singapore and Thailand.* New York: St. Martin's, 1982.

3. Latin America

Baer, Werner. *The Brazilian Economy: Growth and Development.* New York: Praeger, 1983.

Betancourt, Roger R.; Sheehey, Edmund J.; and Vogel, Robert C. "The dynamics of inflation in Latin America." *American Economic Review* 66, no. 4 (September 1976):688–698.

Brundensies, Claes, and Lundohl, Mots, eds. *Development Strategies and Basic Needs in Latin America: Challenges for the 1980's.* Boulder, Colo.: Westview Press, 1982.

Farley, Rawle. *The Economics of Latin America: Development Problems in Perspective.* New York: Harper & Row, 1972.

Foxley, Alejandro, ed. *Income Distribution in Latin America.* New York: Cambridge University Press, 1976.

Furtado, Celso. *Economic Development of Latin America: Historical Background and Contemporary Problems*, 2d ed. Cambridge Latin American Studies, no. 8. New York: Cambridge University Press, 1976.

Grunwald, Joseph, ed. *Latin America and World Economy: A Changing International Order.* Beverly Hills: Sage Publications for the Center for Inter-American Relations, 1978.

Hunter, John M., and Foley, James W. *Economic Problems of Latin America.* Boston: Houghton Mifflin, 1975.

Odell, Peter R., and Preston, David A. *Economics and Societies in Latin America: A Geographical Interpretation.* New York: Wiley, 1973.

Pearce, Andrew. *The Latin American Peasant.* London: Frank Cass, 1975.

Smith, T. Lynn. *The Race between Population and Food Supply in Latin America.* Albuquerque: University of New Mexico Press, 1976.

Swift, Jeannine. *Economic Development in Latin America.* New York: St. Martin's, 1976.

Syrquin, Moshe, and Tertel, Simon. *Trade, Stability, Technology and Equity in Latin America.* New York: Academic Press, 1982.

Weiskoff, Richard, and Figueroa, Adolfo. "Traversing the social pyramid: A comparative review of income distribution in Latin America." *Latin American Research Review* 11, no. 2 (1976).

Wynia, Gary W. *The Politics of Latin American Development.* New York: Cambridge University Press, 1978.

4. Nutrition and Health

Balderston, Judith B. *et al. Malnourished Children of the Rural Poor: The Web of Food, Health, Education, Fertility and Agricultural Production.* Boston: Auburn House, 1981.

Berg, Alan. "Malnourished people: A policy view." *World Bank Staff Working Paper* (1981).

Berg, Alan, and Muscat, Robert J. *The Nutrition Factor: Its Role in National Development.* Washington, D.C.: Brookings Institution, 1978.

Golladay, Fredrick. "Health issues and policies in the developing countries." *World Bank Staff Working Paper No. 412* (1980).

Ram, Rati, and Schultz, Theodore W. "Life span, health, savings and productivity." *Economic Development and Cultural Change* 7, no. 3 (April 1979).

Reutlinger, Shlomo, and Selowsky, Marcelo. *Malnutrition and Poverty: Magnitude and Policy Options.* Baltimore: Johns Hopkins University Press, 1976.

Reutlinger, Shlomo, and Selowsky, Marcelo. "The economic dimensions of malnutrition in young children." *Finance and Development* 16, no. 2 (June 1979).

CHAPTER 3 Alternative Theories and the Meaning of Development

1. Indicators of Development

Baster, Nancy. *Measuring Development: The Role and Adequacy of Development Indicators.* London: Frank Cass, 1972.

Chenery, Hollis, and Syrquin, Moshe. *Patterns of Development, 1950–1970.* New York: Oxford University Press for the World Bank, 1975.

Kravis, Irving B.; Heston, Alan; and Summers, Robert. *International Comparisons of Real Product and Purchasing Power.* Baltimore: Johns Hopkins University Press for the World Bank, 1978.

Kuznets, Simon. *Modern Economic Growth: Rate, Structure and Spread.* New Haven: Yale University Press, 1966.

Morris, Morris David. *Measuring the Conditions of the World's Poor: The Physical Quality of Life Index.* New York: Pergamon, 1974.

Pyatt, Graham, and Roe, Alan. *Social Accounting for Development Planning.* New York: Cambridge University Press, 1977.

Ram, Rati. "Composite indices of physical quality of life, basic needs fulfillment, and income: A principal component representation." *Journal of Development Economics* 11, no. 2 (1983):227–248.

UNESCO. *The Use of Socio-Economic Indicators in Development Planning.* New York: UNESCO, 1976.

World Bank. *World Development Reports.* Washington, D.C.: World Bank, 1978.

2. Development Goals and Objectives

Adelman, Irma. "Development economics: A reassessment of goals." *American Economic Review* 65, no. 2 (May 1975):302–309.

Chenery, Hollis B. "The structuralist approach to development policy." *American Economic Review* 65, no. 2 (May 1975).

Currie, Lauchlin. "The objectives of development." *World Development* 6, no. 1 (January 1978):1–10.

Flammang, Robert A. "Economic growth and economic development: Counterparts or competitors?" *Economic Development and Cultural Change* 28, no. 1 (October 1979).

Lewis, W. Arthur. *The Theory of Economic Growth.* Homewood, Ill.: Richard D. Irwin, 1955.

Nash, Manning, ed. *Essays on Economic Development and Cultural Change in Honor of Bert F. Hazelitz.* Economic Development and Cultural Change, vol. 25, supplement 1977. Chicago: University of Chicago Press, 1977.

Pugwash Symposium. "The role of self-reliance in alternative strategies for development." *World Development* 5, no. 3 (March 1977):257–266.

Ranis, Gustav *et al.*, eds. *Comparative Development Perspectives.* Boulder, Colo.: Westview Press, 1984.

Reynolds, Lloyd G. *Image and Reality in Economic Development.* Yale University Economic Growth Center Series. New Haven: Yale University Press, 1977.

Richards, P. J. "Target setting for basic needs services: Some possible approaches." *International Labor Review* 120, no. 5 (1981):645–658.

Seers, D., and Joy L., eds. *Development in a Divided World.* Harmondsworth, England: Penguin, 1971.

Sheehan, G., and Hopkins, Mike. "Meeting basic needs: An examination of the world situation in 1970." *International Labor Review* 117, no. 5 (September– October 1978).

Singer, H. W. *The Strategy of International Development: Essays in the Economics of Backwardness.* Edited by Sir Alec Cairncross and Mohinder Pari. White Plains, N.Y.: International Arts and Sciences, 1975.

Streeten, Paul. *The Frontiers of Development Studies.* New York: Wiley, 1972.

Streeten, Paul. *Development Perspectives.* New York: St. Martin's, 1981.

3. Theories of Development

Brenner, Y. S. *Theories of Economic Development and Growth.* New York: Praeger, 1966.

Chenery, Hollis, and Syrquin, Moshe. *Patterns of Development, 1950–1970.* Washington, D.C.: World Bank, 1975.

Chenery, Hollis B. "Interaction between theory and observation." *World Development* 11, no. 10 (1983):853–862.

Fei, John C. H., and Ranis, Gustav. *Development of the Labor Surplus Economy: Theory and Policy.* New Haven: Yale University Press, 1964.

Hirschman, Albert O. *The Strategy of Economic Development.* New Haven: Yale University Press, 1958.

Kelley, Allen C. *et al. Dualistic Economic Development: Theory and History.* Chicago: University of Chicago Press, 1972.

Little, Ian. *Economic Development: Theory, Policy and International Relations.* New York: Basic Books, 1982.

Nafziger, E. Wayne. "A critique of development economics in the U.S." *Journal of Development Studies* 13, no. 1 (October 1976).

Roemer, Michael. "Resource-based industrialization in developing countries: A survey." *Journal of Development Economics* 6, no. 2 (June 1979).

Streeten, Paul. "Development dichotomies." *World Development* 11, no. 10 (1983): 875–980.

4. Dependency Theory, Imperialism, Marxism

Amin, Samir. *Imperialism and Unequal Development.* New York: Monthly Review Press, 1977.

Bagchi, Amuja Kumar. *The Political Economy of Underdevelopment.* Cambridge: Cambridge University Press, 1982.

Baran, Paul A. *The Political Economy of Growth.* New York and London: Modern Reader Paperbacks, 1957.

Cardoso, Fernando Henrique. "The consumption of dependency theory in the United States." *Latin American Research Review* 13, no. 2 (1978).

Dos Santos, Theotonio. "The structure of dependence." *American Economic Review* 60, no. 2 (May 1970):231–236.

Frank, Andre Gunder. *Capitalism and Underdevelopment in Latin America.* New York and London: Modern Reader Paperbacks, 1967.

Frank, Andre Gunder. *On Capitalist Underdevelopment.* London: Oxford University Press, 1975.

Godfrey, Martin, ed. "Is dependency dead?" *IDS Bulletin* 12, no. 1 (1980).

Goodman, David, and Redclift, Michael. *From Peasant to Proletarian: Capitalist Development and Agrarian Transitions.* New York: St. Martin's, 1982.

Goulet, Denis. *The Cruel Choice: A New Concept in the Theory of Development.* Center for the Study of Development and Social Change, Cambridge, Mass. New York: Atheneum, 1971.

Jameson, Kenneth P., and Wilber, Charles K., eds. Special issue: "Socialist models of development." *World Development* 9, nos. 9 and 10 (1981).

Kahl, Joseph A. *Modernization, Exploitation and Dependency in Latin America.* New Brunswick, N.J.: Transaction, 1976.

Lall, S. "Is dependence a useful concept in analysing underdevelopment?" *World Development* 3, nos. 11 and 12 (November–December 1975):799–810.

Palma, Gabriel. "Dependency: A formal theory of underdevelopment or a methodology for the analysis of concrete situations of underdevelopment." *World Development* 6, nos. 7 and 8 (July–August 1978):881–924.

Rhodes, Robert I., ed. *Imperialism and Underdevelopment: A Reader.* New York: Monthly Review Press, 1970.

Sloan, John W. "Dependency theory and Latin American development: Another key fails to open the door." *Inter-American Economic Affairs*, no. 3 (Winter 1977).

Street, James H., and Delmus, James D. "Institutionalism, structuralism and dependency in Latin America," *Journal of Economic Issues* 16, no. 3 (1982):673–690.

Williams, Gavin. "Imperialism and development: A critique." *World Development* 6, nos. 7 and 8 (July–August 1978):925–936.

5. Political Development

Almond, Gabriel A., and Coleman, James S., eds. *The Politics of the Developing Areas.* Princeton, N.J.: Princeton University Press, 1960.

Finkle, Jason L., and Gable, Richard W., eds. *Political Development and Social Change*, 2d ed. New York: Wiley, 1971.

Heeger, Gerald A. *The Politics of Underdevelopment.* New York: St. Martin's, 1974.

Huntington, Samuel. *Political Order in Changing Societies.* New Haven: Yale University Press, 1969.

Uphoff, Norman Thomas, and Ilchman, Warren F. *The Political Economy of Change.* Berkeley and Los Angeles: University of California Press, 1969.

Van Niekerk, A. E. *Populism and Political Development in Latin America.* Rotterdam: Rotterdam University Press, 1974.

CHAPTER 4 Historic Growth and Contemporary Development: Lessons and Controversies

1. History of Development

Adelman, Irma, and Morris, Cynthia Taft. "Growth and impoverishment in the middle of the nineteenth century." *World Development* 6, no. 3 (March 1978).

Bairoch, Paul. *The Economic Development of the Third World since 1900.* Translated from the fourth French edition by Cynthia Postan. Berkeley and Los Angeles: University of California Press, 1975.

Bhatt, V. V. "Economic development: An analytic-historical approach." *World Development* 4, no. 7 (July 1976):583–592.

Bird, Richard M. "Land taxation and economic development: The model of Meiji Japan." *Journal of Development Studies* 13, no. 2 (January 1977).

Furtado, Celso. *Economic Development of Latin America: A Survey from Colonial Times to the Cuban Revolution.* Cambridge: Cambridge University Press, 1970.

Gould, John D. *Economic Growth in History: Survey and Analysis.* London: Methuen, 1972.

Hirschman, Albert O. *The Passions and the Interests: Political Arguments for Capitalism before Its Triumph.* Princeton, N.J.: Princeton University Press, 1977.

Hughes, J. R. T. "What difference did the beginning make?" *American Economic Review* 67, no. 1 (February 1977):15−20.

Moore, Banington, Jr. *Social Origins of Dictatorship and Democracy: Lord and Peasant in the Making of the Modern World.* Harmondsworth, England: Penguin, 1974.

Morawetz, David. *Twenty-Five Years of Economic Development: 1950 to 1975.* Washington, D.C.: World Bank, 1977.

Rimmer, Douglas. "Have-not nations: The prototype." *Economic Development and Cultural Change* 27, no. 2 (January 1979).

Rostow, W. W. *The Stages of Economic Growth: A Non-Communist Manifesto.* Cambridge: Cambridge University Press, 1961.

Sachs, Ignacy. *The Discovery of the Third World.* Cambridge, Mass.: MIT Press, 1976.

Smith, Sheila. "Colonialism in economic theory: The experience of Nigeria." *Journal of Development Studies* 15, no. 3 (April 1979).

CHAPTER 5 Growth, Poverty, and Income Distribution

1. Poverty

Ahluwalia, Montek S.; Carter, Nicholas G.; and Chenery, Hollis B. "Growth and poverty in developing countries." *Journal of Development Economics* 6, no. 3 (September 1979):299−342.

Altimer, Oscar. "The extent of poverty in Latin America." *World Bank Staff Working Paper No. 522* (1982).

Amuzegar, Jahangir. "International growth, equity and efficiency." *Finance and Development* 15, no. 1 (March 1978).

Balogh, Thomas. *The Economics of Poverty*, 2d ed. White Plains, N.Y.: International Arts and Sciences, 1974.

Balogh, Thomas. "Failures in strategy against poverty." *World Development* 6, no. 1 (January 1978).

Chambers, Robert. "Rural poverty unperceived: Problems and remedies." *World Bank Staff Working Paper No. 400* (1980).

Griffin, Keith, and Khan, Azizur Rahman. "Poverty in the Third World: Ugly facts and fancy models." *World Development* 6, no. 3 (March 1978):295−304.

Hasan, Parvez. "Growth and equity in East Asia." *Finance and Development* 15, no. 2 (June 1978):28−32.

Isenman, Paul *et al. Poverty and Human Development.* New York: Oxford University Press, 1982.

Myrdal, Gunnar. *The Challenge of World Poverty: A World Anti-Poverty Program in Outline.* Foreword by Francis O. Wilcox. New York: Pantheon, 1970.

Rodgers, G. B. "A conceptualisation of poverty in rural India." *World Development* 4, no. 4 (April 1976):261−276.

Rondinell, Dennis A., and Ruddle, Kenneth. "Coping with poverty in international assistance policy: An evaluation of spatially integrated investment strategies." *World Development* 6, no. 4 (April 1978).

Sen, Amartya. "Levels of poverty: Policy and change." *World Bank Staff Working Paper No. 401* (1980).

Stamp, Elizabeth. *Growing Out of Poverty.* Oxford: Oxford University Press, 1977.

Streeten, Paul et al. *First Things First: Meeting Basic Human Needs in Developing Countries.* London: Oxford University Press, 1981.

Ward, Barbara et al., eds. *The Widening Gap: Development in the 1970s.* New York: Columbia University Press, 1971.

World Bank. *The Assault on World Poverty: Problems of Rural Development, Education and Health.* Baltimore: Johns Hopkins University Press, 1975.

2. Income Distribution: Principles, Concepts, and Policies

Adelman, Irma. "Growth, income distribution and equity-oriented development strategies." *World Development* 3, nos. 2 and 3 (February–March 1975):67–76.

Adelman, Irma, and Morris, Cynthia Taft. *Economic Growth and Social Equity in Developing Countries.* Stanford, Calif.: Stanford University Press, 1973.

Adelman, Irma, and Morris, Cynthia Taft. "Distribution and development: A comment." *Journal of Development Economics* 1, no. 4 (February 1975):401–402.

Adelman, Irma; Morris, Cynthia Taft; and Robinson, Sherman. "Policies for equitable growth." *World Development* 4, no. 7 (July 1976):561–582.

Ahluwalia, Montek S. "Income distribution and development: Some stylized facts." *American Economic Review* 66, no. 2 (May 1976):128–135.

Ahluwalia, Montek S. "Inequality, poverty and development." *Journal of Development Economics* 3, no. 4 (December 1976):307–342.

Atkinson, A. B. *The Economics of Inequality.* New York: Oxford University Press, Clarendon Press, 1975.

Best, Michael H. "Uneven development and dependent market economies." *American Economic Review* 66, no. 2 (May 1976).

Bornschier, Volker. "World economy, level of development, and income distribution: An integration of different approaches to the explanation of income inequality." *World Development* 11, no. 1 (1983):11–20.

Cairncross, Alec, and Puri, Mohinder, eds. *Employment, Income Distribution and Development Strategy: Problems of the Developing Countries. Essays in Honor of H. W. Singer.* New York: Holmes and Meier, 1976.

Chenery, Hollis et al. *Redistribution with Growth: Policies to Improve Income Distribution in Developing Countries in the Context of Economic Growth.* London and New York: Oxford University Press for the World Bank and the Institute of Development Studies, University of Sussex, 1974.

Cline, W. R. "Distribution and development: A survey of literature." *Journal of Development Economics* 1, no. 4 (February 1975): 359–400.

Faaland, J. "Growth, employment and equity." *International Labor Review* 114, no. 1 (July–August 1976).

Fei, J. C.; Ranis, G.; and Kuo, S. W. Y. "Growth and the family distribution of income." *Quarterly Journal of Economics* (February 1978).

Fields, Gary S. "Who benefits from economic development? A reexamination of Brazilian growth in the 1960s." *American Economic Review* 67, no. 4 (September 1977):570–582.

Fields, Gary S. "A welfare economic approach to growth and distribution in the dual economy." *Quarterly Journal of Economics* 93, no. 3 (August 1979).

Frank, Charles R., Jr., and Webb, Richard C., eds. *Income Distribution and Growth in the Less Developed Countries.* Washington, D.C.: Brookings Institution, 1977.

Horowitz, Irving, ed. *Equity, Income, and Policy.* New York: Praeger, 1977.

Lal, Deepak. "Distribution and development: A review article." *World Development* 4, no. 9 (September 1976):713–724.

Lecaillon, Jacques *et al. Income Distribution and Economic Development.* Geneva: ILO Publication, 1983.

Lecaillon, Jacques, and Germides, D. "Income differentials and the dynamics of development." *International Labor Review* 114, no. 1 (July–August 1976).

McLure, C. E., Jr. "Taxation and the urban poor in developing countries." *World Development* 5, no. 3 (March 1977):169–188.

Mellor, John W. "Food price policy and income distribution in low-income countries." *Economic Development and Cultural Change* 27, no. 1 (October 1978).

Paglin, M. "The measurement and trend of inequality: A basic revision." *American Economic Review* 65, no. 4 (September 1975):598–609.

Paukert, Felix. "Income distribution at different levels of development: A survey of evidence." *International Labor Review* 108, nos. 2 and 3 (August–September 1973).

Robinson, Sherman. "Toward an adequate long-run model of income distribution and economic development." *American Economic Review* 66, no. 2 (May 1976): 122–127.

Rothstein, Robert L. "The political economy of redistribution and self-reliance." *World Development* 4, no. 7 (July 1976):593–612.

Sahota, Gian Singh. "Theories of personal income distribution: A survey." *Journal of Economic Literature* 16 (March 1978).

Singer, H. W. "Dualism revisited: A new approach to the problems of the dual society in developing countries." *Journal of Development Studies* 7, no. 1 (October 1970).

Tinbergen, Jan. *Income Distribution: Analysis and Policies.* Amsterdam: North-Holland; New York: American Elsevier, 1975.

Webb, Richard, and Frank, Charles, Jr. *Income Distribution in Less Developed Countries: Policy Alternatives and Design.* Princeton, N.J.: Princeton University and Brookings Institution, 1975.

3. Income Distribution: Statistics and Measurement

Castro, Alfonso Peter *et al.* "Indicators of rural inequality." *World Development* 9, no. 5 (1981):401–428.

Champernowne, D. G. "A comparison of measures of inequality of income distribution." *Economic Journal* 84, no. 336 (December 1974).

Cowell, F. A. *Measuring Inequality: Techniques for the Social Sciences.* New York: Wiley, 1977.

Kakwani, Nanok C. *Income Inequality and Poverty: Methods of Estimation and Policy Applications.* London: Oxford University Press, 1980.

Pyatt, Graham. "On the interpretation and disaggregation of the Gini coefficients." *World Bank Reprint Series No. 38* (June 1976). Reprinted from *Economic Journal.*

Pyatt, Graham. "On international comparisons of inequality." *American Economic Review* 67, no. 1 (February 1977):71–75.

Russet, Bruce *et al.* "Health and population patterns as indicators of income inequality." *Economic Development and Cultural Change* 29, no. 4 (1981):759–780.

4. Women, Poverty, and Development

Boserup, Esther. *Women's Role in Economic Development*. New York: St. Martin's, 1980.

Buvinic, Mayra, and McGreevey, Lycette, eds. *Women and Poverty in the Third World*. Baltimore: Johns Hopkins University Press, 1983.

Dixon, Ruth B. *Rural Women at Work: Strategies for Development in South Asia*. Baltimore: Johns Hopkins University Press, 1978.

Dwyer, Daisy Hilse. "Women and income in the Third World: Implications for policy." *Population Council Working Paper No. 18* (1983).

Henn, Jeanne Koopman. "Feeding the cities and feeding the peasants: What role for Africa's women farmers?" *World Development* 11, no. 12 (1983):1043–1055.

Wellesley Editorial Committee, ed. *Women and National Development*. Chicago: University of Chicago Press, 1977.

World Bank. *World Development Report 1984*. New York: Oxford University Press, 1984. Part II.

CHAPTERS 6 AND 7 The Population Debate and Economics of Population and Development

1. Population and Development

Anker, Richard; Buvinic, Mayra; and Youssef, Nadia H., eds. *Women's Roles and Population Trends in the Third World*. London: Croom Helm, 1982.

Birdsall, Nancy. "Population and poverty in the developing world." *World Bank Staff Working Paper No. 404* (1980).

Birdsall, Nancy. "Analytical approaches to the relationship of population growth and development." *Population and Development Review* 3, nos. 1 and 2 (March–June 1977):63–102.

Bulatao, Rodolfo A., and Lee, Ronald P. *Determinants of Fertility in Developing Countries*. New York: Academic Press, 1983.

Caldwell, John C. *Theory of Fertility Decline*. New York: Academic Press, 1982.

Cassen, R. H. "Population and development: A survey." *World Development* 4, nos. 10 and 11 (October–November 1976):785–830.

Coale, Ansley J., ed. *Economic Factors in Population Growth*. New York: Halsted Press, 1976.

Demeny, Paul. "On the end of the population explosion." *Population and Development Review* 5, no. 1 (March 1979):141–162.

Easterlin, Richard A., ed. *Population and Economic Change in Developing Countries*. Chicago: University of Chicago Press, 1980.

Faaland, Just, ed. *Population and the World Economy in the 21st Century*. New York: St. Martin's, 1982.

Farooq, Ghozi. "Population, human resources, and development planning." *International Labor Review* 120, no. 3 (1981):335–351.

Finkle, Jason L., and Crane, Barbara B. "The politics of Bucharest: Population, development, and the new international order." *Population and Development Review* 1, no. 1 (September 1975):87−114.

Hauser, Philip M. *World Population and Development: Challenges and Prospects.* Syracuse, N.Y.: Syracuse University Press, 1979.

Hawthorn, G., ed. *Population and Development.* London: Frank Cass, 1979.

King, Timothy, ed. *Population Policies and Economic Development.* Baltimore: Johns Hopkins University Press for the World Bank, 1974.

Mauldin, W. Parker, and Berelson, B. "Conditions of fertility decline in developing countries, 1965−75." *Studies in Family Planning* 9, no. 5 (May 1978).

McNicoll, Geoffrey L. "Community-level population policy: An exploration." *Population and Development Review* 1, no. 1 (September 1975):1−22.

Repetto, Robert. *Economic Equality and Fertility in Developing Countries.* Baltimore: Johns Hopkins University Press, 1979.

Ridker, Ronald G., ed. *Population and Development: The Search for Selective Interventions.* Baltimore: Johns Hopkins University Press, 1976.

Rodgers, Gerry. "Population growth, inequality and poverty." *International Labor Review* 122, no. 4 (1983):443−460.

Teitelbaum, Michael S. "Population and development: Is a consensus possible?" *Foreign Affairs* 52, no. 4 (July 1974).

Todaro, Michael P. "Development policy and population growth: A framework for planners." *Population and Development Review* 3, nos. 1 and 2 (March−June 1977):23−44.

World Bank. *World Development Report 1984.* New York: Oxford University Press, 1984. Part II.

CHAPTER 8 Unemployment: Issues, Dimensions, and Analyses

1. Employment and Labor

Bairoch, Paul. *Urban Unemployment in Developing Countries: The Nature of the Problem and Proposals for Its Solution.* Geneva: International Labor Office, 1976.

Bequele, Assefa, and Freedman, David H. "Employment and basic needs: An overview." *International Labor Review* 118, no. 3 (May−June 1979).

Berry, Albert. "Open unemployment as a social problem in urban Colombia: Myth and reality." *Economic Development and Cultural Change* 23, no. 2 (January 1975):276−291.

Bhagwati, J. "Main features of the employment problem in developing countries." *Indian Economic Journal* 19, nos. 4 and 5 (April−June 1972).

Bruton, Henry J. "Economic development and labor use: A review." *World Development*, 1973. Also published in Edgar O. Edwards (ed.), *Employment in Developing Nations.* New York: Columbia University Press, 1974.

Cairncross, Alec, and Puri, Mohinder, eds. *Employment, Income Distribution and Development Strategy: Problems of the Developing Countries. Essays in Honor of H. W. Singer.* New York: Holmes and Meier, 1976.

Chakraborty, A. K. "The causes of educated unemployment in India." *Economic Affairs* 20, no. 7 (July 1975).

Dovering, Folke. "Underemployment, slow motion, and x-efficiency." *Economic Development and Cultural Change* 27, no. 3 (April 1979):485−490.

Durand, John D. *The Labor Force in Economic Development.* Princeton, N.J.: Princeton University Press, 1975.

Edwards, Edgar O. *Employment in Developing Nations: Report on a Ford Foundation Study.* New York and London: Columbia University Press, 1974.

Fei, J. C. H., and Ranis, G. "A model of growth and employment in the open dualistic economy: The cases of Korea and Taiwan." *Journal of Development Studies* 2, no. 2 (January 1975).

Herve, Michel E. A. "Employment and industrialization in developing countries." *Quarterly Journal of Economics* 80, no. 1 (1966).

Hopkins, Michael. "Trends in employment in developing countries, 1960–80 and beyond." *International Labor Review* 122, no. 4 (1983):461–478.

International Labor Office. *Education and the Employment Problem in Developing Countries.* Geneva: ILO, 1973.

International Labor Office. *Employment in Africa: Some Critical Issues.* Geneva: ILO, 1973.

International Labor Office. *Employment Growth and Basic Needs: A One-World Problem. Report of the Director-General of the International Labor Office, Tripartite World Conference on Employment, Income Distribution and Social Progress and the International Division of Labor.* Geneva: ILO, 1976.

Jolly, Richard, ed. *Third World Employment Problems and Strategy: Selected Readings.* Harmondsworth, England: Penguin, 1973.

Krueger, Anne O. "Alternative trade strategies and employment in LDC's." *American Economic Review* 68, no. 2 (May 1978):270–74.

Kuzmin, S. A. "An integrated approach to development and employment." *International Labor Review* 115, no. 3 (May–June 1977).

Kuzmin, S. A. "Structural change and employment in developing countries." *International Labor Review* 121, no. 3 (1982):315–326.

Lewis, W. A. "Summary: The causes of unemployment in less developed countries and some research topics." *International Labor Review* 101, no. 5 (May 1970).

Morawetz, D. "Employment implications of industrialization in developing countries: A survey." *Economic Journal*, September 1974.

Ndegwa, Philip, and Powelson, J. P., eds. *Employment in Africa: Some Critical Issues.* Geneva: International Labor Office, 1974.

Pack, H. "The employment–output trade-off in LDC's: A microeconomic approach." *Oxford Economic Papers* 26, no. 3 (November 1974).

Sen, Amartya Kumar. *Employment, Technology and Development.* Oxford, England: Clarendon Press, 1975.

Stewart, Frances, ed. *Employment, Income Distribution and Development.* London: Frank Cass, 1975.

Turnham, David, with assistance from Ian Jaeger. *The Employment Problem in Less Developed Countries: A Review of Evidence.* Paris: Development Center of the Organization for Economic Cooperation and Development, 1971.

2. Technology

Baer, Werner. "Technology, employment and development: Empirical findings." *World Development* 4, no. 2 (February 1976):121–130.

Baron, C. "Appropriate technology comes of age: A review of some recent literature and aid policy statements." *International Labor Review* 117, no. 5 (September–October 1978).

Berry, R. A. "Factor proportions and urban employment in developing countries." *International Labor Review* 109, no. 3 (March 1974).

Bhalla, A. S., ed. *Technology and Employment in Industry: A Case Study Approach.* Geneva: International Labor Office, 1976.

Dahlman, Carl, and Westphal, Larry. "The transfer of technology." *Finance and Development* 20, no. 4 (1983):6-9.

Das, Ram. *Appropriate Technology: Precepts and Practices.* New York: Vantage, 1981.

Eckaus, Richard S. *Appropriate Technologies for Developing Countries.* Prepared for the Panel on Appropriate Technologies for Developing Countries. Washington, D.C.: National Academy of Sciences, 1977.

Goulet, Denis. *The Uncertain Promise: Value Conflicts in Technology Transfer.* New York: IDOC, 1977.

Hawrylyshyn, Oli. "Capital-intensity biases in developing country technology choice." *Journal of Development Economics* 5, no. 3 (September 1978).

James, Jeffrey. "Growth, technology and the environment in less developed countries: A survey." *World Development* 6, no. 718 (July-August 1978).

Nelson, Richard R. "Less developed countries—Technology transfer and adaptation: The role of the indigenous science community." *Economic Development and Cultural Change* 23, no. 1 (October 1974):61-78.

Pack, H., and Todaro, M. P. "Technology transfer, labor absorption and economic development." *Oxford Economic Papers* 21, no. 3 (1969).

Schumacher, E. F. *Small Is Beautiful: Economics as If People Mattered.* New York: Harper & Row, 1974.

Singer, Hans. *Technologies for Basic Needs.* Geneva: International Labor Office, 1977.

Srinivasan, Mangalam. *Technology Assessment and Development.* New York: Praeger, 1982.

Stewart, F. "Choice of technique in developing countries," *Journal of Development Studies* 9, no. 1 (October 1972).

Stewart, Frances. *Technology and Underdevelopment.* Boulder, Colo.: Westview Press, 1977.

White, Lawrence J. "The evidence on appropriate factor proportions for manufacturing in less developed countries: A survey." *Economic Development and Cultural Change* 27, no. 1 (October 1978).

CHAPTER 9 Urbanization and Migration: Internal and International

1. Rural—Urban Migration

Connell, John et al. *Migration from Rural Areas: The Evidence from Village Studies.* New York, London, and Melbourne: Oxford University Press, 1976.

Fields, G. S. "Rural—urban migration, urban unemployment and under-employment, and job-search activity in LDCs." *Journal of Development Economics* 2, no. 2 (June 1975).

Findlay, Sally. *Planning for Internal Migration.* Washington, D.C.: U.S. Department of Commerce, 1977.

Harris, J. R., and Todaro, M. P. "Migration, unemployment, and development: A two-sector analysis." *American Economic Review* 60, no. 1 (March 1970): 126-142.

Mazumdar, Dipak. "The rural—urban wage gap, migration, and the shadow wage." *Oxford Economic Papers*, November 1976.

Oberai, A. S. *State Policies and Internal Migration*. New York: St. Martin's, 1983.

Peek, P., and Gaude, J. "The economic effects of rural—urban migration." *International Labor Review* 114, no. 3 (November—December 1976).

Rhoda, Richard. "Rural development and urban migration: Can we keep them down on the farm?" *International Migration Review* 17, no. 61 (1983):34—64.

Sabot, Richard H. *Migration and the Labor Market in Developing Countries*. Boulder, Colo.: Westview Press, 1982.

Todaro, M. P. "A model of labor migration and urban unemployment in less developed countries." *American Economic Review* 59, no. 1 (March 1969):138—148.

Todaro, M. P. *Internal Migration in Developing Countries: A Review of Theory, Evidence, Methodology and Research Priorities*. Geneva: International Labor Office, 1976.

Todaro, M. P. "Urban job expansion, induced migration and rising unemployment: A formulation and simplified empirical test for LDC's." *Journal of Development Economics* 3, no. 3 (September 1976):211—225.

Yap, Lorene Y. L. "The attraction of the cities: A review of migration literature." *Journal of Development Economics* 4, no. 3 (September 1977).

2. Urban Development

Beier, George; Churchill, Anthony; Cohen, Michael; and Renand, Bertrand. "The task ahead for the cities of the developing countries." *World Development* 4, no. 5 (May 1976):363—410.

Davis, Kingsley. "Asia's cities: Problems and options." *Population and Development Review* 1, no. 1 (1975):71—86.

Gilbert, Alan, and Gugler, Josef. *Cities, Poverty and Development*. London: Oxford University Press, 1982.

International Labor Office. *Urban Unemployment in Developing Countries*. Geneva: ILO, 1973.

Linn, Johannes F. "The costs of urbanization in developing countries." *Economic Development and Cultural Change* 30, no. 3 (1982):625—648.

Linn, Johannes F. *Cities in the Developing World: Policies for Their Equitable and Efficient Growth*. London: Oxford University Press, 1983.

Lipton, Michael. *Why Poor People Stay Poor: Urban Bias in World Development*. Cambridge, Mass.: Harvard University Press, 1976.

Safa, Helen I., ed. *Towards a Political Economy of Urbanization in Third World Countries*. New York: Oxford University Press, 1982.

Sethuramen, S. V. *The Urban Informal Sector in Developing Countries: Employment, Poverty and Environment*. Geneva: International Labor Office, 1981.

Stark, Obed. "On modelling the informal sector." *World Development* 10, no. 5 (1982):413—416.

Todaro, Michael, and Stilkind, Jerry L. *City Bias and Rural Neglect: The Dilemma of Urban Development*. New York: Population Council, 1981.

United Nations. "Patterns of urban and rural population growth." *Population Studies* 68 (1980).

World Bank. "Urban poverty in developing countries: A World Bank analysis." *Population and Development Review* 1, no. 2 (December 1975):339—345.

3. International Migration

Center for Migration Studies. "International migration and development." *International Migration Review*, Special Issue, vol. 16, no. 60 (1982).

Chaney, Elsa. *Women in International Migration: Issues in Development Planning.* Washington D.C.: U.S. Agency for International Development, 1980.

International Center for Research on Women. *Women in Migration: A Third World Focus.* Washington, D.C.: U.S. Agency for International Development, 1979.

Seralgeldin, Ismail *et al. Manpower and International Labor Migration in the Middle East and North Africa.* London: Oxford University Press, 1983.

Stein, Barry N., and Tomasi, Sylvano M., eds. "Refugees today." *International Migration Review* 15, nos. 53 and 54 (1981).

Swamy, Gurushri. "International migrant workers' remittances: Issues and prospects." *World Bank Staff Working Paper No. 481* (1981).

CHAPTER 10 Agricultural Transformation and Rural Development

1. Agrarian Reform

Alexander, Robert J. *Agrarian Reform in Latin America.* Edited by Samuel L. Baily and Ronald T. Hyman. New York: Macmillan, 1974.

Alier, Juan Martinez. *Haciendas, Plantations and Collective Farms.* London: Frank Cass, 1977.

Barraclough, Solon, ed. *Agrarian Structure in Latin America.* Lexington, Mass.: D.C. Heath, 1973.

Deere, Carmen Diana. "A comparative analysis of agrarian reform in El Salvador and Nicaragua 1979." *Development and Change* 13, no. 1 (1982):1–42.

Dorner, Peter. *Land Reform and Economic Development.* Harmondsworth, England: Penguin, 1972.

Foland, F. M. "Land reform and economic development." *World Politics* 2, nos. 4 and 5 (April–May 1974).

Griffin, Keith. *Land Concentration and Rural Poverty.* London: Macmillan, 1976.

International Labor Office. *Poverty and Landlessness in Rural Asia.* Geneva: ILO, 1977.

King, Russell. *Land Reform: A World Survey.* Leicester, England: University of Leicester, 1977.

Moise, Edwin E. *Land Reform in China and North Vietnam.* Chapel Hill: University of North Carolina Press, 1983.

Rahman, Mustaqur, ed. *Agrarian Egalitarianism.* Dubuque, Iowa: Kendall/Hunt.

United Nations. *Progress in Land Reform.* Sixth Report. New York: United Nations, 1976.

University of Wisconsin Land Tenure Center. *Agrarian Reform in Latin America: An Annotated Bibliography.* Economics Monograph Series, no. 5. Madison: University of Wisconsin Press, 1975.

White, Christine Pelzer, and White, Gorden, eds. "Agriculture, the peasantry and socialist development." *IDS Bulletin* 13, no. 4 (1982).

World Bank. *Land Reform.* Washington, D.C.: World Bank, 1974.

2. Rural Development

Adams, Dale W. "Mobilizing household savings through rural financial markets." *Economic Development and Cultural Change* 26, no. 3 (April 1978):547–560.

Boserup, Ester. *Woman's Role in Economic Development.* New York: St. Martin's, 1970.

Chuta, Enyinna, and Sethuramen, S. V. *Rural Small Scale Industries and Employment in Africa and Asia.* Geneva: International Labor Office, 1983.

Ghai, Dharam *et al.*, eds. *Agrarian Systems and Rural Development.* New York: Holms and Meier, 1979.

Gow, David, and Vansont, Jerry. "Beyond the rhetoric of rural development participation: How can it be done?" *World Development* 11, no. 5 (1983):427–446.

Johnston, Bruce F., and Meyer, Anthony J. "Nutrition, health, and population in strategies for rural development." *Economic Development and Cultural Change* 26, no. 1 (October 1977):1–24.

Paine, Suzanne. "Balanced development: Maoist conception and Chinese practice." *World Development* 4, no. 4 (April 1976):277–304.

World Bank. *Rural Development.* Sector Policy Paper. Washington, D.C.: World Bank, 1975.

Yudelman, Montague. "Integrated rural development projects: The bank's experience." *Finance and Development* 14, no. 1 (March 1977).

3. Agricultural Development

Berry, R. A., and Cline, W. *Agrarian Structure and Productivity in Developing Countries.* Baltimore: Johns Hopkins University Press, 1979.

Bhattacharjee, J. P. "External assistance for food and agricultural development in the Third World." *World Development* 5, nos. 5 and 7 (May–July 1977):633– 640.

Brown, Lester R. *Seeds of Change: The Green Revolution and Development in the 1970's.* New York: Praeger for the Overseas Development Council, 1970.

Croll, Elizabeth J. "Production versus reproduction: A threat to China's development strategy." *World Development* 11, no. 6 (1983):467–482.

Dixon, Ruth B. "Counting women in the agricultural labor force." *Population and Development Review* 8, no. 3 (1982):539–566.

Ghai, Dharam, and Radwan, Samu. *Agrarian Policies and Rural Poverty in Africa.* Geneva: International Labor Office, 1983.

Griffin, Keith. *The Political Economy of Agrarian Change.* Cambridge, Mass.: Harvard University Press, 1974.

Hayami, Yujiro, and Ruttan, Vernon W. *Agricultural Development: An International Perspective.* Baltimore: Johns Hopkins University Press, 1971.

Hsu, Robert C. *Food for One Billion: China's Agriculture since 1949.* Boulder, Colo.: Westview Press, 1982.

Hunter, Guy. *Modernizing Peasant Societies: A Comparative Study in Asia and Africa.* New York and London: Oxford University Press for the Institute of Race Relations, 1969.

International Labor Office. *Mechanization and Employment in Agriculture: Case Studies from Four Continents.* Geneva: ILO, 1974.

Mellor, John W. *The Economics of Agricultural Development.* Ithaca, N.Y.: Cornell University Press, 1966.

Poleman, Thomas T., and Freebairn, Donald K., eds. *Food, Population and Employment: The Impact of the Green Revolution.* New York and London: Praeger, 1973.

Reutlinger, Shlomo. "Malnutrition: A poverty or a food problem?" *World Development,* no. 8 (August 1977):715–724.

Reynolds, Lloyd G., ed. *Agriculture in Development Theory*. New Haven: Yale University Press, 1975.

Sarma, J. S. *Agricultural Policy in India: Growth with Equity*. International Development Research Centre, 1982.

Schultz, T. W. *Transforming Traditional Agriculture*. New Haven: Yale University Press, 1964.

Schutjer, Wayne A. "Agricultural development policy and demographic transition." *Journal of Developing Areas* 12, no. 3 (April 1978).

Thornbecke, E. "Sector analysis and models of agriculture in developing countries." *Food Research Institute Studies* 12, no. 1 (1973).

4. Agricultural Credit

Adams, Dale W., and Graham, Douglas H. "A critique of traditional credit projects and policies." *Journal of Development Economics* 8, no. 3 (1981):347–366.

Baum, Warren C. "Agricultural credit and the small farmer." *Finance and Development* 13, no. 2 (June 1976).

Donald, Gordon. *Credit for Small Farmers in Developing Countries*. Boulder, Colo.: Westview Press, 1976.

Kato, Yuzuru. "Sources of loanable funds of agricultural credit institutions in Asia." *Developing Economies* 10 (1972).

Ladman, Jerry R. "Some empirical evidence in unorganized rural credit markets." *Canadian Journal of Economics* 19 (November 1971).

Lele, Uma J. *Role of Credit and Marketing Functions in Agricultural Development*. Washington, D.C.: International Economic Association, 1972.

CHAPTER 11 Education and Development

1. Education

Alatas, Syes Hussein. *Intellectuals in Developing Societies*. London: Frank Cass, 1977.

Becker, G. *Human Capital*. New York: Columbia University Press, 1975.

Blaug, Mark. *Education and the Employment Problem in Developing Countries*. Geneva: International Labor Office, 1974.

Colclough, Christopher. "The impact of primary schooling and economic development." *World Development* 10, no. 3 (1982):167–186.

Coombs, P. H., with Ahmed, M. *Attacking Rural Poverty: How Nonformal Education Can Help*. Baltimore: Johns Hopkins University Press, 1974.

Dore, Ronald P. *The Diploma Disease: Education, Qualification, and Development*. Berkeley and Los Angeles: University of California Press, 1976.

Edwards, E. O., and Todaro, M. P. "Educational demand and supply in the context of growing unemployment in less developed countries." *World Development* 1, nos. 3 and 4 (March–April 1973):107–117.

Harbison, Frederick H. *Human Resources as the Wealth of Nations*. New York, London, and Toronto: Oxford University Press, 1973.

Jallade, Jean-Pierre. "Education finance and income distribution." *World Development* 4, no. 5 (May 1976):435–444.

Kelly, Gail P., and Elliott, Carolyn M., eds. *Women's Education in the Third World: Comparative Perspectives*. Albany: State University of New York Press, 1982. Chapter 12.

Noor, Abdun. "Education and basic human needs." *World Bank Staff Working Paper No. 450* (1981).

Psacharopoulos, George. "Schooling, experience and earnings: The case of an LDC." *Journal of Development Economics* 4, no. 1 (March 1977):39—48.

Ritzen, J. J. M. *Education, Economic Growth and Income Distribution*. Amsterdam: North-Holland, 1977.

Schultz, T. W. "Investing in poor people: An economist's view." *American Economic Review* 55, no. 2 (May 1965).

Simmons, John. "Retention of cognitive skills acquired in primary school." *Comparative Education Review* 20 (February 1976).

Simmons, John, ed. *The Education Dilemma: Policy Issues for Developing Countries in the 1980s*. Oxford: Pergamon, 1980.

World Bank. *Education*. Sector Working Paper. Washington, D.C.: World Bank, 1974.

CHAPTER 12 Trade Theory and Development Experience

1. Trade and Exchange

Anjaria, S. J. *et al.* "Protectionism." *Finance and Development* 20, no. 1 (1983):2—6.

Balassa, Bela. "Trade in manufactured goods: Patterns of change." *World Development* 9, no. 3 (1981):263—278.

Diaz-Alejandro, Carlos F. "International markets for LDC's: The old and the new." *American Economic Review* 68, no. 2 (May 1978):364—369.

Findlay, Ronald. "Economic development and the theory of international trade." *American Economic Review* 69, no. 2 (May 1979):186—190.

Love, James. "Concentration, diversification and earnings instability: Some evidence on developing countries' exports of manufactures and primary products." *World Development* 11, no. 9 (1983):787—794.

Maizels, Alfred *et al. Exports and Economic Growth of Developing Countries*. New York: Cambridge University Press, 1969.

Michaely, Michael. *Foreign Trade Regimes and Economic Development*. New York: Columbia University Press, 1975.

Morton, Kathryn, and Tulloch, Peter. *Trade and Developing Countries*. New York and Toronto: Wiley, 1977.

Smith, Sheila, and Toye, John. "Introduction: Three stories about trade and poor economies." *Journal of Development Studies* 15, no. 3 (April 1979).

2. International Economics

Balogh, T., and Balacs, P. "Fact and fancy in international economic relations." *World Development* 1, nos. 3 and 4 (March—April 1973):71—106.

Chenery, Hollis B. "Restructuring the world economy." *Foreign Affairs* 53 (January 1975).

Cline, William R. *International Monetary Reform and the Developing Countries*. Washington, D.C.: Brookings Institution, 1976.

Helleiner, G. K., ed. *A World Divided: The Less Developed Countries in the International Economy*. New York: Cambridge University Press, 1976.

Kahn, Herman. *World Economic Development*. Boulder, Colo.: Westview Press, 1979.

Meier, Gerald M. *The International Economics of Development: Theory and Policy.* New York and London: Harper & Row, 1968.

Sura, Ariel Buira. "Recession, inflation and the international monetary system." *World Development* 9, nos. 11 and 12 (1981):1115−1128.

United Nations. *The Future of the World Economy.* New York: United Nations, 1976.

Williamson, John. *The Open Economy and the World Economy.* New York: Basic Books, 1983.

CHAPTER 13 The Balance of Payments and Commercial Policy

1. Trade Policies

Baldwin, Robert E. *Nontariff Distortions of International Trade.* Washington, D.C.: Brookings Institution, 1970.

Bhagwati, Jagdish N. "Market disruption, export market disruption, compensation and GATT reform." *World Development* 4, no. 12 (December 1976):989−1020.

Cline, William. "Can the East Asian model of development be generalized?" *World Development* 10, no. 2 (1982):81−90.

Corden, W. M. *The Theory of Protection.* Oxford: Clarendon, 1971.

Johnson, Harry G., ed. *Trade Strategy for Rich and Poor Nations.* Toronto: University of Toronto Press, 1971.

Keesing, Donald B. "Trade policy for developing countries." *World Bank Staff Working Paper No. 353* (1979).

Meier, Gerald M. *Problems of Trade Policy.* New York: Oxford University Press, 1973.

Murray, Tracy. *Trade Preferences for Developing Countries.* New York: Halsted, 1977.

Streeten, Paul, ed. *Trade Strategies for Development: Papers of the Ninth Cambridge Conference on Development Problems, September 1972.* Cambridge University Overseas Studies Committee. New York: Wiley, 1973.

Yeats, Alexander. *Trade and Development Policies: Leading Issues for the 1980s.* New York: St. Martin's, 1981.

2. Commodities

Behrman, Jere R. *International Commodity Agreements: An Evaluation of the UNCTAD Integrated Commodity Programme.* NIEO Series, no. 9. Washington, D.C.: Overseas Development Council, 1977.

Brook, Ezriel M., and Grilli, Enzo R. "Commodity price stabilization and the developing world." *Finance and Development* 14, no. 1 (March 1977).

Brown, C. P. *Primary Commodity Control.* New York: Oxford University Press, 1975.

Duncan, Ron, and Lutz, Ernst. "Penetration of industrial country markets by agricultural products from developing countries." *World Development* 11, no. 9 (1983): 771−786.

Frank, Isaiah. "Toward a new framework for international commodity policy." *Finance and Development* 13, no. 2 (June 1976).

Grilli, Enzo R., ed. "The outlook for primary commodities." *World Bank Commodity Working Paper No. 9* (1982).

McNicol, David L. *Commodity Agreements and Price Stabilization.* Lexington, Mass.: Lexington Books, 1978.

Ridker, Ronald G. *Changing Resource Problems of the Fourth World.* Baltimore: Johns Hopkins University Press, 1976.

Singh, Shamsher. "The international dialogue on commodities." *Resources Policy,* June 1976.

Varon, Bension, and Takeuchi, Kenji. "Developing countries and non-fuel minerals." *Foreign Affairs* 52, no. 3 (April 1974).

Wilson, Peter. "The consequences of export instability in developing countries." *Development and Change* 14, no. 1 (1983):39−60.

3. Economic Integration

Balassa, Bela. *The Theory of Economic Integration.* Homewood, Ill.: Richard D. Irwin, 1961.

Barnouin, Jack P. "Trade and economic cooperation among developing countries." *Finance and Development* 19, no. 2 (1982):24−27.

El Agraa, Ali M. *International Economic Integration.* New York: St. Martin's, 1982.

Machlup, Fritz. *A History of Thought on Economic Integration.* New York: Columbia University Press, 1977.

Morawetz, David. *The Andean Group: A Case Study in Economic Integration among Developing Countries.* Cambridge, Mass.: MIT Press, 1974.

Nsouli, Saleh M. "Monetary integration in developing countries." *Finance and Development* 18, no. 4 (1981):41−45.

Switzer, Kenneth A. "The Andean group: A reappraisal." *Inter-American Economic Affairs* 26, no. 4 (Spring 1973).

Willmore, Larry N. "Trade creation, trade diversion and effective protection in the Central American Common Market." *Journal of Development Studies* 12, no. 4 (July 1976).

4. Import Substitution

Baer, Werner. "Import substitution and industrialization in Latin America: Experiences and interpretations." *Latin American Research Review* 7, no. 1 (Spring 1972).

Hirshman, Albert C. "The political economy of import-substituting industrialization in Latin America." *Quarterly Journal of Economics,* February 1968.

Little, I. M. D. "Import controls and exports in developing countries." *Finance and Development* 15, no. 3 (September 1978).

Maitra, P. "Import substitution and changing import structure in an underdeveloped country." *Economic Affairs* 15, no. 4 (April 1970).

5. Industrial Development

Anderson, Dennis. "Small industries in developing countries: A discussion of issues." *World Development* 10, no. 11 (1982):913−948.

Cukor, Gyorgy. *Strategies for Industrialization in Developing Countries.* New York: St. Martin's, 1974.

Gulhati, Ravi, and Sekhar, Uday. "Industrial strategy for late starters: The experience of Kenya, Tanzania and Zambia." *World Development* 10, no. 11 (1982): 949−972.

Hensley, R. J. "Industrial organization and economic development." *Economica Internationale* 28, nos. 3 and 4 (August–November 1975).

Roemer, Michael. "Dependence and industrialization strategies." *World Development* 9, no. 15 (1981):429–434.

Schmitz, Hubert. "Growth constraints in small scale manufacturing in developing countries." *World Development* 10, no. 6 (1982):429–450.

World Bank. *Industry*. Sector Working Paper. Washington, D.C.: World Bank, April 1972.

CHAPTER 14 Foreign Investment and Aid: Old Controversies and New Opportunities

1. Foreign Aid

Abbott, G. C. "Two concepts of foreign aid." *World Development* 1, no. 9 (September 1973).

Chenery, Hollis B., and Carter, Nicholas G. "Foreign assistance and development performance, 1960–1970." *American Economic Review* 63, no. 2 (May 1973).

Dacy, D. C. "Foreign aid, government, government consumption, saving and growth in less developed countries." *Economic Journal* 85, no. 339 (September 1975).

Goulet, Denis, and Hudson, Michael. *The Myth of Aid: The Hidden Agenda of the Development Reports*. Prepared by the Center for Development and Social Change, International Documentation on the Contemporary Church. New York: Orbis Books, 1971.

Hamsell, Sven, and Nordberg, Olle. "The gap in international resource transfers." *Development Dialogue*, no. 1 (1981):5–13.

Iqbal, Zubair. "Arab concessional assistance, 1975–81." *Finance and Development* 20, no. 2 (1983):31–35.

Isenman, Paul J., and Singer, H. W. "Food aid: Disincentive effects and their policy implications." *Economic Development and Cultural Change* 25, no. 2 (January 1977).

Leipziger, Danny M. "Lending versus Giving: The economics of foreign assistance." *World Development* 11, no. 4 (1983):329–336.

Michaely, Michael. "Foreign aid, economic structure, and dependence." *Journal of Development Economics* 9, no. 3 (1981):313–330.

Pearson, Lester B. *Partners in Development: Report of the Commission on International Development*. New York: Praeger, 1969.

Seers, Dudley. "Why visiting economists fail." *Journal of Political Economy* 70, no. 4 (August 1962).

Williams, Maurice J. "The aid programs of the OPEC countries." *Foreign Affairs* 54, no. 2 (January 1976).

2. Foreign Investment

Brecker, Richard, and Bhagwati, Jagdish. "Foreign ownership and the theory of trade and welfare." *Journal of Political Economy* 89, no. 2 (1981):497–511.

Killick, T. "The benefits of foreign direct investment and its alternatives: An empirical exploration." *Journal of Development Studies* 9, no. 2 (January 1973).

Lall, S. "Less-developed countries and private foreign direct investment: A review article." *World Affairs* 2, nos. 4 and 5 (April–May 1974).

Reuber, Grant L. *Private Foreign Investment in Development*. Oxford: Oxford University Press, 1973.

Stamp, M. "Has foreign capital still a role to play in development?" *World Development* 2, no. 2 (February 1974).

3. Multinational Corporations

Agmon, Tamir, and Kindleberger, Charles P., eds. *Multinationals from Small Countries*. Cambridge, Mass.: MIT Press, 1977.

Ball, George W., ed. *Global Companies: The Political Economy of World Business*. Englewood Cliffs, N.J.: Prentice-Hall for the American Assembly, 1975.

Barnet, Richard J., and Muller, Ronald E. *Global Reach: The Power of the Multinational Corporations*. New York: Simon and Schuster, 1974.

Bergsten, C. Fred; Hersh, Thomas; and Moran, Theodore H. *American Multinationals and American Interests*. Washington, D.C.: Brookings Institution, 1978.

Caves, Richard. *Multinational Enterprise and Economic Analysis*. London and New York: Cambridge University Press, 1982.

Chen, Edward. "The role of MNC's in the production and transfer of technology in host countries." *Development and Change* 12, no. 4 (1981):579−600.

Deo, S. "The multinational corporations and the developing countries." *Economic Affairs* 20, no. 8 (August 1975).

Drucker, Peter F. "Multinationals and developing countries: Myths and realities." *Foreign Affairs* 2, no. 2 (February 1974).

Dunning, J. H. "Multinational enterprises and trade flows of less developed countries." *World Development* 2, no. 2 (February 1974).

Helleiner, Gerald K. "Transnational enterprises in the manufacturing sector of the less developed countries." *World Development* 3, no. 9 (September 1975).

International Labor Office. *The Impact of Multinational Enterprises on Employment and Training*. Geneva: ILO, 1976.

Lall, Sanjaya. "The emergence of Third World multinationals." *World Development* 10, no. 2 (1982):127−146.

Meller, Patricio, and Mizala, Alejandra. "U.S. multinationals and Latin American manufacturing employment absorption." *World Development* 10, no. 2 (1982): 115−126.

Morley, Samuel A., and Smith, Gordon W. "The choice of technology: Multinational firms in Brazil." *Economic Development and Cultural Change* 25, no. 2 (January 1977).

Streeten, P. "Policies towards multinationals." *World Development* 3, no. 6 (June 1975):393−398.

United Nations. *Multinational Corporations in World Development*. New York: United Nations, 1973.

Vernon, Raymond. *Storm over the Multinationals: The Real Issues*. Cambridge, Mass.: Harvard University Press, 1977.

Watanabe, Susumu. "Multinational enterprises, employment and technology adoption." *International Labor Review* 120, no. 6 (1981):693−710.

4. U.S. Policy

Connell-Smith, Gordon. *The United States and Latin America: An Historical Analysis of Inter-American Relations*. New York: Halsted, 1974.

Dominquez, Jorge I., ed. *Economic Issues and Political Conflict: U.S.—Latin American Relations*. Boston: Butterworth, 1982.

Martin, Edwin M., and Fowler, Henry H. *The United States and the Developing Countries*. Boulder, Colo.: Westview Press, 1977.

Overseas Development Council. *U.S. Foreign Policy and the Third World, Agenda 1983*. New York: Praeger, 1983.

Slater, Jerome. "The United States and Latin America: The new radical orthodoxy." *Economic Development and Cultural Change* 25, no. 4 (July 1977).

CHAPTER 15 Development Planning: Theory and Practice

1. Planning

Aharoni, Yair. *Markets, Planning and Development: The Private and Public Sectors in Economic Development*. Cambridge, Mass.: Ballinger, 1977.

Amin, Galal A. "Project appraisal and income distribution." *World Development* 6, no. 2 (February 1978):139—152.

Blitzner, Charles R.; Clark, P.; and Taylor, L., eds. *Economy-Wide Models and Development Planning*. London: Oxford University Press, 1975.

Cave, Martin, and Hare, Paul. *Alternative Approaches to Economic Planning*. New York: St. Martin's, 1981.

Centre for Development Planning, Projections and Policies. "Implementation of development plans: The experience of developing countries in the first half of the 1970's." *Journal of Development Planning*, United Nations, New York, 1977.

Chenery, Hollis B. "The structuralist approach to development policy." *American Economic Review* 65, no. 2 (May 1975):310—316.

Chenery, Hollis B. *et al.*, eds. *Studies in Development Planning*. Harvard Economic Studies, vol. 136. Cambridge, Mass.: Harvard University Press, 1971.

Cook, Wade D., and Kuhn, Tillo E. *Planning Processes in Developing Countries: Techniques and Achievements*. Amsterdam: North Holland, 1982.

Davis, Kemal *et al. General Equilibrium Models for Development Policy*. New York: Cambridge University Press, 1982.

Griffin, Keith B., and Eros, John L. *Planning Development*. Development Economics Series. Reading, Mass.: Don Mills, 1971.

Hilhost, Joseph G. M. "Strategies and regional planning in Latin America: Some reflections." *Development and Change* 12, no. 4 (1981):525—546.

International Labor Office. *Planning Techniques for a Better Future*. Geneva: ILO, 1976.

Khalid, R. O. "Planning and the budget process: An introduction." *Finance and Development* 15, no. 2 (June 1978).

Killick, T. "The possibilities of development planning." *Oxford Economic Papers* 41, no. 4 (October 1976).

Lewis, W. Arthur. *Development Planning: The Essentials of Economic Policy*. New York: Harper & Row, 1966.

Lisk, F. "Conventional development strategies and basic-needs fulfillment." *International Labor Review* 115, no. 2 (March—April 1977).

Mirrlees, J. A. "Social benefit-cost analysis and the distribution of income." *World Development* 6, no. 2 (February 1978):131—138.

Roemer, Michael. "Planning by 'revealed preference': An improvement upon the traditional method." *World Development* 4, no. 9 (September 1976):775–783.

Spulber, Nicholas, and Horowitz, Ira. *Quantitative Economic Policy and Planning: Theory and Models of Economic Control.* New York: Norton, 1976.

Tinbergen, Jan. *Development Planning.* Translated from the Dutch by N. D. Smith. New York and Toronto: McGraw-Hill, 1967.

Todaro, Michael P. *Development Planning: Models and Methods.* New York: Oxford University Press, 1971.

Waterston, Albert. *Development Planning: Lessons of Experience.* Baltimore: Johns Hopkins University Press, 1972.

White, Gordon. "Socialist planning and industrial management: Chinese economic reforms in the post-Mao era," *Development and Change* 14, no. 4 (1983): 483–514.

2. Project Analysis

Bhatt, V. V. "On a development bank's selection criteria for industrial projects." *Economic Development and Cultural Change* 25, no. 4 (July 1977):639–656.

Harberger, Arnold C. *Project Evaluation: Collected Papers.* Markham Economics Series. Chicago: Markham, 1973.

Lal, Deepak. *Methods of Project Analysis: A Review.* Baltimore: Johns Hopkins University Press, 1974.

Little, I. M. D., and Mirrlees, James A. *Project Appraisal and Planning for Developing Countries.* New York: Basic Books, 1974.

Little, I. M. D., and Scott, M. F. G. *Using Shadow Prices.* New York: Holmes and Meier, 1976.

Misham, E. J. *Cost-Benefit Analysis.* New York: Praeger, 1976.

Organization for Economic Cooperation and Development. *Manual of Industrial Project Analysis in Developing Countries. Vol. 1: Methodology and Case Studies.* Paris: Development Center of the Organization for Economic Cooperation and Development, 1968.

Palmer, Ingrid. "Women's issues and project appraisal." *IDS Bulletin* 12, no. 4 (1981):32–39.

Squire, Lyn, and van der Tak, Herman C. *Economic Analysis of Projects.* A World Bank Research Publication. Baltimore: Johns Hopkins University Press for the World Bank, 1975.

United Nations. *A Guide to Practical Project Appraisal: Social Benefit-Cost Analysis in Developing Countries.* New York: United Nations Industrial Development Organization, 1978.

CHAPTER 16 Monetary and Fiscal Policy: The Role and Limitations of the State

1. Fiscal Policy and Inflation

Aghevli, Bijan B., and Khan, Mohsin S. "Government deficits and the inflationary process in developing countries." *IMF Staff Papers* (September 1978).

Balassa, Bela. "Structural adjustment policies in developing countries." *World Development* 10, no. 1 (1982):23–38.

Dornbusch, Rudiger. "Stabilization policies in developing countries: What have we learned?" *World Development* 10, no. 9 (1983):701−708.

Galbis, Vincente. "Inflation: The Latin American experience 1970−79." *Finance and Development* 19, no. 3 (1982):22−26.

Heller, Peter S. "A model of fiscal behavior in developing countries: Aid, investment and taxation." *American Economic Review* 65, no. 3 (June 1975):429−445.

Kaldor, Nicholas. "Will underdeveloped countries learn to tax?" *Foreign Affairs*, January 1963.

Kean, Mohsin, and Knight, Malcom. "Some theoretical and empirical issues relating to economic stabilization policies in developing countries." *World Development* 10, no. 9 (1982):709−730.

Pazos, Felipe. "Chronic inflation in Latin America." *Challenge* 20, no. 2 (May−June 1977).

Rothstein, Robert L. "Politics and policy-making in the Third World: Does a reform strategy make sense?" *World Development* 4, no. 8 (August 1976):695−708.

Saini, Krishon. "The monetarist explanation of inflation: The experience of six Asian countries." *World Development* 10, no. 10 (1982):871−884.

Tanzi, Vito. "Fiscal disequilibrium in developing countries." *World Development* 10, no. 12 (1982):1069−1082.

Tanzi, Vito. "Tax increases and the price level." *Finance and Development* 19, no. 3 (1982):27−30.

Toye, J. F. J., ed. *Taxation and Economic Development.* London: Frank Cass, 1979.

Wachter, Susan M. *Latin American Inflation: The Structuralist Monetarist Debate.* Lexington, Mass.: D.C. Heath, 1976.

Wang, T. N., ed. *Taxation and Development.* New York: Praeger, 1976.

2. Banking and Finance

Bhatt, V. V., and Meerman, J. "Resource mobilization in developing countries: Financial institutions and policies." *World Development* 6, no. 1 (January 1978).

Cairncross, Alec. *Inflation, Growth and International Finance.* Albany: State University of New York Press, 1975.

Desai, V. "Role of banks in economic growth." *Economic Affairs* 21, no. 6 (June 1976).

Friedman, Irving S., and Costanzo, G. A. *The Emerging Role of Private Banks in the Developing World.* New York: Citicorp, 1977.

Leff, N. H. "Rates of return to capital, domestic savings, and investment in the developing countries." *Kyklos* 28, no. 4 (1975).

Newlyn, W. T. *The Financing of Economic Development.* Oxford: Oxford University Press, 1977.

Saladin, Peter. "The link between the creation of Special Drawing Rights (SDRs) and development finance." *Development Dialogue*, no. 1 (1981):38−46.

Tun Wai, U. *Financial Intermediaries and National Savings in Developing Countries.* Praeger Special Studies in International Economics and Development. New York: Praeger, 1972.

Williams, David. "Opportunities and constraints in international lending." *Finance and Development* 20, no. 1 (1983):24−28.

World Bank. *Development Finance Companies.* Sector Policy Paper. Washington, D.C.: World Bank, April 1976.

3. Military and Development

Ball, Nicole. "Defense and development: A critique of the Benoit study." *Economic Development and Cultural Change* 20, no. 1 (1983):507−524.

Nawaz, Shuja. "Economic impact of defense expenditures." *Finance and Development* 20, no. 1 (1983):34−36.

Thorsson, Inga. "Guns and butter: Can the world have both?" *International Labor Review* 122, no. 4 (1983):397−410.

**CHAPTER 17 Development Issues in the 1980s:
Energy, Food, Debt, and the Economic Order**

1. Energy

Eden, Richard. *Energy Economics: Growth, Resources and Policies.* Cambridge: Cambridge University Press, 1982.

Ghadar, Fariborz. *The Evolution of OPEC Strategy.* Lexington, Mass.: Lexington Books, 1977.

Kalymon, B. A. "Economic incentives in OPEC oil pricing policy." *Journal of Development Economics* 2, no. 4 (December 1975).

Nunnenkamp, P. "The impact of rising oil prices in economic growth of developing countries in the seventies." *Kyklos* 35, no. 4 (1982):633−647.

Powelson, John P. "The oil price increase: Impacts on industrialized and less-developed countries." *Journal of Energy and Development* 3, no. 1 (Autumn 1977).

Rovani, Yves. "Energy transition in developing countries." *Finance and Development* 20, no. 4 (1983):24−27.

Vernon, Raymond, ed. *The Oil Crisis.* New York: Norton, 1976.

Williams, Maurice J. "The aid programs of the OPEC countries." *Foreign Affairs* 54, no. 2 (January 1976).

2. World Food Problems

Aziz, Sartaj. "The world food situation and collective self-reliance." *World Development* 5, nos. 5 and 7 (May−July 1977).

Bigman, David. *Coping with Hunger: Toward a System of Food Security and Price Stabilization.* Cambridge, Mass.: Ballinger, 1982.

Clay, Edward, and Singer, Hans, eds. "Food as aid: Food for thought." *IDS Bulletin* 14, no. 2 (1983).

De Castro, Josue. *The Geopolitics of Hunger.* Introduction by Jean-Pierre Berlan. New York and London: Monthly Review Press, 1977.

Islam, Nural. "The hungry, crowded and competitive world." *World Development* 5, no. 8 (August 1977):699−706.

Kay, Cristobal. "A cross-section analysis of food insecurity in developing countries: Its magnitude and sources." *Journal of Development Studies* 18, no. 2 (1982): 185−204.

Meerman, Jacob, and Cochrane, Susan Hill. "Population growth and food supply in sub-Saharan Africa." *Finance and Development* 19, no. 3 (1982):12−17.

Poleman, Thomas T. "World food: Myth and reality." *World Development* 5, nos. 5 and 7 (May−July 1977):383−394.

Reutlinger, Shlomo, and Knapp, Keith. "Food security in food deficit countries." *World Bank Staff Working Paper No. 393* (1980).

Schertz, Lyle P., and Bernston, Byron L. "The new politics of food." *World Development* 5, nos. 5 and 7 (May–July 1977):623–632.

Sinha, Radha, ed. *The World Food Problem: Consensus and Conflict*. Gilford, Conn.: Pergamon, 1978.

Williams, Maurice J. "Prospects for eliminating hunger in the face of world-wide economic recession." *International Labor Review* 121, no. 6 (1982):657–670.

3. Debt Problems

Hope, Nicholas C. "Developments in and prospects for the external debt of the developing countries: 1970–80 and beyond." *World Bank Staff Working Paper No. 488* (1981).

Hope, Nicholas C., and Klein, Thomas. "Issues in external debt management." *Finance and Development* 20, no. 3 (1983):23–26.

IMF Staff. "Debt rescheduling: What does it mean?" *Finance and Development* 20, no. 3 (1983):26–30.

Jorge, Antonio *et al.* (eds.). *Foreign Debt and Latin American Economic Development*. New York: Pergamon, 1983.

McDonald, Donogh C. "Debt capacity and developing country borrowing: A survey of the literature." *International Monetary Fund Staff Paper* 29, no. 4 (1982): 603–646.

Roett, Riordan. "Democracy and debt in South America: A continuous dilemma." *Foreign Affairs* 62, no. 3 (1984):694–720.

Sanchez, Arnau, and Carlos, Juan, eds. *Debt and Development*. New York: Praeger, 1982.

4. IMF and Stabilization

Bogdanowicz-Bindert, Christine. "Portugal, Turkey and Peru: Three stabilization programs under the auspices of the IMF." *World Development* 11, no. 1 (1983): 65–70.

Bura, Ariel. "IMF financial programs and conditionality." *Journal of Development Economics* 12, nos. 1 and 2 (1983):111–135.

Dell, Sidney. "Stabilization: The political economy of overkill." *World Development* 10, no. 8 (1982):597–612.

Killick, Tony, and Chapman, M. "Much ado about nothing: Testing the impact of IMF stabilization programmes in developing countries." London: Overseas Development Institute, 1982.

Nowzod, Bahram. *The IMF and Its Critics*. Princeton, N.J.: Princeton University Press, 1981.

Williamson, John. *The Lending Policies of the International Monetary Fund*. Washington, D.C.: Institute for International Economics, 1982.

Williamson, John. *IMF Conditionality*. Washington, D.C.: Institute for International Economics, 1983.

5. The New International Economic Order

Amuzegar, Jahangir. "The North–South dialogue: From conflict to compromise." *Foreign Affairs* 54, no. 3 (April 1976).

Bauer, P. T., and Yamey, B. S. "Against the new economic order." *Commentary*, April 1977.

Bhagwati, Jagdish N. *The New International Economic Order: The North–South Debate.* Cambridge, Mass.: MIT Press, 1977.

Center for Development Planning, Projections and Policies. "Salient features of economic cooperation among developing countries." *Journal of Development Planning*, United Nations, New York, 1978.

Green, R. H., and Singer, H. W. "Toward a rational and equitable new international economic order: A case for negotiated structural changes." *World Development* 3, no. 6 (June 1975):427–444.

Hamrell, Sven, and Nordberg, Olie, eds. "The international monetary system and the new international order." *Development Dialogue*, no. 2 (1980).

Leontief, Wassily *et al. The Future of the World Economy: A United Nations Study.* New York: Oxford University Press, 1977.

Lewis, W. Arthur. *The Evolution of the International Economic Order.* Princeton, N.J.: Princeton University Press, 1978.

Singh, Jyoti Shankar. *A New International Economic Order: Toward a Fair Redistribution of the World's Resources.* Praeger Special Studies in International Economics and Development. New York: Praeger, 1977.

Streeten, Paul. "Approaches to a new international economic order." *World Development* 10, no. 1 (1982):1–18.

Tinbergen, Jan, coordinator. *RIO: Reshaping the International Order: A Report to the Club of Rome.* New York: Dutton, 1978.

Ul Haq, Mahbub. *The Poverty Curtain: Choices for the Third World.* New York: Columbia University Press, 1976.

UNESCO. "Towards a new international economic and social order." *International Social Science Journal* 28, no. 4 (1976).

United Nations. *Declaration on the Establishment of a New International Economic Order, Resolutions of the General Assembly at its Sixth Special Session, April 9–May 2, 1974.* New York, 1974.

van Dam, Ferdinand. "North–South negotiations." *Development and Change* 12, no. 4 (1981):481–504.

AUTHOR INDEX

SUBJECT INDEX